黄海勇引渡案
法理聚焦

赵秉志 主编

江苏人民出版社

图书在版编目(CIP)数据

黄海勇引渡案法理聚焦/赵秉志主编. —南京：
江苏人民出版社,2019.8
 ISBN 978-7-214-16781-1

Ⅰ.①黄⋯ Ⅱ.①赵⋯ Ⅲ.①引渡法-研究-中国
Ⅳ.①D922.144

中国版本图书馆 CIP 数据核字(2019)第 203576 号

书　　名	黄海勇引渡案法理聚焦
主　　编	赵秉志
责任编辑	朱　超
责任监制	王列丹
装帧设计	许文菲
出版发行	江苏人民出版社
出版社地址	南京市湖南路1号A楼,邮编:210009
出版社网址	http://www.jspph.com
照　　排	江苏凤凰制版有限公司
印　　刷	江苏凤凰通达印刷有限公司
开　　本	718毫米×1000毫米　1/16
印　　张	35.75　插页1
字　　数	518千字
版　　次	2019年11月第1版　2019年11月第1次印刷
标准书号	ISBN 978-7-214-16781-1
定　　价	98.00元

(江苏人民出版社图书凡印装错误可向承印厂调换)

关注重大典型案例　促进境外追逃追赃

——《黄海勇引渡案法理聚焦》序言

赵秉志*

作为新中国成立以来最为复杂的引渡案件,黄海勇走私、引渡案得到了我国国家领导人的高度重视和有关方面的不懈关注。从1998年黄海勇出逃到2016年他被引渡回国,对黄海勇追逃历时18年,引渡历时8年,期间历尽曲折,该案不仅穷尽了秘鲁国内的引渡程序,而且被提交到美洲人权委员会和美洲人权法院。该案是美洲人权法院成立以来首次就引渡逃犯案件作出判决,是我国专家证人首次在国际人权法院出庭并首战告捷,也是我国首次从拉美国家成功引渡犯罪嫌疑人。正如我国外交部所言,黄海勇引渡案的成功,将会对我国今后在拉美国家乃至世界范围内的追逃追赃工作产生直接影响,具有重要的标志性意义。党的十八大以来,以习近平同志为核心的党中央高度重视反腐败追逃追赃工作。在党的十九大报告中,习近平总书记明确强调"不管腐败分子逃到哪里,都要缉拿归案、绳之以法",表达了我们党和国家将追逃追赃进行到底的坚强决心和历史担当。在此背景下,系统研究黄海勇引渡案的法理问题和诉讼程序,从中探索和努力揭示我国反腐败追逃追赃相关工作的经验教训,对于推动我国境外追逃追赃法治实践的发展与完善具有重要意义。

北京师范大学刑事法律科学研究院(简称"北师大刑科院")是在教育部

---

* 北京师范大学刑事法律科学研究院教授、法学博士、博士生导师,中国刑法学研究会会长、国际刑法学协会副主席暨中国分会主席,G20反腐败追逃追赃研究中心学术委员会主任暨研究员。

和中央政法领导机关支持下而由北京师范大学重点建设的专门从事刑事法学研究的综合性学术研究机构。北师大刑科院一贯密切关注中国刑事法治建设领域的重大事件,注重研究刑事司法实践中的典型疑难案例。对这些典型疑难案例的深入研究,不仅丰富了我国刑法学研究的内容,促进了刑法学相关理论的发展,而且对于推动我国刑事司法、立法和刑事法治建设的进步起到了积极作用。为了全面、深入研究黄海勇引渡案的相关法理问题,进一步推动我国刑事法学理论研究的深入发展和反腐败追逃追赃实践的开展,在北师大刑科院的支持下,我们决定编辑出版这本《黄海勇引渡案法理聚焦》,并纳入笔者主编的"中国疑难刑事名案法理研究"系列出版。

基于较为全面反映黄海勇引渡案所涉及到的事实、理论和法律问题的考虑,我们将《黄海勇引渡案法理聚焦》一书分为"专题研究"、"百家争鸣"、"媒体报道"、"资料选编"、"判决文书"和"延伸阅读"六个部分,纳入有关文论和资料。

"专题研究"部分收录了笔者和张磊教授(北师大刑科院国际刑法研究所副所长,G20反腐追逃追赃研究中心副主任)合作的"黄海勇引渡案法理问题研究"一文。笔者曾经作为秘鲁政府邀请的3位出庭专家证人之一,到美洲人权法院巡回法庭就黄海勇引渡案出庭作证。本文结合笔者出庭作证的切身经历,在对黄海勇引渡案的基本案情进行梳理的基础上,对于该案在秘鲁国内以及美洲人权委员会、美洲人权法院的诉讼程序进行了详细研究,并对引渡程序中涉及到的法理问题(死刑问题、酷刑问题,境外羁押能否折抵国内刑期问题等)进行了分析和研究,力图较为全面地还原黄海勇引渡案的整个过程,并深入挖掘该案涉及到的法理问题。

"学术争鸣"部分收录了研究黄海勇引渡案的4篇代表性论文。其中,现任中国外交部驻印度尼西亚棉兰总领馆总领事的孙昂先生的《美洲人权法院黄海勇引渡案述评——兼论"外交承诺"的法理和实践》一文,作者结合其本人到美洲人权法院法庭出庭作证的经历,针对黄海勇案件的诉讼程序,特别是其中所涉及的引渡承诺问题进行了详细研究,颇有见地和启迪意义。中国社会科学院国际法研究所柳华文研究员的《美洲人权法院引渡第一案的意义及其启示》一文,对于黄海勇引渡案的意义,美洲人权法院审理黄海勇引渡案中控辩双方的基本观点，以及其中涉及的死刑、酷刑等问题进行研究，并探讨了对我国的相关启示。柳华文研究员也曾经受秘鲁政府的邀请，作为专家证人向美洲人权法院提交了有关中国人权法律保护状况的书面证词，该文的写作以作者参与美洲人权法院庭审书面作证的真实经历为基础，为研究黄海勇引渡案提供了难得的第一手资料，具有重要的学术价值。而以研究国际暨区际刑事司法合作见长的时任最高人民检察院反贪总局检察官（现为中央纪委国家监委研究室副局级纪检监察员）陈雷博士的《引渡在国际追逃追赃中的作用发挥——黄海勇引渡案的启示》一文，以黄海勇引渡案为视角，对于引渡在国际追逃追赃中的作用进行了深入研究；北师大刑科院硕士研究生罗翊乔的《被外交部称为"新中国成立以来最复杂的引渡案"有多复杂？》一文，对于黄海勇在秘鲁的引渡程序进行了详细探究。这两篇专论对于了解和研究黄海勇引渡案也具有参考作用。

近年来，围绕黄海勇引渡案媒体曾进行了广泛的跟踪报道，本书"媒体报道"部分选取其中代表性的 8 篇报道，力图从多个视角展现黄海勇引渡案的全貌。

在美洲人权法院审理黄海勇案件中，笔者与时任中国外交部境外追逃与国际执法合作特别协调员、外交部条约法律司参赞（现任中国外交部驻印度尼西亚棉兰总领馆总领事）孙昂先生曾经受秘鲁政府邀请一起到美洲人权法院出庭作证，中国社会科学院国际法所柳华文研究员也受邀请向法院提交了书面证词。在法庭作证时，笔者和孙昂参赞首先进行了个人陈述，然后依次回答了法庭各方的问题。本书收录了我们二人在美洲人权法庭上的个人陈述和被询问的问题，以及柳华文研究员所提交的书面证词。此外，笔者接到秘鲁政府到美洲人权法院出庭作证的邀请之后，在我国中央纪委、外交部、海关总署等部门的指导下，在本人所在单位几位同事（张磊教授、袁彬教授、何挺副教授）的协助下，为作证进行了充分准备，先后撰写了 20 余万字的准备材料，最后凝练为《赵秉志为赴美洲人权法院就黄海勇案作证所准备的主要材料》，作为笔者到美洲人权法院作证的主要依据，我们也将该资料收入到本书当中。上述资料对于国际社会了解中国的刑事司法制度，以及今后我国专家证人到国际人权法庭作证具有参考价值，因而在"资料精选"

部分我们也将这些材料纳入，以飨读者。

判决文书是研究典型案件最为珍贵的资料，为了全面反映黄海勇案的全貌，本书收录了三个相关的判决书：一是美洲人权法院诉黄海勇案判决书。2015年6月美洲人权法院就黄海勇诉秘鲁政府一案作出有利于中国主张的判决，为顺利引渡黄海勇奠定了坚实基础。本书"判决文书"部分收录了该判决书（英文），对于深度研究和了解黄海勇引渡案乃至美洲人权法院的相关主张与实践都具有参阅价值。二是黄海勇走私普通货物案一审判决书。2019年6月12日，武汉市中级人民法院对于黄海勇走私普通货物案作出一审判决，黄海勇提出上诉后又撤回上诉，判决遂生效。该判决的生效，意味着这起中国最为复杂的引渡案终于落下帷幕，该判决也创制了境外羁押期限折抵国内判决刑期的先例，具有重要意义。三是潘子牛走私普通货物案二审判决书。潘子牛是黄海勇的同案犯，由湖北省高级人民法院于2014年8月作出二审判决，该判决所认定的相关犯罪事实与黄海勇的判决有密切关系，对于理解黄海勇案也极具参考价值，所以也将该判决书收录。

习近平总书记高度重视我国现阶段的反腐败追逃追赃法治工作，近年来围绕反腐败追逃追赃问题发表了一系列重要讲话，提出了一系列新的重要理论、重要论断、重要观点，从而形成了习近平反腐败追逃追赃的思想。而十八大以来，我国反腐败追逃追赃不断取得新成就，开创新局面，根本原因就在于以习近平同志为核心的党中央的坚强领导，就在于习近平总书记关于反腐败追逃追赃思想的科学指导。所以，研究习近平反腐败追逃追赃思想就具有重要的理论和实践意义。在"延伸阅读"部分，收录了笔者和张磊教授新近所撰写的"习近平反腐败追逃追赃思想研究"一文（该文系笔者承担的教育部阐释党的十九大精神专项任务"习近平反腐败追逃追赃思想研究"最终成果），以期对推动我国反腐败追逃追赃理论的研究的有所助益。

黄海勇引渡案涉案金额巨大，追逃历程漫长曲折，历经秘鲁国内司法系统和美洲人权司法机构，是我国国际刑事司法合作中的标志性经典案例。我们希望，通过聚焦本案的法理问题，使社会各界全面了解黄海勇引渡案所涉及到的实体法、程序法、刑事政策、外交理念等问题，从而为推动我国反腐败追逃追赃的全面开展，乃至推进我国刑事法治的发展进程，作出有益的贡献。

最后,我们衷心感谢多位专家学者慷慨同意将他们的论文和文章收入本书,从而增强了本书的理论深度和信息容量。特别感谢孙昂先生、柳华文研究员同意将他们作证的相关资料输入本书,他们的支持极大地提高了本书的价值。我也要诚挚感谢在我参与黄海勇引渡案工作和活动中曾给予我支持和帮助的中央纪委、外交部、海关总署等方面的领导和同志,感谢北师大刑科院的几位年轻同仁的协助,尤其要感谢张磊教授协助我编辑本书所作的贡献。我们还要衷心感谢江苏人民出版社对本书编辑出版的鼎力支持。

2019 年 6 月谨识

目 录
contents

[专题研究]

003〉 黄海勇引渡案法理问题研究　　　　　　　　　　　赵秉志　张　磊

[学术争鸣]

067〉 美洲人权法院黄海勇引渡案述评
　　　——兼论"外交承诺"的法理和实践　　　　　　　　　　孙　昂
100〉 美洲人权法院引渡第一案的意义及其启示　　　　　　　柳华文
116〉 引渡在国际追逃追赃中的作用发挥
　　　——成功引渡黄海勇都有什么启示　　　　　　　　　　陈　雷
122〉 黄海勇引渡案：回顾、探析与启示　　　　　　　　　　罗翊乔

[媒体报道]

151〉 潜逃十八年走私犯罪嫌疑人被成功引渡押解回国　　海关总署网站
153〉 专家：中国从拉美引渡嫌犯对国际追逃有借鉴意义
　　　　　　　　　　　　　　　　　　　　李　晔　陈　敏　王子辰
155〉 我国首次成功从"拉美"引渡嫌犯回国　　　　　　　　蔡岩红
157〉 新中国最复杂的引渡案内幕　　　　　　　　　　　　　刘　星
162〉 北师大教授应秘鲁邀请作证　成功引渡嫌犯　　　　　张恩杰
165〉 中国专家出庭"最复杂引渡案"始末　　　　　　　　　冯　彬
172〉 赵秉志教授出席国际法庭作证的中国逃犯黄海勇引渡案我方获胜
　　　　　　　　　　　　　　　　　　　　　　　　京师刑事法治网
174〉 赵秉志教授等应邀参加"10·7"专案（黄海勇引渡案）引渡工作研
　　　讨会　　　　　　　　　　　　　　　　　　　　京师刑事法治网

[资料精选]

179〉 赵秉志出席美洲人权法院黄海勇引渡案庭审个人陈述及被询问之

问题

185〉赵秉志为赴美洲人权法院就黄海勇案作证所准备的主要材料

230〉孙昂出席美洲人权法院黄海勇引渡案庭审个人陈述及被询问之问题

238〉柳华文就黄海勇引渡案向美洲人权法院提交的书面证词

[判决文书]

271〉INTER-AMERICAN COURT OF HUMAN RIGHTS CASE OF WONG HO WING *V.* PERU JUDGMENT OF JUNE 30 2015*

497〉黄海勇走私普通货物案一审判决书

514〉潘子牛走私普通货物案二审判决书

[延伸阅读]

529〉习近平反腐败追逃追赃思想研究　　　　　　　赵秉志　张　磊

---

* 美洲人权法院黄海勇诉秘鲁案判决书。

专题研究

黄海勇引渡案法理问题研究

赵秉志* 张 磊**

一、概述

（一）为什么要关注黄海勇引渡案

黄海勇，中国重大走私案首犯。曾任深圳裕伟贸易实业有限公司法人代表、深圳市亨润国际实业有限公司董事、总经理，湖北裕伟贸易实业有限公司法人代表、武汉丰润油脂保税仓库有限公司董事长、香港宝润集团有限公司董事。

1996年8月至1998年5月期间，黄海勇伙同他人，利用其经办的多家公司与武汉市对外经济贸易发展公司等多家公司相互勾结、虚构事实，向海关骗领3本《进料加工手册》，逃避海关监管，共同进口保税毛豆油10.74万吨在境内销售牟利，案值12.15亿元，偷逃税款7.17亿元。案发后，黄海勇于1998年8月出逃，先后逃至美国、秘鲁等国。2008年10月，黄海勇在秘鲁被秘鲁警方逮捕，后中国政府向秘鲁政府提出引渡黄海勇的请求。2016年7月17日凌晨，黄海勇自秘鲁被成功押解回国。① 至此，被誉为建国以来最复杂引渡案件的黄海勇引渡案暂告一段落。反思黄海勇引渡案，有以下

---

* 北京师范大学刑事法律科学研究院教授、法学博士、博士生导师，中国刑法学研究会会长、国际刑法学协会副主席暨中国分会主席，G20反腐败追逃追赃研究中心学术委员会主任暨研究员。

** 北京师范大学刑事法律科学研究院教授、法学博士、博士生导师，G20反腐败追逃追赃研究中心副主任暨研究员。

① 《潜逃十八年走私犯罪嫌疑人被成功引渡押解回国》，载 http://www.gov.cn/xinwen/2016—07/18/content_5092299.htm。

理由值得我们关注：

首先，本案走私普通货物涉案金额巨大，犯罪嫌疑人滞留境外时间漫长。黄海勇伙同他人涉嫌走私10.7万吨毛豆油，偷逃税款7.17亿元，涉案金额巨大。他从1998年8月出逃，到2016年7月被引渡回国，在境外滞留18年，引渡他耗时8年（从2008年11月到2016年7月）。在引渡黄海勇的过程中，虽然秘鲁政府一直积极同我国政府开展引渡合作，而且两国之间一直具有良好的外交关系，可为什么双方的引渡程序还耗费将近8年时光？值得我们思考。

其次，美洲人权委员会和美洲人权法院介入了本案。引渡黄海勇，是中国和秘鲁政府之间的国际刑事司法合作，可是案件为什么会被提交到美洲人权委员会，并还要由美洲人权法院审理？以后我国和他国再开展类似的引渡合作案件，是否也有可能被提交到国际人权审判机构（如欧洲人权法院）等？我们应当如何应对？

再次，本案系中国专家证人首次到国际人权法庭出庭作证。在美洲人权法院审理黄海勇引渡案中，秘鲁政府邀请了三位专家证人出庭作证，其中两位证人来自中国。那么在该案中，为什么会邀请中国专家证人出庭作证？专家证人作证的主要内容是什么？以后类似案件是否还会邀请中国专家证人出庭作证？也值得我们关注。

复次，本案对于以后中国境外追逃具有重要的借鉴意义。2014年以来，在以习近平为总书记的党中央的领导下，我国掀起了以"天网行动"为代表的境外追逃追赃风暴，并取得了突出成绩。但是迄今为止，还有一些重要的腐败分子逍遥海外，涉案巨额贪腐资金尚未追回。2016年9月，G20杭州峰会通过了《二十国集团反腐败追逃追赃高级原则》，开创性地提出对外逃腐败人员和外流腐败资产"零容忍"、国际反腐败追逃追赃体系和机制"零漏洞"、各国开展反腐败追逃追赃合作时"零障碍"的概念，在构建国际反腐败新格局目标下发出清脆嘹亮的"中国声音"。① 而2016年9月23日在北京师范大学成立的G20反腐败追逃追赃研究中心，则更是第一个面向G20成

---

① 朱基钗、罗宇凡：《G20杭州峰会帷幕落下 反腐大网正在拉开》，载http://www.sd.chinanews.com/2/2016/0907/23601.html。

员国开展反腐败追逃追赃研究的机构,不仅为G20成员国开展相关合作搭建了平台,将来还会为反腐败国际合作规则的制定提供智力支持。① 在此背景下,作为新中国成立以来最复杂的引渡案和继赖昌星遣返案以后我国反腐败国际刑事司法合作的又一典型案例,黄海勇的成功引渡对于以后中国开展境外追逃具有重要的借鉴意义,值得我们重点研究。

最后,本案也反映了中国刑事法治发展的进程。黄海勇引渡案件的成功,不仅是中秘双方国际刑事司法合作的典范,也是中国近年来刑事法治发展进步的结果,是中国刑事法治建设同国际接轨的结果,是中国刑事法治形象不断完善的结果。对于该案件的研究,有利于进一步推动中国刑事法治建设的发展。

基于上述理由,我们选择黄海勇引渡案作为研究对象,试图理清黄海勇引渡案件的基本程序和所涉及的法律问题,从中总结经验教训,从而推动我国境外追逃追赃的法治实践及其理论研究的进一步开展。

(二)黄海勇引渡案的基本案情

由于黄海勇引渡案件不仅涉及秘鲁国内的刑事司法程序,还涉及美洲人权委员会和美洲人权法院的诉讼程序,所以对于本案的基本案情我们分为以下三个阶段进行阐述:

1. 秘鲁国内司法程序

黄海勇1998年外逃以后,在一段时间内消失在人们的视野当中。2001年6月,我国公安部通过国际刑警组织针对黄海勇发布了红色通缉令。2008年10月,黄海勇在秘鲁被秘鲁警方逮捕,同年11月,我国根据《中华人民共和国和秘鲁共和国引渡条约》向秘鲁提出引渡黄海勇的请求。② 基于中秘双方以往良好的外交与合作关系,并经过中国政府的反复努力,秘鲁政府快速回应我国的引渡请求,并积极配合我国开展双边引渡合作。但是,由于秘鲁已经对于普通犯罪废除了死刑(现在只对战争背景下的叛国罪保留有死

---

① 张磊:《二十国集团反腐败追逃追赃研究中心:为反腐败国际合作提供智力支撑》,载《中国纪检监察报》2016年9月24日。
② 《中国和秘鲁引渡条约》第1条规定:"双方有义务根据本条约的规定,应对方请求,相互引渡在一方境内发现的被另一方通缉的人员,以便对其进行刑事诉讼或者执行刑罚。"

刑),①而且自1970年以来一直未执行过死刑,所以当时秘鲁政府要求我国就黄海勇被引渡回国以后不判处死刑作出承诺。2009年12月,经过我国最高人民法院决定,并由外交部代表中国向秘鲁政府作出了对于黄海勇不判处死刑的外交承诺。2010年1月26日,秘鲁最高法院判决同意引渡黄海勇。黄海勇不甘心被引渡,聘请专业律师,以回国存在所谓死刑和酷刑风险为由抗拒引渡。秘鲁最高法院判决以后,黄海勇及其律师即向秘鲁宪法法院提出违宪法申诉。2011年5月,秘鲁宪法法院认为我外交承诺不充分,要求秘鲁政府停止引渡程序,并推翻了秘鲁最高法院同意引渡黄海勇的判决,引渡被迫中止。秘鲁政府虽然随后向秘鲁宪法法院提出了重新审查的请求,但是此请求被秘鲁宪法法院于2013年3月驳回,维持原判。

2. 美洲人权委员会受理案件

在向秘鲁宪法法院申诉的同时,黄海勇及其律师也以"被引渡回国将会面临死刑,其人权将受侵犯"为由向美洲人权委员会提出申诉。2010年11月1日,美洲人权委员会正式受理"黄海勇诉秘鲁政府"案,并一再向美洲人权法院申请给予黄海勇"人身保护令",阻碍秘鲁政府采取引渡行动。2013年7月,美洲人权委员会作出报告,称秘鲁政府对于黄海勇的超期羁押等措施侵犯了黄的人身权利,有违美洲人权公约。因为中国的死刑酷刑状况令人疑虑,秘鲁政府同意引渡黄海勇的决定过于草率。建议秘鲁政府终止引渡、改变或解除对黄海勇采取的临时羁押措施。

3. 美洲人权法院受理案件

2013年10月30日,美洲人权委员会将此案提交给美洲人权法院进行审理。2014年1月29日,美洲人权法院作出决定,要求秘鲁政府在其作出最后判决之前不得引渡黄海勇。2014年9月3日,美洲人权法院巡回法庭在巴拉圭首都亚松森,借用巴拉圭最高法院开庭审理了"黄海勇诉秘鲁政府"一案。2015年6月,美洲人权法院正式作出判决,判定由于引渡黄海勇回国不存在其被判处死刑和遭受酷刑的风险,所以秘鲁政府可以引渡黄海勇回国。至此,黄海勇引渡案获得重大突破,取得了程序上的最大胜利,奠

---

① 《各国死刑存废盘点:亚洲最多 我国55个死刑罪名》,载 http://mt.sohu.com/20150630/n415902060.shtml。

定引渡法律基础。其后,黄海勇又陆续穷尽了秘鲁国内全部法律救济程序,于 2016 年 7 月 17 日被引渡回中国。

(三)黄海勇引渡案件引发的法理问题

关于黄海勇引渡案,主要存在以下几个法理问题:

1. 黄海勇回国为什么采取的是引渡,而不是其他追逃措施?当前我国境外追逃有多种措施,我们为什么采取引渡,而没有采取其他措施?中国和秘鲁之间开展引渡的法律依据是什么?

2. 美洲人权法院和美洲人权法庭为什么会介入到黄海勇案件当中?以往我国境外追逃案件都是国与国之间的刑事司法合作,黄海勇引渡案为什么会涉及美洲人权委员会和美洲人权法庭?这两个机构的性质和功能是什么?

3. 美洲人权法院的专家证人作证制度是怎样的?为什么黄海勇引渡案会有中国专家证人出庭作证?美洲人权法院专家证人作证制度是怎样的?我国专家证人作证的主要内容是什么,在黄海勇引渡案件中发挥了什么作用?

4. 黄海勇的引渡程序是怎样的?作为新中国成立以来最复杂的引渡案,黄海勇案件的引渡程序到底是怎样的?到底经历了怎样的曲折程序?我国政府又是怎样一步步取得引渡程序的胜利的?

5. 黄海勇在境外的羁押能否折抵国内刑期?从 2008 年被秘鲁政府逮捕之后到被引渡回国,黄海勇特被秘鲁政府羁押了 8 年,那么这 8 年羁押期限是否能够在中国法院对于黄海勇判决的刑期中予以折抵?

6. 从黄海勇引渡案中,我们应当吸取的经验教训是什么?研究已经发生的典型案例,是为了更好地警戒未来。黄海勇引渡案是我国最为复杂的引渡案件,具有重大影响,其中既有值得我们反思的教训,更有许多值得我们总结的经验。

二、对黄海勇为什么要采取引渡措施

党的十八大以来,以习近平同志为核心的党中央展开了前所未有的反腐败高潮,其中尤其要求各有关部门要加大反腐败国际追逃追赃力度,不能让境外、国外成为一些腐败分子的"避罪天堂",腐败分子即使逃到天涯海角,也要把他们追回来绳之以法。特别是进入2014年以来,在党中央的领导下,我国也掀起了前所未有的境外追逃追赃风暴:①2014年1月15日,中央纪委第三次全体会议为"反腐败国际合作"作出部署,提出将加大国际追逃追赃力度,决不让腐败分子逍遥法外;2014年7月22日,公安部部署代号为"猎狐2014"的行动,集中开展缉捕在逃境外经济犯罪嫌疑人专项行动,后来延长为"猎狐2015""猎狐2016""猎狐2017"行动;2014年10月10日,中央反腐败协调小组国际追逃追赃工作办公室亮相,标志着我国纪检、政法、金融、外交等八个部门将联手追逃追赃,建立集中统一、高效顺畅的追逃追赃协调运作机制;2015年3月26日,中央反腐败协调小组国际追逃追赃工作办公室决定启动"天网"行动,要求有关部门将从2015年4月开始,综合运用警务、检务、外交、金融等手段,集中时间、集中力量"抓捕一批腐败分子,清理一批违规证照,打击一批地下钱庄,追缴一批涉案资产,劝返一批外逃人员"。② 这些专项行动取得了突出的成绩,截止到2017年8月31日,我国通过"天网行动"先后从90多个国家和地区追回外逃人员3 339人,其中国家工作人员628人,追回赃款人民币93.6亿元。③

总结我国以往的境外追逃措施,主要有引渡、非法移民遣返、异地追诉和劝返,④其中后三者也被称为引渡的替代措施。虽然引渡是出现最早的追逃措施,但是由于引渡面临着诸多限制,迄今为止我们境外追逃的成功案例多是通过非法移民遣返、异地追诉和劝返所取得,引渡回国的成功案例鲜见。如我们通过非法移民遣返程序追回了赖昌星、⑤邓心志、崔自

---

① 张磊:《腐败犯罪境外追逃追赃的反思与对策》,载《当代法学》2015年第3期。
② 《国际追逃追赃启动"天网"行动 集中力量抓捕腐败分子》,http://legal.people.com.cn/n/2015/0326/c188502—26756067.html。
③ 《追逃3 339人追赃93.6亿"百名红通"已有46人到案》,载 http://www.ccdi.gov.cn/xwtt/201709/t20170930_108299.html。
④ 黄风:《境外追逃的四大路径》,载《人民论坛》2011年11月刊。
⑤ 赖昌星是新中国成立以来涉案金额最大的经济犯罪分子,赖昌星遣返案是我国反腐败国际刑事司法合作的成功范例。赖昌星于1999年8月携家人出逃加拿大,经过中加双方的共同努力,赖昌星于2011年7月23日被遣返回国。

力、①曾汉林、②通过异地追诉追回了余振东、③通过劝返追回了胡星、④高山。⑤ 特别是劝返,在境外追逃中发挥了越来越重要的作用。来自最高人民检察院反贪污贿赂总局的数据显示,2013 年我国检察机关从境外追捕归案 16 名贪污贿赂犯罪嫌疑人中,有 12 人系经劝返主动回国投案自首的。⑥ 而在公安部"猎狐 2014"行动中,截至该年度 10 月 29 日从境外缉捕的 180 名在逃经济犯罪嫌疑人中,有 76 名是被劝返的,占总数的 42.2%。⑦ 国际刑警组织中国国家中心局于 2016 年 4 月 22 日集中公布的 100 名红色通缉令人员名单中到案的主要方式是劝返、缉拿、遣返等方式,⑧并没有一名"百名红通"人员是被引渡回来的。那么在开展引渡存在诸多障碍,我国当下的主要追逃措施并非引渡的前提下,为什么针对黄海勇采取了引渡措施?这就值得我们关注和总结。我们认为,黄海勇案件之所以采取引渡途径,主要是基于以下几点原因:

（一）中秘双方具有开展引渡的法律依据

当前,我国境外追逃之所以很少采取引渡,是因为中国与外逃人员的主要目的地国美国、加拿大、澳大利亚等都还没有签署双边引渡条约(中国和

---

① 2003 年邓心志、崔自力涉嫌合同诈骗罪潜逃到加拿大,后二人的难民申请先后被加拿大方面否决。邓心志于 2008 年 8 月 22 日被遣返回国,是首个从加拿大被遣返的经济犯罪嫌疑人。崔自力于 2010 年 1 月 13 日被遣返回国。

② 1997 年 10 月至 1998 年 8 月,曾汉林涉嫌重大合同诈骗犯罪,并于案发前潜逃至加拿大。曾汉林潜逃后,我国公安机关坚持不懈地对其开展境外追逃工作,迅速向加方提出缉捕、遣返请求,并及时提供曾汉林涉嫌犯罪的相关证据材料。2011 年 2 月 17 日,曾汉林非法移民诉讼审理终结并被加拿大遣返回国。参见邹伟:《经济案疑犯曾汉林潜逃加拿大 12 年被遣返回国》,载 http://news.sina.com.cn/c/2011—02—18/190721977702.shtml.

③ 2001 年 10 月,涉嫌挪用巨额资金的中国银行开平支行行长余振东潜逃境外。2002 年 12 月,余振东在洛杉矶被美方执法人员拘押,2004 年 2 月因非法入境、非法移民及洗钱三项罪名被美法院判处 144 个月监禁。根据余振东与美方达成的辩诉交易协议,美国政府把余振东遣送回中国以前,应从中国政府得到关于余振东在中国起诉和监禁的相应保证,即:假如余振东在中国被起诉的话,应当被判处不超过 12 年刑期的有期徒刑,并不得对余进行刑讯逼供和判处死刑。2004 年 4 月 16 日,美方将余振东驱逐出境并押送至中国。这是第一个由美方正式押送移交中方的外逃经济犯罪嫌疑人。2006 年 3 月 31 日,江门市中级人民法院以贪污罪、挪用公款罪判处余振东有期徒刑 12 年,并处没收其个人财产 100 万元。

④ 胡星是原云南省交通厅副厅长,涉嫌受贿,案发后于 2007 年 1 月 19 日潜逃国外,2 月 18 日被劝返回国。

⑤ 高山是原中国银行哈尔滨河松街支行行长,在伙同商人李东哲骗取客户巨额存款后,于 2004 年 12 月 30 日出逃加拿大。2012 年 8 月,经过中加双方的共同努力,高山自愿回国自首。

⑥ 常红:《我国过去 5 年抓获 6694 名外逃贪污贿赂嫌犯》,载 http://news.sina.com.cn/c/2014—10—29/112931063085.shtml.

⑦ 《公安部"猎狐"百天:180 人落网》,载 http://news.xinhuanet.com/yzyd/local/20141103/c_1113095006.htm

⑧ 《"百名红通人员"30 人到案 都是怎么追回来的》,载 http://www.lawtv.com.cn/jujxw/guonei/2016—06—26/64071.html.

澳大利亚虽然2007年9月已经签署引渡条约,但是尚未生效),而这些国家又都坚持(或者在一定程度上坚持)条约前置主义,即以双边条约关系作为开展引渡合作的前提条件,所以中国和这些国家间很难顺利开展引渡合作。但是这种障碍在中国和秘鲁之间并不存在,中秘两国之间于2001年10月5日就签署了双边引渡条约,该条约第1条之规定,双方有义务根据本条约的规定开展引渡合作。在此前提之下,我国在2008年11月向秘鲁方面提出引渡黄海勇的请求,可谓于法有据,名正言顺,并且得到秘鲁方面的积极回应与配合。

除了中国和秘鲁之间的双边条约之外,两国相关的国内法也是双方合作的重要依据。同时,由于该案又被黄海勇方面提交给美洲人权委员会和美洲人权法院,所以本案引渡的法律依据除了中秘《引渡条约》、中秘国内法之外,本案引渡的依据还有美洲人权委员会和美洲人权法院的相关程序性规定。

1. 中秘《引渡条约》

中国与秘鲁于2001年11月5日签订了《引渡条约》(2003年4月5日生效,共计22条)。该条约主要规定了可以引渡的罪行,应当或者可以拒绝引渡的理由,引渡的国内法条件,提出引渡申请的条件和要求,引渡申请的程序、通讯和信息渠道等内容。结合黄海勇案,中秘引渡条约中有以下内容需要特别关注:(1)中秘双方具有根据对方请求开展引渡合作的义务,这是双方围绕黄海勇案件开展引渡合作的前提。中秘引渡条约在第1条就明确规定双方有"根据对方要求引渡境内所有人员,从而对其采取刑事程序或执行判决"的义务。在黄海勇被秘鲁逮捕之后,选择何种途径将黄海勇带回中国是双方必须作出的重要选择,正因为有了中秘引渡条约的存在,双方才得以围绕本案开展引渡合作,如果没有中秘引渡条约,也许采取的将是其他途径。① (2)中秘双边引渡条约没有明确规定被请求引渡罪行涉及死刑问题时应该如何处理。本案中,死刑问题是黄海勇能否被顺利引渡的关键,也是黄海勇方面赖以对抗引渡的主要凭借,更是秘鲁司法机关、美洲人权委

---

① 当前公认的追逃途径除了引渡之外,还有非法移民遣返、异地追诉和劝返。参见黄风:《境外追逃的四大路径》,载《人民论坛》2011年11月刊。

员会和美洲人权法院关注的重点问题之一,所以判决书中专门提出双边条约中关于死刑问题的规定,为下文围绕死刑问题展开的诉讼程序奠定基础。

2. 中国和秘鲁国内法的相关规定

引渡分为主动引渡和被动引渡。主动引渡,也称为请求引渡或者从外引渡,是指一国请求将犯罪嫌疑人、被告人或被判刑人引渡回国的活动,是请求国的行为。被动引渡也称为被请求引渡或者向外引渡,指一国向请求国引渡犯罪嫌疑人、被告人或被判刑人的活动,是被请求国的行为。① 在各国国内法关于引渡程序的规定中,一般都包括了主动引渡程序和被动引渡程序,以调整本国分别作为请求国和被请求国与他国所开展的引渡活动。在中秘双方围绕黄海勇案件所开展的引渡程序中,中国是请求国,秘鲁是被请求国,双方的引渡合作,就要依据中国法律中的主动引渡程序和秘鲁法律的被动引渡程序展开。因此,除了双边引渡条约之外,两国国内法律中关于引渡程序的规定也是双方开展引渡合作的法律依据。

第一,中国的主动引渡程序

中国的引渡程序主要由《中华人民共和国引渡法》(以下简称《引渡法》)所调整,该法共计 55 条,分为四章,除了第一章总则和第四章附则以外,第二章"向中华人民共和国请求引渡"(调整被动引渡程序)和第三章"向外国请求引渡"(调整主动引渡程序)是其主要内容。在本案中,中国主要适用的是第三章的相关内容,该章共计五条(第 47—51 条),主要规定向外国提起引渡的国内程序,紧急情况下在提起引渡请求前请求外国先行羁押,引渡请求所需要的文书材料,引渡中的追诉承诺和量刑承诺,被请求引渡人和相关财物的接收等问题。

中国《引渡法》第 47 条具体规定了向外国提出引渡请求的一般程序:"请求外国准予引渡或者引渡过境的,应当由负责办理有关案件的省、自治区或者直辖市的审判、检察、公安、国家安全或者监狱管理机关分别向最高人民

---

① 黄风:《国际刑事司法合作的规则与实践》,北京大学出版社 2008 年版,第 19 页。

法院、最高人民检察院、公安部、国家安全部、司法部提出意见书,并附有关文件和材料及其经证明无误的译文。最高人民法院、最高人民检察院、公安部、国家安全部、司法部分别会同外交部审核同意后,通过外交部向外国提出请求。"根据该条之规定并结合中国实践,中国向外国提出引渡程序基本流程如下:(1) 具体办理案件的地市一级审判、检察、公安、国家安全或者监狱管理机关(建议引渡机关)向省、自治区、直辖市一级相应机关建议引渡;(2) 省、自治区、直辖市一级机关(提议引渡机关)就下一级机关提出的引渡建议经过审核后向中央相应机关提议引渡(或者就自己负责办理的需要引渡的案件直接向中央相应机关提议引渡);(3) 中央相应机关(申请引渡机关)就省、自治区、直辖市相应一级机关的引渡提议审核后向外交部提出申请(或者就其负责办理的需要引渡的案件直接向外交部提出申请);(4) 外交部(提出引渡机关)接到中央机关的引渡请求后报国务院批准;(5) 国务院(批准引渡机关)批准后,由外交部向被请求国提出引渡请求;(6) 外交部向驻被请求国的使馆转递引渡请求并发出有关指示;(7) 中国(请求国)驻被请求国的使馆向驻在国外交部提交引渡请求。

在本案中,负责办理案件的是武汉海关缉私局,由于其直接受中国海关总署缉私局(中国公安部第 24 局)的垂直领导,所以由该局(提议引渡机关)直接向公安部提出引渡请求,①公安部(申请引渡机关)经过审核之后向外交部提出引渡申请,由外交部(提出引渡机关)在报请国务院(批准引渡机关)批准后向秘鲁提出引渡请求。②

第二,秘鲁的被动引渡程序

秘鲁的引渡程序主要由秘鲁《宪法》、秘鲁《刑事诉讼法》等法律规定。在引渡黄海勇过程中,主要障碍并且耗时最长的是秘鲁的被动引渡程序。结合黄海勇案件,该程序程序有以下特点值得注意:

(1) 秘鲁的被动引渡程序是混合程序,包括司法程序和政治程序(politi-

---

① 在我国,海关缉私局是海关机构的重要组成部分,也是公安机关的一个组成部分,是走私犯罪的侦查机关,同时接受海关和公安机关的领导。
② 严格来说,中国国内的主动引渡程序也是黄海勇引渡程序的重要组成部分,应当是本文的研究对象,但是由于笔者研究资料欠缺,所以本文着重对于中国主动引渡程序的法律规定进行论述,实际操作也应当是严格依法进行的。

cal stage)两个阶段。秘鲁《宪法》(2009 年 9 月秘鲁宪法法院颁布)第 37 条规定:"只能由行政部门在得到最高法院同意后,按照法律和国际条约规定及对等原则进行引渡。"①所以,秘鲁的被动引渡首先由秘鲁最高法院作出决定,然后再由秘鲁政府作出决定,只有在两者都同意的前提下,才能成功引渡。

(2) 引渡合作必须坚持双重犯罪原则和可引渡犯罪原则。双重犯罪原则(double criminality)和可引渡犯罪(extradition offence)原则是各国开展引渡合作的两个重要原则。前者要求引渡请求所指行为依照请求国和被请求国法律均构成犯罪,②后者要求引渡所涉及的犯罪必须是可引渡的犯罪,即引渡的犯罪应当达到一定的严重程度(被判处一定刑罚),从而值得对其开展引渡合作。③ 秘鲁《刑事诉讼法》也就引渡的双重犯罪原则和可引渡的犯罪进行了规定:"引渡申请基于的事实在申请引渡国和秘鲁均不构成犯罪,或者依据两国法律规定,不应当判处最高 1 年或者 1 年以上徒刑的,则对引渡申请予以拒绝。"④根据该规定,请求国提起引渡所涉嫌的犯罪必须在请求国和秘鲁均构成犯罪,并且至少都应判处一年以上徒刑,否则应当拒绝引渡。

(3) 对于可能被判处死刑的犯罪,在请求国做出不判处死刑的保证之前,应当拒绝引渡。死刑不引渡原则是当前国际社会开展引渡合作时所坚持的一项基本原则,该原则要求对于被引渡人可能判处或者执行死刑情况下拒绝引渡。所以,如果被请求引渡人在请求国可能被判处死刑,在请求国做出不判处死刑的保证之前,秘鲁应当拒绝引渡。对此,秘鲁《刑事诉讼法》也进行了明确规定:被请求引渡人在请求引渡国可能被判处死刑,并且请求国未提供不对其判处死刑承诺的情况下,应当拒绝引渡。⑤

---

① 《世界各国宪法》编辑委员会编译:《世界各国宪法(美洲大洋洲卷)》,中国检察出版社 2012 年版,第 223 页。
② 黄风:《国际刑事司法合作的规则与实践》,北京大学出版社 2008 年版,第 7 页。
③ 黄风:《国际刑事司法合作的规则与实践》,北京大学出版社 2008 年版,第 9 页。
④ 秘鲁《刑事诉讼法》第 517 条第 1 款。参见,《世界各国刑事诉讼法》编辑委员会编译:《世界各国刑事诉讼法(美洲卷)》,中国检察出版社 2016 年版,第 173 页。
⑤ 秘鲁《刑事诉讼法》第 517 条第 3 款。参见,《世界各国刑事诉讼法》编辑委员会编译:《世界各国刑事诉讼法(美洲卷)》,中国检察出版社 2016 年版,第 173 页。

3. 美洲人权委员会和美洲人权法院的相关程序规定

美洲人权委员会和美洲人权法院是根据《美洲人权公约》所建立的美洲人权体系的组成部分,两者构成了美洲国家组织最重要的区域性人权保障机制。① 本案中,黄海勇及其律师于 2009 年 3 月 27 日向美洲人权委员会提出申诉。美洲人权委员会经过审查后,于 2010 年 11 月通过 151/102 号受理报告受理了黄海勇诉秘鲁政府案。2013 年 10 月 30 日,美洲人权委员会将该案件提交给美洲人权法院,要求美洲人权法院对该报告中所提到的侵权情况进行审查,明确秘鲁政府所应承担的法律责任,并命令秘鲁政府执行该报告中的建议。② 所以,本案在被提交给美洲人权法院之后,将由该法院居中审判,美洲人权委员会(作为黄海勇的代表)及黄海勇作为原告一方,而秘鲁政府作为被告一方,这是本案当事各方的基本利益框架。

(二)难以实施其他追逃措施

1. 难以进行劝返

劝返是在逃犯发现地国家司法执法机关的配合下,通过发挥法律的震慑力和政策的感召力,促使外逃人员主动回国接受处理的一种措施,③ 具有追逃国的主导作用、国家强制力为后盾、程序的多样性以及缉拿方式的软柔性、有效性和及时性等特点,劝返强调通过对犯罪嫌疑人说服教育,晓之以理,动之以情,摆明利害关系,促使其心理上发生转变,心悦诚服地随办案人员回国,整个过程没有任何强硬色彩,完全出于犯罪嫌疑人自愿。④ 而在黄海勇案件中,黄海勇一直通过各种措施和我国对抗,抗拒被引渡回国。在此前提之下,他显然不会接受劝返回国自首。而且,黄海勇在被秘鲁方面逮捕之后进行羁押,我方并没有太多机会接触黄海勇并对其进行劝说,更降低了劝返的可能性。

2. 没有必要采取非法移民遣返和异地追诉

作为引渡的替代措施,非法移民遣返(也被称为移民法的替代措施)指

---

① 关于美洲人权委员会和美洲人权法院的详细情况,我们将在下文详述。
② 美洲人权法院判决书第 4 段。
③ 《"百名红通人员"30 人到案 都是怎么追回来的》,载 http://www.lawtv.com.cn/jujxw/guonei/2016—06—26/64071.html。
④ 张磊:《从胡星案看劝返》,载《国家检察官学院学报》2011 年第 2 期。

将不具有合法居留身份的外国入境者遣送回国,是遣返国为维护本国安全和秩序而单方面做出的决定。① 异地追诉(也被称为刑事法的替代措施)指在难以开展引渡合作的情况下,协助逃犯发现地国依其本国法律对逃犯提起诉讼的特殊的国际司法合作形式。② 两者都是双方在无法诉诸正式的引渡程序或者引渡遇到不可逾越的法律障碍的情况下采取的替代性措施。黄海勇案件中,一方面,中秘双方已经启动引渡合作,秘鲁方面积极配合中方引渡请求,所以没有必要再采取其他引渡替代措施;另一方面,不论非法移民遣返,还是异地追诉,都需要秘鲁方面启动相应的非法移民程序,或者是刑事诉讼程序,需要中方向秘方提供大量证据,在中方没有向秘方提供这些证据的前提下,秘方也难以启动相应程序。

综上,我国当前境外追逃很少采取引渡措施的主要原因是引渡存在法律上的困难,或者犯罪嫌疑人经过劝说愿意投案自首而没有必要再进行引渡。而在黄海勇案件中,一方面引渡不存在法律上的障碍,另一方面劝返、非法移民遣返、异地追诉并不现实或者不可能,所以采取引渡是最为有效也是最为现实的措施。

三、黄海勇案在秘鲁的诉讼程序及分析

黄海勇在 1996 年 8 月至 1998 年 5 月在中国实施了严重的走私罪行后潜逃境外,2001 年 6 月,中国通过国际刑警组织的红色通缉令对于黄海勇进行全球通缉。2008 年 10 月 27 日上午,黄海勇从美国入境秘鲁,在秘鲁利马市的"豪尔赫·查韦斯国际机场(Jorge Chávez International Airport)"被捕,后秘鲁警方将其移交给秘鲁卡亚俄常设刑事法院(Permanent Criminal Court of El Callao)管辖,黄海勇被关押在秘鲁卡亚俄临时监狱。

秘鲁《刑事诉讼法》中针对外国当局指控人员的羁押规定了"临时逮捕或预引渡"的强制措施。根据该规定,临时逮捕主要是针对两类人员适用:一是相关国家中央机关正式提出引渡申请的人员;二是被他国追捕而试图

---

① 赵秉志、张磊:《赖昌星案件法理问题研究》,载《政法论坛》2014 年第 4 期。
② 黄风著:《引渡问题研究》,中国政法大学出版社 2006 年版,第 120 页。

进入本国的被请求引渡人。正式的逮捕请求都应当提交给国家检察长办公室,由其立即转交具有管辖权的预审法官,同时通知相应的省检察院。只要被指控的犯罪事实在秘鲁也可能构成犯罪,并且会被判处 1 年以上的监禁,就可以签发临时逮捕令。一旦执行临时逮捕,预审法官应当在 24 小时内听取被捕人员的陈述,如果被捕人员未委托可以信任的律师,还可以为其指定官方的辩护律师。① 另外,中秘《引渡条约》对此也进行了规定:"在紧急情况下,在提交引渡请求之前,请求方可以请求羁押被指控的人员"。② 黄海勇就是根据该临时逮捕制度而被羁押,并由此开始了长达八年的引渡程序。下文笔者将以美洲人权法院黄海勇诉秘鲁案判决书(INTER-AMERICAN COURT OF HUMAN RIGHTS CASE OF WONG HO WING V. PERU JUDGMENT OF JUNE 30,2015,以下简称"判决书")③中所描述的关于黄海勇的引渡程序为主要依据,④对于黄海勇在秘鲁,以及在美洲人权委员会和美洲人权法院的诉讼程序进行研究。本部分将黄海勇在秘鲁的引渡程序分成五个阶段分别进行分析:

(一)自黄海勇被逮捕到秘鲁最高法院做出第一次判决(2008 年 10 月至 2009 年 1 月)

1. 黄海勇被逮捕后的各方反应

(1)基本程序。⑤

黄海勇被秘鲁警方逮捕之后,黄海勇方面和中国方面都及时做出了反应:

---

① 秘鲁《刑事诉讼法》第 523 条,参见《世界各国刑事诉讼法》编辑委员会编译:《世界各国刑事诉讼法(美洲卷)》,中国检察出版社 2016 年版,第 175 页。
② 中秘《引渡条约》第 9 条。
③ 美洲人权法院判决书分为十三个部分:案情介绍与争议情况;法院程序;权力;初步反对意见;临时措施;前期考虑;证据;证明的事实;生命、人身安全权利以及与保障权利的义务有关的不遣返原则;与尊重和确保权利义务有关的司法保护和司法担保权;与尊重和保障权利的义务有关的人身自由和人身安全权利;赔偿;判决结果。
④ 严格意义上来说,黄海勇的引渡程序从 2008 年 11 月黄海勇被秘鲁警方逮捕开始,一直到 2016 年 7 月黄海勇被引渡回国为止,前后历时近 8 年时间。但是由于本文以美洲人权法院黄海勇诉秘鲁案美洲人权法院判决书中所描述的引渡程序为研究对象,所以本文针对的引渡程序是从 2008 年 11 月到 2015 年 6 月美洲人权法院作出判决的将近 7 年时间。2015 年 6 月以后到 2016 年 7 月 1 多的时间里,黄海勇又陆续穷尽了秘鲁国内的救济程序,但是由于相关资料欠缺,所以本文从略。
⑤ 美洲人权法院判决书第 60—63 段。

第一,黄海勇方面。在黄海勇被逮捕的第二天即 2008 年 10 月 28 日,卡亚俄刑事法庭对于黄海勇案进行了预审,黄海勇则在律师的陪同下发表声明,声称如果因为被指控的罪行被遣返回中国,他将有可能被执行或适用死刑,所以要求秘鲁当局给予其特殊待遇,以保障其人权,并且要求在秘鲁接受审判。2008 年 12 月 10 日,在卡亚俄刑事法庭举行的公开听证会上,黄海勇及其律师再次提出,本案适用的条款是规定了死刑的中国刑法第 151 条,①也就是说黄海勇被遣返回国以后有可能被判处死刑。

第二,中国方面。在黄海勇被秘鲁警方逮捕的 5 天后即 2008 年 11 月 3 日,中国公安部第 24 局根据中秘《引渡条约》以黄海勇涉嫌违反中国《刑法》第 153、154、191、389 和 390 条,构成走私普通货物罪、洗钱罪和行贿罪为由,②向秘鲁方面提出引渡黄海勇的请求,同时要求秘鲁当局采取必要的措施,确保继续羁押黄海勇,以便于此后开展引渡程序。该引渡请求还指出黄海勇涉案金额超过 7.17 亿元人民币,并且其中的 404.8 万美元已经被从中国转出,同时还附上了中国《刑法》的相关法条规定、批准逮捕书以及逮捕证等内容。但是判决书也明确指出,在中国的提出引渡请求及其附件中,并不包括中国《刑法》第 151 条规定的内容,根据该条之规定,黄海勇所涉嫌的走私普通货物罪可能被判处死刑。

(2) 法理评析。

黄海勇被逮捕之后双方的反应具有以下特点:

第一,在反应时间上。双方都较为迅速,说明之前都作了充分的准备。特别是黄海勇及其律师,在黄海勇被逮捕第二天的听证会上即明确发出声明,对抗引渡。而中方则在黄海勇被捕的 5 天后即向秘鲁方面提出了引渡请求。虽然中方反应的时间略晚于黄海勇方面,但是考虑到消息的传递、时差、各机关协调配合,准备引渡材料等都需要时间,所以能够在 5 天之后即将

---

① 当时的中国《刑法》第 153 条规定,走私普通货物、物品行为情节特别严重的,根据刑法第 151 条第 4 款的规定处罚。第 151 条第 4 款针对该条第 1、2 款规定的犯罪规定了无期徒刑或者死刑,并没收财产。所以,根据当时的中国《刑法》,走私普通货物、物品罪是可以判处死刑的。只不过该条的死刑由第 153 和 151 条共同规定。

② 中国《刑法》第 153 和 154 条,是关于走私普通货物、物品罪的规定,第 191 条是关于洗钱罪的规定,第 389 和 390 条是关于行贿罪的规定。

引渡材料准备妥当并提交给秘鲁方面,已经难能可贵。

第二,在声明的内容上。黄海勇方面在第一次声明中就直接抛出死刑问题作为自己的救命稻草,以回国后将有可能被执行或适用死刑为由对抗引渡。不仅如此,在一个月后的引渡听证会上再次明确提出本案所适用的条款是中国《刑法》第151条,这说明其不仅有所准备,而且较为准确地把握住对抗引渡的关键点。在此后的几年中,黄海勇方面就紧紧抓住死刑问题,为双方引渡合作造成了巨大麻烦,大大延缓了引渡程序的进程。相比之下,中方虽然也按照双边条约的要求提交了引渡材料,附上了相关刑法条文的内容和诉讼文书的复印件,但并没有提交关于走私普通货物罪可能被判处死刑的中国《刑法》第151条的法律条文。而正是这一点,不仅被判决书明确指出中方提交材料缺少关键性条文,而且(如后所述)也被黄海勇方面作为攻击我方的理由。

2. 秘鲁最高法院的第一次判决

(1) 基本程序。①

2009年1月6日,本案被提交到秘鲁最高法院。2009年1月19日,秘鲁最高法院第二临时刑事法庭就黄海勇引渡案举行了听证会。在听证会上,黄海勇方面和中方围绕死刑问题再次展开了交锋:

第一,中国方面对黄海勇涉嫌的犯罪事实作出进一步的解释。在听证会的当天,法庭收到了中国武汉海关缉私局提交的报告,该报告针对黄海勇在中国所涉嫌的犯罪事实作了进一步解释,指出黄海勇是和他人一同犯罪,并提出了其他同案犯所适用的刑法条文。但判决书还是明确指出,中国武汉海关的报告依然没有提到该罪行可能适用死刑的问题。

第二,黄海勇方面提交了中国《刑法》第151条和第153条的译文。在听证会,黄海勇的律师提交了书面辩词和中国《刑法》第151和153条的译文,并向法庭说明,根据中国《刑法》这两条的规定,涉案金额"超过50万元(如本案)的走私罪",应当根据该法第151条第4段规定予以处罚,而且"情节十分严重的,将被处以无期徒刑或者死刑"。

---

① 美洲人权法院判决书第63—64段。

2009年1月20日,秘鲁最高法院第二临时刑事法庭做出本案引渡程序中首次咨询判决(first advisory decision),主要包括以下内容:

第一,中国针对黄海勇以逃避关税罪(the offenses of evasion of customs,在中国《刑法》中被称为走私普通货物罪)和行贿罪提出引渡请求是正确的,这符合两国之间《引渡条约》的规定,同时指出,对于逃避关税罪,引渡仅适用于"中国《刑法》第153条第一段规定"(for the criminal offense established in the first paragraph of article 153 of the Chinese Criminal Code.)的情况下。

第二,中国针对黄海勇以洗钱罪提出引渡是不当的,因为秘鲁刑法中并不存在洗钱罪,这不符合秘鲁引渡所遵循的双重犯罪原则。

(2)法理评析。

本阶段中,黄海勇方面和中方在听证会上分别进一步提出自己的主张,秘鲁最高法院在此基础上作出了判决,本阶段有以下特点:

第一,黄海勇方面在之前抛出死刑问题并向法庭指出本案适用中国《刑法》第151条的基础上,本阶段直接向法庭提交了该条文的译文(也就是走私普通货物罪可能被判处死刑的依据),用于证明自己前述的可能被判处死刑的危险。客观来说,黄海勇方面不仅抓住了本案引渡问题的要害,而且一再提交和补充相应的证明材料及其译文,紧紧揪住死刑问题不放,用于支持自己的论点,抗拒引渡。而对比之下,中方在此阶段虽然进一步解释了黄海勇是共同犯罪,其同案犯可能适用的刑法条款,说明黄海勇回国后可能被判处的刑罚,但还是没有针对本案的死刑问题进行直接回应。法庭判决书显然也注意到这一点,明确指出中国武汉海关的报告依然没有提到该罪行可能适用死刑的问题。

第二,秘鲁最高法院的首次咨询判决对于中国的引渡请求进行了评价,在肯定中方以逃避关税罪和行贿罪提出引渡请求的基础下,将围绕走私普通货物罪的引渡限制在不判处死刑的前提下,同时以双重犯罪原则否定了中方就洗钱罪提出的引渡请求。应当说,严格依照中国和秘鲁的法律规定,秘鲁最高法院的该判决是比较客观的。因为当时的中国《刑法》的确针对走私普通货物罪规定了死刑,而且如果秘鲁刑法中没有规定洗钱罪的话,以洗钱罪为由向秘鲁方面提交引渡请求就有违背引渡的双重犯罪原则之嫌。

(二) 从秘鲁最高法院第一次判决到其第二次判决(2009年1月至2010年1月)

1. 秘鲁最高法院的第一次判决后双方反应

(1) 基本程序。①

在秘鲁最高法院作出第一次咨询判决不到一周后,即2009年1月26日,黄海勇的兄弟就以"存在侵犯黄海勇生命和人身安全的某种迫在眉睫的威胁"为由,针对秘鲁最高法院第二临时法庭的法官提出第一次人身保护请求,并要求释放黄海勇。其提出请求的主要依据仍然是死刑问题,并明确指出中国"出于恶意,引渡请求没有附上规定了死刑的 中国《刑法》第151条对应的译文"。另外,他还请求释放黄海勇。

2009年2月2日,中方向秘鲁司法部引渡和被判刑人员移交官方委员会(Official Commission for Extraditions and Prisoner Transfers of the Ministry of Justice) 提交了中国公安部的一份说明(第一次外交照会),明确指出:根据请求引渡黄海勇所涉及犯罪的性质和中国《刑法》的规定,不存在对黄海勇判处无期徒刑或死刑的可能,中国将依据法律以及中秘《引渡条约》对黄海勇追究刑事责任。

2009年2月12日,秘鲁利马第56刑事法庭签发命令,要求在针对黄海勇方面提出的人身保护令的程序作出结论之前,暂时中止引渡程序。但是该命令在2009年4月24日被秘鲁利马高等法院刑事法庭以人身保护令程序中没有关于中止引渡程序的规定为由予以撤销。

2009年2月19日,秘鲁司法部被判刑人员引渡和移交官方委员会对引渡请求出具报告指出:"未收到中国《刑法》第151条的译文,根据资料的译文,第153条第1段提到了该条"。根据以上内容认为,需要"获取译文"。2009年2月24日,中国驻秘鲁大使馆向秘鲁利马第56刑事法庭提交了中国《刑法》第151、153、154、191、389和390条的译文。

2009年4月2日,秘鲁利马第56刑事法庭作出判决,包括以下内容:第一,黄海勇方面提出的人身保护请求成立,但是驳回了释放黄海勇的请求;

---

① 美洲人权法院判决书第65—71段。

第二,以"不具有足够依据"为由宣布秘鲁最高法院于2009年1月20日的咨询判决无效,即认为该判决所依据的事实没有明确并充分地说明为什么不能因为其犯下的可能适用死刑的犯罪而引渡黄海勇。经过一次上诉之后,2009年6月15日该决定得到确认。

2009年8月25日,中国驻秘鲁大使向秘鲁最高法院提交了一份外交照会(第二次外交照会),明确指出,与黄海勇案件类似的案件在中国被判处了15年监禁,所以不存在可能对黄海勇适用死刑的可能。

(2)法理评析。

本阶段的程序有以下特点值得关注:

第一,黄海勇提出了人身保护令申请。人身保护令作为普通法古老的特权令状,是由法院向羁押者签发一份命令,要求羁押者将被羁押者提交法院以审查羁押的合法性。人身保护令在英美法国家被誉为"大自由令状"。[①]该项制度最早起源于英国,自1066年诺曼底公爵征服英国开始,国王为加强司法集权,"要求各地司法机关根据国王的令状并以国王的名义进行审判",人身保护令制度正是在此基础上发展演变而来。随着大英帝国的海外扩张,该项制度作为保障人身自由的重要举措被扩展到世界各地特别是当今的普通法系国家。[②] 在本案中,黄海勇一直利用人身保护令作为自己的救济手段,一再延缓引渡程序的进展。秘鲁利马第56刑事法庭[③]就是审理黄海勇方面提出的人身保护令的法庭。由于该人身保护令是针对秘鲁最高法院的首次咨询判决的,所以该法庭在判决黄海勇方提出的人身保护令成立的同时,还以无充足理由说明黄海勇不能被引渡为依据宣布秘鲁最高法院的首次咨询判决无效。在该判决之后,中国再次向秘鲁发出外交照会,提交了同类案例没有判处死刑而仅仅判处了有期徒刑的说明,再次表明对于黄海用不存在适用死刑的可能性。需要注意的是,之前中国提交的黄海勇同案

[①] 薛竑:《人身保护令制度研究》,西南政法大学2006年博士学位论文,第1页。
[②] 房国宾、黄承云:《两大法系人身保护令制度比较研究》,载《西部法学评论》2008年第5期。
[③] 根据秘鲁法律,当事人可以在秘鲁国内任一法院提出人身保护令申请,不一定在对该案具有管辖权的卡亚俄法院提出人身保护。美洲人权法院判决书中出现的利马第56、42、53法庭等都是审理黄海勇提出的人身保护令申请的初级法院(一审),被驳回后,黄海勇还可向利马高院上诉(二审)。如终审再被驳回,黄海勇可向秘鲁宪法法院提出违宪申诉。秘鲁宪法法院的决定是最终裁决。

犯的判决情况，以及这次提交的案件情况，都是用相关或者相似的案例说明黄海勇不会被判处死刑，而不是直接针对本案作出不判处死刑的承诺，当然在说明本案不会被判处死刑上的力度上也就不如后者，这也许就是后来秘鲁最高法院明确要求在案件增加中方不判处死刑承诺的原因。

第二，中方迟迟没有提交关于中国《刑法》第151条及其译文被黄海勇方面诬蔑为恶意。在提起人身保护请求的同时，黄海勇方面将中国方面所提交的引渡请求中没有包含中国《刑法》第151条关于走私普通货物罪可以判处死刑的规定及其译文作为攻击中方的理由，将中方推断为"以恶意和隐蔽的方式(in a malicious and covert manner)"，即故意不提交该条文，以便于掩盖可能判处黄海勇死刑的事实。

第三，中国公安部在秘鲁最高法院首次判决之后，提交了黄海勇不会被适用死刑的说明，并明确中国将依据法律和中国秘鲁双边条约的规定追究黄海勇的刑事责任。这也被认为是中国向秘鲁方面提交的第一次外交照会。此时，距离黄海勇被逮捕已经过了将近4个月。但需要注意，由于此次提交说明的是中国公安部，并非中国最高人民法院，所以此次提交的说明并不意味着中方正式作出了不判处死刑的承诺。

第四，在秘鲁司法部针对中方提交的报告的回应中，明确强调该报告并没有提交中国《刑法》第151条的译文，中方于5天之后提交了相应条文的译文。这表明，即使是第一外交照会提交了不判处黄海勇死刑的说明，也没有达到对方要求，还是缺少该条文的译文，经过对方的再一次要求以后，中方则又提交了译文。此时，比黄海勇方面明确提交关键性法条及译文已经晚了1个月左右。而且秘鲁司法部的反馈也说明，提交关键法条的译文是此次引渡必不可少的程序。这说明，中方所提交引渡程序材料的把握上，还有待进一步提高。

2. 第二次人身保护令申请与中方不判处死刑的承诺

（1）基本程序。[①]

2009年10月2日，秘鲁最高检察院的检察官通知秘鲁最高法院：表明

[①] 美洲人权法院判决书72—77段。

不赞成秘鲁最高法院同意引渡黄海勇的首次咨询裁决。

2009年10月5日,秘鲁最高法院常设刑事庭举行听证会,命令将资料退还给卡亚俄高级法院刑事法庭,让该法庭"附上已经提交(或者已经请求提交)在被判处死刑之后不执行死刑的担保,并且重新及时举行听证会"。

2009年10月12日,黄海勇的律师以"对黄海勇的生命与人身安全存在某种迫在眉睫的威胁"为由,针对秘鲁最高法院常设刑事庭法官提交了第二份人身保护请求。2010年1月5日,秘鲁利马第53刑事法庭经过审理认为该请求不当,因为其提出的请求已经在2009年4月2日的判决中进行了分析,后上诉后又被驳回。

2009年12月9日,秘鲁最高法院常设刑事庭举行引渡听证会。2009年12月11日,中国驻秘鲁大使馆通知该刑事庭(中方发出的第三次外交照会):中国最高人民法院已经决定,如果黄海勇先生被引渡回国并判刑,将不对其执行死刑,"即便根据法律其罪行足以判处死刑"。

2009年12月15日,秘鲁最高法院常设刑事法庭进行公开审理,宣布10月5日的听证会无效,双方当事人可以围绕中国所提交外交承诺发表自己的观点。

2009年12月21日,秘鲁最高法院常设刑事庭重新举行引渡听证会,法庭命令在案件卷宗中添加中国《刑法》第151条的译文,以及2009年12月11日中国驻秘鲁大使馆公文中提到的最高人民法院的承诺。2009年12月29日,中国重新提交了《刑法》第151条的译文(中方发出的第四次外交照会)。

(2)法理评析。

本阶段诉讼程序具有以下特点:

第一,由于秘鲁最高检察院也不赞成秘鲁最高法院的首次咨询裁决,秘鲁最高法院将案件退给了卡亚俄高等法院,要求其附上中国不执行死刑的担保,这说明迄今为止,虽然中方已经提交了数个关于本案不会适用死刑的说明,但是一直没有明确作出不判处死刑的承诺。对此,中方在两个月后的2009年12月11日向秘鲁最高法院正式提交了不判处死刑的承诺。也促使秘鲁最高法院在4天后也就是12月15日宣布撤销把案件退回卡亚俄法院的裁决,让双方围绕中国提交的不判处死刑的承诺发表自己的观点。这也进一步证明,中国作出充分的不判处死刑的承诺是本案的关键环节,如果没有该承诺,诉讼程序就会继续搁置,如果有了承诺,诉讼程序就会顺利推进。

第二,黄海勇方面再次以其生命受到威胁(也就是死刑问题)为由提出了人身保护令请求,但是后来被驳回。这应该也是黄海勇方面的诉讼策略,其一再提出人身保护令,是其拖延诉讼程序的重要战术,不论最终结果如何,都会造成诉讼程序的耽搁和延长。

第三,在秘鲁最高法院临时法庭继续举行引渡听证会的时候,中国提交了本国最高人民法院所作出的不判处死刑的承诺。这是中国正式根据中国《引渡法》第50之规定①就本案作出不判处死刑的承诺,向对方明确表示,即使根据黄海勇的罪行依法应当被判处死刑,其最终也不会被判处死刑。事实上,根据当时的中国《刑法》第151条之规定,并结合黄海勇的涉案事实,他客观上是存在被判处死刑的可能的。而中方不判处死刑承诺的作出,则正式表明,不论原本依照立法是否应当判处死刑,黄海勇最终都不会被判处死刑。

第四,秘鲁最高法院引渡听证会上还要求在法庭卷宗中(case file)中添加中国《刑法》第151条的译文,以及2009年12月11日中国驻秘鲁大使馆公文中提到的中国最高人民法院的承诺。这也表明,在本案法庭卷宗中并没有这两份案件材料。中国最高人民法院的承诺由于是刚刚提交,尚未存入卷宗当中可以理解,但是为什么在2009年2月中方已经提交给秘鲁方面的刑法第151条的译文尚未纳入卷宗当中,美洲人权法院判决书没有说明。笔者理解,是因为当时提交给的是秘鲁利马第56法庭,而并非秘鲁最高法院,所以卷宗当中没有。即便如此,中方在得到秘鲁方面的要求之后,即在8天之后再次提交了该条的译文。

---

① 中国《引渡法》第50条规定:"被请求国就准予引渡附加条件的,对于不损害中华人民共和国主权、国家利益、公共利益的,可以由外交部代表中华人民共和国政府向被请求国作出承诺。对于限制追诉的承诺,由最高人民检察院决定;对于量刑的承诺,由最高人民法院决定。在对被引渡人追究刑事责任时,司法机关应当受所作出的承诺的约束。"

(三)从秘鲁最高法院第二次判决到秘鲁宪法法院作出判决(2010年1月至2011年6月)

1. 秘鲁最高法院的第二次咨询判决

(1) 基本程序。①

2010年1月27日,秘鲁最高法院常设刑事庭发布第二次咨询判决,包括以下内容:(1) 批准关于中国《刑法》第153、154、389和390条规定的逃避关税罪和行贿罪产生的引渡请求。(2) 虽然逃避关税罪规定有死刑,但是2009年12月8日中国最高人民法院已经做出了不判处死刑的承诺,所以应当认为黄海勇不存在被判处死刑的风险。(3) 以不符合双重犯罪原则宣布中方以洗钱罪提出引渡的请求无效。(4) 秘鲁最高法院判决引渡黄海勇的条件是:"中国当局作出不会判处其死刑的承诺;在对被引渡人作出判决时将判决内容通知秘鲁政府。"

2010年2月9日,黄海勇的律师针对秘鲁总统、司法部和外交部提交了第三份人身保护请求,后被秘鲁利马第42专业刑事法庭宣布无效,上诉后于4月14日被驳回,理由是在引渡期间,总统、司法部和外交部没有发布任何侵权或威胁黄海勇的决定,也没有对其的造成任何侵害。黄海勇的律师随后又提出违宪上诉,2011年5月24日该上诉得到了秘鲁宪法法院的支持。

2011年2月22日中国驻秘鲁大使通知秘鲁司法部(第五次外交照会),除了不判处死刑的承诺以外,中国政府正式承诺将邀请秘鲁政府派遣观察员参加黄海勇被引渡回国后的审判,并对判决的执行情况进行监督。2011年2月25日中国通过了《刑法修正案(八)》(2011年5月1日生效),中国方面2011年4月6日将《刑法修正案(八)》获批的情况通知了秘鲁宪法法院。

(2) 法理评析。

本阶段诉讼程序有以下特点:

第一,秘鲁最高法院作出了第二次判决:(1) 批准了针对逃避关税罪(走私普通货物罪)和行贿罪的引渡申请,但基于不符合双重犯罪原则,拒绝了针对洗钱罪提出的引渡申请;(2) 虽然根据走私普通货物罪可能判处死刑,

---

① 美洲人权法院判决书78—80段,第93段。

但是基于中国最高人民法院已经做出的不判处死刑的承诺,秘鲁最高法院相信,黄海勇被引渡回国之后不会被判处死刑;(3)明确黄海勇被引渡回国的条件是:中国当局作出不会判处其死刑的承诺,而且中方在对黄海勇作出判决时,应当将将判决内容通知秘鲁政府。

第二,中方承诺邀请秘鲁方面监督黄海勇回国后的审判。在秘鲁最高法院作出第二次判决1年后,中国向秘鲁方面发出了第五次外交照会,向秘鲁方面承诺,将邀请秘鲁方面派员参加在黄海勇被引渡回国之后的审判,并且对于判决执行情况进行监督。这一方面做出了除了不判处死刑承诺之外的新的外交担保,即邀请秘鲁方面进行监督,而且这也是对于秘鲁最高法院第二次判决中所要求的引渡黄海勇的条件的一个回应。但是,这种回复似乎有点晚,因为是在秘鲁最高法院作出判决的将近一年之后才予以回应。

第三,中方及时向秘鲁方面通知最新立法进展。中国立法机关通过《刑法修正案(八)》废除了包括走私普通货物罪在内的13种经济性、非暴力犯罪的死刑,占死刑全部罪名总数的19.1%;同时原则上免除了审判时已满75周岁老年人死刑的适用。这是中国踏上废除死刑征途步伐的一个起点和迈出的一大步,标志着法学界呼吁已久的限制、废除死刑的主张正式获得了国家立法机关的认可,并进入立法操作层面。① 中国及时将该消息通知了秘鲁方面,从而从立法上明确说明,即使中国未对秘鲁做出不判处死刑的承诺,由于中国刑法的修改,中国法院也不可能对于黄海勇判处死刑。

2. 秘鲁宪法法院的判决及其修正

(1) 基本程序。②

秘鲁最高法院作出判决之后,黄海勇及其律师向秘鲁宪法法院提起违宪申诉,后秘鲁宪法法院经过审判于2011年5月24日作出判决,包括两个方面的内容:(1)认为中国提供的外交担保不足以保证不会对黄海勇执行死刑。理由是根据联合国的标准,中国死刑的适用存在法外执行、即审即决或任意处决(extrajudicial, summary or arbitrary executions.),而且其死刑适

---

① 参见高铭暄、陈璐著:《〈中华人民共和国刑法修正案(八)〉解读与思考》,中国人民大学出版社2011年版,第3页。
② 美洲人权法院判决书81—84段,第200段。

用受到公众舆论影响过大。(2)中国虽然提交了《刑法修正案(八)》有关的资料,但是该资料并没有通过秘鲁的正式外交程序递交,也没有提到中国《宪法》是否承认刑法对于被告人有利的溯及力问题。因此也不能被理解为不适用死刑的担保。在此基础上,秘鲁宪法法院宣布黄海勇的人身保护请求是正当的,并且命令秘鲁政府放弃将黄海勇引渡回中国。

秘鲁宪法法院的判决作出以后,秘鲁司法部和外交部的公共辩护律师申请秘鲁宪法法院针对已经做出的判决作出进一步的解释。2011年6月9日,秘鲁宪法法院作出决定,明确指出,关于为什么在判决中认为中国提供的外交担保不充分,是因为在作出判决时案件卷宗中并没有公诉人所提到的外交担保,而只包括了关于第八次刑法修正案废除走私罪死刑的情况,但这"不能构成外交担保"。① 外交担保的材料是在判决作出以后的2011年7月7日才纳入卷宗当中的。② 因此,法院没有机会对于走私普通货物罪死刑的废除是否适用于本案,和中国所提供的外交担保进行评估。③ 考虑到以上情况,秘鲁宪法法院认为,判决中的第9条和第10条依据存在实质性的错误,因此,对其进行如下修改:"9. 中国提供的外交担保不足以保证不会对黄海勇先生执行死刑。这是因为案件材料中没有中国提供给秘鲁政府的任何外交担保。④ ……10. 由于本案卷宗中没有外交担保,本庭认为,不能证明中国已经为维护黄海勇先生的生命权提供了必要和

---

① On June 9, 2011, the Constitutional Court issued a decision in which it indicated that, "regarding the request to clarify the reasons why it had considered that the diplomatic assurances offered by the People's Republic of China were insufficient, [it recalled] that at the time the [judgment] was delivered, the case file did not contain any of the diplomatic assurances referred to by the public attorneys who were requesting the clarification". 参见美洲人权法院判决书第84段。

② The diplomatic assurances were incorporated into the case file following the delivery of this judgment on July 7, 2011 参见美洲人权法院判决书第84段。

③ Thus, the Constitutional Court was unable to assess either the annulment of the death penalty for the offense of smuggling ordinary merchandise and it applicability to Wong Ho Wing's situation, or the subsequent diplomatic assurances provided by the People's Republic of China, which this Court has been able to assess. 参见美洲人权法院判决书第203段。

④ [The diplomatic assurances offered by the People's Republic of China are insufficient to ensure that the death penalty will not be imposed on Wong Ho Wing]. This is because, since the case file does not contain any diplomatic assurances provided to the Peruvian State by the Republic of China, it has not been proved that real protection of the right to life has been ensured. 参见美洲人权法院判决书第84段。

充分的担保。"①同时,法庭还认为,虽然法庭在判决之后才了解中国外交担保的内容,但是这并不能改变已经通过的判决,因为其已经获得了宪法上的既判力。②

(2) 法理评析。

从上面的程序可知,秘鲁宪法法院首先作出了判决,然后又通过决定对于做出该判决的理由进行了修改。具体来说,秘鲁宪法法院在2011年5月24日作出的判决中,认为中国死刑适用存在法外执行和任意处决,受到舆论影响较大,中国提交的《刑法修正案(八)》不仅没有通过秘鲁的正式外交程序递交,也没有说明在溯及力上是否适用于黄海勇案件,所以中国提供的外交担保不能够保证对黄海勇不适用死刑,进而拒绝引渡黄海勇。而经过秘鲁司法部等要求作出进一步解释之后,秘鲁宪法法院对于之前判决的主要依据修改为"作出判决之时,外交担保并被纳入案件卷宗当中"。事实上如前所述,中国早在2009年12月11日就将不判处死刑的承诺提交给秘鲁最高法院常设刑事庭。但是关于该外交担保为什么在2011年5月24日作出判决之前没有被纳入秘鲁宪法法院的案件卷宗,直到2011年7月7日才被纳入,判决书并没有明确说明。

(四) 从秘鲁宪法法院作出判决到美洲人权法院作出判决(2011年6月至2013年10月)

1. 基本程序。③

按照秘鲁《刑事诉讼法》规定的引渡程序,在司法程序结束之后引渡程序进入行政程序。在秘鲁宪法法院作出判决之后,秘鲁司法部数次提出违宪上诉,要求对秘鲁宪法法院的判决作出解释。但是2013年3月12日,秘鲁宪法法院裁定,要求对黄海勇先生作出的判决进行解释的请求无效。自此以后,双方对于对秘鲁宪法法院的判决(2011年5月24日)和秘鲁最高法院的第二次咨询判决(2010年1月27日)都没有提出新的上诉,因此两个判

---

① Bearing in mind the inexistence of diplomatic assurances in the case file, this Court finds that it has not been proved that the People's Republic of China has granted the necessary and sufficient guarantees to safeguard the right to life of Wong Ho Wing. 参见美洲人权法院判决书第84段。
② 美洲人权法院判决书第200段。
③ 美洲人权法院判决书第86—91段,第93段,第108—114段。

决同时有效,即认为应当支持引渡的判决和秘鲁宪法法院放弃引渡的判决同时存在。从那时起,秘鲁司法部一直在办理程序,没有作出最终决定。

(1) 中方又发出三次外交照会。

第六次外交照会。2011年6月10日(秘鲁宪法法院对其判决作出解释的第二天),中国向秘鲁司法部发出第六次外交照会,提交了中国《刑法》第12条(关于刑法溯及力问题)的译文,证明中国《刑法》第八次修正案将适用于黄海勇先生一案。

第七次外交照会。2011年12月22日,中国驻秘鲁大使馆向秘鲁外交部发出了第七次外交照会,提交了对于中国《刑法修正案(八)》所适用的案件的解释,解释中明确了以下内容:根据中国《刑法》第12条第1段规定,对于中国《刑法》的追溯效力应当遵循根据行为当时的法律进行判决的原则和从轻判决的原则。对于中国《刑法》生效之前已经宣判的罪行,如果行为当时的法律和现行法律没有变化,适用行为当时的法律。中国《刑法修正案(八)》(2011年5月1日生效)修改了中国《刑法》第153条第1段之规定,黄海勇的罪行发生于该修正案生效之前,但是经该修正案修改后该罪的刑罚轻于修改前的刑罚,所以根据从旧兼从轻原则,对本案应适用中国《刑法修正案八》。2009年12月中国作出的不判处死刑的承诺继续有效,即对黄海勇不适用死刑。

第八次外交照会。2014年8月19日,中国大使馆向秘鲁外交部发出第八次外交照会,包括以下内容:(1) 承诺黄海勇不会遭受酷刑等不人道的待遇。作为《禁止酷刑和其他残忍、非人道或有辱人格的待遇或处罚公约》的缔约国,在2009年作出不判处黄海勇承诺的基础上,中国政府确保黄海勇将不会受到酷刑或其他残忍、非人道或有辱人格的待遇和处罚。中国方面将遵守这一承诺。(2) 保障黄海用的诉讼权利。根据中国《刑事诉讼法》和《律师法》,保障黄海勇聘请律师为其辩护,并可以在不受监视的情况下与其律师会面的权利。中国司法机关应当对黄海勇的审判和预审进行同步录音录像,并可应秘鲁方面的要求供其使用。允许具有执业资格证、可以在中国从事经营的独立的社会医疗机构为黄海勇提供医疗服务。(3) 保障秘鲁方面随时了解和监督黄海勇在中国的诉讼程序。保证秘鲁方面可以了解黄海勇在中国的羁押地点,派遣外交或者领事官员与黄海勇座谈;秘鲁方面可以派遣其外交官员或领事官员旁听对于黄海勇的公开审判;在黄海勇羁押期间,为其提供视频设施,方便秘鲁官员与黄海勇联系。

(2)黄海勇又提出三次人身保护令申请。

第四次人身保护令申请。2011年11月16日,黄海勇的律师针对秘鲁司法部和卡亚俄高等法院提交了第四份人身保护令申请,认为黄海勇临时羁押的材料提交给了司法部,但是随后没有提交给卡亚俄高等法院。2012年5月30日,秘鲁利马第30刑事法庭宣布不予受理,因为这并没有对于黄海勇的宪法权利造成任何损害。

第五次人身保护令申请。2012年3月13日,黄海勇的律师针对秘鲁最高法院开庭审理本案提出第五次人身保护请求。根据2014年12月1日秘鲁政府的通知,该程序尚未有结果。①

第六次人身保护令申请。2013年4月26日,黄海勇的律师又提交了第六份人身保护令,申请要求立即释放黄海勇,并不受任何限制。2013年11月20日,黄海勇再次提出要求改变对自己的羁押状况。2014年3月10日,卡亚俄第七刑事法庭针对黄海勇的该要求作出裁决指出,黄海勇被剥夺自由的时间超过了合理的期限,因此应当改变为较轻的刑事强制措施,但要能够确保其留在秘鲁,直至行政机关对引渡请求作出终审判决。因此,法庭命令将其变为由其弟弟对其监视居住(house arrest),②并于2014年3月24日开始执行。有鉴于此,接受黄海勇第六份人身保护令的法院也于2014年10月24日作出裁决,以黄海勇已经变为监视居住,而且该案件已经提交给美洲人权法院为由驳回申请。

2. 法理评析。

在秘鲁宪法法院作出判决之后,秘鲁司法部虽然数次提起违宪上诉,但是最终还是被驳回。之后,司法部一直没有就引渡程序作出最终裁决。但是中方继续通过外交照会的形式推动引渡程序的开展,而黄海勇方面则通过人身保护令的方式要求释放黄海勇,延缓引渡程序的进行。

---

① Cfr. 2014年12月1日秘鲁政府的书面材料(背景资料,第1159页)。人身保护请求于2013年4月29日得到认可。Cfr. 2013年4月29日批准美洲人权法院判决书(证词,第8517到8520页)。
② The Court ordered "house arrest…… in the custody of his brother." 参见美洲人权法院判决书第113段。当然,这里的"house arrest"能否翻译为"监视居住"还有待于进一步研究,本文暂且将其翻译为"监视居住"。

第一,中国方面。中方首先在秘鲁宪法法院对于判决作出解释的第二天就提交了中国《刑法》第12条的译文,然后又于四个月后再次就中国《刑法修正案(八)》的溯及力问题进行了解释。后又在美洲人权法院开庭审理黄海勇案件(2014年9月3日)的前夕,即2014年8月19日向秘鲁外交部做出了进一步的外交承诺,包括保证黄海勇不遭受酷刑等不人道的待遇的承诺,保证其各项诉讼权利的承诺,以及保证秘鲁方面了解各项诉讼进程并和黄海勇保持联络的承诺。这说明,虽然死刑问题是本案的核心,中国作出不判处死刑承诺是本案的关键问题,但是除此之外,不遭受酷刑,保证其诉讼权利,保证秘鲁的监督权,也是秘鲁重点关注的问题。中国方面所做出的这些的承诺,向秘鲁和美洲人权法院全面展现中国刑事司法的进步,表明中国对黄海勇进行公正审判的决心,为美洲人权法院作出有利于中国的判决奠定基础。

第二,黄海勇方面。人身保护令,是黄海勇延缓引渡程序的重要措施。秘鲁宪法法院判决之后,黄海勇又多次申请人身保护令或者提出人身保护请求。对于不合理的请求,秘鲁相应司法机关予以驳回。但是对于一些合理的请求,秘鲁法院也及时作出处理。应当说,由于本案涉及程序复杂,黄海勇自2008年11月被捕以来一直被羁押,客观上的确存在超期羁押的问题。也正因为如此,在黄海勇提出改变对自己的羁押要求之后,卡亚俄法庭将对其强制措施改变为监视居住。根据判决书显示,到2015年6月判决书作出时,黄海勇已经被羁押5年4个月,监视居住1年3个月。根据秘鲁《刑事诉讼法》第272条之规定,审前羁押不得超过9个月,案情复杂的,不得超过18个月。所以,虽然在此期间秘鲁政府一直在推进相应的诉讼程序,但是超期羁押的客观事实是存在的。那么,对此是否能够在黄海勇回国接受审判后所判处的刑期中予以折抵,就值得关注。

四、黄海勇案在美洲人权委员会和美洲人权法院的诉讼程序及分析

在秘鲁最高法院作出同意引渡黄海勇的首次咨询判决之后,黄海勇方面还将案件提交到美洲人权委员会,并最终提交给美洲人权法院,这两个区

域性人权机构在黄海勇引渡案件中具有重要地位。

（一）美洲人权委员会和美洲人权法院

1. 美洲人权委员会

美洲人权委员会是美洲国家组织①系统中两个促进和保护人权的机构之一。1959年在智利首都圣地亚哥举行的第五届外交部长协商会议（Consultation of Ministers of Foreign Affairs）上通过决议，决定依照《美洲国家组织宪章》选举成立美洲人权委员会。1960年，美洲国家组织常设委员会批准《美洲人权委员会规约》，标志着美洲人权委员会的正式成立。1978年7月，《美洲人权公约》生效，并在其第7章中确认了美洲人权委员会履行《公约》的职责。1980年，《美洲人权委员会程序规则》通过。因此，美洲人权委员会实际上行使的是《美洲国家组织宪章》《美洲人权公约》两个公约的职能。除了这两个国际公约以外，美洲人权委员的组织机构和职能，还由《美洲人权委员会规约》和《美洲人权委员会程序规则》进行了详细规定。

根据上述国际公约之规定，美洲人权委员会根据对象的不同具有不同的职权：(1) 对于美洲国家组织的成员国，该委员会的职能主要有：发展人权意识；向各成员国政府提出改进保护人权措施的建议；要求成员国提交关于人权问题的报告；向成员国提供咨询等。② (2) 对于《美洲人权公约》的缔约国，除了(1)中的职权之外，还具有针对公约规定的申诉和来文采取行动；就依据公约所提起的案件在美洲人权法院出庭；对尚未提交美洲人权法院的案件，如认为必要可以要求法院采取它认为适当的临时措施；等等。③ (3) 对于非《美洲人权公约》的缔约国，该委员会的职能除了(1)中列举的职权外，还包括对于《美洲人的权利和义务宣言》相关条款④所涉及的人权保护情况给予特别注意；对于来文以及其他相关信息加以审查并在认为合适的

---

① 美洲国家组织（Organization of American States—OAS）最初是由美国和拉美国家于1890年建立的美洲共和国国际联盟。1948年在波哥大举行的第九次美洲会议通过了《美洲国家组织宪章》，联盟遂改称为"美洲国家组织"。该组织的宗旨是加强美洲大陆的和平与安全；确保成员国之间和平解决争端；成员国遭到侵略时，组织声援行动；谋求解决成员国间的政治、经济、法律问题，消除贫困，促进各国经济、社会、文化合作；控制常规武器；加速美洲国家一体化进程。现在有正式成员35个。参见中华人民共和国外交部网站，http://wcm.fmprc.gov.cn/pub/chn/pds/gjhdq/gjhdqzz/lhg_40/t4571.htm
② 《美洲人权委员会规约》第18条。
③ 《美洲人权委员会规约》第19条。
④ 《美洲人的权利和义务宣言》第1、2、3、4、18、25和26条。

时候提出建议；等等。① 秘鲁既是美洲国家组织的成员国，也是《美洲人权公约》的缔约国，所以美洲人权委员会可以针对秘鲁实施上述(1)和(2)规定的职权。

美洲人权委员会共有 7 名委员，由美洲国家组织大会从成员国政府所提名的候选人选出，以个人身份任职，不代表任何国家。委员会成员从当选之日起享有外交人员的特权与豁免权。② 美洲人权委员会设有秘书处，协助和支持美洲人权委员会的各项工作。③

2. 美洲人权法院

美洲人权法院是除美洲人权委员会外美洲人权区域保护的另一个重要机构，其职能是根据《美洲人权公约》管辖美洲国家(实际上主要是拉美国家)有关人权的案件和相关法律事务。美洲人权法院的成立也与《美洲人权公约》的生效有密切关系，1978 年 7 月《美洲人权公约》生效后，美洲人权法院正式建立。随后，分别于 1979 年 10 月通过了《美洲人权法院规约》(以下简称《规约》)，1980 年 8 月通过了《美洲人权法院程序规则》，前者规定了法院的管辖权和组织结构，后者规定了法院审理案件的具体程序，从而奠定了该法院运行的法律基础。《规约》第 1 条明确规定了法院的性质和目的："美洲人权法院是一个法律自主机构，其目的是适用和解释《美洲人权公约》。该法院根据公约和规约的规定行使职权。"美洲人权法院规模较小，仅由 7 名法官组成。法官必须是美洲国家组织成员国的国民，但是仅以个人身份当选，不得有两名法官为同一国家的国民。④

美洲人权法院的主要职能，是通过行使诉讼管辖权和咨询管辖权等方式来实施《美洲人权公约》：(1) 诉讼管辖权。该法院的诉讼管辖权是指审理和裁决有关成员国是否侵犯人权的权力，该法院的诉讼管辖权分为两种，即对缔约国间控告的管辖权和对个人申诉的管辖权。不论是缔约国还是个人提出控告，诉讼管辖权的被告只能是国家。该法院诉讼管辖权的特点是其

---

① 《美洲人权委员会规约》第 20 条。
② 《美洲人权公约》第 12 条。
③ 《美洲人权公约》第 40 条。
④ 赵海峰、窦玉前：《美洲人权法院——在困难中前进的区域人权保护司法机构令》，载《人民司法》2005 年第 12 期。

仅接受成员国或者人权委员会提交的案件,个人无权直接向其提交申诉,由美洲人权委员会作为受害者个人的代表在法庭上出现。对于国家间指控的案件,该委员会也应当出庭。①而且,在美洲人权法院行使诉讼管辖权之前,需要穷尽《美洲人权公约》所规定的美洲人权委员会的有关指控程序。也就是说,该法院行使诉讼管辖权的前提是美洲人权委员会的审查程序已经结束,诉至法院的指控和申诉必须首先经过美洲人权委员会的审查,只有在委员会无法解决的情况下才提交给法院。(2)咨询管辖权。咨询管辖权主要是澄清人权文件的法律标准,以及判定国家的法律和实践与这些标准是否相符,咨询管辖权的提请主体包括美洲国家组织的成员国和《美洲国家组织宪章》第10章所载的机关。

虽然美洲人权法院成立初期面临管辖权缺乏普遍性、美洲的政治机构对该法院的支持不够、法官素质不高等问题,但是自成立以来,该法院在监督各国实施公约,采取临时措施、监督判决的执行等方面都做了很多工作,对于拉美各国人权保护的发展也起到了重要作用。正如美洲人权法院院长、秘鲁前司法部长暨前外交部长迭戈·加西亚-萨扬所说,"美洲人权法院的法律体系已经在诉讼和解决拉美地区人权保护的不同方面占据着重要位置,大大促进和推动了保障人权的国内诉讼程序,使法律手段更加民主化,在具体案件处理中,也不再仅仅只是追求令受害人满意,而是为推动维护权利的基本改革,为消除侵犯人权的行为而斗争,为人类的逐渐进步而斗争。"②与此同时,美洲人权法院还致力于开展文化得多样性,政府信息公开,对于弱势群体的保护等工作的开展,对于美洲尤其是南美人权的保护产生了积极的影响。③

3. 秘鲁与美洲人权委员会、美洲人权法院的关系

秘鲁是美洲国家组织的成员国,也是《美洲人权公约》的缔约国,所以对于秘鲁发生的违反《公约》的相关案件,这两个区域性人权组织都有权进行

---

① 赵海峰、窦玉前:《美洲人权法院——在困难中前进的区域人权保护司法机构介》,载《人民司法》2005年第12期。
② 迭戈·加西亚-萨扬:《泛美人权法庭的实践》,载《光明日报》2010年10月21日。
③ 《泛美人权法庭庭长:推动文化多样性的保护》,载 http://www.cnr.cn/2010tfzt/rqlt/st/201010/t20101019_507193156.html。

管辖。这也是黄海勇及其律师能够以个人名义将秘鲁政府诉至美洲人权委员会,美洲人权委员会经过审查之后,又将案件提交给美洲人权法院的原因。

4. 美洲人权法院的专家证人制度

黄海勇引渡案件的一个亮点是中国专家证人到美洲人权法院作证,为成功引渡黄海勇发挥了重要作用。而中国专家证人出庭作证的依据,就是美洲人权法院的专家证人作证制度,该制度主要是由《美洲人权法院程序和证据规则》(以下简称《程序规则》)规定的。根据《程序规则》之规定,"专家证人(expert witness)"是指拥有特定的科学、艺术、技术或实践知识或经验,可以依其特定领域的知识或经验向法院就争议问题提供信息的人。《程序规则》对于担任专家证人的资格并没有进行明确规定,但却明确规定了丧失专家证人的条件。[①] 根据《程序规则》,缔约国和美洲人员委员会、受害人及其代理人以及被告国都可以提出专家证人,同时必须提交专家证人的简历、联系信息和作证的目的。一方提出专家证人名单以后,该法院需要将该名单发送给另一方,另一方如果有异议应当在 10 日以内提出。首席法官应当将异议通知给专家证人,让专家证人对此发表评论。法院在收到一方符合要求的变更专家证人的请求后,在征求另一方意见以后可以接受变更请求。

在专家证人出庭作证的庭审程序中,首先由美洲人权委员会宣读起诉书,然后由首席法官传唤作证者到庭。在法庭确定专家证人的身份以后进行询问之前,专家证人应当宣誓,保证其将诚实和认真地履行其职责。对于专家证人的询问首先由提供专家证人的一方进行,然后由另一方询问。

为了保护专家证人,各国不能因对法庭作出的陈述、意见或法律抗辩而起诉专家证人,也不能对他们的家人施加压力。专家证人应当出庭作证,如果被传唤出庭的专家证人无正当理由没有出庭或者拒绝作证,或者法院认为其行为违反了之前的宣誓,法院应当通知对专家证人有管辖权的国家,以便于该国依照国内法对其采取措施。

在得知美洲人权法院将要开庭审理黄海勇引渡案件以后,秘鲁政府积

[①] 如,与一名受害人是四代以内直系或者旁系血亲或收养关系;在国内层面或者美洲促进与保护人权机制内与案件事实相关的程序中,曾为一名受害人的代理人;与提供自己作为专家证人的一方有密切联系或曾经为其下属,法院认为可能影响公正;曾经为美洲人权委员会工作人员,了解争议案件的情况;曾经在争议案件中作为被告方的代理人;以前以任何身份在任何机构参与过争议案件等。

极准备应诉,并与中国政府沟通,希望中方提出专家证人人选,到美洲人权法庭出庭作证。同时要求相关专家证人应当具有独立身份,避免对外产生中国政府直接介入的印象。中国政府经过认真筛选,最终确定由北京师范大学刑事法律科学研究院院长暨中国刑法学研究会会长赵秉志教授、时任外交部境外追逃与国际执法合作特别协调员孙昂参赞(现任中国外交部驻印度尼西亚棉兰总领馆总领事)和中国社会科学院国际法研究所所长助理柳华文教授作为专家证人,并得到秘鲁政府的许可和美洲人权法院的批准。

2014年9月3日,美洲人权法院在巴拉圭首都亚松森的巴拉圭最高法院开庭,审理中国政府向秘鲁政府提出引渡申请的涉嫌走私普通货物罪的中国公民黄海勇引渡案。赵秉志教授、孙昂参赞和秘鲁前司法部长托马博士作为秘鲁政府邀请的3位专家证人到庭作证,并分别承担了不同的作证任务:

赵秉志教授的作证及各方对其盘问主要围绕与本案相关的中国刑事司法程序和实体问题以及赵秉志教授曾出庭作证的中加遣返赖昌星案件的有关情况而进行。赵秉志教授首先围绕个人简况、与本案相关的中国刑事诉讼程序和中国《刑法修正案(八)》进行了自我陈述,然后依次接受了秘鲁政府方面、美洲人权委员会代表、黄海勇的律师的盘问以及法庭的发问,各方共计向赵秉志教授提出 61 个问题,[①]包括黄海勇案件可能涉及的我国刑事诉讼程序,我国《刑法修正案(八)》的主要内容,我国死刑问题,赖昌星遣返案件的相关问题等,涵盖我国刑事法治发展状况的多个方面。

孙昂参赞的作证及各方对其的盘问则主要围绕中国引渡法制与实践以及中加遣返赖昌星的外交承诺而进行。孙昂参赞首先围绕中国对外开展引渡合作的三种方式,中国引渡合作中的不判处死刑的外交承诺等问题进行了自我陈述,然后依次接受了秘鲁政府方面,黄海勇的律师,美洲人权委员会代表的盘问以及法庭的发问,各方共计向孙昂参赞提出问题 52 个,[②]涉及中国的引渡制度,中国不判处死刑外交承诺的作出,中国外交承诺的执行状

[①] 其中秘鲁政府律师雷阿尼奥先生的问题11个,黄海勇律师路易斯·拉马斯普丘先生的问题16个,美洲人权委员会专员詹姆斯·路易斯·卡夫罗里先生的问题16个,法庭五位法官的问题18个。

[②] 其中秘鲁政府律师多奈雷斯女士的问题16个,黄海勇的律师路易斯·拉马斯普丘先生和米格尔·安赫尔·索里亚·富尔特先生的问题共计14个,美洲人权委员会专员詹姆斯·路易斯·卡夫罗里先生和西尔维亚·塞拉诺·古斯曼女士的问题共计11个,法庭五位法官的问题11个。

况,赖昌星遣返案中的外交承诺等问题。

秘鲁前司法部长托马博士的作证及各方对其的盘问主要围绕与本案相关的中秘引渡条约和秘鲁相关国内法律问题而进行。

秘鲁政府邀请的另一位中方专家证人中国社会科学院国际法研究所研究员柳华文作为未出庭的专家证人,经美洲人权法院同意提交了有关中国人权法律保护状况的书面证词。该证词主要涉及中国人权政策的制定、中国人权白皮书中关于司法工作中人权保障的规定,中国在人权领域与联合国的合作,中国在调查和惩处酷刑行为方面的新进展,中国对于被羁押人人权的保障等问题。

(三)黄海勇在美洲人权委员会和美洲人权法院的基本程序。[①]

1. 在美洲人权委员会的诉讼程序(2009年3月至2013年10月)

2009年3月27日,黄海勇首次向美洲人权委员会提出请求。2010年11月,美洲人权委员会通过151/102号受理报告接受了该案。2013年7月18日,根据《美洲人权公约》第50条,美洲人权委员会通过第78/13号背景报告(以下称"背景报告"),就本案得出了一系列结论,认为秘鲁政府侵犯了黄海勇的人身自由权、生命权、人身安全权利、司法保障与司法保护的权利,具体包括三部分:(1)自2008年10月27日被秘鲁羁押后,任意和过度地剥夺黄海勇的自由,涉嫌超期羁押;(2)在引渡程序中,部分违规行为侵犯了黄海勇的人身安全;(3)2011年5月24日,秘鲁宪法法院已经命令秘鲁行政机关放弃引渡黄海勇,但并没有得到执行,违反了司法保护权。

在此基础上,美洲人权委员会还向秘鲁政府提出了一系列建议:(1)采取必要的措施尽快根据《秘鲁刑事诉讼法》终止引渡程序,严格遵守2011年5月24日秘鲁宪法法院的判决对引渡申请作出裁决,同时,秘鲁政府应当确保其主管机构均不得延误履行该判决。(2)对黄海勇的临时逮捕措施进行审查。特别要指出的是,与黄海勇人身自由相关的所有司法决定的执行,均应当严格遵守《背景报告》描述的例外性、必要性和相称性原则。

2013年7月30日,美洲人权委员会将《背景报告》发送给秘鲁政府,给

[①] 美洲人权法院判决书第2—14段。

予其两个月的时间对履行建议的情况进行通报。2013年9月30日，秘鲁政府提交了一份报告，介绍了为履行这些建议而采取的措施。

2. 在美洲人权法院的诉讼程序（2013年10月至2015年6月）

2013年10月30日，美洲人权委员会将本案提交给美洲人权法院，①要求美洲人权法院对《背景报告》中所包含的侵权情况，对秘鲁政府所应承担的责任得出结论，另外还要求命令秘鲁政府执行该报告中的建议。2013年12月9日，美洲人权法院将该案件被提交的情况通知了秘鲁政府和黄海勇的律师。

2014年2月5、6和9日，黄海勇的律师向美洲人权法院提交了申请书、辩词和证词。2014年5月6日，秘鲁向美洲人权法院提交其初步反对意见书、向美洲人权委员会提交关于本案的答复、向黄海勇方面提交申请书和辩词的意见。在向美洲人权委员会的答复中，秘鲁政府以"尚未走完内部程序"为由提出了初步反对意见：(1) 在2009年3月黄海勇首次向美洲人权委员会提出申请的时候，黄海勇案件并没有用尽国内上诉程序，所以秘鲁政府的所谓超期羁押并非没有缘由。(2) 在美洲人权委员会决定受理本案时，并没有考虑到黄海勇代表所提出的人身保护要求正在办理手续的程序中。也就是说，黄海勇的"引渡程序正在办理"，秘鲁行政机关到现在都没有做出决定。对此，美洲人权委员会认为，秘鲁政府应当对受理期间未用尽内部上诉程序的例外情况提交说明。黄海勇律师也认为，行政机关的决定"超过四年"都未有结果，因此，存在"引渡决定不合理拖延"的情况。美洲人权法院经过审议，驳回了秘鲁政府的初步反对意见。

2014年7月28日，美洲人权法院审理本案的审判长签发命令，召集秘鲁政府、黄海勇律师和美洲人权委员会举行听证会，听取各方的意见。2014年9月3日，美洲人权法院在巴拉圭首都亚松森市举行了听证会，②2014年

---

① 美洲人权法院审理该案的有6名法官：Humberto Antonio Sierra Porto（审判长）；Roberto F. Caldas（副审判长）；Manuel E. Ventura Robles（法官）；Alberto Pérez Pérez（法官）；Eduardo Vio Grossi（法官），Eduardo Ferrer Mac-Gregor Poisot（法官）。

② 出席听证会的有：a) 美洲委员会：James Louis Cavallaro, Commissioner and Silvia Serrano Guzmán and Erick Acuña, Advisers of the Executive Secretariat; b) 受害人方：Luis Lamas Puccio 和 Miguel Ángel Soria Fuerte, c) 秘鲁政府：Luis Alberto Huerta Guerrero, Special Supranational Public Prosecutor, Agent, and Sofia Janett Donaires Vega and Carlos Miguel Reaño Balarezo, lawyers of the Special Supranational Public Prosecutor's Office.

10月3日,当事人与美洲人权委员会分别提交其书面最终辩词和意见。2015年6月24日,法院开始考虑作出判决。

2015年6月30日,美洲人权法院就本案作出判决,包括以下内容:(1)如果秘鲁引渡黄海勇,黄海勇不存在被适用死刑的可能性以及遭受酷刑的危险,秘鲁也不会因为违反《美洲人权公约》第4、5条和《美洲地区预防和惩治酷刑公约》第13条第4段规定的相关义务而承担责任。(2)秘鲁政府对于黄海勇的羁押措施超出了合理期限,侵犯了黄海勇的人身自由权,为此应当在接到本判决书1年之内,赔偿黄海勇3万美元,同时支付黄海勇的律师2.8万美元的成本和费用。并强调,支付给律师的成本和费用也是赔偿的一部分,因为黄海勇基于秘鲁政府应当承担国际责任的行为而在国内和国际采取的行为都应当获得赔偿。(3)秘鲁政府因为没有尽到应尽职责而导致引渡程序拖延至今,秘鲁必须尽快在引渡程序中作出最终决定。(4)自本判决通知之日起,秘鲁政府应当在6个月之内发布本判决书,并在1年内向美洲人权法院提交介绍其为执行判决而采取的措施的报告。(5)关于原告方的其他主张,不予支持。①

(四)法理评析

1. 美洲人权法院最终做出有利于中方的判决

在经过1年8个月(从2013年10月30日至2015年6月30日)的漫长审理之后,美洲人权法院对于本案作出了判决。判决书第329条对于本案的问题做出了最终处理,该条虽然分为17个部分,分别对于相关问题作出了最终裁决,但是其核心主要包括3部分内容:(1)如果秘鲁方面判决将黄海勇引渡给中国,黄海勇不存在被判处死刑或者遭受酷刑等不公正待遇的风险,秘鲁政府也不会为此承担相应的国际责任。这里需要注意的是,美洲人权法院的判决书并不是直接判决秘鲁是否引渡黄海勇,而是针对黄海勇回国后可能面临的情况作出裁判,最终是否引渡的裁判还将由秘鲁方面做出。(2)裁判秘鲁方面需要对黄海勇的超期羁押承担责任,秘鲁政府应当在接到判决书1年内承担相应的赔偿责任。具体来说,由于超期羁押侵犯了黄海勇

---

① 美洲人权法院判决书第329、302、306、317、322、323段。

的人身自由权,秘鲁政府需要赔偿黄海勇3万美元,同时支付给黄海勇的律师2.8万美元的成本和费用。并强调支付给律师的成本和费用也是赔偿的一部分,因为黄海勇是基于秘鲁政府的不当行为而聘请律师采取诉讼行为的。(3)由于秘鲁政府没有尽到应尽职责,致使引渡程序拖延至今,所以命令秘鲁必须尽快在引渡程序中作出最终决定。

从该判决我们可以看出,美洲人权法院一方面围绕死刑、酷刑等问题进行评估,认可了中方做出的包括不判处死刑在内的外交承诺;另一方面,也指出秘鲁政府的超期羁押客观存在,秘鲁政府应当为此承担相应的责任,并督促秘鲁政府尽快做出判决。这也反映出,为了配合中国的引渡请求,秘鲁方面的确付出了巨大代价。该判决的做出,标志着中国在黄海勇引渡问题上取得了实质性的胜利,虽然之前秘鲁宪法法院针对中国的外交承诺问题提出了质疑,但是美洲人权法院最终认可了中国的外交承诺,从而为秘鲁方面最终做出有利于中国的判决奠定了基础。此后虽然黄海勇方面依然心有不甘、不屈不挠地继续利用秘鲁国内程序对抗引渡,但最终还是被引渡回国。

2. 中国专家证人的证言对于做出有利于中方的判决起到重要作用

在本案的审理中,专家证人发挥了重要作用,判决书也进行了专门描述:"法院还收到了黄海勇以及证人 Kin Mui Chan 与 He Long Huang 在公证人面前作出的声明,以及 Carmen Wurst de Landázuri、Ben Saul 和 Geoff Gilbert、Huawen Liu 和 Jean Carlo Mejía Azuero 专家的意见。对于听证会期间获得的证据,法院听取了专家赵秉志、孙昂和 Víctor Oscar Shiyin García Toma 的意见。"[①]这些专家证人特别是中方专家证人的证言,对于本案判决的作出发挥了重要作用。

第一,对于专家证人证言的肯定。

判决书中多次引用中方专家证人的证言,对于最终作出有利于中方的判决作出了贡献。

中国刑法学研究会会长赵秉志教授的证言对于证明黄海勇不会被判处

---

① 美洲人权法院判决书第37段。

死刑发挥了重要作用。判决书曾经3次引用专家证人赵秉志教授的证言：(1)强调黄海勇不可能被判处死刑。"如根据中国刑事法专家赵秉志的说法，在《刑法修正案（八）》出台之前，根据黄海勇的罪行，对其的量刑为第三档即10年以上有期徒刑至无期徒刑或死刑。但是，《刑法修正案（八）》于2011年5月生效以后，就不可能针对黄海勇所涉嫌的走私普通货物罪判处死刑"；①而且"由于他的同案犯被判处了13年有期徒刑，因此，法庭在对其量刑时，将考虑其同案犯适用同种的刑罚和相同幅度的量刑。"②(2)向法庭解释中国刑法第12条的溯及力问题，强调《刑法修正案（八）》可以适用于黄海勇案件。"根据专家证人赵秉志在听证会上的解释，以及德国马克斯—普朗克研究所的司法报告③和标准内容，中国《刑法》第12条规定了有利于被告人的刑事追溯原则"，④这就意味着，对于黄海勇可以适用刑法修正案八的规定。(3)关于外交担保，"赵秉志专家强调，《刑法修正案（八）》之后，即使未提供不判处死刑的外交担保，也不会对走私普通货物罪判处死刑。"⑤

孙昂参赞的证言对于说服法庭相信中国提供的外交担保的拘束力问题卓有成效："法院注意到专家证人孙昂的意见，他说，根据中国《引渡法》第50条，在中国外交部提供外交担保之后，这些担保对中国所有司法机构都是有效力的。法庭认为，在本案的特殊情况下，担保以及提供的监测方法是充分的。"⑥由此可见，对于说服美洲人权法院巡回法庭相信中国外交担保的效力或拘束力，孙昂参赞的证言功不可没。

柳华文研究员所提交的书面证言，对于法庭排除黄海勇回国后遭受酷刑或残忍、非人道或有辱人格折磨的危险的可能也发挥了重要作用。如判决书提到："秘鲁政府在卷宗中所提供的中国专家柳华文的意见，强调了在

---

① 美洲人权法院判决书第147段。
② 美洲人权法院判决书第148段。
③ 根据上述报告，"合法性原则（法无明文不为罪，罪刑法定原则），中国刑法承认：根据《刑法》第12条第1节，第12条第1段禁止在一项新的刑法规定中进行追溯应用，除非新规定所包含的处罚更有利（温和法律原则）。换言之，如果新的规定更有利，则必须强制执行"。同时解释称，目前，"根据中国刑法，黄海勇先生一案不适用死刑，因为没有一项罪行是引渡中所通缉的"。《中国刑法专家对黄海勇先生洗钱、行贿、走私和海关欺诈一案的报告》（背景资料，第820页）。
④ 美洲人权法院判决书第149段。
⑤ 美洲人权法院判决书第151段。
⑥ 美洲人权法院判决书第186段

维护酷刑与其他残忍、非人道或有辱人格虐待禁令,以及排除严刑逼供方面的改善情况,或是新的控制、通报和监管情况,以及在中国羁押人员受到的待遇情况。"①

而反观黄海勇所提供的专家证人 Geoff Gilbert、CarmenWurst 和 Ben Saul 的证言,判决书几乎没有提到,这也再次说明,在专家证人方面,秘鲁政府方面的证人特别是来自中方的证人证言,对于说服法庭最终作出有利于引渡的判决起到了至关重要的作用。

第二,对于对方专家证人意见的反驳

虽然本案中专家证人的证言起到了重要作用,但双方也都对于对方专家证人的证言进行了质疑,这些质疑对于我们以后进一步改进专家证人作证有一定的借鉴意义。如秘鲁政府则要求驳回黄海勇方面 Geoff Gilbert、CarmenWurst 和 Ben Saul 的专家意见。秘鲁政府认为:(1) 专家 Geoff Gilbert 从专业背景和经验上都不足,另外,还反对采纳该专家对黄海勇先生一案使用的背景资料。(2) 质疑 Carmen Wurst 的专家意见,秘鲁政府对其使用的方法提出异议,怀疑报告的质量及其应有的科学的严谨性。(3) 对于 Ben Saul 的专家意见,秘鲁政府对其报告所使用的背景资料、分析论证方法以及尚未答复秘鲁方面任何问题的情况表示质疑。对于秘鲁政府的质疑意见,法院也表示将在评估本案背景证据时适当考虑这些意见。②

五、对于黄海勇走私普通货物案判决的评价

2019 年 6 月 12 日,武汉市中级人民法院对黄海勇案作出一审判决:"被告人黄海勇犯走私普通货物罪,判处有期徒刑十五年(刑期从判决执行之日起计算。判决执行以前先行羁押的,羁押一日折抵刑期一日,即自 2008 年 10 月 30 日起至 2023 年 10 月 29 日止)"。黄海勇提出上诉后又撤回上诉,判决遂生效。至此,中国最为复杂的这起引渡案终于落下帷幕。通过研究黄海勇案的判决,我们发现有以下亮点值得研讨和肯定:

---

① 美洲人权法院判决书第 175 段。
② 美洲人权法院判决书第 51 段。

（一）将黄海勇在秘鲁被羁押的刑期予以折抵具有重要意义

1. 关于黄海勇在境外的羁押期限应否折抵其国内刑期

在本案中，黄海勇于2008年10月被秘鲁警方逮捕后即被羁押（2014年3月被改为监视居住）。也就是说，从其被逮捕直到2016年被引渡回国，黄海勇已经被羁押了将近8年。那么，黄海勇在秘鲁被羁押的8年能否折抵他被引渡回国以后被判处的刑期？这个问题就值得研究。

我国刑法中有犯罪嫌疑人先行羁押期限折抵刑期的规定，但是要以被告人被判处有期自由刑为前提。如果被告人被判处无期徒刑，由于无期徒刑的性质而无法进行刑期折抵。我国刑法典第41、44、47条具体规定了有期自由刑的折抵问题。根据该规定，判决以前先行羁押的，羁押1日折抵管制刑期2日，折抵拘役或有期徒刑1日。虽然我国刑法典上述规定中的"先行羁押"没有明确是否包含"域外先行羁押"的情况，但作为中国刑法的规定，一般理解是该规定应当只适用于在中国国内的羁押。关于域外羁押期限能否折抵回国后判处的有期自由刑的问题，我国刑法、刑事诉讼法和引渡法中都没有明确规定，理论上和实务中都有对此予以否定的主张。但在赵秉志教授准备到美洲人权法院出庭作证而进行相关问题研究的过程中，我们就主张，从法理上来讲，对于秘鲁方面基于我国请求而对黄海勇进行的域外羁押，应当折抵其回国后被判处的有期自由刑。我们持此一主张的主要理由如下：

（1）黄海勇被秘鲁警方羁押是基于我国的引渡请求而被采取的剥夺其人身自由的强制措施。

我国《引渡法》第14条规定："请求国请求引渡，应当作出如下保证……请求国提出请求后撤销、放弃引渡请求，或者提出引渡请求错误的，由请求国承担因请求引渡对被请求引渡人造成损害的责任。"该条规定实际上体现了"引渡请求国应当承担被请求国根据本国引渡请求所采取的一切措施的法律后果"的精神实质，那么，基于中国请求而采取的羁押等刑事强制措施所产生的法律后果，自然也应当由中国承担。黄海勇案件中，武汉海关走私犯罪侦查局于2001年3月16日对黄海勇签发逮捕证，同年6月26日中国警方通过国际刑警组织签发红色通报，希望各成员国逮捕黄海勇并引渡给中国。2008年10月27日,秘鲁警方根据该红色通报逮捕黄海勇,黄海勇随后被羁押。所以,黄海勇在秘鲁被执行的羁押实际上是中国以引渡为目的而请求秘鲁所采取的刑事强制措施,中国应当承认并承担该羁押所产生的相应法律后果。

(2) 符合罪刑法定原则有利于被告人的实质内涵。

作为刑法的基本原则,罪刑法定原则是资产阶级反对封建刑法的罪刑擅断中产生的,它以保障公民自由、限制国家刑罚权的行使为己任,其基本内容是法无明文规定不为罪,法无明文规定不处罚,其实质内涵是行为时法无明文的即"不定罪、不处罚"。时至今日,罪刑法定原则已成为当代各国刑法乃至国际刑法规范中被普遍认可和广泛采纳的第一基本原则,并对整个刑事法治具有纲举目张的作用,其地位和功能不容挑战。在刑事诉讼当中,罪刑法定原则的基本精神体现为"有利于被告人",这不仅因为罪刑法定原则自身的终极目标就是保护人权,而且也由被告人在刑事诉讼中的弱势地位所决定。罪刑法定原则的派生原则如禁止类推、从旧兼从轻原则、禁止不定期刑等,均体现了有利于被告人的精神内涵。在本案中,黄海勇在域外已经被羁押将近8年,虽然羁押的执行者是秘鲁政府,但是秘鲁政府是基于中国的引渡请求而将黄羁押,黄海勇也是因为自己涉嫌在中国所实施的走私犯罪而被羁押,这种羁押与其在中国被逮捕而进行的羁押并没有实质的区别。从罪刑法定原则"有利于被告人"基本精神出发,应当将其在秘鲁的将近8年的羁押期限在其被判处的刑期中予以折抵。

(3) 在国际条约中有域外羁押期限折抵所判处刑期的立法先例可资借鉴。

虽然我国国内立法中迄今尚没有关于境外羁押能否折抵国内刑期的相关规定,但是我国同他国签订的双边引渡条约中却已有类似规定,这样的规定分为两类:① 明确规定境外羁押时间应当折抵回国后被判的刑期。如《中华人民共和国和突尼斯引渡条约》第14条"移交被请求引渡人"中明确规定:"如果同意引渡,缔约双方应当商定移交的地点、时间,被请求方应通知请求方被请求引渡人受到羁押的时间,以便折抵该人的刑期。"② 虽然没有明确规定,但是暗含着境外羁押时间可以折抵回国后被判出的刑期。如《中华人民共和国和秘鲁引渡条约》第 11 条"移交被引渡人"规定："如果被请求方同意引渡,双方应当商定执行引渡的时间、地点等有关事宜。同时,被请求方应当将被引渡人移交前已被羁押的时间通知请求方。"这种规定虽然没有明确说明境外羁押时间可以折抵回国的刑期,但是却要求双方在移交被引渡人的时候"被请求方应当将被引渡人移交前已被羁押的时间通知请求方",这本身就说明,被请求方有义务将其已经羁押被引渡人的时间告诉请求方,请求方也有义务了解被请求人已经被羁押的时间,以便于为后续的相关诉讼程序作为参考,而参考的一个重要内容就应当是能否折抵被判处的刑期。

综上,我们认为,黄海勇回国后如果被判处有期自由刑,他在秘鲁被羁押期限应当考虑折抵其回国后所判的有期徒刑刑期,这是合乎法理与情理的,其具体折抵方法可以参考中国刑法第 41、44、47 条之规定;当然,如果黄海勇被判处的是无期徒刑,则没有刑期折抵问题。

2. 一审判决将黄海勇在秘鲁被羁押的刑期予以折抵具有重要意义

关于上述刑期折抵问题,武汉中级人民法院 2019 年 6 月 12 日做出的判决认定："(……判决执行以前先行羁押的,羁押一日折抵刑期一日,即自 2008 年 10 月 30 日起至 2023 年 10 月 29 日止)"。如前所述,2008 年 10 月 30 日正是黄海勇在秘鲁被逮捕的时间,此后黄海勇一直处于秘鲁警方的羁押和监管之下,2016 年 7 月 13 日黄海勇被秘鲁政府引渡给我国,同年 7 月 17 日,被武汉海关缉私局押解回中国被执行逮捕。黄海勇被我国公安机关执行逮捕后羁押的时间,根据我国刑法规定应当在被判决的刑期内予以折抵。但是对于被秘鲁政府逮捕后予以羁押将近 8 年的期限(2008 年 10 月至 2016 年 7 月)是否能够折抵,我国国内法中并没有明确规定。对此,我们已在前文中从多个角度论证了黄海勇在秘鲁被羁押的时间应当折抵国内刑期的法理依据。

武汉市中级人民法院能够在我国国内法律没有明确规定的前提下,根据法理最终判决对于黄海勇在秘鲁的羁押时间予以折抵,具有重要的意义:(1)创制了境外羁押期限折抵国内判决刑期的先例。黄海勇案是我国第一个对于境外羁押期限进行折抵的案件。随着我国境外追逃案件的日益增多,我国会有更多的案例面临境外羁押期限能否折抵国内刑期的问题,本案的判决将为此后的类似案件创制先例。(2)推动我国刑法关于刑期折抵问题的完善。我国刑法没有规定境外羁押期限能否折抵国内判决刑期,随着时代的发展,这种规定越来越不能适应司法实践的需要。虽然如前所述,我国所缔结的部分双边条约中也有折抵刑期的规定,但这些双边条约仅仅适用于缔约国之间,并不具有普遍的适用意义。本案的判决是一个重要契机,将为我国修改刑法,明确规定境外羁押期限可以折抵我国国内判决的刑期奠定实践基础。(3)充分体现罪刑法定原则有利于被告人的精神内涵。如前所述,罪刑法定原则的一个基本精神内涵是"有利于被告人"。本案中秘鲁根据中方的引渡请求,基于黄海勇在中国所实施的走私犯罪,对其执行逮捕并羁押近8年时间,从罪刑法定原则"有利于被告人"基本精神内涵出发,将黄海勇在秘鲁的羁押期限折抵其在国内被判处的刑期,向世界昭示着我国刑事法治充分尊重与保障犯罪嫌疑人和被告人的各项权益,对国内法律没有明确规定的问题,将作出有利于被告人的裁决。(4)鼓励在境外被羁押的外逃人员尽早回国自首。随着我国追逃追赃国际合作的全面展开,将有更多的犯罪嫌疑人基于我国的请求而被他国逮捕、羁押,进而被引渡回国,那么这类犯罪嫌疑人在境外被羁押的期限(引渡程序一般都较为漫长)如果不能折抵其回国后被判处的刑期,将有利于鼓励更多犯罪嫌疑人及时回国自首,从而有利于提高我国境外追逃效率。

(二)对于黄海勇走私犯罪金额的认定应当与同案犯潘子牛的判决保持一致

对于黄海勇涉案的犯罪金额,本案判决认定:"公诉机关指控被告人黄海勇犯走私普通货物罪的犯罪事实成立,但指控的犯罪数额有误,应按照湖北省高院人民法院对同案犯潘子牛走私普通物案终审判决确定的走私金额认定。"根据上述认定,黄海勇的涉案金额有两种说法,分别是公诉机关武汉市人民检察院的指控金额710645040.44元和武汉市中级人民法院法院最终的认定金额379524829.28元。本案中,同案犯潘子牛是黄海勇的下属,两人涉嫌共同实施走私犯罪,之前我国法院对于潘子牛的涉案罪行已经做出生效判决。黄海勇犯罪金额的认定,与该判决中所认定的潘子牛的犯罪金额具有密切关系。

对于潘子牛走私普通货物案,武汉市中级人民法院于 2012 年 10 月 17 日作出一审判决,认定潘子牛犯走私普通货物罪,偷逃国家税款人民币 710645040.44 元,判决潘子牛判处有期徒刑 13 年。后潘子牛不服,提出上诉。2014 年 8 月 15 日,湖北省高级人民法院就该案作出二审判决,认为一审判决所认定的部分犯罪事实不清,证据不足,所认定的犯罪金额有误,潘子牛涉嫌走私偷逃应缴税款应为 379524829.28 元,最终二审判决维持一审判决中对潘子牛的定罪部分以及财物处置部分,撤销一审判决中对上诉人潘子牛的量刑部分,判决潘子牛犯走私普通货物罪,判处有期徒刑 10 年。

本案中,黄海勇和潘子牛两人在涉案的五家公司分别担任董事长、总经理或董事等职务,两人都应对涉案单位所实施的全部走私犯罪负刑事责任。在潘子牛的犯罪事实已经由湖北省高级人民法院作出终审判决的前提下,应当以该判决所认定的事实为准。所以本案公诉机关以潘子牛案一审判决中所认定(并且已经被二审判决所改变的)的潘子牛的犯罪金额作为指控黄海勇的犯罪金额,并不妥当。武汉市中级人民法院将湖北省高院人民法院对潘子牛走私普通物案终审判决确定的走私犯罪金额 379524829.28 元,认定为黄海勇的犯罪金额,我们认为是正确的。

(三)对于犯罪单位的刑事责任不再追诉并不能免除犯罪自然人的刑事责任

我国刑法典第 31 条规定:"单位犯罪的,对单位判处罚金,并对其直接负责的主管人员和其他直接责任人员判处刑罚。"据此,我国刑法对于单位犯罪实行双罚制,不仅依法追究犯罪单位的刑事责任,还要依法追究单位中相关自然人即直接负责的主管人员和其他直接责任人员的刑事责任。在黄海勇案件中,涉案的若干公司均由黄海勇担任董事长兼法人代表(或董事、总经理),黄海勇应当对于这些公司所实施的走私犯罪行为承担刑事责任。正如一审判决所认定的:深圳市亨润国际实业有限公司、深圳裕伟贸易实业有限公司、深圳市裕伟实业发展有限公司、湖北裕伟贸易实业有限公司和武汉丰润油脂保税仓库有限公司未经海关许可并且未补缴应缴税款,擅自将批准进口的进料加工保税毛豆油在境内销售牟利,偷逃应缴税款共计人民币 379524829.28 元,其行为均构成走私普通货物罪,且数额特别巨大。黄海勇作为上述单位直接负责的主管人员,应对上述单位所犯走私普通货物罪承担罪责,其行为已构成走私普通货物罪,且犯罪情节特别严重。

基于我国刑法对于单位犯罪的双罚制,上述涉案公司和黄海勇都应当对走私行为承担相应的刑事责任。鉴于上述涉案单位均因为被吊销营业执照而不复存在,对其无法追究刑事责任,因此一审判决依法对上述涉案单位不再追诉。但是,对于单位不再追究刑事责任,并不能免除黄海勇作为单位直接负责的主管人员所应当承担的刑事责任,所以一审判决依然依法追究了黄海勇的刑事责任。

(四)具有坦白的法定情节并不意味着一定要从轻处罚

量刑情节是指某种行为已经构成犯罪的前提下,法院对犯罪人裁量刑罚时应当考虑的据以决定刑罚轻重或者免除刑罚处罚的各种情况。量刑情节根据不同标准分为不同种类,以刑法是否做出明文规定可以分为法定量刑情节和酌定量刑情节,以情节对量刑轻重产生的影响可以分为从宽情节和从严情节。对于不同量刑情节的适用,在具体案件中应当综合进行考量。本案中,黄海勇虽然具备坦白的法定可以从宽情节,但由于其又同时具备犯罪情节特别严重等酌定从严情节,法院经过衡量最终对其不予以从轻处罚。

我国《刑法修正案(八)》增设了刑法典第67条第3款:"犯罪嫌疑人虽然不具有前两款规定的自首情节,但是如实供述自己罪行的,可以从轻处罚;因其如实供述自己罪行,避免特别严重后果发生的,可以减轻处罚"。根据该款之规定,坦白成为法定的从宽情节,犯罪嫌疑人虽然不具有自首情节,但只要如实供述自己的罪行,就可以对其从轻处罚。由于如实供述自己罪行而避免特别严重后果发生的,可以减轻处罚。本案中,黄海勇归案后认罪坦白,符合坦白的成立条件,可以从轻处罚。而具体是否从轻处罚,就要综合考虑本案的其他情节。事实上,黄海勇虽然具备坦白的情节,但其偷逃应缴税达到3亿多元,案发以后潜逃至境外18年,这些都是酌定的从重情节。审判机关在综合考虑黄海勇案的法定从宽情节和酌定从重情节之后,最终对其不予以从宽处罚,符合我国刑法的相关规定及其立法精神。

六、黄海勇案件的经验与反思

从黄海勇 2008 年 11 月被羁押,到美洲人权法院 2016 年 7 月被引渡回国,黄海勇案件跌宕起伏,历尽波折。经过我国和秘鲁政府的不懈努力,终于促使美洲人权法院做出有利于我方的判决,最终将黄海勇引渡回国,这是我国引渡合作史上的里程碑,具有重大标志性意义。对于此案我们可以得出以下启示:

(一)咬定青山不放松,持之以恒开展境外追逃

黄海勇引渡案,境外追逃 18 年,引渡程序 8 年,其间不仅经过了秘鲁地方法院、秘鲁最高法院、秘鲁宪法法院,而且被提交到美洲人权委员会和美洲人权法院。在此过程中,黄海勇及其律师一再利用死刑问题、人身保护令等措施为引渡设置障碍。中秘两国相关部门为引渡的顺利进行付出了艰辛努力:(1)中国方面。在中国国家领导人亲自过问、批示和与秘鲁国家领导人商谈下,中方由中央纪委、外交部、中国驻秘鲁使馆、国家海关总署、司法部、最高人民法院、最高人民检察院、武汉海关以及有关高等院校的专家证人组成工作团队,共同努力,坚持不懈,攻坚克难,不屈不挠,将案件一点点推向前进,为本案的胜利奠定了基础。(2)秘鲁方面。秘鲁政府与中国具有良好的外交关系,在中方的争取和沟通下,秘鲁各相关部门一直对于引渡合作持支持态度。秘鲁总理府、外交部、司法部、内政部、监狱管理局、警察总局等政府部门,最高法院、利马高等法院院、卡亚俄高等法院等司法机构,秘鲁宪法法院、国家检察院等独立机构,秘鲁利马机场管理局等相关机构都曾参与此案,其间秘鲁经历了 2 届政府,5 任外长,4 任最高法院院长,11 任司法部长,12 任内政部长,这些部门和中方一道精诚合作,接续努力,共同开展黄海勇案的引渡工作,其间的曲折与漫长远远超乎想象。

反思引渡黄海勇的过程,我们可以发现,在很多情况下,包括引渡在内的境外追逃说到底就是中方和外逃人员之间的一场毅力的较量,谁能够坚持到最后,胜利就会属于谁。所以,我们在开展境外追逃工作的时候,一定要对于境外追逃的曲折和漫长有着足够的心理准备。2014 年以来,中国开

展了以"天网"行为、"猎狐"行动为代表的境外追逃追赃专项行动,取得了突出的成绩,境外追逃中的最难啃的硬骨头——"百名红通人员",①截止到2017年10月8日也被追回了47名,②表面上看来都是在短短几年内取得的成绩,但是每一个追回的外逃人员都凝聚了中国追逃机构和人员的大量心血,都是中国同他国多年来开展国际合作的结果。特别是与国外合作开展非法移民遣返、异地追诉和引渡合作的案件,一般都不是短时间内能够成功的。如赖昌星案件,从赖昌星1999年出逃到2011年历经12年才被追回。③所以在境外追逃中,我们一方面要妥善采取各种措施,努力在短时间之内将外逃人员尽早缉拿归案,但同时也应当抱着打持久战的决心,特别是对于外逃美国、加拿大、澳大利亚等西方经济、法治发达国家的犯罪嫌疑人,以咬定青山不放松的精神,百折不挠,锲而不舍,有针对性地解决境外追逃中的一个个法律难题,一步步推进案件的进行,直到将犯罪嫌疑人缉拿归案。

(二)积极推进死刑改革,化解对方对于我国死刑问题的误解

死刑问题几乎是我国每一个涉严重犯罪引渡案件都不可回避的问题。作为国际刑事司法合作中的一项基本原则,死刑不引渡是现代引渡制度的产物,并随着人权观念的兴起逐步形成和发展起来。黄海勇所涉嫌的走私普通货物罪,虽然已经于2011年由《刑法修正案(八)》废除了死刑,但死刑问题仍然是黄海勇及其律师用来对抗引渡的主要借口之一,也是美洲人权法院关注的重点问题之一。在美洲人权法院的巡回法庭上,赵秉志教授作为专家证人被询问的61个问题中,涉及死刑的有22个(占了三分之一还多),主要包括黄海勇是否会被适用死刑,中国就黄海勇案件所作出的不判处死刑的外交承诺,以及中国死刑适用的罪名、数量、执行方式等三方面的问题。孙昂参赞被询问的52个问题中,涉及死刑的也有10个(占了将近五分之

---

① 张磊:《从"百名红通人员"归案看我国境外追逃的发展》,载《北京师范大学学报(社会科学版)》2017年第3期。
② 《"百名红通人员"郭欣回国投案》,载 http://www.ccdi.gov.cn/special/ztzz/ztzzjxs_ztzz/201710/t20171009_108429.html
③ 关于赖昌星案件的详细内容,请参见赵秉志、张磊:《赖昌星案件法律问题研究》,载《政法论坛》2014年第4期。

一),涉及中国以往不判处死刑的外交承诺是否得到了履行,保证不判处死刑承诺履行的机制等问题。而且,即使在明确了黄海勇所涉嫌的走私普通货物罪已经被《刑法修正案(八)》废除了死刑之后,美洲人权法院各方还就中国死刑的适用对赵秉志教授、孙昂参赞进行了详细询问,更加说明了死刑问题在黄海勇案件,乃至在涉中国引渡案件中的重要地位。围绕死刑问题,我们需要注意以下几个方面的问题:

1. 积极推进死刑改革

近年来我国努力推进死刑改革,加快限制和废除死刑的步伐,通过《刑法修正案(八)》和《刑法修正案(九)》先后废除了13种和9种罪名的死刑,但是我国现在还对包括贪污罪、受贿罪在内的46种犯罪保留有死刑,对于贪污罪、受贿罪的死缓犯还配置了不得减刑、不得假释的终身监禁制度。当前我国正在全面开展反腐败境外追逃工作,腐败犯罪的死刑问题将是我们无法回避的问题。我们应当顺应世界范围内限制和废除死刑的国际趋势,结合我国国情,切实推进死刑改革进程,尽早废除非暴力犯罪特别是腐败犯罪和经济犯罪的死刑,并为最终废除死刑而努力。在当前我国还不具备完全废除死刑的条件下,如果在引渡、遣返等国际合作中遭遇死刑问题,应当根据案件情况,及时、果断作出并严格信守不判处死刑的承诺,避免死刑成为外逃者的免责盾牌,以尽早将外逃者缉捕归案,切实推动我国境外追逃工作的开展。

2. 直面死刑问题

黄海勇涉嫌的走私普通货物罪,在《刑法修正案(八)》通过之前的《刑法》第153条和第151条中是规定有死刑的,这是客观事实。但是在中国向秘鲁方面提交的引渡请求和随后的各种说明中,却迟迟没有明确提供该条文之规定和相应的译文。例如,在2008年11月黄海勇被逮捕之后,中方在前三次向秘鲁方面提交引渡材料或者说明,[①]均没有提到《刑法》第151条之规定,直到2009年2月19日秘鲁司法部明确要求提供《刑法》第151条及译文之后,中方才于5天后的2月24日提交了该条的规定及译文。而反观黄

---

① 这三次分别是:2008年11月3日中方首次向秘鲁方面提供请求引渡黄海勇的材料;2009年1月中方向秘鲁最高法院提交的关于黄海勇犯罪事实的进一步解释;2009年2月2日中方公安部提交给秘鲁司法部的说明。

海勇方面,在黄海勇被逮捕后的第二天就提出中国《刑法》对走私普通货物罪规定的死刑问题,在两周后举行的听证会上,黄海勇方面再次直接提出本案适用的条款是中国《刑法》第151条,并在2009年2月19日秘鲁最高法院的引渡听证会上提交了该条文及译文。中方对死刑问题的延缓与迟疑(没有及时提交该条的规定及译文),也被黄海勇首次提出人身保护请求的时候,污蔑为"出于恶意而隐瞒"。事实上,不论中方是否提供关于死刑的规定,以及何时提交,都不能掩盖该罪规定有死刑的事实。而且即使中方不明确提出,也会被对方直接提出。所以,既然死刑问题在我国境外追逃中无法回避,那么我们就应当直接面对,在向对方提交的材料中明确说明该罪可能被判处死刑的情况,并尽早做出不判处死刑的承诺,而不应该忽略甚至有意回避此问题,因为我方的任何疏忽或者回避,都可能被外逃人员直接提出,并被对方国家或者国际人权机构理解为故意甚至恶意掩盖对于外逃人员判处死刑的可能性,从而影响我国司法形象,降低追逃成功的可能性。

3. 全面澄清死刑问题

境外追逃中的死刑问题不仅包括死刑立法问题,还包括实践中死刑的实际适用状况。秘鲁宪法法院2011年5月24日判决拒绝引渡黄海勇的理由之一,就是怀疑中国法律中的死刑还可能存在法外执行和任意处决,死刑的适用受到舆论影响较大。所以境外追逃中的死刑问题,并不仅限于某种犯罪是否规定有死刑,还在于中国死刑在实践中的适用状况问题,如死刑适用有没有法外执行,死刑的适用是否存在法外因素等。而这些问题,都和国际社会对于中国司法制度的不了解和误解颇有关系。近年来,国际社会中部分国家对于我国刑事法治建设不断进步、人权保障不断完善的现状视而不见,认为中国根本没有基本的刑事法治制度,犯罪嫌疑人一旦会被引渡(遣返)回国,很可能会遭受酷刑、死刑乃至法外执行等严刑峻法。即使我们把相关法律和案例摆到他们面前,证明中国法治状况的进步与公正,他们还是会执拗地认为法律规定不足以说明问题,司法实践和立法规定存在较大差距,相关案件背后受多种非法律因素的控制与制约。[①] 实际上,近年来我

---

① 赵秉志:《我在加拿大赖昌星聆讯庭上作证》,载《凤凰周刊》2011年第23期。

国刑事法治取得了突破性的进展,我国死刑的适用都是严格依照法律进行,没有任何法外执行。现实中,虽然公众舆论的确对于死刑适用有一定的影响,但也是在法律允许的限度之内。针对这种可能存在的误解乃至曲解,我们在向被请求国提出的引渡材料中,不仅要对于法律是否规定有死刑,是否依法可能判处死刑进行说明,还可以向对方提供证明中国死刑实践中的适用状况,死刑适用标准的说明,以尽量减少对方对于我国死刑制度的误解。当然,这在根本上还要靠我国刑事法治的进步,和对于这些进步的适当宣传,以增强国际社会特别是被请求国对于中国的了解。①

(三)加强自身刑事法治建设,完善国际刑事法治形象

在国际刑事司法合作中,引渡能否顺利进行的一个重要因素,就是被请求国是否认同和信任请求国的刑事司法制度。因此,能否增强国际社会对于我国刑事司法制度的了解与信心,将是我国能否顺利开展引渡合作的关键。在黄海勇案件中,黄海勇及其律师用来对抗引渡的主要理由,除了死刑之外,就是声称黄海勇回国之后很可能会面临酷刑以及非公正的待遇。在美洲人权法院的法庭上,赵秉志教授被询问的涉及中国刑事司法制度的问题有13个(占所有问题的五分之一),具体包括黄海勇被引渡回国之后的刑事诉讼程序,中国无罪判决的比例,中国刑事诉讼是否存在酷刑,中国刑事诉讼中律师的参与程度,引渡程序中特定性原则的适用等。孙昂参赞被询问的涉及中国引渡制度和被引渡人回国之后刑事诉讼程序的问题有23个(占其所有问题的将近二分之一),具体包括中国外交承诺的作出与履行、中国引渡相关程序,中国和他国开展引渡合作的情况等。

美洲人权法院对于中国刑事诉讼程序问题的关注,直接关系到其对于中国刑事司法制度公正性的评价,即中国刑事司法制度是否符合美洲人权法院所认可的国际人权标准,黄海勇在被引渡回中国后能否获得公正的审判和人道的待遇,诉讼权利能否得到充分的保障。近年来,在中央的领导下,我国刑事法治建设取得了长足进展,"国家尊重和保障人权"被写入宪法,人权保障的刑事法治理念逐步得到确立,中国特色社会主义法律体系已

① 张磊:《反腐败零容忍与境外追逃》,法律出版社2017年版,第187页。

经形成,国际社会对于中国刑事法治的了解与信任明显提升,这也是中国近年来境外追逃工作取得突出成绩的重要原因之一。但是客观来说,中国刑事法治建设还有一些需要改进的地方,如部分地方还存在刑讯逼供,司法机构的独立性尚有待进一步提高等等。所以,我们应当积极推进中央所确定的以审判为中心的诉讼制度改革,完善刑事法律制度,保证刑事审判的公开、公平、公正,充分保障犯罪嫌疑人、被告人的诉讼权利,进一步增强国际社会对于中国刑事法治的认同与信心,奠定我国在境外追逃中的自信与底气。

需要注意的是,当前国际社会对于中国刑事司法制度不信任的原因,还在于他们对中国刑事法治发展的状况不完全了解。在赵秉志教授等赴美洲人权法院作证之前,就得知该法庭因为不知道中国已经于2011年废除了走私普通货物罪的死刑而对中国能否遵守不判处黄海勇死刑的承诺信心不足。而在赵秉志教授在美洲人权法院作证接近尾声之时,美洲人权法院的庭长谢拉法官也明确表示:"您所讲的与我们原来所了解的有很大不同,我们将认真研究"。这都反映出美洲人权法院对于中国刑事法治状况的了解不够,进而也增加了他们对引渡中国嫌犯的担心与疑虑。所以,我们在加快我国刑事司法改革、推进刑事法治建设的同时,还要积极加强同外部世界的交流与宣传,使国际社会能够及时而全面地了解我国的社会进步状况,特别是我国刑事法治建设的卓越成就,利用各种机会澄清国际社会对于我国法律和司法制度的误解与偏见,从而推动海外追逃工作的顺利开展。

(四)妥善运用已有成功案例,推动境外追逃的顺利开展

在赵秉志教授、孙昂参赞等人于2014年4月接到将赴美洲人权法院作证的任务的时候,就获知此次作证的一个重要方面就是介绍赖昌星遣返案件的相关情况。这一方面是因为赵秉志教授曾经于2001年8月和10月两次应加拿大政府邀请作为事实证人(实质上是作为专家证人对待)赴加拿大出席了审理赖昌星案件的法庭聆讯并发表了证言,孙昂参赞当时作为中国外交部条约法律司的官员也直接接触了赖昌星案件的材料并参与了有关工作;另一方面是由于两案有极大的相似性,黄海勇案件是美洲人权法院审理的首个涉中国引渡案件,赖昌星遣返案件是该法庭审理黄海勇案件的重要

参考。在准备作证的过程中,赵秉志教授在中纪委、外交部等中央部门的指导和帮助下,在北师大刑事法律科学研究院几位年轻学者的协助下,①有针对性地回忆、整理了他所参与的赖昌星遣返案件的有关情况。在美洲人权法院审理黄海勇案件过程中,法庭各方询问赵秉志教授关于赖昌星案件的问题共有 10 个,询问孙昂参赞的关于赖昌星案件的问题也有 10 个,包括加拿大为什么同意遣返赖昌星,赖昌星的定罪量刑,赖昌星案件中的外交承诺,黄海勇案件与赖昌星案件的相似性等。后续的实践证明,我国在赖昌星案件中及时作出并严格遵守不判处死刑的外交承诺,依法对赖昌星进行公正审判,充分保障赖昌星的诉讼权利,允许加方在赖昌星服刑后前去探视等事实,都向美洲人权法院表明,中国具有较为完善的刑事司法制度,中国政府信守承诺、言出必行,对于美洲人权法院作出引渡黄海勇的裁决具有积极的促进作用。

所以,在国际引渡、遣返合作中,我们要妥善运用以往的成功案例,积极宣传外逃人员回国以后所受到的公正待遇、宽大处理,向国际社会和外逃人员表明,中国具有公正的司法制度,完善的诉讼程序,完全能够保证外逃人员的合法权益和诉讼权利,从而一方面增强他国对于中国刑事法治的信心,积极与中国开展引渡合作;另一方面促进外逃人员思想的转变,提高其自觉接受引渡乃至回国自首的可能性。

(五)遵守国际法律规则,提供符合对方要求的证据材料

在法庭上,美洲人权委员会的律师曾经向赵秉志教授询问关于中国向秘鲁提出引渡申请中为什么没有附上证实黄海勇构成犯罪的证据和中国相关法律条文的西班牙文文本的问题。这两个问题,赵秉志教授由于不了解我国向秘鲁提出引渡请求的具体内容,而都如实作了"不了解"的回答。虽然就该问题对方律师并没有纠缠下去,该问题对于整个案件也没有发生实质性影响,但是也反映出引渡合作中被请求方对于引渡提交证据和材料的重视。事实上引渡合作当中,被请求国或者引渡双边条约中都规定了提出

---

① 2016 年 4 月接到出庭作证的任务以后,因为时间紧、作证又涉及多个方面,为了保证圆满完成作证任务,赵秉志教授约请他所在的北京师范大学刑事法律科学研究院的三位青年教师(张磊教授、袁彬教授和何挺副教授)和他一起组成作证工作小组,协助他进行前期资料准备工作。

引渡请求所需的文件(如《中国和秘鲁引渡条约》中就有相关规定①)。但是,由于基层办案机关对国际法律与制度的不熟悉,对于引渡工作的具体标准欠缺经验,在准备、翻译证据和材料方面不熟练,以及嫌疑人出逃后不能及时有效取证等因素,我国往往难以提供符合对方要求的证据材料,一个突出的表现就是引渡请求中关于犯罪事实的描述过于简单,请求材料不包含必要的线索和信息,这样的请求很容易被搁置乃至拒绝。对此来自国际刑事司法合作一线的实务工作人员有过明确论述:在我国引渡请求实践中,因请求书的制作质量和译文质量不高,以及向被请求国提供的相关证据材料不符合被请求引渡国的证据标准,而影响引渡的顺利开展的情况客观存在。主要原因包括:各国法律制度和司法制度差异较大,各国对于引渡请求所附加的证据材料、证据标准有不同要求,没有统一、专业的翻译机构等。② 也有实务工作者称,在相关技术细节上,由于很多案件来自基层,他们对国际司法协作和不同国家的具体标准欠缺经验,在准备、翻译所需证据和材料方面不太熟练。另外,有些嫌疑人出逃后,办案单位难以短时间内有效取证。③ 这都严重影响了境外追逃的效率。例如,2005年5月意大利佛罗伦萨上诉法院裁决拒绝引渡中国公民高明亮的一个理由,就是中方提供的支持引渡请求的证据过于薄弱,不符合基本的证据规则。④ 2015年7月,加拿大温尼伯法院判定程慕阳司法复核成功,将程慕阳的难民申请发回难民署重新考虑和决定的主要原因,也是中方向加方提供的相关证据不全面或者这些证据过于模糊。⑤

客观来说,遵守国际法律制度,提供符合对方要求的证据材料,是刑事司法协助中的技术性问题,只要给予足够重视和充分准备,应该能够克服。所以,我们一定要认真研究引渡被请求国的国际刑事司法合作法律规范和

---

① 《中华人民共和国和秘鲁引渡条约》第7条规定:"引渡请求应当以书面方式提出,并且包括或者附有:……(三)有关案情的说明,包括犯罪行为及后果的概述;(四)有关该项犯罪的刑事管辖权、定罪和刑罚的法律规定……"
② 郭明聪:《关于刑事司法协助几个问题的探讨》,载"10·7"专案引渡工作研讨会"会议资料。
③ 王丽娜、李恩树、蔡婷贻、张舟逸:《盘点境外追逃追赃:薄熙来法国别墅仍未追缴》http://news.china.com/domestic/945/20141201/19034927.html。
④ 黄风主编:《中国境外追逃追赃经验与反思》,中国政法大学出版社2016年版,第133页。
⑤ 陈雷:《如何破解程慕阳案国际执法合作困局》,载《法制日报》2015年7月21日。

制度,提前做好充分准备,一旦需要,一次性及时提出符合要求的引渡请求和包括翻译文本在内的所有证据材料,减少对方因为证据材料问题搁置乃至拒绝我国引渡请求的可能性,从而降低境外追逃追赃中的技术性障碍。

(六)全面提交案件材料,根据要求果断作出外交承诺

美洲人权法院判决书显示,从黄海勇被羁押,到宪法法院做出判决,中方共计提出了八次照会,这些照会中,除了引渡请求之外,还涉及黄海勇与他人共同犯罪的事实,同案犯的判刑情况和所适用的法律及判处的刑罚等等。但是,其中有数次所提交信息都是在对方要求或者提醒之下才提交的。比如,前述的提交中国《刑法》第151条法条及其译文的问题和中国《刑法》第12条的溯及力说明问题,都是在对方提醒之后提交的。这种在对方提醒甚至是数次提醒下提交材料的情境,往往使得中国在引渡程序中处于被动(起码从美洲人权法院判决书的行文上来看是如此)。所以,我们在以后境外追逃向对方提交材料的过程中,可以考虑将有关材料进行打包一次性予以提交,防止在材料的提交上被对方一再提醒补充,甚至被外逃人员提前提交材料而占了先机而处于被动。具体来说,应当提交的要求引渡的材料可以包括三个部分:

第一,双方法律规定的案件材料、翻译文本和相关案件事实。应当根据双边引渡条约规定以及被请求国引渡法律之规定提交引渡材料,①一般包括被请求引渡人的基本情况,相关案情说明,相关法律条文、诉讼文书、证据材料以及相应的翻译文本,特别是相关规定有死刑的法律条文,一定要如实提交。同时要注意根据对方要求提供相应的翻译文本(如秘鲁是西班牙语,就应当提交西班牙文本,需要的话还可以附上英文文本)。相关案件事实包括行为人共同犯罪事实,共同犯罪人在中国的诉讼程序,以及判刑情况,向对

---

① 如中秘《引渡条约》规定第7条就规定:"一、引渡请求应当以书面形式提出,并且包括或者附有:(一)请求机关的名称;(二)被请求引渡人的姓名、年龄、性别、国籍、身份证件、职业、住所地或者居所地等有助于确定被请求引渡人的身份和可能所在地点的资料;如有可能,有关其外表的描述、照片和指纹;(三)有关案情的说明,包括犯罪行为及其后果的概述;(四)有关该项犯罪的刑事管辖权、定罪和刑罚的法律规定;(五)有关追诉时效或者执行判决期限的法律规定。二、除本条第一款规定外,(一)旨在对被请求引渡人进行审判的引渡请求还应当附有请求方主管机关签发的逮捕证的副本;(二)旨在对被请求引渡人执行刑罚的引渡请求还应当附有已经发生法律效力的法院判决书的副本和关于已经执行刑期的说明。三、经适当签署和(或者)盖章的引渡请求及所需文件应当附有被请求方文字的译文。四、根据本条第三款提交的文件免于任何形式的领事认证。"

方说明在中国,根据同案犯的情况不会被判处死刑,诉讼权利会得到充分的保障。当然,引渡程序和刑事司法合作的情况是多变的,也不可能一次提交所有的材料,更不可能一次提交的所有材料均符合对方的标准,但是我们应当尽早全面做好准备,即使遇到不符合对方要求或者缺少相应材料的情况,也应当快速反应,在第一时间补充相关材料,从而在国际合作中处于主动,彰显中方对于该案的重视程度,提高国际司法合作的效率。

第二,外交承诺。从黄海勇案我国向秘鲁方面陆续作出的三个包含有外交担保的照会(分别为2009年12月,2011年2月22日,2014年8月19日)可以看出,在开展引渡合作过程中,被请求国所关注的关键问题除了犯罪嫌疑人是否会被判处死刑之外,还包括犯罪嫌疑人是否会遭受酷刑等残忍和非人道的待遇,诉讼权利能否得到充分保障,请求国能否保证被请求国对于案件进展的知情权和监督权等问题。这说明,引渡合作中的外交担保不仅包括不判处死刑或者不执行死刑的承诺,而且包括承诺不会遭受酷刑等非人道的待遇,承诺保障外逃人员充分享有的诉讼权利,承诺外逃人员在执行刑罚的时候享有医疗服务,承诺在案件审判的时候邀请对方参加庭审,对于案件执行情况进行监督等等。虽然外交担保一般是基于对方的要求作出承诺或者担保,①而不宜在对方未提出请求的情况下主动承诺,甚至一次性打包承诺。但是我们同样要尽早准备,与国内有关部门提前做好沟通工作,力争做到"提前充分准备,按需及时承诺",一旦对方要求,各部门快速行动,精诚合作,尽早做出恰当的承诺和担保,以推动引渡程序的顺利开展。

第三,刑法修正案的溯及力问题。秘鲁宪法法院在2011年5月的判决中,拒绝中国引渡请求的一个理由是"没有提到中国《宪法》是否承认刑法对于被告人有利的溯及力问题"。由于《刑法修正案(八)》生效于2011年5月,而黄海勇的相关犯罪主要实施于1996—1998年间,确实存在中国《刑法修正案(八)》是否适用于本案的问题。客观来说,根据中国《刑法》第12条,中国刑法在溯及力问题上采取的是从旧兼从轻原则,所以《刑法修正案(八)》当

---

① 比如,秘鲁最高法院在2010年1月作出第二次咨询判决的时候,就提出黄海勇的引渡条件之一是"在对黄海勇做出判决的时候,将判决的内容通知秘鲁政府",此后的2月22日中方通过外交照会向秘鲁司法部承诺邀请秘鲁政府派遣观察员参加对于黄海勇的审判,并对判决执行情况进行监督。

然可以适用于黄海勇案件,即不判处死刑。这虽然在我国刑事法领域是一个常识性问题,但是对于并不熟悉中国刑法规定的美洲国家来说,却是陌生的。如果中国《刑法》不坚持从旧兼从轻原则,即使《刑法修正案八》废除死刑,对于黄海勇依然可以适用死刑。所以,虽然中国已经于2009年12月向秘鲁做出了不判处黄海勇死刑的承诺,也已经于2011年4月就将《刑法修正案(八)》对于走私普通货物罪死刑的废止情况通知了秘鲁方面,但如果没有提到该修正案的溯及力问题,那么秘鲁宪法法院对于中国是否判处黄海勇死刑的问题存在疑惑也在情理之中。所以,我方在秘鲁宪法法院做出判决之后的2011年12月,即通过外交照会的形式向秘鲁方面进一步解释了中国《刑法》第12条关于溯及力的规定。总之,在以后的境外追逃的司法协助中,在向对方提交关于相关犯罪死刑废除材料的时候,不仅要提交相关刑法修正案的材料,还要注意提交关于修正案的溯及力问题的材料,以便对于已经废除了死刑的修正案的溯及力的问题进行明确说明。

(七)保持客观公正,如实向国际社会证明中国刑事法治的进步

如前所述,美洲人权法院审理本案的一个突出特点是专家证人出庭作证,特别是中方的专家证人,在法庭上的表现得到了判决书的专门赞许,为法庭最终作出有利于我方的判决发挥了重要作用。我们也可以预见,在以后的境外追逃案件中,会有更多的外逃犯罪嫌疑人在穷尽所在国司法程序之后,为了拖延诉讼程序,很有可能将案件提交给区域性人权机构进行审理,也会有更多的专家证人走向国际法庭,捍卫我国的司法尊严和法治声誉。所以,从本案专家证人出庭作证的实践中汲取有益经验,对于以后我国专家证人到国际人权机构出庭作证具具有重要意义。具体来说,总结本案专家证人作证,有以下两点值得注意:(1)所选取的专家证人一定要具有丰富的相关司法经验和阅历。根据《美洲人权法院程序和证据规则》(简称《程序规则》)之规定,"专家证人(expert witness)"是指拥有特定的科学、艺术、技术或实践知识或经验,可以依其特定领域的知识或经验向法院就争议问题提供信息的人。在美洲人权法院的法庭上,秘鲁政府反驳黄海勇方专家证人证言的一个主要理由,就是对方专家不具有与其作证相关的专业背景和实践经验。所以,所选取的专家证人一定要具备与作证相符合的良好的

专业背景,充分的知识储备和丰富的实践经验,从而在资质上提高其证言的可信性。(2) 充分做好各种准备。在秘鲁政府对于对方证人的质疑当中,还包括了对于对方所提交报告所使用的案例,其分析方法,以及没有回答秘鲁政府所提出的所有问题等。也就是说,在法庭上,专家证人可能遇到对方对自己的各种质疑。所以,专家证人在作证时,应当有充分的准备,不论对方问题如何刁钻,都要不卑不亢,予以适当的回答。

(八)做好充分准备,妥善应对引渡中的程序性意外

美洲人权法院判决书显示,在本案诉讼程序中至少出现过两次由于缺少案件材料而影响程序进行甚至判决结果的情况:第一次是2009年12月21日,秘鲁最高法院常设刑事法庭在引渡听证会上,要求在案件卷宗中增加中国刑法第151条的译文。① 但如前所述,中国早在2009年2月24日,就通过驻秘鲁使馆向利马第56法庭递交了包括中国《刑法》第151条在内的相关刑法条文的译文。② 第二次是2011年6月9日,秘鲁宪法法院针对该法院2011年5月24日的判决所做出的解释,指出基于在本案卷宗中没有中方向秘鲁作出的不判处死刑的外交承诺的相关材料,认为不能证明中国已经做出了不判处黄海勇死刑的担保。③ 同样如前所述,中国早在2009年12月11日,即向秘鲁最高法院刑事法庭提交了中方的量刑承诺。关于在这两种情况下,为什么案件卷宗中没有中方之前已经提交的材料和文件,美洲人权法院判决书中并没有说明,也没有相关资料佐证,所以笔者也无从得知。④ 但至少说明,在引渡程序中,不论是基于何种原因,任何技术性甚至程序性问题都可能影响案件的程序进程甚至最终判决。所以,在不了解甚至不充分熟悉对方司法体系和诉讼程序的前提下,我们对于境外诉讼的困难和复杂应当有足够的心理预期,在可能的情况下,应及时了解并提醒对方司法机关将案件材料向相关机关予以转交。同时,每次提交案件材料之时,都准备

---

① the Chamber ordered that the translation of article 151 of the Criminal Code of the People's Republic of China should be requested and added to the case file,参见美洲人权法院判决书第77段。
② 美洲人权法院判决书第69段。
③ 美洲人权法院判决书第84段。
④ 笔者只能推断为,在第一种情况下,中方提交译文的对象是利马第56法庭,而不是秘鲁最高法院刑事庭,所以该庭的案件卷宗当中并没有该译文。在第二种情况下,中方之前的外交担保是提交给秘鲁最高法院,而不是秘鲁宪法法院,所以秘鲁宪法法院的案件卷宗当中没有该外交担保。

多份材料作为备用,以便于在由于对方司法机关之间交流不畅而导致案件卷宗中缺少相关材料的时候,予以及时补充,从而保证诉讼程序不间断并能够高效进行。

(九)积极同西方国家缔结双边条约,为境外追逃追赃提供法律依据

双边条约和协定是我国开展国际刑事司法协助的重要依据。中国和秘鲁之所以能够顺利引渡黄海勇,中秘引渡条约是一个重要的法律基础。虽然到目前为止中国已与近 60 个国家签署了 79 项司法协助条约,与 46 个国家签署了引渡条约,①但是与我国外逃犯罪分子的主要目的国加拿大、美国等西方发达国家都没有签订专门的引渡条约。中国、加拿大、美国虽然都是《联合国反腐败公约》的缔约国,根据加拿大 1999 年《引渡法》,国际公约也可以成为开展引渡合作的依据,但是中加之间尚没有通过国际公约开展引渡合作的先例。美国则拒绝利用国际公约作为开展引渡合作的依据。所以,依据国际公约开展引渡合作还存在一定障碍。在此背景下,积极发展同发达国家的合作关系,争取缔结双边条约,将是推动我国国际刑事司法协助的重要渠道。

令人振奋的是,最近中国和加拿大之间在双边条约和协定的缔结方面有了突破性进展。2016 年 9 月 22 日,在李克强总理访问加拿大期间,中加两国外长正式签署了《中华人民共和国和加拿大关于分享和返还被追缴资产的协定》,这是我国就追缴转移到境外的犯罪所得同他国缔结的第一项专门协定,是我国深化司法领域国际合作的重要举措,②也是中加双方刑事司法执法合作的一个重要里程碑。事实上,关于赃款赃物的查找、冻结、没收和移交问题,1994 年中加之间签订的《中华人民共和国和加拿大关于刑事司法协助的条约》第 17 条即进行了规定,③但这些规定过于原则,实践中的可

---

① 徐宏:《中加签署合作协定,跨境追赃新添利器》,载 http://pic.beelink.cn/html/201609/content_305405.htm.
② 徐宏:《中加签署合作协定,跨境追赃新添利器》,载 http://pic.beelink.cn/html/201609/content_305405.htm.
③《中华人民共和国和加拿大关于刑事司法协助的条约》第十七条赃款赃物规定:"一、一方可以根据请求,尽力确定因发生在另一方境内的犯罪而产生的赃款赃物是否在其境内,并将调查结果通知该另一方。为此,请求方应向被请求方提供以确认赃款赃物在被请求方境内的情况和资料。二、被请求方一旦发现前款所述赃款赃物,则应采取其法律所允许的措施对赃款赃物予以冻结、扣押或没收。三、在法律允许的范围内,被请求方可以根据请求方的请求将上述赃款赃物移交给请求方。但此项移交不得侵害与这些财物有关的第三者的权利。四、如果上述赃款赃物对被请求方境内其他未决刑事案件的审理是必不可少的,被请求方得暂缓移交。五、双方应在各自法律允许的范围内,在向被害人进行补偿的有关诉讼中相互协助。"

操作性不强。而此次《中华人民共和国和加拿大关于分享和返还被追缴资产的协定》则对于中加双方返还和分享被追缴的犯罪资产提供了更为详细、具体和具有操作性的依据。《协定》的内容主要包括分享和返还两个方面，规定对于被转移到他国的犯罪所得是应当返还还是分享，要根据该犯罪所得是否能够认定合法所有人分别予以认定：如果一方（资产流入国）的法院认定犯罪所得属于另一方（资产流出国）或其境内的企业、个人合法所有，犯罪所得将依法返还给另一方。如果无法认定犯罪所得的合法所有人，一方没收后可依法与另一方分享没收资产，分享比例根据另一方提供的协助大小确定。除了对于分享和返还的对象进行明确规定外，《协定》还详细规定了资产分享和返还的具体程序和途径。① 这些规定为两国在返还和分享犯罪所得方面提供了具有操作性的法律依据，对于提高资产流入国配合资产流出国开展追赃国际合作的积极性具有重要意义。

除了追赃国际合作之外，中加之间在追逃国际合作方面也取得重要进展。据媒体报道，加拿大总理办公室网站上的一份联合公报显示，加拿大已经同意与中国进行协商，签署一份双边引渡条约。而长久以来，加拿大一直对此类条约持抵制态度。② 随着近年来中加双方人员流动更加频繁，交往更为密切，双方开展引渡合作的愿望更加迫切。在此背景之下，中加双方在引渡谈判上有了重大转机，对于中加国际刑事司法合作的开展来说，无疑是一个重大利好消息。据媒体称，在接下来的几个月里，双方将就引渡条约进行深入的讨论，当前两国不存在重大的政治和法律障碍，并且已经建立了良好的合作基础。③

《中华人民共和国和加拿大关于分享和返还被追缴资产的协定》的签订，是中加国际刑事司法合作的一个重要进展，完全符合两国共同愿望和共同利益。我们期待，以该《协定》的签订为契机，中加能够在《引渡条约》、《移管被判刑人条约》等双边条约签订上尽快取得实质性进展，并以中加合作为

---

① 汪闽燕：《中加签订关于分享和返还被追缴资产的协定》，载《法制日报》2016年9月23日。
② 《加拿大同意与中国协商引渡条约转变抵制态度》，载 http://news.163.com/16/0922/00/C1HDSLUO00014JB5_all.html。
③ 《加拿大同意与中国协商引渡条约转变抵制态度》，载 http://news.163.com/16/0922/00/C1HDSLUO00014JB5_all.html。

范本,推动我国与其他外逃人员主要目的国(如美国、澳大利亚、新西兰等西方发达国)在类似协定、条约的谈判和签订上取得突破,从而进一步完善我国司法执法对外合作体制,推动我国境外追逃追赃的全面开展。

(十)加强对于国际人权法庭规则的了解,做好充足的应诉准备

黄海勇引渡案被称为中国最复杂的引渡案件,该案不仅历经了秘鲁最高法院和宪法法院等国内司法系统,而且还被黄海勇及其律师申诉至美洲人权委员会,并最终提交至美洲人权法院进行审理。美洲人权委员会和美洲人权法院是根据《美洲人权公约》建立的泛美人权体系的两个主要的人权机构,分别有自己的人权保护机制和程序规则,两个机构特别是美洲人权法院的裁决,将对于引渡黄海勇具有决定性意义。因此,对于这两个国际组织的机构设置、程序规则的了解,对我们成功引渡黄海勇具有重要意义。

我国的专家证人之所以能够在美洲人权法院的巡回法庭上,面对各方的问题沉着冷静,妥善回答,就因为他们在接到作证任务以后,就在外交部等部门的指导、帮助下,查阅了大量的关于美洲人权委员会、美洲人权法院、秘鲁司法体系的相关资料,提前进行熟悉了解,为法庭作证的顺利进行奠定了基础。近年来,越来越多的外逃人员将人权问题作为对抗引渡和遣返的理由,除了向在逃国家的司法系统提起诉讼以外,还将案件提交到区域性人权机构,如美洲人权法院,欧洲人权法院等。我们应当全面了解区域性人权机构的性质、运作和程序规则,做好充分的应诉准备,才能在未来境外追逃中,知己知彼,百战不殆。

七、结　语

黄海勇引渡案的成功,归根到底是我国国内刑事法治发展和人权保障进步的结果。我国每一个引渡案件的开展,都是对我国法治发展程度和人权保障进程的综合检验,也将对我国今后引渡合作的开展产生示范性影响。黄海勇引渡案是美洲人权法院成立以来首次就引渡逃犯案件作出判决,是秘鲁首次同非欧洲国家开展引渡,是我国首次在国际人权法院出庭并首战告捷,也是我国首次从拉美国家成功引渡犯罪嫌疑人,将会对我国今后在拉

美国家的追逃工作产生直接影响,并可能在一定程度上影响我国在欧洲方向的追逃工作,具有重要的标志性意义。经过中纪委、外交部、海关总署等多个部门8年来乃至更长时间持续不懈的共同努力,黄海勇终于被成功引渡回国。但是黄海勇案件并没有结束,在后续对黄海勇的刑事诉讼程序中,我们一定要严格遵循法治程序,充分保障黄海勇的各项诉讼权利,兑现之前我国作出的外交承诺,用铁的事实向秘鲁政府、美洲人权法院乃至整个国际社会表明,中国政府值得信赖,中国法治值得信赖,中国刑事司法制度能够充分保障犯罪嫌疑人的权益,从而提升中国的国际刑事法治形象,增强国际社会对于中国刑事法治的信心,实现我国国际刑事司法合作工作的良性循环。相信黄海勇案件必将成为今后他国与我国开展引渡合作所"遵循的先例",在我国乃至全球国际刑事司法合作实践中留下光辉的一页。

(本文主要内容曾在《法律适用》2017年第3期和《法学杂志》2018年第1、2期发表)

学术争鸣

美洲人权法院黄海勇引渡案述评

——兼论"外交承诺"的法理和实践

孙 昂*

■ 一、秘鲁国内司法机关对黄海勇案的前期审理①

中国公民黄海勇（Wong Ho Wing）②涉嫌走私普通货物罪，偷逃税款7亿余元人民币。黄海勇1998年8月外逃出境，长期栖身美国，并通过婚姻关系取得美国永久居民身份（"绿卡"）。2001年，中国政府通过国际刑警组织对黄海勇发布红色通缉令（也称"红色通报"）。2008年10月27日，黄海勇赴秘鲁探视其弟，在利马机场入境时触发红色通缉令，被秘鲁警方逮捕。当日，警方将黄海勇案移交秘鲁卡亚俄刑事法院。次日，黄海勇由其律师陪同出庭，以"被遣返回国可能适用死刑"为由，请求"在秘鲁审判"此案。

11月，中国政府根据中国和秘鲁引渡条约③启动引渡程序，照会秘方，请求秘鲁引渡黄海勇。

秘鲁引渡程序采取"行政初审—司法复核—行政决定"模式。行政初审的决定由国家检察长办公室和外交部等组成的政府引渡委员会作出。在司法复核阶段，案件经一审法院审理后交最高法院复核。最高法院拒绝引渡

---

* 中国驻印度尼西亚棉兰总领事。曾先后担任联合国难民事务高级专员办公室（"难民署"）驻缅甸若开邦副驻地官员、联合国安理会基地组织制裁委员会法律专家、外交部境外追逃和国际执法合作特别协调员、条约法律司副司长。本文只代表作者本人的看法，不代表作者目前和曾经任职的机构的立场。

① 本文案情部分主要引自美洲人权法院黄海勇案判决词。其中的中方材料，除了中秘引渡条约的约文，均由用西班牙语写成的判决词转译。待中方相关材料公布后，以公布的官方材料为准。关于秘鲁的引渡等法律制度，主要根据笔者在办理黄海勇案过程中多次向秘鲁政府主管官员口头了解所获信息整理。

② Wong Ho Wing 是秘鲁政府、法院和美洲人权法院对"黄海勇"音译。

③ 中国和秘鲁引渡条约2001年11月5日签署，2003年4月5日生效。在这项条约谈判时，笔者是中方代表团成员之一。

的判决有法律约束力,引渡不得进行;最高法院同意引渡的判决无法律约束力,系授权政府决定是否同意引渡。政府接到最高法院同意引渡的判决后,以最高行政决议的形式做出是否同意引渡的行政决定。

与引渡程序有关的是人身保护令之诉。人身保护令制度适用于任何形式的羁押,依引渡请求实施逮捕后,如被请求引渡人申请人身保护令并获准,将重获人身自由,从而在事实上终止引渡程序。秘鲁法律体系中的人身保护令之诉经普通法院一审和上诉审后,由宪法法院终审。

2008年11月14日,卡亚俄刑事法院收到中方递交的引渡请求书。中方以黄海勇涉嫌走私普通货物罪、洗钱罪和行贿罪请求引渡。请求书附有中国刑法相关条款(但未附刑法第一五一条关于走私普通货物罪情节十分严重的,处以无期徒刑或死刑的内容)。2009年1月19日,秘鲁最高法院审理黄海勇引渡案。同日,法院收到中方递交的补充材料,包括刑法第一五一条。次日,最高法院作出判决,认为黄海勇案情符合中秘引渡条约,同意以走私罪①和贿赂罪予以引渡。法院同时提出,该案走私罪应仅适用"中国刑法第一五三条第一款"(该款不含死刑)。

1月26日,黄海勇提起人身保护令之诉,以其"生命和人身完整性②受到迫在眉睫的威胁"为由,要求获释,并声称中方"出于恶意,引渡请求书未附中国刑法第一五一条相关部分的译文,而该部分规定,走私罪可能被判处死刑"。

2月2日,中方照会秘方,照会附中国公安部第二十四局向秘鲁引渡委员会所作声明:"根据中华人民共和国刑法,(黄海勇)不存在适用无期徒刑或死刑的可能。"(照会一)③2月12日,利马第五十六刑事法院裁定,在完成人身保护令之诉前,中止黄海勇引渡程序。秘鲁政府对裁定提出上诉。4月24日,最高法院裁定:鉴于中止引渡并非人身保护令的法定程序,下级法院

---

① 黄海勇涉嫌的走私普通货物罪,在秘鲁刑法中称"偷逃海关关税罪"。根据国际引渡法,引渡所针对的行为必须根据请求方和被请求方法律均构成犯罪,但在双方法律中该行为的罪名是否相同,可以忽略不计。
② 在国际人权法上,"侵犯生命"通常指死刑,"侵犯人身完整性"通常指酷刑等可能造成肉体和/或精神伤害的行为。
③ 在办理黄海勇引渡案过程中,中方多次照会秘方。此处的"照会一"和后续依次编号的照会,均在不同程度上与"外交承诺"有关,为叙述有序,作此编号。与"外交承诺"无关的其他照会,不列入这一序号。本文照会编号与美洲人权法院黄海勇案判决词中对中方照会的编号不尽一致。

中止黄海勇引渡程序的裁定无效。①

在这一过程中,秘鲁政府引渡委员会 2009 年 2 月 19 日对黄海勇引渡案出具报告,其中对死刑问题表示:即使可能适用死刑,只要中方承诺不适用死刑或承诺判处死刑后不予执行,中秘引渡条约允许引渡。② 2 月 24 日,中方向利马第五十六刑事法院递交中国刑法第一五一条、第一五三条、第一五四条、第一九一条、第三八九条和第三九零条的西班牙语译文。8 月 25 日,中方向秘鲁最高法院递交照会,表示与黄海勇案相似的案件,在中国所判刑罚为 15 年有期徒刑,因此,不存在对黄海勇适用死刑的可能(照会二)。

10 月 5 日,最高法院将案件发还卡亚俄刑事法院,要求其附上中方关于不判处死刑的承诺后重新审理。12 月 9 日,最高法院审理黄海勇引渡案。12 月 11 日中方照会秘鲁最高法院,表示"中华人民共和国最高人民法院已经做出如下决定:如果将黄海勇从秘鲁引渡回中国,并且法院通过审理判定有罪,即便其罪行已经构成死刑,法院也不会对其判处死刑"(照会三)。12 月 21 日,秘鲁最高法院再次审理黄海勇引渡案,要求在诉讼文件中增加中国刑法第一五一条译文和中方关于不判死刑承诺的照会。12 月 29 日,中方照会秘鲁最高法院,递交刑法第一五一条译文和中国最高人民法院上述决定的复印件和译文(照会四)。

2010 年 1 月 27 日,秘鲁最高法院就黄海勇引渡案作出第二次判决,表示中方不判死刑的承诺表明,"即使被请求引渡人在请求引渡国被判死刑或类似刑罚,也不存在(被执行死刑)的任何实质性风险",并判决同意引渡。同时,法院认定洗钱罪不符合双重犯罪原则,不同意就该项犯罪实施引渡。③

在秘鲁最高法院审理黄海勇引渡案的过程中,黄海勇以其"生命与人身完整性受到迫在眉睫的威胁"为由,于 2009 年 10 月 12 日第二次提起人身保护令之诉。该诉于 2010 年 1 月 5 日和 6 月 30 日分别在一审和上诉中被驳

---

① 秘鲁最高法院这一判决的意思是,作为两项平行的诉讼程序,人身保护令之诉在法律不能直接影响引渡之诉。当然,如果黄海勇在人身保护令之诉中获胜,将获得释放,在事实上使得引渡无法继续进行。
② 中秘引渡条约对死刑问题的处理详见下文。
③ 根据国际引渡法的"特定原则",如果被请求国拒绝就某项犯罪引渡逃犯,逃犯仍可因其他犯罪而被引渡,但引渡后,请求国不得就被请求国拒绝引渡的犯罪起诉和审判逃犯或者执行刑罚。

回。黄海勇遂基于其第二次人身保护令之诉提起违宪之诉。秘鲁最高法院第二次判决同意引渡后,黄海勇以秘鲁总统、司法部和外交部侵权为由,于2010年2月9日第三次提起人身保护令之诉。该诉于2月25日和4月14日分别在一审和上诉中被驳回。其中上诉法院认为,处理黄海勇引渡案的过程"不存在总统、司法部和外交部的侵权或威胁"。黄海勇随即基于其第三次人身保护令之诉提起违宪之诉。

在此期间,中方2011年2月22日照会秘鲁司法部:"除了不判处极刑,中国政府还正式承诺,邀请秘鲁政府派遣观察员,届时旁听对黄先生进行的审理,并且对判决的执行情况进行监督"(照会五)。

在秘鲁宪法法院审理黄海勇提起的违宪之诉的过程中,2011年5月1日,中国刑法修正案(八)生效,走私普通货物罪的死刑被废除。中方于2011年4月6日通过外交照会将该修正案的相关情况告知秘鲁宪法法院(照会六)。

2011年5月24日,秘鲁宪法法院对违宪之诉作出判决,认为中方的承诺不足以保证不对黄海勇执行死刑;中方文件没有说明刑法修正案(八)对走私普通货物罪规定的较轻刑罚有无追溯效力。据此,宪法法院判令"秘鲁政府放弃将黄海勇引渡回中华人民共和国"。2011年6月10日中方照会秘方,递交中国刑法第十二条译文,表明中国刑法修正案(八)适用于黄海勇案(照会七)。

2011年12月22日,中方照会秘方,表示根据中国最高人民法院的决定(已通过2009年12月11日照会告知秘方),中方向秘方做出正式承诺:如果黄海勇被引渡回中国,即使被判处死刑,也不会对其执行死刑。[①] 中

[①] 在这一承诺中,"被判处死刑,也不会对其执行死刑"的表述,不源自中国法律。中国法律并没有判处死刑后确保不予执行的机制。即使被引渡人被判处"死刑缓期执行",根据刑法第五十条,"判处死刑缓期执行的,在死刑缓期执行期间……如果故意犯罪,情节恶劣,报请最高人民法院核准后执行死刑"。中国引渡实践中的"被判处死刑,也不会对其执行死刑"的表述,是源自国际引渡法的常见做法。如前引中法引渡条约第三条规定的,"引渡请求所针对的犯罪依照请求方的法律应当判处死刑"的,应当拒绝引渡,"除非请求方作出被请求方认为足够的保证不判处死刑,或者在判处死刑的情况下不予执行"。国际引渡法之所以如此表述,是因为许多国家的外交承诺不能约束法院。通过外交途径作出不判处死刑的承诺后,法院仍有可能判处被引渡人死刑。此时,往往需要通过国家元首行使死刑赦免权来确保被引渡人"被判处死刑,也不会对其执行死刑"。考虑到中国法律没有判处死刑后确保不予执行的机制,在对外承诺"被判处死刑,也不会对其执行死刑"时,往往需要同时承诺不判处死刑,如中法引渡条约第三条和黄海勇案"照会八"。在实践中,中方将实际履行承诺中的"不判处死刑",而没有必要再考虑如何履行承诺中的"被判处死刑,也不会对其执行死刑"。这种看似多余的做法是外交实践中常见的,并非画蛇添足,其功能详见下文的分析。

方这一承诺依然有效。2011年5月1日,中国刑法修正案(八)生效,废除了黄海勇涉嫌的走私普通货物罪的死刑。照会附有相关法律条款、最高人民法院对刑法修正案(八)的说明以及这两份文件的西班牙语译文(照会八)。

2012年2月9日,秘鲁司法与人权部部长请求最高法院基于"中华人民共和国刑法修正案(八)已经生效,废除走私普通货物罪死刑的规定"做出新判决。最高法院于2月21日和3月14日两次开庭审理黄海勇引渡案,但均因"缺少资料",没有做出新的判决。

至此,秘鲁国内各法院对黄海勇案的审理暂时告一段落。根据美洲人权法院此后的认定,截至此时,黄海勇案的法律状态是:秘鲁最高法院2010年1月27日同意引渡的判决有效,宪法法院2011年5月24日命令秘鲁政府放弃引渡的判决也有效。黄海勇引渡案陷入了秘鲁国内法的"僵局"。

黄海勇案司法程序陷入僵局后,中秘两国政府并没有因此停止针对黄海勇的引渡合作。2011年12月,中方再次请求秘方引渡黄海勇。秘鲁警方根据请求,对黄海勇实施羁押(后改为监视居住),化解了黄海勇潜逃的风险。

二、美洲人权委员会和美洲人权法院介入黄海勇案

2009年3月27日,黄海勇向美洲人权委员会呈文,请求其介入案件。

美洲人权委员会依《美洲人权公约》设立。公约授权委员会审议个人来文。调查案件后,委员会可在有关各方间进行调解,以达成和解。如无法和解,委员会可以提出报告(无法律约束力),并将案件提交到美洲人权法院,请法院做出有法律约束力的判决。

2013年7月18日,美洲人权委员会就黄海勇案提出报告,认定秘鲁政府侵犯了黄海勇根据《美洲人权公约》享有的人身自由权、生命权、人身完整权等,对黄海勇造成损害,秘鲁政府应当为此承担责任;要求秘鲁政府严格履行秘鲁宪法法院2011年5月24日关于不得引渡的判决,尽快终止引渡程序;充分赔偿黄海勇因其权利被侵犯而遭受的损害。

秘鲁政府拒绝接受报告内容。美洲人权委员会遂于2013年10月30日将"黄海勇诉秘鲁共和国案"提交到美洲人权法院,请求法院根据委员会报告所述,认定秘鲁政府侵犯黄海勇的各项权利,判令秘鲁政府履行报告各项建议,并承担相应的国际责任,作出赔偿。

美洲人权委员会还于2010年2月至2014年3月期间,13次申请美洲人权法院采取临时措施,阻止引渡黄海勇。美洲人权法院批准了各次申请,命令秘鲁政府在完成美洲人权公约框架内的各项程序前,不得向中国引渡黄海勇(美洲人权法院的命令对秘鲁有法律约束力)。

2013年12月9日,美洲人权法院将受理案件一事通知秘鲁政府和黄海勇。秘鲁政府准备应诉,并邀请中方专家出庭支持应诉。笔者以国际引渡法专家身份接受了秘方的出庭邀请。考虑到该案还涉及中国刑法制度和中国人权总体状况,著名刑法学家、北京师范大学赵秉志教授和著名国际人权法学家、中国社会科学院国际法研究所柳华文教授也加入了中方诉讼团队。三人均以个人专家身份作证。

2014年2月5日、6日和9日,黄海勇分别向美洲人权法院提交诉状、陈述和证据。5月6日,秘鲁政府向法院提交初步答辩,不认为其侵犯了黄海勇的任何权利。7月28日,法院决定公开审理本案,以听取秘鲁政府、黄海勇和美洲人权委员会三方代表的陈述,并决定传唤秘鲁政府提出的三名中国籍专家和一名秘鲁籍专家(前司法部长托马博士)。法院随后决定,赵秉志教授、托马博士和笔者出庭口头作证,柳华文教授向法院提交书面证词。

2014年9月3日,美洲人权法院借用巴拉圭最高法院审判大厅公开审理黄海勇引渡案。

开庭前,柳华文教授向法院提交了书面证词,陈述中国人权政策的制定、中国人权白皮书关于司法工作中保障人权的内容、中国在人权领域与联合国机构的合作、中国在调查和惩处酷刑行为方面的进展以及中国对在押人员的人权保障等。

在法庭审理中,赵秉志教授、托马博士和笔者作了陈述,并接受了秘鲁政府代表、美洲人权委员会的两名代表、黄海勇的两名律师和多名法官的询问。中国外交部拉美司的姚雯敏女士担任本案中文和西班牙文之间的口译。中国海关总署缉私局费继恒副处长作为黄海勇案经办人之一,也随中方诉讼团队前往巴拉圭,就案情等事项向中方诉讼团队提供信息和其他协助。

赵秉志教授首先就个人简况、与本案相关的中国刑事诉讼程序和中国刑法修正案(八)作了陈述,然后回答了各方提出的 60 余个问题,包括黄海勇引渡案涉及的中国刑事诉讼程序、中国刑法修正案(八)的主要内容、中国的死刑制度、赖昌星遣返案(赵秉志教授曾在该案中出庭作证)的相关问题等,涵盖我国刑事司法制度的多个方面。

托马博士的陈述和答问主要围绕中秘引渡条约和秘鲁相关国内法律问题展开。

笔者首先就中国引渡法律和实践特别是在引渡案件中不判死刑的外交承诺等问题作了陈述,然后回答了各方提出的 50 余个问题,涉及中国的引渡制度、中国不判死刑和禁止酷刑的外交承诺、中国履行外交承诺的状况特别是赖昌星遣返案中的外交承诺(笔者参与了起草该案部分外交承诺的工作)的履行情况等问题,其中的重点是"外交承诺"问题(本文以下的评析也因此主要围绕"外交承诺"展开)。

三、中方关于不判死刑的外交承诺

在美洲人权法院受理黄海勇案前,中方通过外交途径先后八次照会秘方,主要就黄海勇引渡后的量刑问题作出说明和承诺。美洲人权法院受理该案后,中方 2014 年 8 月 19 日再次照会秘方承诺不判死刑:"中国政府于 2009 年承诺:根据最高人民法院的决定,不对黄海勇适用死刑……中方将遵守这一承诺"(照会九)。①

通过外交途径承诺不判死刑,是国际引渡法晚近出现的一种特殊安排,所适用的情势是:被请求国已经废除死刑或对引渡所涉犯罪不适用死刑,请求国仍保留死刑、且对引渡所涉犯罪仍可适用死刑。

---

① "照会九"还有其他内容,其述评详见下文。

在本案中,秘鲁仅允许对战时的叛国罪和恐怖主义犯罪判处死刑。其宪法第一四零条规定:"仅法律以及秘鲁为当事国的条约中规定的战争时的叛国罪和恐怖主义犯罪适用死刑。"① 而在中国刑法修正案(八)生效前,黄海勇涉嫌的走私普通货物罪的最高刑是死刑。

2003年4月5日生效的中秘引渡条约没有对如何处理死刑问题直接作出规定,只是在条约第五条"引渡的国内法条件"项下表示:"只有在不违反被请求国法律体系时,才能进行引渡。"秘鲁刑事诉讼法典第五一七条规定,如果"请求引渡的罪行在请求引渡国可以适用死刑,并且请求引渡国未提供不执行死刑的担保",应当拒绝引渡。为了在"不违反被请求国法律体系"的情况下顺利推进黄海勇引渡案,中方在2009年12月11日的"照会三"首次作出了对黄海勇不判死刑的外交承诺。

这一外交承诺的法律依据是中国引渡法第五十条:"被请求国就准予引渡附加条件的,对于不损害中华人民共和国主权、国家利益、公共利益的,可以由外交部代表中华人民共和国政府向被请求国作出承诺。对于限制追诉的承诺,由最高人民检察院决定;对于量刑的承诺,由最高人民法院决定。在对被引渡人追究刑事责任时,司法机关应当受所作出的承诺的约束。"这一条款包括三项内容,结合黄海勇案分别叙述如下:

一是在"不损害中华人民共和国主权、国家利益、公共利益"的情况下方可向被请求国作出承诺。在本案中,鉴于秘鲁对走私普通货物罪不适用死刑,中方面前的选项有二:一是承诺不判死刑,争取将黄海勇引渡回国受审;二是不作承诺,秘方将依其国内法拒绝引渡,黄海勇将逍遥法外。两相权衡,笔者认为,前一选项更符合中国的"国家利益、公共利益"。同时,中方的承诺系依主权自主作出,且此种承诺已经以隐含的方式体现在中秘引渡条约之中,因此,这一承诺"不损害中华人民共和国主权"。

二是承诺由外交部代表中国政府向被请求国作出。基于国际法和普遍的外交实践,承诺的具体形式既可以是中国外交部代表中国政府向被请求国驻中国大使馆发出外交照会;也可以是中国驻被请求国大使馆根据中国

---

① 1993年秘鲁宪法,www.congreso.gob.pe/ntley/ConstitucionP.htm,最后访问时间:2017年12月10日。

外交部的指令,代表中国政府向被请求国主管部门发出外交照会。两种途径效力相同。在特定案件中选择哪一途径,由中方单方面决定(如果对方对途径问题无具体要求),或者由双方协商确定(如果对方对途径问题提出具体要求)。从笔者多年从事引渡/遣返逃犯工作的实践看,两种途径都用过。在黄海勇案中,关于死刑问题和其他问题的历次承诺,基本上是通过中国驻秘鲁大使馆向秘鲁主管机关发出外交照会。

三是关于量刑的外交承诺依中国最高人民法院的决定作出,对中国司法机关有法律约束力。在国际引渡法上,外交照会对司法机关有无法律约束力,没有统一的法理和实践。中国和法国引渡条约第三条"应当拒绝引渡的理由"项下规定:"引渡请求所针对的犯罪依照请求方的法律应当判处死刑"的,应当拒绝引渡,"除非请求方作出被请求方认为足够的保证不判处死刑,或者在判处死刑的情况下不予执行"(第七款)。这一条款大体反映了国际引渡法的普遍实践,即对请求方关于不判死刑的承诺,由被请求方判断是否"足够"。之所以需要作出判断,原因就在于各国外交承诺对司法机关的量刑决定并非都有法律约束力。中国引渡法第五十条的上述规定,在很大程度上澄清和解决了这一问题。① 只有在最高人民法院作出不判死刑的决定后,外交部才能代表中国政府向被请求国作出承诺。② 在这种情况下,中国司法机关受外交承诺的约束,系应有之义。

尽管中国法律对不判死刑的外交承诺有明确的规定,在庭审过程中,美洲人权委员会专家古斯曼女士依然向笔者发问:"你说中国作出的不判死刑的外交承诺得到了100%的履行,你的信息来源为何?有什么机制能防范引渡后不会被秘密处决?"马克格雷格尔法官也向笔者发问:"有无第三方介入制度以确保中国作出的不判死刑承诺得到履行?如果出现违反外交承诺的

---

① 中国引渡法关于量刑(主要是不处死刑)承诺的规定,从国际实践看,是十分独特的。截至2000年该法通过时,尚未见到其他国家法律有类似的规定。中国引渡法在制度层面较好地解决了"不判处死刑"的"承诺"是否"足够"的问题。
② 根据这一规定来分析中方历次照会的性质,在最高人民法院就黄海勇案作出不判处死刑的决定之前发出"照会一"和"照会二"不构成"外交承诺",只是对中国相关法律和司法实践的说明。"照会九"所指的"中国政府于2009年做出承诺:根据最高人民法院的决定,不对黄海勇适用死刑",应指"照会三"。"照会四"不是一项独立的"外交承诺",是对"照会三"的补充。

情况,有无中国国内司法程序可以保障外交承诺的履行?"①

那么,不判死刑的外交承诺作出后,到底能不能在中国法律体系中确保得到履行?中国引渡法第五十条规定:"对于量刑的承诺,由最高人民法院决定。"据此,如果死刑案件由最高人民法院复核,可以预期最高人民法院了解相关承诺并会予以履行。但引渡法2000年生效时,死刑案件并非全部由最高人民法院核准。② 根据最高人民法院的决定对外作出不判死刑承诺后,会不会出现高级人民法院在其职权范围内核准并执行死刑的情况?应该不会。首先,引渡法规定:"在对被引渡人追究刑事责任时,司法机关应当受所作出的承诺的约束。"这里的司法机关包括各级司法机关,不限于作出量刑决定的最高人民法院。其次,笔者认为,2000年引渡法作为特别法修正了当时的其他相关法律。如果在作出不判死刑的外交承诺后,高级人民法院依然核准死刑判决,为执行引渡法,最高人民法院有权干预,对死刑判决依法作出改判或指示下级法院改判。2006年死刑复核权统一收归最高人民法院行使后,就不判死刑的外交承诺而言,这一问题不再存在。③

笔者认为,对于死刑以外的其他量刑承诺,特别是高级人民法院或中级人民法院为终审法院的案件,这一问题依然存在。因此,仍应将引渡法视为特别法,修正相关各法,授权最高人民法院在下级法院未履行外交承诺时,依法干预。

---

① 在美洲人权法院作证过程中各方向笔者提出的问题,系根据赵秉志教授的现场记录整理。关于死刑问题,黄海勇的律师索里亚富尔特在庭审中还根据"大赦国际"组织提供的信息向笔者表示:"你刚才说,在所有涉及死刑的案件中,中国作出的不判处死刑的外交承诺都得到了履行。就我所知,至少在3起案件中,中国政府作出了不判处死刑的承诺,但是,他们引渡到中国后,都被处死了。他们分别是王建业、洛桑丹增和方勇,分别涉及泰国、美国和加拿大。"这些说法明显与事实不符。美洲人权法院在黄海勇案判决词也表示:"法院指出,代表并没有提供这些说法的证据。"

② 1983年9月2日之前,人民法院组织法规定:死刑案件由最高人民法院核准。1983年9月2日,六届全国人大常委会第二次会议决定将人民法院组织法修改为"死刑案件除由最高人民法院判决的以外,应当报请最高人民法院核准。杀人、强奸、抢劫、爆炸以及其他严重危害公共安全和社会治安处死刑的案件的核准权,最高人民法院在必要的时候,得授权省、自治区、直辖市的高级人民法院行使。"1996年和1997年,全国人大常委会先后修改刑事诉讼法和刑法,两部法律均明确规定:死刑由最高法院核准。但因人民法院组织法未同步修改,2000年引渡法生效时,死刑复核权未统一收归最高人民法院行使。

③ 2006年10月31日,十届全国人大常委会第二十四次会议表决通过关于修改人民法院组织法的决定,将人民法院组织法的第十三条修改为:"死刑除依法由最高人民法院判决的以外,应当报请最高人民法院核准。"

四、中方关于禁止酷刑的外交承诺

从法理逻辑和诉讼策略角度看,中方在黄海勇案中的禁止酷刑承诺,有四个问题需要讨论:一是对黄海勇承诺禁止酷刑的必要性;二是对黄海勇承诺禁止酷刑的有效性;三是需承诺的具体事项;四是承诺的事项与中国法律的兼容性。

(一)对黄海勇承诺禁止酷刑的必要性。中秘引渡条约没有关于酷刑问题的条款,不过,根据条约第二十条"与其他条约的关系"规定,"本条约不影响缔约双方根据任何其他条约享有的权利和承担的义务"。中国和秘鲁都是《联合国禁止酷刑和其他残忍、不人道或有辱人格的待遇或处罚公约》的缔约国。公约第三条第一款规定了不推回原则:"如有充分理由相信任何人在另一国家将有遭受酷刑的危险时,任何缔约国不得将该人驱逐、推回或引渡至该国。"

有意思的是,关于与其他条约的关系,《禁止酷刑公约》规定:"本公约各项规定不妨碍任何其他国际文书或国家法律中关于禁止残忍、不人道或有辱人格的待遇或处罚、或有关引渡或驱逐的规定"(第十六条第二款)。两项条约规定互不影响/妨碍,这是不是陷入了逻辑循环?不是。就不推回原则而言,应该理解为中秘引渡条约不影响中秘两国在《禁止酷刑公约》下承担的不推回义务。如果中秘引渡条约在禁止酷刑的事项上有比《禁止酷刑公约》更严格的条款,假设中秘引渡条约规定,"如有充分理由相信被请求引渡人在请求国将有遭受酷刑和其他残忍、不人道或有辱人格的待遇或处罚的危险时,请求国应当拒绝引渡该人",即将不推回原则的适用范围从"酷刑"扩展到"其他残忍、不人道或有辱人格的待遇或处罚",则应适用中秘引渡条约,而非《禁止酷刑公约》。现实是,中秘引渡条约在禁止酷刑方面未作任何直接规定,因此,在引渡黄海勇案中,应当适用禁止酷刑公约第三条。

另外,禁止酷刑也可因其他法律渊源(如国内法和区域性国际公约)的规定而成为引渡合作中需要解决的事项。中国引渡法就规定:"外国向中华人民共和国提出的引渡请求,有下列情形之一的,应当拒绝引渡:……被请求引渡人在请求国曾经遭受或者可能遭受酷刑或者其他残忍、不人道或者有辱人格的待遇或者处罚的"。①《美洲地区预防和惩治酷刑公约》第十三条第四款也规定:"如果存在生命危险,可能被处以酷刑,受到残忍、不人道或有辱人格的对待,或者受到被请求引渡国特别或特设法庭的审判,则不得引渡或遣返被请求引渡人。"②

综合以上各项法律制度,在中国和秘鲁的引渡合作中,存在"遭受酷刑的危险"构成拒绝引渡的法定理由。③ 换言之,在黄海勇引渡案中提出"酷刑"问题,从法律上讲,是可以的;从实务上讲,在预料中。

果不其然,在美洲人权法院审理黄海勇案的过程中,酷刑问题是焦点之一。仅对笔者提出的涉及酷刑的问题就包括:中国已经作出的外交承诺包含禁止酷刑和不人道待遇的内容吗?加拿大方面为什么(就赖昌星案)向中国提出禁止酷刑的要求?赖昌星被遣返回国后,他本人及其家人是否受到酷刑及不人道对待?你如何确认赖昌星未遭受酷刑,你与赖昌星见面了吗?(以上是黄海勇的律师索里亚富尔特的提问)中国政府作出的禁止酷刑承诺与不判死刑承诺是一样的吗?(以上是美洲人权委员会专家古斯曼女士的提问)

如上所述,柳华文教授已经接受邀请,准备向美洲人权法院提交证词,全面介绍中国人权事业的进步,包括在反对酷刑领域的进步。在此情况下,是否有必要针对黄海勇本人专门作出禁止酷刑的外交承诺?

中国人权事业的进步包括在反对酷刑领域的进步有目共睹。但是,国际上仍有一些人"不客观、不公正"地看待中国人权状况,包括中国反对酷刑的现状。以联合国禁止酷刑委员会为例。2008年,禁止酷刑委员会针对中

---

① 中国引渡法将不推回原则的适用范围从"酷刑"扩展到"其他残忍、不人道或有辱人格的待遇或处罚"。在引渡实践中,如果中国是被请求国,在不推回原则上,应适用中国引渡法,而非《禁止酷刑公约》。
② 秘鲁是这项美洲公约的缔约国,中国不是,从直接的法律意义上讲,这项公约仅约束秘鲁,不约束中国。但由于秘鲁受该公约约束的事实,中国会受到公约的间接影响。这一法理也适用于国内法,中国引渡法的有关规定不直接适用于外国,但在引渡合作中,因中方依中国引渡法行事,中国引渡法将在事实上影响外方。
③ 例如,向禁止酷刑委员会递交的《中华人民共和国执行〈禁止酷刑和其它残忍、不人道或有辱人格的待遇或处罚公约〉情况的第六次报告》曾表示:"中国与外国缔结的引渡条约一般规定,该条约不妨碍缔约双方根据多边公约所承担的义务和享有的权利,如《中华人民共和国和保加利亚共和国引渡条约》。因此,中外引渡条约不影响本条的适用。"该报告全文见中国外交部官方网址:http://www.fmprc.gov.cn/web/ziliao_674904/tytj_674911/tyfg_674913/t4832.shtml,最后访问时间:2017 年 12 月 10 日。

国履行《禁止酷刑公约》的情况发布了报告。① 对于禁止酷刑委员会的这一份报告,中国外交部发言人表示:中方对报告中的不实指责、诬蔑攻击和无理要求表示不满和反对。发言人说,我们认为这样一个报告总体上不客观、不公正。个别委员对中国的偏见根深蒂固,无视中国政府在保护人权、反对酷刑领域所做出的努力和取得的积极进展,将道听途说的消息、甚至无稽之谈加入报告中。对于这样一份报告,我们当然不能接受。②

在美洲人权法院开庭审理黄海勇案时,禁止酷刑委员会这份"总体上不客观、不公正"的报告仍然是其针对中国的最新报告。在庭审中,美洲人权委员会专家古斯曼女士还当庭向笔者发问:你如何评论联合国对中国酷刑问题的评论(指禁止酷刑委员会2008年对中国履约情况的评论)。根据美洲人权法院黄海勇案判决词,法院在该案审理过程中确实参考了禁止酷刑委员会2008年对中国履约情况的报告。

除了禁止酷刑委员会的报告,国际性人权法院在涉及酷刑问题的案件中,还往往参考美国国务院针对各国发布的"国别人权报告"以及大赦国际、人权观察等非政府组织提供的材料。③ 禁止酷刑委员会的报告尚且"总体上不客观、不公正",美国国务院、大赦国际、人权观察的材料在法庭审理中的作用更是可想而知。

面对这一形势,中方一方面通过柳华文教授的证词,向美洲人权法院全面介绍中国人权状况,包括中国反对酷刑的情况;另一方面,依然有必要针对黄海勇本人作出禁止酷刑的外交承诺。这样做的法理逻辑(legal reasoning)是:柳华文教授的证词向美洲人权法院表明,中国人权事业的进步特别是在反对酷刑领域的进步,足以保证黄海勇引渡回中国后不会遭受酷刑。假如美洲人权法院根据其收到的其他材料,认为中国人权事业的进步包括在反对酷刑领域的进步,尚不足以确保黄海勇引渡回中国后不会遭受酷刑,

---

① 禁止酷刑委员会报告,CAT/C/CHN/CO/4.
② 中国外交部官方网址:http://www.fmprc.gov.cn/ce/cegv/chn/rqrd/hractivities/t624641.htm,最后访问时间:2017年12月10日。
③ Othman (Abu Qatada) v. The United Kingdom, European Court of Human Rights, Application no. 8139/09. 判决详见联合国难民署官方网址:http://www.refworld.org/cases,ECHR,4f169dc62.html,最后访问时间:2017年12月10日。

中方愿意通过外交途径针对黄海勇本人承诺禁止酷刑,以表明无论酷刑现象是否在中国全面禁绝,中方有决心、有能力确保黄海勇在引渡后不会遭受酷刑。

（二）对黄海勇承诺禁止酷刑的有效性。如果中方针对黄海勇本人作出禁止酷刑的外交承诺,究竟会不会使美洲人权法院认定黄海勇引渡回中国后,不存在遭受酷刑的危险？黄海勇案是美洲人权法院审理的第一起引渡案,在法院对该案作出判决之前,我们无从知道法院的立场。但在引渡/遣返案件中承诺禁止酷刑,却是常见的外交实践。能否根据其他国际机构对这一问题的观点来预测美洲人权法院的立场？

在准备赴美洲人权法院出庭作证的过程中,笔者全面梳理了其他国际机构在承诺禁止酷刑一事上的观点。事实证明,这一做法有其意义。因为美洲人权法院在黄海勇案中确实参考了其他国际机构的观点。黄海勇案判决书表示:"本院(指美洲人权法院)认为,应当考虑欧洲(人权)法院在此领域广泛采用的法理,以及依《公民权利和政治权利国际公约》所设的人权事务委员会、依《禁止酷刑和其他残忍、不人道或有辱人格的待遇或处罚公约》及其任择议定书所设的禁止酷刑委员会的观点和决定。"

不过,关于禁止酷刑的外交承诺,各个国际机构观点不一,在一定程度甚至相互对立。有代表性的分别是联合国禁止酷刑委员会[①]的观点和欧洲人权法院的观点。

自1980年代成立以来,禁止酷刑委员会就高度关注存在酷刑危险时不推回原则的适用(《禁止酷刑公约》第三条)。委员会成立后制订的第一号"一般性意见"就是关于公约第三条的。但1997年制订第一号一般性意见

---

① 将禁止酷刑委员会称为"联合国禁止酷刑委员会"可能会有一些争议。因为,禁止酷刑委员会是根据《禁止酷刑公约》设立的条约机构,只对《禁止酷刑公约》缔约国有职权,它不是联合国的组成部分。但另一方面,《禁止酷刑公约》是在联合国框架内谈判、制订的(有时也被称为"联合国禁止酷刑公约"),禁止酷刑委员会的工作由联合国人权事务高级专员办公室辅助和支持,禁止酷刑委员会的正式文件,多印有联合国的标记。另外,根据《禁止酷刑公约》第二十三条,禁止酷刑委员会各成员"根据《联合国特权和豁免公约》有关章节的规定,应享有为联合国服勤的专家的便利、特权和豁免"。在便利、特权和豁免问题上,公约没有说比《联合国特权和豁免公约》有关章节,而是直接说"根据《联合国特权和豁免公约》有关章节的规定,应享有"。从上述意义上讲,将禁止酷刑委员会称为"联合国禁止酷刑委员会"并无大碍。而从本文的主题而言,鉴于禁止酷刑委员会与其他两个联合国机构(联合国人权事务高级专员办公室和联合国难民事务高级专员办公室)的观点有明显的关联性,将禁止酷刑委员会称为"联合国禁止酷刑委员会"更为贴切。

时,委员会似乎并不重视与不推回原则直接相关的"外交承诺"问题。第一号一般性意见根本就没有提及"外交承诺"问题。

"9·11事件"后,外交承诺大量地用于美国等西方国家向中东国家遣返恐怖嫌犯。这引起了一些国际机构包括禁止酷刑委员会的高度关注。艾哈迈德·阿奇扎(Ahmed Agiza)案是禁止酷刑委员会在"外交承诺"领域影响最大的案例。阿奇扎曾在瑞典寻求避难。"9·11事件"后不久,2001年11月,在获得埃及政府作出的禁止酷刑外交承诺后,阿奇扎被瑞典政府遣返回原籍国埃及。遣返工作由美国中央情报局操办,使用中央情报局的飞机。尽管外交承诺包含瑞典外交官进行探视的安排,阿奇扎在埃及监狱还是遭到了殴打和电击。2005年5月,禁止酷刑委员会认定瑞典违反了《禁止酷刑公约》第三条的义务,并认为"获取外交承诺,特别是在其没有强制实施机制的情况下,不足以防范明显的危险"。①

此后,禁止酷刑委员会又对外交承诺发表了一系列负面意见。例如,在审议德国履约报告时,禁止酷刑委员会表示:如果有充分理由相信任何人在另一国家将有遭受酷刑和虐待的危险,在引渡和遣返案件中,都应避免寻求和接受外交承诺,因为此种外交承诺,即使对监督措施作出了安排,仍然可能无法保证相关人员前往上述国家后不会遭受酷刑和虐待。② 在审议美国履约报告时,禁止酷刑委员会表示:注意到释放并向原籍国遣返关押在关塔那摩美军基地的涉恐人员之前,美国从涉恐人员的各原籍国获得了禁止酷刑的外交承诺。禁止酷刑委员会进而表示,非政府来源的报告表明,一些涉恐人员获释后遭到了虐待。为此,禁止酷刑委员会敦促美国确保被驱逐、遣返或引渡的人员(包括恐怖嫌犯),不会面临遭受酷刑或其他残酷、不人道或有辱人格的待遇或处罚的危险。③

近年来,禁止酷刑委员会的这一态度趋于强硬。2014年,禁止酷刑委员会在第五十五届会议上决定修订关于公约第三条的第一号一般性意见。经过第五十六、五十七、五十八和五十九届会议,委员会在2017年4—5月举行

---

① 禁止酷刑委员会文件,CAT/C/34/D/233/2003.
② 禁止酷刑委员会文件,CAT/C/DEU/CO/5.
③ 禁止酷刑委员会文件,CAT/C/60/R.2.

的第六十次会议上完成了对这项一般性意见修订草案的一读。一读草案增设了全新的第四部分:"外交承诺"。其中第一段(全文的第十九段)解释了"外交承诺"的含义,第二段(全文的第二十段)表示:"(禁止酷刑)委员会认为,如有充分理由相信他/她(指被遣返人员)将有遭受酷刑的危险,将要接收被遣返人员的公约缔约国签发外交承诺,就违反了公约第三条规定的'不推回'原则,它们(指外交承诺)不应被用作损害这一原则的法律漏洞。"①

禁止酷刑委员会的观点在联合国框架内获得了一些支持。在委员会对阿奇扎案发表意见后不久,2005年8月,联合国酷刑问题特别报告员诺瓦克就表示:"外交承诺不足以保护被遣返的人员","外交承诺规避不推回义务"。②同年11月16日,联合国大会在关于酷刑或其他残酷、不人道或有辱人格的待遇或处罚的决议中表示:"承认使用外交承诺不免除各国根据国际人权法、人道主义法和难民法承担的义务,特别是不推回原则。"③在同年12月10日(国际人权日)的致辞中,联合国人权事务高级专员阿尔布尔表示:"寻求'外交承诺'来消除酷刑危险的趋势令人担忧……有许多理由来怀疑这些承诺的价值……即使一些监督机制在遣返后发挥了作用,一些政府与另一些政府通过达成法律上无约束力的协议来处理有法律约束力的多项联合国文件中的核心问题,这威胁并架空国际人权法的内容。"④

2010年5月,联合国人权事务高级专员办公室又与其他机构合作⑤发表了题为"防止酷刑:给各国人权机构的实用指南"的长文,⑥表示:"不推回原则显示了对酷刑和其他形式虐待的绝对禁止。在近年的实践中,明知有关人员被遣返后将有遭受酷刑或虐待的危险,一些国家仍寻求外交承诺,这损害了(上述原则)。这一做法被用于所谓的反恐战争,遣送国寻求接收国承诺:所涉人员不会遭受酷刑或其他形式的虐待。这违反了不推回原则,是不

---

① 禁止酷刑委员会文件,CAT/C/DEU/CO/3—5.
② 2005年8月23日"联合国新闻简报"(Press Release).
③ 联合国大会文件 A/C. 3/60/L. 25/Rev. 1.
④ 转引自酷刑受害者国际康复委员会网址:http://irct.org/media-and-resources/latest-news/article/203,最后访问时间:2017年12月10日。
⑤ 与人权高专办合作发表此文的分别是 the Association for the Prevention of Torture (APT)和总部设在澳大利亚的 Asia Pacific Forum of National Human Rights Institutions。
⑥ 联合国人权高专办官方网址:http://www.ohchr.org/Documents/Countries/NHRI/Torture_Prevention_Guide.pdf,最后访问时间:2017年12月10日。

能允许的。"

禁止酷刑委员会的观点还在一定程度上影响到了美洲人权保护体系。美洲人权委员会2006年7月呼吁美国关闭关塔那摩美军基地,(在遣返在押人员时)要"确保不使用外交承诺来规避不推回义务"。[①] 美洲人权委员会的这一表态对黄海勇案尤其不利。一则美洲人权委员会本来就直接参与美洲人权法院对黄海勇案的审理,二则美洲人权委员会与美洲人权法院同属美洲人权保护体系,前者对后者的影响不容轻视。

与上述形成对比的是,欧洲人权法院等国际机构在一定程度上和一定条件下接受禁止酷刑的外交承诺。

2012年1月17日,欧洲人权法院对其受理的首个涉及禁止酷刑外交承诺的案件——乌斯满诉英国案作出判决。[②] 乌斯满是一位伊斯兰教神职人员,他1993年自约旦来到英国,并获准在英国避难。"9·11事件"后,乌斯满被认定为拉登在欧洲的首席代表,被英国视为国家安全的威胁。在将乌斯满遣返回约旦的过程中,英国从约旦获得禁止酷刑的外交承诺。遣返案后上诉至欧洲人权法院。欧洲人权法院在判决中注意到联合国禁止酷刑委员会认为约旦存在着广泛而常见的酷刑现象。对此,法院提出了一个尖锐的问题:"接收国普遍的人权状况能否排除接受任何承诺?"法院的结论是:"一国的普遍状况只有在极为罕见的情况下才能使承诺不具有任何份量。"法院还表示,它从未制订"这样一项绝对的规则"——"不履行多边义务(指各人权公约项下的义务)的国家,就不能相信它会遵守双边承诺。"法院认为,英国和约旦作出了真诚的努力,以寻求和提供透明而详细的承诺,从而确保乌斯满返回约旦后不会受到虐待。约旦的外交承诺[③]足以保证乌斯满免受酷刑和其他残忍、不人道或有辱人格的待遇或处罚。英国可以寻求并

---

① "人权观察"网站:https://www.hrw.org/news/2006/11/10/diplomatic-assurances-against-torture,最后访问时间:2017年12月10日。
② Othman (Abu Qatada) v. The United Kingdom, European Court of Human Rights, Application no. 8139/09. 判决详见联合国难民署官方网址:http://www.refworld.org/cases,ECHR,4f169dc62.html,最后访问时间:2017年12月10日。
③ 与通常的外交承诺采用接收国致遣送国的外交照会这一形式不同,约旦就乌斯满案向英国作出的外交承诺采用了约旦和英国签订"谅解备忘录"的形式。但这并不没有从法律上改变其作为"外交承诺"的性质。

依赖于约旦提供的承诺。①

联合国难民署也为禁止酷刑的外交承诺留出了一定的空间。难民署在2006年8月发布的"联合国难民署关于外交承诺与国际难民保护的照会"中表示："接收国针对特定人员作出外交承诺②……构成决策时的评估因素之一。但此种承诺不影响遣送国根据习惯国际法以及其作为全球性和区域性国际人权条约的缔约国所承担的义务……现在已经明确的是,只有此种承诺有效地消除了所涉人员受保障的权利被侵犯的危险,遣送国才算履行了其国际义务。"③

总之,禁止酷刑的外交承诺是当今国际法上一个悬而未决的问题,尚无关于这一问题的成熟制度,在双边和多边国际条约中也几乎看不到与此相关的条款(相比之下,关于不处死刑承诺,国际法已有相对成熟的制度,许多条约也有明文规定)。这为推测美洲人权法院对禁止酷刑承诺的立场增加了难度。也许美洲人权法院会像欧洲人权法院那样接受禁止酷刑承诺,或者会像禁止酷刑委员会那样排斥禁止酷刑承诺。在这一不确定情况下,从诉讼策略角度讲,对黄海勇作出禁止酷刑承诺依然是合适的选项。这毕竟为秘鲁检察官和中方证人在美洲人权法院的庭审中说服法官、应对黄海勇的律师和美洲人权委员会专家的诘难准备了更多的可用之"牌"。④

基于上述考虑,中方"照会九"在承诺不判死刑的同时,明确表示："作为《禁止酷刑和其他残忍、不人道或有辱人格的待遇或处罚公约》的缔约国,中国政府确保黄海勇不会受到酷刑或其他残忍、不人道或有辱人格的待遇和处罚。中方将遵守这一承诺。"

(三)中方需在"禁止酷刑"项下承诺的具体事项。如上所述,对于不判死刑的承诺,"照会九"仅仅原则性地表示："根据最高人民法院的决定,不

---

① 乌斯满案详情参见拙著《国际反恐前沿:恐怖主义挑战国际法》,黑龙江教育出版社2013年版。
② 《关于难民地位的公约》第三十三条第一款规定："任何缔约国不得以任何方式将难民驱逐或送回("推回")至其生命或自由因为他的宗教、种族、国籍、参加某一社会团体或具有某种政治见解而受威胁的领土边界。"在实践中,联合国难民署所指的"外交承诺",通常既包括不判死刑的外交承诺,也包括禁止酷刑的外交承诺。
③ 联合国难民署官方网址:Http://www.refworld.org/pdfid/44dc81164.pdf,最后访问时间:2017年12月10日。
④ 美洲人权法院黄海勇引渡案秘鲁政府诉讼团队负责人韦尔塔检察官后来向笔者表示:这份照会(指承诺禁止酷刑的"照会九")就像"王炸"。一出手,对方就被炸蒙了。

对黄海勇适用死刑……中方将遵守这一承诺。"从以下引述的一些国际机构的表态来看,对于禁止酷刑,仅仅作这样的原则性表态可能是不够的。

联合国人权事务高级专员阿尔布尔在2005年国际人权日(12月10日)致辞中表示:"不判处或执行死刑的承诺容易监督。我认为,当涉及酷刑和虐待时,情况就不同了。"①在反恐中保护人权和基本自由独立专家于2006年2月16日向联合国人权理事会提交报告表示:"涉及适用死刑或军事法庭审判的承诺可以明确加以核查,与此不同,针对酷刑和其他虐待的承诺,需要有能力和独立的人员执续不断的警觉。"②联合国难民署2006年8月发布的"联合国难民署关于外交承诺与国际难民保护的照会"表示:"一般而言,如果外交承诺旨在确保所涉人员引渡后不被判处死刑……其可适用与否的评估相对简明。在此种情况下,被引渡人会被提交正式的程序,请求国对承诺的遵守可予监督。"③概括起来,在这些国际机构眼中,不判死刑承诺相对简明易行,禁止酷刑承诺则不然。

这些国际机构的看法在一定程度上反映到了美洲人权法院对黄海勇案的审理中。美洲人权委员会专家古斯曼女士就曾在庭审中向笔者发问:中国作出的禁止酷刑承诺与不判死刑承诺是一样的吗?

应该承认,与不判死刑承诺相比,禁止酷刑承诺确实有其特殊之处。以中国为例,承诺不判死刑是因为中国刑法没有废除死刑,并且引渡针对的犯罪可适用死刑,换言之,如果没有不判死刑的外交承诺,引渡后依法判处被引渡人死刑并执行死刑,无论在国际法上,还是在中国国内法上,都是合法的。如果中方承诺了不判死刑,司法机关就要受其约束。可以预期这一承诺在引渡完成后会得到切实履行。

而酷刑不仅是国际法禁止的,也是中国法律禁止的。《禁止酷刑公约》第二条第一款规定:"每一缔约国应采取有效的立法、行政、司法或其他措施,防止在其管辖的任何领土内出现施行酷刑的行为。"中国刑法禁止刑讯

---

① 转引自酷刑受害者国际康复委员会网址:http://irct.org/media-and-resources/latest-news/article/203,最后访问时间:2017年12月10日。
② 联合国文件:E/CN.4/2006/94.
③ 联合国难民署官方网址:Http://www.refworld.org/pdfid/44dc81164.pdf,最后访问时间:2017年12月10日。

逼供和体罚、虐待被监管人员,对因刑讯逼供、暴力取证、体罚虐待被监管人员犯罪致人伤残、死亡的,可以判处死刑、无期徒刑或十年以上有期徒刑。然而,在国际法和国内法均明令禁止的情况下,酷刑现象在中国并未绝迹。①因此,仅仅表示"中国法律禁止酷刑,中国是《禁止酷刑公约》缔约国,中方将履行公约义务",在引渡案件中,有时不足以让被请求方认为消除了被引渡人在中国遭受酷刑的危险。

为了解决这一问题,从国际上常见的做法看,在外交照会中除了明确承诺禁止酷刑外,还需要就承诺的履行作出保障性安排。

为了争取赢得美洲人权法院的黄海勇引渡案,中方禁止酷刑承诺的具体内容,一方面需要立足于中国国内法(不超出中国国内法允许的范围)和中国参加的国际条约(特别是《禁止酷刑公约》),另一方面,也要参考相关国际实践。

欧洲人权法院在乌斯满诉英国案中对禁止酷刑承诺是否有效提出了11项判断标准:(1)是否已向本法院披露承诺的各项条款;(2)承诺是具体的,还是泛泛的、含糊的;(3)承诺由何人作出,对该国是否有约束力;(4)如果承诺是中央政府作出的,地方政府是否会遵守;(5)承诺针对的待遇在接收国是否合法;(6)承诺是否由缔约国作出(指作出承诺的国家是否加入了相关国际人权公约);(7)两国关系的强弱,包括接收国以往遵守同类承诺的纪录;(8)遵守承诺能否通过外交或其他监督机制予以核实;(9)接收国有无禁止酷刑的有效机制,包括它是否愿意与国际监督机制(含国际人权非政府组织)合作,它是否愿意调查关于酷刑的指控并惩戒应对酷刑承担责任的人

---

① 笔者在中国外交部条约法律司从事《禁止酷刑公约》相关工作时,曾向联合国禁止酷刑委员会主席询问:"就你所知,目前世界上的酷刑现象是否仅存在于部分国家?"他答道:"酷刑现象目前存在于世界上所有国家,只是程度和形式不同而已。"酷刑现象在中国亦未绝迹。例如,根据向禁止酷刑委员会递交的《中华人民共和国执行〈禁止酷刑和其它残忍、不人道或有辱人格的待遇或处罚公约〉情况的第六次报告》提供的信息,2007年,因刑讯逼供被中国人民法院判有罪的50人,因暴力取证罪被判有罪的27人,因虐待被监管人被判有罪的77人;2008年,因刑讯逼供被判有罪的63人,因暴力取证罪被判有罪的34人,因虐待被监管人被判有罪的97人;2009年,因刑讯逼供被判有罪的60人,因暴力取证罪被判有罪的2人,因虐待被监管人被判有罪的88人;2010年,因刑讯逼供被判有罪的60人,因暴力取证罪被判有罪的2人,因虐待被监管人被判有罪的34人;2011年,因刑讯逼供被判有罪的36人,因暴力取证罪被判有罪的1人,因虐待被监管人被判有罪的26人。

员；(10) 所涉人员曾否在接收国遭受虐待；(11) 承诺的可靠性是否已经由遣送国国内法院审查。

事实证明，欧洲人权法院对乌斯满诉英国案的判决在禁止酷刑承诺一事上对美洲人权法院审理黄海勇案有直接影响。美洲人权法院在黄海勇案判决词中逐字引用了欧洲人权法院上述判决中列出的这 11 项标准，并根据这 11 项标准和其他一些因素，评估了中方禁止酷刑外交承诺的有效性。

除了欧洲人权法院，联合国酷刑问题特别报告员也对此提出了若干判断标准。他认为，有效的禁止酷刑承诺至少应包括：能够立即接触律师、对讯问过程全程录音录像并记录在场人员姓名和身份、及时获得独立的医疗检查、不得断绝其与外界的通讯、不得关押在秘密地点。[①]

在欧洲人权法院和联合国酷刑问题特别报告员提出的禁止酷刑承诺有效性的各项标准中，"承诺针对的待遇在接收国是否合法"和"及时获得独立的医疗检查"两项值得特别关注。

欧洲人权法院提出的"承诺针对的待遇在接收国是否合法"，指外交照会中承诺不予实施的待遇依接收国国内法是否合法。言下之意是，如果所涉待遇在接收国国内法中是非法的，那么，在外交承诺之外，还有一层国内法的制约，所涉人员遭受这一待遇的可能性就会相应降低；反之，如果所涉待遇在接收国国内法中是合法的，那就少了一层制约，发生的概率就会相应增加。

在美洲人权法院黄海勇案的庭审中，卡尔达斯法官向笔者的提问就涉及"合法待遇"问题："中国是否规定囚犯有强迫劳动的义务？"

罪犯参加生产劳动，是中国监狱法有明文规定的，[②]是一种"合法待遇"。若罪犯中有好逸恶劳者拒绝从事生产劳动，监狱管理方如何履行监狱法的规定，确保能够"组织罪犯从事生产劳动"？这里有许多解释、想象、误解甚至故意曲解的空间，如果在庭审中不能妥善回答这个问题，法庭有可能认为

---

① 转引自联合国难民署官方网址：Http://www.refworld.org/pdfid/44dc81164.pdf，最后访问时间：2017 年 12 月 10 日。
② 中国监狱法第四条规定："监狱……组织罪犯从事生产劳动，对罪犯进行思想教育、文化教育、技术教育"。

中国"合法地"存在着某种被《禁止酷刑公约》所禁止的"待遇或处罚"。①

因此，在根据中国监狱法对卡尔达斯法官的问题直截了当地回答"是"之后，笔者对这个问题作了进一步的回应："我的工作使我有机会参观世界上许多国家的监狱。若按劳动与否，各国监狱可以分为囚犯需参加劳动的和囚犯不参加劳动的两大类。在我的印象中，参加劳动的囚犯状态要好一些。毕竟劳动是人的生活常态，而囚禁在小小的监舍里长年无所事事于身心均不利。另外，劳动还能使囚犯学习劳动技能，有助于他们出狱后谋生。"卡尔达斯法官进一步问道："如果囚犯拒绝劳动，会有何后果？""如果因身体不适等原因不参加劳动，自然是允许的。如果没有特殊原因，他们依法应参加劳动。"卡尔达斯法官追问道："如果囚犯坚持不参加劳动，会有何后果？""那就违反了监狱管理规定，会有相应后果。比如，在申请减刑、假释时，就会受到负面影响。"至此，卡尔达斯法官停止了追问。②

这个问题超出了笔者事先准备的范围，但事后回忆起来，当时在法庭上的即兴回答，没有出现被动或不利的局面，至少没有让美洲人权法院误以为黄海勇回到中国服刑后，由于中国监狱管理特有的制度，他会遭受某种"残忍、不人道或有辱人格的待遇或处罚"。

联合国酷刑问题特别报告员提出的"及时获得独立的医疗检查"这一问题，也受到其他国际机构的高度重视。禁止酷刑委员会曾表示：就禁止酷刑而言，独立的医疗检查是基本的法律保障，在押人员声称遭受酷刑和虐待时，能接触独立的医生尤其重要。③

联合国大会2000年12月4日第55/89号决议通过的"有效调查和记录酷刑和其他残忍、不人道或有辱人格待遇或处罚的原则"认可医疗人员在调查和记录酷刑方面的独特作用。"原则"建议：各国的酷刑调查人员"应能咨

---

① 中国的监狱管理制度，特别是"监狱……组织罪犯从事生产劳动，对罪犯进行思想教育、文化教育、技术教育"这一特点，许多西方国家官员不了解，甚至存有一些误解和偏见。为了消除他们的误解和偏见，在近年的引渡条约和刑事司法协助条约谈判过程中，如果西方国家的谈判代表团在北京有时间的话，笔者总是会建议他们去中国的监狱参观。"百闻不如一见"，这样的参观活动，往往能够在一定程度上增加西方国家官员对中国监狱管理制度的了解，消解他们误解和偏见。
② 这段问答系根据笔者的回忆整理而成的。
③ 联合国毒品与犯罪问题办公室官方网址：https://www.unodc.org/documents/justice-and-prison-reform/EGM-Uploads/IEGM_Brazil_Jan_2014/CAT_observations_to_SMR_－_18.12.2013，最后访问时间：2017年12月10日。

商公正的医疗专家或其他专家,或有权委托这些专家进行调查"。"参与调查酷刑或不当待遇的医疗专家,其行为在任何时候均应符合最高的道德标准,尤应在进行任何检查之前取得知情同意。检查应符合既定的医疗执业标准,特别是,检查应在医疗专家的控制下并在安全人员及其他政府官员不在场的情况下保密进行。医疗专家应立即如实编写书面报告。"

在深入研究关于禁止酷刑承诺的国际实践的基础上,为了最大限度地争取美洲人权法院认可中方的外交承诺,"照会九"对禁止酷刑承诺作了全面、系统的陈述:"(1)……①作为《禁止酷刑和其他残忍、不人道或有辱人格的待遇或处罚公约》的缔约国,中国政府确保黄海勇不会受到酷刑或其他残忍、不人道或有辱人格的待遇和处罚。中方将遵守这一承诺。(2)秘鲁方面可以探访黄海勇的羁押场所。根据秘方要求,中方将尽快安排探访黄海勇的羁押场所,包括其生活的房间,并安排黄海勇与秘鲁驻华外交官或领事官员面谈。秘方官员可由秘方挑选的一名译员陪同。(3)如有必要,根据秘方要求,中方将提供视频设施,以便于黄海勇在羁押期间与秘鲁驻华外交官或领事官员联系。(4)根据中国刑事诉讼法和律师法,黄海勇有权指定一名中国执业律师为其辩护,也有权拒绝其委托的律师的辩护,另行挑选其他律师。黄海勇可以在不受监视的情况下与其律师会面。(5)秘方可派遣其驻华外交官或领事官员旁听根据中国刑事诉讼法和刑法对黄海勇案进行的公开审理。(6)黄海勇回到中国后,中国司法机关将对其审判和审讯进行同步录音录像,并且记录出席审判和审讯黄海勇时的所有参与人的身份。这些录音和录像可以根据秘鲁方面的要求供其查询。(7)根据中国监狱法和看守所条例,(包括黄海勇在内的)所有服刑人员和在押人员均可获得必要的医疗服务。根据秘鲁方面的合理要求,中国方面允许具有执业资格、可以在中国大陆执业的独立社会医疗机构为黄海勇提供医疗服务。鉴于医疗服务报告的隐私性质,秘鲁方面需要经过黄海勇同意后方可了解报告的内容。"

与此前中方历次外交照会相比,"照会九"大大增加了禁止酷刑承诺的

---

① 省略部分仅涉及不判死刑承诺。

内容,特别是保障性措施(照会的 2—7 项均为保障性措施)。①

(四)承诺的事项与中国法律的兼容性。中方"照会九"新增加的承诺事项,包括各项保障性措施,均是中国法律要求或允许的。

关于秘方探访黄海勇的羁押场所。这是国际引渡法框架内的特殊安排,不同于领事探视权。② 领事探事权限于探视领事官员的本国国民,并且领事探事权受国际法保护,除非所涉在押人员明示反对,接受国不得妨碍领事探视权的行使。③ 而按"照会九",秘方可以探视不是其国民的黄海勇,联系方式也不限于实地探视。中方将提供用于联系的视频设施。这些特殊安排不是秘鲁根据国际法或中国法律享有的权利,但也不为中国法律所禁止。中国的羁押场所,经中国政府主管部门同意,可以在领事探视之外,安排外国政府官员参观。④

关于秘方获取录音录像。在黄海勇案"照会九"之前,中国法律法规就已经要求司法执法机关在办案时录音录像,以防止非法取证(酷刑是非法取证的主要手段之一)。最高人民检察院 2005 年 11 月发布《人民检察院讯问职务犯罪嫌疑人实行全程同步录音录像的规定(试行)》,要求人民检察院在讯问犯罪嫌疑人时,对讯问全过程实施不间断的录音、录像。公安部 2012 年 12 月发布修订后的《公安机关办理刑事案件程序规定》,要求对讯问过程录音或者录像,并且要不间断进行,保持完整性,防止非法取证。⑤

关于"独立社会医疗机构"为黄海勇提供服务。除了监管场所的常规医疗服务,监狱和看守所附属医疗机构以外的"独立社会医疗机构"参与监管场所医务工作也是中国法律法规允许的。根据公安部《关于切实加强和改进公安监管场所医疗卫生工作的通知》,对未配备医师的公安监管场所,由

---

① 美洲人权法院在审理黄海勇案时也清楚地注意到了这一点,判决词表示:"中华人民共和国提供的承诺正在逐渐变化。起初,这些承诺是为了应对适用死刑的危险,但 2014 年提供的最新承诺与所声称的酷刑或其他残忍、不人道或有辱人格的待遇有关。"
② 根据《维也纳领事关系公约》的规定,"领事官员有权探访受监禁、羁押或拘禁之派遣国国民,与之交谈或通讯,并代聘其法律代表。领事官员并有权探访其辖区内依判决而受监禁、羁押或拘禁之派遣国国民。但如受监禁、羁押或拘禁之国民明示反对为其采取行动时,领事官员应避免采取此种行动。"(第三十六条第一款)
③ 接受国可以对领事探视权制定法律规章,但维也纳公约要求"此项法律规章务须使本条所规定之权利(指'领事探视权')之目的得以充分实现"(第三十六条第二款)。
④ 例如,2011 年 1 月,美国、英国等 47 个国家的 69 名驻华使领馆警务联络官参观了北京市第一、第二看守所。见《中华人民共和国执行〈禁止酷刑和其它残忍、不人道或有辱人格的待遇或处罚公约〉情况的第六次报告》。
⑤ 《中华人民共和国执行〈禁止酷刑和其它残忍、不人道或有辱人格的待遇或处罚公约〉情况的第六次报告》。

医院(诊所)承担公安监管场所日常医疗卫生工作;要通过建立"所院协作"机制,积极探索公安监管场所医疗工作社会化模式。① 通知所说的"医疗工作社会化"在一定意义上就是让"独立社会医疗机构"参与监管场所的医务工作。

此外,"照会九"还承诺秘方可派遣其驻华外交官或领事官员旁听对黄海勇案进行的公开审理,黄海勇委托中国执业律师为其辩护,并可在不受监视的情况下与其律师会面等。这些承诺也都是中国法律要求或允许的。

各项承诺均符合中国法律,这不仅表明中国政府相关部门是在法治原则下办理黄海勇引渡案,而且增强了中方外交承诺的可信度。因为,假如中方外交承诺包含中国法律不允许的事项,在法庭辩论中很容易受到对方诘难:不合法的承诺如何能在中国法律的框架内得到履行?如果听任法庭辩论沿这一路径进行,则不仅可能使法庭认为中方对这一具体事项的承诺缺乏可信度,并且可能进而影响中方外交承诺的整体可信度。

五、美洲人权法院的判决和后续程序

2015年9月16日,美洲人权法院对黄海勇案作出判决。对于死刑问题,法院表示:"根据(中国)刑法的从轻追溯原则,认为在废除走私(普通货物)罪死刑后,即使黄海勇先生被引渡回中国,也不存在对其依法适用死刑的实质性危险。"

判决表明,中方"照会七""照会八"以及赵秉志教授在庭审中的证词,② 让法官们充分而清楚地了解并理解了中国刑法修正案(八)废除了走私普通货物罪的死刑,并且这一规定将适用于黄海勇案。在这一基础上,法官们得出了完全符合中国法律和实践的结论。

法院在判决中没有分析中方的不判死刑承诺,只是表示:中国刑法修正

---

① 参见卫生部、公安部《关于切实加强和改进 公安监管场所医疗卫生工作的通知》(公通字〔2009〕60号)。
② 从实际效果看,赵秉志教授的证词全面而有效,起到了预期的作用。遗憾的是,在赵秉志教授作证时,法庭书记官要求笔者留在证人等候室,不得旁听。因此,失去了旁听的机会,也使得本文难以对赵秉志教授的证词作更详细的引述和讨论。希望在赵秉志教授发表其证词后,有学习和讨论的机会。

案(八)生效后,"已经消除了黄海勇先生被起诉并处以死刑的可能性,因此,为了确定黄海勇先生目前是否处于危险境况,不需要分析所提供的不判死刑外交承诺是否充分"。

从总结经验的角度回溯此案,在美洲人权法院开庭前中方发出的"照会九"有无必要再提及不判黄海勇死刑的外交承诺?在严格的法律意义上,刑法修正案(八)生效后,就没有必要继续承诺对黄海勇不判死刑。但是,"照会九"重申"中国政府于2009年承诺:根据最高人民法院的决定,不对黄海勇适用死刑……中方将遵守这一承诺",这也不是不可以。正如笔者在美洲人权法院庭审中向法庭表示的:"在许多引渡案件中,中方承诺不判死刑是不必要的。因为在这些案件中,引渡所针对的犯罪在中国刑法上没有死刑这一刑罚。当然,对于这样的案件,如果被请求国要求中方作出不判死刑的承诺,中方也可以考虑在外交照会中写明不判死刑。"

作为诉讼策略,"照会九"重申不判死刑承诺是谨慎而必要的步骤。这一承诺和刑法修正案(八)一起,构成不判黄海勇死刑的"双保险"。① 正如高空走钢丝的演员,其高湛技艺是第一道保险,身上系的安全绳是第二道保险。在不出意外的情况下,第一道保险足矣。万一出现意外,第二道保险也可确保万无一失。美洲人权法院是一审终审,设计应诉方案须以万无一失为目标。如果在今后的案件特别是重大案件中再次出现类似的情况,笔者依然会建议采用这一"双保险"模式,以提高胜诉概率。

在酷刑问题上,美洲人权法院表示:"由于本案提供了外交承诺,法院认为,对于所声称的黄海勇先生将面临违反《美洲人权公约》第五条规定的虐待的危险所存在的任何疑问,2014年中国方面提供的最新外交承诺是令人满意的……根据本案的特定情况,承诺以及提供的监督方法是充分的……没有证据证明引渡黄海勇先生将面临违反酷刑或其他残忍、不人道或有辱人格待遇禁令的真实的、可预见的危险。"

这一结论来之不易!

---

① 在中国刑法修正案(八)生效后、发出"照会九"之前,中方2011年12月22日致秘方的"照会八",也是一种"双保险"。该照会除了说明中国刑法修正案(八)废除了走私普通货物罪的死刑,还表示:"根据中国最高人民法院的决定,中方向秘方做出正式承诺:如果黄海勇被引渡回中国,即便被定罪为死刑,也不会对其执行死刑。中方的该承诺仍然有效。"

鉴于国际社会对禁止酷刑承诺有不同观点,特别是对这类承诺能否得到切实履行、能否有效消除酷刑风险有争议,笔者在作证过程中,通过主动陈述、回答法官和秘鲁检察官的提问、反驳黄海勇的律师和美洲人权委员会专家的诘难,全力争取让法官们确信,中方的外交承诺,包括禁止酷刑的外交承诺,是真诚的、可信的、有历史记录为证的。在庭审中各方向笔者提出的50多个问题中,与中国外交承诺的可信性相关的问题达20个之多。除了10个与赖昌星案有关的问题之外,还包括:中国政府在引渡案件中对外国作出的外交承诺,是否对所有中国政府机关都有约束力?中国政府在引渡案件中作出的外交承诺的约束力在中国法律中有无保障?在你的职业生涯中接触到的中国就引渡对外国作出的外交承诺,履行的情况如何?是否可以说中国就引渡对外国作出的外交承诺是可信、有效的?如果中国就引渡对外国作出的外交承诺没有得到履行,有何种后续解决争议程序可资利用?(以上是秘鲁多奈雷斯检察官的提问)中方作出外交承诺后,是否允许联合国相关机构跟进?(以上是黄海勇的律师索里亚富尔特的提问)你说若外交承诺的履行出现问题,可通过外交途径解决,那么,是否也可通过司法途径解决?有什么机制能防范被引渡回国后不会被秘密处决?(以上是美洲人权委员会专家古斯曼女士的提问)如果出现违反外交承诺的情况,有无中国国内司法程序保障外交承诺的履行?(以上是马克格雷格尔法官的提问)若被引渡者不多,很容易跟踪他们的状况,请告诉我们,这些人有无在狱中死亡的?(以上是卡尔达斯法官的提问)

值得一提的是,柳华文教授的书面证词,虽然着眼于从宏观和全局角度介绍中国人权事业的进步,包括中国反对酷刑的立场和进展情况,未直接涉及禁止酷刑的外交承诺,但这一证词对美洲人权法院认可中方禁止酷刑的外交承诺,有着特殊的法律意义。

在禁止酷刑承诺问题上,联合国禁止酷刑委员会曾多次表达这样的观点:如果有充分理由相信,引渡和遣返后所涉人员有遭受酷刑和虐待的危险,遣送国应避免寻求和接受外交承诺(参见针对美国和德国履约情况的前述表态),接收国若签发外交承诺,就违反了《禁止酷刑公约》规定的不推回原则(见委员会对其第一号一般性意见的一读修订草案)。这一观点在国际社会有一定的影响和接受度。其法理逻辑是，如果根据一国的人权总体状况，确实存在遭受酷刑的危险，就不得通过承诺禁止酷刑来引渡或遣返。美洲人权委员会专家古斯曼女士对笔者的提问"你如何评价联合国对中国酷刑问题的评论"就存在着将庭审引向联合国禁止酷刑委员会上述法理逻辑的意图和风险。

这时，中方诉讼团队的"组合拳"发挥了作用。柳华文教授的书面证词对中国人权事业特别是反对酷刑工作总体进展的阐述，有助于规避联合国禁止酷刑委员会不认可禁止酷刑承诺的法理逻辑。因为，禁止酷刑委员会的法理逻辑的适用前提是：有充分理由相信在引渡和遣返后所涉人员有遭受酷刑和虐待的危险。根据国际社会通常接受的量化标准，要达到禁止酷刑委员会所指的危险程度，发生酷刑或虐待的概率须超过50%（more likely than not）。柳华文教授的证词足以让任何不带成见的人相信：尽管中国的人权状况未臻尽善尽美，酷刑现象也未绝迹，但不存在黄海勇引渡后有超过50%的概率遭受酷刑或其他虐待的情况。规避了禁止酷刑委员会不认可禁止酷刑承诺的法理逻辑之后，美洲人权法院在庭审中能够将围绕酷刑问题辩论，聚焦在中方对黄海勇个人所作的禁止酷刑承诺是否完整、是否可信上。

如果用数字来形象地描述中方诉讼团队是如何解决黄海勇引渡案中的酷刑问题，那就是，柳华文教授有效地证明了黄海勇引渡后遭受酷刑和其他虐待的概率不可能超过50%，而"照会九"对禁止酷刑及一系列保障措施的外交承诺，加上笔者在庭审中对中国外交承诺可信度的阐述，促使美洲人权法院相信，黄海勇引渡后遭受酷刑和其他虐待的概率低到不应影响其引渡。

最终，美洲人权法院6名法官组成的合议庭①以5票赞成、1票反对作出判决："黄海勇不会依法被判处死刑，并且也未表明引渡会使当事人面临真实的、可预见的有悖于人身完整待遇（指酷刑）的个人风险，因此，如果引渡黄海勇先生，国家（指秘鲁）不必因为违反确保其生命权和人身完整权的义

---

① 在法庭由6名法官组成的情况下，如果出现3比3，则获法庭庭长支持的一方胜诉。

务而承担责任,也不必为没有根据《美洲地区预防和惩治酷刑公约》第十三条第四款规定的不推回义务而承担责任。"

一言以蔽之,在引渡问题上,美洲人权法院判黄海勇败诉。判决公布的当晚,秘鲁总统即签署同意引渡黄海勇的最高行政决议。秘鲁警方立刻据此羁押了黄海勇。

中国派出由外交部、海关总署、公安部等部门组成的联合工作组第一时间赶赴秘鲁准备接收。但黄海勇的律师也在第一时间三线同时出击:一是向美洲人权法院提出临时措施申请,要求中止引渡;二是向秘鲁法院提起人身保护令之诉;三是向秘鲁法院起诉,要求将黄海勇的羁押改为监视居住。在黄海勇案出现三项新的未决诉讼的情况下,引渡工作再次受阻。秘鲁卡亚俄高院裁定:在上述三项法律程序全部完成前,中止引渡。

虽然引渡工作出现波折,但美洲人权法院的胜诉基本扫清了本案的法律障碍,案件大局已定。2015年10月,美洲人权法院驳回黄海勇提出的临时措施请求。2016年2月,秘鲁卡亚俄高院驳回将羁押改为监视居住的诉讼请求。5月,秘鲁宪法法院驳回黄海勇的人身保护令之诉。至此,三项法律程序全部终结。秘鲁卡亚俄高院遂解除中止引渡的禁令。中方联合工作组再赴秘鲁。

不料,黄海勇以程序性事由(要求秘鲁政府向美洲人权法院报告判决执行情况)再次要求美洲人权法院干预引渡。美洲人权法院要求秘鲁政府在向法院报告判决执行情况前中止引渡。秘鲁卡亚俄高院据此再次命令中止引渡。

2016年6月,在秘鲁政府按要求向美洲人权法院做出报告后,美洲人权法院裁定秘鲁政府完全保障了黄海勇的司法救济权,可以引渡。2016年7月,秘鲁卡亚俄高院根据美洲人权法院最新裁决解除中止引渡黄海勇的禁令。中方第三次派出联合工作组赴秘鲁。7月12日,在完成相关法律手续后,秘鲁警方将黄海勇从监狱押至利马国际机场,与中方联合工作组办理交接手续。国际刑警组织中国国家中心局的警官与秘鲁警方在机场签署移交协议,接收黄海勇。

2016年7月14日,黄海勇被押解回国。

六、美洲人权法院黄海勇引渡案的法律意义

黄海勇是中国从美洲国家引渡的第一名逃犯。成功引渡黄海勇是多种因素合力的结果。在政治上,中国人权、法治取得长足进步。中国和秘鲁双边关系良好,高层交往不断。秘鲁是第一个与中国缔结引渡条约的美洲国家。在黄海勇引渡案启动后,中方通过多种途径做秘方工作,特别是先后几任中国驻秘鲁大使和大使馆其他外交官接力做工作,前后八年,推动秘鲁政府在本案最困难、最关键的时刻毫不动摇地与中方全力合作,最终为这起引渡案画上圆满的句号。

在法律上,美洲人权法院黄海勇引渡案至少具有以下三个方面的意义:

(一)对黄海勇引渡案所涉人权问题,美洲人权法院具有最高法律权威。美洲人权法院判秘鲁胜诉,既扫清了黄海勇引渡案在美洲人权保护体系中的障碍,也打破了该案在秘鲁国内司法程序中因最高法院和宪法法院意见对立而形成的僵局。秘鲁宪法法院后来对黄海勇案作出于我方有利的改判,其基础就是美洲人权法院于我方有利的判决。反之,假如美洲人权法院在该案中判决不得引渡黄海勇,即使秘鲁宪法法院重审黄海勇人身保护令之诉并作出于我方有利的判决,依然因受制于美洲人权法院的判决,而不能引渡黄海勇。

在美洲人权保护体系中,美洲人权法院的判决只适用于本案,不构成普通法意义上的"先例/判例"。但是,美洲人权法院于我方有利的判决,为今后该法院审理同类案件提供了参考,将大大降低我方在该法院办理同类案件的难度。反之,假如美洲人权法院在黄海勇案中作出不利于我方的判决,同类案件的律师可以轻易地"复制"黄海勇案,以相同或相似的理由请求美洲人权法院阻止受其管辖的国家①向中国引渡逃犯。极有可能发生的后果是,中国不仅无法引渡黄海勇,也无法引渡藏身拉丁美洲和加勒比地区的其他逃犯。如果将目光放得更远一些,藏身其他国家的中国逃犯,在中国司法

---

① 美洲人权法院管辖的国家包括拉丁美洲和加勒比地区的绝大多数国家。

执法机构的追捕压力之下,也可能转而藏身美洲人权法院管辖的国家。甚至中国境内的犯罪分子,为了逃避法律制裁,闻讯后也会千方百计逃往拉丁美洲和加勒比地区。这将在中国境外追逃的"天网"上捅出一个大窟窿。

(二)如上所述,在引渡/遣返案件中能否使用禁止酷刑的"外交承诺",各个国际机构分歧明显。美洲人权法院的判决为国际社会认同禁止酷刑承诺增加了砝码。换言之,美洲人权法院对黄海勇案的判决不仅在拉丁美洲和加勒比地区形成了于我方有利的案例,对于全球围绕禁止酷刑承诺的争论,也增加了于我方有利的声音,有助于推动更多的国家和国际机构认同禁止酷刑承诺。

如果对各个国际机构在禁止酷刑承诺上的分歧作更深层次的分析,就会发现,美洲人权法院判决的意义远不限于此。

在黄海勇案之前,对禁止酷刑承诺分属两个不同阵营的国际机构,一方主要是联合国人权事务高级专员办公室和禁止酷刑委员会,它们不认同禁止酷刑承诺;另一方是欧洲人权法院和联合国难民署,它们在一定程度上和一定条件下认同禁止酷刑承诺。

虽然在禁止酷刑承诺上,欧洲人权法院和联合国难民署的各项文件均中规中矩地阐述各自的法律观点和法理逻辑,但不排除这两个机构的立场有更深层的政治考量。

首先来看欧洲人权法院。欧洲人权法院在乌斯满诉英国案中所面临的难题是许多西欧国家共有的:来自中东的涉恐人员威胁国家安全,必须在刑满释放或无法定罪(往往是因为证据不足)时将他们遣返回原籍国。而在一些西欧国家眼里,这些中东国家往往有这样那样的人权问题,包括存在酷刑现象。如果仅仅因为在西欧国家眼里这些中东国家存在酷刑现象,就无法遣返来自这些中东国家的涉恐人员,将严重威胁其滞留国家的安全。并且,由于申根免签证安排给西欧国家带来的人员跨境流动便利,这些涉恐人员可能对整个西欧构成安全威胁。在审理涉及禁止酷刑承诺的案件时,欧洲人权法院不得不解决这一难题。从政治上讲,这个难题的解决路径只有一条,这就是欧洲人权法院在乌斯满诉英国案判决词中所直言不讳的:在反恐斗争中,"必须"允许各国遣返那些非其国民、被其视为国家安全威胁的人员。① 要在法律上实现这一目标,一个选项就是接受禁止酷刑承诺。同时,为维护欧洲人权法院的形象,再对这一承诺附加严格的条件。这就是欧洲人权法院对乌斯满诉英国案判决的深层背景。

联合国难民署的境况与欧洲人权法院相近。近年有大批来自中东、非洲国家的人员偷渡西欧各国。他们中有一些人被西欧国家接受为政治难民,获得避难甚至定居的机会,另一些人则被西欧国家认定为非法经济移民,不予接收。在一些西欧国家眼里,这些非法经济移民的原籍国多有这样那样的人权问题,包括存在酷刑现象。如果仅仅因为在西欧国家眼里这些中东、非洲国家存在酷刑现象,就无法遣返来自这些国家的非法经济移民,可能对西欧各国的社会稳定造成严重的问题。假如联合国难民署拒绝认同禁止酷刑承诺,坚持绝对的不推回原则,势必无法遣返这些非法经济移民,这是西欧各国无法接受的。在这一背景下,就不难理解联合国难民署为什么会认同禁止酷刑承诺,同时为这类承诺附加多项条件。②

与欧洲人权法院和联合国难民署不同,联合国人权高专办和禁止酷刑委员会就其职责而言,没有遣返涉恐人员和遣返非法经济移民的压力。在这一背景下,它们对禁止酷刑承诺持负面立场,也不出乎意料。

在这一问题上,美洲人权法院又处在何种境况中?由于黄海勇涉嫌的是走私普通货物罪,不会对藏身地国的国家安全和社会稳定带来多少威胁。因此,单纯从所处境况而言,美洲人权法院近联合国人权高专办和禁止酷刑委员会,而远欧洲人权法院和联合国难民署。换言之,从上述角度看,直到作出判决那一刻,美洲人权法院拒绝认同禁止酷刑承诺的可能性始终存在。在这一境况下,美洲人权法院最终在黄海勇案判决中认同禁止酷刑承诺,实属不易。美洲人权法院的判决,在区域层面,明确了在其管辖下的拉丁美洲

---

① Othman (Abu Qatada) v. The United Kingdom, European Court of Human Rights, Application no. 8139/09. 判决详见联合国难民署官方网址:http://www.refworld.org/cases, ECHR, 4f169dc62.html,最后访问时间:2017 年 12 月 10 日。
② 在分析欧洲人权法院和联合国难民署对禁止酷刑承诺所持观点的政治考量时,笔者依据的主要是在联合国难民署(1994—1997 年)和联合国安理会反恐机构(2008—2013 年)的工作经历,特别是在这两个机构工作时大量阅读的各类文献以及与各国政府、各国际机构工作交流所获得的信息。限于篇幅,在本文中恕不一一引述。

和加勒比地区,禁止酷刑承诺可以用于引渡/遣返案件;①在全球层面,进一步提高了禁止酷刑承诺的接受度,有助于最终形成国际法上的禁止酷刑承诺制度,意义重大。

(三)黄海勇案是中华人民共和国成立以来,中方第一次参与国际人权法院的诉讼,也是中方第一次参与国际性法院的诉讼。

本案的直接当事方是秘鲁政府和黄海勇,但本案的争议焦点是中国的人权状况、刑法司法制度以及引渡法律和实践。中方诉讼团队虽然以专家证人身份参与诉讼,但他们的书面和口头证词帮助美洲人权法院的法官们了解和理解,并在相当程度上接受和认同中国的人权状况、刑事司法制度以及引渡法律和实践。正如美洲人权法院黄海勇案合议庭庭长谢拉法官对中方证人所说的:"您所讲的与我们原来所了解的有很大不同,我们将认真研究。"中方诉讼团队的工作,对最终以5比1的明显优势赢得黄海勇引渡案发挥了独特而不可替代的作用。

中方团队参与美洲人权法院的诉讼,包括出庭前的准备工作和庭审时陈述和答问,不仅为中方今后再度介入美洲人权法院的诉讼积累了有益的经验(也有一些教训)。而且,由于各个国际性法院的诉讼有一定的相通之处,中方在黄海勇案中首次参与国际性法院的诉讼并胜诉,这其中所获得的经验,也可供今后参与其他国际性法院诉讼时参考。

(本文原载于《中国国际法年刊》2017年卷)

---

① 在美洲人权法院对黄海勇引渡案作出判决后,有多个拉丁美洲国家的外交官在不同场合对笔者表示:作为美洲人权法院审理的第一起引渡案件,他们一直高度关注此案,特别是法院能否接受,以及在何种条件下接受引渡案件中的禁止酷刑的外交承诺。他们多认为,美洲人权法院对黄海勇引渡案的判决,特别是该法院认可禁止酷刑外交承诺的立场,将便利美洲国家间开展引渡合作,有利于在本地区打击跨国犯罪。

美洲人权法院引渡第一案的意义及其启示

柳华文*

国际合作追逃追赃是中国反腐败工作的重要组成部分。随着经济全球化的发展以及交通和通讯的日益便利,腐败案件中追逃追赃的任务越来越突出。在2014年1月召开的中央纪委第三次全会上,习近平总书记的重要讲话吹响了境外追逃腐败分子的号角。他指出:"不能让国外成为一些腐败分子的'避罪天堂',腐败分子即使逃到天涯海角,也要把他们追回来绳之以法,5年、10年、20年都要追,要切断腐败分子的后路。"①2014年10月,中共18届4中全会决定提出:"加强反腐败国际合作,加大海外追赃追逃、遣返引渡力度。"②

近年来,人权问题常常成为中国对外追逃遣返引渡的障碍。③ 中国福建公民黄海勇是经济犯罪嫌疑人,不是腐败犯罪,但是他所经历的引渡过程中的国内和国际诉讼过程典型反映了中国对外追逃工作、包括反腐败境外追逃工作面临的挑战和问题。在2014年9月举行的美洲人权法院的庭审过程中,中国专家首次在国际人权法庭出庭,协助秘鲁政府应诉,并且成功反驳了原告的相关主张。2015年6月,法院判决由于不存在死刑和酷刑风险可以将其引渡回中国。④

---

* 中国社会科学院国际法研究所副所长、研究员,中国社会科学院人权研究中心执行主任。
① 引自人民网:http://cpc.people.com.cn/xuexi/n/2015/1010/c385474—27680631.html,最后访问时间:2016年3月20日。
② 引自中国社会科学网:http://www.cssn.cn/fx/fx_ttxw/201410/t20141030_1381703.shtml,最后访问时间:2016年3月20日。
③ 张毅:《引渡中的法律障碍透析》,《中国司法》2005年第4期,第80页。
④ 判决官方文本为西班牙语。*Caso Wong Ho Wing vs. Peru*, Sentencia de 30 de Junio de 2015, Serie C No. 297, Corte Interamericana de De Derechos Humanos,美洲人权法院网站:http://www.corteidh.or.cr/docs/casos/articulos/seriec_297_esp.pdf,最后访问时间:2016年3月20日。该判决在后文中简称"判决"。

实际上,国际司法机构审理引渡中的人权问题的历史并不长,1989年欧洲人权法院审理的索艾林案(Soering v. the United Kingdom)是这一国际实践的起源。① 黄海勇诉秘鲁案则是美洲人权法院关于引渡框架下国家义务的首个案例,②对于该法院和美洲国家组织成员国以及欧洲人权法院等区域性人权司法机构和欧美一些发达国家具有一种启示作用。作为案例,美洲人权法院在此案中总结和运用的法理在国际法和国内法上具有重要的影响。

一、基本案情

上世纪90年代末,中国福建公民黄海勇因在中国犯下走私普通货物罪、涉案金额巨大,受到中国司法机关追究。③ 他先是逃往美国,后来逃到秘鲁。中国政府根据《中华人民共和国和秘鲁共和国引渡条约》向秘鲁提出引渡要求。在历经数年,用尽秘鲁国内从地方法院到最高法院、从刑事法院到宪法法院的救济手段后,该案被提交到美洲人权委员会。

根据《美洲人权公约》建立(以下简称《公约》)的 美洲人权委员会和美洲人权法院是美洲国家组织最重要的区域性人权保障机制。委员会设在位于美国华盛顿特区的美洲国家组织总部,而法院设在哥斯达黎加的首都圣何塞。

美洲人权委员会目前例行的工作程序是,申诉个案在审查之后一律提交美洲人权法院审理。2010年11月1日,美洲人权委员会正式受理此案。2013年10月30日美洲人权委员会将"黄海勇诉秘鲁"案提交给美洲人权法院。④ 根据法院的程序规则 ,被指称的受害者、被诉的国家是案件的当事

---

① 郝鲁怡:《引渡中的人权问题研究》,《国际法研究》2015年第6期,第52页。
② Inter-American Court of Human Rights, *Inter-American Court of Human Rights-Annual Report 2015*, 2015, p. 100.
③ 从有关新闻报道中,可以看到部分涉及黄海勇的案情,如《失职损失5亿错误还是犯罪? 原武汉海关关长翻供》,新华网:http://news.xinhuanet.com/newscenter/2002—08/13/content_522542.htm,访问时间:2016年4月10日。
④ *Wong Ho Wing v. Peru*, Inter-American Court of Human Rights, Case No. 12794.

方。人权委员会仅在程序上可以在为当事方,但是它更是以美洲人权体系的"公诉人"的身份出庭工作。①

美洲人权委员会认为,黄海勇自 2008 年 10 月 27 日在秘鲁被拘捕以来,已经并继续成为武断和过分剥夺人身自由的受害者。秘鲁当局的有关措施缺乏正当程序基础,在"临时逮捕"名义下延续了长达 5 年而无最终结论。在不同的引渡阶段,秘鲁当局在办案、寻求以及评估中国提供的保证方面有一系列过失和不当(omissions and irregularities)。这不仅是对正当程序(due process)的多方面的违反,而且在考虑到死刑和酷刑行为可能发生的风险的情况下,也没有遵守保障黄海勇生命权、人道待遇权的公约义务。② 在人权委员会的报告中,委员会认定,秘鲁侵犯黄的人身自由、生命、人道待遇、公正审判和司法保护权。委员会建议秘鲁采取必要措施保证引渡程序尽快结束,根据秘鲁刑事诉讼法典的规定,严格遵循 2011 年 5 月 24 日秘鲁宪法法院的裁决,拒绝引渡黄海勇。③

早在 2013 年 11 月 22 日的新闻公报中,人权委员会就指出,该案首次使美洲人权法院有机会,就引渡案件和裁决中必须适用的标准形成案例法;特别是,法院将可以就引渡申请国关于死刑和酷刑风险所做的外交或者其他种类的保证发表意见。④

《关于人的权利和义务的美洲宣言》(简称《美洲人权宣言》)1948 年 5 月 2 日由第九届美洲国家国际会议通过,比联合国《世界人权宣言》早了 7 个月。《美洲人权宣言》在序言中强调:"人的权利的国际保护应当成为演进中的美洲法律的主要指南"。而这也越来越成为几十年来的美洲人权制度和机制发展过程的一种写照。因此,美洲人权法院在审理黄海勇案的过程中,将充分关注对于人权的保障,而国家实现公诉的权力、打击犯罪的任务并非它的首要关注;而重要的平衡点,就是现行相关国际法的适用。

---

① [美]托马斯·伯根索尔等著,黎作恒译:《国际人权法精要》(第 4 版),法律出版社 2010 年版,第 204 页。
② *File to the Court of the Inter-American Court of Human Rights on the Case No. 12794*, the Inter-American Commission on Human Rights, October 30, 2013.
③ *Merits Report No. 78/13*, Inter-American Commission on Human Rights, July 18, 2012.
④ Inter-American Commission on Human Rights, Press Release No. 93/13.

二、庭审情况

2014年9月3日,美洲人权法院以巡回法庭的形式在巴拉圭首都亚松森的巴拉圭最高法院开庭,审理黄海勇诉秘鲁案。此次美洲人权法院的庭审,由该法院7位法官中的5位法官组成法庭。北京师范大学刑事法律科学研究院院长暨中国刑法学研究会会长赵秉志教授、中国外交部条约法律司孙昂参赞和秘鲁前司法部长托马博士作为秘鲁政府邀请的三位专家证人,经美洲人权法院批准到庭作证。笔者当时作为中国社会科学院国际法研究所研究员、中国社会科学院人权研究中心副主任兼秘书长应秘鲁政府邀请并经法院同意,担任专家证人并各法院提供经过公证的书面证词。根据法院工作规则,专家证人是否出庭作证,由法院根据需要确定。①

法庭全天听取了秘鲁政府方面的3位专家证人的证词,并由各方进行了盘问和辩论。赵秉志教授的作证及各方对其盘问主要围绕以下问题进行:与本案相关的中国刑事司法程序和实体问题,赵秉志教授曾出庭作证的中加遣返赖昌星案件有关情况。孙昂参赞的作证及各方对其的盘问则主要围绕中国引渡法制与实践以及中加遣返赖昌星的外交承诺而进行。秘鲁前司法部长托马博士的作证及各方对其的盘问主要围绕与本案相关的中秘引渡条约和秘鲁相关国内法律问题而进行。在自我陈述之后,专家证人依次接受了秘鲁政府方面、美洲人权委员会代表、黄海勇的律师的质证以及法庭的发问。

美洲人权委员会美国籍委员卡瓦利阿罗和黄海勇聘请的两名律师在交叉询问和辩论中,肆意攻击中国司法制度和人权状况,污蔑中国政府在西藏、新疆"迫害"当地少数民族、"迫害""法轮功",以中国人权状况恶劣为由,要求法院阻止秘鲁政府向中国引渡黄。黄的律师还向法院声称,西方国家因不满中国人权状况而拒绝向中国移交嫌犯,要求法院参照办理。

孙昂严词驳斥了委员会和黄的律师的不实之词,介绍了中国司法制度

---

① Héctor Faúndz Ledesma, *The Inter-American System for the Protection of Human Rights*, 3rd edtion, Inter-American Institute of Human Rights, 2008, p. 704.

和人权事业的新发展，以我国近年与法国、意大利、西班牙、葡萄牙和澳大利亚签订引渡条约以及从加拿大遣返赖昌星和自美国遣返余振东为例，说明我国与西方国家之间已就引渡和遣返逃犯成功开展合作。

笔者向法院提交的书面证词主要是有针对性的证明中国的法治和人权保障情况。

法庭对出庭作证的专家证人表示感谢，并特别表示赵秉志教授和孙昂参赞的作证对他们了解中国刑事法制与实践很有帮助。在当天下午三位专家证人作证结束之后，参与庭审的三方又进行了辩论和陈述。

按照惯例，一般在庭审后的半年到一年左右的时间里，美洲人权法院会作出裁判。

三、法院的相关判决及其法理主张

前已述及，2015年6月，美洲人权法院正式作出判决，判定秘鲁政府可以引渡黄海勇回中国，不存在死刑和酷刑的风险。

（一）控辩双方的相关主张和法院确定的审理任务

法院强调了引渡的重要性，以及相关国家合作的义务。它在判决中正确地指出："这关系到各国的共同利益，因为可以使犯有某些罪行的人员能够被绳之以法。"① 同时，法院强调，在引渡程序的框架内，或者其他的国际司法合作方式下，《美洲人权公约》的成员国应当遵守公约规定的人权义务。因此，"在引渡程序中，应当遵守相关国家在人权方面的国际义务，以及应有的程序的要求，同时，这一法律手段不能被用作逃避惩罚的途径。"②

为了确定引渡黄海勇将使秘鲁政府承担的责任，法院要专门分析秘鲁关于保证自称的受害人的生命和人身安全权利的义务，以及在面对声称会威胁到这些权利的辩护时遵守不予推回原则的义务。

具体来说，在本案中，原告方声称，对黄海勇而言，有三种不同程度的危险：一个是因请求引渡的罪行而执行死刑的危险，一个是被秘密执行死刑的

---

① 判决第119段。
② 判决第119段。

危险,还有一个是遭受酷刑或残忍、非人道或有辱人格的对待的危险。原告方代表指出,"中华人民共和国向秘鲁政府提交的所谓不执行死刑的担保不可信";由于中国存在所谓"有实施酷刑的背景",秘鲁政府"也应当要求提供不会遭受酷刑或残忍、非人道或有辱人格的对待的担保";而且,"担保本身不能对避免残忍对待提供应有的保护",秘鲁政府应当对中国的人权现状和黄海勇先生的特殊情况进行分析。①

秘鲁政府则坚持认为其履行了与尊重并保障黄海勇生命权、人身安全和司法保障相关的国际义务。秘鲁政府强调,最高法院和宪法法庭均评估了迄今为止其决定采纳的担保。遗憾的是,美洲人权委员会没有对这些方面进行评估。秘鲁政府强调,法院应当考虑在法院起诉时的情况,并且对委员会和原告过期或者至少不完整的信息来源进行谨慎的评估。另外,秘鲁政府指出,虽然《美洲人权公约》和《美洲地区预防和惩治酷刑公约》为了防范和处罚酷刑的不遣返原则,只要推断(不是没有证据的单纯的断言)相关人员可能面临生命危险或可能遭受酷刑、非人道或有辱人格的待遇,就适用不遣返的原则,但是在本案中,推断没有得到证实。秘鲁政府强调,其最高法院已经收到中国外交部门和最高人民法院提交的不执行死刑的担保,并且将其视为一项不可回避的承诺。另外,秘鲁政府特别指出,"请求国现在的背景并非像委员会和代表试图确认的那样"。②

美洲人权法院认定,尊重并保障权利的一般义务衍生出特殊的义务,可以根据权利主体的特殊保护需求确定这些义务,这种需求可以根据其个人的情况或是其所处的具体情况确定。法院认为,在本案中,秘鲁政府在面对黄海勇的引渡请求时,有义务保障《美洲人权公约》第4条(生命权)和第5条(人身安全权利)中指出的权利,以及与第1条第1款有关的权利,加上《美洲地区预防和惩治酷刑公约》第13条规定的不遣返原则。这可以从联合国普遍性人权机制和欧洲区域性人权机制的法理与案例中获得支持。③

原告方声称的是一种可能发生的风险。法院认为,由于《美洲人权公

---

① 判决第122段。
② 参见判决第123段。
③ 判决第125、131至135段、143段。

约》的最终目的是实现人权的国际保护,因此,应当允许在发生侵权之前对这种案例进行分析。因此,需要法院对相关人员被引渡后发生这些伤害的可能性做出论断。在这个意义上,由于尚未完成引渡,法院应当有条件地审查秘鲁政府的责任,从而确定,如果被引渡,是否将侵犯所谓的受害人的生命权和人身安全权利。①

(二)法院对涉及引渡的死刑风险的判断

美洲人权法院指出,原告方代表对请求国违反程序风险的主张主要指的是所谓的严刑逼供和缺少《美洲人权公约》所要求的保护,甚至最终导致强制执行死刑。因此,法院在与酷刑以及残忍、非人道或有辱人格待遇风险相关的问题上审查了所辩称的风险,以及所辩称的强制执行死刑的风险,如有必要,将针对请求国可能出现的公然拒绝司法的情况进行相应的考量。②

法院认为,在分析黄海勇在请求国可能面临的风险时,应该考虑并评估目前可用的所有信息,包括在秘鲁最高法院二审之后中国立法的进展情况,以及在秘鲁宪法法庭作出判决之后中国提交的外交担保。要考虑终审判决时存在的危险情况,如有必要,还应当分析所声称的侵犯司法保护权的情况。③

黄海勇被通缉的罪行之一——普通货物走私罪,在其被羁押和被请求引渡时,按当时的中国刑法,是适用死刑的。但是2011年5月1日,同年2月颁布的中国《刑法修正案(八)》开始施行。根据专家证人赵秉志在庭审过程中的解释和德国马克思—普朗克研究所的司法报告,中国《刑法》第12条承认有利于当事人的刑事追溯原则。因此,请求引渡黄海勇的走私罪消除了判处死刑的可能。④

针对原告方所谓存在"秘密执行死刑的危险",法院强调,美洲人权委员会和相关代表并没有对所谓的该项危险提供具体的信息。"一般来说,作为与请求国执行死刑相关的背景因素,委员会和代表指出,对执行死刑的数据和统计都不是公开的,据说是作为国家机密处理的,没有分类的数据指出被

---

① 判决第142段。
② 判决第136段。
③ 判决第141、154段。
④ 判决第147至149段。

秘密执行死刑的人员的数量,对此,请求国自身也是确认了的。不过,本庭认为,根据该信息,不能推断出黄海勇先生如果被引渡到中国就可能面临真实的、可以预见的人身危险。"①正因为在中国普通货物走私罪从法律上不适用死刑,法院认为不论原告方提到的有关中国适用死刑的犯罪的报告以及适用死刑的犯罪数量,还是秘鲁方面强调的中国在这方面的进展或者改善,都是无效信息,或者与法院在本案中的评估要求不相符合。②

（三）法院对涉及引渡的酷刑风险的判断

法院认为,在审查可能面临剥夺一个人的生命或者自由权危险而适用不推回原则时,要确定的这种危险应当是真实的、可以预见的结果。因此,在程序义务上,秘鲁政府应当进行单独的审查,核实并评估。如果相关人员陈述可信、确凿或者证明可能面临的危险情况,就当遵守不遣返原则。③

法院参考了联合国和欧洲区域人权机制的法理。在这方面,联合国人权事务委员会已经采用了实际危险标准,即,结果是必然并且可以预见的结果;而联合国禁止酷刑委员会已经指出,危险必须是可以预见的、真实的和个人的。欧洲人权法院也已经表达了该标准,并且指出,应当有根据地提供理由,从而确信的确存在违反酷刑与残忍对待禁令的真实的危险。法院同意这些标准,并且认为,"为了确定是否存在残忍对待的危险,应当审查将申请人遣返至接收国后可以预见的后果,同时,考虑该国的整体情况,以及申请人的个人情况"。④

在审查所辩称的在请求国的危险时,法院应当审查认为存在所辩称的危险的国家的情况,并且将提交的信息与《美洲人权公约》规定的标准进行对比,不过,法院指出,这并不意味着对请求国国家情况的判定,也不意味着确定请求国的相关责任。⑤

判决认为,在审查被引渡人在目的国可能面临的危险情况时,引渡考虑该国的实际情况,而不仅仅是官方报告的情况,而仅仅批准条约并不能确保

---

① 判决第121、153段。
② 判决第154段。
③ 判决第129、155、156段。
④ 判决第157、160段。
⑤ 判决第169段。

不会遭受酷刑。同时,虽然国内存在一些确保人权或禁止酷刑和其他非残忍、非人道或有辱人格折磨的标准,但这不足以确保实现适当的保护,防止有悖于《公约》的情况发生。另外,法院指出,在分析目的国可能存在的危险情况时,仅仅参考该国整体的人权状况是不够的,需要证明被引渡人的特殊情况(在这些情况下其将面临真实的、可以预见的个人危险,并且在被引渡后遭受酷刑或残忍、非人道或有辱人格折磨的危险),例如,隶属于一个受迫害组织、请求国之前存在酷刑或残忍折磨的先例、导致请求引渡的罪行等,取决于目的国的特殊情况。①

法院引用了欧洲人权法院的判词:"仅仅参考某个国家人权情况的整体情况,不能找到驳回引渡的依据。如果法庭可以使用的资料介绍了整体情况,一个特殊案例中的申请人的具体主张,应当参考能够证明其害怕受到残忍对待的个人情况,用其他证据来佐证。仅在一些最极端的案例中,法庭不需要这些个人情况的证据;在这些案例中,目的国整体的暴力情况的强度,会使遭返至该国的人毫无疑问地面临违反《欧洲人权公约》第 3 条规定的实际的危险。"②

法院注意到,在引渡程序的卷宗中有国际非政府组织的新闻和报告,指出并收集了中国违反酷刑和其他残忍、非人道或有辱人格对待禁令的做法。③ 法院还认为,在审查一个人在引渡目的地国的管辖范围内可能面临的人权危险时,可以使用国内来源的报告,也可以使用国际组织或者非政府组织的报告。④

在本案中,对于可能存在的酷刑或残忍、非人道或有辱人格折磨的危险,美洲人权委员会和代表辩称,不同的国际组织和代表(如联合国禁止酷刑委员会和前联合国酷刑或其他残忍、非人道或有辱人格折磨问题报告专员曼弗雷德·诺瓦克)以及非政府组织(如"国际大赦"组织和"人权观察"组

---

① 判决第 172、173 页。
② 欧洲人权法院案例,尼所穆克宏·杜拉亚尔诉俄罗斯案,第 31890/11 号,2013 年 10 月 3 日判决书,第 110 段。另见:德斯阿克斯贝尔格诺夫诉乌克兰案,第 12343/10 号。2011 年 2 月 10 日判决书,第 37 段;玛塔库洛夫和阿斯卡洛夫诉土耳其案,第 46827/99 和 46951/99 案。2005 年 2 月 4 日判决书,第 73 段。
③ 判决第 161 段。
④ 判决第 171 段。

织等)已经表达了对酷刑相关法规缺陷的关注,并且对严刑逼供、中国的羁押情况以及缺乏对酷刑责任人的调查、起诉和处罚情况持续进行了指控。但是,法院认为,委员会和代表所依据的信息指的是中国整体的人权情况。根据这些情况,不足以认为黄海勇将面临违反酷刑或其他残忍、非人道或有辱人格虐待的真实的、可预见的个人危险。代表和委员会均没有提供辩词、证据或依据来证明,这种整体情况将根据黄海勇的特殊情况对其带来个体和具体的人身危险。代表提到的有关所谓被指控犯有恐怖主义罪行的人员、人权捍卫者、政治犯以及维吾尔族人员的人权情况,与黄海勇先生一案没有丝毫关系。①

同时,法院确认,2014年中国方面提供的最新的防止酷刑危险的外交担保是"令人满意的"。②

综上,法院判定:目前,请求引渡黄海勇的走私普通货物犯罪不存在依法适用死刑的可能;另外,没有证据证明引渡黄海勇将使其面临违反酷刑或其他残忍、非人道或有辱人格虐待禁令的真正的、可以预见的人身危险。因此,法院的结论是,在目前的情况下引渡黄海勇,秘鲁政府没有违反《美洲人权公约》与其第1.1条有关的第4条和第5条载明的确保其生命权和人身安全权利的义务,也没有违反《美洲地区预防和惩治酷刑公约》第13条第4款规定的不遣返义务。③

(四)法院确定本案可以使用的证据

美洲人权法院注意到关于证据材料的时间要求。它认同欧洲的司法机构在引渡问题上惯用的法理,即为了确定一个国家的责任,应当对被请求国在引渡时可以了解或应当了解的信息进行分析,如果没有发生引渡,则应当对欧洲司法机构进行审查之时可用的信息进行分析。④

当后发生的证据与更早出现的事实材料所显示的事实有不同或者有差异的时候,显然应该以后面产生的证据为准。本案中原告方无视中国法治与人权进步的具体事实,提供的证据或者不具有相关性,或者不符合法院审

---

① 判决第175、176段。
② 判决第177—186段。
③ 判决第187、188段。
④ 判决第140、141段。

理案件当时的中国法治与人权的状况。在这里,时间因素是考量证据的重要方面。

本案中,秘鲁政府对美洲人权委员会使用的、作为所谓的请求国人权的危险情况依据的某些信息提出了异议。具体指出"委员会引用的某些人权机构以及联合国某些专题报告员发现的情况,都是多年以前的情况,不能反映今天的现实"。在确定中国的相关情况时,法院判定,它应当考虑秘鲁政府的这项意见。①

本案的审理因为当事方声称的是可能面临的侵犯人权的风险,举证时以人证为主。法院在判决中专门列明,"法院还收到了声称的受害人黄海勇以及证人 Kin Mui Chan 与 He Long Huang 在公证人面前作出的声明(证明),以及 Carmen Wurst de Landázuri、Ben Saul 和 Geoff Gilbert、柳华文和 Jean Carlo Mejía Azuero 作为专家的意见。对于听证会期间获得的证据,法院听取了专家赵秉志、孙昂和 Víctor Oscar Shiyin García Toma 的意见。"②

法院在多处提到了秘鲁政府推荐并获得法院认可的专家证人的证言。赵秉志教授关于中国刑法的证言为法院认定。③ 柳华文研究员的证言也获得关注。比如,法院在判决正文中提道:"秘鲁政府在卷宗中提供了专家柳华文的意见,强调了在维护酷刑与其他残忍、非人道或有辱人格虐待的禁令,以及排除严刑逼供方面的改善情况,或是新的控制、通报和监管情况,以及在中国羁押人员受到的待遇情况。"④判决在注释中专门提道:"上述专家强调,《刑法》、《刑事诉讼法》和《人民警察法》明文禁止酷刑和虐待,新《刑事诉讼法》已经明确了排除非法获得证据(例如,通过酷刑或其他暴力行为和威胁获得证据)的法规。另外证言称,有多项标准明确了调查对羁押人员非法取证或严刑逼供以及体罚应当遵循的步骤,如《刑事诉讼法》、《行政检察法》、《人民警察、公安机关纪检委员会管理法》和《人民检察法》。另外澄清说,有快速通信途径可以指控或投诉酷刑或虐待,如调查和审讯过程使用录音和录像方法,经常对羁押人员进行体检,也强调了为了防止酷刑而正在推

---
① 判决第170段。
② 判决第37段。
③ 判决第147—149段、151段,注199、201、202、203、207。
④ 判决第175段。

动使用的方案。"①

又比如,法院在判决中提道:"委员会表示,没有司法机制来执行上述担保。不过,法院注意到专家孙昂的意见,他说,根据中国《引渡法》第 50 条,'在中国外交部提供外交担保之后,这些担保对中国所有司法机构都是有效力的'。法庭认为,在本案的特殊情况下,担保以及提供的监测方法是充分的。"②

判决中较少使用大量文字引用专家意见,中国专家证言获得引用,并且有肯定的判定。这说明,此次中国专家证人参与诉讼是非常成功和有效的。

四、案例意义与价值

（一）本案是美洲人权法院引渡第一案

判决承认,本案是美洲法院在引渡程序框架内对《公约》成员国义务进行第一次宣判。对此,秘鲁政府对"引渡"作狭义理解,反对首开先河地应用到驱逐出境、避难或驱逐的案例中。但是,法院不同意这一意见,而是作了扩张的解读。法院指出,保障生命权与人身安全权利的义务,以及面对酷刑和其他形式的残忍、非人道或有辱人格的对待的危险,或是生命权危险时的不遣返原则,"适用于将一名人员遣返至另一国的所有方式,包括引渡"。③

虽然称为第一案,也可以说它在美洲人权法界具有开创性的意义。而且,因为本案在审理和判决过程中,相当程度上参考了联合国人权条约机构处理相关申诉的个案和欧洲人权法院受理相关案件的法理,所以本身在实质上并非全然地创新;更为准确地说,它是处理相关引渡、遣返案件与人权保障关系时的当下国际法法理的最新的总结与体现。

（二）本案对其他国际人权司法机构的影响

美洲人权法院认为,应当考虑欧洲区域性的国际法院相关问题广泛采用的法理,以及联合国《公民权利和政治权利国际公约》框架下人权事务委

---

① 判决注 233。
② 判决第 186 段。
③ 判决第 130 段。

员会和《禁止酷刑和其他残忍、非人道或有辱人格的待遇或处罚公约》及其任择议定书框架下禁止酷刑委员会的观点和决定。① 法院的态度如此明确,表明了虽然从法律上说,美洲、欧洲和非洲等区域性人权机构和组织互不隶属,它们与联合国等普遍性国际组织的人权机制在法律上各自独立,但是作为人权国际保护的权威和专业机构,它们在国际人权法的法理上具有相通性、一致性。至少,客观上,这些机构和机制在努力追求和保持一种整体性和统一性。黄海勇诉秘鲁案体现了这一点。

美洲人权法院在黄海勇诉秘鲁案的判决中大量引用了欧洲人权法院的案例的判决及其推理逻辑和观点,也引用了联合国人权条约机构的推理逻辑和观点,体现国际法作为一个整体发挥作用的特点和趋势。② 实际上,这反映的正是美洲人权法院近年来工作的一个特点。它一贯引用自己的先例,同时也常常提及其他人权机构的调查和决定,其中包括联合国人权事务委员会、特别报告员、禁止酷刑委员会以及欧洲人权法院的判例法。③ 法院曾引用《维也纳条约法公约》第31条第2款和第3款来支持它的这种作法,并将其解释为需要考虑相关的整个国际制度。④ 它也曾指出:"总体来看,当代人权条约,特别是《美洲人权公约》,都不是传统类型的那种为了缔约国之间的利益而实现对待交换的多边条约。"⑤

反过来,美洲人权法院在本案的判决,也必将对其他区域性国际人权司法机构和人权机制的工作产生相互借鉴和影响的作用。这种借鉴和影响,并非严格的法律义务,从形式上说,不存在有法律根据的法律效力,而是理论和参考意义上的辅助渊源,应该说是实质上的重要的价值和意义。

(三)本案对国内司法机构处理人权问题的影响

黄海勇在美洲人权法院判决之后,在秘鲁国内做了最后一次努力,再次将案件诉至秘鲁宪法法院。但是美洲人权法院的判决对作为《美洲人权公约》的缔约国以及接受法院管辖权的秘鲁的国内司法机构来说,具有重要的

---

① 判决第131段。
② 参见柳华文:《论法律作为一个整体促进人权》,《人权》2013年第5期,第10—15页。
③ [美]托马斯·伯根索尔等著,黎作恒译:《国际人权法精要》(第4版),第216页。
④ Case of Tibi, Judgment of the Inter-American Court of Human Rights, September 7, 2004.
⑤ Case of La Cantuta, Judgment of the Inter-American Court of Human Rights, November 29, 2006.

影响;从以往的经验来看,包括秘鲁在内的相关国家拒绝履行法院判决的情形是罕见的。① 2016年5月23日,秘鲁宪法法院重审此案后最终判定,秘鲁政府可以引渡黄海勇回中国。② 这最终扫除了引渡黄海勇回中国的法律障碍,也是秘鲁通过完成国内法律程序,作为缔约国实施美洲人权法院判决的重要行动。

本案的判决是终局性的裁决,对当事人和当事国家来说具有法律约束力,对于美洲人权委员会和接受美洲人权法院管辖的国家来说同样具有重要的法律效力。美洲人权法院的对于美洲国家国内立法、司法的影响越来越大,甚至在特殊情况下,有人以《美洲人权公约》为根据在国内进行诉讼。③ 对于这些国家以外国家的效力,主要是基于人权法宗旨与原则以及相关法理的统一性而产生的参考与参照的意义。

相关事项并不复杂,因此目标和宗旨既定的情况下,处理问题的关键在于运用同样的法理和逻辑推理标准,对具体国家和具体个案进行适用和判断。

不能说再遇有类似事实的案件,都可以做出引渡或者遣返不违反相关国家批准、加入的国际人权条约产生的保障人权的义务,但是可以肯定的是,相关的判断必须考虑适用较为统一的法理和逻辑标准。

而且,对于同一个国家来说,在没有明确、可信的相反的证据证明的情况下,不应该做出相反或者明显不同的判断。

(四)本案对于国际社会的影响和启示

在国际社会,原则上,人权的国际保护已经成为法律和实践两方面的现实。但是,如何具体地开展国际间的人权交流与合作,特别是开展具体的行动,是不无争议的,也远远谈不上发达。在欧洲、美洲的区域性人权机制下,人权的国际关注和司法干预走得相对较远,也较为典型。

更为经常的,我们看到,美国、英国等西方国家自设话语权,定期发布他

---

① Héctor Faúndz Ledesma, *The Inter-American System for the Protection of Human Rights*, pp. 853—855.
② 2016年5月23日,秘鲁宪法法院判决第01522-2016-HC号。
③ Héctor Faúndz Ledesma, *The Inter-American System for the Protection of Human Rights*, p. 941.

国的人权国别报告,对他国的人权保障一般和专门领域的状况品头论足。一些西方非政府组织,如"大赦国际""人权观察"等,同样是作讽人权卫士,通过公开发布报告的形式批评包括大量发展中国家在内的各国的人权状况。

目前的国际社会是以民族国家为基本单位的,国界本身也是当下国际社会治理的现实边界。在全球化的今天,各国之间无疑会发生更频繁和深刻的互动,而且比以往任何时候都更需要沟通、交流、了解和信任。如何判断这其中的人权因素,考虑到何种程度才是客观、公正、正常、正确的?国际司法协助、引渡与遣返中的人权因素和问题就典型地反映了这种需求。

本案中美洲人权法院的法官们在判决中较为严格遵守了当下国际法、包括国际人权法的相关法理,审慎、客观地评估各种证据材料和各方主张,体现了较强的专业精神。

值得注意的是,虽然判决中提及了国际组织及其特别报告员、一些非政府组织对中国反酷刑状况的批评,提到了原告方提出的发生在中国国内的一些所谓的严重侵犯人权的个案,但是法院坚守严格的法律逻辑,认真评估相关材料与本案的真实关系。这并非容易。任何时候,法律推理都不应该简单地感情用事,更不能带着偏见和歧视性的态度来判断。法院没有给予这些批评和个案多少权重,说明他们冷静的头脑和在国际司法程序上的慎重。

中国作为发展中人口大国,近年来经济发展和社会进步迅速,法治和人权事业不断取得进步。这也是美洲人权法院判决原告方相关主张无效的重要基础。这也可以对那些不分青红皂白、一味诋毁和抹黑中国的外国政府和非政府组织形成一种启示:应对中国怀有善意,尊重事实,至少不能将政治对抗和法律以外的因素带入司法程序。

■ 五、结论和建议

在联合国层面,受理酷刑申诉的场合除了联合国《禁止酷刑公约》及其议定书的条约机构禁止酷刑委员会之外,还有《公民权利和政治权利国际公约》的条约机构人权事务委员会等。① 中国已经签署但是尚未批准《公民权利和政治权利国际公约》；中国虽然批准了《禁止酷刑公约》，但是没有接受有关个人申诉的程序。基于中国关于人权条约的一贯立场，联合国的条约机构不能受理来自中国国内的个人申诉案件。

但是，当中国公民因为腐败等犯罪行为逃至国外，却可以因为所在国是相关国际人权公约的缔约国并且接受有关条约机构或者区域性人权司法机构的管辖权，提起反对遣返或者引渡的个人人权申诉或者诉讼。

这种申诉或者诉讼本身在宗旨上是为了更好地通过个案保障人权，但是实际上却容易被滥用，当作拖延和阻挠遣返或者引渡的法律手段。加上当事人利用所在国国内司法程序所做的拖延和阻挠，极大地增加了中国境外追逃的时间、物力和人力成本。即使中国和相关国家之间在外交等政治领域取得较强的互信，比如黄海勇案所涉及的秘鲁——两国外交关系良好并且已经签订引渡条约多年，法律领域的诉累仍然可能是程度惊人的耗时、耗力。

因此，客观上，必须重视境外追逃、遣返引渡工作中的人权因素，逐渐提升中国国内相关工作的应对经验和水平。随着中国国内法治和人权事业的进步，应该更好的加强国际交流与合作，并努力让国际社会包括相关国家的行政和司法部门了解和信任中国的法治与人权保障水平，为境外追逃创造更为有利的环境和条件。

中国境外追逃追赃工作是反腐工作中的重要环节和内容，需要在案例积累的基础上，不断总结和推进。② 黄海勇诉秘鲁案典型地反映了境外追逃特别是遣返、引渡工作中遇到的人权因素。美洲人权法院的司法判决反映了国际人权法在相关领域的法理发展，更表现出来该区域性人权司法机构相关的权威性和专业性。我们参与诉讼的成功经验值得总结，其案例价值值得推广。

（本文原载于《东南大学学报》2016 年第 6 期）

---

① 王强军：《酷刑：非法移民遣返的瓶颈——兼评赖昌星遣返案》，载赵秉志、张磊编著：《赖昌星案件的罪与罚》，中国台湾新学林出版股份有限公司 2015 年版，第 223 页。
② 参见黄风主编：《中国境外追逃追赃：经验与反思》，中国政法大学 2016 年版。

引渡在国际追逃追赃中的作用发挥

——成功引渡黄海勇都有什么启示

陈 雷*

2016年7月17日,涉嫌偷逃税7亿元人民币、潜逃境外18年之久的重大走私案犯罪嫌疑人黄海勇从秘鲁被引渡回国,成为我国首次从遥远的拉美国家引渡回国的逃犯。这是我国自"天网行动"和"猎狐行动"以来,遵循和利用国际司法合作规则,运用引渡措施,几经曲折,成功地开展国际追逃追赃的又一典型案例。为我国今后在世界各国开展以引渡为主要手段的国际追逃,尤其是我国贪官外逃的重点国家深入推进国际追逃追赃工作,积累了丰富和宝贵经验。笔者认为,成功引渡黄海勇主要有以下三方面的启示。

一、以积极的态度研究和运用引渡手段开展国际追逃追赃

引渡是国际司法合作的重要制度,是世界各国普遍认可的国际追逃的重要措施。如果一个国家(即被请求引渡国)接受另一个国家引渡逃犯的请求(即引渡请求国),经该国引渡审查或审理程序决定引渡逃犯的,在国际法意义上产生引渡义务,该国有责任将逃犯移交给引渡请求国。引渡合作的法律依据主要有两个方面:一是两国间缔结的引渡条约或共同批准加入的含有引渡条款的国际公约(特别声明不适用的除外)。如果两国没有缔结引渡条约或公约,经双方协商同意,也可以依据"互惠原则"开展个案引渡合作;二是各国的引渡法。对于引渡案件的审查,如是否符合引渡条件,有无

---

* 中央纪委国家监委研究室副局级纪检监察员、原最高人民检察院反贪总局检察官。

拒绝引渡的情形等,以及是否同意引渡准予并作出决定等,由主权国家独立地作出,属于国内法调整范畴。

我国与秘鲁不仅分别制订了本国的引渡法,两国还于 2001 年 11 月 5 日签署了引渡条约(2003 年 4 月 5 日生效)。《中国和秘鲁引渡条约》是两国间开展黄海勇案引渡合作的重要法律依据。犯罪嫌疑人黄海勇伙同他人于 1996 年至 1998 年间,在深圳、武汉、上海三地的公司骗领毛豆油进料加工手册、成立虚假保税仓库,倒卖免税毛豆油 10.7 万吨,共计偷逃税款 7 亿余元人民币。案发后,黄海勇等犯罪嫌疑人经香港潜逃至美国。2001 年 6 月我国通过国际刑警组织对黄海勇发布红色通报,当得知他曾入境秘鲁的行踪后,及时向秘鲁警方提出执法合作请求。2008 年 10 月黄海勇再次入境秘鲁时被秘鲁警方抓获。考虑到秘鲁警方无法依据国际刑警发布的红色通报,将黄海勇直接移交我国,因此引渡合作是最佳选择。依据我国《引渡法》第 47 条规定,海关总署缉私局通过公安部作为引渡黄海勇的请求机关制作了引渡请求书,并依据我国《引渡法》第 4 条第 1 款和《中国和秘鲁引渡条约》第 6 条规定的外交联系途径,于同年 11 月我国向秘鲁提出引渡请求。

该案给我们的主要启示之一,我国在开展国际追逃追赃实践中,应当以积极的态度研究并善于运用引渡合作机制。目前,我国已与 45 个国家缔结了引渡条约(其中 32 项已经生效),在我国批准加入的《联合国反腐败公约》(缔约国 180 个)和《联合国打击跨国有组织犯罪公约》等国际刑法公约中均设有引渡条款,许多缔约国允许通过公约的引渡条款开展追逃国际合作,其中就包括了我国贪官外逃较为突出的国家,如加拿大等国。但是,与我国积极缔结双边引渡条约和批准加入含有引渡条款国际公约相比,目前实务部门在办案实践中,真正研究和运用引渡手段开展国际追逃工作并不多,一些引渡条约缔结后,从来就没有适用过。客观原因很多,包括不了解不熟悉引渡合作机制,国际法律障碍较多,办案时间长,办案效果不能很快体现出来,合作成本高等,但主观上不积极主动,不善于研究和运用引渡机制开展国际追逃是主要原因。

二、排除和克服引渡合作的法律障碍

锲而不舍，穷追猛打，严肃认真对待和解决国际追逃过程中存在问题，努力排除和克服国际法律障碍，是成功开展国际追逃工作的重要经验。自2008年11月我国启动引渡黄海勇程序，秘鲁政府接受我国的引渡请求后，两国密切合作，我国向秘鲁检方提交了大量的证实黄海勇涉嫌在中国犯罪的有效证据材料，6次派出工作组赴秘鲁开展执法合作，同时耐心细致向秘鲁各级层作好解释说明工作。一是旗帜鲜明地表明我国将黄海勇缉捕归案的决心，二是向秘鲁方详细介绍黄海勇的犯罪事实以及适用的法律，以及我国保障犯罪嫌疑人各项法律权利有关法律制度，取得了积极效果。

为抗拒引渡，犯罪嫌疑人黄海勇聘请了秘鲁最著名的"人权律师"，在引渡审理程序过程中，一是诬称其被引渡将面临"人权"问题，回国审判面临"酷刑"，以博取不了解中国司法状况的西方人士，包括司法界人士的"同情"；二是穷尽所有的法律手段，与秘鲁检方打"程序战"。由于秘鲁国内法允许在秘鲁引渡诉讼程序结束后，被引渡人可以向美洲人权委员会申诉，还可以向美洲人权法院上诉。因此，犯罪嫌疑人黄海勇在律师的帮助下，自2010年1月秘鲁最高法院判决同意向我方引渡后，不断地提起上诉、申诉诉讼。两度将案件上诉至秘鲁宪法法院、两度申诉至美洲人权委员会、两度上诉至美洲人权法院，案件被拖入旷日持久的法律战。在此过程中，引渡工作曾一度面临极为困难、复杂的局面，秘鲁宪法法院和美洲人权委员会曾作出不利于引渡决定，迫使引渡程序，几度中止、搁置。

为扭转不利局面，在关键的美洲人权法院的诉讼中，中秘两国调整应对策略，加强执法合作，一方面，向法庭提供了大量的涉及中国人权状况、司法制度等翔实的证据资料；另一方面，由中秘两国法学家和政府官员组成的专家证人出庭作证，提供证词，支持秘鲁政府诉讼团队，化解了对方律师的刁难发问，有力地证明了黄海勇涉嫌在中国犯罪，而且他被引渡回中国不会面临任何"人权"问题。2015年9月16日，美洲人权法院作出裁决，由秘鲁政府决定是否引渡黄海勇。2016年5月23日，秘鲁国家宪法法院裁决同意秘鲁政府向中国引渡犯罪嫌疑人黄海勇。7月14日中秘两国签署引渡交接文件，7月17日黄海勇被押解回国。

　　该案给我们的另一个启示是，应当努力克服和排除引渡等国际追逃的各种国际法律障碍。在国际引渡立法和实践中，基于保护本国公民利益、保护人权、维护人道主义的需要，以及在死刑适用、政治犯罪和军事犯罪等方面，各国的引渡法都会设置一定的限制条件，从而形成了拒绝引渡的原则、理由和情形。如"本人公民不引渡原则""政治犯罪不引渡原则""军事犯罪不引渡原则""违反人权保护不引渡原则""违反人道主义或存在酷刑情形不引渡原则"等。而作为被请求引渡人的逃犯，在对抗引渡的过程中，往往也会聘请律师以此为"法律依据"，千方百计地抗拒或逃避引渡。目前，在我国国际追逃实践中，面临的主要障碍是所谓的"人权"和"酷刑"问题，客观上我国存在着死刑制度，而西方一些对我国政治制度、司法制度不了解，并怀有偏见、抱有成见的人，抑或以所谓"人权卫士"自居的人，大肆攻击、诽谤我国"人权状况"，作为攻击我国社会制度的借口，一些外国律师也借题发挥。因此，我国在开展引渡合作实践中，应当善于研究如何克服拒绝引渡的情形的出现，除了在事实和证据方面提供扎实、确凿、充分的合作依据外，还应当有针对性在真实、全面地介绍我国法律制度、司法制度，尤其是公民所享有的政治权利、民主权利、诉讼权利等人权发展状况。在赖昌星遣返案件中，赖昌星的律师马塔斯以中国存在所谓的"人权"和"酷刑"等问题，作为对抗加拿大移民局的遣返理由，但我国向加拿大执法当局提供大量的中国人权发展状况，加方采信中国政府意见，马塔斯的企图以失败告终，赖昌星最终还是被强制遣返。而黄海勇聘请的律师也深知此套路，而且该引渡案比赖昌星遣返案难度更大的是，秘鲁国内法引渡程序结束后，黄海勇还可以向美洲区域性国际人权组织申诉和上诉，我国也从来没有遇到这样的引渡诉讼案件，黄海勇及其律师认为其胜算的比率显然高于赖昌星遣返的机会。但中方在认真研究了秘鲁的引渡程序制度，密切配合秘鲁司法当局启动的引渡程序，除提供了大量翔实的诉讼证据资料外，还提供足以让秘鲁司法当局和美洲人权法院信服的中国人权真实的状况，包括中方证人出庭作证。为最终成功引渡黄海勇奠定了坚实的基础。

三、研究和利用好国际司法合作规则,提高引渡合作的质量和成效

引渡制度是当今最具有典型意义的国际司法合作制度,既是国际法的内容之一,在国际法中具有重要的地位和作用;也是国内法中的一个部门法,是国家开展引渡合作的重要法律依据。在引渡制度长期发展中,形成了许多国际社会普遍认可、并为各国引渡法吸收的司法合作规则,如双重犯罪原则、本国公民不引渡原则、死刑犯罪不引渡原则、人权保护原则、或引渡或起诉原则等。在引渡合作实践中,引渡请求国(嫌犯出逃国)和被引渡请求国(嫌犯逃往国)还形成了相互尊重国家主权和司法主权原则、支持配合引渡诉讼原则、尊重和遵守引渡决定原则、移交被引渡人原则等。这些共同的引渡合作的国际规则,我们要认真加地研究和运用。

与此同时,鉴于引渡审查审理程序属于被引渡请求国(嫌犯逃往国)国内法程序,我们还要认真加以研究和利用好,采取相应的合作对策。在黄海勇引渡案中,尽管早在2010年1月秘鲁最高法院就判决同意向中国引渡黄海勇,但黄海勇及其聘请律师以《美洲人权公约》可以管辖美洲国家有关人权的案件和相关法律事务的规定为依据,向美洲人权委员会提出申诉,提出了中国刑事法治中的"死刑"和"酷刑"问题,该委员会于2013年7月据此作出报告,要求秘鲁政府停止引渡黄海勇,并对中国的死刑和"酷刑"状况表示担忧。在该引渡案几乎功亏一篑之时,中秘两国经紧急磋商,决定将该案提交给美洲人权法院审理,两国开展了更加密切的执法合作以应对黄海勇对抗引渡。在开庭审理前,我国的法律专家就中国人权状况、刑事司法制度和引渡制度撰写12万字的作证材料提供法庭审理参考。为配合庭审,支持秘鲁政府的诉讼团队,应秘鲁政府邀请我国著名刑法学家赵秉志教授和秘鲁前司法部长托马博士等作为出庭专家证人出庭作证,向美洲法院提交证词。这些具体有效的合作手段,是黄海勇引渡案成功的关键。

该案给我们的再一个启示是,研究和利用好国际司法合作规则,努力提高追逃国际合作的质量和成效。我国应当更加认真探索和研究运用引渡合

作机制,外交部要进一步发挥好引渡中央机关的作用,公安部、最高检等实务部门要善于运用引渡措施开展国际追逃追赃。在开展引渡和遣返等国际追逃实践中,我国不仅要按照国际合作的要求提供证实逃犯涉嫌犯罪扎实而有效证据资料和法律文书,还应当积极配合相关国家进行的引渡或遣返等诉讼,尊重和遵守相关国家的诉讼程序规则、原则和要求,必要时可安排我国的办案人员、法律专家出席外国法庭,支持、配合该国检控、移民等诉讼团队开展的引渡和遣返程序。在我国引渡和遣返实践中,有许多成功案件,但也有一些失败案例,究其原因的根本,就在于是否认真地按照上述要求去做。如果努力去做了,成效的把握就很大。

(本文原载于《中国检察官》2017年第4期下)

黄海勇引渡案：回顾、探析与启示

罗翊乔*

2016年7月17日涉嫌偷逃税款7.17亿元人民币、潜逃境外18年之久的重大走私案犯罪嫌疑人黄海勇从秘鲁被引渡回中国，这被我国外交部称为"新中国成立以来最复杂的引渡案"，亦是《中秘引渡条约》签署以来第一个成功的案例。

《中秘引渡条约》于2001年11月5日签署，2003年4月5日开始生效。根据该条约第1条的规定，双方有义务根据本条约的规定，应对方请求，相互引渡在一方境内发现的被另一方通缉的人员，以便对其进行刑事诉讼或者执行刑罚。中秘两国拥有良好的外交关系且签订了双边引渡条约，本以为引渡黄海勇不会有太大问题，但引渡过程之曲折、耗时之长久、程序之繁杂皆属我国引渡实践之罕见。纵观全案，真可谓是一波三折，跌宕起伏。

一、案情回顾

（一）黄海勇其人其事

黄海勇，曾任深圳市亨润国际实业有限公司总经理、深圳裕伟贸易实业有限公司法人代表、湖北裕伟贸易实业有限公司法人代表、香港宝润集团有限公司董事、武汉丰润油脂保税仓库有限公司董事长。[①]

黄海勇案发，要从19年前说起。1998年8月武汉海关调查局接到群众

---

* 北京师范大学法学院硕士生。
① 赵秉志、张磊："黄海勇引渡案法理问题研究"，载《法律适用》2017年第4期。

举报:有人在武汉地区非法倒卖免税进口毛豆油牟利。武汉海关立即成立由关长莫海涛为组长的调查组。但随着调查的日益深入才意外地发现:莫海涛正是这起案件的幕后保护伞。

1996年8月至1997年1月,黄海勇伙同公司同事潘子牛以深圳国际实业有限公司和武汉对外经济贸易发展有限公司的名义,在武汉海关先后申领到C47006100042、C47006100175、C47007100051毛豆油进料加工手册,每册项下2万吨,共计6万吨。莫海涛直接同意以上3本进料加工手册的批准备案。随后,黄海勇等人在上海、天津转关时进口毛豆油6万吨。在未经海关的许可下,擅自将这6万吨毛豆油倒卖给上海、天津、武汉的5家公司。① 这种手段,就是海关术语中所说的"飞料",即经免税进口并在国内加工的原料,本应该返销国外,但却在国内倒卖牟利,以此来偷逃税款。

1997年1月至5月,黄海勇和潘子牛,将香港宝润集团有限公司以假合资的形式,与武汉某集团有限公司共同成立武汉丰润油脂保税仓库有限公司。在莫海涛的非法支持下,二人获审批建立了武汉丰润油脂保税仓库。但其实,这是一个"四无虚假仓库",即无库址、无面积、无设施、无监管人员。随后,黄海勇等人又以保税的名义将从上海转关武汉、计入保税仓库监管的约4.64余万吨毛豆油"飞料"走私给武汉市3家油脂公司。②

1997年3月至1998年3月,黄海勇持西藏外经贸厅签发的无效毛豆油进口许可证,在武汉海关先后将3.16余万吨毛豆油予以低价补税。③ 1996年至1998年的两年间,在莫海涛等人的帮助下,黄海勇伙同潘子牛,违反相关法律法规,走私了10.64余万吨毛豆油,偷逃税款共计7.17亿元人民币。

案发后,黄海勇经香港潜逃至美国。后来,投奔了在秘鲁经商的弟弟。

(二)引渡请求初获认可

2001年6月我国海关缉私部门通过公安部协调国际刑警组织对黄海勇

---

① 参见湖北省高级人民法院:"潘子牛走私普通货物、物品罪二审刑事判决书",载 http://wenshu.court.gov.cn/content/content? DocID=3790a6af-e0c5-40ff-a983-64f6608441bd&KeyWord=%E6%BD%98%E5%AD%90%E7%89%9B,最后访问日期:2017年10月20日。
② 参见吕佳臻:"黄海勇:新中国最复杂引渡案嫌犯",载《法律与生活》2016年第18期。
③ 参见王向葵、常云润、尹晔斌:"关长徇私,两年中失税5亿——武汉海关原关长莫海涛堕落纪实",载《检察风云》2002年第7期。

发布红色通报,在全球范围内进行缉捕。后来发现黄海勇在秘鲁曾有过入境记录,公安机关立即向国际刑警组织秘鲁国家中心局提出执法合作请求。2008年10月27日,当黄海勇从美国回到秘鲁查韦斯国际机场时,被秘鲁国际刑警成功抓获。同一天,警方把他带到了秘鲁卡亚俄刑事法院。

2008年11月14日我国根据《引渡法》第4条第1款和《中秘引渡条约》第6条之规定,通过外交联系途径,向秘鲁提出了引渡请求。根据这份请求,黄海勇涉嫌的罪名分别是由《刑法》第153条、第154条、第191条、第389条和第390条规定的走私普通货物罪、洗钱罪和行贿罪。

在秘鲁,对外国的引渡请求是由司法部门和行政部门实行双重审查。根据秘鲁《刑事诉讼法》第七卷第二编引渡的相关规定,引渡事务由司法部牵头处理,外交部组成的官方委员会提交报告后,由政府通过部长理事会作出最终决定。但是,在政府作出上述决定之前,必须听取最高法院刑事庭的意见,只有在最高法院作出同意引渡的咨询性裁决后,政府才能决定引渡,然后由国家检察长办公室通过外交渠道通知请求引渡国,并在对请求引渡国作出的照会中表明同意引渡的附加条件。

在秘鲁司法系统中,法院共分为四级,最高法院是全国最高的司法机关,其次是设在法律规定的各司法区首府的高等法院,再次是包含民事法庭、刑事法庭和特别法庭的设于地方的初级法院,最后是村镇上的调解法院。各级法院的法官均通过全国或地方司法官员委员会挑选和任命。最高法院行使终审权,首席大法官是司法机关的最高领导,全体会议是司法机关的最高审议机关。①

2009年1月6日案件被提交至秘鲁最高法院。1月19日秘鲁最高法院第二临时刑事分庭召开引渡庭审。同一天,收到了一份中国武汉海关走私调查局的报告,阐明了黄海勇被指控的行为和适用的法律。1月20日秘鲁最高法院第二临时刑事分庭发布了第一次咨询性裁决,认为针对黄海勇的引渡请求满足了《中秘引渡条约》所规定的条件,秘鲁可以就黄海勇的逃税和贿赂行为同中国开展引渡合作。

---

① 参见秘鲁《宪法》第四章国家机构的规定。

(三) 死刑问题突然作梗

2009年1月26日黄海勇的弟弟提交了一份人身保护令申请来反对秘鲁最高法院的判决,声称这是对他哥哥生命权和人身完整权的侵害;指责中国的引渡请求以"恶意和隐蔽"的方式没有附上中国《刑法》第151条的相关翻译,而该条款包含了对走私罪的死刑适用。① 根据秘鲁《刑事诉讼法》第517条的规定,如果被请求引渡人在引渡后可能被判处死刑,并且请求国未提供不对其判处死刑的保证,秘鲁应当拒绝有关的引渡请求。

2月10日秘鲁司法部引渡和罪犯移转委员发布了关于引渡请求的报告,指出确实没有收到关于中国《刑法》第151条的相关译文。因此,有必要获得相关译文,而且中国必须提供相应的外交承诺,即保证不对黄海勇判处死刑。两天后,秘鲁利马第56刑事法院下令暂时中止引渡程序,直到人身保护令程序结束为止。秘鲁司法部公诉人对此提出了上诉。

10月2日秘鲁最高检察院的检察官通知最高法院:不赞成最高法院同意引渡黄海勇的第一次咨询性裁决。三天后,最高法院常设刑事法庭举行了公开审理,裁定将案卷重新发回卡亚俄刑事法院,理由是该法院在审理过程中没有遵守关于死刑承诺的要求。12月15日秘鲁最高法院常设刑事法庭进行公开审理,宣布撤销之前作出的裁定,并通知双方当事人就中国的外交照会提供论据。

2010年1月27日秘鲁最高法院常设刑事法庭发布了第二次咨询性裁决,决定仍然接受中国针对黄海勇逃税和贿赂行为提出的引渡请求,认为引渡黄海勇没有适用死刑和相似处罚的真实危险。同时,不同意关于洗钱行为的引渡请求,因为它不符合秘鲁《刑事诉讼法》规定的双重犯罪原则。

随后,秘鲁宪法法院受理了黄海勇律师提出的上诉申请,并于2011年5月24日作出判决认为:中国提供的外交保证不足以充分确保对黄海勇不适用死刑。该判决表示中国没有在联合国证明其对生命权予以实际保护,并听信某些人权组织的说法,认为中国容许所谓的"法外处决、简易处决和任意处决"。该判决还指责中国法院有时候判处死刑"不是根据客观事实,而

---

① 《刑法修正案(八)》颁布之前,按照当时我国《刑法》第151和153条的规定,走私情节特别严重的,可以判处无期徒刑或者死刑。

是受公众舆论的影响"。宪法法院还认为,中国的《刑法修正案(八)》不是通过外交程序正式提交的,而且中方没有说明该修正案对死刑的废止是否产生有利于被告人的溯及力。

最终,秘鲁宪法法院作出判决:秘鲁政府不得向中国引渡黄海勇。

(四)开释与否僵持不下

秘鲁宪法法院是解释宪法并监督宪法实施的最高机构,独立于任何其他国家机关,仅按照秘鲁《宪法》和《宪法法院组织法》的规定行使职权。法院由7位法官构成,任期5年,不允许连任,由国会选举产生。法院的目的在于裁决合宪性事项,拥有以下职权:第一,唯一有权审理违宪诉讼;第二,有权审理根据《宪法》和其他法律授权的权限或职权相冲突的案件;第三,享有审理不保护公民权利案件的最终权力。法院作出裁定或判决时采用简单大多数投票规则,即要求至少5位法官的一致同意,方可作出确认或驳回违宪诉求的裁决。①

面对宪法法院的不利判决,秘鲁政府和司法机关并没有放弃引渡黄海勇的初衷,并且继续寻求采用宪法法院未禁止的方式实现与中国的引渡合作,为此,在数年的时间中一直维持着对黄海勇的引渡羁押或限制人身自由措施。

为了反对秘鲁最高法院同意引渡的判决以及抗议秘鲁行政部门不执行秘鲁宪法法院的判决和超期羁押问题,黄海勇及其家人和律师采取了诸多措施,其中最主要的是六份人身保护令申请。

人身保护令是秘鲁的宪法保障措施之一。秘鲁《宪法》第200条第1款规定:"当任何一个当局、官员或任何人的行动或失职,损害或威胁个人自由或相关宪法性权利时,均可以提出人身保护令。"

2009年10月12日黄海勇的律师基于"黄海勇的宪法性权利遭受侵害"为由提交了第二份人身保护令申请来反对秘鲁最高法院赞成引渡的咨询性裁定。但秘鲁主管机关决定不予受理。

2010年2月9日黄海勇的律师提交了第三份人身保护令申请,向秘鲁

---

① 参见胡建淼:《世界宪法法院制度研究》,中国法制出版社2013年版,第384—388页。

总统、司法部和外交部发难。2月25日秘鲁利马第42特别刑事法院宣布不予受理。紧接着,律师又提出了上诉。4月14日法院再次确认不予受理,因为秘鲁总统、司法部和外交部在此期间没有发布任何侵犯或威胁黄海勇权利的决定,也没有造成客观和具体的损害。

2011年11月16日黄海勇的律师提交了第四份人身保护令申请,向秘鲁司法部和最高法院反对黄海勇一直处于临时羁押状态,且行政部门没有遵循宪法法院的判决作出拒绝中国引渡请求的决定。后在2012年5月30日秘鲁最高法院宣布不予受理,因为羁押措施是根据相关法律规定适用的,法院有权决定延长期限。

2012年3月13日黄海勇的律师提交第五份人身保护令申请,反对秘鲁最高法院再次开庭审理,以及指责秘鲁政府迟迟不作出拒绝引渡请求的决定。后被秘鲁最高法院驳回。

2013年4月26日黄海勇的律师提交了第六份人身保护令申请,要求立即释放黄海勇并不受任何管制。2014年10月24日秘鲁法院宣布不予受理,因为引渡逮捕措施已经变更为监视居住。

(五)人权组织推波助澜

根据秘鲁《宪法》第205条的规定:"一旦国内司法机关提供的所有司法途径全部被使用或拒绝,若当事人认为其宪法性权利仍受到损害,可向依照秘鲁所参加的国际条约所组成的国际法院或国际机构提起诉讼。"

为抗拒引渡,黄海勇聘请了秘鲁著名的律师,几乎穷尽了所有法律手段,展开旷日持久的"程序战":将案件两度上诉至秘鲁最高法院、两度上诉至秘鲁宪法法院。2009年3月27日黄海勇及其律师在向秘鲁最高法院上诉的同时,以"引渡回中国会遭受死刑和酷刑"为由申诉至美洲人权委员会。2010年11月1日美洲人权委员会正式受理了此案。

美洲人权委员会于1959年成立,当时主要是《美洲国家组织宪章》体系下的一个专门机构。1978年7月18日《美洲人权公约》生效,1979年10月《美洲人权委员会规约》通过,这两个文件使其正式成为《美洲人权公约》的监督执行机构。1980年通过的《美洲人权委员会程序规则》详细规定了基本的组织结构、功能和职权范围。因此,美洲人权委员会既能够监督缔约国履行公约义务的情况,受理国家间的相互指控,又能够对特定国家开展调查和接受被侵犯合法权利的个人申诉。① 而且,可以提出申诉的申请主体特别广泛,任何个人或经成员国承认的非政府组织,均可以控告某一缔约国侵犯了其《美洲人权公约》所规定的权利。秘鲁既是《美洲人权公约》的缔约国,也是美洲国家组织的成员国,所以接受美洲人权委员会和美洲人权法院的管辖。

美洲人权委员会由各成员国政府提名的候选人名单中选择七人组成,任期四年,只能连任一次,其主要职责是促进尊重和保护人权。当成员国内任何人的合法权利遭受到侵犯,并已经穷尽了国内法规定的救济方法之后,可向委员会递交包含谴责或控诉某一成员国的请愿书;然后委员会核对事实,进行调查,有关各国应向其提供一切必要的便利;最后委员会在尊重公约所承认的人权基础上对问题进行友好解决,并公布委员会报告。②

2013年6月18日美洲人权委员会作出报告认为:自黄海勇2008年10月27日在秘鲁被捕以来,"临时逮捕"持续长达5年而无最终结论,已严重侵犯了受害人黄海勇的人身自由。秘鲁当局在办案及评估中国提交的外交保证过程中有一系列的过失和不当。这不仅违反了正当程序原则,而且也没有遵守保障黄海勇生命权、人道待遇权、人身自由和司法保护权的《美洲人权公约》义务。③

美洲人权委员会同时表达了对中国"死刑"和"酷刑"状况的担忧,建议秘鲁政府尽快采取必要措施结束引渡程序,开展对黄海勇临时羁押必要性的审查,对他合法权利的侵害做出赔偿。最后,还要求严格执行秘鲁宪法法院2011年5月24日所做出的裁决和遵守秘鲁《刑事诉讼法》的相关规定,④拒绝引渡黄海勇。

2013年10月30日,在美洲人权委员会的支持下,"黄海勇诉秘鲁"案被提交至美洲人权法院审理。美洲人权法院是在《美洲人权公约》和《美洲人

---

① 参见刘杰敏、张晓明:"美洲区域性人权保护机制析论",载《华南理工大学学报(社会科学版)》2012年第1期。
② 参见《美洲人权公约》第六章美洲国家间人权委员会的规定。
③ 参见《美洲人权公约》第二章公民和政治权利的规定。
④ 《秘鲁共和国刑事诉讼法》第517条第3款第4项规定:"被申请引渡人在申请引渡国可能被判处死刑,并且申请引渡国未提供不对其判处死刑的保证,应当拒绝其引渡申请。"

权法院规约》的框架下于1979年正式成立的,后者和1980年通过的《美洲人权法院程序规则》详细规定了法院的组织结构、管辖权和审理案件的程序规则。法院主要通过行使诉讼管辖权和咨询管辖权来实施和解释《美洲人权公约》,诉讼管辖是指审理和裁决有关成员国是否侵犯了个人的人权,咨询管辖是指判定国家的立法和司法活动是否符合相关人权保护规定的法律标准。① 在本案中,被告方是秘鲁政府,原告方是"受害人"黄海勇,美洲人权委员会则以维护黄海勇"合法权利"的名义站在原告一方参与诉讼。

美洲人权法院由各缔约国提出的候选人名单中选举七名法官组成,任期六年,只能连任一次,管辖提交至法院的有关公约各项规定的解释和实施的案件以及通过特别协议承认法院管辖权的案件。法院的主要职能是:发现公约所保护的权利或自由受到侵犯后,作出裁决以保证受害一方享有其被侵犯的权利或自由,并对受害一方给予公平的补救或赔偿,紧急情况下,还可以采取必要的临时性措施。法院的判决是终局性的,不得上诉。如对判决的内容有异议,可以在收到判决书之日起九十日内提出请求,然后法院作出合理的解释。最后,各缔约国必须服从法院的判决,并按照国内的程序予以执行。②

(六)中秘合作坚持不懈

在这里需要特别说明的是,自2011年5月24日秘鲁宪法法院作出不得引渡黄海勇的判决之后,秘鲁行政部门始终掌握着该引渡案件的处理进程,而且一直没有作出是否引渡的最终决定。

按理说,在宪法法院作出不得引渡的判决后行政部门应当立即决定拒绝相关引渡请求,但秘鲁政府却没有这样做,而是认为对宪法法院的判决可做狭义解释,继续考虑绕开死刑问题引渡黄海勇。2011年11月25日秘鲁司法部的代表指出:秘鲁宪法法院不得引渡的决定只适用于黄海勇的偷逃关税和走私行为,而不适用于行贿行为,因为针对后一行为中国法律并没有规定适用死刑的可能性。2012年2月9日秘鲁司法部请求秘鲁最高法院发

---

① 参见赵海峰、窦玉前:"美洲人权法院——在困难中前进的区域人权保护司法机构",载《人民司法》2005年第12期。
② 参见《美洲人权公约》第七章美洲国家间人权法院的规定。

布一份补充咨询性裁决。2月20日秘鲁司法部的代表又提出上诉,要求宪法法院就其判决作出解释。

关于酷刑问题,秘鲁政府认为某些个人和组织抹黑中国人权保障制度和刑事司法制度的说法并不符合中国的现实情况。2011年5月9日秘鲁政府通过驻华大使馆邀请北京师范大学刑事法律科学研究院黄风教授出具了一份《中国法律对犯罪嫌疑人和被告人权利的保护专家意见书》,具体阐述了中国法律关于罪刑法定和无罪推定原则、保障被告人诉讼权利的各项制度以及严禁刑讯逼供和排除非法证据的规定。

中国主管机关也做出大量的努力。由中央纪委、外交部、公安部、司法部和海关总署组成的黄海勇案引渡工作组,先后6次赴秘鲁与其相关部门协商执行引渡工作。中国驻秘鲁大使馆和引渡工作组齐心协力,向秘方提供了大量扎实、合法、有效的证据材料,并耐心细致做好秘鲁各级机关的解释说明工作。一方面,旗帜鲜明地展示了要将黄海勇引渡回国的决心;另一方面,积极介绍中国相关的法律制度,以促进秘鲁政府和司法部门的理解和支持。[①]

在2008年中国向秘鲁提出引渡请求时,黄海勇所涉嫌的走私普通货物罪是很有可能被判处死刑的。虽然《中秘引渡条约》中并未规定"死刑不引渡"或者"免除死刑的承诺"等条款,但是由于秘鲁早已经对普通犯罪废除了死刑且近些年来一直未实际执行过死刑,[②]再加上秘鲁作为《美洲人权公约》缔约国所承担的国际人权义务,遂要求中国作出不对黄海勇适用死刑的承诺,否则将不予引渡。对此,中国先后向秘鲁发送了八份外交照会。

2009年2月2日中国公安部向秘鲁司法部引渡和罪犯移转委员会发送了第一次照会,表示根据中国《刑法》的规定,不可能对黄海勇适用无期徒刑或者死刑;中国司法机关在审理案件时会严格遵守相关法律和《中秘引渡条约》。2月24日中国驻秘鲁大使馆将中国《刑法》第151条、第153条、第154条、第191条、第389条和第390条的译文发送给秘鲁利马第56刑事法院。

---

① 刘星:"新中国最复杂的引渡案内幕",载 http://news.hexun.com/2016-07-27/185168783.html,最后访问日期:2017年9月27日。
② 参见赵秉志、张磊:"黄海勇引渡案法理问题研究",载《法律适用》2017年第4期。

8月25日中国驻秘鲁特命全权大使向秘鲁最高法院发送了第二次外交照会,表示根据中国的司法实践,类似的案件,包括同样的涉案金额和行为,被判处了15年有期徒刑,并且没有对黄海勇适用死刑的可能性。

12月11日中国驻秘鲁特命全权大使向秘鲁最高法院发送了第三次外交照会,表示中国最高人民法院已经决定,如果黄海勇在中国被判决有罪,即使他的行为按照法律规定应该被判处死刑,法院也不会判处死刑。此外,大使还表示,如果引渡请求被允许,他全权承诺不会对黄海勇适用死刑。

12月29日中国驻秘鲁特命全权大使向秘鲁最高法院常设刑事分庭发送了第四次外交照会和中国最高人民法院决定的副本和译文,重申不会对黄海勇判处死刑,无论是死刑立即执行还是缓期两年执行。

2011年2月22日中国驻秘鲁大使向秘鲁司法部发送了第五次外交照会,表示中国政府承诺在对黄海勇进行法庭审理时将邀请秘鲁政府派观察员到场并监督对判决的执行情况。

4月6日中国主管机关向秘鲁宪法法院发送了《刑法修正案(八)》,其中规定了废除走私普通货物罪的死刑,并于2011年5月1日开始生效。

6月10日中国驻秘鲁大使向秘鲁司法部发送了第六次外交照会和中国《刑法》第12条关于溯及力的译文,正式确认《刑法修正案(八)》关于废止走私罪死刑的规定适用于黄海勇案件。

12月22日中国驻秘鲁大使馆向秘鲁外交部发送了第七次外交照会指出:早在2009年12月11日中方就根据最高人民法院的决定向秘鲁作出了正式承诺,不会对黄海勇适用死刑。这项承诺会持续有效。

2014年8月19日中国驻秘鲁大使馆向秘鲁外交部发送了第八次外交照会,除了重申之前作出的承诺,还表示:(1)将来羁押黄海勇的地点可供秘方访问。按照秘方的要求,中方也将尽快组织对羁押地点的考察以及黄海勇与秘方外交或领事官员的会见,并可以有一个秘方翻译人员陪同。(2)如有需要,视频会议设施可供使用,以便黄海勇可以联系秘方外交或领事官员。(3)根据中国《刑事诉讼法》和《律师法》的规定,黄海勇有权聘请律师替他辩护,也有权更换律师,且与律师的会见不受监督。(4)根据中国《刑事诉讼法》和《刑法》的规定,秘方可以派外交或领事官员出席黄海勇的公开庭审。(5)黄海勇被引渡回国后,中国司法机关会对审前和审时同步录音录像,并记录期间所有在场人员的身份。如有需要,也会提供给秘方。(6)根据中国《监狱法》和《看守所条例》的规定,黄海勇有权获得必要的医疗服务。按照秘方的要求,中国将允许一个独立的社会医疗机构为黄海勇提供医疗服务。(7)中国外交部条约法律司和秘鲁驻华大使馆会就上述全部事项保持沟通渠道。①

(七)据理力争美洲法院

1. 专家证人法庭雄辩

2014年9月3日美洲人权法院在巴拉圭共和国的最高法院开庭审理此案。此次庭审由该法院7位法官中的5位组成法庭。应秘鲁政府的邀请并经美洲人权法院的批准,北京师范大学刑事法律科学研究院院长暨中国刑法学研究会会长赵秉志教授、中国外交部条约法律司孙昂参赞和秘鲁前司法部部长托马博士作为专家证人出庭作证,中国社会科学院国际法研究所柳华文研究员提供了经过公证的书面证词。

法庭听取了3位专家证人的证词,并由秘鲁政府方面、美洲人权委员会代表、黄海勇律师以及法庭依次对他们进行质证和发问。其中,赵秉志教授的证词主要围绕与本案有关的中国刑事司法程序和实体法律问题;孙昂参赞的证词主要围绕中国引渡法治实践以及中加两国遣返赖昌星案的外交承诺;托马博士的证词主要围绕与本案有关的《中秘引渡条约》和秘鲁国内法律问题;柳华文研究员的书面证词主要是证明中国的法治和人权保障状况。法庭对出庭作证的专家证人表示了感谢,并认为赵秉志教授和孙昂参赞的作证对他们了解当前中国的刑事法治状况很有帮助。在当天下午三位专家证人作证结束之后,参与庭审的三方又进行了激烈的辩论。②

2. 三大问题争议不断

实际上,庭审中主要涉及三大核心问题:死刑、酷刑和超期羁押。

关于死刑问题,主要围绕三个方面展开。第一,针对原告方提出"黄海

---

① 美洲人权法院:"黄海勇诉秘鲁案判决书",载http://www.corteidh.or.cr/cf/jurisprudencia2/ver_expediente.cfm?nId_expediente=203&lang=en,最后访问日期:2017年10月15日。

② 参见柳华文:"美洲人权法院引渡第一案的意义及其启示",载《东南大学学报(哲学社会科学版)》2016年第6期。

勇所涉嫌的罪名有可能被判处死刑"的说法,法庭经审理认为黄海勇如果被引渡回中国并没有适用死刑的真正风险(real risk):(1) 2011 年 5 月 1 日生效的《刑法修正案(八)》废除了走私普通货物罪的死刑。(2)中国的几次外交照会以及专家证人赵秉志教授和德国马普所的司法报告也都指出了中国《刑法》第 12 条关于刑法溯及力"从旧兼从轻"的有利于被告人原则;第二,针对原告方提出"中国存在私下或秘密执行死刑的危险,并且不公开执行死刑的数据和信息,都是作为国家机密处理"的说法,法庭认为,美洲人权委员会和黄海勇的律师都没有提供具体的材料或证据以佐证其论据,不能凭此推断黄海勇如果被引渡到中国就会面临个人的、真实的、可预见(individual, real and foreseeable)的危险;第三,针对原告方提出"关于在中国可能被判处死刑的罪名数量和程序的报告,来佐证黄海勇声称的生命权遭受威胁"的说法,法庭认为,由于死刑不适用于在中国走私普通货物的行为,所以这种资料是无关紧要的,法庭没有义务去评估这个报告。最终,法庭判定:黄海勇没有被适用死刑的可能性。

关于酷刑问题,主要围绕三个方面展开。第一,针对原告方提出"黄海勇的人身自由和健康权存在风险"的说法,法庭援引了欧洲人权法院的评判标准,即"为了确定是否存在酷刑的危险,不仅要审查申请人被引渡回国后可以预见的后果,还要考虑该国的整体情况以及申请人的个人状况",并认为没有充分的理由使其相信存在真实的危险;第二,针对原告方提出的"可能遭受酷刑和其他残忍、不人道或有辱人格的待遇或处罚"的说法,法庭通过调查中国的风险状况和提供的外交保证后认为,美洲人权委员会和黄海勇的律师都没有提供辩词、证据和依据来证明引渡会给黄海勇带来具体的人身特定危险(personal, individual and specific risk);第三,针对原告方提出的有关恐怖组织人员、人权卫士、政治罪犯和维族群体的人权情况,法庭认为这些与黄海勇案没有关系。法庭还认为中国提供的外交保证是"令人满意"的,同时是充分和有效的。最终,法庭判定:没有证据表明引渡黄海勇会使其面临酷刑和其他残忍、不人道或有辱人格的待遇或处罚的真实的、可以预见的人身危险。

关于超期羁押问题,针对原告方提出"秘鲁行政机关不但没有遵守宪法法院的判决和尽到相关的审慎义务,而且采取了一系列拖延措施,持续六年没有作出最终决定,违反了合理的时间要求。"法庭通过审查秘鲁行政机关的行为以及未能遵守合理时间的原因认为,虽然这个案件是复杂的,原告方一直在采取救济措施来不断上诉和申诉,但是引渡程序持续了六年以上,在整个过程中行政机关几乎没有重视过决定的拖延对黄海勇的人身自由和其他合法权利所造成的影响,而且黄海勇确实被长期剥夺或限制了人身自由(羁押5年半和监视居住1年)。最终,法庭判定:秘鲁行政部门的引渡决定超出了合理的时间,违反了《美洲人权公约》的相关规定,①侵害了黄海勇的合法权利。

2015年6月30日美洲人权法院正式作出判决:第一,秘鲁的羁押措施超出了合理时间限度,构成对黄海勇人身自由权的侵犯,为此应赔偿黄海勇及其律师共计五万八千美元。关于原告方的其他主张,不予支持。第二,如果秘鲁引渡黄海勇,没有适用死刑的可能性以及遭受酷刑的危险,也不会违反《美洲人权公约》规定的相关义务。第三,秘鲁必须尽快在引渡程序中作出最终决定。

2016年5月23日,秘鲁政府决定向中国引渡犯罪嫌疑人黄海勇。同年7月14日中秘两国有关执法部门在秘鲁签署引渡交接文件。由于我国与秘鲁没有直达航班,也为了保证"归途的绝对安全",黄海勇被我国押解小组安排乘坐智利和俄罗斯航空公司的航班,途径古巴、俄罗斯,最终成功引渡回国。②

二、法律问题探析

(一)条约和法律依据

1.《中秘引渡条约》

结合本案,根据《中秘引渡条约》的规定,主要涉及以下方面:第一,双

---

① 《美洲人权公约》第8条第1款规定:"人人都有权在适当的保证下和一段合理的时间内由事前经法律设立的独立公正的主管法庭进行审讯,以判定对该人具有犯罪性质的任何控告,或决定该人的民事、劳动、财政或具有任何其他性质的权利和义务。"

② 参见冯彬:"中国专家出庭'最复杂引渡案'始末",载《廉政瞭望》2016年第20期。

方有义务根据本条约的规定,应对方请求,相互引渡在一方境内发现的被另一方通缉的人员,以便对其进行刑事诉讼或者执行刑罚;第二,为进行刑事诉讼而请求引渡,根据双方法律均构成犯罪,且均可判处一年以上有期徒刑或者其他更重的刑罚,属于可引渡的犯罪;第三,如果被请求方认为,为支持引渡请求所提供的材料不充分,可以要求在三十天内提交补充材料。如果请求方提出合理要求,这一期限可以延长十五天;第四,被请求方应当根据本国法律规定的程序处理引渡请求,并且迅速将决定通知请求方;第五,本条约不影响缔约双方根据任何其他条约享有的权利和承担的义务。①

2. 中国《引渡法》

结合本案,根据《引渡法》的规定,主要涉及以下方面:第一,主要目的是为了保障引渡的正常进行,加强惩罚犯罪方面的国际合作,保护个人和组织的合法权益,维护国家利益和社会秩序;第二,中国和外国之间的引渡,通过外交途径联系,外交部为指定的进行引渡的联系机关;第三,被请求国就准予引渡附加条件的,对于不损害中国主权、国家利益、公共利益的,可以由外交部代表中国政府向被请求国作出承诺。对于限制追诉的承诺,由最高人民检察院决定;对于量刑的承诺,由最高人民法院决定。在对被引渡人追究刑事责任时,司法机关应当受所作出的承诺的约束。②

(二)秘鲁引渡制度

1. 引渡的范围和条件

(1)被告人、被判决人作为在国外所实施的犯罪行为的实施者或参与者,无论是秘鲁居民、游客或过境者,只要位于秘鲁国境内,就都可以被引渡,以接受请求国的调查、审判以及履行已判处的刑罚。(2)若被请求引渡人在请求国可能被判处死刑,并且请求国未提供不对其判处死刑的保证,则应当拒绝引渡请求。(3)引渡请求未满足相应条件或者提供内容不完整的,中央机关依有管辖权机关的申请,在外交部的协调下,要求请求引渡国对申请和提供的文件进行修改、完善。

---

① 参见《中华人民共和国和秘鲁共和国引渡条约》第1、2、8、10、20条的规定。
② 参见《中华人民共和国引渡法》第1、4、50条的规定。

2. 引渡的具体程序

(1) 秘鲁国家检察长办公室收到引渡请求后，如果请求国要求临时羁押，预审法官就可以对被请求引渡人下达引渡的逮捕令；(2) 预审法官在传唤省级检察官后，听取被请求引渡人的陈述，陈述之前，应当事先告知其逮捕的原因以及引渡请求的细节；(3) 在15日内，预审法官传唤被申请引渡人及其辩护人、省级检察官、使馆代表开庭审理，组织提交证据，听取各方陈述和意见，最后将审理记录提交至最高法院刑事庭；(4) 最高法院刑事庭召集各方开庭审理后，在5日内作出咨询性裁决并在3日内送交至司法部；(5) 部长理事会以最高裁决的形式作出是否引渡的决定，再由国家检察长办公室通过外交渠道通知请求引渡国，并在对其作出的外交照会中表明同意引渡的附加条件；(6) 自发出通知之日起，请求引渡国需在30日内完成引渡工作。①

(三) 秘鲁宪法法院

1. 与最高法院的区别

秘鲁最高法院及其下级法院属于普通法院，通常只裁决民事、刑事以及行政案件，不能涉及国家基本宪法原则争议的处理，其主要职责是把既有的法律适用于具体的案件，因此工作具有很强的技术性。而宪法法院不同于普通法院，主要表现在三个方面：第一，主要职责不同。宪法法院的主要职责是根据本国的历史和国情来解释宪法，并监督宪法的实施；第二，法官地位不同。宪法法院的法官不能担任最高法院的职务，并享有与立法机关成员相同的权力、特权和豁免权；第三，法律效力不同。宪法法院的裁决具有终局性且最高的法律效力。例如在本案的审理过程中，第一审和第二审都是由最高法院审理的，而宪法法院则是根据黄海勇的特别上诉来进行最后审。

2. 宪法法院的受案范围

根据宪法法院所受理案件的保护目标不同，可以把受案类型分为三类：

(1) 保护宪法权利案件

这类案件是对宪法权利的司法审查，主要为了保护秘鲁《宪法》第一章

---

① 参见秘鲁《刑事诉讼法》第513—522条之规定。

所规定的人的基本权利,例如公民的人身自由权、人身完整权、生命权、健康权、不被驱逐权等等。当个人的宪法性权利遭受到国家机关、官员或其他人的职责或行为的侵害或威胁时,即可自行或委托辩护律师提起此类诉讼。本案即属于这种情况。

(2) 违宪案件

审理此类案件的原则是宪法至上,即宪法优于其他法律和法规,主要是为了维护宪法在整个法律体系中的最高地位和权威。当具有法律效力的规范在重要方面或根本上与宪法相抵触,或这些法律规范没有以宪法规定的形式被批准却公布或发表时,即可发生违宪诉讼。与前者不同的是,仅以下主体能够提起诉讼:总统、总检察长、1/4 国会议员、5 000 名公民;若被指控的是地方条例的话,还包括地区 1% 的公民、地区主席和大学教授。

(3) 权限冲突案件

审理此类案件主要是为了决定国家机关对应的职权以及取消其无权作出的决定或行为。当国家机关没有按照或者超出宪法的规定行使职权,从而妨碍了宪法授权给其他机关的职权时就会提起此类诉讼。

3. 对宪法法院的评价

虽然根据宪法的规定,秘鲁宪法法院是一个独立的机构,可实际上却并非如此。有学者指出,秘鲁行政机关经常出于自己的政治目的任命或罢免某些法官,直接或间接地操控着司法系统,法官们不能依据宪法独立行使所赋予的职权,经常受制于实权在握的行政机关。所以,宪法法院的独立性很难得到保证。[①]

(四)《美洲人权公约》

1. 公约概况

1969 年 11 月 22 日,12 个国家在哥斯达黎加圣约瑟城签订的《美洲人权公约》于 1978 年 7 月 18 日开始生效。公约共 11 章,82 条。其中第一章规定了各缔约国应尊重该公约所承认的各项权利和自由,并保证在它们管辖下的所有人都能自由地、全部地行使这些权利和自由。第二章专门规

---

① 胡建淼:《世界宪法法院制度研究》,中国法制出版社 2013 年版,第 384—392 页。

定了公民的各项权利,包括生命权、人道待遇权、自由权和司法保护权等等。

该公约是继《欧洲人权公约》之后的第二个区域性人权保障公约,是在人权保护的呼声日益高涨的背景下所制定的一部区域性人权宣言书。该公约在序言部分就明确规定:希望在本半球,在民族制度的范围内,巩固以尊重人的基本权利为基础的个人自由和社会正义的制度;承认人的基本权利的来源并非由于某人是某一国家的公民,而是根据人类人格的属性,因此以公约形式来加强或补充美洲国家国内法提供的保护而对上述权利给予国际性保护是正当的。

2. 公约的特点

(1) 人权内容的全面性

公约在第二章用很长的篇幅对公民应受保护的权利做了细致且全面的规定,具体包括法律人格权、生命权、人道待遇权、不受奴役权、个人自由权、公平审判权、受赔偿权、享有私生活权、良心和宗教自由权、思想和发表意见的自由权、答辩权、集会权、结社权、家庭权、姓名权、儿童权、国籍权、财产权、迁徙和居住自由权、参加政府权、平等保护权、司法保护权。

(2) 法官可以充分发表意见

我国法院在法庭评议时,采取少数服从多数原则,评议笔录不公开,且在判决书中不允许附上法官不同的意见。这与公约的规定大不相同。根据公约第 66 条的规定:如法院作出地判决不能全部或部分地代表各位法官的一致意见,任一法官都有权在该判决中附上其不同的或单独的意见。例如在本案中,就有 Alberto 和 Eduardo 两位法官发表了自己不同的见解,并附在了黄海勇判决书正文之后。这种制度设计更加有利于发挥司法独立、法官独立的作用,也更加有利于保护人权。

(3) 可操作性强

公约第一部分是有关人权的实体性规定,第二部分则是有关对人权保护的程序性规定。例如向人权委员会或法院提起申诉或起诉的主体、审查要件以及裁决的公开等内容都作了详细的规定。由此可见,公约并不是一部口号式的宣言书,而是一部具有很强操作性的人权保护公约。

3. 对《美洲人权公约》的评价

有学者指出,由于美洲地区各国的经济发展水平和人权保护的程度具有很大的差距,因此公约的具体内容很难在短期内得到具体落实。不可否认,公约的实施情况不是特别尽如人意,但我们也不能因此而全面否定其价值。事实上,公约在几十年的时间里,还是对保护和促进美洲地区的人权方面起到了一些积极作用的。①

(五)量刑承诺问题

1. 量刑承诺的含义

何谓"量刑承诺"? 目前在学界或相关法律法规中还没有统一或明确的定义。有学者认为,量刑承诺是指由请求引渡犯罪嫌疑人的国家司法机关向被请求引渡的国家作出引渡该犯罪嫌疑人回国受审后减轻刑事处罚的决定,包括原本应该判处死刑而不被判处死刑或判处死刑不予执行的许诺或保证。② 还有的学者认为,量刑承诺是指为了推动引渡的顺利开展,请求引渡国向被请求引渡国作出的关于对被请求引渡人在回国受审后予以减轻处罚的承诺的制度。③ 笔者基本支持这两种观点,认为量刑承诺是指请求引渡国向被请求引渡国主动或被动作出的关于被请求引渡人在定罪、量刑事项上所作出的承诺。量刑承诺分为两种:一种是承诺不适用死刑,即不判处死刑或不执行死刑,包括死刑立即执行和缓期两年执行;另一种是承诺减轻处罚,即缩短羁押刑期或变更刑罚执行方式。

2. 量刑承诺与外交保证的区分

自2009年2月2日至2014年8月19日,中国共向秘鲁发送八份外交照会。其中第一、二、三、四、六和七份属于量刑承诺,第五和第八份属于外交保证。那么这两者是如何区分出来的呢? 笔者认为,一言以蔽之,看内容是否属于定罪、量刑抑或直接相关。也即,如果是有关具体罪名、刑罚轻重、死刑适用以及溯及力等问题,则属于量刑承诺;如果是有关人权保障、执行刑罚、监督机制以及其他不属于量刑承诺的问题,则属于外交保证。由此看

---

① 参见胡建淼:《外国宪法:法规及评述》,北京大学出版社2004年版,第102—106页。
② 参见陈雷、薛振环:《论我国引渡制度的量刑承诺——兼论死刑不引渡原则的变通或例外适用》,载《法学杂志》2010年第1期。
③ 参见张磊:《境外追逃中的量刑承诺制度研究》,载《中国法学》2017年第1期。

来,外交保证与量刑承诺相比,范围更加广,内容更加多,且具有一定的兜底性。

3. 量刑承诺的审查标准

在2008年中国向秘鲁提出引渡请求时,黄海勇所涉嫌的走私普通货物罪是很有可能被判处死刑的。为了顺利将黄海勇引渡回国,中国通过几次外交照会作出了"不适用死刑"的量刑承诺,最终获得了秘鲁和美洲人权法院的审查认可,并被认定是"可靠的、有效的、可检验的"(solid、significant and verifiable)的充分承诺(sufficient guarantee)。① 对此,笔者将量刑承诺的审查标准总结为两方面——充分性和有效性。

(1) 量刑承诺的充分性(sufficient)

"充分性"可谓是衡量能否成功引渡最为关键的因素,也是被请求国严格审查的标准。"充分性"有着国际法和双边条约法依据。1990年《联合国引渡示范条例》第4条(d)项规定,如果按照被请求国的法律应判处死刑,可以拒绝引渡,除非该国作出被请求国认为是充分的保证。② 《中华人民共和国和西班牙王国引渡条约》、《中华人民共和国和澳大利亚引渡条约》和《中华人民共和国和法兰西共和国引渡条约》也都规定了,③除非请求方作出被请求方认为"足够的"保证,否则将拒绝引渡。

"充分性"应该由国家指定的专门机关负责审查。如英国《2003年引渡法》第94条规定由国务大臣(Secretary of State)负责接受关于不判处或不执行死刑的"书面保证",并且审查它是否"适当";意大利《刑事诉讼法典》第698条第2款规定由司法部长和对引渡请求进行司法审查的法院来审查保

---

① 参见美洲人权法院:《黄海勇诉秘鲁案判决书》,载http://www.corteidh.or.cr/cf/jurisprudencia2/ver_expediente.cfm?nId_expediente=203&lang=en,最后访问日期:2017年10月15日。

② 《联合国引渡示范条例》第4条拒绝引渡之任择理由(d)项规定:"被请求国的法律作为请求引渡原因的罪行应判处死刑,除非该国作出被请求国认为是充分的保证,表示不会判处死刑,或即使判死刑,也不会予以执行"。

③ 《中华人民共和国和西班牙王国引渡条约》第3条第8项规定:"根据请求方法律,被请求引渡人可能因引渡请求所针对的犯罪被判处死刑,除非请求方作出被请求方认为足够的保证不判处死刑,或者在判处死刑的情况下不执行死刑。"《中华人民共和国和澳大利亚引渡条约》第3条第6项规定:"根据请求方法律,被请求引渡人可能因引渡请求所针对的犯罪被判处死刑,除非请求方保证不判处死刑,或者在判处死刑的情况下不执行死刑。"《中华人民共和国和法兰西共和国引渡条约》第3条第7项规定"引渡请求所针对的犯罪依照请求方的法律应当判处死刑,除非请求方作出被请求方认为足够的保证不判处死刑,或者在判处死刑的情况下不予执行。"

证是否是"充足的"。① 具体到本案中,按照秘鲁《刑事诉讼法》第522条第1款的规定,则是由秘鲁部长理事会以最高裁决的形式作出最终能否引渡的决定。

(2) 量刑承诺的有效性(significant)

"有效性"主要是指量刑承诺的效力问题,即请求国成功引渡后是否受约束,以及在多大程度上受量刑承诺的约束。"有效性"标准在我国《引渡法》第50条中有着明确的规定:"在对被引渡人追究刑事责任时,司法机关应当受所作出的承诺的约束。"而且条文中用的是"应当",而不是"可以"。这表明了量刑承诺作出之后,在全国范围内具有相应的约束力,各级司法机关都必须在量刑承诺的范围内起诉、审判和执行。

"有效性"还包括被请求人引渡回国后的执行评估情况。如果请求国作出不适用死刑的承诺,最后又判处死刑或执行死刑,那么这就是个完全无效的量刑承诺;如果请求国一开始遵守了承诺,然后又违背了承诺,那么这就是个相对无效的承诺。"有效性"的实施评估不是几个月或者几年就能够完成的,而是常态性、持续性和终局性的,直到被请求人的刑罚执行完毕。

(3) 充分性和有效性的关系

"充分性"和"有效性",既紧密相关,又相互区别,二者相辅相成,共同构成了量刑承诺的审查标准。但二者的功能却是大相径庭的。"充分性"主要是指引渡前量刑承诺的作出,是事前标准,是关乎能否开展引渡的决定性因素;"有效性"主要是指引渡后量刑承诺的兑现,是事后标准,是关乎量刑承诺的效力和执行情况的评估性因素。

(六) 外交保证问题

1. 外交保证的含义

同量刑承诺一样,"外交保证"截止到目前也还没有统一或明确的定义。美洲人权法院认为,外交保证是各国在引渡过程中作出的真诚的常见做法,包括请求引渡国向被请求引渡国所作出的承诺和保证,要求被请求引渡人

---

① 黄风:"国际引渡合作规则的新发展",载《比较法研究》2006年第3期。

必须根据被请求引渡国所承担的国际人权义务来接受对待和惩罚。① 有外国学者认为,外交保证是指国家间通过签订移送协定来保障被移送人将按照国际标准受到对待。② 联合国难民事务高级专员办事处(UNHCR)在《关于外交保证和国际难民保护的说明》中认为,外交保证是指接受国承诺将有关的人根据派遣国规定的条件或更普遍地遵守国际法规定的人权义务来对待。③ 对此,笔者认为,外交保证是指请求引渡国向被请求引渡国主动或被动作出的关于承担国际法或国际人权义务等事项上所作出的保证。具体到本案中,即秘鲁通过要求中国作出外交保证的方式,将其自身所承担的《美洲人权公约》义务转嫁给中国。

2. 外交保证的审查标准

在黄海勇案中,美洲人权法院援引了欧洲人权法院关于"奥斯曼诉英国"(Othman v. The United Kingdom)案中所确定的审查标准——外交保证的质量及其可靠性(quality and reliability),同时量化了具体的评估因素。笔者认为这套评估体系对中国的引渡实践大有裨益,将来我们再作出外交保证时可以予以参考和对照,其详细内容如下:a. 保证条款是否已经披露给法院。b. 保证内容是具体的还是普遍的、模糊的。c. 保证是谁作出的以及能否约束请求国。d. 如果请求国中央政府作出了保证,是否可以期望地方当局遵守。e. 保证是否涉及请求国合法或非法的待遇。f. 保证是否由条约的缔约国作出。g. 请求国和被请求国之间双边关系的时间和程度,以及请求国遵守类似保证的记录。h. 是否可以通过外交手段或其他监督机制客观地核实遵守保证的情况,包括提供不受约束的路径给被请求人的律师。i. 请求国是否存在有效地反对酷刑制度,包括是否愿意与国际人权监督机构合作,比如国际人权 NGO 组织,以及是否愿意调查酷刑指控并惩罚相关负责人。j. 被请求人是否曾在请求国遭受过虐待。k. 保证的可靠性是否接

---

① 参见美洲人权法院:《黄海勇诉秘鲁案判决书》,载 http://www.corteidh.or.cr/cf/jurisprudencia2/ver_expediente.cfm?nId_expediente=203&lang=en,最后访问日期:2017 年 10 月 15 日。
② 参见科尔杜拉·德勒格:《移送被拘留者:法律框架、不推回原则及当前的挑战》,载红十字国际委员会东亚地区代表处翻译:《红十字国际评论》2008 年文选 2010 年版,第 275 页。
③ 参见联合国难民事务高级专员办事处:《关于外交保证和国际难民保护的说明》,载 http://www.refworld.org/docid/44dc81164.html,最后访问日期:2017 年 10 月 22 日。

受过请求国法院的审查。①

3. 外交保证的实质内涵

首先,外交保证不是单纯的政治性声明,它不仅具有正式的法律效力,而且存在国际道义上的拘束。若请求国违反了保证的内容,那么它将承受日后类似承诺不被认可从而导致引渡请求被拒绝的风险,也会倍受国际舆论的压力。②

其次,外交保证是国际上通行且常见的做法,通过上述量化的标准,带给被请求人在防止死刑、酷刑和其他残忍、不人道待遇或处罚以及其他相应合法权利的程序保障,同时也有利于提高外交保证的质量和可靠性。

最后,只有在辅以独立且有效的实施监督机制,外交保证才能消除被请求人的、真实的、可预见的(individual, real and foreseeable)危险和威胁,③同时才能得到被请求国的支持和认可。例如,在"查哈尔诉英国"(Chahal v. The United Kingdom)案中,印度作出了不包含具体监督机制的承诺。④ 欧洲人权法院认为该承诺无法保证查哈尔的人权,因此英国如果同意遣返将违反《欧洲人权公约》。再如"奥泽瑞诉瑞典"(Mohammed Alzery v. Sweden)案中,埃及承诺:"将依照埃及宪法、法律的规定保证被遣返人的人权"。⑤ 联合国人权事务委员会也认为该承诺没有包含有效的实施监督机制,因此无法消除个人所受到的威胁,所以瑞典的驱逐行为违反了《公民权利和政治权利国际公约》。而在黄海勇案中,美洲人权法院经审理认为中国提供的第 8 份外交照会是详细的,包含具体的监督执行机制,符合上述确定的审查标准,可以消除受害者风险状况的任何担忧。

---

① 参见美洲人权法院:《黄海勇诉秘鲁案判决书》,载 http://www.corteidh.or.cr/cf/jurisprudencia2/ver_expediente.cfm?nId_expediente=203&lang=en,最后访问日期:2017 年 10 月 15 日。
② 参见朱慧兰:《论引渡承诺的性质和效力——以"黄海勇诉秘鲁案"为视角》,载《湖北警官学院学报》2017 年第 2 期。
③ 参见朱慧兰《国际刑事司法协助中承诺免除死刑问题研究》,载《武大国际法评论》2016 年第 1 期。
④ 参见欧洲人权法院:《查哈尔诉英国案判决书》,载 http://hudoc.echr.coe.int/eng?i=001-58004,最后访问日期:2017 年 10 月 15 日。
⑤ 参见联合国人权事务委员会:《奥泽瑞诉瑞典案决议》,载 http://www.refworld.org/cases,HRC,47975afa21.html,最后访问日期:2017 年 10 月 15 日。

三、对我国境外追逃的启示

从 2008 年 11 月我国依据《中秘引渡条约》向秘鲁政府提出引渡请求,到 2016 年 7 月黄海勇成功引渡回国,在整个引渡程序中,我国几乎经历了秘鲁国内和美洲人权保护机构的所有法律程序。从中,我们积累了丰富的办案经验,特别是在案件办理过程中,我国中央纪委、海关、外交、公安等多个部门通力合作,形成了良好的跨部门引渡工作协作配合机制,[①]进一步提升了打击外逃犯罪分子的国际合作水平,对我国在拉美国家的追逃工作产生了直接影响,有利于我国今后境外追逃追赃工作的实践。

(一)努力缔结双边条约和国际公约,积极构建国际刑事司法合作新秩序

引渡是境外追逃的主要路径之一,也是世界各国普遍认可的重要措施。而双边引渡条约无疑是两国开展引渡的前提和法律依据。正如本案一样,中国之所以能够成功引渡黄海勇,主要是因为签署了《中秘引渡条约》,双方之间没有法律障碍。截止到 2017 年 4 月,我国已经与 48 个国家签署了双边引渡条约,与 59 个国家签订了刑事司法协助类条约,与 90 多个国家(地区)和国际组织签署了 120 余项检务合作协议或谅解备忘录,并加入了《联合国反腐败公约》《联合国打击跨国有组织犯罪公约》等国际公约,[②]可谓是"硕果累累"。但是,我国尚未与美国、加拿大等西方发达国家签订引渡条约,所以外逃犯罪分子也多是逃往这些国家,以至于办起案来困难重重。

因此,一方面,我们要积极探索加入国际公约和组织,努力推动和世界各国的刑事司法合作,加快双边引渡条约、刑事司法协助条约的谈判、缔结和履约进程,尤其是同西方发达国家和地区;另一方面,我们也要秉持合作共赢的理念,加强与联合国、G20 集团、亚太经合组织、金砖国家等国际组织

[①] 参见胡涛:《黄海勇引渡归案,十八载悬念尘埃落定》,载 http://www.iis.whu.cn/index.php?id=1829,最后访问日期:2017 年 10 月 18 日。

[②] 参见中央纪委监察部网站:《近距离走进中央追逃办:带您了解反腐败国际追逃追赃的"台前幕后"》,载 http://www.ccdi.gov.cn/special/ztzz/ztzzjxs_ztzz/201704/t20170425_97795.html,最后访问日期:2017 年 4 月 25 日。

和国家的联系,利用好"一带一路"国际合作高峰论坛的东道主地位,倡导设置国际交流合作平台和议题,不断增强国际话语权和规则制定权,积极构建国际刑事司法合作新秩序。

(二)加快废除死刑步伐,加强刑事司法制度建设

近年来,我国一直在努力推进死刑改革,不断加快限制适用和废除死刑的步伐,刑罚体系方面取得了长足进步,如《刑法修正案(八)》减少了13个死刑罪名,《刑法修正案(九)》再次减少了9个死刑罪名。在社会各界,也一直存在着全面废除死刑的声音。但是,我国目前仍是世界上保留死刑的五十多个国家之一,迄今为止仍有46种死刑罪名。① 死刑问题和"死刑不引渡"原则一直是我国同其他国家开展引渡和刑事司法合作不可逾越的障碍与鸿沟。如在本案中,3位专家证人在美洲人权法院被问到涉及中国死刑方面的问题就达30多个。

因此,一方面,我们应当继续坚持少杀、慎杀、逐步减少适用死刑罪名的刑事政策,顺应世界各国全面废除死刑的趋势和潮流,切实推进死刑改革进程,尽早废除非暴力型犯罪尤其是腐败犯罪和经济犯罪的死刑,并最终达到全面废除死刑;②另一方面,在当前我国还保留死刑的情况下,要进一步减少死刑的判决和执行,借鉴其他废除死刑国家的立法经验,加强刑事司法制度建设,完善我国的刑罚结构和体系。同时,在引渡、遣返等国际合作中,根据实际情况,可以作出充分的外交承诺或担保;在将外逃人引渡回国后,也应当遵守相应承诺,以彰显我国恪守承诺、值得信赖的"国际名片"。

(三)不断完善人权保障机制,大力提升国际法治形象

改革开放以来,我国高度重视保障人权问题,先后批准或加入了《消除对妇女一切形式歧视公约》《消除一切形式种族歧视国际公约》《禁止酷刑和其他残忍、不人道或有辱人格的待遇或处罚公约》等20多项国际人权公约,宪法、刑法、刑事诉讼法等国内法律法规也都以"尊重和保障人权"为原则加以修改和完善。尤其是党的十八届四中全会审议通过了《中共中央关于全面推进依法治国若干重大问题的决定》,强调要依法保障公民权利,健全公

---

① 参见赵秉志、张磊:《黄海勇引渡案法理问题研究》,载《法律适用》2017年第4期。
② 同上。

民权利救济渠道,为中国人权事业的发展提供了重要的政治保证。① 但是,我们还应该清醒地认识到:虽然我国在保障人权问题上取得了巨大的成就,但与西方发达国家相比,仍有很大的进步空间。如我国虽然签署了《公民权利和政治权利国际公约》,但尚未批准和生效;国内人权立法和执法机构等领域还存在一些法律空白和违法行为。

因此,一方面,我国应适当接受西方国家和国际人权组织对中国人权状况的合理批评和建议,结合中国具体的实际情况,把依法治国原则和保障人权原则有机地统一起来,努力完善人权保障制度和执行监督机制,将保障人权贯穿于立法、司法、执法、守法的全过程;另一方面,还要加强国际人权保障方面的交流与合作,扩大舆论宣传的影响和传播,努力让国际社会更加了解和信任真实的中国人权保障状况。同时,还应恪守引渡承诺,促进两国之间的理解,尽量避免因政治制度或意识形态的差异而造成困境和障碍。这样,有利于树立中国"信守承诺"的国际形象,增强国际社会对我国司法制度的信任,从而实现境外追逃的良性循环。

(四)正确认识并完善引渡承诺制度,充分调动相关部门的能动性和积极性

有学者主张引渡承诺实际上是人权与主权的博弈,损害了本国的司法主权,同时也违反了法律面前人人平等的原则。② 对此,笔者认为引渡承诺是一国自愿作出的主权让渡,并非遭受了他国的侵害。而且,正是为了实现法律面前人人平等和惩治犯罪的需要,所以才利用作出引渡承诺这一措施来追捕并追诉已经逃往国外的犯罪分子。但是,我国虽然在《引渡法》和若干引渡条约中确立了有关量刑承诺的条款,但却没有对这一程序以及引渡承诺制度作出更加具体的规定。例如,引渡承诺的作出主体、前提、条件、效力和适用范围。这就使得我国司法机关和外交部门无章可循,只能靠个案的积累,逐步探索。此外,我国在本案中作为请求引渡国,在具体过程中,理应保持主动。如果外交部门积极同秘鲁政府联系和商洽,主动询问其中存在的问题,司法机关协助配合并予以快速解决,那么引渡程序可能就不会这

---

① 李宏:《不断推进法治中国的人权事业新发展》,载《光明日报》2017年4月13日第004版。
② 参见温耀原:《论引渡中的主权与人权》,载《法学杂志》2013年第5期。

么长久和复杂。

因此,一方面,正确认识引渡承诺制度,公正客观地评价引渡承诺的负面影响,妥善处理国家主权、适用法律平等与引渡承诺之间的关系,制定出一套内容具体和实用性强的量刑承诺实施细则。至于作出引渡承诺所坚持的原则或者说最低限度,笔者认为可以参照《引渡法》第 49 和 50 条的规定①;另一方面,在今后的引渡过程中,尤其是在主动引渡中,应进一步提高外交部门和司法机关的能动性和积极性,合理利用各方面的资源,减少各部门之间的隔阂,加强主管部门之间的相互联系和配合,不能"九龙治水,各管一段"。此外,如需作出引渡承诺,外交部门应主动与被请求国沟通,提高办事效率,加强两国磋商和互信,避免在程序上走弯路、走错路,②从而浪费国家的人力、物力、财力以及司法资源。

(五)加强对国际人权机构的了解,不断提升办案人员的实战经验

在本案中,不仅历经了秘鲁国内司法程序,而且还牵涉到美洲人权法院和美洲人权委员会两大国际人权机构。黄海勇的律师和美洲人权委员会的代表蓄意打起"程序战"并抛出种种难题,企图以此来抗拒引渡回国,虽然大都被有效化解,如针对"死刑不引渡"原则,我国做出了不判处死刑的外交承诺;针对"死刑"和"酷刑"问题,中秘两国 3 位专家证人出庭作证,并提供了大量证据材料和报告,但是从本案的具体过程和我国的应对措施上来看,也反映了我国对国外和国际人权机构的法律制度和规则还不是充分的了解,并且无法有效应对。

因此,一方面,在国际形势日趋复杂的今天,我们要遵守国际法律制度和国际司法合作规则,在法治的轨道上开展境外追逃追赃工作,不能让外逃分子钻法律的漏洞来逃避追捕和审查;另一方面,我国也要加强对办案机关的教育和培训,尤其是基层的办案人员,要加快学习和掌握国际法律制度,

---

① 《中华人民共和国引渡法》第 49 条规定:"引渡、引渡过境或者采取强制措施的请求所需的文书、文件和材料,应当依照引渡条约的规定提出;没有引渡条约或者引渡条约没有规定的,可以参照本法第二章第二节、第四节和第七节的规定提出;被请求国有特殊要求的,在不违反中华人民共和国法律的基本原则的情况下,可以按照被请求国的特殊要求提出。"第 50 条规定:"被请求国就准予引渡附加条件的,对于不损害中华人民共和国主权、国家利益、公共利益的,可以由外交部代表中华人民共和国政府向被请求国作出承诺。对于限制追诉的承诺,由最高人民检察院决定;对于量刑的承诺,由最高人民法院决定。"
② 参见黄风:《我国主动引渡制度研究:经验、问题和对策》,载《法商研究》2006 年第 4 期。

探索和研究国际人权和司法机构的组织架构和程序规则,总结和归纳成功案例的经验和教训,不断提升办案人员的实战能力和经验,以此来促进我国的境外追逃追赃工作迈入新的台阶。

结语

　　黄海勇引渡案是在中央反腐败协调小组国际追逃追赃工作办公室的统一协调下,在最高人民法院、最高人民检察院、公安部、司法部等有关部门的大力支持和协助下,外交部和海关总署通力合作成功办理的经典案例。① 同时,也是我国同秘鲁开展引渡执法合作的成功个案,彰显了我国打击外逃犯罪分子的决心和信心,为我国在拉美地区开展引渡执法工作打下了良好基础,为我国今后同欧美国家和国际人权组织处理涉华人权问题积累了宝贵经验,有助于国际社会了解中国当前的刑事司法和人权保障状况,加深了国外对我国法治和人权状况的理解和信任,有助于推动我国在拉美地区乃至全世界的追逃追赃工作。

（本文部分内容曾在《民主与法制周刊》2017 年第 28 期发表）

---

① 中国海关总署:《潜逃十八年走私犯罪嫌疑人被成功引渡押解回国》,载 http://www.customs.gov.cn/publish/portal0/tab65603/info808774.htm,最后访问日期:2017 年 10 月 15 日。

媒体报道

潜逃十八年走私犯罪嫌疑人被成功引渡押解回国[*]

海关总署今日（7月17日）向外通报，武汉海关缉私局侦办的"10·7"毛豆油走私案主犯黄海勇于7月17日凌晨自秘鲁被成功引渡押解回国。

1998年8月，武汉海关调查局根据群众举报，对黄海勇等人在武汉地区非法倒卖免税进口毛豆油走私牟利一事展开调查。1999年9月，该案移交至新成立的武汉海关走私犯罪侦查分局（现武汉海关缉私局）立案侦查，查明1996年至1998年间，黄海勇团伙利用其在深圳、武汉、上海三地的公司骗领毛豆油进料加工手册、成立虚假保税仓库，倒卖免税毛豆油10.7万吨，共计偷逃税款达7亿余元人民币。案发后，黄海勇等3名主要犯罪嫌疑人经香港潜逃至美国。该案引起了当时国务院领导的高度关注，要求海关总署不惜代价彻查。

多年来，海关从未放弃对涉案犯罪嫌疑人的追逃工作。2001年6月海关缉私部门通过公安部协调国际刑警组织对黄海勇发布红色通报，在全球范围内进行缉捕。在发现黄海勇曾入境秘鲁的行踪后，海关缉私部门通过公安部及时向国际刑警组织秘鲁国家中心局提出执法合作请求，2008年10月黄海勇再次入境秘鲁时被秘方国际刑警抓获，同年11月中方即向秘方提出引渡请求，自此我国政府相关部门与秘方政府及有关执法部门开始了长达8年的引渡程序磋商。2010年1月，秘鲁最高法院判决同意向我方引渡。但黄海勇随后多次利用两国法律制度差异给执行引渡判决设置障碍，包括以回国后存在死刑和酷刑风险为借口将引渡案上诉至泛美人权委员会和美洲人权法院，企图逃避法律制裁。

---

[*] 原载海关总署网站 http://www.customs.gov.cn/customs/302249/302425/635444/index.html，最后访问日期2019年6月19日。

该引渡案是在中央反腐败协调小组国际追逃追赃工作办公室的统一协调下,在最高人民法院、最高人民检察院、公安部、司法部等有关部门的大力支持和协助下,外交部和海关总署通力合作成功办理的经典案例。中央纪委、外交部、公安部、司法部和海关总署组成黄案引渡工作组先后6次赴秘鲁与秘方有关部门协商执行引渡工作。我驻秘鲁大使馆全力为引渡工作提供支持和帮助,驻秘使馆3任大使始终高度重视,向秘方强调中国政府打击违法犯罪的坚定决心,积极介绍中国相关法律制度,增进秘鲁政府和有关执法部门的理解和支持,为最终成功引渡发挥了重要作用。外交部根据最高人民法院、最高人民检察院依据我国法律作出的决定,向秘鲁政府作出关于保障人身权利等外交承诺,对秘方和美洲人权法院最终准予引渡起到了关键作用。公安部将黄海勇列入"猎狐行动"境外重点追逃人员名单,体现我国境外追逃追赃工作的决心和力度。为促使美洲人权法院做出于我有利判决,国内知名法律专家赴美洲人权法院出庭作证,推动该法院对我国刑事司法制度和人权保障作出正确的认识,为公正判决扫除了障碍。为支持配合引渡工作,司法部及时通过中秘刑事司法协助渠道,对黄海勇转移至秘鲁的犯罪资产向秘方提出予以调查追缴的刑事司法协助请求。

经过各方的不懈努力和艰苦工作,2015年9月,美洲人权法院做出裁决:在充分保障黄海勇穷尽秘鲁国内全部司法程序的基础上,由秘鲁政府决定是否引渡黄海勇。2016年5月23日,秘鲁国家宪法法院公布裁决结果,同意秘鲁政府向中国引渡犯罪嫌疑人黄海勇,7月14日,中秘两国有关执法部门在秘鲁签署引渡交接文件,黄海勇终被我成功引渡。

此案是公安部"猎狐行动"及海关境外追逃追赃重要成果,创造了中国追逃引渡多项第一:首次从拉美国家成功引渡犯罪嫌疑人、中秘引渡条约签署以来首个成功引渡案例、首起美洲人权法院审理涉及中国的引渡案件、首个中国在美洲人权法院胜诉的引渡案例。此次成功引渡,为我今后在拉美地区开展引渡执法合作提供了宝贵经验借鉴,对我境外追逃追赃工作具有重要意义。

此案再次反映出海关对逃犯"一追到底",严厉打击走私的坚强决心,无论犯罪嫌疑人逃到哪里,终将受到法律的严厉制裁。

专家:中国从拉美引渡嫌犯对国际追逃有借鉴意义*

李 晔 陈 敏 王子辰

新华社北京 7 月 18 日电(李晔 陈 敏 王子辰)7 月 17 日凌晨,境外潜逃 18 年的走私案嫌犯黄海勇自秘鲁被成功引渡押解回国,这是中国首次从拉美国家成功引渡犯罪嫌疑人。专家认为本案树立了良好的先例,同时也是中拉关系健康发展的重要体现。

作为秘鲁政府邀请的非出庭专家证人,直接参与此案的中国社会科学院人权研究中心副主任柳华文表示,美洲人权法院的法官在本案判决中较为严格遵守了当下国际法、包括国际人权法的相关法理,审慎、客观地评估各种证据材料和各方主张,体现了较强的专业精神。

黄海勇一案是首例由美洲人权法院审理的涉及中国的引渡案件,也是首例依据中秘引渡条约的成功案例。柳华文说:"中国近年来经济发展和社会进步迅速,法治和人权事业不断取得进步。这也是美洲人权法院判决原告方相关主张无效的重要基础。"

中国社科院拉美所政治室助理研究员谭道明认为此案影响深远。他指出,中国通过中秘司法协助的途径成功引渡犯罪嫌疑人,树立了良好的先例,也积累了重要的成功经验。本案同时也是近年来中拉整体合作顺利推进、中拉关系健康发展的一个重要体现。

上世纪 90 年代末,黄海勇勾结时任武汉海关关长莫海涛,通过倒卖毛豆油牟利,共计逃税款 7 亿余元人民币并潜逃境外。2008 年 11 月中国政府向秘方提出引渡要求,自此中国政府相关部门与秘方开始了长达 8 年的引渡程

---

* 原载 http://xhpfm.news.zhongguowangshi.com:8091/v300/newshare/982402?channel=zhongsou,最后访问日期 2019 年 6 月 18 日。

序磋商。2015年9月美洲人权法院作出裁决:在充分保障黄某穷尽秘鲁国内司法程序的基础上,由秘鲁政府决定是否引渡。今年5月23日,秘鲁国家宪法法院公布裁决结果,同意秘鲁政府向中国引渡犯罪嫌疑人黄某。

"中国政府通过司法途径对黄海勇进行依法追逃、依法引渡,体现了中方对秘鲁等拉美国家的国内、国际法律体系的高度尊重。近年来中国不仅强调法治建设,同时也尊重他国的国内法和相关国际法规则。"谭道明说。

中国与外国开展引渡合作的历史虽然不长,但发展迅速。自2000年中国通过《中华人民共和国引渡法》起,中国已与52个国家缔结了各类司法合作方面的双边条约共计84项,为打击跨国犯罪与追逃奠定重要基础。

但由于规制范围、效力有限,签署的双边引渡条约数量不足、质量不高,一些西方国家对中国的政治偏见和歧视导致引渡问题上的双重标准,相关当事国在引渡过程或结果中收益的经济考量等问题,中国引渡制度的实现仍存在多重阻碍。

柳华文指出,黄海勇引渡案反映的境外追逃,特别是遣返、引渡工作中遇到的种种因素,不仅有助于国际社会了解中国刑事法制与实践,为中国当前反腐败法治中的海外追逃实践提供了宝贵经验和成功案例,而且对中国今后在拉美国家的追逃工作有直接的借鉴意义,甚至可能在一定程度上影响中国在欧洲方向的追逃工作。

他同时提出,在国际政治交往方面,中国应积极缔结双边引渡条约,推动建立区域性或多边性引渡机制并继续推进双边协商的引渡合作机制。在与引渡有关的审判及程序上,中国应推进司法体制改革,完善审判制度并构建腐败犯罪的财产追回程序,为境外追逃创造更为有利的环境和条件。

我国首次成功从"拉美"引渡嫌犯回国[*]

蔡岩红

7月17日凌晨1时10分,一架航班缓缓靠停在北京首都机场二号航站楼208号廊桥。十分钟后,一个身着黄色T恤、个头不高的男子,在身着便衣的武汉海关缉私警的押解下走下飞机。此人便是涉嫌偷逃税7亿元人民币、潜逃境外18年,由武汉海关缉私局侦办的"10·7"毛豆油走私案嫌犯黄海勇。此人也是我国首次成功从拉美国家引渡的犯罪嫌疑人。

"我们此次行程40多个小时,将黄海勇从秘鲁押解回国。此案再次反映出海关严厉打击走私的坚强决心,无论犯罪嫌疑人逃到哪里,终将受到法律的严厉制裁。"参与此次押解任务的武汉海关缉私局副局长彭正德用沙哑的声音告诉记者。

据了解,1998年8月,武汉海关调查局根据群众举报,对黄海勇等人在武汉地区非法倒卖免税进口毛豆油走私牟利一事展开调查。1999年9月,该案移交至新成立的武汉海关走私犯罪侦查分局(现武汉海关缉私局)立案侦查。经查,1996年至1998年间,黄海勇团伙利用其在深圳、武汉、上海三地的公司骗领毛豆油进料加工手册、成立虚假保税仓库,倒卖免税毛豆油10.7万吨,共计偷逃税款达7亿余元人民币。案发后,黄海勇等3名主要犯罪嫌疑人经香港潜逃至美国。

2001年6月海关缉私部门通过公安部协调国际刑警组织对黄海勇发布红色通报,在全球范围内进行缉捕。在发现黄海勇曾入境秘鲁的行踪后,海关缉私部门通过公安部及时向国际刑警组织秘鲁国家中心局提出执法合作

---

[*] 原载《法制日报》2016年7月17日。

请求。2008年10月黄海勇再次入境秘鲁时被秘方国际刑警抓获,同年11月中方即向秘方提出引渡请求。

自此我国政府相关部门与秘方政府及有关执法部门开始了长达8年的引渡程序磋商。2010年1月,秘鲁最高法院判决同意向我方引渡。但黄海勇随后多次利用两国法律制度差异给执行引渡判决设置障碍,包括以回国后存在死刑和酷刑风险为借口将引渡案上诉至泛美人权委员会和美洲人权法院。

2015年9月,美洲人权法院作出裁决:在充分保障黄海勇穷尽秘鲁国内全部司法程序的基础上,由秘鲁政府决定是否引渡黄海勇。2016年5月23日,秘鲁国家宪法法院公布裁决结果,同意秘鲁政府向中国引渡犯罪嫌疑人黄海勇,7月14日,中秘两国有关执法部门在秘鲁签署引渡交接文件,黄海勇终被我成功引渡。

新中国最复杂的引渡案内幕*

刘 星

嫌疑人潜逃18年,此案历时8年,历经秘鲁国内和美洲人权体系所有法律程序,被中国外交部称为是"新中国成立以来的最复杂的引渡案"

7月17日凌晨,由外交部牵头,中央纪委、公安部和海关总署派员参加的押解小组成功将涉嫌重大走私犯罪的嫌疑人黄海勇从秘鲁引渡押解回国。黄海勇,涉嫌走私普通货物罪,偷逃税款7.17亿元人民币,于1998年8月出逃,潜逃境外18年。

此案历时8年,历经秘鲁国内和美洲人权体系所有法律程序,被中国外交部称为是"新中国成立以来的最复杂的引渡案",也是公安部"猎狐行动"及海关境外追逃追赃重要成果;创造了中国追逃引渡多项第一:首次从拉美国家成功引渡犯罪嫌疑人,中秘引渡条约签署以来首个成功引渡案例,首起美洲人权法院审理涉及中国的引渡案件,首个中国在美洲人权法院胜诉的引渡案例,中国首次在国际人权法院出庭。

武汉海关原关长的"朋友"

黄海勇是武汉海关原关长莫海涛的莫逆之交。上世纪90年代,年富力强的莫海涛"年轻有为",是中组部跟踪培养的干部,因为在深圳海关工作成绩突出,40岁即被破格提拔为正厅级,1996年6月,他调任武汉海关任关长。而莫海涛放纵的走私人员都是在深圳海关的"好"朋友、旧相识,黄海勇、潘子牛、杨改清即是莫海涛的莫逆之交。

黄海勇起初并不认识莫海涛。据被莫海涛亲切称为"杨子"的杨改清供

---

* 原载《法治周末》2016年7月27日。

述,1995年7月,莫海涛受深圳惠威公司杨改清请求,未经拍卖程序,擅自决定销售给黄海勇1.3万吨海关罚没原糖,事后,黄分给杨200多万元。

莫海涛武汉赴任后,黄、潘、杨三人也如影随形,跟到武汉。武汉海关货管处原副处长王绩成(已判刑)证实,黄海勇到武汉,每次都有莫的爱人同行。"朋友"们的聚餐通常由莫海涛召集,黄海勇买单,地点则多是亚洲大酒店、江汉饭店等地。莫海涛说:"吃饭不过只是沟通一下感情而已。"

而"吃饭"显然别有意味。据武汉海关工作人员证实,黄海勇经常到货管处办事,人送外号"黄党组",意即莫黄关系非同一般,所以黄海勇办事常常能一路绿灯,畅通无阻。

1996年8月至1998年12月期间,黄海勇、潘子牛在武汉海关先后申领到毛豆油、羊毛条进料加工手册。其中莫海涛直接同意批准C47006100042号加工手册备案。

经湖北省检察院专案组查实,黄、潘用进料加工手册,先后在上海、天津转关时进口毛豆油6万吨,未经海关许可,擅自将6万吨毛豆油飞料(即将本应加工完毕后返销国外的产品在国内销售)。

1997年3月,黄海勇持一份无效的西藏进口许可证(只有海关总署签发的才有效)向武汉海关申请低价内销补税,莫海涛认为"打个擦边球也可以",同意使用该许可证,并说"总署有什么事我去当面解释",接受企业的低价报关。仅此一项,就造成国家损失税款1.5亿元。

1997年1月,黄海勇等人以香港宝润集团公司与武汉某集团公司合资的名义,向武汉海关提交设立油脂保税仓库的报告。在莫海涛支持下,武汉丰润保税仓库设立成为"无库址、无面积、无设施"的"三无"虚假仓库。

随后,黄海勇等人又将保税仓库监管的4.7万吨毛豆油飞料走私。经查实,武汉某集团公司在武昌白沙洲的确有个油库,但保存的全是国家储备油,没有一滴油是武汉海关的。莫海涛事后承认,"仅凭企业申请,没有相关的文件材料,没有进行实地考察,先申请后补办手续是违反程序的"。

1998年4月,黄海勇等人以加工名义将500吨羊毛条假结转到湛江,并在武汉海关将500吨羊毛条备案核销,致使国家损失税款653万余元。

1998年8月,武汉海关调查局根据群众举报,对黄海勇等人在武汉地区非法倒卖免税进口毛豆油走私牟利一事展开调查。1999年9月,该案移交至新成立的武汉海关走私犯罪侦查分局(现武汉海关缉私局)立案侦查。

黄海勇背后的莫海涛也很快浮出水面,2002年11月27日,湖北省武汉市中级人民法院公开宣告一审判决:认定武汉海关原关长莫海涛犯玩忽职守罪,判处有期徒刑3年。

历经美洲所有引渡程序

案发后,黄海勇等3名主要犯罪嫌疑人经香港潜逃至美国。多年来,海关从未放弃对涉案犯罪嫌疑人的追逃工作。2001年6月,海关缉私部门通过公安部协调国际刑警组织对黄海勇发布红色通报,在全球范围内进行缉捕。在发现黄海勇曾入境秘鲁的行踪后,及时向国际刑警组织秘鲁国家中心局提出执法合作请求。2008年10月,黄海勇再次入境秘鲁时被秘方国际刑警抓获,同年11月中方即向秘方提出引渡请求,自此中国政府相关部门与秘方开始长达8年的引渡程序磋商。

2010年1月,秘鲁最高法院判决同意向中方引渡,但黄海勇为抗拒引渡,诬称其被引渡回国会面临"人权"问题,并聘请了秘鲁最著名的"人权律师",用尽了所有法律手段,两度将案件上诉至秘鲁最高法院、两度上诉至秘鲁宪法法院、两度申诉至美洲人权委员会、两度上诉至美洲人权法院,案件被拖入旷日持久的法律战。

在此过程中,引渡工作曾一度面临极为困难、复杂的局面,秘鲁宪法法院和美洲人权委员会作出的不利于引渡的决定迫使引渡程序几度中止、搁置。

由于黄海勇聘请律师以中国刑事法治中的"死刑"和"酷刑"问题向美洲人权委员会提出申诉;美洲人权委员会于2013年7月作出报告,要求秘鲁政府停止引渡黄海勇,并对中国的"死刑"和"酷刑"状况表示担忧。

随后,黄海勇引渡案提交给美洲人权法院。美洲人权法院是除美洲人权委员会外美洲人权区域保护的另外一个重要机构,其职能是根据《美洲人权公约》管辖美洲国家(实际上主要是拉美国家)有关人权的案件和相关法律事务。

为扭转不利局面,在关键的美洲人权法院的诉讼中,应秘鲁政府邀请,中国组成专家团队，撰写12万多字的作证材料，就中国的人权状况、刑事司法制度和引渡制度向美洲人权法院提交证词、出庭作证，与秘鲁政府诉讼团队密切配合，一一化解了对方律师的刁难发问，有力地证明了黄海勇被引渡回中国不会面临任何"人权"问题。

2014年9月3日，美洲人权法院在巴拉圭首都亚松森的巴拉圭最高法院开庭，审理中国政府向秘鲁政府提出引渡申请的涉嫌走私普通货物罪的中国公民黄海勇引渡案。此次庭审由该法院7位法官中的5位组成法庭。

北京师范大学刑事法律科学研究院院长暨中国刑法学研究会会长赵秉志教授、中国外交部条约法律司孙昂参赞和秘鲁前司法部长托马博士作为秘鲁政府邀请的3位专家证人，经美洲人权法院批准到庭作证。

法庭全天听取了秘鲁政府方面的3位专家证人的证词，并由各方进行了盘问和辩论。赵秉志教授主要围绕与本案相关的中国刑事司法程序和实体问题以及中加遣返赖昌星案件的有关情况进行了作证，回答了各方盘问；孙昂参赞则主要围绕中国引渡法制与实践以及中加遣返赖昌星的外交承诺进行。

秘鲁前司法部长托马博士的作证及各方对其的盘问主要围绕与本案相关的中秘引渡条约和秘鲁相关国内法律问题而进行。在当天下午3位专家证人作证结束之后，参与庭审的3方又进行了辩论和陈述。按照惯例，庭审结束后一年左右宣判。

2015年9月17日，美洲人权法院的法庭作出了秘鲁政府胜诉的裁判：在充分保障黄海勇穷尽秘鲁国内全部司法程序的基础上，由秘鲁政府决定是否引渡。2016年5月23日，秘鲁国家宪法法院公布裁决结果，同意秘鲁政府向中国引渡犯罪嫌疑人黄海勇，7月14日，中秘两国有关执法部门在秘鲁签署引渡交接文件，黄海勇终被中方成功引渡。

国际追逃的宝贵经验

黄海勇出逃18年，最终被引渡回国，再次表明，只要各国有合作打击犯罪的强烈政治意愿、只要有扎实有效的法律应对就一定能够克服各种障碍。

此次成功引渡，为我国今后处理国际人权司法机构审理涉华引渡案件积累了宝贵经验；为我国在拉美地区开展引渡执法合作打下良好基础；并可能在一定程度上影响我国在欧洲方向的追逃工作。

据介绍,8年间,该引渡案在中央反腐败协调小组国际追逃追赃工作办公室的统一协调下,中央纪委、外交部、公安部、司法部和海关总署组成黄案引渡工作组先后6次赴秘鲁与秘方有关部门协商执行引渡工作。

引渡工作组与秘鲁政府举行磋商,在向秘鲁政府提交含有大量扎实、有效的证据材料引渡请求书的同时,耐心细致地做秘鲁各层级的解释说明工作,一方面,旗帜鲜明地表明将黄海勇缉捕归案的决心;一方面,向秘方详细介绍黄海勇的犯罪事实、适用的法律,以及我国保障犯罪嫌疑人各项法律权利有关法律制度。

中国驻秘鲁大使馆全力为引渡工作提供支持和帮助,驻秘使馆3任大使始终高度重视,向秘方强调中国政府打击违法犯罪的坚定决心,积极介绍中国相关法律制度,增进秘鲁政府和有关执法部门的理解和支持,为最终成功引渡发挥了重要作用。

外交部根据最高人民法院、最高人民检察院依据我国法律作出的决定,向秘鲁政府作出关于保障人身权利等外交承诺,对秘方和美洲人权法院最终准予引渡起到了关键作用。

为支持配合引渡工作,司法部及时通过中秘刑事司法协助渠道,对黄海勇转移至秘鲁的犯罪资产向秘方提出予以调查追缴的刑事司法协助请求。

为促使美洲人权法院作出对中国有利的判决,国内知名法律专家赴美洲人权法院出庭作证,推动该法院对我国刑事司法制度和人权保障作出正确的认识,为公正判决扫除了障碍。此举也加深了国家间对法治、人权的理解和信任,有助于国际社会了解中国刑事法制与实践。

北师大教授应秘鲁邀请作证　成功引渡嫌犯[*]

张恩杰

昨日,第一个面向二十国集团反腐败追逃追赃的研究中心在北京师范大学成立。昨日上午,中共中央书记处书记、中央纪委副书记赵洪祝出席了研究中心的揭牌仪式。

据悉,该研究中心将通过专题研究、学术研讨和培训等多种形式开展工作,为二十国集团成员国开展反腐败追逃追赃合作创造交流平台,推动建立以追逃追赃务实合作为内容的国际反腐败新秩序。

记者获悉,除了北师大的专家外,该中心研究队伍还包括了中纪委、最高法、最高检等单位具有反腐败研究专长、熟悉反腐败追逃追赃事务的专家成员。

中纪委等多单位专家为中心成员

北京师范大学国际反腐败教育研究中心秘书长、研究员彭新林参加了昨天的揭牌仪式,他向《法制晚报》记者透露,G20反腐败追逃追赃研究中心能在华设立,是建立在我国近年来深入开展反腐败斗争、高度重视反腐败务实国际合作、反腐败追逃追赃取得显著成绩的基础之上的。当然,这也与G20成员国对我国关于反腐败追逃追赃合作倡议的广泛认可、理解,以及我国开展的反腐败国际合作行动、我国在国际反腐败领域的重要地位和影响力密切相关。

据了解,该研究中心是第一个面向G20成员国开展反腐败追逃追赃研究的机构,之前在其他国家尚未设立相应的机构。

---

[*] 原载《法制晚报》2016年9月24日。

"之所以会选择在北京师范大学成立这样一个研究机构,是因为北师大在反腐败国际追逃追赃方面有很强的研究实力,拥有比较专业的学者,同时也培养了很多国际刑法等领域的硕士、博士和博士后,对反腐败国际追逃追赃问题有着比较集中的研究。"彭新林如此解释说。

据其介绍,该研究中心专家成员既包括北师大在反腐败追逃追赃研究方面有专长的学者,也有中央纪委监察部、最高人民法院、最高人民检察院、中国人民银行、司法部、公安部、外交部以及地方司法机关具有反腐败研究专长、熟悉反腐败追逃追赃事务的专家等。此外,中心还会吸纳G20国家的海外专家。

拒绝涉腐人员入境将成研究重点

记者注意到,在此前G20杭州峰会上通过的《二十国集团反腐败追逃追赃高级原则》里,"注意到外逃腐败人员和资产造成的损害,各国应视情采取措施拒绝成为腐败人员与腐败资产的避风港"成为一项重要内容。对此,彭新林研究员称,这项内容将成为他们研究的重点领域,如引渡、司法协助、资产返还立法和实践等,跨国商业贿赂、投资移民政策等。

"我国在国际追逃方面存在一定的法律障碍,各国政治制度、价值观念和法律制度上都有差异;高昂的追逃成本也是制约国际追逃工作开展的一大瓶颈;互联网、信息科技、技术侦查等技术措施运用有限,技术装备存在不足,国际追逃经验也不够丰富,这些短板得想办法攻克。"彭新林如是说。

据了解,截至2015年3月,我国已与39个国家签署了引渡条约,与52个国家签订了刑事司法协助类条约。彭新林表示,"目前我国尚未和美国、加拿大、澳大利亚等国家签署引渡条约,只能通过劝返、司法协助等方式。而当前我国公布的100名红色通缉令人员中。已经归国的有1/3,而这其中有近五成是通过劝返得以实现的。"

今年4月,国际追逃追赃工作办公室宣布启动"天网2016"。"天网2016"由多个专项行动组成,包括继续由公安部牵头开展"猎狐行动"、最高检牵头开展职务犯罪国际追逃追赃专项行动、央行会同公安部开展打击利用离岸公司和地下钱庄向境外转移赃款专项行动;中组部、外交部、公安部和中央纪委开展出国(境)证照违规问题专项治理行动等。这次"天网"行动是去年3月追逃办启动"天网"行动的延续。

昨日,北师大刑科院国际刑法研究所副所长张磊副教授向法晚记者透露,今年7月17日凌晨,由外交部牵头、中央纪委和海关总署派员参加的押解小组成功将涉嫌重大走私犯罪的嫌疑人黄海勇从秘鲁引渡回国。

而在此之前的2014年9月3日,应秘鲁政府邀请,北师大刑科院院长暨中国刑法学研究会会长赵秉志教授等组成专家团,就中国的刑事司法制度、引渡制度和人权状况到位于巴拉圭首都亚松森的美洲人权法院巡回法庭上出庭作证,与秘鲁政府诉讼团队密切配合,回答了来自法庭各方的询问。2015年9月16日,美洲人权法院作出判决,完全支持引渡黄海勇。

据了解,黄海勇涉嫌走私普通货物罪,偷逃税款7.17亿元人民币,于1998年8月出逃。2001年,我国通过国际刑警组织对黄海勇发布红色通报。2008年10月,秘鲁警方根据国际刑警组织红色通报逮捕黄海勇,我国立即根据2001年签署的《中秘引渡条约》请求引渡黄海勇。

"为抗拒引渡,黄海勇聘请了秘鲁最著名的律师,诬称其被引渡回国会面临死刑问题和所谓的'人权'问题,几乎用尽了所有法律手段:将案件两度上诉至秘鲁最高法院、两度上诉至秘鲁宪法法院,然后又申诉至美洲人权委员会,后被美洲人权委员会提交给美洲人权法院,案件被拖入旷日持久的法律战。在此过程中,对黄海勇的引渡工作曾经面临极大困难,秘鲁宪法法院和美洲人权委员会都曾作出不利于引渡的裁判,使得引渡程序几度中止、搁置。"张磊如此分析说。

他称,在此情况下,赵秉志教授等作为秘鲁政府邀请的专家证人,经美洲人权法院批准到庭就中国的刑事司法制度、引渡制度和人权状况等问题进行作证,为成功引渡黄海勇发挥了重要作用。

据悉,此案历时8年,历经秘鲁国内和美洲人权体系所有法律程序,堪称是新中国成立以来最为复杂的引渡案件。黄海勇也是我国首次从拉美国家成功引渡的犯罪嫌疑人,为我国今后处理国际人权司法机构审理涉华引渡案件积累了宝贵经验,为我国在拉美地区开展引渡执法打下良好基础,对国际追逃追赃工作具有重要意义。

中国专家出庭"最复杂引渡案"始末[*]

冯 彬

事隔两年半,赵秉志仍然记得,2014年4月,我国外交部条法司有关负责人专门到北京师范大学刑事法律科学研究院,介绍将在美洲人权法院开庭的涉嫌走私普通货物罪的中国公民黄海勇引渡案,邀请赵秉志作为秘鲁政府方面的专家证人出庭作证,支持我国的海外追逃工作。深知这是一项艰巨而有意义的任务,赵秉志当时毫不犹豫地答应下来。

由中国法律专家作为秘鲁政府的专家证人,到国际法庭上就中国刑事法治状况出庭作证,中秘有关部门认为,赵秉志无疑是最合适的人选。作为中国刑法学研究会会长、知名刑法教授和曾经担任过福建远华特大走私系列案件2名被告辩护人的刑事律师,他曾受加拿大政府公民移民部的邀请,于2001年8月和10月两赴加拿大,在赖昌星难民资格聆讯庭上作证,对成功遣返赖昌星发挥了重要作用。

■ 走私案发 嫌疑人远逃海外

黄海勇案发,始于18年前。

1998年8月,武汉海关调查局接到举报,有人在武汉地区非法倒卖免税进口毛豆油走私牟利;而海关总署自查账目时,也发现了10.7万吨毛豆油的走私问题。

武汉海关立即成立调查组,由关长莫海涛任组长。但随着调查深入却

---

[*] 原载《廉政瞭望》2016年第20期。

发现，莫正是这起案件背后的保护伞。

1996年，黄海勇等人用莫海涛同意批准的进料加工手册，先后在上海、天津转关时进口毛豆油6万吨，未经海关许可，擅自将6万吨毛豆油"飞料"在国内走私（即将本应加工完毕后返销国外的产品在国内销售）。

1997年1月，在莫海涛支持下，黄海勇等人设立起"无库址、无面积、无设施"的保税仓库。随后，他们又将保税仓库监管的4.7万吨毛豆油飞料同样在国内销售走私。

黄海勇等走私倒卖的毛豆油，共计偷逃税款7亿余元人民币。

案发后，莫海涛落网，并于2002年11月因玩忽职守罪获刑3年。而黄海勇早已闻风而逃，先到美国，随后投奔了在秘鲁经商的弟弟。

2001年6月，海关缉私部门通过公安部协调国际刑警组织发布红色通报，全球缉捕黄海勇，在发现黄海勇曾入境秘鲁的行踪后，即向国际刑警组织秘鲁国家中心局提出执法合作请求。2008年10月，黄海勇再次入境秘鲁时被秘方国际刑警抓获，1个月后，中方提出引渡黄的请求。秘鲁最高法院也在2010年判决同意向中方引渡黄海勇。

"由于中秘的外交关系很好且有双边引渡条约，在正常情况下，引渡黄海勇问题应该不大，"北师大刑事法律科学研究院国际刑法研究所副所长、G20反腐败追逃追赃研究中心副主任张磊曾研究过赖昌星遣返案，他认为同前者相比，中秘两国已于2001年签署了引渡条约，引渡黄海勇本不应该存在太多障碍。

"然而，引渡并没有想象中那么顺利。"

比赖昌星更"赖"

为了抗拒引渡，黄海勇声称其回国会面临"人权"问题，并聘请了秘鲁著名的"人权律师"，将案件两度上诉至秘鲁最高法院、秘鲁宪法法院，甚至以黄海勇"被引渡回国将会面临死刑，其人权将受侵犯"为由向美洲人权委员会提出申诉。

2013年7月，美洲人权委员会作出报告，建议秘鲁政府停止引渡黄海勇,并对中国的"死刑"和"酷刑"状况表示担忧。

"死刑不引渡是国际刑事司法合作中的一项基本原则,而酷刑更在各国法律体系中都不被认可。"张磊说,外逃人员正是利用这一点,想尽办法拖延时间。

比如1999年外逃的赖昌星。他在加拿大一"赖"就是12年,从提出难民申请到被遣返回国,几乎将该国法律程序走了个遍。期间他甚至以为自己要被遣返回国,以头撞柱,使案件重回加拿大司法程序。

"抗拒引渡也以金钱为基础。"张磊说,一些外逃人员会用转移到境外的资金聘请顶级律师,比如为赖昌星辩护的就是在北美名声大噪的人权律师大卫·马塔斯,而外逃加拿大的原中国银行哈尔滨河松街支行行长高山也曾聘请此人。

黄海勇则利用相似的手段,通过美洲人权委员会将秘鲁政府告上美洲人权法院,形成了新中国成立以来最复杂的引渡案件。

"以往的引渡、遣返或者劝返,再复杂也是两国之间的事,而这起涉及中秘双方的案件,被提交到了区域性的人权机构,就有了格外的艰巨和特殊的意义。"赵秉志告诉记者。

为扭转不利局面,秘鲁政府邀请中国法律专家作为秘鲁政府的专家证人到美洲人权法院出庭作证。最终,中国外交部敲定,并经美洲人权法院批准,由赵秉志和外交部条法司参赞孙昂远赴美洲人权法院出庭作证,中国社科院研究员柳华文则作为非出庭证人,向法庭提交书面证词。同时秘鲁方面推荐的该国前司法部长托马也获批作为专家证人,与中国专家一同出庭作证。

"上庭作证的时间虽然并不长,但为此做的准备工作却是大量的。"赵秉志告诉记者。

为了为作证做好充分准备,2014年6月9日起,中国作证团队前往美洲人权法院所在国和秘鲁进行作证前的沟通。

第一站,哥斯达黎加——美洲人权法院总部所在地。中方代表团一行8人来到这里,就案件基本情况,和此次庭审的操作规程、证人注意事项等与美洲人权法院方面座谈。

6月11日,代表团到达秘鲁,与秘鲁外交部、司法人权部等部门继续沟通、交流。"光是外交保障方面就谈了一整天。"赵秉志说,为了在庭审时达到最默契配合,这次中秘双方的交流内容涉及引渡的方方面面,包括作证的要点,中国《刑法修正案(八)》的效力,赖昌星遣返案的细节等问题,"甚至谈到黄海勇在秘鲁关押的时间能否从其被引渡回国后将被判处的刑期中扣除的问题"。

为作证认真准备

归国后,作证团队开始分头准备。赵秉志约请他所在研究院的三名青年教师袁彬、张磊、何挺和他一起组成作证工作小组,进行前期资料准备。预设问题的同时,开始起草证词。

"无论是加拿大难民聆讯庭还是美洲人权法院,都是以西方的视角看中国的法治状况。"赵秉志介绍,赖昌星被成功遣返,一个重要因素就是其涉嫌的走私普通货物罪在《刑法修正案(八)》中废除了死刑,而且此前我国最高司法机关也通过外交部向加拿大政府作出了赖被遣返回国不会被判处死刑的量刑承诺。不过,中国的死刑问题仍然是黄海勇及其律师用来对抗引渡的主要借口之一,也是法院关注的重点问题之一。

"在赵老师带领下,我们根据个人擅长领域分工进行准备。"张磊说,准备过程中,相对容易操作的是秘鲁方面的问题,因为我方毕竟是作为秘鲁政府的证人出庭作证,"对手"黄海勇的律师和美洲人权委员会所可能提出的问题,则要花大力气去研究。

"他们会想尽办法提出有利于本方观点的问题,甚至是充满火药味的质疑。"张磊介绍,2001年赵秉志在加拿大出庭作证时,赖昌星的律师曾向法庭和赵秉志提交了一份在中国杂志上刊登文章的英译本,内容为全国人大内司委的一个调研报告的简介,其中列举了中国1996年刑事诉讼法实施后律师办理刑事案件中遇到的比较突出的问题。对方律师明确询问赵秉志,这些问题是不是中国律师实务中的状况?希望以此来攻击中国的司法制度状况。

赵秉志审核对比中英文版本后发现，对方提交的英文本只翻译了我国律师执业存在问题方面的叙述，而对该文章开头从宏观上肯定我国法律改革和司法改进的部分只字未提，遂明确指出该翻译文本是断章取义，是片面的、不客观的。赵的意见受到法庭重视，法庭裁决因译文不客观而不接受对方律师的这份材料，并表示赵也不必回答该问题，轻松化解了对方的"杀招"。

有赖昌星案中作证的这些经验，作证工作小组的准备就更加细致和具有针对性。那段时间，团队时常会讨论到深夜，多次梳理、整理的各种材料粗略统计亦有几十万字。

近3个月后，赵秉志和孙昂等远渡重洋，将赴国际法庭，为中国的法治正名。

黄海勇引渡案，将在美洲人权法院临时设置于亚松森（巴拉圭首都）的巴拉圭最高法院的巡回法庭开庭。

"由于我国与巴拉圭尚未建立外交关系，当晚到了亚松森，都还不确定能否顺利入境。"同行人员告诉赵秉志，此前，我国驻巴西的外交人员就曾被巴拉圭拒绝入境。好在通过我国驻巴西圣保罗总领事馆全力协助，作证团队于8月31日深夜顺利入境亚松森。

■ 遭遇"挖坑"，为中国法治正名

"由于中西方思维和法治的差异，以及秘鲁方面对于引渡提交证据和材料的重视，之前经中秘双方沟通后我们准备的作证资料几乎都被秘方推翻而要重来。"赵秉志笑言，幸亏自己此前的功课做得还行，加上多年经验，能够一边交流和归纳问题，一边调整思路和准备新的作证提纲，中方作证小组连续两整天都在酒店与秘鲁方面沟通和准备，而且每晚都要"加班"到深夜。

为提高交流效率与质量，外交部为中方作证小组派出了白雪和姚雯敏两名西班牙语翻译。他们曾多次担任我们党和国家领导人会见、出访时的西班牙语翻译。

2014年9月3日，美洲人权法院成立以来首个引渡案开庭，同时也是中国专家证人首次在国际人权法院出庭作证。这一刻,中方等了8年。

庭审期间,秘鲁司法和人权部、黄海勇律师、美洲人权委员会、法庭分别向证人发问,其中不乏双方现场交锋。

如黄海勇的律师问:"未经审判,你何以判定他犯了走私罪?"

赵秉志从容回答:"按照中国刑事诉讼法,在法院作出有罪判决并生效前,不能认定任何人构成犯罪。我是说黄海勇涉嫌构成走私普通货物罪,他是否有罪要等他回国经法院审判之后作结论。"

再如美洲人权委员会的律师问:"你在参与的引渡案件中,都是持的支持引渡的观点,对吗?"

赵秉志答:"……在本案中,我应秘鲁政府邀请,作为专家证人向法庭说明中国刑事法治情况,以及与黄海勇案有关的刑诉程序、刑法修改情况。我已宣誓要如实作证,我不是一贯支持引渡,只是在作证中帮法庭了解中国的刑事法治情况……"

"这个问题就是陷阱,想证明我在主观上支持引渡中国人,从而削弱证明力。"赵秉志解释。

法庭上针对赵秉志提出的问题共有61个,涉及死刑的有22个。主要包括黄海勇是否会被适用死刑,中国就黄海勇案件作出的不判处死刑的外交承诺,以及中国死刑适用的罪名、数量、执行方式等问题。

事实上,近年来我国推进了死刑改革,加快限制和废除死刑的步伐,分别通过《刑法修正案(八)》和《刑法修正案(九)》先后废除了13种和9种罪名的死刑。

"我去作证前,就得知法庭由于不了解中国已废除了走私普通货物罪的死刑,而对中国能否遵守不判处黄海勇死刑的承诺信心不足。"赵秉志坦言,当前国际社会对中国刑事法治状况还缺乏了解。

而作证接近尾声时,美洲人权法院巡回法庭庭长谢拉表示:"您(赵秉志)所讲的与我们原来所了解的有很大不同,我们将认真研究"。

2015年9月,美洲人权法院作出裁决:在充分保障黄海勇穷尽秘鲁国内全部司法程序的基础上,由秘鲁政府决定是否引渡黄海勇。

"就像赖昌星案对该案起到的示范效应一样,接下来黄海勇案也能对更多的引渡案提供借鉴。"赵秉志举例说,当年高山已拿到了加拿大永久居住权,如果一直抗拒回国,会比赖昌星拖更长时间,但在赖案震慑下,高山回国自首。他感慨,其实,任何外逃人员回来,背后都是我国相关执法部门长时间的不懈努力。而中国综合国力提升,司法改革带来的刑事法治形象的改善,更有助于实现我国海外追逃追赃方面国际刑事司法合作工作的良性循环。

张磊清楚地记得,2016年7月17日早晨,他收到了赵秉志的微信:"黄海勇回来了!"那一刻,北京的天很蓝!

当时,由于我国与秘鲁没有直达航班,也为了"保证归途的绝对安全",黄海勇被我国相关部门押解小组安排乘坐智利和俄罗斯航空公司的航班途径古巴、俄罗斯,成功引渡回国。等待他的,将是我国司法机关依法公正的审判。

赵秉志教授出席国际法庭作证的中国逃犯黄海勇引渡案我方获胜*

（一）

2014年9月3日，美洲人权法院在巴拉圭首都亚松森的巴拉圭最高法院开庭，审理中国政府向秘鲁政府提出引渡申请的涉嫌走私普通货物罪的中国公民黄海勇引渡案。北京师范大学刑事法律科学研究院院长暨中国刑法学研究会会长赵秉志教授、中国外交部条约法律司孙昂参赞和秘鲁前司法部长托马博士作为秘鲁政府邀请的3位专家证人，经美洲人权法院批准到庭作证。

在中秘按双边引渡条约商议引渡涉嫌重大走私犯罪主犯黄海勇的过程中，黄为抗拒引渡，聘请律师以中国刑事法治中的"死刑"和"酷刑"问题向美洲人权委员会提出申诉；美洲人权委员会于2013年7月作出报告，要求秘鲁政府停止引渡黄海勇，并对中国的死刑和"酷刑"状况表示担忧。随后，黄海勇引渡案提交给美洲人权法院审理。此次即是美洲人权法院开庭专门审理秘鲁政府的引渡主张。

美洲人权法院是除美洲人权委员会外美洲人权区域保护的另外一个重要机构，其职能是根据《美洲人权公约》管辖美洲国家（实际上主要是拉美国家）有关人权的案件和相关法律事务。此次美洲人权法院的庭审，由该法院7位法官中的5位法官组成法庭。法庭全天听取了秘鲁政府方面的3位专家证人的证词，并由各方进行了盘问和辩论。赵秉志教授的作证及各方对其盘问主要围绕与本案相关的中国刑事司法程序和实体问题以及赵秉志教授曾出庭作证的中加遣返赖昌星案件的有关情况而进行，赵秉志教授在自

---

* 原载京师刑事法治网，http://ccls.bnu.edu.cn/criminal/info/showpage.asp? ProgramID＝&pkID＝47523&keywor 最后访问日期2019年7月8日。

我陈述之后,依次接受了秘鲁政府方面、美洲人权委员会代表、黄海勇的律师的盘问以及法庭的发问;孙昂参赞的作证及各方对其的盘问则主要围绕中国引渡法制与实践以及中加遣返赖昌星的外交承诺而进行。赵秉志教授和孙昂参赞围绕上述问题提供了客观、鲜明、充分的证言。秘鲁前司法部长托马博士的作证及各方对其的盘问主要围绕与本案相关的中秘引渡条约和秘鲁相关国内法律问题而进行。法庭对三位专家证人的作证予以感谢,并特别表示赵秉志教授和孙昂参赞的作证对他们了解中国刑事法制与实践很有帮助。在当天下午三位专家证人作证结束之后,参与庭审的三方又进行了辩论和陈述。当天庭审结束后,秘鲁政府方面对三位专家证人的作证给予了充分肯定和高度评价。秘鲁政府邀请的另一位非出庭专家证人中国社科院国际法研究所研究员柳华文则经法庭同意于庭前向法庭提交了有关中国人权法律保护状况的书面证词。

据悉,按照惯例,本次庭审后的半年到一年左右,美洲人权法院的法庭将会作出裁判。此次庭审是泛美人权体系和美洲人权法院首次审理引渡案件,法庭的裁判将直接影响此案最终走向即中秘引渡黄海勇能否成功,也会对我国今后在拉美国家的追逃工作产生直接影响,并可能在一定程度上影响我国在欧洲方向的追逃工作。

(二)

美洲人权法院于2014年9月3日开庭审理黄海勇引渡案一年有余后,2015年9月17日,中国外交部得到消息:美洲人权法庭终于作出了裁决:要求引渡黄海勇的秘鲁政府和中国政府一方获胜!这是一项历史性的判决,是美洲人权法院成立以来首次就引渡逃犯案件作出判决,也是中国首次在国际人权法院出庭并首战告捷!至此,逃犯黄海勇即将踏上被引渡回国的路程。这次成功的在国际法庭上的追逃引渡实践,也给我国当前反腐败法治中的海外追逃实践提供了宝贵的经验和成功的典型案例。

9月17日当天,外交部条法司副司长孙昂即及时向赵秉志教授通报了此次国际法庭庭审获胜的佳音;10月6日,国家海关总署缉私局许文荣副局长率该局一处主要负责同志邀请赵秉志教授和柳华文教授就此案的获胜裁判及其意义等进行了座谈。

赵秉志教授等应邀参加"10·7"专案(黄海勇引渡案)引渡工作研讨会*

2016年7月17日,涉嫌重大走私犯罪的嫌疑人黄海勇被从秘鲁引渡回国,这是我国境外追逃工作的重大成果。我国领导人和中央有关部门对该案的追逃追赃工作高度重视,当年朱镕基总理和中央政法委罗干书记曾做过专门批示,习近平总书记2015年曾为此案与秘鲁时任总统奥良塔·乌马拉专门进行沟通,中央纪委王岐山书记也高度关注此案引渡工作的进展,中央纪委、外交部、海关总署、公安部、司法部、最高人民法院、最高人民检察院等部门密切配合、协同作战,经过长期坚持不懈的努力,终于使这起新中国成立以来最复杂的引渡案完美收官。该案(也被称为"10·7"专案)追逃历时18年、引渡历时8年,是我国首次从拉美国家成功引渡犯罪嫌疑人,是美洲人权法院首次审理涉中国引渡案件,也是我国政府官员和学者首次在国际人权法庭出庭作证。2014年9月3日,北师大刑科院院长暨中国刑法学研究会会长赵秉志教授、时任外交部条法司参赞(现任外交部条法司副司长)孙昂和秘鲁前司法部长托马博士作为秘鲁政府邀请的3位专家证人,经美洲人权法院批准到庭作证。秘鲁政府邀请的另一位非出庭专家证人中国社科院国际法研究所所长助理柳华文研究员经法庭同意向法庭提交了有关中国人权法律保护状况的书面证词。四位专家证人的证言(证词)对于成功引渡黄海勇发挥了重要作用。

为了全面总结"10·7"专案引渡工作,给今后开展境外追逃工作积累经验,海关总署缉私局于2016年8月11—12日在武汉海关组织召开"10·7"

---

* 原载京师刑事法治网,http://ccls.bnu.edu.cn/criminal/info/showpage.asp?ProgramID=&pkID=47523&keywor 最后访问日期2019年7月7日。

专案引渡工作研讨会。来自中纪委国际合作局、外交部条法司暨拉美司、海关总署缉私局、最高人民法院国际合作局、最高人民检察院国际合作局、司法部司法协助外事司、公安部国际合作局、北京师范大学、中国社会科学院国际法研究所、中国驻秘鲁大使馆、武汉海关缉私局、湖北省公安厅的领导、专家30余人参加了会议。国家海关总署缉私局刘晓辉局长首先致辞,对与会代表的到来表示欢迎。然后海关总署缉私局费继恒副处长通报了"10·7"专案引渡工作情况,接着与会各部门代表分别发言,总结本部门在参与该案办理过程中的经验和体会。刑科院院长赵秉志教授应邀与会,并结合自己作为专家证人参与美洲人权法院巡回法庭庭审的经历,作了题为"关于进一步推动我国境外追逃工作的几点思考——我在黄海勇引渡案美洲人权巡回法庭上出庭作证的体会"的主题发言,充分肯定"10·7"专案重大意义的同时,也提出我国境外追逃的若干建议,得到与会者的好评。会议最后,刘晓辉局长进行了总结,对各部门在办理"10·7"专案过程中所提供的协助表示感谢。此次研讨会对于总结"10·7"专案的经验,推动海关部门乃至我国反腐败境外追逃工作的开展具有重要意义。刑科院国际刑法研究所副所长张磊副教授陪同赵秉志教授参加了上述活动。

资料精选

赵秉志出席美洲人权法院黄海勇引渡案庭审个人陈述及被询问之问题

时间:2014年9月3日上午9:15—11:00
地点:巴拉圭首都亚松森市,巴拉圭最高法院

一、宣誓

我郑重宣誓:我将凭荣誉和良心忠实履行专家证人的职责(大意,原文为西班牙文)。

二、陈述

尊敬的各位法官:

我是秘鲁政府邀请的来自中国的专家证人赵秉志,下面我先介绍一下我个人的简况,并对法庭审理黄海勇先生引渡案所需要了解的中国刑事法相关情况予以概要介述。

(一)我的个人简况

我叫赵秉志,1988年获得法学博士学位,并在中国重点大学担任刑法学教授已22年,兼任中国刑法学研究会会长。我自1988年起作为专家一直参与中国立法机关起草、修改刑法的工作,并参与了本案涉及的中国《刑法修正案(八)》的起草工作;我作为中国最高法院、最高检察院的咨询专家多年来一直参与重要司法活动的咨询和重大疑难案件的研究。我自1985年起作为兼职律师办理了上百件各类刑事案件,并曾应加拿大政府邀请作为证人

于2001年8月10日和10月23日两次在加拿大审理赖昌星案的聆讯法庭上作证,加拿大法庭认可并采纳了我的证词。

(二)与本案相关的中国刑事法治情况

中国现代意义上的刑事法治建设始于20世纪70年代末,经过30多年的发展,已经建立了一个较为完备的刑事法律体系,而且形成了与西方发达国家法治发展程度大体接近的崇尚法治、尊重人权、追求公平正义的现代刑事法治理念。现介绍与本案相关的中国刑事诉讼法和刑法两个方面的情况如下:

1. 相关刑事诉讼程序

本案黄海勇先生如果按照中秘两国引渡条约被引渡回中国,他将依照中国《引渡法》和刑法、刑事诉讼法的规定进入中国相应的刑事诉讼程序。中国现行刑事诉讼法颁布于1979年,并于1996年、2012年进行了两次重大修订,从而建立了一个较为完备的刑事程序法治体系,主要表现在两个方面:一是明确规定了审判独立、审判公开、无罪推定、保障辩护权、两审终审制、法律面前人人平等等现代刑事程序法治原则,有力地保障了刑事诉讼程序的公平、公正、公开的运行。二是规定了科学合理的刑事诉讼程序,包括适用于普通刑事案件的六大程序(立案、侦查、起诉、一审、二审、执行)和适用于特定案件的死刑复核、审判监督(再审)程序以及针对未成年人等的特别程序,各种程序都有其严格合理的期限要求,各种程序相互配合又相互制约,为案件的正确处理提供制度保障。

刑事诉讼参与的各方,在审前阶段主要包括侦查机关、检察机关、犯罪嫌疑人及其辩护人、被害人及其代理人、证人、鉴定人等;在审判阶段主要包括公诉机关、法院、被告人及其辩护人、被害人及其代理人、证人、鉴定人等。

在中国刑事诉讼制度中,审判公开制度、完善的辩护制度和严格的证据规则尤为重要:(1)审判公开即法院审理案件和宣告判决向社会公开,允许公民旁听,允许记者采访报道。(2)辩护制度包括被告人有权随时委托辩护人及赋予辩护律师在刑事诉讼中广泛的权利。(3)关于证据规则,不仅规定要"重证据、不轻信口供","证据经过查证属实,才能作为定案的根据","严禁刑讯逼供和以威胁、引诱、欺骗以及其他非法方法收集证据,不得强迫任何人证实自己有罪",而且确立了非法证据排除规则。

本案黄先生若被引渡回中国进入刑事诉讼程序,会受到公正的程序处遇。

2.《刑法修正案(八)》的重要修正及其溯及力

中国立法机关 2011 年 2 月 25 日通过并于同年 5 月 1 日起生效的《刑法修正案(八)》,对中国刑法典作了多方面重要的修改完善,《刑法修正案(八)》通过后其内容被全面纳入了刑法典。《刑法修正案(八)》也对本案所涉及的走私普通货物罪作了极其重要的修正,即废止了该罪的死刑,使该罪的法定最高刑降低为无期徒刑,而其法定最低刑仍维持为一个月的拘役。

对《刑法修正案(八)》之前发生而未审结的案件是否适用《刑法修正案(八)》,根据中国刑法典第 12 条关于刑法溯及力采取"从旧兼从轻"原则的规定,应当适用较轻的法律即《刑法修正案(八)》,即对黄海勇走私普通货物案应当适用《刑法修正案(八)》,黄海勇若构成此罪,其可能判处的最重的刑罚应为无期徒刑而不是死刑。

以上是我的简要陈述,请法庭审查并予以采纳。下面我愿意如实回答各方的提问。

谢谢。

三、被询问之问题[*]

(一)秘鲁政府司法和人权部国家检察司律师 Sr. Carlos Miguel Reano 发问

1. 黄海勇若被引渡回中国,之后的刑事诉讼程序是怎样的?
2. 黄海勇案件的刑事审判是否公开?各方参与人有哪些?
3. 黄海勇案的审判机关是谁?黄若不服一审判决,可否提起上诉?黄若上诉向哪个机关提起?哪个机关对其案件二审?
4. 辩护律师何时可介入诉讼?被告人的辩护律师有哪些诉讼权利?
5. 走私普通货物罪的量刑是怎样的?若因此罪被判处无期徒刑,是否

---

[*] 根据赵秉志教授在美洲人权法院法庭上的记录整理。

可能减刑?

6. 犯罪嫌疑人自被调查之日起,他的羁押情况如何?判决生效后羁押期间,是否有机制可去检查、监督其关押条件?

7. 中国刑法中的走私普通货物罪是否已取消死刑?这一取消规定是否适用于黄海勇案?

8. 黄海勇的同案共犯潘子牛的审判是否适用了《刑法修正案(八)》?对其判了什么刑罚?是否被判处了死刑?

9. 你是否应加拿大政府邀请出席了赖昌星案件的法庭审理?为什么加拿大同意向中国遣返赖昌星?

10. 赖昌星被起诉的罪名是什么?对他的定罪量刑是怎样的?

11. 对比黄海勇案与赖昌星案,若黄被引渡回中国,其司法操作程序是否会与赖案相似?中国是否提供同样的外交承诺?

(二)黄海勇的律师 Luis Lamas Puccio 发问

1. 黄海勇案与赖昌星案相似,为什么黄未被起诉?

2. 黄海勇还未经审判,你何以判定他犯了走私罪?

3. 作为刑法教授,你是支持死刑还是反对死刑?

4. 请告诉我们,近两年来,中国有多少人被判处死刑?

5. 请告诉我们中国执行死刑的数字?

6. 你一再提到黄海勇的罪行,黄海勇构成犯罪了吗?

7. 你了解中国向秘鲁政府提出引渡黄海勇申请的内容吗?

8. 那你解释一下为什么这个引渡申请中没有附上证实黄海勇构成犯罪的证据?

9. 请你介绍一下中国刑法中的死刑与无期徒刑有什么区别?二者不是差不多吗?

10. 中国执行死刑用什么方式?

11. 枪决是射击犯人头部,对吗?

12. 在赖昌星案中,中国向加拿大提出引渡赖昌星的申请,有无附上英文版的中国刑法?

13. 那么为什么中方向秘鲁提出引渡黄海勇的申请中没有中国相关法

律条文的西班牙文文本?

14. 中国哪个机构可以向外国作出不判处死刑等外交承诺?

15. 最高人民法院作出这类决定,是否会受到外交部的影响?

16. 如果是《刑法修正案(八)》通过之前黄海勇在中国受审,他会被判处什么刑罚?

(三)美洲人权委员会 James Louis Cavallaro 发问:

1. 你在自述中说你作为律师办理过 100 多件案件,你办的都是刑事案件吗?

2. 你参与办理刑事案件的身份?有无作为检控律师参与办理刑案的?

3. 你参与的刑事案件的审判结果?法院有无采纳你的意见?

4. 中国刑事司法中有没有无罪的判决?

5. 那么你能告诉我们中国刑事司法中有罪无罪的比例是多少?

6. 如果我们说中国刑事司法中 99% 的案件审判都是有罪的结论,你对此如何评价?

7. 中国现行刑法中还有多少死刑罪名?

8. 有哪些严重的暴力犯罪适用死刑较多?

9. 中国的 55 种死刑罪名中有多少非暴力犯罪?

10. 那就是说有 20 多种非暴力犯罪可被判处死刑?

11. 请举例非暴力犯罪中哪些罪名被实际适用死刑?

12. 刑事诉讼中如果发现了新的证据,可否启动案件的重新审判?

13. 中国刑事诉讼的侦查和检察阶段,是否有酷刑发生?

14. 除参与赖昌星案件外,你还参与过其他引渡案件的作证吗?

15. 你在参与的引渡案件中,都是持的支持引渡的观点,我这样说对吗?

美洲人权委员会 Silvia Serrano Guzman 接着发问:

16. 中国刑事诉讼中的上诉程序是怎样提起的?诉讼过程中有侵犯权利的问题可否提出?

(四)法庭发问

Eduardo Ferrer Mac-Gregor Poisot 法官:

1. 中国判处死刑最常见的罪名是什么?

2.《刑法修正案（八）》生效后，还有哪些非暴力犯罪被判处死刑？

3. 中国刑法第 151 条包括哪些罪名？最重的刑罚是什么？

Eduardo Vio Grossi 法官：

1. 根据中秘两国引渡条约和中国法律，是否会发生要求引渡时的罪名与后来引渡被申请人回国后的罪名不一致的情况？

2. 你这样说，有无法律依据？

3. 如果黄海勇被引渡回中国，他不会被判处死刑，对吗？

Manuel E·Ventura Robles 法官：

1. 在赖昌星案件中，中国是否向加方正式提出了引渡申请？

2. 中方向加方就赖昌星案件作出的外交承诺，与中方向秘鲁就黄海勇案作出的外交承诺一样吗？

Roberto F·Caldas 法官：

1. 你是否了解最近中国最近一次对走私罪判处死刑的案件？

2. 若黄海勇被引渡回国受审，他会被判处无期徒刑，对吗？会还是不会？

3. 若黄海勇被引渡回国受审，是否会由审判潘子牛的同一法院审判？

Humberto Antonio Sierra porto 庭长：

1. 根据你的证词，我理解中国在赖昌星案件和黄海勇案件中作出的外交承诺都是由中国最高法院决定，再由中国外交部对外作出的，是这样的，对吗？

2. 中国最高法院作出不判处死刑决定的根据何在？

3. 二审是由省级高级法院作出判决的，如果最高法院对省高级法院的二审裁判有不同意见，怎么协调？

4. 在引渡案件中，若省高级法院二审终审时作出的判决违背了最高法院不判处死刑的承诺，怎么协调？

5. 引渡嫌疑人回国受审时，所审判的罪名是否会与引渡申请不一致或者多出其他罪名？

6. 引渡后发现嫌疑人原来还有其他罪行，也不会追加起诉吗？

7. 在赖昌星案件中，中方的外交承诺允许加方在中方判决赖昌星之后去探视他，你认为有此必要吗？

赵秉志为赴美洲人权法院就黄海勇案作证所准备的主要材料

巴拉圭·亚松森

2014年9月3日

目次

一、中华人民共和国刑事司法体系整体状况

（一）中国处理引渡回国案件的一般刑事司法流程。

1. 向外国提出引渡请求的程序

2. 引渡回国之后的司法程序

（二）有权审理黄海勇案件的司法机关和诉讼进行的地点。

1. 什么级别、什么地方的机构会管辖此案？

2. 什么机构会接收被引渡回国的黄海勇？

（三）中国国内法律规定的刑事诉讼主要阶段和法定期限。

1. 第一阶段：立案

2. 第二阶段：侦查

3. 第三阶段：审查起诉

4. 第四阶段：第一审

5. 第五阶段：第二审

6. 第六阶段：执行

7. 关于黄海勇被引渡前在秘鲁被羁押的时间可否在中国所判刑期中折抵。

（四）中国刑事诉讼的原则。

1. 侦查权、检察权、审判权由专门机关依法行使原则

2. 严格遵守法律程序原则

3. 以事实为根据、以法律为准绳原则

4. 人民法院、人民检察院依法独立行使职权原则

5. 分工负责、互相配合、互相制约原则

6. 人民检察院依法对刑事诉讼实行法律监督原则

7. 犯罪嫌疑人、被告人有权获得辩护原则

8. 未经人民法院依法判决，对任何人都不得确定有罪原则

9. 审判公开原则

10. 两审终审原则

（五）详细说明中国刑事诉讼整个过程的公开或不公开性，以及参与的诉讼各方。

（六）中国法律有关上诉问题的规定。

1. 上诉审的提起

2. 上诉理由

3. 上诉不加刑原则

4. 上诉审的管辖法院和检察院

5. 审理期限

6. 上诉审的程序

7. 上诉审的宣判

8. 上诉审裁判的效力

（七）是否存在如人身保护令或庇护等快速司法保护机制？

（八）检察院的职权或在刑事诉讼全过程中承担该职权的机关？

1. 审查批准逮捕

2. 羁押必要性审查

3. 审查起诉

4. 通过其他方式对侦查机关的侦查活动进行监督

5. 出庭支持公诉

6. 二审抗诉及出席二审法庭

7. 再审抗诉

8. 对刑罚执行活动进行监督

（九）被起诉人的法律代表（律师）的介入和职权。

1. 委托辩护律师

2. 何时可以委托辩护律师？

3. 法律援助辩护

4. 辩护律师的诉讼权利

（十）在被判无期徒刑的情况下，是否存在再审的可能性？

（十一）确定被起诉人或被判决人关押的有关准则？以及负责执行该关押决定的机关？

1. 审前羁押（预防性关押）

2. 已决羁押

（十二）中国监禁制度的核心内容。

二、与黄海勇案直接有关的事项

（一）指控黄海勇并由此向秘鲁提出引渡请求的事实及罪名（洗钱、走私）。

1. 涉嫌走私普通货物的案件事实与性质

2. 涉嫌洗钱的案件事实与性质

（二）对这些罪名比较区分，重点介绍申请引渡黄海勇时适用刑法中对每项罪名的刑罚和修改法律后现行法律规定的刑罚；提出引渡黄海勇申请的法律依据？

1. 涉嫌的走私普通货物、物品罪的罪名及其刑罚

2. 涉嫌的洗钱罪及其刑罚

3. 提出引渡申请的法律依据

（三）当走私罪可判处死刑时，中国是否有被执行死刑的案例？

（四）中国《刑法修正案（八）》的修法范围和司法效力？除了走私罪，还有哪些罪名也涉及该修正案？推动《刑法修正案（八）》削减死刑罪名的主要原因是什么？

1.《刑法修正案（八）》的修法范围

2. 推动《刑法修正案（八）》削减死刑罪名的主要原因

（五）阐述中国刑法包括《刑法修正案（八）》的修法过程，推动修改法律

和其他重要事项进程的主要依据是什么？

1. 《刑法修正案（八）》的修法过程

2. 推动修改法律和其他重要事项进程的主要依据

（六）当前已有多少案件适用于《刑法修正案（八）》？其中有多少走私案件？

（七）根据中国国内法律，阐述有利于被起诉人的溯及力问题，指出如被引渡，其对于黄海勇案是否适用？并由此确定不会对其适用死刑。

（八）黄海勇案同谋的刑事诉讼情况，是否对其适用了《刑法修正案（八）》？

1. 对于涉案单位的查处

2. 对于涉案个人的查处

（九）死刑改革问题。

1. 中国死刑制度的演进

2. 中国对死刑适用的限制措施

3. 中国政府没有趋于扩大执行死刑范围的政策

（十）说明中国加大力度打击法律机构内部存在的腐败问题的情况。

三、黄海勇面临的后续司法进程

（一）赖昌星案件的诉讼程序如何？其被判决和执行的罪名是什么？

1. 赖昌星案是引渡还是遣返？其基本程序是怎样的？

2. 赖昌星案件的诉讼程序

3. 赖昌星被判决和执行的罪名

4. 赖昌星走私普通货物罪的涉案金额远远大于黄海勇案件

5. 赖昌星审判时《刑法修正案（八）》的实施情况

（二）赖昌星案件是否曾运用上诉机制？是否有代理人？

一、中华人民共和国刑事司法体系整体情况

（一）中国处理引渡回国案件的一般刑事司法流程。

1. 向外国提出引渡请求的程序

中国向外国提出引渡请求或者引渡过境请求的，被称为主动引渡。中

国《引渡法》第47条规定了向外国提出引渡请求的一般程序:"请求外国准予引渡或者引渡过境的,应当由负责办理有关案件的省、自治区或者直辖市的审判、检察、公安、国家安全或者监狱管理机关分别向最高人民法院、最高人民检察院、公安部、国家安全部、司法部提出意见书,并附有关文件和材料及其经证明无误的译文。最高人民法院、最高人民检察院、公安部、国家安全部、司法部分别会同外交部审核同意后,通过外交部向外国提出请求。"根据该条之规定并结合我国实践,我国向外国提出引渡程序基本流程如下:

(1) 具体办理案件的地市一级审判、检察、公安、国家安全或者监狱管理机关(建议引渡机关)向省、自治区、直辖市一级相应机关建议引渡;

(2) 省、自治区、直辖市一级机关(提议引渡机关)就下一级机关提出的引渡建议经过审核后向中央相应机关提议引渡(或者就自己负责办理的需要引渡的案件直接向中央相应机关提议引渡);

(3) 中央相应机关(申请引渡机关)就省、自治区、直辖市相应一级机关的引渡提议审核后向外交部提出申请(或者就其负责办理的需要引渡的案件直接向外交部提出申请);

(4) 外交部(提出引渡机关)接到中央机关的引渡请求后报国务院批准;

(5) 国务院(批准引渡机关)批准后,由外交部向被请求国提出引渡请求;

(6) 外交部向驻被请求国的使馆转递引渡请求并发出有关指示;

(7) 中国(请求国)驻被请求国的使馆向驻在国外交部提交引渡请求。

中国《引渡法》第48条还就提出引渡请求前,请求外国对被请求引渡人先行采取强制措施的程序进行了规定:"在紧急情况下,可以在向外国正式提出引渡请求前,通过外交途径或者被请求国同意的其他途径,请求外国对有关人员先行采取强制措施。"根据该条,最高人民检察院、公安部、国家安全部、司法部如果认为本系统内有需要先行采取强制措施的,在正式提出引渡请求前,经过上述单位审查同意,可以通过外交途径或者被请求国同意的其他途径,请求外国对有关人员先行采取强制措施,然后再正式提出引渡请求。

2. 引渡回国之后的司法程序

中国《引渡法》第51条规定:"公安机关负责接收外国准予引渡的人以及

与案件有关的财物。对于其他部门提出引渡请求的,公安机关在接收被引渡人以及与案件有关的财物后,应当及时转交提出引渡请求的部门;也可以会同有关部门共同接收被引渡人以及与案件有关的财物。"根据该条,犯罪嫌疑人被引渡回国之后:(1)由公安机关(或者会同有关部门)接收被引渡人以及与案件有关的财物;(2)对于其他部门提出引渡请求的,公安机关应当及时转交给提出引渡请求的部门,然后进入中国相应的刑事诉讼程序。

(二)有权审理黄海勇案件的司法机关和诉讼进行的地点。

1. 什么级别、什么地方的机构会管辖此案?

中国《刑事诉讼法》第20条规定:"中级人民法院管辖下列第一审刑事案件:(1)危害国家安全、恐怖活动案件;(2)可能判处无期徒刑、死刑的案件。"黄海勇及其走私集团在1996至1998年期间大肆走私毛豆油,偷逃税款达7.17亿人民币,涉嫌走私普通货物罪和洗钱罪,根据中国《刑法》第153条的规定有可能被判处无期徒刑,所以在级别上应当由中级人民法院管辖。

中国《刑事诉讼法》第24条规定:"刑事案件由犯罪地的人民法院管辖。"黄海勇案件的主要犯罪地是武汉市,按照地域管辖原则应当由武汉市的人民法院管辖,即应当由武汉市中级人民法院管辖。综上,黄海勇案件应当由武汉市中级人民法院以及与该法院相对应的武汉市人民检察院、武汉市公安局(武汉海关缉私局)管辖)管辖。

2. 什么机构会接收被引渡回国的黄海勇?

根据中国《引渡法》第51条关于"公安机关负责接收外国准予引渡的人以及与案件有关的财物"的规定,公安机关(海关缉私局)会接收引渡回国的黄海勇。根据上述关于黄海勇案件地域管辖和级别管辖的阐述,应当由武汉市公安局(武汉海关缉私局)负责接收引渡回国的黄海勇。

(三)中国国内法律规定的刑事诉讼主要阶段和法定期限。

中国刑事诉讼法对普通刑事案件规定了立案、侦查、审查起诉、第一审、第二审和执行六个诉讼阶段。对于被告人被判处死刑立即执行和死刑缓期两年执行的案件则另行规定了死刑复核程序。在侦查、审查起诉、第一审、第二审四个阶段,对于犯罪嫌疑人、被告人被羁押的,规定了明确的办案羁押期限。

1. 第一阶段：立案

立案是中国刑事诉讼的第一个阶段，指公安机关、人民检察院或者人民法院对于报案、控告、举报、自首以及自己发现的材料，依据管辖范围进行审查，以判明有无犯罪事实和应否追究刑事责任，并决定是否作为刑事案件进行侦查或审判的诉讼活动和诉讼阶段。只有经过立案才正式启动刑事诉讼程序。

2. 第二阶段：侦查

侦查是指侦查机关对已经立案的刑事案件，依法进行专门调查工作和采取有关的强制性措施，以收集、调取、核实案件证据材料，查明案情，确定是否移送审查起诉的诉讼阶段。完整的侦查阶段，始于侦查机关作出立案决定之后，终于侦查终结，其结果是或者撤销案件，或者移送审查起诉。

在侦查阶段，对于犯罪嫌疑人被羁押的案件，规定了明确的办案期限（即羁押期限）。一般情况下，侦查羁押期限不得超过2个月，但案情复杂、期限届满不能终结的案件，可以经上一级人民检察院批准延长1个月（《刑事诉讼法》第154条）。另外还有两种延长侦查羁押期限的例外情形：(1) 对于交通十分不便的边远地区的重大复杂案件、重大的犯罪集团案件、流窜作案的重大复杂案件和犯罪涉及面广，取证困难的重大复杂案件，经省级人民检察院批准或者决定，可以延长2个月（《刑事诉讼法》第156条）；(2) 对犯罪嫌疑人可能判处10年有期徒刑以上刑罚，依照上述第一种情形延长期限届满，仍不能侦查终结的，经省级人民检察院批准或者决定，可以再延长2个月（《刑事诉讼法》第157条）。此外，如果在侦查期间，发现犯罪嫌疑人另有重要罪行的，自发现之日起需要重新计算侦查羁押期限（《刑事诉讼法》第158条）。即侦查阶段的审前羁押期限一般不超过2个月，最多不超过7个月，若发现另有重要罪行可再延长。

在侦查阶段，侦查机关讯问犯罪嫌疑人是侦查取证的一种措施，通过讯问能获得证据、查清案件事实，但同时讯问的过程也需要进行规范，以保障犯罪嫌疑人的合法权利不受侵犯。中国《刑事诉讼法》从多个方面对讯问程序进行了规范，包括：(1) 要求讯问应当在看守所内进行。拘留后，应当立即将被拘留人送交看守所，至迟不得超过24小时（《刑事诉讼法》第83条）；逮

资料精选

捕后,应当立即将被逮捕人送交看守所(《刑事诉讼法》第91条)。犯罪嫌疑人被送交看守所羁押后,侦查人员对其进行讯问,应当在看守所内进行(《刑事诉讼法》第116条)。(2)首次讯问的时间。侦查机关对于被拘留和逮捕的犯罪嫌疑人,必须在被拘留、逮捕后的24小时内进行讯问,在发现不应当拘留、逮捕时,必须立即释放犯罪嫌疑人(《刑事诉讼法》第84条、92条)。(3)严禁刑讯逼供和以威胁、引诱、欺骗以及其他非法方法收集证据,不得强迫任何人证实自己有罪。采用刑讯逼供等非法方法收集的犯罪嫌疑人、被告人供述应当予以排除(《刑事诉讼法》第50条、54条)。(4)明确讯问的过程。侦查人员在讯问犯罪嫌疑人的时候,应当首先讯问犯罪嫌疑人是否有犯罪行为,让他陈述有罪的情节或者无罪的辩解,然后向他提出问题。对与本案无关的问题,犯罪嫌疑人有拒绝回答的权利(《刑事诉讼法》第118条)。讯问笔录应当交犯罪嫌疑人核对,对于没有阅读能力的,应当向他宣读。如果记载有遗漏或者差错,犯罪嫌疑人可以提出补充或者改正。犯罪嫌疑人承认笔录没有错误后,应当签名或者盖章。侦查人员也应当在笔录上签名。犯罪嫌疑人请求自行书写供述的,应当准许(《刑事诉讼法》第120条)。(5)讯问过程中的同步录音录像。侦查人员在讯问犯罪嫌疑人的时候,可以对讯问过程进行录音或者录像;对于可能判处无期徒刑、死刑的案件或者其他重大犯罪案件,应当对讯问过程进行录音或者录像。对讯问的录音或录像,应保证完整性(《刑事诉讼法》第121条)。

3. 第三阶段:审查起诉

审查起诉是指人民检察院对侦查机关侦查终结移送起诉的案件进行全面审查,以便决定是否将犯罪嫌疑人交付人民法院审判的诉讼阶段。审查起诉的结果是决定提起公诉或者不起诉。

在审查起诉阶段,检察机关应当在1个月以内作出是否起诉的决定,重大复杂的案件,可以延长0.5个月,因此,审查起诉阶段的办案期限一般不超过1.5月(《刑事诉讼法》第169条)。对于需要补充侦查的案件,应当在1个月以内补充侦查完毕,以2次为限,补充侦查完毕再次移送检察机关审查起诉的,重新计算审查起诉的期限(《刑事诉讼法》第171条)。即审查起诉阶段的办案期限最长不超过6.5个月。

4. 第四阶段：第一审

第一审是指人民法院对人民检察院提起公诉、自诉人提起自诉的案件进行初次审判时的阶段。中国普通刑事案件的第一审程序主要包括以下五个阶段：(1) 开庭。开庭是正式进行法庭审判前的准备阶段，在这一阶段，审判长需要查明当事人是否到庭，宣布案由，宣布合议庭的组成人员、书记员、公诉人、辩护人、诉讼代理人、鉴定人和翻译人员的名单，告知当事人有权对合议庭组成人员、书记员、公诉人、鉴定人和翻译人员申请回避，告知被告人享有辩护权利(《刑事诉讼法》第185条)。(2) 法庭调查。法庭调查是在审判人员主持下，控辩双方和其他诉讼参与人的参加下，当庭对案件事实和证据进行审查、核实的诉讼活动，可以对被告人、被害人发问，询问证人、鉴定人、出示物证和宣读有关笔录。法庭调查是以直接言词的形式，由控辩双方对对方所出示的证据进行交叉质证，以确定哪些证据可以作为定案依据的过程。所有证据只有在法庭上调查核实后才能作为定案的依据，因而法庭调查是法庭审判的核心环节(《刑事诉讼法》第186—192条、193条第1款)。(3) 法庭辩论。法庭辩论是在法庭调查的基础上，控辩双方就被告人的行为是否构成犯罪、犯罪的性质、罪责轻重、证据是否确实充分，以及如何适用刑法等问题，进行互相争论和反驳(《刑事诉讼法》第193条第2款)。(4) 被告人最后陈述。在法庭辩论终结后，由被告人进行最后的陈述，这一阶段不可被省略，这也是中国刑事诉讼法赋予被告人的一项重要诉讼权利(《刑事诉讼法》第193条第3款)。被告人最后陈述只要不超出本案范围，一般不能限制其发言时间或打断其发言。(5) 评议与宣判。被告人最后陈述完毕后，审判长宣布休庭，由合议庭进行评议。评议由审判长主持，秘密进行。评议如果存在分歧意见，应当按照多数人的意见作出决定。评议之后进行宣判，分为当庭宣判和定期宣判两种。当庭宣判是在评议作出决定后，立即复庭由审判长宣告判决结果。当庭宣判的，应当在5日内送达判决书。定期宣判是在评议作出决定后，另行确定日期宣告判决。定期宣判的，应当在宣判后立即送达判决书(《刑事诉讼法》第195、196条)。

在第一审阶段，一般情况下人民法院应当在受理案件后2个月内宣判，至迟不得超过3个月，即第一审期间的羁押期限一般不超过3个月(《刑事诉讼法》第202条)。另外还有两种例外情形：(1) 对于可能判处死刑的案件或者附带民事诉讼的案件，以及交通十分不便的边远地区的重大复杂案件、重大的犯罪集团案件、流窜作案的重大复杂案件或犯罪涉及面广，取证困难的重大复杂案件，经上一级人民法院批准，可以延长3个月；(2) 因特殊情况还需要延长的，报请最高人民法院批准延长(《刑事诉讼法》第202条)，每次可延长1—3个月(最高人民法院《关于适用〈中华人民共和国刑事诉讼法〉的解释》第173条第2款)，但此种延长的例外情形较少适用。即第一审阶段羁押期限最长不超过6个月，但特殊情况下根据需要可报请最高人民法院批准再行延长。

一审判决的种类主要包括以下几种：A. 案件事实清楚，证据确实、充分，依据法律认定被告人有罪的，应当作出有罪判决；B. 依据法律认定被告人无罪的，应当作出无罪判决；C. 证据不足，不能认定被告人有罪的，应当作出证据不足、指控的犯罪不能成立的无罪判决(《刑事诉讼法》第195条)。

5. 第五阶段：第二审

第二审又称上诉审，是指第二审人民法院根据上诉人的上诉或者人民检察院的抗诉，就第一审人民法院尚未发生法律效力的判决或裁定认定的事实和适用的法律进行审理时所应当遵循的阶段。在中国刑事诉讼程序中，上诉审分为开庭审理和不开庭审理两种方式。对于下列案件，应当组成合议庭，开庭审理：(1) 被告人、自诉人及其法定代理人对第一审认定的事实、证据提出异议，可能影响定罪量刑的上诉案件；(2) 被告人被判处死刑的上诉案件；(3) 人民检察院抗诉的案件；(4) 其他应当开庭审理的案件(《刑事诉讼法》第223条第1款)。第二审人民法院开庭审理的程序，基本上参照第一审程序进行。不开庭审理的方式，也需要组成合议庭，通过讯问被告人以及听取其他当事人、辩护人和诉讼代理人的意见等方式，最终作出裁判(《刑事诉讼法》第223条第2款)。

在第二审阶段，第二审人民法院受理上诉、抗诉案件，应当在2个月以内审结(《刑事诉讼法》第232条)。另外还有两种例外情形：(1) 对于可能判处死刑的案件或者附带民事诉讼的案件，以及交通十分不便的边远地区的重大复杂案件、重大的犯罪集团案件、流窜作案的重大复杂案件或犯罪涉及面广,取证困难的重大复杂案件,经省级人民法院批准,可以延长 2 个月;(2)因特殊情况还需要延长的,报请最高人民法院批准延长(《刑事诉讼法》第 232 条),每次可延长 1—3 个月(最高人民法院《关于适用〈中华人民共和国刑事诉讼法〉的解释》第 173 条第 2 款),但此种延长的例外情形较少适用。即第二审阶段羁押期限最长不超过 4 个月,但特殊情况下可以根据需要报请最高人民法院批准再行延长。

6. 第六阶段:执行

执行,是指人民法院将已经发生法律效力的判决、裁定交付执行机关,将其所确定的内容依法付诸实施的阶段。执行是刑事诉讼的最后一个阶段。

此外,对于死刑案件还专门规定死刑复核程序。死刑复核程序是法院对被判处死刑的案件予以审查核准的特殊审判程序,体现了中国法律对于死刑适用的慎用和严格适用的态度。根据中国刑事诉讼法的规定,判处死刑立即执行的案件由最高人民法院统一进行核准。最高人民法院复核死刑案件,应当讯问被告人,辩护律师提出要求的,应当听取辩护律师的意见(《刑事诉讼法》第 240 条)。判处死刑缓期两年执行案件则由省一级的高级人民法院进行复核。

7. 关于黄海勇被引渡前在秘鲁被羁押的时间可否在中国所判刑期中折抵。

根据中国法律规定,先行羁押期限折抵刑期以被告人被判处有期自由刑为前提。如果被告人被判处无期徒刑,由于无期徒刑的性质而无法进行刑期折抵。中国《刑法》第 41、44、47 条规定了有期自由刑的折抵问题。根据该规定,判决以前先行羁押的,羁押 1 日折抵管制刑期 2 日,折抵拘役或有期徒刑 1 日。虽然上述规定中的"先行羁押"没有明确是否包含"域外先行羁押"的情况,但作为中国《刑法》的规定,该规定应当只适用于在中国国内的羁押。

关于域外羁押期限与回国后判处的有期自由刑的折抵问题,中国法律没有明确规定。虽然中国《刑法》第 10 条规定"凡在中华人民共和国领域外犯罪,依照本法应当负刑事责任的,虽然经过外国审判,仍然可以依照本法追究,但是在外国已经受过刑罚处罚的,可以免除或者减轻处罚。"但在黄海勇案件中,因为黄海勇在秘鲁尚未受过刑罚处罚(而只是受到羁押),因此不能适用该条之规定。

虽然中国法律没有明确规定域外羁押期限与回国后所判有期自由刑的折抵问题,但我们认为,从法理上来讲,基于中国(请求国)请求而进行的域外羁押,可以考虑折抵回国后被判处的有期自由刑。中国《引渡法》第14条规定:"请求国请求引渡,应当作出如下保证……请求国提出请求后撤销、放弃引渡请求,或者提出引渡请求错误的,由请求国承担因请求引渡对被请求引渡人造成损害的责任。"该条规定实际上体现了"引渡请求国应当承担被请求国根据本国引渡请求所采取的一切措施的法律后果"的精神实质,那么基于中国请求而采取的羁押等刑事强制措施所产生的法律后果,自然也应当由中国承担。黄海勇案件中,武汉市海关走私犯罪侦查局(2003年之后,经国务院批准,海关总署走私犯罪侦查局更名为海关总署缉私局,下属的武汉海关走私犯罪侦查局更名为武汉海关缉私局)于2001年3月16日对黄海勇签发逮捕证,同年6月26日中国警方通过国际刑警组织签发红色通报,希望各成员国逮捕黄海勇并引渡给中国。2008年10月27日,秘鲁警方根据该红色通报拘捕黄海勇,黄海勇随后被羁押。所以,黄海勇在秘鲁被执行的羁押实际上是中国以引渡为目的而请求秘鲁所采取的刑事强制措施,中国可以考虑承认并承担该羁押所产生的相应法律后果。

因此,黄海勇回国后如果被判处有期自由刑,在秘鲁被羁押期限可以考虑折抵回国后所判刑期,具体折抵方法可以参考中国刑法第41、44、47条之规定;但如果被判处无期徒刑,则没有刑期折抵问题。

(四)中国刑事诉讼的原则。

中国刑事诉讼法规定了一系列原则,以保障刑事诉讼的顺利进行,主要包括:

1. 侦查权、检察权、审判权由专门机关依法行使原则

对刑事案件的侦查、拘留、执行逮捕、预审,由公安机关负责。检察、批准逮捕、检察机关直接受理案件的侦查、提起公诉,由人民检察院负责。审

判由人民法院负责。除法律特别规定的以外,其他任何机关、团体和个人都无权行使这些权力(《刑事诉讼法》第3条第1款)。

2. 严格遵守法律程序原则

人民法院、人民检察院和公安机关在进行刑事诉讼活动时,必须严格遵守刑事诉讼法和其他有关法律的规定,不得违反法律规定的程序和规则,更不得侵害各方当事人和其他诉讼参与人的合法权益。违反法律程序严重的,应当依法承担相应的法律后果(《刑事诉讼法》第3条第2款)。

3. 以事实为根据、以法律为准绳原则

以事实为根据,就是将客观存在的情况作为处理案件的根据,处理案件不能违背已经查明的事实,也不能在没有查明事实的情况下武断来处理案件。以法律为准绳,就是指公安司法机关对案件的实体问题和程序问题作出处理,必须以刑法、刑事诉讼法和其他相关法律的规定为标准和尺度(《刑事诉讼法》第6条)。

4. 人民法院、人民检察院依法独立行使职权原则

人民法院依照法律规定独立行使审判权,人民检察院依照法律规定独立行使检察权,不受行政机关、社会团体和个人的干涉(《刑事诉讼法》第5条)。

5. 分工负责、互相配合、互相制约原则

"分工负责",是指人民法院、人民检察院和公安机关在刑事诉讼中根据法律有明确的职权分工,应当在法定范围内行使职权,各司其职。"互相配合",是指人民法院、人民检察院和公安机关进行刑事诉讼,应当在分工负责的基础上,相互支持,通力合作,使案件的处理能够上下衔接,协调一致,共同完成查明案件事实,追究、惩罚犯罪的任务。"互相制约",是指人民法院、人民检察院和公安机关进行刑事诉讼,应当按照诉讼职能的分工和程序上的设置,相互约束,相互制衡,以防止发生错误或及时纠正错误(《刑事诉讼法》第7条)。

6. 人民检察院依法对刑事诉讼实行法律监督原则

人民检察院是国家的法律监督机关,在刑事诉讼活动中,有权对公安机关的立案侦查、法院的审判和执行机关的执行活动是否合法进行监督。这

种监督贯穿于刑事诉讼活动的始终(《刑事诉讼法》第 8 条)。

7. 犯罪嫌疑人、被告人有权获得辩护原则

人民法院、人民检察院和公安机关应当保障犯罪嫌疑人、被告人和其他诉讼参与人依法享有的辩护权和其他诉讼权利(《刑事诉讼法》第 14 条)。

8. 未经人民法院依法判决,对任何人都不得确定有罪原则

确定被告人有罪的权力由人民法院统一行使,其他任何机关、团体和个人都无权行使。人民法院判决被告人有罪,必须严格依照法定程序,在保障被告人享有充分的辩护权的基础上,依法组成审判庭进行公正、公开的审理(《刑事诉讼法》第 12 条)。

9. 审判公开原则

详见下面(五)部分。

10. 两审终审原则

两审终审,是指一个案件经过两级人民法院审判即告终结的制度,对于第二审人民法院作出的终审判决、裁定,当事人等不得再提出上诉,人民检察院不得按照上诉审程序提出抗诉(《刑事诉讼法》第 10 条)。两审终审原则保证两级法院审理案件,有助于保障案件审理的正确与公正。

(五)详细说明中国刑事诉讼整个过程的公开或不公开性,以及参与的诉讼各方。

中国刑事诉讼的审前阶段(即侦查和审查起诉阶段)以不公开进行为原则,但刑事诉讼的进展情况对于犯罪嫌疑人及其近亲属则是公开的。例如,在拘留之后,除无法通知或者涉嫌危害国家安全犯罪、恐怖活动犯罪若通知可能有碍侦查的情形以外,均应当在 24 小时以内通知被拘留人的家属。有碍侦查的情形消失以后,应当立即通知被拘留人的家属(《刑事诉讼法》第 83 条);在逮捕之后,除无法通知的以外,应当在 24 小时以内,通知被逮捕人的家属。

审前阶段的诉讼参与各方主要包括侦查机关(通常为公安机关)、检察机关、犯罪嫌疑人、犯罪嫌疑人的辩护人、被害人、证人、鉴定人等其他诉讼参与人。

中国刑事诉讼审判程序适用审判公开原则,即人民法院审理案件和宣

告判决向社会公开,允许人民群众旁听,允许新闻记者采访报道。这一原则也是中国宪法所规定的一项基本原则(《宪法》第 125 条)。中国刑事诉讼法也规定了审判公开的例外情形,包括:(1) 有关国家秘密或个人隐私的案件,不公开审理;(2) 涉及商业秘密的案件,当事人申请不公开审理的,可以不公开审理;(3) 审判时被告人不满 18 周岁的案件,不公开审理(《刑事诉讼法》第 11 条、183 条、274 条)。对于上述不公开审理的案件,不公开的范围仅限于法庭审理阶段,宣判仍然要公开进行(《刑事诉讼法》第 196 条第 1 款)。鉴于黄海勇案件的具体情况,显然并不属于上述三类不公开审理的案件,因而该案的审理应当会公开进行。

审判阶段的诉讼参与各方主要包括公诉机关(检察机关)、人民法院、被告人、被告人的辩护人、被害人、证人、鉴定人等其他诉讼参与人。

(六) 法律有关上诉问题的规定。

1. 上诉审的提起

上诉审的提起有两种方式:上诉和抗诉。其中上诉权是被告人享有的一项重要诉讼权利,中国刑事诉讼法明确规定,对被告人的上诉权,不得以任何借口加以剥夺或限制(《刑事诉讼法》第 216 条第 3 款);同时,被告人的辩护人和近亲属在征得被告人同意后也可以提起上诉(《刑事诉讼法》第 216 条第 1 款)。

另外一种提起上诉审的方式,是与作出一审裁判的法院同级的人民检察院认为该法院作出的判决、裁定确有错误时,应当向上一级人民法院提出抗诉(《刑事诉讼法》第 217 条)。

2. 上诉理由

关于被告人提起上诉的理由没有规定任何限制,只要在法定期限内提出上诉,不论理由是否充分,都会引起上诉审程序。而检察机关的抗诉,只有在有充分的根据认定原裁判"确有错误"时才能提起(《刑事诉讼法》第 217 条)。

3. 上诉不加刑原则

为了充分保障被告人的上诉权,使其能够没有顾虑地行使其上诉权,中国刑事诉讼法的上诉审程序规定了上诉不加刑原则,即第二审人民法院审判只有被告人单方上诉的案件,不得以任何理由加重被告人刑罚的一项审判原则。但若是检察院同时提起抗诉的案件,则不受上诉不加刑原则的限制。第二审人民法院审理被告人或者他的法定代理人、辩护人、近亲属上诉的案件,不得加重被告人的刑罚。第二审人民法院发回原审人民法院重新审判的案件,除非有新的犯罪事实,人民检察院补充起诉的以外,原审人民法院也不得加重被告人的刑罚(《刑事诉讼法》第226条)。

4. 上诉审的管辖法院和检察院

上诉审的管辖法院是一审法院的上级法院,具体到黄海勇案件中,如果由主要犯罪地的武汉市中级人民法院进行一审,则上诉审的管辖法院是湖北省高级人民法院。对于人民检察院提出抗诉的案件或者第二审人民法院开庭审理的公诉案件,应当由与第二审人民法院同级的人民检察院派员出席法庭(《刑事诉讼法》第224条),具体到黄海勇案件中则是湖北省人民检察院。

5. 审理期限

第二审人民法院受理上诉、抗诉案件,应当在2个月以内审结。对于可能判处死刑的案件或者附带民事诉讼的案件,以及交通十分不便的边远地区的重大复杂案件、重大的犯罪集团案件、流窜作案的重大复杂案件或犯罪涉及面广,取证困难的重大复杂案件,经省级人民法院批准,可以延长2个月。即第二审案件的审理期限可达到4个月。若因特殊情况还需要延长的,报请最高人民法院批准延长(《刑事诉讼法》第232条)。

6. 上诉审的程序

在中国刑事诉讼程序中,上诉审分为开庭审理和不开庭审理两种方式。对于下列案件,应当组成合议庭,开庭审理:(1)被告人、自诉人及其法定代理人对第一审认定的事实、证据提出异议,可能影响定罪量刑的上诉案件;(2)被告人被判处死刑的上诉案件;(3)人民检察院抗诉的案件;(4)其他应当开庭审理的案件(《刑事诉讼法》第223条第1款)。第二审人民法院开庭审理的程序,基本上参照第一审程序进行。不开庭审理的方式,也需要组成合议庭,通过讯问被告人以及听取其他当事人、辩护人和诉讼代理人的意见等方式,最终作出裁判(《刑事诉讼法》第223条第2款)。

7. 上诉审的宣判

第二审法院对不服第一审判决的上诉、抗诉案件进行审理后,应按案件的不同情况作出裁判:(1)原判决认定事实正确和适用法律正确、量刑适当的,应当裁定驳回上诉或抗诉,维持原判。(2)原判决认定事实没有错误,但适用法律有错误或者量刑不当的,例如,混淆了罪与非罪的界限,认定犯罪性质不准,罪名不当,量刑畸轻、畸重,或者重罪轻判、轻罪重判等,第二审法院应当撤销原判,重新判决,并在判决中阐明改判的根据和理由。(3)原判决事实不清楚或者证据不足的,既可以由二审法院查清事实后改判,也可以裁定撤销原判,发回原审人民法院重新审判。(4)发现一审法院有违反法律规定的诉讼程序的情形的,应当裁定撤销原判,发回原审人民法院重新审判(《刑事诉讼法》第 225 条、227 条)。

8. 上诉审裁判的效力

中国刑事诉讼实行两审终审制,即一个案件经过两级人民法院审判即告终结的制度。第二审人民法院作出的判决或裁定,除死刑案件外,都是终审的判决和裁定,一经宣告即发生法律效力,被告人不得再行上诉,检察机关也不得按照二审程序提起抗诉(《刑事诉讼法》第 10 条、233 条)。

(七)是否存在如人身保护令或庇护等快速司法保护机制?

中国刑事诉讼中目前没有人身保护令程序。但对于羁押期间和侦查活动可能侵犯犯罪嫌疑人、被告人的基本权利,规定有其他的保护措施。

中国宪法和检察院组织法规定,检察机关是与法院并列的司法机关,检察机关代表司法机关审查批准逮捕、对是否有必要继续进行羁押进行审查并对侦查机关的侦查活动是否合法进行监督(《宪法》第 129 条、131 条;《人民检察院组织法》第 5 条)。

在中国刑事诉讼程序中,除了检察机关以外,还有其他主体可以对审前羁押与侦查活动提出质疑和进行监督:一是犯罪嫌疑人、被告人及其辩护人和其他利害关系人可以对审前羁押和侦查活动中的不当行为提出申诉和控告(《刑事诉讼法》第 115 条);二是人大代表、专家学者等人员可以以"特邀监督员"的形式,巡查监督看守所的看管活动,并对其中的不当处遇或侵犯权利的行为提出意见(公安部监所管理局 2011 年 9 月 13 日印发《看守所特邀监督员巡查监督工作规定》)。

(八)检察院的职权或在刑事诉讼全过程中承担该职权的机关?

在中国刑事诉讼中,检察机关承担以下职责:

1. 审查批准逮捕

根据中国刑事诉讼法的规定,检察机关享有批准逮捕的权力,对于侦查阶段报送逮捕的案件,检察机关的侦查监督部门必须作出批准逮捕或不批准逮捕的决定(《刑事诉讼法》第88条)。人民检察院审查批准逮捕,可以讯问犯罪嫌疑人;有下列情形之一的,应当讯问犯罪嫌疑人:A. 对是否符合逮捕条件有疑问的;B. 犯罪嫌疑人要求向检察人员当面陈述的;C. 侦查活动可能有重大违法行为的(《刑事诉讼法》第86条)。之所以要求检察机关在审查批准逮捕时讯问犯罪嫌疑人,目的在于通过讯问犯罪嫌疑人对侦查机关的侦查活动进行监督,避免不必要的审前羁押,保障犯罪嫌疑人的权利。审查批准逮捕同时也是对侦查机关侦查活动的一种监督。

2. 羁押必要性审查

在批准逮捕以后,检察机关有权根据案件的具体情况对是否有必要继续进行审前羁押进行羁押必要性审查。人民检察经审查认为不需要继续羁押的,应当建议有关机关予以释放或者变更强制措施。有关机关应当在10日内将处理情况通知人民检察院(《刑事诉讼法》第93条)。上述规定有助于减少或缩短不必要的审前羁押,保障犯罪嫌疑人、被告人的人身自由权利。

3. 审查起诉

对于侦查终结后侦查机关报请提起公诉的案件,由检察机关的公诉部门进行审查,以决定是否提起公诉。检察机关在审查起诉时应当讯问犯罪嫌疑人(《刑事诉讼法》第170条),对于犯罪嫌疑人没有犯罪事实,或者犯罪情节、依照刑法规定不需要判处刑罚或者免除刑罚的,人民检察院可以作出不起诉决定(《刑事诉讼法》第167条、170、173条)。人民检察院认为犯罪嫌疑人的犯罪事实已经查清,证据确实、充分,依法应当追究刑事责任的,应当作出起诉决定,按照审判管辖的规定,向人民法院提起公诉,并将案卷材料、证据移送人民法院(《刑事诉讼法》第172条)。

4. 通过其他方式对侦查机关的侦查活动进行监督

检察机关还可以通过受理犯罪嫌疑人、被告人及其辩护人等的申诉或控告等方式对侦查机关的侦查活动进行监督,要求侦查机关纠正其违法行为(《刑事诉讼法》第115条第2款)。

5. 出庭支持公诉

公诉人受人民检察院指派,出庭支持公诉,主要目的在于代表国家指控、揭露和证实犯罪,提请人民法院对被告人依法审判。具体的职责包括宣读起诉书、讯问被告人、对证人与鉴定人等进行发问、出示物证、与被告人及其辩护人进行辩论等(《刑事诉讼法》第186—193条)。

6. 二审抗诉及出席二审法庭

地方各级人民检察院认为本级人民法院第一审的判决、裁定确有错误的时候,应当向上一级人民法院提出抗诉(《刑事诉讼法》第217条)。被害人及其法定代理人不服地方各级人民法院第一审的判决的,也可以请求人民检察院提出抗诉(《刑事诉讼法》第218条)。对于检察机关抗诉的案件以及第二审人民法院决定开庭审理的公诉案件,同级人民检察院都应当派员出席法庭(《刑事诉讼法》第224条)。

7. 再审抗诉

最高人民检察院对各级人民法院已经发生法律效力的判决和裁定,上级人民检察院对下级人民法院已经发生法律效力的判决和裁定,如果发现确有错误,有权按照审判监督程序向同级人民法院提出抗诉(《刑事诉讼法》第243条第3款)。

8. 对刑罚执行活动进行监督

作为国家的法律监督机关,人民检察院依法对执行活动的合法性进行监督。例如,人民法院在交付执行死刑前,应当通知同级人民检察院派员临场监督(《刑事诉讼法》第252条规定);人民检察院对决定暂予监外执行、减刑、假释以及罪犯在服刑期间又犯罪等情况实行监督(《刑事诉讼法》第255、256、262条);人民检察院对执行机关执行刑罚的活动是否合法实行监督。如果发现有违法的情况,应当通知执行机关纠正(《刑事诉讼法》第265条)。

（九）被起诉人的法律代表（律师）的介入和职权。

关于被追诉人的法律代表及其职权，中国刑事诉讼法作了明确而全面的规定。

1. 委托辩护律师

明确规定犯罪嫌疑人、被告人除自己行使辩护权以外，还可以委托1—2位律师担任辩护人（《刑事诉讼法》第32条第1款）。

犯罪嫌疑人、被告人完全可以按照自己的意愿来委托辩护律师，犯罪嫌疑人、被告人被羁押的，也可以由其监护人、近亲属代为委托辩护人（《刑事诉讼法》第33条第3款）。

2. 何时可以委托辩护律师？

明确规定犯罪嫌疑人在刑事诉讼开始时就可以委托辩护律师。犯罪嫌疑人自被侦查机关第一次讯问或者采取强制措施之日起，有权委托辩护律师，侦查机关在第一次讯问犯罪嫌疑人或者对犯罪嫌疑人采取强制措施的时候，负有告知犯罪嫌疑人有权委托辩护人的义务（《刑事诉讼法》第33条第1款、第2款）。这一规定也就意味着，犯罪嫌疑人在被羁押期间甚至羁押之前就可以获得辩护律师提供的法律帮助。

3. 法律援助辩护

中国刑事诉讼法明确规定了法律援助辩护。犯罪嫌疑人、被告人因经济困难或者其他原因没有委托辩护人的，本人及其近亲属可以向法律援助机构提出申请。对符合法律援助条件的，法律援助机构应当指派律师为其提供辩护。犯罪嫌疑人、被告人可能被判处无期徒刑、死刑，没有委托辩护人的，人民法院、人民检察院和公安机关应当通知法律援助机构指派律师为其提供辩护（《刑事诉讼法》第34条）。中国法律援助辩护包括了从侦查到审判的完整阶段，这意味着在审前羁押阶段，犯罪嫌疑人就可以获得免费的律师帮助。

4. 辩护律师的诉讼权利

中国刑事诉讼法明确规定了辩护律师的各项权利及其行使，这些规定对于保障犯罪嫌疑人、被告人的辩护权具有重要意义。

(1) 辩护律师在审前羁押期间的主要权利。

A. 阅卷权。辩护律师自人民检察院对案件审查起诉之日起，可以查阅、摘抄、复制本案的案卷材料,无须获得办案机关许可(《刑事诉讼法》第38条)。案卷材料是指包括诉讼文书和证据材料在内的案卷中的所有材料。人民检察院和人民法院应当为辩护人查阅、摘抄、复制案卷材料提供便利和充分的时间。在侦查阶段,辩护律师虽然不享有阅卷权,但也可以向侦查机关了解犯罪嫌疑人涉嫌的罪名和案件有关情况,以准备辩护(《刑事诉讼法》第36条)。辩护律师在侦查期间可以向侦查机关了解的事项包括:犯罪嫌疑人涉嫌的罪名,当时已查明的该罪的主要事实,犯罪嫌疑人被采取、变更、解除强制措施的情况以及侦查机关延长侦查羁押期限等情况。

B. 会见通信权。辩护律师可以同在押的犯罪嫌疑人、被告人会见和通信。辩护律师要求会见在押的犯罪嫌疑人、被告人的,只需要携带律师执业证书、律师事务所证明和委托书或者法律援助公函,看守所应当及时安排会见,保证辩护律师在48小时以内见到在押的犯罪嫌疑人、被告人。辩护律师会见在押的犯罪嫌疑人、被告人,可以了解有关案件情况,提供法律咨询等;自案件移送审查起诉之日起,可以向犯罪嫌疑人、被告人核实有关证据。辩护律师会见犯罪嫌疑人、被告人时不被监听(《刑事诉讼法》第37条)。

C. 调查取证权。辩护律师经证人或者其他有关单位和个人同意,可以向他们收集与本案有关的材料;辩护律师经人民检察院或者人民法院许可,并且经被害人或者其近亲属、被害人提供的证人同意,可以向他们收集与本案有关的材料。辩护律师还可以申请人民检察院、人民法院代为调查取证以及申请人民检察院和人民法院调取未随案移送的证明犯罪嫌疑人、被告人无罪或罪轻的证据(《刑事诉讼法》第41条)。

D. 申请解除期限届满的强制措施的权利。犯罪嫌疑人、被告人及其法定代理人、近亲属或者辩护人对于人民法院、人民检察院或者公安机关采取强制措施期限届满的,有权要求解除强制措施,包括解除羁押予以释放(《刑事诉讼法》第97条)。

E. 提出意见权。辩护律师有权在不同诉讼阶段向办案机关提出辩护意见,有关办案机关必须听取(《刑事诉讼法》第36条、159条、170条、223条第2款)。

F. 申诉控告权。辩护律师认为公安机关、人民检察院、人民法院及其工作人员阻碍其依法行使诉讼权利的,有权向同级或者上一级人民检察院申诉或者控告。人民检察院对申诉或者控告应当及时进行审查,对情况属实的,通知有关机关予以纠正(《刑事诉讼法》第47条)。

G. 保密权。辩护律师对于在执业活动中知悉的委托人的有关情况和信息,有权予以保密(《刑事诉讼法》第46条)。

(2) 辩护律师在法庭审理阶段的主要权利包括:

辩护律师能够充分参与并发挥作用,享有参加法庭调查和辩论的权利。在法庭调查阶段,辩护人在公诉人讯问被告人后经审判长许可,可以向被告人发问(《刑事诉讼法》第186条第2款);经审判长许可,可以对证人、鉴定人发问(《刑事诉讼法》第189条);法庭审理中,辩护人有权申请通知新的证人到庭,调取新的物证,重新鉴定或者勘验(《刑事诉讼法》第192条第1款)。在法庭辩论阶段,辩护人可以对证据和案件情况发表意见并且可以和控方展开辩论(《刑事诉讼法》第193条第2款)。

(十) 在被判无期徒刑的情况下,是否存在再审的可能性?

中国刑事诉讼法规定了审判监督程序作为一种特殊的救济程序。审判监督程序是对已经发生法律效力的裁判,发现在认定事实或适用法律上确有错误,依法提起并对案件进行重新审理的特别审判程序。案件的当事人及其法定代理人、近亲属在原审裁判生效后,可以向人民法院或人民检察院提出申诉(《刑事诉讼法》第241条)。如果申诉满足下列条件之一,人民法院应当重新进行审判:(1) 有新的证据证明原判决、裁定认定的事实确有错误,可能影响定罪量刑的;(2) 据以定罪量刑的证据不确实、不充分、依法应当予以排除,或者证明案件事实的主要证据之间存在矛盾的;(3) 原判决、裁定适用法律确有错误的;(4) 违反法律规定的诉讼程序,可能影响公正审判的;(5) 审判人员在审理该案件的时候,有贪污受贿,徇私舞弊,枉法裁判行为的(《刑事诉讼法》第242条)。具体到黄海勇案件中,黄海勇若被定罪判刑,他在服刑期间可以自行或者由其近亲属向有关人民法院和人民检察院提出申诉,申诉也可以委托律师代为进行。申诉并没有明确的时间限制,在原审判决生效后的10年、20年甚至30年以后都可以提出。

人民法院按照审判监督程序重新审判案件,由原审人民法院审理的,应当另行组成合议庭进行。参与过本案第一审、第二审、复核程序审判的合议庭组成人员，不得参与本案的再审程序的审判。人民法院按照审判监督程序重新审判的案件，如果原来是第一审案件，应当依照第一审程序进行审判，所作的判决、裁定，可以上诉、抗诉；如果原来是第二审案件，或者是上级人民法院提审的案件，应当依照第二审程序进行审判，所作的判决、裁定，是终审的判决、裁定(《刑事诉讼法》第245条)。人民法院按照审判监督程序重新审判的案件，应当在作出提审、再审决定之日起3个月以内审结，需要延长期限的，不得超过6个月(《刑事诉讼法》第247条第1款)。

案件经过重新审理后，应按案件的不同情况作出裁判：(1)原判决、裁定认定事实和适用法律正确、量刑适当的，应当裁定驳回申诉或者抗诉，维持原判决、裁定。(2)原判决、裁定定罪准确、量刑适当，但在认定事实、适用法律等方面有瑕疵的，应当裁定纠正并维持原判决、裁定。(3)原判决、裁定认定事实没有错误，但适用法律有错误，或者量刑不当的，应当撤销原判决、裁定，予以改判。(4)依照第二审程序审理的案件，原判决、裁定事实不清或者证据不足的，可以在查清事实后改判，也可以裁定撤销原判，发回原审人民法院重新审判。(5)原判决、裁定事实不清或者证据不足，经审理事实已经查清的，应当根据查清的事实依法裁判；事实仍无法查清，证据不足，不能认定被告人有罪的，应当撤销原判决、裁定，判决宣告被告人无罪(最高人民法院《关于适用〈中华人民共和国刑事诉讼法〉的解释》第389条)。

（十一）确定被起诉人或被判决人关押的有关准则？以及负责执行该关押决定的机关？

1. 审前羁押（预防性关押）

关于审前羁押，中国刑事诉讼法规定了拘留和逮捕两种羁押性的强制措施。

拘留是在侦查过程中，遇有紧急情况下，依法临时剥夺现行犯或者有重大犯罪嫌疑者的人身自由的一种强制措施。拘留的审前羁押期限一般情况下最多为14日，对于流窜作案、多次作案、结伙作案的，拘留的羁押期限可以延长至最多37日，之后检察机关必须作出批准逮捕或不批准逮捕的决定，如果不批准逮捕,则会立即释放犯罪嫌疑人或者转为取保候审、监视居住等非羁押性强制措施(《刑事诉讼法》第89条)。如果批准逮捕,则在逮捕后会继续进行羁押。

逮捕是一种较长时间的剥夺人身自由的强制措施。中国刑事诉讼法规定了三种逮捕条件。(1)对有证据证明有犯罪事实,可能判处徒刑以上刑罚的犯罪嫌疑人、被告人,采取取保候审尚不足以防止发生下列社会危险性的,应当予以逮捕:A.可能实施新的犯罪的;B.有危害国家安全、公共安全或者社会秩序的现实危险的;C.可能毁灭、伪造证据,干扰证人作证或者串供的;D.可能对被害人、举报人、控告人实施打击报复的;E.企图自杀或者逃跑的。(2)对有证据证明有犯罪事实,可能判处十年有期徒刑以上刑罚的,或者有证据证明有犯罪事实,可能判处徒刑以上刑罚,曾经故意犯罪或者身份不明的,应当予以逮捕。(3)被取保候审、监视居住的犯罪嫌疑人、被告人违反取保候审、监视居住规定,情节严重的,可以予以逮捕(《刑事诉讼法》第79条)。中国刑事诉讼法对逮捕后的审前羁押期限按照诉讼阶段分别进行了规定(详见上文对中国刑事诉讼主要诉讼阶段的介绍),下表对逮捕后审前羁押和审判阶段羁押的期限予以列明。

表1 中国《刑事诉讼法》规定的逮捕后审前和审判阶段羁押期限

审前阶段（至少13.5个月）	侦查阶段（至少7个月）	一般情形	2个月
		案情复杂、期限届满不能终结,经上一级人民检察院批准	延长1个月
		交通十分不便的边远地区的重大复杂案件、重大的犯罪集团案件、流窜作案的重大复杂案件和犯罪涉及面广,取证困难的重大复杂案件,经省级人民检察院批准或者决定	再延长2个月
		对犯罪嫌疑人可能判处10年有期徒刑以上刑罚,经省级人民检察院批准或者决定	再延长2个月
		发现犯罪嫌疑人另有重要罪行的	自发现之日起重新计算侦查羁押期限
	审查起诉阶段（至少6.5个月）	一般情形	1个月
		重大复杂的案件	延长0.5个月
		需要补充侦查的案件(补充侦查以2次为限)	最长不超过6.5个月

续表

审判阶段（至少10个月）	一审阶段（至少6个月）	一般情形	2个月，至迟不超过3个月
		可能判处死刑的案件或者附带民事诉讼的案件，以及交通十分不便的边远地区的重大复杂案件、重大的犯罪集团案件、流窜作案的重大复杂案件或犯罪涉及面广，取证困难的重大复杂案件，经上一级人民法院批准	延长3个月
		因特殊情况还需要延长的，报请最高人民法院批准延长	每次可延长1—3个月
	二审阶段（至少4个月）	一般情形	2个月
		可能判处死刑的案件或者附带民事诉讼的案件，以及交通十分不便的边远地区的重大复杂案件、重大的犯罪集团案件、流窜作案的重大复杂案件或犯罪涉及面广，取证困难的重大复杂案件，经省级人民法院批准	延长2个月
		因特殊情况还需要延长的，报请最高人民法院批准延长	每次可延长1—3个月

中国《刑事诉讼法》还规定，对于犯罪嫌疑人、被告人被羁押的案件，不能在上述规定的侦查羁押、审查起诉、一审、二审期限内办结的，对犯罪嫌疑人、被告人应当予以释放；需要继续查证、审理的，对犯罪嫌疑人、被告人可以取保候审或者监视居住（《刑事诉讼法》第96条）。

审前羁押一般在办案机关所在区、县的看守所，由公安机关执行。

2. 已决羁押

对被判处死刑缓期二年执行、无期徒刑、有期徒刑的罪犯，由公安机关依法将该罪犯送交监狱执行刑罚。对被判处有期徒刑的罪犯，在被交付执行刑罚前，剩余刑期在3个月以下的，由看守所代为执行（《刑事诉讼法》第253条第2款）。服刑人员一般会被送至其户籍所在地的监狱进行服刑，以便家属探监和回归社会。

在黄海勇案件中，他若被定罪判刑后有可能被送至其户籍所在地广东省下属的监狱服刑，其服刑监狱的管理机构为广东省司法厅下属的监狱管理局。

（十二）中华人民共和国监禁制度的核心内容。

根据中国监狱法规定，中国监狱依法收押改造经人民法院判处死刑缓期二年执行、无期徒刑、有期徒刑的罪犯。中国监狱实行部、省两级管理，以省为主的管理体制。司法部监狱管理局主管全国监狱工作，直接管理部直属监狱。各省（区、市）监狱管理局直接管理本辖区的监狱。中国监狱认真贯彻"惩罚与改造相结合、以改造人为宗旨"的监狱工作方针，坚持把降低刑满释放人员重新违法犯罪率作为衡量监管工作的"首要标准"，坚持把教育改造罪犯作为监狱工作的中心任务，健全教育改造制度和工作体系，积极创新教育改造模式和方式方法。长期以来，中国监狱始终坚持严格公正文明执法，确保罪犯在公平公正的法制环境下接受教育改造；采取多项措施，实现监狱持续安全稳定，确保在安全稳定的环境下对罪犯实施教育改造。中国监狱全面推行一周五天劳动教育、一天课堂教育、一天休息的教育改造模式，大力加强对罪犯的道德、法制、文化、管理、劳动教育，广泛开展心理咨询、心理矫治和个别化教育，广泛开展监狱（监区）文化建设，充分利用社会资源开展社会帮教，罪犯教育改造质量不断提高；普遍开展罪犯职业技能培训，建立完善劳动培训制度，提高罪犯刑满释放后适应社会的能力。①

中国法律规定了服刑人员在服刑期间的权利，包括：罪犯的人格不受侮辱，其人身安全、合法财产和辩护、申诉、控告、检举以及其他未被依法剥夺或者限制的权利不受侵犯（《监狱法》第7条）。关于如何保障其权利，还规定了具体的监督机制和救济途径则包括：（1）服刑人员可以向监狱的上级管理机构写信反映问题，而且这些信件不受检查（《监狱法》第47条）。（2）对于监管人员在刑罚执行期间的违法行为，服刑人员及其家属可以向驻监检察室的检察官控告、举报。检察机关作为法律监督机关，负有对刑事案件判决、裁定的执行和监狱等刑罚执行机关的活动是否合法进行监督的责任。对于服刑人员及其家属的控告、举报，驻监检察室应当依法受理（《监狱法》第6条、《人民检察院监狱检察办法》第6章）。

---

① 以上内容摘自中国司法部监狱管理局邵雷局长于2013年12月4日在河南郑州举行的"中英监狱管理研讨会"上的发言，可参见司法部网站http://www.moj.gov.cn/jyglj/content/2014-03/25/content_5393650.htm?node=253。

二、与黄海勇案直接有关的事项

（一）特别提及指控黄海勇并由此向秘鲁提出引渡请求的事实及罪名（洗钱、走私）。

1. 涉嫌走私普通货物的案件事实与性质

根据中国海关总署提供的资料,1996—1998 年间,黄海勇以自己任法人代表的 4 家公司和其余 9 家公司共同合谋,于 1996 年 8 月、12 月和 1997 年 1 月采取虚假手段向武汉海关分三次骗领进料加工均为 2 万吨毛豆油的 C47006100042 号手册(简称 42 号手册)、C47006100175 号进料加工手册(简称 175 号手册)和 C47007100051 号手册(简称 51 号手册),此后分别利用上述 42 号手册、175 号手册、51 号手册进口毛豆油 19 925 吨、19 942 吨、20 000 吨。此外,黄海勇走私集团还以丰润保税库名义进口毛豆油 47 560 吨。即黄海勇走私集团共计走私进口毛豆油 10.74 万余吨,毛豆油完税价格 498 039 063 元,偷逃应缴税款 7.17 亿元。上述 10.74 万吨保税毛豆油逃避海关监管,且未经海关许可并在境内全部倒卖。

黄海勇采取欺骗手段在进口货物的过程中偷逃应缴税款,其行为涉嫌构成中国《刑法》第 153 条的走私普通货物罪。黄海勇走私普通货物,偷逃应缴税款 7.17 亿元,远远高于中国走私货物"偷逃应缴税额特别巨大"的认定标准(即个人偷逃应缴税额 50 万元以上、单位偷逃应缴税额 250 万元以上,参见最高人民法院法《关于审理走私犯罪案件适用法律有关问题的通知》),依照中国刑法,对其应当判处"十年以上有期徒刑或者无期徒刑,并处偷逃应缴税额一倍以上五倍以下罚金或者没收财产",并对构成走私普通货物罪的单位判处罚金(《刑法》第 153 条)。

2. 涉嫌洗钱的案件事实与性质

根据中国海关总署提供的资料,1998 年 8 月 20 日,黄海勇将走私赃款中的 404.6 万美元通过香港华侨商业银行分三次转移至境外。其中汇往美国洛杉矶 17.8 万美元,汇往美国纽约 257.9 万美元,汇往秘鲁首都利马 128.9 万美元。

黄海勇的这一行为属于明知是走私犯罪所得,"通过转账或者其他结算方式协助资金转移"(《刑法》第191条),其行为涉嫌构成中国《刑法》第191条的洗钱罪。由于黄海勇涉嫌洗钱的数额高达404.6万美元,数额特别巨大,属于"情节严重"的洗钱行为,因此其洗钱罪一旦成立将可能被判处"五年以上十年以下有期徒刑,并处洗钱数额百分之五以上百分之二十以下罚金"(《刑法》第191条)。

(二)对这些罪名比较区分,重点介绍申请引渡黄海勇时适用刑法中对每项罪名的刑罚和修改法律后现行法律规定的刑罚;提出引渡黄海勇申请的法律依据?

1. 涉嫌的走私普通货物、物品罪的罪名及其刑罚

关于走私普通货物、物品罪,中国2011年《刑法修正案(八)》第27条规定:"将刑法第一百五十三条第一款修改为:'走私本法第一百五十一条、第一百五十二条、第三百四十七条规定以外的货物、物品的,根据情节轻重,分别依照下列规定处罚:(一)走私货物、物品偷逃应缴税额较大或者一年内曾因走私被给予二次行政处罚后又走私的,处三年以下有期徒刑或者拘役,并处偷逃应缴税额一倍以上五倍以下罚金。(二)走私货物、物品偷逃应缴税额巨大或者有其他严重情节的,处三年以上十年以下有期徒刑,并处偷逃应缴税额一倍以上五倍以下罚金。(三)走私货物、物品偷逃应缴税额特别巨大或者有其他特别严重情节的,处十年以上有期徒刑或者无期徒刑,并处偷逃应缴税额一倍以上五倍以下罚金或者没收财产。'"与刑法典原第153条关于走私普通货物、物品罪的规定相比,《刑法修正案(八)》对走私普通货物、物品罪主要作了以下修改:

第一,废止了走私普通货物、物品罪的死刑。中国刑法典原第153条第1款第1项规定,走私货物、物品,"情节特别严重的,依照本法第一百五十一条第四款的规定处罚"。而中国刑法典原第151条第4款规定:"犯第一款、第二款罪,情节特别严重的,处无期徒刑或者死刑,并处没收财产。"即中国1997年刑法典中对走私普通货物、物品罪规定有死刑。《刑法修正案(八)》删除了这一规定,废止了走私普通、货物罪的死刑。

第二,调整了走私普通货物、物品罪的定罪量刑标准。《刑法修正案

(八)》调整了刑法典原第 153 条第 1 款关于走私普通货物、物品罪法定刑的排列顺序并将其对应的偷逃应缴税额的数额分别修改为"数额特别巨大"、"数额巨大"和"数额较大"。

据此,走私货物、物品偷逃应缴税额特别巨大或者有其他特别严重情节的,处 10 年以上有期徒刑或者无期徒刑,并处偷逃应缴税额 1 倍以上 5 倍以下罚金或者没收财产。在黄海勇所在公司构成走私货物、物品罪时,对其公司可判处罚金。

2. 涉嫌的洗钱罪及其刑罚

关于洗钱罪,经 2006 年《刑法修正案(六)》修正的刑法典第 191 条规定:"明知是毒品犯罪、黑社会性质的组织犯罪、恐怖活动犯罪、走私犯罪、贪污贿赂犯罪、破坏金融管理秩序犯罪、金融诈骗犯罪的所得及其产生的收益,为掩饰、隐瞒其来源和性质,有下列行为之一的,没收实施以上犯罪的所得及其产生的收益,处五年以下有期徒刑或者拘役,并处或者单处洗钱数额百分之五以上百分之二十以下罚金;情节严重的,处五年以上十年以下有期徒刑,并处洗钱数额百分之五以上百分之二十以下罚金:(一)提供资金账户的;(二)协助将财产转换为现金、金融票据、有价证券的;(三)通过转账或者其他结算方式协助资金转移的;(四)协助将资金汇往境外的;(五)以其他方法掩饰、隐瞒犯罪所得及其收益的来源和性质的。""单位犯前款罪的,对单位判处罚金,并对其直接负责的主管人员和其他直接责任人员,处五年以下有期徒刑或者拘役。"据此,明知是走私犯罪所得及其产生的收益而仍然采取各种方式将资金汇往境外以掩饰、隐瞒其性质和来源的,可构成洗钱罪,情节严重的,将会被处以 5 年以上 10 年以下有期徒刑,并处洗钱数额 5%以上 20%以下罚金。

3. 提出引渡申请的法律依据

中国《引渡法》和《中华人民共和国和秘鲁共和国引渡条约》(以下简称"《中秘引渡条约》")是中方向秘鲁提出引渡黄海勇请求所依据的主要法律,双方所依据的主要条款包括但不限于下列条款:

(1)《引渡法》第 3 章(第 47 条至 51 条)为"向外国请求引渡",该章规定了中国向外国请求引渡的具体程序,中国可以依据该章之规定向秘鲁方面请求引渡黄海勇。

(2)《中秘引渡条约》第1条为"引渡义务",根据该条中秘双方有义务应对方的请求相互开展引渡合作,

(3)《中秘引渡条约》第2条为"可引渡的犯罪",根据该条,只有在引渡请求所针对的行为根据双方法律均构成犯罪,并均可判处1年有期徒刑以上刑罚或者其他更重的刑罚,才能同意引渡。黄海勇所实施的行为涉嫌走私普通货物罪、洗钱罪,根据中秘双方法律均构成犯罪,并被均可判处1年以上有期徒刑的刑罚。

(4)《中秘引渡条约》第3条为"应当拒绝引渡的理由",根据该条,在下列情况下应当拒绝引渡:A. 被请求方认为引渡请求所针对的犯罪是政治犯罪,或者被请求方已经给予被请求引渡人受庇护的权利;B. 被请求方有充分理由认为引渡请求是基于不正当的追诉目的;C. 根据请求方的法律,请求针对的犯罪仅是军事犯罪;D. 根据请求方的法律,由于时效已过或者赦免等原因,被请求引渡人已经被免予追诉或者免予执行刑罚;E. 被请求方已经对被请求引渡人就引渡请求所针对的犯罪做出终审判决或者终止诉讼程序;F. 根据请求方的法律,引渡请求所涉及的案件属于受害人告诉才处理的案件。黄海勇案件所涉及的犯罪不是政治犯罪、军事犯罪,引渡请求不是基于不正当的追诉目的,也不符合上述任何应当拒绝引渡的理由。

(5)《中秘引渡条约》第4条为"可以拒绝引渡的理由",规定了下列理由作为可以拒绝引渡的理由:A. 被请求方根据本国法律对引渡请求所针对的犯罪具有管辖权,并且对被请求引渡人就该犯罪正在进行刑事诉讼或者准备提起刑事诉讼;B. 被请求方认为由于被请求引渡人的年龄、健康或其他个人原因,引渡不符合人道主义考虑。黄海勇案件中,秘鲁方面并没有以上述理由拒绝引渡。

(三)当走私罪可判处死刑时,中国是否有被执行死刑的案例?

在《刑法修正案(八)》生效之前,中国对走私普通货物偷逃应缴税额在50万元以上,情节特别严重的,依法可判处犯罪分子死刑(《刑法》第153条)。在实践中,中国确实有对个别走私普通货物情节特别严重的犯罪分子适用死刑的案例。例如,中国曾对广东湛江"9898"特大走私、受贿系列案中

的走私集团首要分子林春华(走私成品油44船75.38万余吨,价额9.9亿余元,从中偷逃应缴税额3.47亿余元)适用了死刑。2007年中国对福建石狮张永记、邱宗闽(走私香烟酒偷逃应缴关税人民币967 079 100.93元)适用了死刑。

但从目前查询到的资料情况看,中国之前只对极个别的犯走私普通货物罪的犯罪分子执行了死刑,有的犯走私普通货物罪的犯罪分子虽被判处了死刑但同时被宣告了缓期二年执行。例如,中国1999年对广东省湛江市淇兴实业公司总经理林柏青(走私小麦、油菜籽等共偷逃应缴税款6041万元)就以犯走私普通货物罪判处死刑缓期二年执行,2002年对汕头和发(集团)有限公司储运部经理兼东海港务有限公司集装箱部负责人陈少伟(参与走私108次,偷逃应缴税额人民币5亿多元)也以犯走私普通货物罪,判处了死刑缓期二年执行。这些犯罪分子最终都没有被执行死刑。

(四) 中国《刑法修正案(八)》的修法范围和司法效力?除了走私罪,还有哪些罪名也涉及该修正案?推动《刑法修正案(八)》削减死刑罪名的主要原因是什么?

1.《刑法修正案(八)》的修法范围

《刑法修正案(八)》是中国近年来修法幅度最大也是最为全面的一次刑法修正,修改范围广泛,包括从宽和从严两个方面。其中,在从宽方面,该次刑法修正主要从五个方面体现了立法的从宽要求:(1) 取消13种经济性、非暴力犯罪的死刑;(2) 对已满75岁的人犯罪从宽,包括对已满75周岁的人犯罪从轻或者减轻处罚、对已满75周岁的人原则上不适用死刑以及对已满75周岁的人适用缓刑从宽;(3) 对未成年人犯罪进一步从宽,包括对未成年人犯罪适用缓刑从宽、未成年人犯罪不成立累犯、被判处5年有期徒刑以下刑罚的未成年人免除前科报告义务;(4) 对怀孕的妇女适用缓刑从宽;(5) 将坦白罪行由以前的司法中酌情适用的从宽情节上升为法定从宽情节。

在从严方面,中国主要是为了配合死刑的削减和限制适用,对死缓、无期徒刑和有期徒刑采取了适当从严的立法修正:(1) 规范并限制死缓犯的减刑,规定死缓犯有重大立功表现的,2年期满后由原来的减为15年以上20年以下延长至减为25年有期徒刑,同时增加了限制因累犯和因故意杀人、强奸、抢劫、绑架、放火、爆炸、投放危险物质或者有组织的暴力性犯罪被判处死缓的犯罪分子的减刑;(2)普遍延长了无期徒刑的实际执行刑期,将无期徒刑犯的实际执行最低刑期由原来的10年提高到13年;(3)有条件地提高了有期徒刑数罪并罚的刑期,将有期徒刑数罪并罚的最高刑期由原来的20年,调整为有期徒刑数罪并罚的总和刑期在35年以上的,最高可到25年。

在死刑罪名削减方面,《刑法修正案(八)》废止了13种经济性、非暴力性犯罪的死刑,其中除了走私普通货物、物品罪,还包括8种破坏市场经济秩序罪,即走私文物罪(《刑法》第151条第4款),走私贵重金属罪(《刑法》第151条第4款),走私珍贵动物、珍贵动物制品罪(《刑法》第151条第4款),票据诈骗罪(《刑法》第194条第1款),金融凭证诈骗罪(《刑法》第194条第2款),信用证诈骗罪(《刑法》第195条),虚开增值税专用发票、用于骗取出口退税、抵扣税款发票罪(《刑法》第205条),以及伪造、出售伪造的增值税专用发票罪(《刑法》第206条);1种侵犯财产罪,即盗窃罪(《刑法》第264条);3种妨害社会管理秩序罪,即传授犯罪方法罪(《刑法》第295条),盗掘古文化遗址、古墓葬罪(《刑法》第328条第1款),以及盗掘古人类化石、古脊椎动物化石罪(《刑法》第328条第2款)。

2. 推动《刑法修正案(八)》削减死刑罪名的主要原因

推动《刑法修正案(八)》削减死刑罪名的主要原因有三个方面:

(1)中国实现和谐社会、促进社会稳定与发展的需要。和谐社会建设被作为了中国现阶段社会发展的目标。和谐社会也是法治社会,健全、理性、高效的社会主义法治是实现和谐社会构想的基石。这对中国死刑制度改革提出了新的要求,要求其从构建和谐社会的宏伟目标出发,积极发挥作用,不断巩固和谐社会建设的成果,促进社会的稳定与发展。

(2)中国不断加强人权保障并顺应民众人权观念发展变化的需要。中国重视人权保障工作。2004年3月,"国家尊重和保障人权"被明确写入了中国宪法修正案,从而使中国人权保障上升到了宪政的高度。之后,中国政府提出将"加强人权保障,促进人权事业全面发展"作为中国第12个五年(2011—2015年)规范发展的目标之一。在中国政府和中国社会各界的不懈努力下,中国未来的人权事业必将得到全面发展。这也对与人权事业休戚相关的中国死刑制度改革提出了进一步的要求。同时,随着改革开放的不断深入和国家对人权保障的加强,中国民众的权利意识和法治观念与以往相比得到了前所未有的加强。人民群众要求司法机关适用死刑的要求并不是很强烈,对已经出现的某些错误适用死刑的情形会给予一定的批评。即便对某些严重刑事犯罪的行为人,如果犯罪人确实存在值得原谅的因素,民众也普遍持宽容态度。中国民众的这种人权观念的发展变化和对死刑问题的关注,对当代中国死刑制度的改革提出了新的进一步的要求。

(3)中国顺应死刑国际发展潮流的体现。废止死刑是国际死刑发展的主要潮流,目前世界上绝大多数国家都在法律上或者事实上废止了死刑。这一现象还有进一步扩大的趋势。在此背景下,中国需要顺应国际社会死刑的发展潮流,改革其过于宽泛的死刑制度。同时,限制与废止死刑不仅为多数国家的立法和司法所采纳,而且也被联合国诸多国际公约、欧洲人权公约、美洲人权公约等国际法律文件所认可。1966年12月联合国通过的《公民权利和政治权利国际公约》第6条明确规定,死刑只适用于"最为严重的犯罪"。1989年12月15日联合国第43届大会通过的《旨在废止死刑的〈公民权利和政治权利国际公约〉第二任择议定书》第2条则进一步规定:"本议定书缔约国管辖范围内,任何人不得被处死刑。"此外,一些区域性国际条约也都对死刑作了严格的限制性规定。迄今,中国政府已经签署或者加入了包括《公民权利和政治权利国际公约》、《禁止酷刑和其他残忍、不人道或有辱人格的待遇或处罚公约》在内的20多部人权类国际公约。中国有义务按照其参与、认可的相关国际条约的要求对死刑制度作进一步的改革。

(五)阐述中国刑法包括《刑法修正案(八)》的修法过程,推动修改法律和其他重要事项进程的主要依据。

1.《刑法修正案(八)》的修法过程

中国刑法典的制定始于1979年,之后中国根据社会发展的需要通过了25部单行刑法,并在107部非刑事法律中设置了附属刑法规范。1997年3月14日,中国根据社会和法治建设的需要,在对1979年刑法典进行全面、系统修订的基础上,颁布了一部全新的刑法典。之后,为了适应社会发展的需要，中国又先后进行了9次重要的刑法立法活动，出台了1部单行刑法和8个刑法修正案；同时还通过了9个刑法立法解释文件。

《刑法修正案（八）》是2011年2月25日由中国国家立法机关——全国人民代表大会常委会①通过，其修法活动始于2009年下半年。经过1年多的立法调研并在广泛征求相关部门、全国和地方人大代表以及有关专家学者等方面意见的基础上，全国人大常委会的立法起草机关——法制工作委员会拟定了《刑法修正案（八）（草案）》。该草案先后于2010年8月16日、2010年12月20日和2011年2月23日由全国人大常委会进行了3次立法审议，并通过网站、与有关部门座谈、地方调研、向法律院校发出征求意见函等方式，进一步广泛征求了社会各方面的意见。我本人所在的北京师范大学刑事法律科学研究院也在意见征求之列，我们还为此专门提交了草案修改完善的建议报告。在此基础上，中国全国人大常委会通过了《刑法修正案（八）》。根据规定，该修正案已于2011年5月1日起开始施行。

2. 推动修改法律和其他重要事项进程的主要依据

总体上看，推动中国修改法律和其他重要事项进程的主要依据有以下几个方面：一是应对中国社会发展过程中的新情况、新问题的现实需要；二是弥补法律规范疏漏的需要；三是贯彻落实相关刑事政策的需要，如《刑法修正案（八）》删除了13种基本不用、备而少用的死刑罪名，调整了死刑与无期徒刑、有期徒刑之间的结构关系，就是为了积极贯彻宽严相济的基本刑事政策；四是借鉴、吸收国际先进经验并与有关国际公约相协调的需要。中国已经签署或者批准了的一些国际条约，如联合国《公民权利和政治权利国际公约》《联合国反腐败公约》等，对中国刑法完善提出了新的要求。中国刑法典需要与这些国际公约的规定相协调。《刑法修正案（八）》关于削减死刑罪名、设置老年人犯罪从宽暨免死制度以及增设对外国公职人员、国际公共组织官员行贿罪等方面的规定，就积极了借鉴、吸收了国际社会的先进立法经验，贯彻了相关国际公约。

---

① 中国的全国人民代表大会和全国人民代表大会常务委员会共同行使国家立法权。全国人民代表大会制定和修改刑事、民事、国家机构的和其他的基本法律。全国人民代表大会常务委员会制定和修改除应当由全国人民代表大会制定的法律以外的其他法律；在全国人民代表大会闭会期间，对全国人民代表大会制定的法律进行部分补充和修改，但是不得同该法律的基本原则相抵触（《立法法》第7条）。

（六）当前已有多少案件适用了《刑法修正案（八）》？其中包括多少走私案件？

中国《刑法修正案（八）》因修法内容全面、涉及方面广泛，自2011年5月1日施行以来，已经进行了大量的诉讼和审判。根据中国海关提供的数据，自2011年5月至2014年6月，中国法院一审共审结走私普通货物、物品案件2606件，共判决4866人，没有任何被告人被判处死刑（既没有被判处死刑立即执行，也没有被判处死刑缓期二年执行）。这些案件都与黄海勇案件类似，并且都适用了《刑法修正案（八）》。因此，黄海勇被引渡回国后，中国也必定会对其走私普通货物、物品的行为适用《刑法修正案（八）》。

（七）根据中国国内法律，阐述有利于被起诉人的溯及力问题，指出如被引渡，其对于黄海勇案是否适用？并由此确定不会对其适用死刑。

在刑法的溯及力上，中国采取的是有利于被告人的从旧兼从轻原则，即新法原则上没有溯及力，但新法不认为是犯罪或者处刑较轻的，则要按照新法处理（《刑法》第12条）。与1997年《刑法》关于走私普通货物罪的规定相比，《刑法修正案（八）》关于取消走私普通货物罪死刑的规定，既属于新的法律，也属于"处刑较轻"的法律。根据从旧兼从轻原则，对于发生在《刑法修正案（八）》之前但在《刑法修正案（八）》实施后可能涉及判处死刑的走私普通货物犯罪，都应适用《刑法修正案（八）》的规定而不能对被告人判处死刑（包括不能判处死刑缓期二年执行）。

本案中，黄海勇走私普通货物的行为虽然发生在《刑法修正案（八）》颁行之前，但因《刑法修正案（八）》废止了走私普通货物罪的死刑，与刑法典原有规定相比，属于"处刑较轻的"法律，对黄海勇应适用《刑法修正案（八）》修法的规定，依法不可能判处其死刑。

（八）黄海勇案同谋的刑事诉讼情况，是否对其适用了《刑法修正案（八）》？

关于黄海勇同案犯的查处情况，据中国有关司法机关提供的材料，目前多数同案犯都未进入审判阶段，少数同案犯已经判决且其审判时间都是在《刑法修正案（八）》生效以前，都不存在适用《刑法修正案（八）》的情形。其具体查处情况如下：

1. 对于涉案单位的查处

黄海勇案的涉案单位包括黄海勇的4家公司和其余9家公司。这些公司目前均未被司法处理,根据其参与走私的情况,可将其大体可分为两类:第一类是7家涉嫌走私普通货物的策划、组织、实施单位,包括深圳亨润国际实业有限公司(策划、组织单位)、深圳裕伟贸易实业有限公司(策划、组织单位)、湖北裕伟贸易实业有限公司(策划、组织单位)、武汉丰润油脂保税仓库有限公司(策划、实施单位)、上海润丰油脂食品有限公司(策划、组织单位)、武汉市对外经济贸易发展公司(策划单位)和武汉油脂集团(策划、实施及购油单位)。第二类是6家涉嫌参与走私普通货物的单位,包括上海金环国际贸易有限公司(提供仓储、付汇、发油及购油单位)、上海汇荣油脂储运有限公司(仓储单位)、广东鹤山华侨商品供应公司(提供国内增值税发票和帐号单位)、武汉华捷油脂有限公司(提供假证明及购油单位)、武汉沙鸥高级食用油总厂(提供假证明及购油单位)和上海油脂集团公司进出口分公司(购油单位)。

2. 对于涉案个人的查处

黄海勇的涉案同案犯目前共11人,对其查处大体可分为四类:(1)已经判决4人。即潘子牛(深圳市亨润国际实业有限公司、深圳市裕伟实业发展有限公司董事、总经理,湖北裕伟贸易实业有限公司总经理,香港宝润集团有限公司董事),被武汉市中级人民法院以犯走私普通货物罪,判处13年有期徒刑;李汉忠(武汉油脂集团法人代表),2000年7月被武汉市中级人民法院以挪用公款罪判处有期徒刑6年;李福财(广东鹤山华侨商品供应公司副总经理),2000年12月,被江门市中级人民法院以虚开增值税发票罪判处有期徒刑14年;文有佳(武汉华捷油脂有限公司总经理),2001年7月被武汉市东西湖区人民法院以挪用资金罪判处有期徒刑1年,缓刑2年。(2)存疑不起诉(即因证据不足而未被起诉)的5人。即冯楠杰(武汉丰润油脂保税仓库有限公司总经理暨武汉油脂集团副总经理),2003年1月被武汉市人民检察院存疑不起诉;周永生(上海润丰油脂食品有限公司总经理),2003年1月被武汉市人民检察院存疑不起诉;刘卓尔(上海润丰油脂食品有限公司副经理),2003年1月被武汉市人民检察院存疑不起诉;杨永昌(上海金环国际贸易有限公司法人代表),2003年1月被武汉市人民检察院存疑不起诉;纪顺英(武汉油脂集团副总经理),2003年1月被武汉市人民检察院存疑不起诉。(3)在逃1人。即邵辉(湖北裕伟贸易实业有限公司暨武汉丰润油脂保税仓库有限公司副总经理),已逃往美国,并取得绿卡,目前被通缉。(4)取保候审1人。即冯福亨(广东鹤山华侨商品供应公司法人代表),2011年12月被抓获,现取保候审。

(九)死刑改革问题。

1. 中国死刑制度的演进

与世界其他国家和地区一样,中国古代曾长期将死刑作为社会治理的重要手段。近现代以来,中国逐渐加强了对死刑的控制。新中国领导人毛泽东同志曾明确提出要严格死刑的适用,对于"可杀可不杀的,一律不杀"。中国1979年《刑法》只对28种犯罪规定了死刑,其中有一半属于危害国家根本利益的国事罪,实践中极少适用死刑,其余绝大部分则都属于严重的暴力性犯罪;1979年的《刑法》和《刑事诉讼法》也明确规定死刑案件一律由最高人民法院核准或判决。之后随着改革开放的深入,中国进入了社会快速转型期,新型犯罪不断涌现,严重犯罪频发,犯罪的数量也急剧增加。出于加强社会治理的现实考虑,中国在十多年间主要通过单行刑法的方式增设了多种犯罪的死刑,可以适用死刑的罪名数量迅速增加,至1997年修订《刑法》之前,中国的死刑罪名数量已增至72种;同时,中国自1980年起也通过相关法律和司法解释把部分普通刑事案件的死刑核准权下放到省级高级法院行使。出于对死刑适用扩张的担忧,中国1997年全面修订的《刑法》开始对死刑采取限制的态度,在立法上对死刑适用的条件、对象和程序作了限制,死刑罪名数量也减至68种。中国1996年底修订的《刑事诉讼法》将死刑案件的核准权重申规定由最高人民法院统一行使。但随后最高人民法院根据《人民法院组织法》的规定仍将部分死刑案件的核准下放至高级人民法院,死刑适用所受到的实体与程序限制仍然有限,死刑适用的数量有所反弹。进入21世纪以后,基于相关国际公约的要求、世界社会普遍废止死刑的趋势以及中国人权与法治建设的需要,在法学界的推动和国家决策领导层的支持下,死刑改革问题受到了中国立法和司法机关前所未有的重视,中国立法机关和司法机关通过一系列立法和司法改进措施,严格限制了死刑适用的条件、对象和程序,并将死刑罪名的数量缩减至55种。

2. 中国对死刑适用的限制措施

中国现阶段的死刑适用是受到了严格的实体和程序限制。具体体现在:

其一,死刑适用的条件限制。中国《刑法》第48条规定:"死刑只适用于罪行极其严重的犯罪分子。"其中,"罪行极其严重"是指犯罪的客观危害、犯罪分子的主观恶性和人身危险性均极其严重,实践中主要是指严重危害国家安全、公共安全或者人身安全的暴力犯罪。而且对于罪行极其严重的犯罪分子,只要是依法可不立即执行的,就不应当判处死刑立即执行(最高人民法院2010年《关于贯彻宽严相济刑事政策的若干意见》第29条)。

其二,死刑适用的对象限制。这主要体现在三个方面:(1)犯罪的时候不满18周岁的人和审判的时候怀孕的妇女,不适用死刑(《刑法》第49条第1款)。同时,中国司法机关对"审判的时候怀孕的妇女"作了从宽解释,既包括人民法院审理案件的时候被告人正在怀孕,也包括案件起诉到人民法院之前被告人怀孕但作了人工流产的情况(最高人民法院研究室1991年3月18日《关于如何理解"审判的时候怀孕的妇女不适用死刑"问题的电话答复》和最高人民法院1998年8月7日《关于对怀孕妇女在羁押期间自然流产审判时是否可以适用死刑问题的批复》)。(2)审判的时候已满75周岁且不是以特别残忍手段致人死亡的人不适用死刑(《刑法》第49条第2款)。(3)对犯罪的精神障碍人、又聋又哑和盲人原则上也不能适用死刑(《刑法》第18、19条)。

其三,严格死刑案件的核准程序。中国全国人大常委会2006年10月31日通过《关于修改〈中华人民共和国人民法院组织法〉的决定》,明确规定死刑案件的核准权归最高人民法院行使。在此基础上,中国最高人民法院自2007年1月1日起将此前下放至高级人民法院的部分死刑案件核准权全部收归最高人民法院统一行使(最高人民法院《关于统一行使死刑案件核准权有关问题的决定》),从而有利于统一并严格死刑案件的适用标准。

其四,严格死刑案件二审的审理程序。与一般刑事案件不同,中国最高司法机关规定,对一审判处死刑立即执行的案件,二审必须采取开庭的方式进行审理(最高人民法院、最高人民检察院《关于死刑第二审案件开庭审理程序若干问题的规定(试行)》),这有利于保障被告人充分行使其诉讼权利,也有利于更好地查明案件事实,防止错判。

其五,严格死刑适用的证据标准。中国对死刑案件采取了更为严格的证据标准,要求案件事实必须排除一切合理怀疑,取证程序必须排除任何非法取证的可能(最高人民法院、最高人民检察院、公安部、国家安全部和司法部《关于办理死刑案件审查判断证据若干问题的规定》)。

其六,死刑执行制度的严格限制。在中国,对于应当判处死刑的犯罪分子,如果不是必须立即执行的,可以判处死刑同时宣告缓期2年执行(《刑法》第48条第1款)。这类犯罪分子只要在2年考验期内没有故意犯罪就可在2年期满后减为无期徒刑或者有期徒刑。

中国刑法立法和刑事司法对死刑适用的上述严格限制,体现了中国慎用死刑的态度和政策。

3. 中国政府没有趋于扩大执行死刑范围的政策

如前所述,中国历来重视对死刑的政策控制。早在新中国成立之初,中国就在积极的死刑实践中逐渐形成了"保留死刑,严格控制死刑"或称"保留死刑,坚持少杀,防止错杀"的死刑政策,并在1979年第一部刑法典制定时得到切实体现和强调。

21世纪初,中国政府提出了构建和谐社会和实行宽严相济的基本刑事政策,中国的死刑政策被进一步调整为"保留死刑,严格控制和慎重适用死刑"。在此政策的指导下,中国死刑立法和司法都取得了积极进展,不仅死刑适用的标准更为严格、死刑罪名进一步减少,而且死刑适用的数量大幅下降。在此基础上,2013年11月中共十八届三中全会通过的《中共中央关于全面深化改革若干重大问题的决定》在确立"推进法治中国建设"的重大国策之下,进一步明确提出要"逐步减少适用死刑罪名",从而把死刑制度的深入改革作为法治中国建设进程中的一项重大任务。这也是中国首次明确提出要"减少死刑适用"。据此,中国将进一步推动减少死刑的执行范围。据悉,正在起草中的中国《刑法修正案(九)》会进一步限制死刑并削减死刑罪名。中国不存在扩大死刑执行范围的刑事政策和立法、司法趋势。

（十）中国加大力度打击法律机构内部存在的腐败问题情况。

中国政府将腐败视为妨碍实现法治国家和社会和谐稳定的重大问题，重视加强对腐败行为的打击。早在新中国成立初期，中国政府就通过严惩腐败高官刘青山、张子善（这二人是当时天津市的最高负责人）表明了其反腐败的坚强决心。进入改革开放以后，中国政府在发展社会经济的同时，也注重打击腐败犯罪。中国最近一届政府换届以后，对腐败犯罪的治理得到了明显加强。中共十八大报告强调，对腐败行为要坚持"老虎""苍蝇"一起打，既坚决查处领导干部违纪违法案件，又切实解决发生在群众身边的不正之风和腐败问题。2013年，中共中央发布了《建立健全惩治和预防腐败体系2013—2017年工作规划》，提出要加大查处腐败违法犯罪行为的力度。自中共十八大以来，中国政府查处一系列具有重大影响的高官腐败案件。据初步统计，仅2014年上半年（截至2014年8月），中国政府就查处了20多名省部级高官，其中还包括原中共中央政治局常委、中央政法委书记周永康，查处的其他腐败官员更是数以万计。

在加强打击腐败犯罪的过程中，中国政府也十分注重惩治司法机构内部存在的腐败问题。中国最高领导人习近平曾在中国高层政法工作会议上明确提出要"坚持严格执法公正司法"，"让暗箱操作没有空间，让司法腐败无法藏身"，彰显了中国反对司法腐败的坚强决心。为加强和改进新形势下的司法工作，2014年6月，中国最高人民法院专门出台了30条意见重点治理法院腐败违纪。近年来，中国也依法惩治了一大批司法腐败案件。其中既有原最高人民法院副院长黄松有等省部级高官，也有负责具体司法案件的基层法官和检察官。经过对司法腐败犯罪的治理，中国司法的廉洁性、公正性、公开性得到了进一步提升，减少了腐败等案外因素对司法审判的干预。

三、黄海勇面临的后续司法进程

（一）赖昌星案件的诉讼程序如何？其被判决和执行的罪名是什么？

1. 赖昌星案是引渡还是遣返？其基本程序是怎样的？

在赖昌星案件中，由于加拿大在引渡问题上坚持条约前置主义立场，而中加双方当时还没有双边引渡条约,所以没有采取引渡程序,而是采取非法移民遣返程序。根据加拿大《移民和难民保护法》及相关法律,遣返赖昌星经过了难民身份确认程序和遣返前的风险评估程序两个阶段:

(1) 难民身份确认程序

加拿大难民制度主要包括该国公民与移民部(Citizenship and Immigration Canada,简称 CIC)和移民及难民事务委员会(Immigration and Refugee Board of Canada,简称 IRB)两个机构。CIC 对移民及难民事务负有全面的责任,所有难民申请都首先提交给 CIC 审查。IRB 则是独立行政法庭,其职能具有准司法的性质,负责对移民和难民事务作出公平裁决,CIC 和 IRB 两者职能上彼此独立,工作上相互合作。根据加拿大《移民与难民保护法》,在加拿大申请难民需要经过行政程序和司法程序。行政程序包括:(1) 向 CIC 提出申请;(2) 经 CIC 审查,认为其有资格得到 IRB 的听证,将其申请提交 IRB 的公约移民甄别处进行听证审查,根据结果决定是否赋予其难民资格;(3) 如申请人不服该决定,可向 IRB 的复议处提出复议。至此,难民身份确认的行政程序结束。当事人如果对复议决定还不服,只能通过司法程序救济:(1) 就复议决定向联邦法院提起诉讼;(2) 若对联邦法院的判决不服,可以向联邦上诉法院提出上诉;(3) 对联邦上诉法院的判决不服的,还可以将案件提交到最高法院。赖昌星案的难民身份确认程序,主要围绕赖昌星在中国实施的犯罪行为是否政治犯罪,是否具有难民身份而展开。

1999 年 8 月赖昌星和妻子曾明娜持有香港护照潜逃加拿大。2000 年 11 月 23 日,赖昌星签证过期,CIC 以非法移民罪将赖昌星夫妇拘捕,准备作为非法移民驱逐出境。赖昌星以回国将会受到迫害甚至被判处死刑等理由申请"难民资格"。IRB 于 2001 年 7 月 3 日开始对此案进行难民听证。在听证过程中,CIC 邀请了 3 位专家证人(美国的 Jerome Cohen 教授、加拿大的杨诚(Vincent Yang)博士和 Charles Berrtun 博士),和 4 位来自中国的事实证人(参与赖昌星集团远华走私案查处的吴建平警官、李永军检察官,负责李纪周案件起诉工作的王忠华检察官,和时任中国人民大学法学院教授的赵秉志博士)出席了聆讯庭,提供了较为有力的关于中国司法制度和远华案审判基本公正、依法的证言。其中赵秉志教授于 2001 年 8 月 10 日、10 月 23

日两次赴加拿大出席赖昌星案件聆讯庭作证,接受了CIC律师和赖昌星代理律师的交叉询问,以及聆讯庭审裁官的询问,取得了良好的作证效果。需要说明的是,赵秉志教授虽然名义上是事实证人,但在听证中实际上是按照专家证人对待的。加拿大公民与移民部方面本来希望邀请赵秉志教授主要以专家证人的身份出庭作证,但按照加拿大的法律,对专家证人作证在对方持异议的情况下需要较长的辩论时间,为保证及时邀请赵秉志教授到庭作证,加拿大公民与移民部改为邀请赵秉志教授以事实证人的身份出庭作证。经过漫长的听证,IRB认为赖昌星夫妇犯下了严重的非政治罪行,不具备获得难民身份的资格,于2002年6月21日驳回其难民申请。至此,行政程序结束。但是赖昌星又于2002年8月26日向加拿大联邦法院提出起诉,请求法院推翻IRB的裁决,进入司法救济程序。2004年2月3日加拿大联邦法院驳回赖昌星难民申请的司法复议请求,维持IRB的裁决。赖昌星又陆续上诉至加拿大联邦上诉法院、最高法院,2005年4月、9月联邦上诉法院、最高法院陆续驳回其上诉,维持了IRB对赖昌星"不授予难民资格"的裁决,否定了赖昌星的难民身份。

(2)遣返前的风险评估程序。

根据加拿大的法律,当事人难民身份被否定以后,如果要遣返还要进行遣返前的风险评估程序。对于评估结果,行为人可以提出司法复议。如果对于结果还是不满,被评估人可以一直上诉下去,使得风险评估程序进入"上诉——评估——再上诉——再评估"的循环。

赖昌星案件中的遣返前的风险评估程序主要是围绕中国酷刑、死刑和司法状况,以及中方对赖昌星不判处死刑承诺的可信性。2006年5月CIC对于赖昌星的风险评估完成,认为赖昌星被遣返后没有生命危险,决定将其遣返回中国。2006年6月16日,加拿大边境服务局将赖昌星从其居所拘捕至温哥华市一家监狱。赖昌星见状以为自己是要被送往机场,遂以头撞柱,试图逃避遣返。赖昌星及其律师随后就遣返后的风险评估问题再提出异议,向加拿大联邦法院提出延缓执行遣返令。2007年4月5日,加拿大联邦法院对赖昌星案作出判决,宣布此前CIC发出的遣返令无效,接受赖昌星提出对遣返前风险评估进行司法复核的申请。由此,赖昌星又成功地回到了加拿大复杂的司法程序中。2011年7月21日加拿大联邦法院驳回赖昌星关于暂缓执行遣返令的申请,下令立即执行遣返令。至此,赖昌星遣返案的所有法律程序均已结束,2011年7月23日,赖昌星终于被遣送回国。

2. 赖昌星案件的诉讼程序

经过中国和加拿大双方的共同努力,赖昌星于2011年7月23日被遣返回中国,中国福建省厦门海关缉私局当即依法对其执行逮捕,并会同厦门市人民检察院对其涉嫌的走私普通货物罪和行贿犯罪开展侦查,2011年12月下旬侦查终结,移送检察机关审查起诉。2012年2月6日,厦门市人民检察院以赖昌星涉嫌走私普通货物罪、行贿罪向厦门市中级人民法院依法提起公诉。同年4月6日厦门市中级人民法院依法公开开庭审理。厦门市中级人民法院于同年5月18日作出了一审定罪量刑的判决。后赖昌星没有提起上诉。

3. 赖昌星被判决和执行的罪名

2012年5月18日厦门市中级人民法院作出了一审判决:认定赖昌星犯走私普通货物罪,判处无期徒刑,剥夺政治权利终身,并处没收个人全部财产;犯行贿罪,判处有期徒刑15年,并处没收个人财产人民币2千万元。决定执行无期徒刑,剥夺政治权利终身,并处没收个人全部财产。赖昌星的违法犯罪所得予以追缴。

4. 赖昌星走私普通货物罪的涉案金额远远大于黄海勇案件

赖昌星案件是新中国成立以来最大的经济犯罪案件,涉案金额巨大。据统计,1995年12月至1999年5月,赖昌星走私集团走私香烟、汽车、成品油、植物油、化工原料、纺织原料及其他普通货物,涉案金额共计人民币273.9亿元,偷逃应缴税额139.9亿元。远远超过黄海勇案件的涉案金额(12.2亿元)和逃税金额(7.17亿元)。

5. 赖昌星审判时《刑法修正案(八)》的实施情况

在赖昌星案件起诉(2012年2月6日)和开庭(2012年4月6日)期间,《刑法修正案(八)》已经生效(该修正案2011年2月25日通过,同年5月1日生效),该修正案对于赖昌星涉嫌的走私普通货物罪进行了修改。《刑法修正案(八)》对走私普通货物罪的修改主要包括两个方面:(1)废止了走私普通货物、物品罪的死刑,(2) 对走私普通货物、物品罪的定罪量刑标准进行了修改,调整了该罪法定刑的排列顺序并将其对应的偷逃应缴税额的数额分别修改为"数额特别巨大"、"数额巨大"和"数额较大"(《刑法》第 153 条)。而对于赖昌星涉嫌的行贿罪,《刑法修正案(八)》没有修改,保持了 1997 年《刑法》关于行贿罪的相关规定(《刑法》第 389 条、390 条)。

(二)赖昌星案件是否曾运用上诉机制?是否有代理人?

2012 年 5 月 18 日厦门市中级人民法院对赖昌星案件作出了一审判决之后,赖昌星在拥有上诉权利并且可以上诉的情况下,自愿认罪服判,没有提起上诉。在该案件中,赖昌星委托了北京市潮阳律师事务所律师杨晓红、裘叶作为自己的辩护人。在一审开庭中,两位辩护人到庭参加诉讼,充分发表了辩护意见。赖昌星的辩护权利得到了充分地行使。

需要注意的是,虽然赖昌星一审宣判之后没有上诉,但并不能否认其所享有的上诉权利。在中加之间另一个著名的遣返案件——邓心志遣返案中,被告人邓心志在一审宣判后行使上诉权,二审减轻其原判刑罚。作为首个从加拿大被遣返的经济犯罪嫌疑人,邓心志于 2008 年 8 月 22 日被遣返回国。2009 年 5 月 6 日,北京市第一中级人民法院一审开庭审理该案,同年 6 月 4 日,邓心志被以合同诈骗罪判处无期徒刑。数日后,邓心志的辩护律师赵小鲁、苏衍庆代其提起上诉。同年 9 月 22 日,北京市高级人民院二审裁判采纳了辩护律师的意见,以邓心志"具有自愿接受遣返及归案后如实供述主要犯罪事实的自首情节"为由改判为有期徒刑 15 年。此案中,被告人邓心志及其辩护人充分行使了辩护权、上诉权,并从无期徒刑改判为有期徒刑 15 年。由此,我们可以推断,如果赖昌星行使上诉权,其上诉权将会得到充分保障,同时也并不能排除其根据案件情况被改判的可能性。

纵观赖昌星案件的诉讼过程,从 2011 年 7 月赖昌星被遣返回国,厦门海关缉私局依法对其执行逮捕,并会同厦门市人民检察院依法就赖昌星案件进行侦查,到 2012 年 5 月 18 日厦门市中级人民法院依法公开宣判,再到赖昌星进入监狱服刑,中国司法机关坚持依法、公正、文明办案,依法保障赖昌星、其他涉案人及赖昌星的辩护律师行使诉讼权利,充分听取了赖昌星及其辩护律师的意见,他们的各项诉讼权利均受到良好的保障,赖昌星没有受到酷刑和其他不人道的对待和处罚。

　　黄海勇案件与赖昌星案件具有极大的相似性,但是黄海勇案件涉案金额要远远低于赖昌星案,黄海勇的犯罪情节也远没有赖昌星案件严重。而且,随着近年来中国刑事诉讼制度的日渐完善,我们可以预见,如果黄海勇被引渡回国接受审判,其辩护权、上诉权等诉讼权利也将得到与赖昌星同样甚至更为充分、有效的保障。

孙昂出席美洲人权法院黄海勇引渡案庭审个人陈述及被询问之问题

时间:2014年9月3日上午11:20—13:30
地点:巴拉圭首都亚松森市,巴拉圭最高法院

一、宣誓

我郑重宣誓:我将凭荣誉和良心忠实履行专家证人的职责(大意,原文为西班牙文)。

二、个人陈述

法官先生:

请允许我介绍一下中国引渡制度的概况。

为了打击跨国犯罪行为,将企图逃避惩罚的犯罪分子绳之以法,中国依据中国法律和相关国际法与有关国家开展引渡合作。

中国对外开展引渡合作共有三种方式:

一是根据双边引渡条约进行引渡合作。截至目前,中国已与38个国家签订了引渡条约,其中29项条约已生效。中国对外签订的第一项是1993年8月26日的中国和泰国间的引渡条约。我本人参加了这项引渡条约的谈判。在美洲,中国已经与秘鲁、巴西、墨西哥和阿根廷签订了引渡条约。在这四个美洲国家中,中国和秘鲁之间最早签订了引渡条约。这项条约于2001年11月5日签订,我本人参加了这项引渡条约的谈判。

中国对外开展引渡合作第二种方式是根据多边条约中的引渡条款进行引渡合作。截至目前,中国参加的全球性国际公约中,有20多项含有引渡条约,如《联合国打击跨国有组织犯罪公约》以及《联合国反腐败公约》等。我本人参加了这两项公约的谈判和后续履约工作。

中国对外开展引渡合作是第三种方式是在缺乏条约基础的情况下,根据本国《引渡法》,依据互惠原则进行引渡合作。例如,中国公民金先生在2001年1月11日参与组织72人偷渡,他被韩国警方抓获时,在他携带的纸箱中查出2公斤冰毒。同年7月2日,中国外交部照会韩国驻华使馆,提出引渡请求,并做出互惠承诺。2002年3月28日,韩国驻华使馆照会外交部,表示韩国政府决定将金某某引渡至中国。2002年4月11日,中韩间完成对金的引渡。我本人参加了这起引渡案件的处理。

除了上述三种引渡方式,中国还通过遣返方式将中国籍逃犯从外国遣返回中国。这种方式适用于逃犯以非法移民身份在外国逗留的情况。这种方式不是常规的引渡程序,但能起到将逃犯遣返回中国、接受审判的实际效果。因此,我们也将它称为变相引渡(de facto extradition)。例如,中国公民余振东1992年至2001年间贪污挪用巨额公款,案发后潜逃至美国。2002年12月,根据中国的请求,美国拘留了余振东。2004年4月16日美国将余振东遣返回中国。2006年3月31日,余振东被中国法院判处监禁。我本人参加了这起遣返案件。

中国与38个国家签订了引渡条约,并且通过其他方式与一些其他国家开展引渡和遣返逃犯的合作。这表明中国与这些国家之间在引渡和遣返逃犯领域存在着相互信任。这种信任是国家之间开展引渡和遣返逃犯合作的基础。

为了依法办理引渡案件,中国立法机构全国人大常委会于2000年12月28日通过了《引渡法》。同日,该法公布施行。这标志着中国引渡法律制度的正式建立,为中国与其他国家开展引渡合作提供了法律基础。

中国《引渡法》和中国与外国签订的引渡条约规定了引渡的一些原则,这些原则也是公认的国际法原则。它们包括政治犯罪不引渡原则、禁止歧视原则、禁止酷刑原则、双重犯罪原则和一事不二理原则。因时间所限,我只解释前两项原则。

政治犯罪不引渡原则是指如果因政治犯罪而请求引渡，应当拒绝引渡。

禁止歧视原则是指如果被请求引渡人可能因其种族、宗教、国籍、性别、政治见解等原因而被提起刑事诉讼或者执行刑罚，或者被请求引渡人在司法程序中可能由于上述原因受到不公正待遇的，应当拒绝引渡。

中国《引渡法》第50条还针对"外交承诺"作了专门的规定。在以往的一些案件中，中国政府曾作出过外交承诺，这些外交承诺主要涉及不判处死刑。

关于死刑，世界各国可分为两类，一类已经废除死刑或者尚未废除死刑，但实际上已经不再执行死刑。另一类保留死刑，并依法执行死刑。中国属于后一类国家。

在许多引渡案件中，中方承诺不判死刑是不必要的。因为在这些案件中，引渡所针对的犯罪在中国刑法上没有死刑这一刑罚。当然，对于这样的案件，如果被请求国要求中方作出不判死刑的承诺，中方也可以考虑在外交照会中写明不判死刑。在这种情况下，中方外交照会关于不判死刑的表述，与其说是一项承诺，不如说是向被请求方说明中国刑法的相关规定。在另一些案件中，引渡所针对的犯罪，在中国刑法上确实还有死刑这一刑罚。针对这种情况，中方在部分案件中作出了不判死刑的外交承诺。

关于中国政府作出的不判死刑的外交承诺，有以下几点希望特别提出来，请法院注意：

第一，在引渡案件中，中国政府不会主动承诺不判死刑，只有在对方国家要求中方承诺不判死刑时，中方才会考虑作出这一承诺。这在中国《引渡法》中有明确规定。

第二，并不是只要对方国家提出不判死刑的要求，中国政府就会作出这样的承诺。根据中国《引渡法》的规定，如果对方国家要求中国政府作出不判死刑的承诺，只有在中国政府认为，作出这一承诺"不损害中华人民共和国主权、国家利益、公共利益"，中方才可以作出承诺。

第三，中国政府在引渡案件中对外作出的不判死刑的承诺，只能由外交部代表中国政府向对方国家作出。这里的"由外交部代表中国政府作出承诺",通常是指由中国驻外国大使馆向对方国家外交部发出外交照会,或者是中国外交部向对方国家驻中国大使馆发出外交照会。正因为如此,在引渡案件中的承诺,也称为"外交承诺"。与中国外交部或中国大使馆无关的其他机构和人员作出的任何表态,包括承诺,都不是中国《引渡法》所讲的"外交承诺"。

第四,在中国外交部作出不判死刑承诺之前,必须由中国最高人民法院作出不判处死刑的决定。根据最高人民法院的这一决定,外交部才能对外作出不判处死刑的承诺。

第五,中国作出的关于不判死刑的外交承诺,在引渡后的审判中,对于司法机关有约束力。这是中国《引渡法》第 50 条明确规定的。另外,关于不判死刑的外交承诺,首先必须由最高人民法院作出不判死刑的决定。这也对各级法院起到了约束作用。因为在中国,死刑案件都须经过最高人民法院的复核(review)。

第六,正因为上述两个方面的制度安排,在实践中,中国作出的不判死刑的外交承诺都得到了很好的执行。从未发生过中国作出不判死刑的外交承诺之后,而被引渡人被判执行死刑的案例。

关于中国政府作为不判处死刑的外交承诺,一个著名的案例就是中国从加拿大遣返赖昌星。

1990 年代,赖昌星伙同他人从境外向中国大规模走私、行贿,涉案金额超过 40 亿美元,偷逃税款超过 15 亿美元,严重破坏了中国正常的经济秩序,给国家造成巨大经济损失。1999 年,赖昌星逃至加拿大。中国要求加拿大将赖昌星遣返回中国。在遣返的过程中,中国政府向加拿大作出不判处赖昌星死刑的外交承诺。加拿大政府接受了中方的承诺。加拿大法院也认为,基于加拿大政府从中国政府得到的有效保证,赖昌星遣返回中国没有风险,支持将赖昌星遣返回中国(见加拿大法院 IMM - 4373 - 11 号判决)。2011 年 7 月 23 日,经过加拿大政府和法院的多轮审核,赖昌星被遣返回中国。2012 年 5 月 18 日,中国法院判处赖昌星无期徒刑(life imprisonment),没有他判处死刑。

赖昌星的案件与黄海勇的案件有许多相似之处,因为两人都是涉嫌走私罪和行贿罪。中国就赖昌星案向加拿大作出过不判处死刑、禁止酷刑并允许加拿大外交官了解赖昌星审判和服刑情况的外交承诺,加拿大政府和法院接受了中国政府的这些外交承诺,向中国遣返了赖昌星。中国就黄海勇案向秘鲁作出过不判处死刑的外交承诺,秘鲁政府和法院也接受了中国政府的外交承诺,同意向中国遣返了黄海勇。我认为,中国政府就黄海勇案所作的外交承诺应足以使黄海勇被引渡至中国后,不会被判处死刑,他的各项权利能得到充分的保障。因此,希望法院在审理黄海勇案时,能够参考赖昌星案的相关情况。

三、被询问之问题*

(一)秘鲁政府国家检察司律师 Sra. Sofia Donaires Vega 发问

1. 中国请求外国引渡逃犯,这些请求多数被接受了,还是被拒绝了?
2. 中国请求外国引渡逃犯的案件,多数涉及哪些罪名?
3. 中国请求外国引渡走私和行贿嫌犯的案件,多少被接受了,多少被拒绝了?
4. 在中国请求外国引渡逃犯而被外国拒绝的案件中,外国政府提出的拒绝理由是什么?
5. 中国请求外国引渡逃犯的案件,有没有因为外国不信任中国政府而拒绝引渡?
6. 在这些涉及死刑的案件中,对方是否都要求中国作出不判死刑的承诺?中国都接受了对方的要求,还是没有接受?
7. 在涉及死刑的案件中,中国作出的不判决死刑的外交承诺是否得到了履行?
8. 在引渡和变相引渡的案件中,被申请引渡国提出的外交承诺包括哪些?
9. 中国政府在引渡案件中对外国作出的外交承诺,是否对于所有中国

---

* 根据赵秉志教授在美洲人权法院法庭上的记录整理。

政府机关都有约束力？

10. 中国政府在引渡案件中作出的外交承诺的约束力在中国法律中有无保障。

11. 在你的职业生涯中接触到的中国就引渡对外国作出的外交承诺，执行的情况如何？

12. 是否可以说中国就引渡对外国作出的外交承诺是可信的，是有效的？

13. 如果中国就引渡对外国作出的外交承诺没有得到执行，有何种后续解决争议的程序可资利用？

14. 能否简要介绍一下赖昌星案？我们知道这是一起变相引渡案件，是这样的吗？

15. 赖昌星涉嫌走私罪，在中国要求加拿大遣返赖昌星时，中国《刑法》对走私罪还保留了死刑，因此，中国根据加拿大的要求作出了不判处赖昌星死刑的外交承诺。而不判处赖昌星死刑的决定是由中国最高法院作出的。情况是这样的吗？

16. 考虑到赖昌星遣返案中，中国执行了不对其判处死刑的外交承诺，在黄案中，是否予以同样的外交承诺并确保其实行？

（二）黄海勇的第2位律师 Miguel Angel Soria Fuerte 发问

1. 你刚才说，在所有涉及死刑的案件中，中国作出的不判决死刑的外交承诺都得到了履行。然而，就我所知，至少在3起案件中，中国政府作出了不判决死刑的承诺，但是，在他们引渡到中国后，都被处死了。他们分别是王建业、洛桑丹增和方勇，分别涉及泰国、美国和加拿大。

2. 中国已作出的外交承诺包含禁止酷刑和不人道待遇的内容吗？

3. 中国有无引渡西藏人或维族人回国的案件？

4. 在引渡维族人的案件中，中国有没有承诺不判处死刑？

5. 中国是从哪个国家引渡这个维族人的？是什么罪名？

6. 2013年末，23个维族人被关在关塔那摩美军监狱，为什么没有人把这些人引渡回中国受审？而是把他们关在其他地方了？

7. 他们为什么在关塔那摩被关押了11年之久，而不是把他们引渡回中国受审?

8. 你参与了赖昌星案件的引渡工作了吗?

9. 在赖昌星案件中,中国向加方提出了哪些外交承诺?

10. 赖昌星案件是加方向中国提出了外交承诺的要求吗?

11. 加方为什么要向中国提出禁用酷刑的要求?

12. 赖昌星被遣返回国后,他本人及其家人是否受到酷刑及不人道待遇?

13. 你如何能确认赖昌星未受到酷刑?你与赖昌星见面了吗?

14. 中方作出外交承诺后,是否允许联合国的相关机构跟踪?

(三)美洲人权委员 James Louis Cavallaro 发问

1. 中国引渡法中是否规定回国受审不会超出请求引渡的罪名?

2. 请详细解释引渡法的这一规定及其实施。

3. 你所说的"特定原则"是中国引渡法的规定还是中秘引渡条约的规定?

4. 如果被引渡人回国后又犯了新罪,是可以对此罪审判的,对吗?

5. 如果被引渡人回国后又犯了死罪,可以判他死刑吗?

美洲人权委员会 Silvia Serrano Guzman 接着发问

6. 你作证提供信息的材料来源于何处?

7. 你说中国作出的不判处死刑的外交承诺得到了 100% 的执行,你的来源是哪里?

8. 中国作出禁止酷刑的承诺与不判处死刑的承诺是一样的吗?

9. 你如何评价联合国对中国酷刑问题的评论?

10. 你说若外交承诺履行有问题时通过外交途径解决,那是否有司法途径解决?

11. 有什么机制能防范被引渡回国后不会被秘密处决?

(四)法庭发问

Eduardo Ferrer Mac-Gregor Poisot 法官:

1. 有无第三方介入制度以确保中国作出的不判处死刑的承诺之执行?

2. 如果出现违反外交承诺的情况,有无中国国内司法程序保障外交承诺的执行？

Eduardo Vio Grossi 法官：

1. 根据中秘引渡条约第 10 条，有无秘鲁国内司法决定与秘鲁国家决定不一致的情况？

2. 中国引渡案件中，从中方提出引渡申请，到对方决定是否接受申请，时间一般是多久？

3. 中秘引渡条约第 18 条关于知会司法情况的规定，如何得到执行？

Manuel E·Ventura Robles 法官：

1. 请确认中国对被引渡回国人的审判只能是引渡申请时的罪名吗？

Roberto F·Caldas 法官：

1. 请告诉我们中国一共引渡了多少人回国受审？

2. 是否可以说中国引渡回国受审的不超过 50 人？

3. 若被引渡者不多，很容易跟踪他们的状况，请告诉我们这些人有无在狱中死亡的？

4. 中国对赖昌星案件的外交承诺是否可以同样适用于黄海勇案？

5. 中国是否规定服刑者有强制劳动的义务？

6. 如果犯人拒绝劳动，会有何效果？

柳华文就黄海勇引渡案向美洲人权法院提交的书面证词

2014 年 9 月

姓名：柳华文

国籍：中国

职业履历简述：中国社会科学院国际法研究所所长助理、研究员；中国社会科学院人权研究中心副主任、秘书长。

一、中国的人权政策在国家层面由哪个机构制定，是否隶属于某个中央部委，其他部分如司法部分是否也要执行？

中华人民共和国成立以后，曾经只提保障公民权利，而不使用"人权"这一术语。1991 年，中国国务院新闻办发布第一个人权白皮书，标志着中国政府也开始正式使用"人权"这一术语。2004 年，"尊重和保障人权"写进中国宪法，使人权保障成为宪法原则。2007 年，"尊重和保障人权"首次载入作为执政党的中国共产党的章程。

应该说所有政府部门的工作都与人权有关，但是为了更好的、有目的地推动人权事业，2009 年 4 月 13 日和 2012 年 6 月 11 日，根据国务院授权，国务院新闻办先后发布了《国家人权行动计划（2009—2010 年）》和《国家人权行动计划（2012—2015 年）》。这是从专门人权角度所做的国家级的工作规划。其起草是由跨部门国家人权行动计划联席会议机制负责的，该联席会议机制也负责计划的监督和评估工作。联席会议的成员来自国家立法、司法和行政部门，也包括几个全国性的社会组织。具体包括全国人大常委会法制工作委员会、全国政协社会和法制委员会、最高人民法院、最高人民检察院、国家发展和改革委员会、教育部、国家民族事务委员会、民政部、司法部、人力资源和社会保障部、卫生部、中国残疾人联合会、中国人权研究会等50多家单位。

国家人权行动计划是在中国政府各有关部门和社会各界广泛参与下制定的。在国家人权行动计划联席会议机制领导下,起草工作邀请了来自中国社会科学院、上海社会科学院、北京大学、南开大学、山东大学、中国政法大学、武汉大学、中国人民大学、中央党校等高校和研究机构的专家组成专家小组参与本计划的起草制定工作。在计划起草制定过程中,多次召开联席会议,与政府各有关部门进行反复研究;多次召开座谈会,邀请中国法学会、中华全国律师协会、中国法律援助基金会、中华环境保护基金会、中国教育学会、中国妇女发展基金会、中国扶贫基金会、中国残疾人福利基金会、中国人权发展基金会等20多个单位参加,广泛征求各社会团体、非政府组织、高等院校、研究机构以及社会各界的意见,反复讨论和修订。

中国起草实施国家人权行动计划是响应1993年世界人权大会通过的《维也纳人权行动宣言和纲领》的积极举措。

2009年底,联席会议机制组织开展首个行动计划的中期评估工作,责成各有关部门和单位对2009年度行动计划执行情况作出报告,组织有关单位和专家学者有针对性地进行调查研究,并召开了"《国家人权行动计划(2009—2010年)》执行情况中期评估会议",对前期的落实情况进行评估检查,对如何完成行动计划下一阶段的目标任务提出意见和建议,作出相应部署。中期评估工作有力地推动了行动计划的全面落实。

2010年11月,联席会议机制启动了行动计划终期评估工作,对计划的完成情况展开全面、科学的评估。终期评估工作分调研、评估、总结三个阶段。2010年11—12月,国务院新闻办公室组织新闻单位、人权专家赴上海、四川等地进行调研,听取各界人士的意见和建议,形成了调研报告。中国人权研究会先后五次组织人权专家和非政府组织代表赴北京、天津、山东、广东、福建、浙江等地,就《行动计划》的落实情况进行实地调研,提出意见和建议。在此基础上,联席会议机制责成各有关部门和单位对各自所涉行动计划任务的执行、落实与完成情况进行自我评估,提交了书面评估材料。联席会议机制组织中央国家机关有关部门和单位、人民团体、非政府组织以及南开大学、上海社会科学院、中国社会科学院、中央党校等高校和科研机构的人权专家成立了评估小组，汇集各方面资料，对行动计划的执行情况进行认真的评估总结。在评估过程中，联席会议机制和评估小组多次召开工作会议，对照行动计划中各项指标，对各部门、各单位的自我评估情况进行逐条核实和研究，并通过信函、通话等多种方式广泛征求联席会议机制成员单位和社会各界的意见和建议，最后形成了《〈国家人权行动计划（2009－2010年）〉评估报告》。

在2012年发布的第二个国家人权行动计划，更加强调计划的实施和监督工作。它对实施和监督做了专章规定，特别强调，中央和国家机关各有关部门、各级地方政府应高度重视，结合各部门工作职责和各地区特点，采取切实有效的措施完成行动计划确定的各项目标任务。国家人权行动计划联席会议机制开展阶段性调研、检查和终期评估，并公布评估报告。特别是要发挥社会组织在人权保障中的建设性作用；将《行动计划》作为人权教育和培训的重要内容，切实提高实施《行动计划》的自觉性；鼓励新闻媒体在《行动计划》的宣传、实施和监督方面发挥积极作用。

中国是一个发展中人口大国，过去也曾经历过法治被忽视和破坏带来的深刻的经验教训，改革开放以来，中国大力倡导依法治国和保障人权，特别是进入新的世纪以来，发展变化很快，进步明显。

二、中国的人权白皮书是什么性质的文件，如何撰写，发布情况如何？

中国国务院新闻办公室发布的人权白皮书是中国政府发布的系统介绍中国人权领域相关政策、立场和发展状况的重要文件。

起草发布人权白皮书的目的是，及时总结中国在人权领域的取得成就、遇到的问题和挑战，在全社会倡导尊重和保障人权的社会文化，向全社会公告，同时接受全社会的监督。

1991年11月2日，国务院新闻办公室发表《中国的人权状况》白皮书，是第一个人权白皮书。它向国内外正式表明中国政府对人权的态度、立场、基本政策和实践情况，具有较高的权威性。它一经发布，就在国内法学界引发了关于人权问题的讨论热潮，极大地促进了国内的人权工作。

自第一个人权白皮书发表以来，国务院新闻办相继发表了 30 多个与人权有关的白皮书，其中有的白皮书一般性介绍中国人权状况和中国人权事业新发展，有的专门介绍西藏、新疆等具体地区的人权状况，还有针对知识产权、司法改革等问题的专题性白皮书和针对妇女、儿童、老年人等特殊群体权益保障的白皮书。它们具体、动态地记录和展现了中国人权事业的发展进程。

最近的人权白皮书是 2013 年 5 月 14 日发布《2012 年中国人权事业的进展》和 2014 年 5 月 26 日发布的《2013 年中国人权事业的新进展》。人权白皮书的发布有内容更加丰富、频率更快的态势。

中国人权白皮书的起草由国务院新闻办牵头负责，国家各个部委、最高立法和司法部门提供各自的材料，总结人权领域的工作成就、出现的不足以及下一步的工作方向。在汇总了各个部门的材料之后，国务院新闻办组织一个由政府和学者等参加的起草组，邀请人权领域的全国性的社会组织的专家、学者等参加起草，最终形成正式发布的白皮书。

三、中国人权白皮书在司法工作中的人权保障有哪些反映？

（一）2012 年 10 月 9 日《中国的司法改革》白皮书

每一部综合性的人权白皮书中都有司法工作中的人权保障的内容。值得注意的是，2012 年 10 月 9 日发表的《中国的司法改革》白皮书全面、系统地介绍了中国司法改革的基本情况和主要成就。这个白皮书有十个突出内容概括介绍如下。

1. 防止冤错案

中国的司法改革抓住容易发生执法问题的薄弱环节，加强权力运行的监督制约，为防止冤错案提供了制度保障。

首先是严禁刑讯逼供和非法取证。中国修改刑事诉讼法，完善刑事证据制度,确立了非法证据排除规则,明确采用刑讯逼供和其他非法手段搜集的证据,应当予以排除。

二是强化证人出庭作证。证人出庭作证对于提高庭审质量、有效减少冤错案有重要意义。为鼓励证人出庭作证,建立完善了证人保护制度,明确了证人保护的范围、规定了具体的保护措施、建立了证人出庭作证补助等制度。新刑诉法有以下相关规定:

第六十一条 人民法院、人民检察院和公安机关应当保障证人及其近亲属的安全。

对证人及其近亲属进行威胁、侮辱、殴打或者打击报复,构成犯罪的,依法追究刑事责任;尚不够刑事处罚的,依法给予治安管理处罚。

第六十二条 对于危害国家安全犯罪、恐怖活动犯罪、黑社会性质的组织犯罪、毒品犯罪等案件,证人、鉴定人、被害人因在诉讼中作证,本人或者其近亲属的人身安全面临危险的,人民法院、人民检察院和公安机关应当采取以下一项或者多项保护措施:

(一)不公开真实姓名、住址和工作单位等个人信息;

(二)采取不暴露外貌、真实声音等出庭作证措施;

(三)禁止特定的人员接触证人、鉴定人、被害人及其近亲属;

(四)对人身和住宅采取专门性保护措施;

(五)其他必要的保护措施。

证人、鉴定人、被害人认为因在诉讼中作证,本人或者其近亲属的人身安全面临危险的,可以向人民法院、人民检察院、公安机关请求予以保护。

人民法院、人民检察院、公安机关依法采取保护措施,有关单位和个人应当配合。

第六十三条 证人因履行作证义务而支出的交通、住宿、就餐等费用,应当给予补助。证人作证的补助列入司法机关业务经费,由同级政府财政予以保障。

有工作单位的证人作证,所在单位不得克扣或者变相克扣其工资、奖金及其他福利待遇。

三是保障并强化犯罪嫌疑人、被告人的辩护权。将犯罪嫌疑人委托辩护律师的时间由起诉阶段提前到侦查阶段,并充分保障了辩护律师的执业权利。扩大了法律援助的范围,将原来仅在审判阶段提供的法律援助,拓展到侦查、审查起诉阶段。

四是加强对诉讼活动的法律监督。规定检察机关对侦查人员以非法方法搜集证据的,依法进行调查核实,提出纠正意见。实行在押人员约见检察官制度,进一步畅通发现冤错案的渠道。

五是推进执法规范化建设。通过修改刑事诉讼法,完善了拘留、逮捕后送押和讯问制度,侦查人员对被羁押人的讯问应当在看守所内进行。全面推行侦查讯问过程录音录像制度。看守所与住所检察室联网,对侦查讯问和监管活动进行实时、动态监督。完善在押人员投诉和调查机制,建立在押人员约见民警、看守所负责人制度,及时调查、处理在押人员投诉、控告。

六是加强司法活动的社会监督。进一步完善诉讼当事人、参与人的权利义务告知制度,深化司法公开,以公开促公正。通过完善人民陪审员制度,探索建立人民监督员制度,拓宽群众参与和监督司法活动的渠道。

2. 司法公开透明

人民法院将审判公开延伸到立案、庭审、执行、听证、文书、审务等各个方面。

白皮书指出,面对社会矛盾多发、案件数量大、新情况新问题层出不穷的状况,中国司法机关在加强自身建设的同时,全面推进司法公开,让司法权力在阳光下运行,在社会各界的有效监督下公开、公平、公正地行使。

扩大公开的事项和内容——白皮书显示,人民法院将审判公开延伸到立案、庭审、执行、听证、文书、审务等各个方面。人民检察院依法充分公开办案程序、复查案件工作规程、诉讼参与人在各诉讼阶段的权利和义务、法律监督结果。公安机关、司法行政机关将主要职责、执法依据、执法程序、执法结果及警务工作纪律等向社会广泛公开。

丰富公开的形式和载体——白皮书指出,司法公开从各部门分散发布,转变为统一的信息服务窗口集中发布。公开载体从传统的公示栏、报刊、宣传册等,拓展到网站、博客、微博客、即时通信工具等网络新兴媒介。建立健全新闻发言人和新闻发布例会制度,及时发布司法信息。

强化公开的效果和保障——白皮书指出,加强裁判和检察、公安业务文书的说理和论证,邀请民众、专家参与公开听证、论证过程,开通民意沟通电子邮箱,设立全国统一的举报电话,建立部门负责人接待日,加强司法公开的人力物力保障,确保了司法公开的有序推进和良好效果。

随着社会的发展,公众对于司法的关注度越来越高。中国全面实行审判公开,除涉及国家秘密、个人隐私和未成年人刑事案件之外,其他案件的审理都向社会公众公开,允许旁听。

除此之外,为保障当事人的合法权益和社会公众的知情权、监督权,还完善了以下制度。

一是健全司法公开制度。人民法院实行六项公开,将立案、庭审、执行、听证、文书、审务向社会公开。人民检察院实行检务公开,对不起诉案件、刑事申诉案件依法实行公开审查、公开听证、公开答复。公安机关实行警务公开,推出刑事案件立案和破案回告、消防事故责任公开认定、交通事故公开处理等制度。

二是建立了人民法院、人民检察院、公安机关的新闻发言人制度,通过设立举报电话、设置沟通民意的信箱、公开服务窗口,通过公示栏、报刊、网站、微博等,及时通报重大信息,回应社会关切。

三是完善人民陪审员制度,拓宽人民陪审员的选任来源,增强人民陪审员的代表性。

四是探索建立人民监督员制度,依照监督程序对人民检察院办理职务犯罪案件过程中容易出现问题的立案、撤案、逮捕、不起诉等环节进行监督、评议。

3. 推进量刑规范化

明确量刑步骤,细分法定刑幅度,明确量刑情节的量化标准

白皮书指出,近年来,中国司法机关积极推进量刑规范化改革,建立案例指导制度,加强案件管理,有力促进了司法行为的规范化。

白皮书说,由于中国经济社会发展不平衡、司法人员司法能力存在差异、地方保护主义观念尚未根除等原因,司法裁量权的行使不透明、司法行为不规范等现象依然存在。

白皮书指出,为了规范量刑活动,中国最高人民法院在总结试点经验的基础上,制定了《人民法院量刑指导意见(试行)》和《关于规范量刑程序若干问题的意见(试行)》。明确量刑步骤,细分法定刑幅度,明确量刑情节的量化标准。对于公诉案件,人民检察院依法提出量刑建议,当事人和辩护人、诉讼代理人可以提出量刑意见。在法庭审理中,建立相对独立的量刑程序,对与定罪、量刑有关的事实、证据进行调查、辩论。人民法院在刑事裁判文书中说明量刑理由。这些改革进一步规范了量刑裁判权,保障了量刑活动的公开与公正。

此外,白皮书还指出,近年来,中国司法机关选择法律适用问题比较典型的案例作为指导性案例予以发布,供各级司法人员处理类似案件时参照。案例指导制度促进了司法自由裁量权的规范行使,加强了法律适用的统一性。

4. 慎重适用死刑

白皮书指出,自 2007 年死刑案件核准权统一由最高人民法院行使以来,中国死刑适用标准更加统一,判处死刑的案件逐步减少。

白皮书指出,中国保留死刑,但严格控制和慎重适用死刑。中国刑法规定死刑只适用于极少数罪行极其严重的犯罪分子,并规定了严格的适用标准。2011 年颁布的《刑法修正案(八)》取消了 13 个经济性非暴力犯罪的死刑,①占死刑罪名总数的 19.1%,规定对审判时已年满七十五周岁的人一般不适用死刑,并建立死刑缓期执行限制减刑制度,为逐步减少死刑适用创造法律和制度条件。

白皮书强调,死刑直接关系到公民生命权的剥夺,适用死刑必须慎之又慎。从 2007 年开始,由最高人民法院统一行使死刑案件的核准权。中国实行死刑第二审案件全部开庭审理,完善了死刑复核程序,加强死刑复核监督。最高人民法院复核死刑案件,应当讯问被告人,辩护律师提出要求的,应当听取辩护律师的意见。最高人民检察院可以向最高人民法院提出意

---

① 这 13 个经济性非暴力犯罪的罪名是:走私文物罪,走私贵重金属罪,走私珍贵动物、珍贵动物制品罪,走私普通货物、物品罪,票据诈骗罪,金融凭证诈骗罪,信用证诈骗罪,虚开增值税专用发票、用于骗取出口退税、抵扣税款发票罪,伪造、出售伪造的增值税专用发票罪,盗窃罪,传授犯罪方法罪,盗窃古文化遗址、古墓葬罪,盗掘古人类化石、古脊椎动物化石罪。

见。死刑复核程序的改革,确保了办理死刑案件的质量。

5. 遏制刑讯逼供

司法人员在办案过程中不得强迫任何人证实自己有罪。

白皮书介绍,2012年修改的刑事诉讼法明确规定,司法人员在办案过程中不得强迫任何人证实自己有罪,保障犯罪嫌疑人、被告人供述的自愿性。采用刑讯逼供等非法方法收集的犯罪嫌疑人、被告人供述和采用暴力、威胁等非法方法收集的证人证言、被害人陈述,应当予以排除;收集物证、书证不符合法定程序,可能严重影响司法公正,不能补正或者作出合理解释的,应当予以排除,并明确了非法证据排除的具体程序。公安机关、人民检察院、人民法院在侦查、审查起诉和审判阶段发现有应当排除的非法证据的,都应当予以排除。

我国完善拘留、逮捕后送押和讯问制度。白皮书指出,拘留后应当立即将被拘留人送看守所羁押,至迟不得超过24小时。逮捕后应当立即将被逮捕人送看守所羁押;侦查人员对被羁押人的讯问应当在看守所内进行。结合司法机关执法信息化建设,在讯问、羁押、庭审、监管场所实行录音录像。全面推行侦查讯问过程录音录像制度,明确规定对可能判处无期徒刑、死刑的案件或者其他重大犯罪案件,讯问过程必须进行录音录像;录音或者录像应当全程进行,保持完整性。

6. 保障辩护权

为落实中国宪法规定的辩护权而建立的辩护制度,是中国刑事诉讼的一项基本制度,体现了国家对生命、自由等人权的尊重。白皮书指出,近年来,中国改革和完善辩护制度,改变过去司法实践中"重打击、轻保护"的观念,强调保障人权,保障犯罪嫌疑人、被告人及时获得辩护。

白皮书介绍,中国1979年制定的刑事诉讼法规定,被告人在法院审判阶段才有权委托辩护人。1996年修改的刑事诉讼法明确规定,犯罪嫌疑人在侦查阶段就可以聘请律师提供法律帮助,案件侦查终结移送检察机关后有权委托辩护人。2012年修改的刑事诉讼法进一步明确规定,犯罪嫌疑人自被侦查机关第一次讯问或者被采取强制措施之日起,有权委托辩护人,被告人有权随时委托辩护人。犯罪嫌疑人、被告人在押期间要求委托辩护人的,人民法院、人民检察院和公安机关应当及时转达其要求,犯罪嫌疑人、被告人的监护人、近亲属也可以代为委托辩护人。

白皮书介绍,2006年至2011年期间,全国律师共为2 454 222件刑事案件提供了辩护,比2001年至2005年期间增长了54.16%。

白皮书介绍,2007年修订的律师法,对律师参与诉讼特别是刑事诉讼应当享有的权利进行了补充和强化。规定律师在法庭上发表的代理、辩护意见,除危害国家安全、恶意诽谤他人、严重扰乱法庭秩序的言论外,不受法律追究。这些举措促进了律师辩护职能的有效行使。

白皮书介绍,及时会见在押犯罪嫌疑人、被告人,并查阅案卷材料和调查取证,直接关系到辩护律师在刑事诉讼中辩护职能的发挥。2012年修改的刑事诉讼法规定,除极少数案件外,辩护律师持律师执业证书、律师事务所证明和委托书或者法律援助公函,即可会见在押的犯罪嫌疑人、被告人;辩护律师会见犯罪嫌疑人、被告人时不被监听。辩护律师在审查起诉阶段,即可查阅、摘抄、复制本案案卷材料。辩护人有权申请人民检察院、人民法院调取公安机关、人民检察院收集的证明犯罪嫌疑人、被告人无罪或者罪轻的证据材料。同时规定,辩护人认为公安机关、人民检察院、人民法院及其工作人员阻碍其依法行使诉讼权利的,有权向同级或者上一级人民检察院申诉或者控告。人民检察院对申诉或者控告应当及时进行审查,情况属实的,通知有关机关予以纠正。

7. 提高国家赔偿救助标准

白皮书指出,近年来,国家刑事赔偿标准随经济社会发展不断提高,侵犯公民人身自由权每日赔偿金额从1995年的17.16元人民币,上升到2012年的162.65元人民币。

白皮书指出,中国确立国家赔偿制度,对国家机关和国家机关工作人员行使职权时给公民、法人和其他组织的合法权益造成的损害,国家依法予以赔偿。2010年修改的国家赔偿法健全了国家赔偿工作机构,畅通了赔偿请求渠道,扩大了赔偿范围,明确了举证责任,增加了精神损害赔偿,提高了赔偿标准,保障了赔偿金及时支付,进一步完善了行政赔偿、刑事赔偿和非刑事司法赔偿制度。2011年,各级法院审结行政赔偿案件(一审)、刑事赔偿案件、非刑事司法赔偿案件共计 6 786 件;其中,审结刑事赔偿案件 868 件,赔偿金额 3 067 万余元人民币,与 2009 年相比,分别增长 16.04%、42.9%。

白皮书说,近年来,中国积极探索建立对刑事被害人的救助制度,对遭受犯罪行为侵害、无法及时获得有效赔偿、生活陷入困境,特别是因遭受严重暴力犯罪侵害,导致严重伤残甚至死亡的刑事被害人或其近亲属,由国家给予适当资助。各地根据经济社会发展状况,确定刑事被害人救助的具体标准和范围,并将刑事被害人救助工作与落实法律援助、社会保障等相关制度相衔接,完善了刑事被害人权益保障体系。2009 年至 2011 年,司法机关共向 25 996 名刑事被害人发放救助金 3.5 亿余元人民币,提供法律援助 11 593 件。

(二)2014 年 5 月 26 日《2013 年中国人权事业的进展》白皮书

2014 年 5 月 26 日发表了最新的《2013 年中国人权事业的进展》白皮书。

其中特别提到,多措并举防范冤假错案,遏制刑讯逼供,公民人身自由与生命健康权利更有保障。

在审判公开方面,最高人民法院发布《关于推进司法公开三大平台建设的若干意见》和《关于人民法院在互联网公布裁判文书的规定》,全面推进审判流程公开、裁判文书公开、执行信息公开三大平台建设,增进公众对司法裁判的知情了解。中国法院庭审直播网建成,各级法院全年直播案件庭审 4.5 万次。济南市中级人民法院通过微博全程直播薄熙来案庭审情况,受到广泛、积极关注。各类互联网信息服务网站为公众有效获取信息提供服务的水平大大提高。

白皮书强调:"生命健康权、人身自由权、人格尊严权等人身权利的保护状况,是衡量一个国家人权保护水平的最重要的标尺之一。"2013 年,中国废止劳动教养制度,采取专项行动打击拐卖犯罪、查找解救被拐妇女儿童,依法惩处严重侵害公民人身权利的犯罪,完善冤假错案防止、纠正机制,多措并举保障犯罪嫌疑人、被告人和被羁押人的人身权利,加大安全生产、食品药品等重点领域执法力度,公民人身权利得到切实保障。

防止和纠正冤假错案的措施进一步加强。2013 年,公安部发布《关于进一步加强和改进刑事执法办案工作,切实防止发生冤假错案的通知》等文件,深化错案预防制度机制建设,加强对执法办案全方位、全过程、即时性监督,从源头上防止冤假错案的发生。

最高人民检察院发布《关于切实履行检察职能,防止和纠正冤假错案的若干意见》,健全检察环节错案发现、纠正、防范和责任追究机制;严把事实关、证据关、程序关和法律适用关,对侦查机关不应当立案而立案的,督促撤案 25 211 件;对滥用强制措施、违法取证、刑讯逼供等侦查活动违法情形,提出纠正意见 72 370 件次;对证据不足和不构成犯罪的,决定不批捕 100 157 人、不起诉 16 427 人。保障犯罪嫌疑人诉讼权利和律师执业权利,监督纠正指定居所监视居住不当 606 件,监督纠正阻碍辩护人行使诉讼权利案件 2 153 件。加强羁押必要性审查,对不需要继续羁押的 23 894 名犯罪嫌疑人建议释放或者变更强制措施。注重保障被羁押人员合法权益,监督纠正刑罚执行和监管活动中的违法情形 42 873 件次;督促清理久押不决案件,监督纠正超期羁押 432 人次。

2012 年 12 月 20 日,最高人民法院发布关于适用刑事诉讼法的司法解释共 548 条,这是新中国成立以来条文最多的司法解释。非法证据排除、上诉不加刑等保护当事人各项诉讼权利的原则得以细化落实。2013 年 10 月 9 日,最高人民法院发布了《关于建立健全防范刑事冤假错案工作机制的意见》,坚持疑罪从无原则,规定对定罪证据不足的案件,应当依法宣告被告人无罪;采用刑讯逼供等非法方法收集的供述,应当排除;未在规定的办案场所讯问取得的供述,未依法对讯问进行全程录音录像取得的供述,以及不能排除以非法方法取得的供述,应当予以排除。确保无罪的人不受刑事追究。全年各级法院依法宣告 825 名被告人无罪,并对在申诉中发现的冤假错案,依法予以再审改判。

犯罪嫌疑人、被告人和被羁押者的人身权利得到更好保障。2013 年,公安部制定《公安机关执法办案场所办案区使用管理规定》,规范办案区的使用和管理,严格实行讯问询问过程录音录像制度;实施新的《看守所建设标准》,深入推行看守所医疗卫生社会化,要求所有看守所都要向社会开放,提高执法工作透明度。人民检察院按照"全面、全程、全部"原则,进一步完善了同步录音录像制度,切实保障犯罪嫌疑人的合法权利。

四、中国在人权领域与联合国的合作关系如何？

中国作为发展中大国，也是联合国的创始会员国，安全理事会的常任理事国，一直以积极负责的态度参加联合国的人权活动与工作，努力促进国际人权事业的健康发展，在世界人权事务中发挥着越来越重要的作用。

中国积极参加联合国人权机构的工作。中国从1979年起连续3年派代表以观察员身份列席联合国人权委员会会议。1981年，中国在联合国经济与社会理事会第一届常会上当选为人权委员会成员国，并一直连任该委员会成员。自1984年开始，中国向人权委员会推荐的人权事务专家连续当选为防止歧视和保护少数小组委员会的委员和候补委员。

2006年联合国人权理事会正式成立。同年5月9日中国获选人权理事会理事成员国。并在2009年5月，中国获得人权理事会成员的连任。2013年11月12日，第68届联合国大会在联合国总部举行全体会议，投票改选联合国人权理事会成员。中国获得176票的高票成功当选，任期自2014年至2016年。中国无论作为人权理事会成员还是观察员，均积极深入参与多边人权机制工作，与联合国人权高专办、人权特别机制保持良好合作，及时答复人权特别机制来函，多次接待宗教信仰自由特别报告员、任意拘留问题工作组、酷刑问题特别报告员等特别机制访华。

中国政府高度重视参与联合国人权理事会普遍定期审议工作。除了认真审议其他国家外，我国政府积极筹备和参加对我国的审议工作。2009年是我国首次接受审议。联合国人权理事会第十一次会议于2009年6月2日至18日在日内瓦万国宫举行，会议通过了对中国人权普遍定期审议的报告。

2013年10月22日，人权理事会普遍定期审议工作组在日内瓦开展了对中国的第二次普遍定期审议，备受瞩目。因为报名发言的国家很多，每个国家在会上只有51秒的发言时间。有137个国家的代表、包括50多名大使先后发言，有110多位代表的发言中包括了积极评价中国人权事业成就的内容。10月25日，人权理事会普遍定期审议工作组顺利通过了中国接受第二轮审议的报告。2014年3月20日，联合国人权理事会在日内瓦核可了中国接受第二轮审议的报告。

多年来,中国积极参加国际人权法律文书的起草和制定。中国派代表参与了联合国《儿童权利公约》、《禁止酷刑和其他残忍、不人道或有辱人格的待遇或处罚公约》和《残疾人权利公约》等公约的起草工作。公约之外,中国还参加了《保护民族、种族、语言、宗教上属于少数人的权利宣言》《发展权利宣言》等人权文件的起草。迄今为止,中国已先后加入了20多项国际人权公约和议定书。对于已加入的人权公约,中国政府按规定定期提交有关公约执行情况的报告,履行自己应承担的责任和义务。具体情况请见图表。

我国提交人权条约履约报告情况

公约	公约规定	我国提交报告情况	港澳	审议
经济、社会和文化权利国际公约 ICESCR	一年内首期报告,每五年定期报告	2003年6月(首次)	含港澳	2005年4月
		2010年6月(第二次)	含港澳	2014年4月
消除一切形式种族歧视国际公约 ICERD	一年内首期报告,每两年定期报告	1983年2月(首次)		1983年8月
		1986年6月(第二次)		1986年3月
		1987年12月(第三、四次合并)		1990年8月
		1990年1月(第五至七次合并)		1996年8月
		2000年10月(第八、九次合并)	含港澳	2001年7、8月
		2007年6月(第十至十三次合并)	含港澳	2009年8月
消除对妇女一切形式歧视公约 CEDM	一年内首期报告,每四年定期报告	1983年5月(首次)		1984年3月
		1989年6月(第二次)		1992年1月
		1997年5月(第三、第四次合并)	含香港	1999年2月
		2004年1月(第五、六次合并)	含香港	2006年5月
		2012年1月(第七、八次合并)	含香港	2014年10月
禁止酷刑和其他残忍、不人道或有辱人格的待遇或处罚公约 CAT	一年内首期报告,每四年定期报告	1999年12月(首次)		1990年4月
		1992年10月(第二次) 1996年12月(补充报告)		1993年4月 1996年5月
		1999年5月(第三次)	含香港	2000年5月
		2005年1月(第四、五次合并)	含香港	2008年11月
		2013年3月(第六次)	含香港	2015年11月

续表

公约	公约规定	我国提交报告情况	港澳	审议
儿童权利公约 CRC	两年内首期报告，每五年定期报告	1995年3月（首次）		1996年5月
		2003年6月（第二次）	含香港	2005年9月
		2010年6月（第三、四次合并）	含香港	2013年9月
儿童权利关于买卖儿童、儿童卖淫和儿童色情制品问题的任择议定书 CRC-SC	两年内首期报告，此后随公约	2005年4月（首次）	含澳门	2005年9月
儿童权利公约关于儿童卷入武装冲突问题的任择议定书 CRC-AC	两年内首期报告，此后随公约	2010年11月（首次）		2013年9月
残疾人权利公约 CRPD	一年内首期报告，每四年定期报告	2010年8月（首次）	含港澳	2012年9月

中国在国际人权领域的日益活跃，并获得国际社会的积极肯定和赞誉。2003年11月，中国承办了联合国亚太经社理事会关于制定《残疾人权利公约》的政府间会议，会议通过了《北京宣言》。1995年9月，中国成功地在北京举办了联合国第四次妇女大会和非政府组织妇女论坛。中国还参与推动第二个"亚太残疾人十年（2003—2012年）"活动。2003年12月，第五十八届联合国大会主席朱里安·亨特向中国残疾人联合会主席邓朴方颁发了"联合国人权奖"。

中国还积极开展人权领域的交流。中国与许多西方国家就人权问题进行了多轮对话，邀请了众多联合国和其他国家的人权官员和专家访华，并派出代表团赴一些国家就国际人权领域的有关问题交换意见和看法。

五、联合国禁止酷刑委员会对中国的履约评价，如何理解？

作为《禁止酷刑公约》的条约机构，联合国禁止酷刑委员会经常对各国持尖锐的批评态度，而且极少能看到积极的肯定。这是酷刑这一主题决定的。不论过去还是现在,世界各地的反酷刑形势不容乐观。反酷刑不是一劳永逸的工作,不论发达国家还是发展中国家,都需要时时保持警惕。

不仅对中国有许多批评意见,对其他国家一样,包括美洲地区的许多国家。但不能仅仅因为有这些批评,其他国家就可以以此为理由,拒绝向这些国家引渡被指控犯罪的人。

中国的情况也是类似。联合国禁止酷刑委员会在审议中国的履约报告之后,提出了大量有价值的意见和建议。同时,因为有政治、意识形态方面的因素,存在一些国际非政府组织提供了片面、甚至不真实的信息,联合国禁止酷刑委员会对中国履约报告的审议引用这样的信息来源,使相关结论具有了意识形态和政治对抗的因素,引起了中国政府的抗议。①

虽然有这方面的实质为抗议的评论,但是中国政府还是本着友好、合作、严肃、认真的态度,对委员会的结论性意见进行了法律技术角度的回应和解答。② 这个称为"中华人民共和国政府对禁止酷刑委员会的结论和建议的评论"的文件英文版长达 20 页。

关于《结论性意见》第 31 段("缔约国关于执法人员实施酷刑或虐待的指控很少被调查或起诉,对一些实施酷刑的行为只施以纪律或行政处分""缔约国应确保及时、有效和公正地调查所有关于酷刑和虐待的指控"),中国政府认为,本段所述的情况是不符合事实。<u>首先</u>,在中国,被羁押者对其遭受的酷刑或虐待进行指控和举报的渠道是畅通的。被羁押者或其家属可以通过口头、书面、电子邮件或者约见派驻检察官等多种方式向看守所或其上级主管机关或检察机关进行控告,其他人也可以向上述单位进行举报。每个监区都有检察机关和看守所设置的供被羁押者投递控告和举报信件的信箱,并且每个监室都装有受虐待报警系统。此外,公安机关警务督察部门依据《公安机关督察条例》受理核查公众通过信函、电话等方式对民警违法违纪行为的举报和投诉。<u>其次</u>,中国有关执法机关会根据职权主动去发现发生在监管场所的酷刑或虐待行为。除监管场所的上级主管机关定期或不定期检查外,公安机关的督察民警还可以进入监管场所开展现场督察,检察机

---

① UN Document,CAT/C/CHN/CO/4, 12 December 2008.
② UN Document,CAT/C/CHN/CO/4ADD. 2, 18 December 2009.

关还会深入到监区、监室、提讯室、会见室进行实地检查,主动去发现看守所是否存在酷刑或虐待行为。第三,中国的《刑法》《刑事诉讼法》《人民警察法》等明确禁止对公民包括违法犯罪嫌疑人实施酷刑和虐待。对于发现的酷刑行为,有关执法机关都会依法予以严肃处理。对于情节较轻的,由行为人的主管机关给予纪律或行政处分;对于情节严重的,由检察机关立案侦查,依法追究行为人的刑事责任。中国公安机关对于发生在少数民警中的滥用强制措施、刑讯逼供、体罚虐待违法犯罪嫌疑人等问题,一直是发现一起,严肃查处一起,涉嫌犯罪的,由检察机关启动刑事责任追究程序;对危害程度及情节等较轻、不构成犯罪的,由监察部门进行独立调查,根据违法程度追究相关人员的行政责任,给予警告、记过、记大过、降级、撤职、开除等行政处分。

根据中国法律,中国的法院、检察机关依法分别独立行使审判权、检察权,对公务人员职务犯罪行为依法追究刑事责任;中国政府的行政监察部门、信访部门也负责受理核查公众对公务人员违法犯罪行为的检举和控告。这些为有关被羁押人员受到酷刑虐待的指控能够依法得到及时、有效和公正的调查、处置,以及对相关责任人员追究法纪责任提供了制度保障。

关于《结论性意见》第32、33段("缔约国尚未将完全符合《公约》所载的酷刑定义纳入其国内法")。中国的法律虽然没有专门规定酷刑的定义,但相关法律中涵盖了《公约》关于酷刑定义的各个方面。对基于任何意图或目的、无论以官方身份或者出于公职人员的同意或默认、对任何人采取的任何形式的酷刑,中国法律都是严厉禁止并予处罚的。

关于《结论性意见》中所说的中国法律中反对酷刑的规定"无法涵盖以官方身份实施酷刑的其他人"的问题,中国政府进行了反驳和说明。首先,中国《刑法》可以适用于实施酷刑行为的各项罪名,都不以行为人的身份、意图、目的为要件。同时,针对官方人员等具有特殊身份的人员犯罪,中国法律还作出了一些专门的规定。比如,《刑法》第238条第4款规定,国家机关工作人员利用职权犯非法拘禁罪的,从重处罚。对于司法工作人员为了获取证据而采取的酷刑行为,《刑法》第247条规定了刑讯逼供罪、暴力取证罪。对于监管人员对被监管人采取的酷刑行为,《刑法》第248条规定了虐待被监管人罪等。这些专门罪名的设置,体现了对国家工作人员犯罪的从严惩治,更为有力地保护了公民的合法权益。此外,中国禁止酷刑的政策和措施不仅针对刑事司法领域,也适用于行政执法领域的公务人员等。对于那些虽然不是国家工作人员,但由于公职人员或其他以官方身份行使职权的人的教唆、同意或者默许而实施上述行为的一般人员,根据中国《刑法》关于共同犯罪的规定,应当作为特定主体犯罪的共犯,适用国家机关工作人员所触犯的罪名进行追究。其次,中国法律规定应予处罚的酷刑行为既包括采取殴打、用刑具等方式造成肉体上痛苦的行为,也包括采取虐待、侮辱等方式造成精神上的痛苦的行为。例如,答复时的《刑事诉讼法》第 43 条规定:"严禁刑讯逼供和以威胁、引诱、欺骗以及其他非法的方法收集证据"。其中,"威胁"就是典型的造成精神痛苦的方法,而"其他非法的方法",则包括了所有能够造成肉体和精神痛苦的方法。《刑法》第 238 条规定,非法拘禁他人或者以其他方法非法剥夺他人人身自由的,构成犯罪;具有殴打、侮辱情节的,从重处罚。根据《刑法》第 247 条、第 248 条的规定,刑讯逼供罪、暴力取证罪和虐待被监管人罪,既包括使用暴力的方法,也包括使用虐待、侮辱等造成精神上剧烈痛苦的方法。公务人员在执行公务过程中采取侮辱、诽谤、非法搜查、非法侵入公民住宅、非法剥夺公民宗教信仰自由或者侵犯少数民族习惯等,对被害人造成精神上痛苦的,依法予以处罚。

在专家证人本人看来,中国刑法当中一直有禁止刑讯逼供的条款,将刑讯逼供行为作为犯罪予以追究和处罚。"刑讯逼供"是中国语言中的一个法律术语,其对应的内容与酷刑相当,而且在中国,它的内涵和外延也是与时俱进的。在这方面,前联合国禁止酷刑特别报告员和禁止酷刑委员会的对中国完善立法的关注和建议可以理解,但是如果解释成中国没有禁止酷刑,这是不正确的,不符合实际情况。

禁止酷刑委员会做出了关于中国缺乏对酷刑的调查和对使用酷刑的行为不予调查的批评和关注。诚然,这些问题在一些地方的一些个案中是存在的,但是这并不是普遍存在的问题。而且,这些也正是中国国内法律界、法学界关注的热点问题。近些年来,这些问题的解决已经有了突出的进展。下面还有专门的介绍。

关于《结论性意见》第17段（"缔约国应汇编关于监督国家一级执行《公约》情况的统计数据"），答复说："《结论》要求提供的统计数据十分详细、复杂，对中国这样一个有着复杂国情的发展中大国来说，完成这些统计工作需要付出巨大的成本，短期内难以实现。但中国政府高度重视委员会的意见，将努力加强在反酷刑领域的调查统计工作。"时至今日，相关统计工作已有进展，后文将相关内容中引用有关的统计数字。

六、联合国酷刑问题特别报告员对中国的访问报告如何评价中国的反酷刑工作？

2006年3月10日，原联合国人权委员会酷刑和其他残忍、不人道或有辱人格的待遇或处罚问题特别报告员曼弗雷德·诺瓦克的报告《对中国的访问》①全面展现了该报告员的访问情况以及他对中国禁止酷刑工作的认识。

我本人在此之前就认识诺瓦克教授，还在2010年在北京翻译出版了他的专著《国际人权制度导论》的中文版，对他的专业素养表示敬重。

报告显示，他在2005年11月20日至12月2日对中国进行了访问。他在报告中说，特别报告员对中国政府、特别是外交部表现出的专业水平、合作精神和共同致力于访问团的目标深表赞赏。原来计划访问山东省和新疆维吾尔自治区伊宁，但是由于时间有限，特别报告员不得不取消了对上述地区的访问，特别报告员对此深表歉意，并感谢外交部和山东省以及伊宁自治州有关领导体谅对行程最后一刻的变更。

特别报告员在内容提要第3段中说："尽管酷刑在减少，特别是在城市地区，但特别报告员相信酷刑在中国仍然普遍存在。他欢迎该国政府愿意承认刑事司法制度中普遍存在酷刑，近年来，在中央和省一级作出了各种努力，反对酷刑和虐待。特别报告员认为，由于这些措施，近年来酷刑做法稳步减少。"

---

① UN Document，E/CN. 4/2006/6Add. 6，10 March 2006.

内容提要第 4 段特别报告员认为"中国持续的酷刑做法有成因",第 5 段说:"羁押场所的基本条件看来总体令人满意,但在同被羁押者交谈时,特别报告员对监狱纪律之严格、恐惧和自我约束之明显印象深刻。"

上述内容,笔者认为特别报告员在短暂的时间内,对中国这样一个地理和人口大国进行的访问,获得的认识难能可贵,同时也有一些局限性。他不可能全部使用他所见所闻来撰写他的报告,而是要结合许多书面信息、特别是访问前后的信息。内容提要第 2 段体现了这一点。

他对中国反酷刑的复杂性有所认识,同时承认中国的酷刑在稳步减少,羁押场所的基本条件总体令人满意,这是难得的对于中国反酷刑工作的理解和肯定。

特别报告员对中国存在的酷刑和反酷刑工作有尖锐的批评,我个人认为这非常符合他的身份,毕竟,他作为反对酷刑问题特别报告员,是要发现问题、批评不足并提出关切的。不过,他的短暂的访问以及由此形成的他个人的报告,在国际法上的法律性质和参考意义需要有适当的评估和认识。不能因为他的报告,就彻底否定中国禁止酷刑工作,甚至是中国的法治环境,报告没有这个意思,也不可能有这样的意思。

中国刑法早就废除政治罪的罪名,令人遗憾的是,特别报告员的报告还在讨论政治罪方面的司法工作。他也关注到中国劳动教养工作中可能存在的酷刑问题,2013 年中国已经正式废止了这一制度。

七、联合国人权理事会对中国的普遍定期审议情况如何?

2009 年,中国接受首轮审议后,中国政府接受了各国提出的 42 条建议,包括继续提高人民生活质量,加大扶贫力度,继续深化司法体制改革,进一步保障少数民族权利,继续帮助其他发展中国家实现发展权等。中国当时承诺:"当再次接受审查时,世界将看到一个经济更加繁荣、民主更加健全、法治更加完善、社会更加和谐、人民更加幸福的中国。"

此后,根据有关意见和建议,中国政府如期执行完毕《国家人权行动计划(2009—2010 年)》,于 2012 年 6 月制定并公布了第二期《国家人权行动计划(2012—2015年)》。中国政府不断加强司法体制建设,并将加强人权保障列为重要目标。2008年底启动的司法体制改革的60项任务目前已全部完成。《刑法修正案(八)》取消了13个经济性非暴力犯罪的死刑。2012年修改的《刑事诉讼法》完善了死刑复核程序和非法证据排除制度,规范了强制措施的适用,规定了在看守所内进行讯问和对讯问过程录音录像制度。2013年正式废止劳教改革制度。

2013年10月22日,人权理事会普遍定期审议工作组会议对中国进行第二轮审议,笔者本人也前往日内瓦旁听了此次审议过程。中国代表团团长吴海龙表现出了谦虚和包容的态度。他说,中国扶贫对象规模仍十分庞大,司法领域依然存在不公现象,执法人员人权意识和依法行政水平仍需提高。

包括约56个大使在内的130多个国家的代表在中国接受审议时发言。因为报名发言的国家实在太多,会议时间有限,每个国家只有51秒的发言时间。超过110个国家在发言中包括了对中国人权状况的积极肯定,赞赏中国在经济社会发展、民主法制建设、特殊群体权利保障、开展国际人权合作领域所取得的显著成就。一些西方国家就司法体制改革、非政府组织管理、与联合国人权机制合作等问题向中国提出了建议。会议表明,无论东西方国家,大多数国家都对中国人权事业的进展有积极和客观的认识。

2013年10月25日工作组顺利通过了由塞拉利昂、阿联酋和波兰三国组成的"三国小组"提交的中国接受第二轮审议的报告。中国代表团副团长、中国驻联合国日内瓦办事处及瑞士其他国际组织代表团临时代办吴海涛在发言中表示,报告中所载建议绝大部分是善意和建设性的。他承诺,中方将予以认真研究,结合国情积极考虑,并在明年3月人权理事会第25届会议前正式反馈立场。

各国在会上共提出252条建议。2014年3月20日,联合国人权理事会在日内瓦核可中国接受第二轮审议的报告时,中国政府正式反馈,经慎重研究和努力,中方决定接受其中204条建议,占建议总数的81%,涉及减贫、教育、司法改革等20多个领域。这体现了中国促进和保护人权的决心和勇气,显示了中方对各国建议的开放、积极和认真态度。

八、中国在预防酷刑方面有哪些新的进展?

中国吸收和采纳了联合国禁止酷刑委员会等国国际人权组织和机构的意见和建议,废止了劳动教养制度。在中国,实行了50多年的劳动教养制度在特定条件下为维护社会治安秩序、确保社会稳定、教育挽救违法人员发挥了积极作用。随着治安管理处罚法、禁毒法等法律的施行和刑法的不断完善,以及相关法律的有机衔接,劳动教养制度的作用逐渐被取代,劳动教养措施的使用逐年减少。自2013年3月起,各地基本停止使用劳动教养。2013年12月28日全国人大常委会通过废止有关劳动教养法律规定的决定,废止了劳动教养制度;并对正在被依法执行劳动教养的人员,解除劳动教养,剩余期限不再执行。

其他预防酷刑的样的进展还包括:

2013年,公安部发布《关于进一步加强和改进刑事执法办案工作,切实防止发生冤假错案的通知》等文件,深化预防制度机制建设,加强对执法办案全方位、全过程、即时性监督,从源头上防止酷刑和冤假错案的发生。

最高人民检察院发布《关于切实履行检察职能,防止和纠正冤假错案的若干意见》,健全检察环节错案发现、纠正、防范和责任追究机制;严把事实关、证据关、程序关和法律适用关,对侦查机关不应当立案而立案的,督促撤案25 211件;对滥用强制措施、违法取证、刑讯逼供等侦查活动违法情形,提出纠正意见72 370件次;对证据不足和不构成犯罪的,决定不批捕100 157人、不起诉16 427人。保障犯罪嫌疑人诉讼权利和律师执业权利,监督纠正指定居所监视居住不当606件,监督纠正阻碍辩护人行使诉讼权利案件2 153件。加强羁押必要性审查,对不需要继续羁押的23 894名犯罪嫌疑人建议释放或者变更强制措施。注重保障被羁押人员合法权益,监督纠正刑罚执行和监管活动中的违法情形42 873件次;督促清理久押不决案件,监督纠正超期羁押432人次。

最高人民法院发布关于适用刑事诉讼法的司法解释共548条,这是新中国成立以来条文最多的司法解释。非法证据排除、上诉不加刑等保护当事人各项诉讼权利的原则得以细化落实。2013年10月9日,最高人民法院发布了《关于建立健全防范刑事冤假错案工作机制的意见》,坚持疑罪从无原则,规定对定罪证据不足的案件,应当依法宣告被告人无罪;采用刑讯逼供等非法方法收集的供述,应当排除;未在规定的办案场所讯问取得的供述,未依法对讯问进行全程录音录像取得的供述,以及不能排除以非法方法取得的供述,应当予以排除。确保无罪的人不受刑事追究。全年各级法院依法宣告825名被告人无罪,并对在申诉中发现的冤假错案,依法予以再审改判。

犯罪嫌疑人、被告人和被羁押者的人身权利得到更好保障。2013年,公安部制定《公安机关执法办案场所办案区使用管理规定》,规范办案区的使用和管理,严格实行讯问询问过程录音录像制度;实施新的《看守所建设标准》,深入推行看守所医疗卫生社会化,要求所有看守所都要向社会开放,提高执法工作透明度。人民检察院按照"全面、全程、全部"原则,进一步完善了同步录音录像制度,切实保障犯罪嫌疑人的合法权利。

九、中国在调查和惩处酷刑方面有哪些新进展?是否有充分及时的调查,调查的结果是如何处理的?违法的官员是否受到了应有的法律追究有无统计数字?

修改后的《刑事诉讼法》规定了人民检察院对非法取证行为的调查程序和人民法院在审理过程中对非法证据排除的调查程序。第55条规定,人民检察院接到报案、控告、举报或者发现侦查人员以非法方法收集证据的,应当进行调查核实。对于确有以非法方法收集证据情形的,应当提出纠正意见;构成犯罪的,依法追究刑事责任。第171条第1款增加规定,人民检察院审查案件,认为可能存在以非法方法收集证据情形的,可以要求公安机关对证据收集的合法性作出说明。第56条规定,法庭审理过程中,审判人员认为可能存在以非法方法收集证据情形的,应当对证据收集的合法性进行法庭调查。当事人及其辩护人、诉讼代理人有权申请人民法院对以非法方法收集的证据依法予以排除。第57条规定,在对证据收集的合法性进行法庭调查的过程中,人民检察院应当对证据收集的合法性加以证明。现有证据材料不能证明证据收集的合法性的,人民检察院可以提请人民法院通知有关侦查人员或者其他人员出庭说明情况;人民法院可以通知有关侦查人员或者其他人员出庭说明情况。有关侦查人员或者其他人员也可以要求出庭说明情况。经人民法院通知,有关人员应当出庭。第58条规定,对于经过法庭审理,确认或者不能排除以非法方法收集证据情形的,对有关证据应当依法予以排除。

根据《行政监察法》和《人民警察法》的规定,公安机关纪委、监察部门可以依法调查民警刑讯逼供、滥用强制措施等侵犯涉案人员人身权利的违法违纪案件。

根据《人民检察院组织法》,中国检察机关内设的反渎职侵权部门担负着查处国家机关工作人员的渎职犯罪和利用职权实施的刑讯逼供或暴力取证等侵犯公民人身权利、民主权利的犯罪的职责。全国各级检察机关共设有反渎职侵权机构3 400多个,专职人员16 000多名,确保任何实施酷刑的行为能得到迅速公正的调查。

检察机关严格执法,依法办理监管民警体罚虐待被监管人、渎职造成被监管人员伤害或者死亡案件,维护正常的监管秩序,保障在押人员合法权益不受侵犯。自2008年至2011年底,检察机关依法办理了虐待被监管人案件158件,涉案共191人。

2008年,广西壮族自治区兴安县看守所监管民警王万安,因指使在押人员虐待另一名在押人员黎某某致死,被检察机关立案侦查并提起公诉。看守所所长盘定龙因试图隐瞒事实被提起公诉。2009年6月,广西南宁市中级人民法院依据《刑法》,以故意杀人罪判处王万安有期徒刑15年,以妨害作证罪判处盘定龙有期徒刑6年。

中国人民法院依法公正、及时审判涉及酷刑的侵犯公民人身权利的案件。2007年,因刑讯逼供被判有罪的50人,因暴力取证罪被判有罪的27人,因虐待被监管人被判有罪的77人;2008年,因刑讯逼供被判有罪的63人,因暴力取证罪被判有罪的34人,因虐待被监管人被判有罪的97人;2009年,因刑讯逼供被判有罪的60人,因暴力取证罪被判有罪的2人,因虐待被监管人被判有罪的88人;2010年,因刑讯逼供被判有罪的60人,因暴力取证罪被判有罪的2人,因虐待被监管人被判有罪的34人;2011年,因刑讯逼供被判有罪的36人,因暴力取证罪被判有罪的1人,因虐待被监管人被判有罪的26人。

十、中国如何保障被羁押人的人权?

中国高度重视改进看守所监管水平,严格防范刑讯逼供和超期羁押,改善羁押和监管条件,改善被羁押人的生活条件,保障被羁押人的合法权益。被羁押人送入看守所后七日内每日进行体表检查。被羁押人被提讯前后和提解出所及送返看守所时,严格实行体表检查制度。

逐步实行被羁押人床位制,推动看守所医疗服务社会化,使被羁押人患病能得到及时治疗。

完善被羁押人投诉和调查机制,建立被羁押人约见民警、看守所负责人和驻所检察官制度,及时受理、调查处理被羁押人投诉、控告。

被羁押人羁押期限即将届满的,看守所书面报告检察院驻看守所检察室,由其对侦查机关是否及时释放被羁押人或者变更强制措施进行监督。2008—2011年,全国检察机关通过监督检查,纠正看守所违法羁押5 473人。

大力打击和防范"牢头狱霸",在每个监室设置报警装置,在押人员被侵犯时能够及时报警;实行在押人员出看守所谈话和跟踪观察访谈制度,了解看守所有无"牢头狱霸"等违法行为;落实主、协管民警监室管理责任制,对因管理松懈,发生"牢头狱霸"致其他在押人员死亡或重伤的,依法依纪追究有关人员责任。建立特邀监督员巡查监督看守所制度,特邀监督员可以在工作期间采取不事先告知的方式对看守所履行职责、执法管理等工作进行监督。2010年,看守所发生事故数量同比下降31.6%。

在全国看守所推行被羁押人视频会见方式,方便家属探视。建立被羁押人的安全风险评估和分别管理制度,加强对被羁押人的心理干预。坚持"教育、感化、挽救"的工作方针,以管理促教育,寓教育于管理之中,充分体现对被羁押人的人性关怀,帮助其重塑积极向上的人生信念和健康文明的生活方式。

2012年6月11日发布的《国家人权行动计划(2012—2015年)》明确要求健全被羁押人权利保障机制:严格落实被羁押人入所体检、定期体表检查、收押权利义务告知、紧急报警等制度。严格执行对犯罪嫌疑人的提讯和还押制度。完善对被羁押人的安全风险评估、心理干预、投诉调查处理以及特邀监督员巡查看守所等制度和工作机制。健全被羁押人员约见派驻检察官、派驻检察官与被羁押人谈话以及检察官信箱等制度,预防并查处监管场所工作人员体罚、虐待、侮辱等侵犯被羁押人权利的行为。

中国制定了一系列规范监狱执法行为、保障罪犯合法权益的规章制度,如《2006至2010年监狱人民警察队伍建设规划纲要》《关于加强警务督察工作的意见》(2006年)《监狱人民警察六条禁令》(2006年)《关于加强监狱安全管理工作的若干规定》(2009年)《全国监狱工作"十二五"时期发展规划纲要》(2011年)和《2011至2015年监狱人民警察队伍建设规划纲要》(2011年)《监狱人民警察违法违纪处分规定》(2012年)等,明确要求监狱人民警察依法、严格、公正、文明执法,切实保障罪犯人格不受侮辱,其人身安全、合法财产和辩护、申诉、控告、检举以及其他未被依法剥夺或者限制的权利不受侵犯。明确规定严禁殴打、体罚、虐待或者指使、纵容他人殴打、体罚服刑人员,对违反规定的监狱人民警察视情节给予记过、记大过、降级、撤职、开除处分,涉嫌犯罪的,移送司法机关追究刑事责任。

中国各级行政、司法机关着重加强制度执行力,开展形式多样的专项执法检查活动,有效遏制和预防刑讯逼供等违法行为。2008年2月,最高人民检察院第十届检察委员会第九十四次会议通过的《人民检察院监狱检察办法》、《人民检察院看守所检察办法》、《人民检察院劳教检察办法》和《人民检察院监外执行检察办法》。

截至2011年底,中国检察机关在大型监狱或监狱集中地区设立83个派出检察院,在监管场所设立3 600多个派驻检察室,对中国95%以上的监狱、看守所实行了派驻检察。中国各级检察机关共有监所检察人员12 000多人,其中直接派驻到监狱、看守所等监管场所的检察人员有9 700多人,派驻监管场所检察制度进一步完善,派驻检察机构成为中国检察机关保障在押人员人权的重要形式和途径。

中国加强对监狱执法的监督检查。2009年开展了全国监狱清查事故隐患、促进安全监管专项活动,对全国监狱的罪犯生活卫生、警戒具使用、牢头狱霸等问题开展检查,排查隐患,督促整改。2011年开展了监狱规范化管理年活动,依据法律法规政策,共制定制度4 810项,修改6 087项,废除3 597项,制度规范化水平进一步提高。同年组织了三次全国范围的安全稳定大检查和隐患排查整治活动,督促整改监狱执法和监管安全中的问题和隐患。

在接受检察机关法律监督的同时,中国监狱全面落实并深化狱务公开,包括罪犯法定的权利和义务,监狱人民警察的法定权利、义务和纪律等执法管理内容。所有监狱通过报刊、广播、电视等新闻媒体,在监狱内设置狱务公开专栏和举报箱,开展狱务咨询等方式,向社会公众公开禁止酷刑等执法管理的法律依据、程序、结果和监督等内容,加强社会对监狱执法管理的监督。

十一、作为学者和专家对中国人权状况有哪些整体性的认识?

中国的高等院校和科研机构中共有30多个人权研究和教育中心,人权研究非常活跃。在这些研究中心中还有3个被教育部列为国家人权教育基地,根据《国家人权行动计划(2012—2015年)》,今年将新增加5个分布在不同地区的国家人权教育基地。

以下本人摘要提出几个在自己近年正式发表的论文和专著中阐述的观点,他们代表了本人对中国人权状况整体性和趋势性的认识。

(一)"尊严论"作为人权保障的基础

中国国内出版《人权》杂志2011年2月第1期发表本人的论文《以"尊严论"解读人权》,总结了中国政府和领导人在不同场合对于人的尊严作为人权保障基础的论断,强调基于人的尊严理解和实现人权的重要意义。

全文分为五个部分,分别是:一、"尊严论"体现国际人权法所强调的人权的根据和基础;二、"尊严论"指导下的人权理念强调政府尊重和保障人权的责任;三、"尊严论"指导下的人权理念强调人权的普遍性和平等性;四、

"尊严论"指导下的人权理念强调尊重权利享有者的主体地位,倾听她或他的声音;五、"尊严论"指导下的人权理念强调对权利主体的赋权。

中国《国家人权行动计划(2012—2015年)》在序言中也明确强调:"切实保障公民的经济、政治、社会和文化权利,促进社会更加公正、和谐,努力使每一个社会成员生活得更有尊严、更加幸福。"

(二)国权刑法向民权(人权)刑法的转变

2011年11月,由中国社会科学文献出版社出版专著《〈联合国禁止贩运人口议定书〉研究——以人权法为视角》,这是中国政府批准联合国反对人口贩运的"巴勒莫认定书"后,笔者从人权法角度结合联合国议定书和中国实践所做的专门研究的成果。

书中提到,中国刑法学界的学者们已经提出,刑法应该从国权刑法——即从关注国家对犯罪的追究和惩罚为主,向民权刑法——即强调以人权保障为核心——转变。笔者的这本书,对贩运人口问题的认识,也正是强调从单纯预防和打击贩运犯罪,发展到强调联合国经社理事会等在贩运问题上所强调的"人权至上"原则,强调保障人口贩运被害人的人权,并加强国际合作。

近年来,中国刑法不断修改,重刑主义已被放弃,恢复性司法,社会综合治理等颇受学界重视。

(三)重视软法和社会建设

本人2012年4月在《人权》杂志第2期发表论文《软法与人权和社会建设》。强调依法治国发展到今天,要回应社会的最新发展,重视软法的意义和作用。不仅国际法上出现了软法的兴起,国内软法现象也很突出。软法一方面是指操作性不强、实施不力的法律;另一方面是指在传统法律概念下或者说在严格的法律意义上只具有法律效果、却不具有法律约束力的规则。

本文强调重视对国际软法的研究和应用,比如联合国人权条约机构通过的《一般性意见》或《一般性评论》,重视它们对于国际人权法的发展、对于国际人权公约国内实施的指导意义。

同时,在国内,保护妇女、儿童、老年人、残疾人的立法过去也被批评为法院很少适用、往往是表面上内容丰富、却难以落实到生活当中的法律。现在强调法治,就要实施所有立法、包括这些社会立法。它们的实施方式与传统法律概念不同,关键不仅仅是司法救济,更重要的是要倚重社会机制建设,要将法律落实到日常生活和社区当中。要做到这一点,软法,包括社会组织的自治规则等,意义重大。人权的实现正是如此,既要强调传统的法律概念和实施机制,更要强调新的软法的意义和社会建设的重要性。

（四）法律以一个整体促进人权

2013年10月,在《人权》杂志第5期发表《论法律作为一个整体促进人权》的论文。在纪念联合国世界人权大会通过的《维也纳人权行动纲领和宣言》通过20周年之际,强调所有人权是一个整体,同时法律也是经一个整体促进人权。

要全面的理解法治和现代意义的法律,重视宪法、法律、部门规章、地方立法,结合国际法和国内法,传统意义上的法律规则和现代社会出现的"软法"规则,成功实现社会治理与人权保障。

（五）人权、发展和法治三位一体

在上述《论法律作为一个整体促进人权》一文以及接受媒体采访、会议等多种场合,笔者发表了人权、发展与法治在现代国家是三位一体的系统工程的思想。这一思想也集中体现在中国政府2013年5月发布的人权白皮书中。

人权与发展密不可分。没有发展,人权不可能获得充分而有效的保障。反过来,尊重和保障人权不仅是以人为本的发展目标,本身又可以促进发展主体积极性、主动性和创造性的发挥,扩大参与,促进发展,并保证发展是健康、公平、协调和可持续性的。

法治与发展也是密切联系的,它要满足国家、社会、家庭和个人等在日常生活和发展进程中对于规则的需求。有的法律是直接规定确认和保障人权的规则,有的则是通过调整社会关系间接地影响人权。我们对于发展的理解以及由此在法治建设过程中的权衡和实践,应当纳入人权的视角。

中国是一个发展中大国。继2004年"国家尊重和保障人权"写入《中华人民共和国宪法》之后,"尊重和保障人权,促进人权事业的全面发展"又写入《国民经济和社会发展第十一个五年规划纲要》,这是中国第一次将人权事业发展纳入国家经济和社会发展总体战略。2007年,"尊重和保障人权"首次载入中国共产党章程。尊重和保障人权成为中国共产党和中国领导人治国理政的重要原则。根据国务院授权,国务院新闻办公室2009年和2012年先后发布我国首个和第二个《国家人权行动计划》,专门从人权角度做出的全国性的政府工作规划,全面、具体地规定我国阶段性的人权事业发展举措和目标。可以说,近年来,我国在法律和政策两个层面,或者说在法治建设和发展战略与规划两个方面,人权主流化进程都获得了极大地推进。

中国的人权观与发展观是密切联系在一起的。一个实例是2013年5月14日国务院新闻办公室发布的我国第十个人权白皮书《2012年中国人权事业的进展》。与以往按照权利分类进行篇章布局不同,最新的白皮书与中国政府对发展的新的理解——发展由经济建设、政治建设、文化建设、社会建设和生态文明建设"五位一体"组成,通常称为科学发展观——保持同步,并将人权的视角纳入发展的各个方面。因此,它的主体内容、前面五章的标题分别是:一、经济建设中的人权保障;二、政治建设中的人权保障;三、文化建设中的人权保障;四、社会建设中的人权保障;五、生态文明建设中的人权保障。它清楚地回答了在我国人权与发展的关系问题。它不仅总结和展示了中国人权事业取得的成就,更进一步宣示了中国政府关于发展人权事业的立场和态度。

人权与发展密不可分,而它们都需要通过法治来推动和保障,所以尊重和保障人权、实现全面可持续发展和法治,就成为中国社会发展中一个有机联系的进程。在这方面,"依法推进"已经被确立为中国制定实施国家人权行动计划的一项首要原则。我国发布的《国家人权行动计划(2012—2015年)》导言中指出:"根据宪法关于'国家尊重和保障人权'的原则,遵循《世界人权宣言》和有关国际人权公约的基本精神,从立法、行政和司法各个环节完善尊重和保障人权的法律法规和实施机制,依法推进中国人权事业发展。"

资料精选

判决文书

INTER-AMERICAN COURT OF HUMAN RIGHTS[*]
CASE OF WONG HO WING[**] V. PERU
JUDGMENT OF JUNE 30 2015[***]

(*Preliminary objection, merits, reparations and costs*)

In the case of *Wong Ho Wing*,

the Inter-American Court of Human Rights (hereinafter "the Inter-American Court," or "the Court"), composed of the following judges:

Humberto Antonio Sierra Porto, President

Roberto F. Caldas, Vice President

Manuel E. Ventura Robles, Judge

Alberto Pérez Pérez, Judge

Eduardo Vio Grossi, Judge, and

Eduardo Ferrer Mac-Gregor Poisot, Judge;

also present,

Pablo Saavedra Alessandri, Secretary, and

Emilia Segares Rodríguez, Deputy Secretary

---

[*] Judge Diego García-Sayán, a Peruvian national, did not take part in the hearing of the case and the deliberation of this Judgment, in accordance with the provisions of Article 19(1) of the Court's Rule of Procedure.

[**] According to the information in the file, the official name of the presumed victim in Chinese is Huang Haiyong, while Wong Ho Wing is a transliteration of his name into English *Cf*. Advisory decision of the Permanent Criminal Chamber of January 27, 2010 (evidence file, folio 164). Despite this, in a statement made in the domestic sphere, Wong Ho Wing indicated that Huang is his surname in Mandarin, while Wong corresponds to the version in Cantonese, but that "they both have the same meaning." Statement made by Wong Ho Wing on September 23, 2013, before representatives of the Public Prosecutor for Money-laundering and the Public Prosecution Service (evidence file, folio 7173). For the purposes of this Judgment, the Court will identify the presumed victim as Wong Ho Wing, as he has been identified in the domestic extradition process, as well as throughout these proceedings before the inter-American human rights system.

[***] 本部分为《美洲人权法院黄海勇诉秘鲁案判决书(2015年6月30日)》,来源于美洲人权法院官方网站,http://www.corteidh.or.cr/docs/casos/articulos/seriec_297_ing.pdf,最后登录日期2018年12月14日。

pursuant to Articles 62(3) and 63(1) of the American Convention on Human Rights (hereinafter "the American Convention" or "the Convention") and Articles 31, 32, 42, 65 and 67 of the Court's Rules of Procedure (hereinafter "the Rules of Procedure" or "the Court's Rules of Procedure"), delivers this Judgment structured as follows:

TABLE OF CONTENTS

I. INTRODUCTION OF THE CASE AND PURPOSE OF THE DISPUTE

II. PROCEEDINGS BEFORE THE COURT

III. JURISDICTION

IV. PRELIMINARY OBJECTION

A. Arguments of the State and observations of the representative and of the Commission

B. Considerations of the Court

V. PROVISIONAL MEASURES

VI. PRELIMINARY CONSIDERATIONS

A. The factual framework of the case

A.1) Arguments of the State and observations of the representative and of the Commission

A.2) Considerations of the Court

VII. EVIDENCE

A. Documentary, testimonial and expert evidence

B. Admission of the evidence

B.1) Admission of the documentary evidence

B.2) Admission of the testimonial and expert evidence

C. Assessment of the evidence

VIII. PROVEN FACTS

A. Extradition Treaty between China and Peru

B. The extradition process in Peru

C. The extradition processin the case of Wong Ho Wing *

C. 1) First stage of the process (from the arrest of Wong Ho Wing until the second advisory decision)

C. 2) Second stage of the process (from the second advisory decision to date)

C. 2. a) Subsequent requests made by Executive Branch

C. 2. b) The actual situation

C. 3) Diplomatic assurances granted by the People's Republic of China in relation to the extradition of Wong Ho Wing

D. The detention of Wong Ho Wing and the remedies filed in this regard

IX. RIGHTS TO LIFE AND PERSONAL INTEGRITY AND PRINCIPLE OF NON-REFOULEMENT, IN RELATION TO THE OBLIGATION TO ENSURE RIGHTS

A. Arguments of the parties and of the Commission

B. Considerations of the Court

B. 1) General considerations on the obligation to ensure rights and the principle of non-refoulement in the face of possible risks to the rights to life, to personal integrity, and to due process in extradition proceedings

B. 2) Nature of the State's international responsibility in this case and information to be considered by the Court

B. 3) Alleged risk of the application of the death penalty in this case

B. 4) Alleged risk of torture and other forms of cruel, inhuman or degrading treatment

B. 4. a) Obligation to consider the arguments concerning the risk of a violation of personal integrity

B. 4. b) Alleged risk to Wong Ho Wing in the requesting State

i) Alleged situation of risk in the requesting State

ii) Diplomatic notes and assurances provided by the People's Republic of China

B. 5) General conclusion on the alleged risk of violation of the rights to life and to personal integrity of Wong Ho Wing if he is extradited

X. RIGHTS TO JUDICIAL PROTECTION AND JUDICIAL GUARANTEES, IN RELATION TO THE OBLIGATION TO RESPECT AND ENSURE RIGHTS

A. Arguments of the parties and of the Commission

B. Considerations of the Court

B. 1) The alleged violation of the right to judicial protection

B. 2) Reasonable time of the extradition process

B. 2. a) Complexity of the matter

B. 2. b) Procedural activity of the interested party

B. 2. c) Conduct of the State authorities

B. 2. d) Effects on the legal situation of the person involved in the proceedings

B. 2. e) Conclusion concerning a reasonable time

B. 3) Other guarantees of due process (right to be heard and right to a defense)

B. 3. a) Arguments of the parties and of the Commission

B. 3. b) Considerations of the Court

XI. RIGHTS TO PERSONAL LIBERTY AND PERSONAL INTEGRITY, IN RELATION TO THE OBLIGATION TO RESPECT AND ENSURE RIGHTS

A. Arbitrary nature of the provisional arrest

A. 1) Arguments of the parties and of the Commission

A. 2) Considerations of the Court

B. The alleged unlawful and arbitrary nature of the detention after the decision of the Constitutional Court

B. 1) Arguments of the parties and of the Commission

B. 2) Considerations of the Court

C. The duration of the provisional arrest

C. 1) Arguments of the parties and of the Commission

C. 2) Considerations of the Court

D. Right to appeal before a competent court

D. 1) Arguments of the parties and of the Commission

D. 2) Considerations of the Court

D. 2. a) Habeas corpus of February 9, 2010

D. 2. b) Release request of October 5, 2011

D. 2. c) Release request of October 18, 2011, and *habeas corpus* of November 16, 2011

D. 2. d) Failure to comply with a reasonable time when deciding these remedies

E. Alleged violation of the right to personal integrity of Wong Ho Wing

XII. REPARATIONS

A. Injured party

B. Measures of integral reparation: restitution and satisfaction

B. 1) Restitution

B. 1. a) Extradition process

B. 1. b) Review of the provisional arrest

B. 2) Satisfaction

B. 2. a) Publication and dissemination of the Judgment

B. 3) Other measures requested

C. Compensation

D. Costs and expenses

E. Method of complying with the payments ordered

XIII. OPERATIVE PARAGRAPHS

I
INTRODUCTION OF THE CASE AND PURPOSE OF THE DISPUTE

1. *The case submitted to the Court.* On October 30, 2013, in accordance with the provisions of Articles 51 and 61 of the American Convention and Article 35 of the Court's Rules of Procedure, the Inter-American Commission on Human Rights (hereinafter "the Inter-American Commission" or "the Commission") submitted the case of *Wong Ho Wing against the Republic of Peru* (hereinafter "the State" or "Peru") to the jurisdiction of the Inter-American Court. According to the Commission, the facts of this case related to a series of presumed violations of the rights of Wong Ho Wing, a national of the People's Republic of China, from the time of his detention on October 27, 2008, and throughout the extradition process that continues to date. According to the Commission, Wong Ho Wing has been and continues to be subjected to an alleged arbitrary and excessive deprivation of liberty that is not justified by procedural requirements. The Commission also concluded that, at different stages of the extradition proceedings, the domestic authorities had presumably been responsible for a series of omissions and irregularities in the processing of the case, which constituted, in addition to presumed violations of several aspects of due process, alleged non-compliance with the obligation to ensure the right to life and to humane treatment of Wong Ho Wing. In addition, it concluded that, since May 24, 2011, the date on which the Peruvian Constitutional Court ordered the Executive Branch to refrain from extraditing Wong Ho Wing, the State authorities had allegedly failed to comply with a court ruling, which was incompatible with the right to judicial protection.

2. *Proceedings before the Commission.* The proceedings before the Commission were as follows:

a) *Petition.* On March 27, 2009, Wong Ho Wing lodged the initial petition before the Commission. [1]

---

[1] *Cf.* Initial petition lodged on March 27, 2009, by Luis Lamas Puccio and Wong Ho Wing (evidence file, folio 753).

b) *Admissibility Report*. On November 1, 2010, the Commission adopted Admissibility Report No. 151/10. [1]

c) *Merits Report*. On July 18, 2013, the Commission adopted Merits Report No. 78/13, pursuant to Article 50 of the Convention (hereinafter "Merits Report"), in which it reached a series of conclusions and made several recommendations to the State:

- *Conclusions*. The Commission concluded that the State was responsible for the violation of the rights to personal liberty, life, humane treatment, judicial guarantees and judicial protection, established in Articles 7, 4, 5, 8 and 25 of the American Convention in relation to the obligations established in Article 1(1) of this instrument, to the detriment of Wong Ho Wing.

- *Recommendations*. Consequently, the Commission made a series of recommendations to the State, including that it:

ⅰ. Order the measures necessary to ensure that the extradition process is brought to a conclusion as soon as possible, in accordance with the procedures set forth in the Peruvian Code of Criminal Procedure, denying the extradition in strict compliance with the Constitutional Court's ruling of May 24, 2011. In compliance with this recommendation the State must ensure that none of its authorities instigates mechanisms that would obstruct or delay enforcement of that ruling.

ⅱ. Order an *ex officio* review of Wong Ho Wing's provisional arrest. In that review the State must take into consideration his legal situation upon the conclusion of the extradition process, in accordance with the terms of the preceding recommendation. In particular, any court decision pertaining to the personal liberty of Wong Ho Wing must be made in strict compliance with the principles of exceptionality, necessity, and proportionality in the terms described in the [Merits] Report.

---

[1] *Cf.* Admissibility Report No. 151/10, *Case of Wong Ho Wing v. Peru*, November 1, 2010 (evidence file, folio 1154).

ⅲ. Make full reparations to Wong Ho Wing for the violations established in the Merits Report.

ⅳ. Within a reasonable period, order measures of non-repetition to ensure that, in extradition processes, the procedures established in the Code of Criminal Procedure are followed to the letter and that the necessary safeguards are in place to ensure that any diplomatic or other assurances offered by the requesting State are obtained and weighed in accordance with the standards set out in th[is] Merits Report.

d) Notification of the State. The Merits Report was notified to the State on July 30, 2013, granting it two months to report on compliance with the recommendations. The State presented a report on the measures taken to comply with the said recommendations on September 30, 2013.

3. *Submission to the Court.* On October 30, 2013, the Commission submitted this case to the Court "in order to obtain justice for the [presumed] victim." The Commission appointed Commissioner José de Jesús Orozco Henríquez and Executive Secretary, Emilio Álvarez Icaza, as delegates, and Elizabeth Abi-Mershed, Deputy Executive Secretary, and Silvia Serrano Guzmán as legal advisers.

4. *Requests of the Inter-American Commission.* Based on the foregoing, the Inter-American Commission asked this Court to conclude and declare the international responsibility of Peru for the violations contained in its Merits Report and to order the State, as measures of reparation, to comply with the recommendations included in that report (*supra* para. 2).

5. *Provisional measures.* In the instant case, starting in May 2010, provisional measures were granted under Article 63(2) of the Convention for the State to refrain from extraditing Wong Ho Wing until the organs of the inter-American human rights system had examined and ruled on the case (*infra* para. 31).

II
PROCEEDINGS BEFORE THE COURT

6. *Notification of the State and the representative*. The submission of the case was notified to the State and to the representative of the presumed victim on December 9, 2013.

7. *Brief with motions, arguments and evidence*. On February 5, 6 and 9, 2014, the lawyer, Luis Lamas Puccio, acting on behalf of the presumed victim (hereinafter "the representative"), presented the brief with motions, arguments and evidence (hereinafter "the motions and arguments brief"), in accordance with Articles 25 and 40 of the Court's Rules of Procedure.

8. *Answering brief*. On May 6, 2014, Peru submitted to the Court its brief with a preliminary objection, answering the Commission's submission of the case, and with observations on the motions and arguments brief (hereinafter "the answering brief"). In this brief, the State filed a preliminary objection owing to the presumed failure to exhaust domestic remedies, described the facts, and contested all the alleged violations.

9. *Observations on the preliminary objection*. On June 27 and 28, 2014, the representative and the Inter-American Commission, respectively, presented their observations on the preliminary objection filed by the State.

10. *Public hearing*. On July 28, 2014, the President of the Court issued an order,① in which he convened the State, the representative, and the Inter-American Commission to a public hearing on the preliminary objection and eventual merits, reparations and costs, in order to hear the final oral arguments of the parties, and the final oral observations of the Commission on those issues. In addition, in this order, he requested that the statements of the presumed victim, two witnesses and five expert witnesses be received by affidavit, and these were presented by the parties and the

---

① Cf. Case of Wong Ho Wing v. Peru. Decision of the President of the Court of July 28, 2014. Available at: http://www.corteidh.or.cr/docs/asuntos/wong_28_07_2014.doc.

Commission on August 18, 25 and 29, 2014, respectively. The representative and the State were given the opportunity to pose questions and make observations to the deponents offered by the other party.① The Commission was able to question one of the State's expert witnesses. Also, in the same order, the President convened three expert witnesses proposed by the State to testify during the public hearing. The public hearing took place on September 3, 2014, during the fifty-first special session of the Court, held in Asunción, Paraguay.② During this hearing, the State presented certain documents and the judges of the Court requested specific helpful information and explanations.

11. *Amicus curiae*. The Court received one *amicus curiae* brief from María Isabel Mosquera Ayala on September 18 and 23, 2014.

12. *Final written arguments and observations*. On October 3, 2014, the parties and the Commission presented their final written arguments and observations, respectively. With their final written arguments, the parties provided some of the helpful information, explanations and evidence requested by the judges of this Court (*supra* para. 10), as well as certain documentation. On November 3, 2014, the Secretariat of the Court, on the President's instructions, asked the parties and the Commission to present any observations they deemed pertinent on this documentation.

13. *Helpful information and evidence*. On November 3, 2014, and March 25, 2015, the President of the Court asked the State and the representative for specific helpful information and documentation. The State

---

① Although, under the second operative paragraphs of the President's order of July 28, 2014, both parties were given the opportunity to pose questions to the deponents whose statements were required by affidavit, the representative did not forward any questions for the deponents proposed by the State and the Commission.

② There appeared at this hearing: (a) for the Inter-American Commission: James Louis Cavallaro, Commissioner and Silvia Serrano Guzmán and Erick Acuña, Advisers of the Executive Secretariat; (b) for the presumed victim: Luis Lamas Puccio and Miguel Ángel Soria Fuerte, and (c) for the State: Luis Alberto Huerta Guerrero, Special Supranational Public Prosecutor, Agent, and Sofía Janett Donaires Vega and Carlos Miguel Reaño Balarezo, lawyers of the Special Supranational Public Prosecutor's Office.

presented the requested information and explanations on November 17 and December 1, 2014, and on April 10, 2015.

14. *Observations on the helpful information and evidence, as well as on the supervening evidence on costs and expenses.* On November 17, 2014, the State and the representative presented their observations on the helpful information, explanations and documentation provided with the final written arguments (*supra* para. 12). On December 19, 2014, the Commission indicated that it had no observations to make on the documentation submitted by the State on November 17 and December 1, 2014, and, on May 4, 2015, it forwarded its observations on the documentation provided on April 10, 2015. The representative did not present observations on the helpful information and documentation submitted by the State on November 17 and December 1, 2014, and April 10, 2015.

15. *Supervening facts.* On April 13, and June 11 and 18, 2015, the representative forwarded information on a request to "change the house arrest" of Wong Ho Wing filed in the domestic sphere on March 3, 2015. On April 20, May 4, and June 19 and 23, 2015, the State and the Commission presented their observations in this regard.

16. *Deliberation of this Judgment.* The Court began its deliberation of this Judgment on June 24, 2015.

III

JURISDICTION

17. The Court is competent to hear this case, in the terms of Article 62(3) of the Convention, because Peru has been a State Party to the American Convention since July 28, 1978, and accepted the contentious jurisdiction of the Court on January 21, 1981.

IV
PRELIMINARY OBJECTION

A. Arguments of the State and observations of the representative and of the Commission

18. The State indicated that "the petition was presented to the [Commission] on March 27, 2009, while an application for *habeas corpus* filed on January 26, 2009, was being processed," and that this application was subsequently "declared partly justified." In addition, at that time, "the extradition was being processed" and, even at the present time, the Executive Branch has not taken a final decision. The State underlined that, according to the Admissibility Report, "the petitioner had exhausted the domestic remedies [⋯] with the ruling [of the Supreme Court] of January 27, 2010," as well as with the application for *habeas corpus*, all of them "decided following the filing of this petition." Furthermore, it noted that, when the Admissibility Report was issued, other applications for *habeas corpus* were awaiting a final decision. ①

20. The Commission observed that the State had filed the objection of failure to exhaust domestic remedies at the appropriate opportunity, during the admissibility stage. However, the Commission argued that it had analyzes the exhaustion of domestic remedies "based on the situation in force when it makes a ruling on admissibility" because, in many cases, the situation regarding compliance with the admissibility requirements changes and/or is updated. Therefore, it examined "compliance with the requirement of exhaustion of domestic remedies [⋯], in light of the evolution of the facts and the information available at that time." The Commission also "took into consideration the length of time taken by the respective authorities to examine [the appli-

---

① Moreover, during the public hearing, the State argued that "the main purpose of the presumed victims and their representatives" is to obtain financial compensation, and they had filed no domestic remedies in this regard using the existing mechanisms. The Court underscores that this argument was presented for the first time during the public hearing, so that it is time-barred.

cations for *habeas corpus*] that, by their nature, should be decided promptly."

22. The representative emphasized that "the situation that should be taken into account in order to establish whether the domestic remedies have been exhausted is the one which exists when deciding on admissibility." Thus, he indicated that this interpretation "has entered the domain of international inter-American custom accepted and not rejected by the American States, including Peru." The representative indicated that, when the Admissibility Report was issued, "the extradition proceedings against Wong Ho Wing had been decided in a single and final court, by the Supreme Court of Peru, and during those proceedings, a series of irregularities had occurred that violated due process. Therefore, not only had the appropriate remedies offered by Peruvian law been exhausted, but also, the exception to the exhaustion of domestic remedies established in Article 46(2) (a) of the American Convention on Human Rights was applicable, because due process of law had not been ensured." Regarding the State's argument that the extradition was still being processed, the representative argued that the decision of the Executive Branch had been pending "for more than four years," so that there had been "an unjustified delay in the extradition decision."

B. Considerations of the Court

23. Article 46(1) (a) of the American Convention establishes that, in order to determine the admissibility of a petition or communication lodged before Inter-American Commission in accordance with Articles 44 or 45 of the Convention, the remedies under domestic law must have been pursued and exhausted in accordance with generally recognized principles of international law. ① Thus, the Court has affirmed that an objection to the exercise of its jurisdiction based on the supposed failure to exhaust domestic reme-

---

① *Cf. Case of Velásquez Rodríguez v. Honduras. Preliminary objections.* Judgment of June 26, 1987. Series C No. 1, para. 85, and *Case of Cruz Sánchez et al. v. Peru. Preliminary objections, merits, reparations and costs.* Judgment of April 17, 2015. Series C No. 292, para. 48.

dies must be presented at the appropriate procedural moment; that is, during the admissibility procedure before the Commission. ①

24. In this regard, it can be seen that, during the admissibility procedure before the Commission, the State argued, in communications received on May 1 and 15, August 13 and December 4, 2009, and January 11, March 1, July 16, August 20 and October 26, 2010, that the requirement of exhaustion of domestic remedies had not been met, because decisions remained pending on the applications for *habeas corpus* filed by the representative. ② Therefore, the Court observes that this preliminary objection was filed at the appropriate procedural moment.

23. The Court notes that, basically, the State has submitted two arguments: (i) that, when the initial petition was lodged, domestic remedies had not been exhausted, and (ii) that, when taking its decision on admissibility, the Commission did not take into account that other applications for *habeas corpus* filed by the representative were being processed (*supra* para. 18).

24. On the first point, the Court notes that the initial petition was lodged before the Commission on March 27, 2009. On March 31 that year, the petition was forwarded to the State. Following numerous submissions of additional information by both parties, on November 1, 2010, the Com-

---

① *Cf. Case of Velásquez Rodríguez v. Honduras. Preliminary objections*, *supra*, para. 85, and *Case of Cruz Sánchez et al. v. Peru*, *supra*, para. 49.

② *Cf.* The State's brief of May 1 and 15, 2009, in which it referred to the application for *habeas corpus* filed on January 26, 2009 (evidence file, folio 668); the State's brief of August 13, 2009, in which it referred to the application for *habeas corpus* filed on January 26, 2009 (evidence file, folio 575); the State's brief of December 4, 2009, in which it referred to the application for *habeas corpus* filed on October 12, 2009 (evidence file, folios 407 to 409); the State's brief of January 11, 2010, in which it referred to the application for *habeas corpus* filed on October 12, 2009 (evidence file, folios 482 to 484); the State's brief of March 1, 2010, in which it referred to the applications for *habeas corpus* filed on October 12, 2009, and February 9, 2010 (evidence file, folios 1028 to 1030); the State's brief of July 16, 2010, in which it referred to the applications for *habeas corpus* filed on January 26, 2009, October 12, 2009, and February 9, 2010 (evidence file, folios 844 to 851); the State's brief of August 20, 2010, in which it referred to the application for *habeas corpus* filed on February 9, 2010 (evidence file, folios 773 to 778), and the State's brief of October 26, 2010, in which it referred to the applications for *habeas corpus* filed on January 26, 2009, October 12, 2009, and February 9, 2010 (evidence file, folios 1189 to 1193).

mission issued the Admissibility Report.① In this report, with regard to the exhaustion of domestic remedies, the Commission decided that:

> [T]he alleged victim first argued the failure to comply with the legal and constitutional requirements for admission of the extradition request throughout the advisory proceeding decided in the final instance by the Supreme Court of Justice on January 27, 2010. Secondly, he submitted two applications for *habeas corpus* against the members of the Second Transitory Criminal Chamber and the Permanent Criminal Chamber of the aforementioned Supreme Court, pointing to alleged defects in the advisory proceeding and an alleged inadequate evaluation of the guarantees provided by the Government of the People's Republic of China that the death penalty would not be imposed. In addition, the presumed victim filed a preventive application for *habeas corpus* against the President of the Republic and the Council of Ministers, which has been pending a final decision from the Constitutional Court on constitutional injury since July 14, 2010.
>
> 40. Based on the foregoing considerations, the [Commission] consider[ed] that the presumed victim [had] exhausted the available remedies under domestic law aiming at rectifying the alleged irregularities in the advisory proceeding decided in final instance by the Permanent Criminal Chamber of the Supreme Court of Justice on January 27, 2010. In this regard, the requirement indicated in Article 46(1) (a) of the American Convention has been met.②

25. As the State mentioned, the decisions that, according to the Commission, exhausted the domestic remedies were adopted after the initial petition had been lodged. However, the Court notes that, by requiring that "admission by the Commission of a petition or communication [...] shall be subject to" the said exhaustion (underlining added), Article 46 of the American Convention,

---

① *Cf.* Admissibility Report No. 151/10, *Case of Wong Ho Wing v. Peru*, November 1, 2010 (evidence file, folios 1145 to 1155).
② Admissibility Report No. 151/10, *Case of Wong Ho Wing v. Peru*, November 1, 2010 (evidence file, folio 1152).

should be interpreted in the sense that exhaustion of the remedies is required when deciding on the admissibility of the petition and not when this is lodged.

26. The Court notes that the lodging of the petition, its notification to the State, and the issue of the Admissibility Report are three distinctoccasions: the first derived from an act of the petitioner, and the other two arising from acts of the Inter-American Commission. ① The Inter-American Commission's Rules of Procedure specifically regulate these stages. ② According to articles 28(h) (now 28(8), 29 and 30 of these Rules of Procedure, before forwarding a petition to the State, an initial processing is made during which the Commission analyzes, among other matters, whether the petition contains information on "any steps taken to exhaust domestic remedies, or the impossibility of doing so as provided in Article 31 of the [said] Rules of Procedure." Once the petition has been forwarded to the State, the admissibility stage starts and, consequently, the adversarial proceedings on whether the petition meets the admissibility requirements, including the requirement of exhaustion of domestic remedies. According to those Rules of Procedure, it is when examining admissibility that the Commission decides whether or not the petition complies with this requirement, or whether any of the exceptions established in the Convention are applicable. Thus, the Commission's Rules of Procedure make a distinction between the time at which the initial processing is carried out, when it only examines whether the petition includes information on "any steps taken to exhaust domestic remedies, or the impossibility of doing so," and the mo-

---

① Cf. *Case of Castillo Petruzzi et al. v. Peru. Preliminary objections.* Judgment of September 4, 1998, Series C No. 41, para. 54. See also: *Exceptions to the Exhaustion of Domestic Remedies (Arts. 46.1, 46.2.a and 46.2.b, American Convention on Human Rights).* Advisory Opinion OC-11/90 of August 10, 1990. Series A No. 11, paras. 37 and 40.

② During the processing of this case before the Commission, the Commission's 2008 Rules of Procedure were in force when the initial petition was received, and the 2009 Rules of Procedure were in force at the admissibility stage (when the Admissibility Report was issued). The articles cited above were the same in both versions. The Commission's Rules of Procedure were subsequently amended in 2011 and 2013, and the latter version is the one currently in force. The separation of the stages mentioned above has been maintained in all the Commission's Rules of Procedure in force during the processing of this case before the inter-American system.

ment when it decides on admissibility, when it determines whether such remedies were exhausted, or applies an exception to this requirement.

27. The Court recalls that the rule of prior exhaustion of domestic remedies was conceived in the interests of the State, because it seeks to exempt it from responding before an international organ for acts it is accused of before it has had the occasion to remedy them by its own means.① Nevertheless, the subsidiary nature of the inter-American system is not affected by the fact that the analysis of compliance with the requirement of exhaustion of domestic remedies is made based on the situation when a decision is taken on a petition's admissibility. To the contrary, if any domestic remedy is pending, the State has the opportunity to resolve the situation alleged during the admissibility stage.

28. In addition, the Court considers that it would be contrary to the principle of procedural economy if petitions were not admitted based on the fact that, at the time of the initial presentation, domestic remedies had not been exhausted and if, when the admissibility of these remedies was analyzed, they had already been exhausted. The European Court of Human Rights (hereinafter "the European Court") has ruled similarly in some cases,② as has

---

① *Cf. Case of Velásquez Rodríguez v. Honduras. Merits.* Judgment of July 29, 1988. Series C No. 4, para. 61, and *Case of Cruz Sánchez et al. v. Peru, supra*, para. 48.

② In general, the European Court has considered that domestic remedies should normally have been exhausted when lodging a petition, but has recognized that this rule is subject to exceptions, so that this exhaustion can be achieved shortly after the lodging of the petition, provided this is before its admissibility is determined. However, the European Court has also emphasized that the rule of exhaustion of domestic remedies should be applied with a certain degree of flexibility and without formalistic interpretations (ECHR, *Case of Ringeisen v. Austria*, No. 2614/65. Judgment of 16 July 1971, para. 89), and has therefore admitted petitions where domestic remedies have not been exhausted when the petition is lodged, but were exhausted when the decision on admissibility was made, even when the exhaustion occurred years later. In this regard, see the cases: ECHR, *Case of Trabelsi v. Belgium*, No. 140/10. Judgment of September 4, 2014, para. 92. In this case, the European Court considered a petition admissible, *inter alia*, considering that, in any case, the extradition process ended before the decision on admissibility (even though this was four years after the presentation of the petition). ECHR, *Case of Enzile Özdemir v. Turkey*, No. 54169/00, January 8, 2008, para. 36. In this case, the European Court admitted a petition lodged five years before the corresponding criminal proceedings had ended, considering that those proceedings were exhausted when the Court examined admissibility. ECHR, *Kopylov v. Russia*, No 3933/04. Judgment of 29 July 2010, para. 119. In this case, the European Court admitted a petition lodged more than four years before the decision that exhausted the remedies, considering that the State's objection of exhaustion of domestic remedies had no purpose when the Court decided on admissibility, because those remedies had been exhausted following the presentation of the initial petition.

the International Court of Justice in relation to access to its jurisdiction. ①

29. On the second point alleged by the State, the Court notes that, at the admissibility stage of the petition, two applications for *habeas corpus* had been filed and decided in relation to the "certain and imminent threat of violation of the rights to life and personal integrity of Wong Ho Wing" (*infra* paras. 65 and 74) and a decision was pending on a third application for *habeas corpus* filed by the presumed victim and his representative (*infra* para. 79). These applications for *habeas corpus* were filed in parallel to the extradition proceedings and could be appropriate as regards some of the alleged violations. However, the Court stresses that the application for *ha-*

---

① In this regard, in 1924, in the case of the *Mavrommatis Palestine Concessions*, the Permanent Court of International Justice established that the fact that it did not have jurisdiction when the application was filed was not a sufficient reason to reject its jurisdiction, if this circumstance was rectified subsequently: "Even assuming that before that time [when the application was filed] the Court had no jurisdiction because the international obligation referred to in Article 11 [of the Mandate for Palestine] was not yet effective, it would always have been possible for the applicant to re-submit his application in the same terms after the coming into force of the Treaty of Lausanne, and in that case, the argument in question could not have been advanced. Even if the grounds on which the institution of proceedings was based were defective for the reason stated, this would not be an adequate reason for the dismissal of the applicant's suit. The Court, whose jurisdiction is international, is not bound to attach to matters of form the same degree of importance which they might possess in municipal law. Even, therefore, if the application were premature because the Treaty of Lausanne had not yet been ratified, this circumstance would now be covered by the subsequent deposit of the necessary ratifications." Permanent Court of International Justice, *Mavrommatis Palestine Concessions*, Judgment of 30 August 1924, Series A, No. 2, p. 34. This opinion was adopted by the International Court of Justice in the cases concerning *the Military and Paramilitary Activities in and against Nicaragua* and the *Application of the Convention on the Prevention and Punishment of Genocide*. In the former, the International Court of Justice established that: "It would make no sense to require Nicaragua now to institute fresh proceedings based on the [1956] Treaty [of Friendship], which it would be fully entitled to do." *Case* concerning *the Military and Paramilitary Activities in and against Nicaragua (Nicaragua v. United States of America), Jurisdiction and Admissibility*, Judgment, I. C. J. 1984 Reports, paras. 80 to 83. In the case of the *Application of the Convention on the Prevention and Punishment of Genocide*, the International Court of Justice established that: "It would not be in the interests of justice to oblige the Applicant, if it wishes to pursue its claims, to initiate fresh proceedings. In this respect it is of no importance which condition was unmet at the date the proceedings were instituted, and thereby prevented the Court at that time from exercising its jurisdiction, once it has been fulfilled subsequently. [… I]t is concern for judicial economy, an element of the requirements of the sound administration of justice, which justifies application of the jurisprudence deriving from the Mavrommatis Judgment in appropriate cases. The purpose of this jurisprudence is to prevent the needless proliferation of proceedings." *Case of the Application of the Convention on the Prevention and Punishment of Genocide (Croatia v. Serbia), Preliminary objections*, Judgment, I. C. J. Reports 2008, paras. 87 and 89, and *Cf. Case of the Application of the Convention on the Prevention and Punishment of Genocide (Bosnia and Herzegovina v. Yugoslavia), Preliminary objections*, Judgment, I. C. J. 1996 Reports, para. 26.

beas corpus is not part of the regular extradition process in Peru① and, thus, the filing of additional remedies by the petitioner could not preclude access to inter-American justice.

30. Based on the foregoing considerations, the Court finds it unnecessary to diverge from the opinion indicated by the Commission in its Admissibility Report in this case. Consequently, the Court rejects the preliminary objection.

V
PROVISIONAL MEASURES

31. On February 24, 2010, the Inter-American Commission, during the proceedings before this organ, asked the Court to adopt provisional measures in favor of Wong Ho Wing. The measures were granted for the first time in May 2010.② Following orders of November 26, 2010, and March 4 and July 1, 2011, that extended their effects,③ they were lifted in October 2011, after the decision of the Peruvian Constitutional Court of May 24 that year ordering the Executive Branch to refrain from extraditing Wong Ho Wing.④ Nevertheless, on June 26, 2012, this Court again granted provisional measures in favor of Wong Ho Wing due to "the State's un-

---

① Cf. Code of Criminal Procedure promulgated by Legislative Decree No. 957 of July 29, 2004, articles 516 to 524. Available at: http://www.leyes.congreso.gob.pe/Documentos/Decretoslegislativos/00957.pdf, cited in the Commission's Merits Report, folio 24. Moreover, in its brief with final arguments, the State itself indicated that "[t]he intervention of the Peruvian Constitutional Court is not established in extradition proceedings."

② Cf. Matter of Wong Ho Wing. Provisional measures with regard to Peru. Order of the Court of May 28, 2010. Previously, the President of the Court had required the State to "refrain from extraditing Wong Ho Wing while the request for provisional measures [had not been] decided by the plenary of the Inter-American Court". Matter of Wong Ho Wing. Provisional measures with regard to Peru. Order of the acting President of the Court of March 24, 2010.

③ Cf. Matter of Wong Ho Wing. Provisional measures with regard to Peru. Order of the Court of November 26, 2010; Matter of Wong Ho Wing. Provisional measures with regard to Peru. Order of the Court of March 4, 2011, and Matter of Wong Ho Wing. Provisional measures with regard to Peru. Order of the Court of July 1, 2011.

④ Cf. Matter of Wong Ho Wing. Provisional measures with regard to Peru. Order of the Court of October 10, 2011.

certainty" about the possibility of extraditing him, based on presumed "new facts." These measures were maintained by orders dated December 6, 2012, February 13, May 22 and August 22, 2013, and January 29 and March 31, 2014. ① In both May 2010 and June 2012, the provisional measures were ordered to allow the inter-American system to examine and rule on this case, as well as to prevent frustration of compliance with an eventual decision by its organs. ② Based on the orders of January and March 2014, the measures remain in force. ③

VI
PRELIMINARY CONSIDERATIONS

32. In his motions and arguments brief, the representative included Wong Ho Wing's wife, daughters and brother as presumed victims of the facts of this case. The Commission did not include these persons as presumed victims in its Merits Report. Consequently, their inclusion was contested by the State. However, in his final written arguments, the representative "withdr[ew this request], preserving the right of those persons to demand their rights within the jurisdiction of the Peruvian State." Therefore, this Court takes note of the said waiver and finds that it is not neces-

---

① Cf. *Matter of Wong Ho Wing. Provisional measures with regard to Peru.* Order of the Court of June 26, 2012, fourth having seen paragraph and *considerandum* 38, and subsequent orders extending their effects: *Matter of Wong Ho Wing. Provisional measures with regard to Peru.* Order of the acting President of the Court of December 6, 2012; *Matter of Wong Ho Wing. Provisional measures with regard to Peru.* Order of the Court of February 13, 2013; *Matter of Wong Ho Wing. Provisional measures with regard to Peru.* Order of the Court of May 22, 2013; *Matter of Wong Ho Wing. Provisional measures with regard to Peru.* Order of the Court of August 22, 2013; *Case of Wong Ho Wing. Provisional measures with regard to Peru.* Order of the Court of January 29, 2014, and *Case of Wong Ho Wing. Provisional measures with regard to Peru.* Order of the Court of March 31, 2014.

② Cf. *Matter of Wong Ho Wing. Provisional measures with regard to Peru.* Order of the Court of May 28, 2010, first operative paragraph; *Matter of Wong Ho Wing. Provisional measures with regard to Peru.* Order of the Court of June 26, 2012, first operative paragraph, and *Case of Wong Ho Wing. Provisional measures with regard to Peru.* Order of the Court of January 29, 2014, *consideranda* 5 and 9.

③ Cf. *Case of Wong Ho Wing. Provisional measures with regard to Peru.* Order of the Court of January 29, 2014, and *Case of Wong Ho Wing. Provisional measures with regard to Peru.* Order of the Court of March 31, 2014.

sary to make any additional observations in this regard.

A. The factual framework of the case

A. 1) Arguments of the State and observations of the representative and of the Commission

33. The State argued that the representative had "not respected the factual framework disputed before the Court [⋯] andunduly s[ought] to expand it to allege the supposed violation of the right to personal integrity." According to the State, the facts included in the Merits Report concerning a supposed violation of the personal integrity of Wong Ho Wing relate to the extradition process and the supposed lack of security owing to the risk of the application of the death penalty and torture, but not to the supposed effects of the deprivation of Wong Ho Wing's liberty as the representative alleges. In addition, in its final written arguments, the State indicated that the representative "alleges facts that differ from those delimited by the [Commission], such as a presumed unlawful detention" and also the applications for *habeas corpus* filed on March 13, 2012, and April 26, 2013, that "are not mentioned by the Commission in the section of the [Merits Report] on the facts of the case." The representative and the Commission argued that the facts indicated by the State were included in the factual framework established in the Merits Report.

A. 2) Considerations of the Court

34. This Court recalls that the factual framework of the proceedings beforeit consists of the facts submitted to its consideration in the Merits Report. Consequently, it is not admissible for the parties to allege new facts that differ from those contained in that report, without prejudice to describing those that may explain, clarify or reject the facts that have been mentioned in the report and submitted to the Court's consideration. ① The

---

① Cf. *Case of the Five Pensioners v. Peru. Merits, reparations and costs.* Judgment of February 28, 2003. Series C No. 98, para. 153, and *Case of Cruz Sánchez et al. v. Peru, supra,* para. 90.

exception to this principle are any facts classified as supervening, provided that these are connected to the facts of the proceedings. ①

35. The Court notes that the representative bases himself on the facts relating to the deprivation of liberty of Wong Ho Wing to argue that, in addition to the presumed violation of personal liberty, his personal integrity had also been violated. These facts are included in the factual framework. ② The State's arguments concerning supposed new facts refer to the representative's legal arguments that, although they differ from the legal conclusions of the Commission, do not refer to new facts. In this regard, the Court recalls its consistent case law according to which the presumed victims and their representatives may mention the violation of rights other than those included in the Merits Report, provided they relate to the facts contained in the said document, because the presumed victims are the holders of all the rights recognized in the Convention. ③ Similarly, the representative's arguments on the unlawfulness of Wong Ho Wing's detention and on the applications for *habeas corpus* filed after the 2011 ruling of the Constitutional Court are legal arguments and not new facts. Although the appeal filed on April 26, 2013, ④ is not mentioned specifically, this Court considers that the fact that, following the ruling of the Constitutional Court, the representative filed numerous remedies to try and obtain Wong Ho Wing's liberty forms part of the factual framework. ⑤ The references to all the remedies that were filed constitute facts that complement and describe in greater detail this factual situation that the Commission in-

---

① Cf. *Case of the Five Pensioners v. Peru*, supra, para. 154, and *Case of Cruz Sánchez et al. v. Peru*, supra, para. 90.
② In this regard, see paragraphs 67 to 141 of the Commission's Merits Report.
③ Cf. *Case of the Five Pensioners v. Peru*, supra, para. 155, and *Case of Cruz Sánchez et al. v. Peru*, supra, note al pie 47.
④ The remedies specifically indicated by the State do not explicitly mention the appeal of April 26, 2013. The appeal of March 13, 2012, is indicated in paragraph 138 of the Commission's Merits Report.
⑤ In this regard, see paragraphs 124 to 131, 133, 134, 138 and 141 of the Commission's Merits Report.

cluded in its Merits Report. The Court also considers that the representative's arguments about supposed pressure placed on Peru and on Wong Ho Wing's family so that the extradition would be granted constitutes factual circumstances that would be part of the extradition process in Peru; accordingly, these are facts that explain or clarify the facts contained in the factual framework established by the Merits Report in this case. Consequently, the Court does not find the State's objection admissible as regards the facts relating to the alleged suffering of Wong Ho Wing, his detention and the remedies filed following the ruling of the Constitutional Court, as well as with regard to the alleged pressure to grant the extradition. Despite the above, in the chapter on the facts, the Court will determine those that it considers proved in the instant case.

36. To the contrary, the Court notes that the facts included in the statements of the presumed victim and his next of kin with regard to Wong Ho Wing's detention conditions, or the treatment received during his deprivation of liberty, as well as the proceedings for money-laundering opened in Peru do not constitute facts that explain, clarify or reject those included in the Merits Report. Consequently, the Court will not take them into account in this case.

VII

EVIDENCE

A. Documentary, testimonial and expert evidence

37. This Court received diverse documents presented as evidence by the Commission and the parties attached to their main briefs (*supra* paras. 3, 7 and 8). The Court also received from the parties documents it had requested as helpful evidence under Article 58 of the Rules of Procedure. In addition, the Court received the affidavits made by the presumed victim, Wong Ho Wing, and the witnesses, Kin Mui Chan and He Long Huang, as well

as the expert opinions of Carmen Wurst de Landázuri, Ben Saul and Geoff Gilbert, Huawen Liu and Jean Carlo Mejía Azuero.① Regarding the evidence provided during the public hearing, the Court heard the expert opinions of Bingzhi Zhao, Ang Sun and Víctor Oscar Shiyin García Toma.

B. Admission of the evidence

B. 1) Admission of the documentary evidence

38. In this case, as in others, this Court admits those documents presented by the parties and the Commission at the appropriate opportunity that were not challenged or contested, and the authenticity of which was not questioned.② The documents requested by the Court or its President and provided by the parties after the public hearing were incorporated into the body of evidence in application of Article 58 of the Rules of Procedure.

39. Regarding the newspaper articles presented by the parties and the Commission, this Court has considered that they may be assessed when they refer to well-known public facts or declarations by State officials, or when they corroborate aspects related to the case.③ The Court decides to admit those documents that are complete or that, at least, allow their source and date of publication to be verified.

40. Also, with regard to some documents indicated by the parties and the Commission by means of electronic links, this Court has established that, if a party provides at least the direct electronic link to the document that it cites as evidence and it is possible to Access it, neither legal certainty nor procedural equality is affected, because it can be located immediately by the Court and by the other parties.④ In this case, neither the other par-

---

① The purpose of these statements was established in the President's order of July 28, 2014 (*supra* note 3).
② *Cf. Case of Velásquez Rodríguez v. Honduras. Merits*, *supra*, para. 140, and *Case of Cruz Sánchez et al. v. Peru*, *supra*, para. 102.
③ *Cf. Case of Velásquez Rodríguez v. Honduras. Merits*, *supra*, para. 146, and *Case of Cruz Sánchez et al. v. Peru*, *supra*, para. 104.
④ *Cf. Case of Escué Zapata v. Colombia. Merits, reparations and costs*. Judgment of July 4, 2007. Series C No. 165, para. 26, and *Case of Cruz Sánchez et al. v. Peru*, *supra*, para. 103.

ties nor the Commission opposed or commented on the content and authenticity of such documents.

41. Regarding the procedural occasion to present documentary evidence, according to Article 57(2) of the Rules of Procedure, in general, it must be presented with the briefs submitting the case, with motions and arguments, or answering the submission of the case, as appropriate.

42. The State presented certain documentation with its final written arguments.① The parties and the Commission were able to present their observations on this information and documentation. The representative asked that the new diplomatic assurances presented by Peru with its final written arguments be "rejected" because they were time-barred. According to the representative, "any guarantee not to impose the death penalty or that there is no risk of being subjected to torture or other cruel, inhuman or degrading treatment or punishment must be presented before the domestic courts and, in this case, before Peru's Supreme Court of Justice and Constitutional Court." The Court considers that these objections of the representative refer to matters relating to the merits of this dispute; hence, it is not appropriate to decide them when examining the admissibility of the evidence.

43. In addition, the Commission "called the Court's attention to the lack of clarity of the nature and purpose of annex 3 of the State's final argu-

---

① The State presented: (Annex 1) information from the Public Prosecution Service on preliminary investigations into money-laundering against Wong Ho Wing, his brother and sister-in-law; (Annex 2) information on the actions taken by the Ombudsman in response to the requests to intervene in favor of WHW; (Annex 3) information on the criminal legislation and the criminal procedural system in the People's Republic of China and the guarantees of due process if Wong Ho Wing were to be extradited; (Annex 4) the second instance judgment in the case of Pan Ziniu; (Annex 5) information from the National Council of the Judicature on the control of the judges who issued the first advisory decision; (Annex 6) video of the hearing before the Constitutional Court; (Annex 7) the additional diplomatic assurances offered by the People's Republic of China to the Peruvian State and presented during the hearing before the Inter-American Court; (Annex 8) the documentation on the request for information of the defense of WHW in the domestic sphere; (Annex 9) the compelte file of the extradition proceedings against Wong Ho Wing, and (Annex 10) the order of December 21, 2009, of the Permanent Criminal Chamber of the Supreme Court.

ments brief." It underlined that "the procedurally acceptable content of that brief is exclusively as the State's final arguments and, in no way, can be understood as a clarification or in the sense of modifying the scope and content of the opinion provided by the said expert witness during the hearing." The Court notes that, in this annex, Peru "present[ed] its point of view with regard to the expert opinion of Professor Bingzhi Zhao," owing to the difficulties of translating Chinese into Spanish, and the explanation of a legal system that differs from that of the States Parties to the Convention, because some concepts did not have an exact translation. This could make it difficult to understand the expert opinion; nevertheless, "the original sense of the information and ideas of the deponent were retained." In this regard, the Court notes that, insofar as it was received on the date on which the time frame for the presentation of the final written arguments expired, it would consider this annex to be an expansion of the State's arguments concerning the issues dealt with by expert witness Bingzhi Zhao during the public hearing. However, these arguments do not form part of the said expert opinion and do not possess the probative value of that opinion.

44. The admissibility of the remaining documents presented by the State with its final written arguments was not contested, and their authenticity and veracity were not questioned. Pursuant to Article 58(a) of its Rules of Procedure, the Court finds it in order to admit those documents, insofar as they may be useful to decide this case, help contextualize other evidence provided to the file, and explain some of the parties' arguments.

45. Also, on November 17 and December 1, 2014, and also on April 10, 2015, the State presented the helpful information and documentation requested by the judges of the Court during the public hearing and by its President subsequently (*supra* para. 13). The parties and the Commission were able to present their observations on this information and documentation and its admissibility was not contested or its authenticity and veracity

questioned. Pursuant to Article 58(a) of its Rules of Procedure, the Court finds it in order to admit these documents, insofar as they may be useful to decide this case.

46. The State opposed the admission of the additional costs requested by the representative in the "complementary motions and arguments brief" presented on February 9, 2014, as well as the requests for costs contained in the brief of August 30, 2013, addressed to the Inter-American Commission, which the representative included among the annexes to his motions and arguments brief. The State argued that any request for costs should be made in the motions and arguments brief, so that the additional costs contained in the two briefs should be rejected. The Court notes that the representative forwarded his motions and arguments brief on February 5, 2014, and sent a complementary brief on February 9, 2014, in which he included additional requests for costs and expenses (*supra* para. 7). The Court notes that the complementary brief was received within the time frame for the presentation of the motions and arguments brief in this case, which expired on February 9, 2014. Therefore, it finds that the latter brief should be considered an integral part of the first brief forwarded by the representative and considers admissible the requests for costs and expenses contained therein. Furthermore, with regard to the brief of August 30, 2013, sent with the annexes to the motions and arguments brief, the Court has verified that it forms part of the file of the processing of this case before the Commission, so that finding it inadmissible would be pointless. Nevertheless, the Court notes that, when determining costs and expenses, it will take into account the requests contained in the representative's motions and arguments brief addressed to the Court (received in communications of February 5, 6 and 9, 2014) and not those included in the brief of August 30, 2013, addressed to the Commission, since the former constituted the appropriate procedural stage for its presentation to this Court in accordance

with Article 40(2) (d) of the Court's Rules of Procedure. This does not preclude the possibility of indicating and providing the evidence of the costs and expenses incurred during the proceedings before the Court subsequently, as indicated *infra*.

47. The representative forwarded, with his final written arguments, vouchers for the expenses he incurred following the submission of the motions and arguments brief. The State argued that these new requests for costs should be declared inadmissible as they were time-barred, because the representative should have made the requests in his motions and arguments brief. The Court recalls that, under Article 57(2) of the Rules of Procedure, evidence of facts that take place following the motions and arguments brief is admissible in the case of the representative of the presumed victim. Therefore, following its consistent practice, the Court admits the documentation on costs and expenses incurred after the presentation of the motions and arguments brief, sent by the representative together with his final written arguments, and incorporates it into the body of evidence.

48. On April 13, and June 11 and 18, 2015, the representative sent information on a request made on March 3, 2015, in the domestic sphere to "change house arrest to an order to appear in court periodically," for the Court to assess it, "because it related to a supervening fact." The State opposed the admission of this information because, in its opinion, the representative had not founded his request satisfactorily and the results of the request "are not included in the matters that are being analyzed by the Court […] in this case." According to the State, the representative did not identify the specific purpose of his request or the provisions of the Rules of Procedure on which he based it. In addition, he did not specify why the request to change the house arrest would represent, "strictly, a 'supervening fact,'" and had failed to indicate what he sought to prove with this documentation, or with which to the disputed issues it was related. In this re-

gard, this Court finds that the documentation forwarded by the representative constitutes updated information on the detention situation of Wong Ho Wing, which is part of the factual framework and purpose of this case. Since it refers to facts that have occurred and remedies filed following the representative's last communication, it constitutes information and evidence of supervening facts; therefore, the Court admits the said information under Article 57(2) of the Rules of Procedure.

B. 2) Admission of the testimonial and expert evidence

49. The Court also finds it pertinent to admit the statements of the presumed victim and the witnesses, and the expert opinions provided during the public hearing and by affidavit, to the extent that they are in keeping with the purpose defined by the President in the order requiring them (*supra* para. 10) and the purpose of this case.

50. The representative asked the Court to reject the expert opinions offered by the State because they were not objective. He argued that, during the hearing, the State had accepted that its agents "had 'levels of coordination' with the expert witnesses that they proposed"; thus, expert witness Ang Sun read his answers to the questions posed by the State. According to the representative, "[t]his situation not only violated the right to defense of [his] client, because he was unable to have the same 'levels of coordination,' but also completely invalidates the opinion of [the] expert witnesses." In addition, specifically with regard to Ang Sun, he argued that the latter had a direct interest in the result of the case, asking the Court more than once to take a prompt decision on Wong Ho Wing's extradition. The Court considers that the representative's observations refer to the scope and probative value that should be granted to these expert opinions, which does not affect their admissibility as part of the body of evidence. The Court will take these observations into account when assessing this evidence in its analysis of the merits of the case.

51. For its part, the State asked the Court to reject the expert opinions of Geoff Gilbert, Carmen Wurst and Ben Saul. According to the State, expert witness Geoff Gilbert did not have the required profile and sufficient experience in the matter covered by his opinion; it also contested the application of the precedents used by the expert witness to the case of Wong Ho Wing. Regarding the expert opinion of Carmen Wurst, the State questioned the methodology used, raising doubts about the quality of the report and its proper scientific rigor, as well as the fact that Ms. Wurst, who was a psychologist, had made a medical diagnosis. In the case of the expert opinion of Ben Saul, the State questioned the precedents used, the analysis made, and that he had not answered one of the questions posed by Peru. On the latter point, the Court recalls that it has asserted that the facat that the Rules of Procedure establish the possibility that the parties may pose written questions to the deponents offered by the other party and, when appropriate, by the Commission, imposes the corresponding obligation of the party that offered the statement to coordinate and take the necessary steps to forward the questions to the deponents and to ensure that they include the respective answers. In certain circumstances, the fact that different questions are not answered may be incompatible with the obligation of procedural cooperation and the principle of good faith that governs the international proceedings. Despite this, the Court has considered that the failure to answer the questions of the other party does not affect the admissibility of a statement and is an aspect that, based on the implications of the silences of a deponent, may have an impact on the probative weight of the respective statement, an aspect that must be assessed when examining the merits of the case.[①] Accordingly, the Court will take these observations into account when assessing the evidence.

[①] Cf. *Case of Díaz Peña v. Venezuela. Preliminary objection, merits, reparations and costs.* Judgment of June 26, 2012. Series C No. 244, para. 33, and *Case of Cruz Sánchez et al. v. Peru, supra*, para. 115.

52. The State also asserted "its most vehement rejection" of the statements made by Wong Ho Wing, his wife and brother, that the extradition request was the result of political persecution. The Court considers that the State's objections refer to the content of these statements and not to their admissibility. The arguments contained in the said statements will be assessed when analyzing the merits of the matter, taking into account the corresponding observations of the State.

C. Assessment of the evidence

53. Based on the provisions of Articles 46, 47, 48, 50, 51, 57 and 58 of the Rules of Procedure, as well as on its consistent case law regarding evidence and its assessment,① the Court will examine and assess the documentary evidence provided by the parties and the Commission, the videos, the statements, testimony, and expert opinions, as well as the helpful evidence requested by this Court and incorporated into the file when establishing the facts of the case and ruling on the merits. To this end, it will abide by the principles of sound judicial discretion, within the corresponding legal framework, taking into account the whole body of evidence and the arguments presented in this case.②

54. Also, in accordance with this Court's case law, the statement made by the presumed victim cannot be assessed in isolation, but rather in the context of all the evidence in the proceedings, insofar as it may provide further information on the presumed violations and their consequences.③

---

① Cf. *Case of the "White Van" (Paniagua Morales et al.) v. Guatemala. Merits.* Judgment of March 8, 1998. Series C No. 37, paras. 69 to 76, and *Case of Cruz Sánchez et al. v. Peru*, supra, para. 129.
② Cf. *Case of the "White Van" (Paniagua Morales et al.) v. Guatemala. Merits*, supra, para. 76, and *Case of Cruz Sánchez et al. v. Peru*, supra, para. 129.
③ Cf. *Case of Loayza Tamayo v. Peru. Merits.* Judgment of September 17, 1997. Series C No. 33, para. 43, and *Case of Cruz Sánchez et al. v. Peru*, supra, para. 131.

VIII
PROVEN FACTS

55. This case relates to the request for the extradition of Wong Ho Wing, a Chinese citizen, and the ensuing extradition proceegings in Peru. In this regard, the relevant facts will be described as regards: (A) the extradition treaty between China and Peru; (B) the extradition proceedings in Peru; (C) the extradition process in the case of Wong Ho Wing, and (D) the detention of Wong Ho Wing and the remedies filed in this regard.

A. Extradition Treaty between China and Peru

56. An extradition treaty exists between the People's Republic of China and Peru that was signed on November 5, 2001, and entered into force on April 5, 2003. It establishes the obligation to extradite "anyone who is in their territory and is required by the other party in order to institute criminal proceedings or execute a judgment against them." In addition, the treaty indicates the offenses that are subject to extradition; the obligatory and discretionary grounds for rejecting an extradition request; the conditions and requirements that an extradition request should meet, as well as the procedure, and communication and information channels in the case of an extradition request from either of the contracting parties. This treaty does not include an express clause on the way to proceed in the case of offenses for which the death penalty is established; however, it does establish as a condition for the extradition that "it [shall] not be contrary to the legal system of the Requested Party."[①] The specific provisions of the Extradition Treaty that are relevant for this case are described in greater detail in the corresponding chapters (*infra* paras. 138 and 239).

[①] Extradition Treaty between the Republic of Peru and the People's Republic of China (evidence file, folios 1633 to 1636), and decision of October 5, 2009, of the Permanent Criminal Chamber of the Supreme Court of Justice, (evidence file, folio 101).

B. The extradition process in Peru

57. In Peru, extradition is carried out by means of "a joint procedure consisting of a jurisdictional stage and a political stage."① According to the Constitution, extradition must be granted by the Executive Branch.② To implement this constitutional provision, the Code of Criminal Procedure establishes that the Government will decide on extradition by means of a "supreme decision issued with the agreement of the Council of Ministers, following a report by an official commission presided by the Ministry of Justice and incorporating the Ministry of Foreign Affairs." However, before the Government decision, "the Criminal Chamber of the Supreme Court is required to intervene to issue an advisory decision." This advisory decision is binding "[w]hen the Criminal Chamber of the Supreme Court issues an advisory decision contrary to extradition," but only advisory when it is "favorable to the return or considers it in order to request a foreign country to grant an extradition," so that "the Government may take the appropriate decision."③

58. However, domestic law conditions the granting of extradition "to the existence of assurances that justice will be imparted correctly in the Requesting State" and that it does not have "political implications" for a third State. In addition, among the reasons for rejecting a request for extradition, the procedural norm establishes that extradition shall not be granted

---

① Statement made by Víctor García Toma during the public hearing held in this case.
② Article 37 of the Peruvian Constitution establishes that: "Extradition shall only be granted by the Executive Branch following a report by the Supreme Court, in compliance with the law and the treaties, and based on the principle of reciprocity. Extradition shall not be granted if it is considered that it has been requested in order to persecute or punish for reasons of religion, nationality, opinion or race. The extradition of those pursued for political offenses or for acts related to such offenses is precluded; this does not include genocide, magnicide and terrorism." 1993 Constitution of Peru. Available at: www.congreso.gob.pe/ntley/ConstitucionP.htm, cited in the Commission's Merits Report, folio 19.
③ Code of Criminal Procedure, promulgated by Legislative Decree No. 957 of July 29, 2004, articles 513 to 515. Available at: http://www.leyes.congreso.gob.pe/Documentos/Decretoslegislativos/00957.pdf, cited in the Commission's Merits Report, folio 24. Similarly, see Statement made by Víctor García Toma during the public hearing held in this case.

when "the act on which the process is founded does not constitute an offense in either the requesting State or Peru, and if neither legislation establishes a criminal sanction of any kind, equal to, or in excess of, one year's imprisonment," or when "[t]he offense for which extradition is requested is punishable by the death penalty in the requesting State and the latter has not provided assurances that this will not be applicable."①

59. In addition, regarding the procedure to be followed, Peruvian procedural law establishes that, once the person whose extradition has been requested has been detained, a preliminary investigation judge will take a statement. In this statement, the person sought "may state whatever he considers appropriate." Subsequently, within no more than 15 days, a public hearing must be convened where evidence and arguments are presented in favor of or against extradition, and the individual sought may again make a statement "if he finds this appropriate." Following this hearing, the file is referred to the consideration of the Criminal Chamber of the Supreme Court, which must issue the advisory decision (*supra* para. 57). When it has received the case file, and before forwarded it to the parties, the Criminal Chamber will convene an extradition hearing, following which it issues the corresponding advisory decision within five days at the most. Three days after this decision has been notified to the parties, the Criminal Chamber must forward it to the Ministry of Justice and, as of this moment, the second stage of the procedure commences before the Executive Branch.② The rules relating to the extradition process in Peru are described in greater detail in the corresponding chapters (*infra* paras. 137, 138 and 240 to

---

① Code of Criminal Procedure, promulgated by Legislative Decree No. 957 of July 29, 2004, articles 516 and 517. Available at: http://www.leyes.congreso.gob.pe/Documentos/Decretoslegislativos/00957.pdf, cited in the Commission's Merits Report, folio 24.

② *Cf.* Code of Criminal Procedure, promulgated by Legislative Decree No. 957 of July 29, 2004, article 521. Available at: http://www.leyes.congreso.gob.pe/Documentos/Decretoslegislativos/00957.pdf, cited in the Commission's Merits Report, folio 24.

242).

C. The extradition process in the case of Wong Ho Wing

60. Since 2001, Wong Ho Wing has been "an international fugitive, [owing to an INTERPOL Red Notice,] wanted by the judicial authorities of Hong Kong, China, for the offense of smuggling that occurred between [August 1996 and May 1998]."① Early on October 27, 2008, Wong Ho Wing was arrested in the "Jorge Chávez International Airport" that serves Lima, when he was entering Peru from the United States of America. That same day, the police brought him before the Permanent Criminal Court of El Callao.②

C. 1) First stage of the process (from the arrest of Wong Ho Wing until the second advisory decision)

61. On October 28, Wong Ho Wing gave a preliminary statement in the presence of his lawyer and asked the Peruvian authorities to accord him "special treatment based on the defense of [his] human rights, [because if he was] returned [to his] country for the offenses that [he was] accused of, [he] could be executed or the death penalty would be imposed" on him. Consequently, he "asked to be tried in [⋯] Peru."③

62. On November 14, 2008, the Seventh Criminal Court of El Callao received the request to extradite Wong Ho Wing from the People's Republic of China (hereinafter also "China" or "the Requesting State"), requiring that "the suspect be held in custody." As established in this request, the acts presumably committed by Wong Ho Wing constituted the "offense of

---

① Note of the Peruvian National Police of October 27, 2008 (evidence file, folio 6). *Cf.* INTERPOL Red Notice entitled "Wanted for Prosecution" (evidence file, folio 8), and arrest warrant dated April 16, 2001 (evidence file, folio 6391).
② *Cf.* Note of the Peruvian National Police of October 27, 2008 (evidence file, folio 6).
③ Preliminary statement made by Wong Ho Wing on October 28, 2008, before the Special Criminal Court of El Callao (evidence file, folio 15).

smuggling ordinary merchandise,① the offense of money-laundering, and the offense of bribery," which are defined in articles 153, 154, 191, 389 and 390 of the Criminal Code of the People's Republic of China. ② According to the request, "the taxes evaded amounted to [more than 717 million yuans]." Furthermore, Wong Ho Wing had allegedly transferred the sum of 4,048 million United States dollars out of China. Among other documents, the applicable articles of the Criminal Code of the People's Republic of China on the statute of limitations, the relevant penalties, and the arrest warrant were attached to the request. ③ These articles did not include article 151 of the Chinese Criminal Code which establishes the possibility of the death penalty for the offense of smuggling (*infra* para. 146). ④

63. On December 10, 2008, a public hearing was held during which Wong Ho Wing and his representative mentioned that the applicable provision was article 151, which established the death penalty. ⑤ Following the procedure established in the Procedural Code (*supra* para. 59), on January

---

① The offense established in article 153 of the Chinese Criminal Code is entitled "smuggling ordinary merchandise." However, this offense is similar to the offense entitle "evasion of customs duty" under Peruvian law. *Cf.* Advisory decision of the Permanent Criminal Chamber of January 27, 2010 (evidence file, folios 168 and 169). Consequently, the offense established in article 153 of the Chinese Criminal Code, for which Wong Ho Wing was required, is referred to with both terms in different documents from the extradition process. Whichever the name used, this is the offense established in article 153 of the Chinese Criminal Code, and the penalty for "very serious" cases is established in article 151 of the Chinese Criminal Code (*infra* para. 146). For the purposes of this Judgment, the Court will use the term that appears in the respective document; nevertheless, it should be understood that both terms, "evasion of customs duty" or "smuggling ordinary merchandise" refer to the same offense established in article 153 of the Chinese Criminal Code.

② *Cf.* Extradition request from General Directorate No. 24 of the Ministry of Public Security of the People's Republic of China of November 3, 2008 (evidence file, folio 29), and Decision of November 14, 2008, of the Second Criminal Court of El Callao (evidence file, folios 1737 and 1738). The request was sent accompanied by a note from the Embassy of the People's Republic of China dated November 13, 2008 (evidence file, folio 35).

③ *Cf.* Extradition request from General Directorate No. 24 of the Ministry of Public Security of the People's Republic of China of November 3, 2008 (evidence file, folio 29), and table (general) with the amount of duty evaded by smuggling (evidence file, folio 8404).

④ *Cf.* Pertinent parts of the Criminal Code of the People's Republic of China provided with the extradition request (evidence file, folio 8406).

⑤ *Cf.* Record of the hearing of December 10, 2008 (evidence file, folios 8477 and 8478).

6, 2009, the case file was referred to the Supreme Court of Justice.① On January 19, 2009, the Second Transitory Criminal Chamber of the Supreme Court of Justice held the extradition hearing.② That same day, a report of the Smuggling Investigation Department of the Wuhan Customs' Office was received from the representative of the People's Republic of China explaining the acts that Wong Ho Wing was accused of, and the applicable law,③ with no mention of the possibility of imposing the death penalty for one of the offenses for which his extradition was requested. In addition, the representative presented his written arguments and provided the translation of the relevant parts of articles 151 and 153 of the Chinese Criminal Code, which reveal that, when the amount defrauded is "more than [500 000] yuans, as in this case," smuggling merchandise and objects is punished in accordance with the provisions of paragraph 4 of article 151 of this law, and this establishes that, "in very serious cases, the accused shall be condemned to life imprisonment or to death."④

64. On January 20, 2009, the Second Transitory Chamber of the Supreme Court of Justice issued the first advisory decision in the extradition proceedings. In this decision, the Supreme Court declared the extradition request admissible for the offenses of evasion of customs duty and bribery, considering that the requirements established in the extradition treaty between the two States had been met, and clarifying that, with regard to the offense of evasion of customs duty, extradition was only in order "for the criminal offense established in the first paragraph of article [153] of the

---

① *Cf.* Record of the Seventh Special Criminal Court of El Callao of January 6, 2009 (evidence file, folio 1942).
② *Cf.* Record of extradition hearing of January 19, 2009 (evidence file, folio 1993).
③ This report indicates that Wong Ho Wing "was responsible for importing soybean oil and re-selling it in China" and explains his alleged participation in the acts, together with other individuals. The document does not indicate the offense of which Wong Ho Wing was accused. However, it does indicate the articles of the Criminal Code applicable to the other individuals who took part in the events. *Cf.* Communication of the representative of the People's Republic of China of January 19, 2009 (evidence file, folios 7801 to 7813).
④ Communication of January 19, 2009 (evidence file, folios 7777 to 7790).

Chinese Criminal Code." At the same time, it declared that extradition for the offense of money-laundering was inadmissible because, at the time that, presumably, "the acts were committed in the country of the individual sought [⋯], this offense was not defined in [Peruvian] criminal law."①

65. Following this decision, on January 26, 2009, Wong Ho Wing's brother filed afirst application for *habeas corpus* against the judges of the Second Transitory Criminal Chamber of the Supreme Court of Justice, "based on the certain and imminent threat of violation of the rights to life and personal integrity of [⋯] Wong Ho Wing." Among other grounds, he indicated that "in a malicious and covert manner, the extradition request [⋯] did not attach the relevant translation of article 151 of the Chinese Criminal Code because this provision contains the death penalty for the offense of smuggling." He also indicated that, in an extradition process in which the offense involved was punished with the death penalty, "it was for the Prosecutor General [⋯] to safeguard the lawfulness of the proceedings by issuing an opinion in the extradition process, and ruling on the admissibility of the request." The application also asked for the release of Wong Ho Wing.②

66. On February 2, 2009, the People's Republic of China submitted an explanation from the Ministry of Public Security to the Official Commission for Extraditions and Prisoner Transfers of the Ministry of Justice of Peru, indicating that, according to "the provisions of the Criminal Code of the People's Republic of China, there is no possibility of imposing life imprisonment or the death penalty on him"③(*infra* para. 92. a).

67. On February 10, the Official Commission for Extraditions and Prisoner Transfers issued its report on the extradition request, indicating that "it ha[d] not received the translation of article 151 of the Criminal

---

① Advisory decision of January 20, 2009 (evidence file, folios 46 to 50).
② *Cf.* Application for *habeas corpus* of January 26, 2009 (evidence file, folios 52, 55, 56 and 59).
③ Brief of General Directorate No. 24 of the Ministry of Public Security of February 2, 2009 (evidence file, folios 67 and 68).

Code of the People's Republic of China, an article [⋯] referred to in the first paragraph of article 153, as revealed by the translation [in the case file]." Consequently, it considered that it was necessary "to receive the [said] translation." In addition, taking into account the precautionary measures granted by the Inter-American Commission, it established that:

> [R]egarding extradition, the treaties signed by Peru allow it to grant extradition even in a case where the death penalty may be applied; [however, it is necessary to be] certain that it will not be applied; in other words, [⋯] the corresponding assurances must have been presented that the death penalty will not be applied, or that it will not be implemented even if it is imposed by the courts of the requesting State.
>
> Although the treaty with the People's Republic of China does not contain an express clause on the death penalty, article 5 of the treaty establishes as a condition for extradition: "Extradition shall only be carried out if it is not contrary to the legal system of the requested party." [⋯]
>
> Thus, according to the communication of the Inter-American Commission on Human Rights, [⋯] the offense would merit the death penalty and, since the case file does not include the requesting State's guarantee not to apply the death penalty, the Judiciary should first be requested to forward this guarantee if this has been presented or, if not, requested to rule on the alert raised by the Inter-American Commission [⋯]; that is, on the possible application of the death penalty. [1]

68. On February 12, 2009, the 56th Criminal Court of Lima ordered the "temporary suspension of the processing of the passive extradition process [⋯] until the constitutional *habeas corpus* proceeding has concluded," taking into ac-

---

[1] Report of the Official Commission for Extraditions and Prisoner Transfers dated February 10, 2009 (evidence file, folios 73 and 74).

count that "the continuation of [the] process before the Council of Ministers and the implementation of the return of the individual whose extradition has been requested to the requesting country was imminent."① The Public Attorney of the Judiciary appealed this decision.② On April 24, 2009, the Second Special Criminal Chamber of the Superior Court of Justice of Lima annulled the decision of February 12, 2009, because the precautionary measures and the suspension were not established by law in *habeas corpus* proceedings.③

69. On February 24, 2009, the Embassy of the People's Republic of China in Peru sent the translation of articles 151, 153, 154, 191, 389 and 390 of the Criminal Code of the People's Republic of China to the 56th Criminal Court of Lima.④

70. On April 24, 2009, the 56th Criminal Court of Lima considered well-founded the application for *habeas corpus*, and declared "invalid the advisory decision [of] January 20, [2009,]" because it "was insufficiently substantiated."⑤ The decision was based on the fact that the advisory decision "does not state clearly and categorically that the accused cannot be extradited to be prosecuted for the supposed perpetration of offenses that require the death penalty."⑥ It also declared inadmissible the request to re-

---

① Decision of February 12, 2009 (evidence file, folio 77).
② This appeal was granted on March 9, 2009, and "the respective file" was prepared. *Cf.* Appeal by the Public Attorney of the Judiciary of March 3, 2009 (evidence file, folios 4415 to 4420), and decision of March 9, 2009 (evidence file, folio 2043).
③ *Cf.* Decision of the Second Special Criminal Chamber (evidence file, folio 8481).
④ *Cf.* Note of the Embassy of the People's Republic of China of February 24, 2009 (evidence file, folios 1627 to 1630).
⑤ Decision of April 24, 2009 (evidence file, folios 89 and 90).
⑥ Decision of April 24, 2009 (evidence file, folio 89). Following this decision, on October 14, 2009, the members of the Second Transitory Criminal Chamber of the Supreme Court of Justice were accused before the National Council of the Judicature "for presumed functional misconduct in the issue of the decision of January 20, 2009." Following the respective investigation, on September 19, 2012, the National Council of the Judicature decided "[t]o conclude the disciplinary procedure [⋯], filing the proceedings and to acquit them of the accusations; ordering that the disciplinary proceedings be filed and the corresponding record annulled," considering that the judges had not failed to analyze the case and motivate their findings appropriately. On November 14, 2012, the National Council of the Judicature declared that an appeal for review that had been filed was unsubstantiated, "and considered that the administrative jurisdiction had been exhausted." Decisions of the National Council of the Judicature of December 11, 2009, August 12, 2010, February 14, 2011, September 19, 2012, and November 14, 2012 (evidence file, folios 7343, 7345, 7348, 7355, 7356, 7364, 7365 and 7373).

lease Wong Ho Wing, indicating that this request was not affected by the annulment of the advisory decision. ① Following an appeal, the decision was confirmed on June 15, 2009. ②

71. On August 25, 2009, the Ambassador of the People's Republic of China sent the Supreme Court of Justice a note in which he indicated that case law existed of similar cases where the sentence had been 15 years' imprisonment, "so that there was no possibility that the death penalty would be imposed on the applicant" (*infra* para. 92. b). ③

72. On October 2, 2009, the Supreme Prosecutor advised the Permanent Criminal Chamber of his opinion that the advisory decision on extradition should be unfavorable. ④

73. On October 5, 2009, the Permanent Criminal Chamber of the Supreme Court of Justice held a public hearing during which it ordered the return of the case file to the judge of the Seventh Criminal Court of the Superior Court of Justice of El Callao, to rectify the failure to comply with the requirement "to attach the certification that the guarantee that the death penalty will not be imposed if he is convicted has been presented or, if not, that it has been requested," and to reschedule the hearing. ⑤

74. On October 12, 2009, the representative of Wong Ho Wing filed asecond application for *habeas corpus* against the judges of the Permanent Criminal Chamber of the Supreme Court of Justice "based on the certain and imminent threat of violation of the rights to life and personal integrity that subsists against [⋯] Wong Ho Wing."⑥ On January 5, 2010, the

---

① *Cf*. Decision of April 24, 2009 (evidence file, folio 90).
② *Cf*. Appeal of April 8, 2009 (evidence file, folios 92 and 93), and decision of the Second Special Criminal Chamber of Lima for proceedings where the accused is in prison of June 15, 2009 (evidence file, folio 6231).
③ *Cf*. Note of August 25, 2009 (evidence file, folios 8272 and 8273).
④ *Cf*. Opinion of the Assistant Supreme Prosecutor of October 2, 2009 (evidence file, folios 7965 to 7967).
⑤ *Cf*. Decision of October 5, 2009, of the Permanent Criminal Chamber of the Supreme Court of Justice (evidence file, folios 101 and 102).
⑥ Application for *habeas corpus* of October 12, 2009 (evidence file, folio 105).

53rd Criminal Court of the Province of Lima considered that this application was inadmissible, finding that what was sought was the inadmissibility of extradition and that the arguments had already been analyzed in the decision of April 24, 2009 (*supra* para. 70). ① On February 4, 2010, the representative filed an appeal against this decision,② which was confirmed on June 30, 2010. ③ The representative filed an appeal based on constitutional injury which was declared inadmissible on August 5, 2011, because the Constitutional Court had already ruled on another constitutional remedy (*infra* paras. 81 to 83). ④

75. On December 9, 2009, a passive extradition hearing was held before the Permanent Criminal Chamber. ⑤ On December 11, 2009, the Embassy of the People's Republic of China in Peru advised the Permanent Criminal Chamber that the People's Supreme Court of the People's Republic of China had decided not to impose the death penalty on Wong Ho Wing, if he was extradited and then convicted, "even if his offense is legally subject to the death penalty"⑥(*infra* para. 92. c).

76. On December 15, the Permanent Criminal Chamber ordered the hearing of October 5, 2009, to be nullified so that the parties could present their arguments concerning the note from the Embassy of the People's Republic of China (*supra* para. 75)⑦

77. On December 21, 2009, a new passive extradition hearing was

---

① *Cf.* Judgment of the 53rd Criminal Court of the Province of Lima of January 5, 2010 (evidence file, folio 161).
② *Cf.* Appeal of February 4, 2010 (evidence file, folios 183 and 184).
③ *Cf.* Judgment of the Superior Court of Justice of Lima of June 30, 2010 (evidence file, folios 1521 to 1526).
④ *Cf.* Judgment of the Constitutional Court of August 5, 2011, and separate opinion of Judges Álvarez Miranda and Vergara Gotelli giving reasons for their vote (evidence file, folios 6416 and 6417).
⑤ *Cf.* Record of the hearing of December 9, 2009, before the Permanent Criminal Chamber of the Supreme Court of Justice (evidence file, folio 8278).
⑥ Note of the Embassy of the People's Republic of China in the Republic of Peru of December 11, 2009 (evidence file, folio 140).
⑦ *Cf.* Decision of the Permanent Criminal Chamber of December 15, 2009 (evidence file, folio 142).

held before the Permanent Criminal Chamber.① On that date, the Chamber ordered that the translation of article 151 of the Criminal Code of the People's Republic of China should be requested and added to the case file, together with the undertaking of the People's Supreme Court mentioned in the Embassy's note of December 11, 2009②(*supra* para. 75). On December 29, 2009, the People's Republic of China again sent the translation of article 151 of the Criminal Code (*supra* para. 69).③

C. 2) Second stage of the process (from the second advisory decision to date)

78. On January 27, 2010, the Permanent Criminal Chamber issued the advisory decision in which it decided, by the legal majority, "the passive extradition request [···] in relation to the offenses of evasion of customs duty and bribery against the People's Republic of China," established in articles 153, 154, 389 and 390 of the Chinese Criminal Code.④ Regarding the punishment for the offense of evasion, the Chamber noted the possibility that the death penalty could be applied to this offense. However, it considered that the decision of the People's Supreme Court of December 8, 2009, "reveals an evident undertaking by the judicial authorities of the People's Republic of China not to impose the death penalty on the individual whose extradition is requested if he is found criminally responsible. Therefore, it should be considered that there is no real risk of the application of the death penalty or a similar sanction to this individual in the requesting State."⑤ It

---

① *Cf.* Record of the hearing of December 21, 2009, before the Permanent Criminal Chamber of the Supreme Court of Justice (evidence file, folio 8303).
② *Cf.* Decision of the Permanent Criminal Chamber of December 21, 2009 (evidence file, folios 144 and 145).
③ This was added to the case file the following day. *Cf.* note from the Ambassador Extraordinary and Plenipotentiary of the People's Republic of China to the Republic of Peru of December 29, 2009 (evidence file, folio 149), and advisory decision of the Permanent Criminal Chamber of January 27, 2010 (evidence file, folio 165).
④ *Cf.* Advisory decision of the Permanent Criminal Chamber of January 27, 2010 (evidence file, folios 169 and 173).
⑤ Advisory decision of the Permanent Criminal Chamber of January 27, 2010 (evidence file, folios 171 and 172).

also declared, unanimously, the inadmissibility of the extradition request in relation to money-laundering, because it ran counter to the principle of double jeopardy.① The Chamber conditioned the return of Wong Ho Wing:

> [T]o the undertaking made by the competent authorities of the People's Republic of China not to impose the death penalty, if he should be convicted; in addition, it should advise the Peruvian State of the sentence handed down to the [individual extradited] when this is delivered.②

79. Following the second advisory decision, on February 9, the representative filed a third application for *habeas corpus* "against the certain and imminent threat of violation of the rights to life and personal integrity [of Wong Ho Wing], against the President of the Republic of Peru, the Ministry of Justice, and the Ministry of Foreign Affairs."③ On February 25, 2010, the 42nd Special Criminal Court of Lima declared the application for *habeas corpus* inadmissible.④ The representative appealed this decision and, on April 14, 2010, the declaration of inadmissibility was confirmed, because there had been no "violation or threat by [the President, Minister of Justice and Minister for Foreign Affairs] during the passive extradition," or any "objective and specific harm to the rights cited," because these persons had not issued the contested decision.⑤ The representative

---

① *Cf.* Advisory decision of the Permanent Criminal Chamber of January 27, 2010 (evidence file, folio 173).
② Advisory decision of the Permanent Criminal Chamber of January 27, 2010 (evidence file, folios 173 and 174).
③ The representative argued that, "from the start, the extradition process [...], has been plagued with a series of grave errors and omissions"; among these, he underlined that: (1) "[t]he extradition request was not accompanied by any evidence in relation to the charges it contained"; (2) "[t]he extradition request was not accompanied either by the provision of the Chinese Criminal Code relating to the offense that was the reason for requesting the extradition, which is punished by the death penalty"; (3) the advisory decision and the "opinion of the Special Supranational Public Attorney "ignore the binding nature of the decision issued by the [Inter-American Commission] that the Government of Peru refrain from extraditing the said Chinese citizen," and (4) the undertaking not to apply the death penalty was delivered "[44] days after the Ambassador was notified, [when] the time limit was [30] days according to article 2 of Supreme Decree No. 016 – 2006 – JUS." Application for *habeas corpus* of February 9, 2010 (evidence file, folios 188 and 191).
④ *Cf.* Judgment of February 25, 2010 (evidence file, folio 214).
⑤ *Cf.* Judgment of the Third Criminal Chamber of the Superior Court of Justice of Lima of April 14, 2010 (evidence file, folios 216 to 224).

filed an appeal based on constitutional injury, which was considered admissible on May 24, 2011 (*infra* paras. 81 to 83).①

80. On May 1, 2011, the eighth amendment to the Chinese Criminal Code entered into force annulling the death penalty for the offense of smuggling for which the extradition of Wong Ho Wing was being requested.② The Chargé d'Affaires of the People's Republic of China advised the Constitutional Court of the adoption of this amendment on April 6, 2011.③

81. On May 24, 2011, the Constitutional Court decided the appeal filed based on constitutional injury (*supra* para. 79) indicating that:

> [T]he diplomatic assurances offered by the People's Republic of China are insufficient to ensure that the death penalty will not be imposed on Wong Ho Wing. This is because, in the United Nations, the requesting State has not demonstrated that it guarantees the real protection of the right to life, because it allows extrajudicial, summary or arbitrary executions. Also, it is known in international circles that the death penalty is not imposed objectively, but is influenced by public opinion.④

82. Regarding the information received about the eighth amendment (*supra* para. 80), the Constitutional Court clarified that this amendment,

---

① *Cf.* Appeal based on constitutional injury of May 4, 2010 (evidence file, folios 6419 to 6423).
② *Cf.* Decision of the Permanent Criminal Chamber of February 15, 2012 (evidence file, folio 2595).
③ *Cf.* Judgment of the Constitutional Court of May 24, 2011 (evidence file, folio 280), and decision of the Constitutional Court of June 9, 2011 (evidence file, folio 295). Regarding the offense of smuggling, the said amendment establishes that "the first clause of article 153 of the Criminal Code is amended as follows: 'Anyone who shall smuggle merchandise and objects that are not mentioned in articles 151, 152 and 347 of this law shall be punished pursuant to the following provision, according to the severity of the offense: (a) Anyone who shall smuggle merchandise and objects involving significant evasion of customs duty or who is a repeat offender with more than two administrative sanctions for smuggling in a year, shall be punished with imprisonment for less than three years or detention and fines of from 100% to 500% of the customs duty evaded; (b) Anyone who shall smuggle merchandise and objects involving a very high evasion of customs duty or in very serious cases, shall be punished with imprisonment for from three to 10 years and fines of from 100% to 500% of the customs duty evaded; (c) Anyone who shall smuggle merchandise and objects involving an extremely high evasion of customs duty, or in extremely serious cases, shall be punished with imprisonment for more than 10 years or life imprisonment and fines of from 100% to 500% of the customs duty evaded, or seizure of personal property." *Cf.* Eighth amendment (evidence file, folio 7555).
④ Judgment of the Constitutional Court of May 24, 2011 (evidence file, folio 279).

"to a great extent, ha[d] modified the Criminal Code of the People's Republic of China for the offense of smuggling ordinary merchandise." However, it specified that:

[T]he case file does not reveal […] that this amendment […] has been communicated officially using the diplomatic procedures of the Peruvian State. Moreover, there is no mention of whether the Constitution of the People's Republic of China recognizes the favorable retroactivity of criminal law. Consequently, the Court f[ound] that the said letter c[ould] not be understood and interpreted as a guarantee of the non-application of the death penalty to the beneficiary of the application. ①

83. Based on the foregoing conclusions, the Constitutional Court declared that the application was admissible and "order[ed] the Peruvian State, represented by the Executive Branch, to refrain from extraditing Wong Ho Wing to the People's Republic of China." In addition, it "urge[d] the Peruvian State, represented by the Executive Branch, to proceed in accordance with the provisions of article 4(a) of the Extradition Treaty between the Republic of Peru and the People's Republic of China. ②

84. The public attorneys of the Ministries of Justice and Foreign Affairs, and the Presidency of the Council of Ministers submitted requests to clarify the judgment of the Constitutional Court. ③ On June 9, 2011, the Constitutional Court issued a decision in which it indicated that, "regarding the request to clarify the reasons why it had considered that the diplomatic assurances offered by the People's Republic of China were insufficient, [it recalled] that at the time the [judgment] was delivered, the case file did not contain any of the diplomatic assurances referred to by the public attorneys who were requesting the clarification"; rather, it only included infor-

---

① Judgment of the Constitutional Court of May 24, 2011 (evidence file, folio 280).
② Judgment of the Constitutional Court of May 24, 2011 (evidence file, folio 281).
③ Cf. Ruling of the Constitutional Court of June 9, 2011 (evidence file, folio 291).

mation on the promulgation of the eighth amendment that annulled the death penalty for the offense of smuggling ordinary merchandise, which did "not constitute diplomatic assurances."① The diplomatic assurances were incorporated into the case file following the delivery of this judgment on July 7, 2011.② On this basis, the Constitutional Court considered that conclusions 9 and 10 of the judgment constituted material errors (*supra* para. 81),③ and therefore amended them as follows:

> [The diplomaticassurances offered by the People's Republic of China are insufficient to ensure that the death penalty will not be imposed on Wong Ho Wing]. This is because, since the case file does not contain any diplomatic assurances provided to the Peruvian State by the Republic of China, it has not been proved that real protection of the right to life has been ensured. Also it is *communis opinio* that the mere risk that the death penalty could be applied in the requesting State prevents the requested State from authorizing extradition. In-

---

① Ruling of the Constitutional Court of June 9, 2011 (evidence file, folios 295 and 296).
② *Cf.* Ruling of the Constitutional Court of June 9, 2011 (evidence file, folio 296).
③ Conclusions 9 and 10 of the judgment of the Constitutional Court of May 24, 2011, established that: "9. In this case, this Court considers that the diplomatic assurances offered by the People's Republic of China are insufficient to ensure that the death penalty will not be imposed on Wong Ho Wing. This is because, in the United Nations, the requesting State has not demonstrated that it guarantees the real protection of the right to life, because it allows extrajudicial, summary or arbitrary executions. Also, it is known in international circles that the death penalty is not imposed objectively, but is influenced by public opinion. Indeed, the Human Rights Council in the Report A/HRC/WG. 6/4/CHN/2, of January 6, 2009, emphasized that '16. In 2005, the Government of China explained to the Special Rapporteur on Extrajudicial, Summary or Arbitrary Executions that the death penalty is applicable only to "extremely serious crimes" and "that one of the factors leading to its use in that context is public opinion."10. Bearing in mind the report cited, this Court finds that the People's Republic of China does not grant the necessary and sufficient guarantees to safeguard the right to life of Wong Ho Wing, because, as revealed by the report of the Human Rights Council of the United Nations, one of the factors to impose the death penalty in that country is public opinion. In addition, it should be recalled that, in the instant case, the extradition of the beneficiary would not be in order, because the principle of reciprocity is not respected, since the offenses based on which the extradition is sought are not punished with the death penalty in the Peruvian State. Consequently, the Peruvian State must comply with its obligation to try Wong Ho Wing in accordance with the provisions of article 4(a) of the Extradition Treaty between the Republic of Peru and the People's Republic of China. Judgment of the Constitutional Court of May 24, 2011 (evidence file, folios 279 and 280).

deed, in the case of Yin Fong, Kwok v. Australia of October 23, 2009, the Human Rights Committee emphasized that: 'It is not necessary to prove [⋯] that the author "will be sentenced to death, but that there is a 'real risk' that the death penalty will be imposed on her.

10. Bearing in mind the inexistence of diplomatic assurances in the case file, this Court finds that it has not been proved that the People's Republic of China has granted the necessary and sufficient guarantees to safeguard the right to life of Wong Ho Wing. ①

85. The Constitutional Court also amended the legal grounds for the recommendation that Wong Ho Wing be tried in Peru, indicating that it was "pursuant to the provisions of article 3 of the [Peruvian] Criminal Code" and not pursuant to article 4(a) of the Extradition Treaty (*supra* para. 83). ②

C. 2. a) Subsequent request made by Executive Branch

86. Following the judgment of the Constitutional Court, the Executive Branch filed various judicial remedies to clarify the way in which this decision should be executed. On November 25, 2011, the representative of the Ministry of Justice presented a brief in the procedure of execution of the judgment of the Constitutional Court, indicating that the prohibition to extradite Wong Ho Wing imposed by the Constitutional Court was "applicable only to the possibility of extradition for the offense of evasion of customs duty or smuggling and not with regard to the offense of bribery, for which the possibility of imposing the death penalty is not established."③ Therefore, it asked the 42nd Special Criminal Court of the Superior Court of Justice of Lima to take the foregoing into account and to rule "that this

---

① Ruling of the Constitutional Court of June 9, 2011 (evidence file, folios 297 and 302).
② *Cf.* Ruling of the Constitutional Court of June 9, 2011 (evidence file, folio 302).
③ Brief of November 25, 2011, filed before the judge of the 42nd Special Criminal Court of the Superior Court of Justice of Lima (evidence file, folio 337).

corresponds to the execution of judgment."① On November 30, 2011, it declared that the "request for clarification (definition) of the scope of the mandate of the Constitutional Court" was inadmissible. ② The representative of the Ministry of Justice appealed this decision and, on February 20, 2012, the "Criminal Chamber for proceedings involving detainees" confirmed this decision. In particular, the Chamber indicated that "under article [4] of the Organic Law of the Judiciary, the content of a judgment is immutable, apart from the exceptions established by law."③ The representative of the Ministry of Justice filed an appeal based on constitutional injury requesting an interpretation of the judgment of the Constitutional Court (*infra* para. 90).④

87. On December 22, 2011, the Embassy of the People's Republic of China forwarded "the documents relating to the pertinent legalprovisions, [including article 12 regarding the retroactivity of criminal law,] and clarification on [the application] of the eighth amendment of the Chinese Criminal Code, issued by the [People's Supreme Court] of the People's Republic of China."⑤ The latter established that:

---

① Brief of November 25, 2011, before the judge of the 42nd Special Criminal Court of the Superior Court of Justice of Lima (evidence file, folio 340).
② Decision of the 42nd Special Criminal Court of the Superior Court of Justice of Lima of November 30, 2011 (evidence file, folio 8492).
③ Appeal of December 12, 2011 (evidence file, folios 2712 to 2715), and decision of February 20, 2012, of the Criminal Chamber for proceedings involving detainees of the Superior Court of Justice of Lima (evidence file, folios 354 to 357).
④ The Ministry of Justice argued that the effects of the constitutional decision cannot be permitted to exceed those of the application for *habeas corpus* filed in the instant case in favor [of] Wong Ho Wing, because the Supreme Court of Justice of the Republic has declared admissible the passive extradition of the Chinese citizen for the offenses of evasion of customs duty and also for the offense of bribery. Nevertheless, as can be appreciated from the arguments presented and the decisions made at the constitutional level, no ruling was made on the possibility of carrying out the extradition for the less serious offense; that is, for the offense of passive bribery. *Cf.* Constitutional remedy of March 19, 2013 (evidence file, folios 8496 and 8497).
⑤ Note of the People's Republic of China of December 22 2011 (evidence file, folios 7479 and 7480). The case file does not reveal the date on which the translation of article 12 on criminal retroactivity was sent, because this translation is dated February 24, 2012. *Cf.* Official translation of article 12 (evidence file, folios 7504 and 7505).

Regarding the retroactive effects of the Criminal Code, according to paragraph [1] of article [12] of the Criminal Code of the People's Republic of China, the principle of sentencingin accordance with the law at the time of the act is followed, and also the principle of applying the lesser punishment; in other words, for offenses that have not been sentenced prior to the entry into force of the Criminal Code, if there has been no change in the status of the punishment between the law at the time of the act and the law in force, the law at the time of the act is applied. If the law in force imposes a lesser punishment, the law in force is applied. Under the eighth amendment, which came into force on May 1, 2011, the first paragraph of article 153 of the Criminal Code was amended. The presumed offenses committed by [Wong Ho Wing] occurred before this amendment came into force and, at the same time, pursuant to the provisions of the amended article, the maximum punishment is less than the maximum punishment before the amendment. Based on the above-mentioned principles, the eighth amendment will be applied in the case of [Wong Ho Wing]. The undertaking made by the Supreme Court of the People's Republic of China not to impose the death penalty on [Wong Ho Wing] remains in effect. ①

88. On February 9, 2012, the Ministry of Justice and Human Rights asked the President of the Supreme Court of Justice to issue a "complementary advisory decision," taking into account "the entry into force of the eighth amendment of the Criminal Code of [the People's Republic of China, which annuls] the death penalty for the offense of smuggling ordinary merchandise."② Accordingly, on February 15, 2012, the Permanent Criminal Chamber ordered that a passive extradition hearing be held on February 21,

---

① Clarification of the case to which the eighth amendment is applicable (evidence file, folio 7512).
② Brief of February 9, 2012, before the President of the Supreme Court of Justice (evidence file, folio 352).

2012①(*infra* para. 89). On March 13, 2012, the representative filed a fifth application for *habeas corpus* against the convening of this hearing. ② According to information provided by the State on December 1, 2014, this procedure is still pending. ③

89. However, the February 21 hearing was annulled due to lack of information on the applicable Chinese legislation. ④ After this information had been obtained, on March 6, the Permanent Criminal Chamber again convened the hearing for March 14, 2012. ⑤ That day, the Criminal Chamber indicated that it was unnecessary to hold the hearing and "pointless, as the matter had been dealt with owing to the issue of a new advisory decision." In this regard, it emphasized that, "in sum, there are two final rulings, one of an advisory nature (by the Judiciary), and the other of a binding nature (by the Constitutional Court) that the Executive Branch must comply with, taking into account the provisions of article [113] of the Code of Constitutional Procedure."⑥

90. Meanwhile, on March 12, 2013, the Constitutional Court decided that the request for interpretation of its mandate with regard to Wong Ho Wing was inadmissible (*supra* para. 86). ⑦ It stressed that, regarding this appeal for interpretation:

> [T]he purpose sought is that, [⋯] with the pretext of "clarifying" one element of its judgment, [the Constitutional Court] "a-

---

① *Cf.* Decision of the Permanent Criminal Chamber of February 15, 2012 (evidence file, folio 2595).
② *Cf.* Application for *habeas corpus* of March 13, 2012 (evidence file, folio 361).
③ *Cf.* The State's brief of December 1, 2014 (merits file, folio 1159). The application for *habeas corpus* was admitted on April 29, 2013. *Cf.* Admissibility decision of April 29, 2013 (evidence file, folios 8517 to 8520).
④ *Cf.* Decision of February 21, 2012 (evidence file, folios 7456 to 7460).
⑤ *Cf.* Note of the Embassy of the People's Republic of China of February 27, 2012 (evidence file, folio 7471), and decision of March 6, 2012, of the Permanent Criminal Chamber of the Supreme Court of Justice (evidence file, folio 359).
⑥ Decision of March 14, 2012 of the Permanent Criminal Chamber (evidence file, folio 373).
⑦ *Cf.* Decision of March 12, 2013, of the Constitutional Court (evidence file, folio 377).

mend" its decision, so that it affirms something that it did not indicate at the time, also affecting the *res judicata* guarantee established in article 139(2) of the Constitution. [...]. That, in this regard, in accordance with the content of both the judgment and the clarification ruling issued by the Constitutional Court, it should be pointed out that in these decisions it did not make an individual or separate analysis of the offenses of which the applicant is accused, not only because this was not in order [...], but also because what was relevant was to determine whether or not the right to life of the beneficiary of the *habeas corpus* proceeding was in danger if the extradition request was declared admissible. ①

C. 2. b) The actual situation

91. Following this last decision, the case file does not show that any new appeals have been filed against the judgment of the Constitutional Court or with regard to the extradition process before the Supreme Court. Consequently, at this time, the advisory decision of the Criminal Chamber of the Supreme Court of January 27, 2010, which finds extradition admissible and a binding *prima facie* ruling of the Constitutional Court of May 24, 2011, ordering the State to refrain from extraditing Wong Ho Wing are both in force simultaneously. Since that time, the process has been in the hands of the Executive Branch, which has not taken a final decision in this regard.

C. 3) Diplomatic assurances granted by the People's Republic of China in relation to the extradition of Wong Ho Wing

92. In this case, the following diplomatic assurances or notes haves been given to Peru by the People's Republic of China progressively, between February 2009 and January 2010, when the second advisory decision

---

① Decision of March 12, 2013, of the Constitutional Court (evidence file, folio 377).

was issued (*supra* para. 78):

 a. First diplomatic note: note of February 2, 2009

General Directorate No. 24 of the Ministry of Public Security of the People's Republic of China[①] presented the following explanation to the Official Commission for Extraditions and Prisoner Transfers of the Ministry of Justice of Peru:

A. Based on the nature of the offenses for which the extradition of Wong Ho Wing is requested and the provisions of the Criminal Code of the People's Republic of China, there is no possibility of imposing on him the punishment of life imprisonment or the death penalty.

B. Chinese justice will impose criminal responsibilities on Wong Ho Wing based on the law and respecting fully the Extradition Treaty between the Governments of China and Peru.[②]

 b. Second diplomatic note: note of August 25, 2009

The Ambassador Extraordinary and Plenipotentiary of the People's Republic of China to Peru sent the Supreme Court of Justice a note indicating that "[c]ase law exists from similar cases" where 15 years' imprisonment has been imposed for acts with the same name, or the same offense, and involving an equally important sum and the amount of duty evaded, and where the *modus operandi* has also been similar, "there was, therefore, no possibility of imposing the death penalty on the person sought."[③]

 c. Third diplomatic note: notes of December 10 and 11, 2009

The Ambassador Extraordinary and Plenipotentiary of the

[①] This explanation was presented by the Consul of the Embassy of the People's Republic of China in Peru to the President of the Commission for Extraditions and Prisoner Transfers (evidence file, folio 1615).

[②] Brief of the General Directorate No. 24 of the Ministry of Public Security of February 2, 2009 (evidence file, folios 67, 68 and 1617).

[③] Brief No. 135/2009 of the Ambassador Extraordinary and Plenipotentiary of the People's Republic of China to Peru addressed to the President of the Supreme Court of Justice of August 25, 2009 (evidence file, folio 2417).

People's Republic of China to Peru informed the Permanent Criminal Chamber of the Supreme Court of Justice that "the People's Supreme Court of the People's Republic of China has taken the following decision: if the extradition from Peru to China is executed, and if [...] Wong Ho Wing is tried by a court and found guilty, the court will not impose the death penalty [...] on [...] Wong Ho Wing, even though his crime is subject to the death penalty by law." In addition, the Ambassador advised that he had "full authorization to undertake that the death penalty would not be imposed on [...] Wong Ho Wing if the extradition request of the Government of the People's Republic of China was found admissible."①

d. <u>Fourth diplomatic note</u>: note of December 29, 2009

The Ambassador Extraordinary and Plenipotentiary of the People's Republic of China to Peru sent the Permanent Criminal Chamber of the Supreme Court of Justice a copy and the translation of the decision issued by the People's Supreme Court, establishing that: "[if he is extradited from Peru to China and if] a court finds that Wong Ho Wing is guilty, the court will not sentence Wong Ho Wing to death (including the immediate death penalty or the death penalty with a temporary two-year suspension) [...], even though his crime islegally subject to the death penalty."②

93. Following the second advisory decision of the Supreme Court of Justice and up until August 2014, the following assurances were provided:

---

① Notes Nos. 200/2009, 201/2009 and 202/2009 sent by the Ambassador Extraordinary and Plenipotentiary of the People's Republic of China to Peru to the President of the Permanent Criminal Chamber of the Supreme Court of Justice and the judge of the Seventh Criminal Court of the Superior Court of Justice of El Callao (evidence file, folios 964, 1116 and 1117).

② Note No. 204/2009 of December 29, 2009, sent by the Ambassador of the People's Republic of China to the Republic of Peru to the President of the Permanent Criminal Chamber of the Supreme Court of Justice (evidence file, folios 1622 and 1624).

e. Fifth diplomatic note: note of February 22, 2011

The Ambassador of the People's Republic of China informed the Minister of Justice of Peru, that "the Government Chino undertakes formally, apart from the commitment not to apply the death sentence [⋯], to invite the Peruvian Government to send observers to be present during the hearings held in [the proceedings] against Mr. Wong and to monitor compliance with the [eventual] judgment."①

f. Sixth diplomatic note: note of June 10, 2011

The Ambassador of the People's Republic of China advised the Minister of Justice, attaching the translation of article 12 of the Chinese Criminal Code, that he officially confirmed that the eighth amendment of the Chinese Criminal Code would be applicable to Wong Ho Wing's case "because a preliminary hearing has not yet been held; which proves that the annulment of the death penalty will be applicable to him; thus, there is no risk that this punishment will be imposed."②

g. Seventh diplomatic note: received on December 22, 2011

The Embassy of the People's Republic of China addressed a communication to the Ministry of Foreign Affairs of Peru (*supra* para. 87), in which it indicated that:

Based on the decision of the Supreme Court of the People's Republic of China, in a note dated December 11, 2009 [⋯], the Chinese party made a formal undertaking to the Peruvian party that the death penalty would not be imposed on [Wong Ho Wing], even if he was tried and convicted following his extradition to China. This undertaking by the Chinese party continues to be in effect.

---

① Note No. 010/2011 of February 22, 2011, sent by the Ambassador of the People's Republic of China to the Republic of Peru to the Minister of Justice of the Republic of Peru (evidence file, folio 5 755).
② Note No. 036/2011 of June 10, 2011, cited in the ruling of the Constitutional Court of June 9, 2011 (evidence file, folio 296).

With the entry into force of the eighth amendment to the Criminal Code of the People's Republic of China on May 1, 2011, the death penalty has been annulled for the offense of smuggling ordinary merchandise in which [Wong Ho Wing] is involved. To demonstrated this, the documents with the pertinent legal provisions are attached to [this note], together with the clarification about the cases to which the eighth amendment of the Chinese Criminal Code issued by the Supreme Court of the People's Republic of China is applicable, and also the official translation into Spanish. ①

h. Eighth diplomatic note: note of August 19, 2014

The Embassy of the People's Republic of China addressed a communication to the Ministry of Foreign Affairs, in which it affirmed the following:

1. In 2009, the Chinese Government gave guarantees that, pursuant to the decision of the People's Supreme Court, the death penalty would not be imposed on Mr. [Wong] and, as a State Party to the Convention against Torture and Other Cruel, Inhuman or Degrading Treatment or Punishment, the Chinese Government guarantees that Mr. [Wong] will not be subjected to torture or other cruel, inhuman

---

① Note of the People's Republic of China of December 22, 2011 (evidence file, folios 7479 and 7480). With this note, the People's Republic of China forwarded to Peru: (i) the "Clarification of the cases to which the eighth amendment of the Criminal Code of the People's Republic of China is applicable," in which the People's Supreme Court indicated that the eighth amendment of the Criminal Code would be applicable to the case of Wong Ho Wing; (ii) the official translation of the eighth amendment of the Criminal Code of the People's Republic of China (evidence file, folios 7504 and 7505). However, (iii) the official translation of articles 87 and 88 of the Criminal Code of the People's Republic of China, concerning the statute of limitations, and (iv) the official translation of article 12, paragraph 1, of the Criminal Code of the People's Republic of China, which recognizes the principle of the retroactivity of the most favorable criminal law seems to have been sent later, on February 24, 2012 (evidence file, folios 7497 to 7505). In addition, on April 19, 2013, the Embassy of the People's Republic of China sent a communication to the Ministry of Justice and Human Rights of Peru, with which it forwarded new certifications of those documents as well as complementary documentation on the inapplicability of the death penalty to Wong Ho Wing, particularly the text of articles 151 and 153 of the Chinese Criminal Code before the amendment. *Cf.* Note No. 26/2013 of April 18, 2013, sent by the Ambassador of the People's Republic of China to the Republic of Peru to the Minister of Justice and Human Rights of Peru (evidence file, folio 3491).

or degrading treatment or punishment. The Chinese party will abide by this undertaking.

2. The information regarding the place where Mr. [Wong] would be detained will be accessible to the Peruvian party. In response to the requests of the Peruvian party, the Chinese party will organize visits to the place where Mr. [Wong] will be detained, including his room, as soon as possible, and meetings between Mr. [Wong] and the Peruvian diplomats or consular officials resident in China. The Peruvian officials may be accompanied by an interpreter chosen by the Peruvian party.

3. If necessary, video conferencing facilities will be available so that Mr. [Wong] may contact the Peruvian diplomats or consular officials resident in China during his detention at the request of the Peruvian party.

4. According to the Code of Criminal Procedure of the People's Republic of China and the Lawyers Act of the People's Republic of China, Mr. [Wong] has the right to authorize a lawyer licensed to practice law in China to defend him. He also has the right to reject the defense of the lawyer he chose and to appoint another one. Mr. [Wong] is allowed to meet with his lawyer without being monitored.

5. The Peruvian party may send its diplomats or consular officials resident in China to observe the open trial in the criminal case against Mr. [Wong] in accordance with the Code of Criminal Procedure of the People's Republic of China and the Criminal Code of the People's Republic of China.

6. After Mr. [Wong] has been returned to China, the Chinese judicial authorities will prepare simultaneous audio and video recordings of the pre-trial and trial interrogations, and will record the identity of all those present during the pre-trial and trial interrogations of Mr. [Wong]. These audio and video recordings will be available to the Pe-

ruvian party as requested.

7. Pursuant to the Prisons Act of the People's Republic of China and the Detention Center Regulations of the People's Republic of China, every detainee has access to any medical care that is required.

In response to a reasonable request from the Peruvian party, the Chinese party will permit an independent social medical institution with a license to operate in the continental part of China, to provide medical care to Mr. [Wong].

Given the private nature of the medical report, the Peruvian party requires the consent of Mr. [Wong] to access the content of the report.

The Treaties and Laws Department of the Ministry of Foreign Affairs of the People's Republic of China and the Peruvian Embassy in China shall be the communication channels for all matters related to the above-mentioned articles. ①

D. The detention of Wong Ho Wing and the remedies filed in this regard

94. Peru's procedural law establishes the mechanism of "provisional or pre-extradition arrest" for the detention of individuals wanted by foreign authorities. According to this law, the provisional arrest is in order mainly when a person is "formally requested by the central authority of the interested country." This request must be sent to the Prosecutor General, who must forward it "immediately to the judge of the competent preliminary investigation, advising the respective provincial prosecutor." It is for the said investigating judge to issue the provisional arrest warrant, "provided that the act which is considered an offense is also considered an offense in Peru and that any type of criminal punishment, equal to or in excess of one year's imprisonment, is not established." Once "the provisional arrest has

---

① Note No. 030/2014 of August 19, 2014, sent by the Embassy of the People's Republic of China in the Republic of Peru to the Ministry of Foreign Affairs of Peru (evidence file, folios 7377 to 7382).

been order, the preliminary investigation judge shall hear the person who has been arrested within 24 hours and will appoint a defense counsel if the person arrested does not appoint a lawyer of his own choice" (*infra* para. 241). The arrest will be lifted if the judge observes that the conditions indicated above do not exist, and "will become an order to appear in court periodically, and the prohibition to leave the country," or will cease "if it is proved that the individual arrested is not the person sought, or when the time limit of 30 days for the formal presentation of the extradition request has expired." The said norm also establishes the possibility of "obtaining provisional release, if the legal time limits established in the treaty or law that supports the extradition request expire, or if the individual sought meets the procedural conditions for this measure," and in this case, "the procedure established for the termination of preventive detention will be followed."①

95. In addition, the Extradition Treaty between China and Peru establishes the possibility that "[i]n urgent cases, before the presentation of the extradition request, the requesting party may request the preventive detention of the person sought."②

96. Wong Ho Wing was arrested on October 27, 2008, in the "Jorge Chávez International Airport", and from there he was transferred to the cells of the Judicial Police of El Callao and brought before a judge (*supra* para. 60). Subsequently, Wong Ho Wing was interned in the Transitory Pre-trial Prison of El Callao.③ In this section, the Court will establish the facts relating to the detention of Wong Ho Wing, which occurred in paral-

---

① Code of Criminal Procedure, promulgated by Legislative Decree No. 957 of July 29, 2004, article 523. Available at: http://www.leyes.congreso.gob.pe/Documentos/Decretoslegislativos/00957.pdf, cited in the Commission's Merits Report, folio 24.
② Extradition Treaty between the Republic of Peru and the People's Republic of China, article 9 (evidence file, folio 1635).
③ *Cf*. Note of the First Criminal Court of the Superior Court of El Callao of October 28, 2008 (evidence file, folio 21), and Note of the Peruvian National Police of October 27, 2008 (evidence file, folio 11)

lel to the extradition process.

97. On October 28, 2008, the special court ordered the provisional arrest of Wong Ho Wing:

> [I]n order to ensure his presence in the country while the corresponding extradition request is processed, because he has not proved that he has a domicile or known employment in the country. ①

98. Wong Ho Wing's defense filed an appeal against this provisional arrest warrant, contesting that he did not have "known employment in the country," because he was the "founder and main shareholder of a company [that] he administers: the [⋯] 'Hotel Maury.'" Also, regarding the domicile, he indicated that "when he is in [Peru], he stays at this hotel." ②

99. On November 6, 2008, the Embassy of the People's Republic of China sent a note asked "the competent Peruvian authorities [to take the necessary steps] to ensure the provisional arrest of [Wong Ho Wing] before the arrival of the Chinese commission that would open the extradition process officially." ③

100. On December 11, 2008, the First Transitory Combined Superior Chamber of El Callao confirmed the arrest warrant decision, indicating that it met the requirements established in paragraphs 1, 4 and 10 of article 523. Regarding the arguments contained in the appeal, it indicated that "it was not incumbent [on the court] to analyze [the procedural risks] in the case of a provisional arrest with a view to extradition; rather, that corresponds to a criminal proceeding instituted in [Peru] for a specific offense, which has not occurred [in this case]." ④

101. On September 18, 2009, the representative presented a releasere-

---

① Provisional arrest warrant of October 28, 2008 (evidence file, folios 18 and 19).
② Appeal filed on October 29, 2008 (evidence file, folio 24).
③ Note of November 5, 2008, received on November 6, 2008 (evidence file, folios 32 and 33).
④ Decision of December 11, 2008, of the First Transitory Combined Superior Chamber (evidence file, folios 43 and 44).

quest to the Second Transitory Criminal Chamber of the Peru's Supreme Court of Justice. ① On September 21, 2009, this Second Criminal Chamber ordered that the request be forwarded "to another Supreme Court for a new ruling," considering that it did not have the required competence. ② The file before this Court does not contain information on whether another court ruled on this request.

102. On August 5, 2010, the representative filed another application for release on bail before the Permanent Criminal Chamber of the Supreme Court of Justice requesting that it impose "an order to appear in court periodically with the prohibition to leave the country, pursuant to [⋯] paragraph 6 [of Article 523]." In this regard, he indicated that, since the advisory decision had already been issued, "during the extradition process that was underway, the circumstances that surrounded it at the outset had changed substantially, which led to the conclusion that, if he is released, he will not abuse of his freedom to flee or to fail to comply with the obligations imposed on him." Accordingly, he stated that "the provisions of paragraph 9 of article 523 of the Code of Criminal Procedure are applicable, not only due to the length of [the deprivation of liberty], but also because [he meets] the conditions required to be granted this type of measure," added to which this provision establishes 'that the person arrested may obtain his provisional release, once the legal time limits established in the [extradition] treaty have expired."③

103. On October 19, 2010, the Chamber declared the request for provisional release inadmissible. ④ The four judges who voted in favor of its inadmissibility indicated, among other arguments, that there was no legal

---

① *Cf.* Release request of September 18, 2009 (evidence file, folio 6405).
② *Cf.* Decision of the Second Transitory Criminal Chamber of the Supreme Court of Justice of September 21, 2009 (evidence file, folio 8532).
③ Request for release on bail of August 5, 2010 (evidence file, folio 227).
④ *Cf.* Decision of October 19, 2010 (evidence file, folio 263).

time limit for detention in extradition processes. ① They also indicated that, in the case of Wong Ho Wing, the proceedings had been delayed owing to the appeals filed by his representative at the domestic and the inter-American level. ② Judge José Neyra Flores added that "the probability that he will avoid prosecution has not disappeared; to the contrary, the risk of his absconding is greater, because the Permanent Criminal Chamber has [now] declared [⋯] the extradition request admissible [⋯]; moreover, the processing of the order given in the said judicial ruling is suspended or pending execution," in compliance with the provisional measures ordered by the Inter-American Court. ③ Meanwhile, the dissenting judges indicated that it was in order to grant the provisional release of Wong Ho Wing because, at that time, there was no risk of his absconding. In addition, they took into account the length of time that the presumed victim had been detained. ④

104. Following the ruling of the Constitutional Court ordering the Executive Branch to refrain from extraditing Wong Ho Wing (*supra* para. 83), on October 5, 2011, his representative asked the Permanent Criminal Chamber for his "immediate release without any restrictions." ⑤ On October 10, 2011, the Criminal Chamber declared that this request should "be submitted [⋯] to the corresponding court." ⑥ On October 18, the representative filed the request before the Seventh Criminal Court of El

---

① *Cf.* Vote of Supreme Justice José Antonio Neyra Flores of October 13, 2010 (evidence file, folios 1608 to 1611); Vote of José Luis Lecaros Cornejo and Jorge Calderón Castillo of September 10, 2010 (evidence file, folio 1598), and Vote of Judge Santa María Morillo of September 30, 2010 (evidence file, folio 1601).

② *Cf.* Vote of Supreme Justice José Antonio Neyra Flores of October 13, 2010 (evidence file, folios 1608 to 1611); Vote of José Luis Lecaros Cornejo and Jorge Calderón Castillo of September 10, 2010 (evidence file, folio 1598), and Vote of Judge Santa María Morillo of September 30, 2010 (evidence file, folio 1602).

③ *Cf.* Vote of Supreme Justice José Antonio Neyra Flores of October 13, 2010 (evidence file, folios 1608 to 1611).

④ *Cf.* Vote of Judges San Martín Castro, Prado Saldarriaga and Príncipe Trujillo of September 10, 2010 (evidence file, folios 1593 and 1594).

⑤ Request dated October 5, 2011 (evidence file, folio 2724).

⑥ Decision of the Permanent Criminal Chamber of October 10, 2011 (evidence file, folio 304).

Callao.①

105. On November 2, 2011, the judge asked the Ministry of Justice to forward the provisional arrest file.② On November 4, the representative asked the Ministry of Justice to forward the file.③ On November 8, the representative asked the Seventh Criminal Court to ask the Ministry of Justice to forward the file.④

106. On November 25, 2011, the Ministry of Justiceforwarded the said file and advised the court of the reasons for the delay in forwarding it.⑤ In this regard, it explained that the "request to send the arrest file was about to be answered [⋯] when another note was received [⋯] forwarding the proceedings regarding the release request that was the reason the file was required." It indicated that, since the extradition request "had not been decided by the Executive Branch," it was necessary to consult the Of-

---

① Cf. Request dated October 18, 2011 (evidence file, folio 306).
② Cf. Note of the Seventh Criminal Court of October 26, 2011, received on November 2, 2011 (evidence file, folio 318).
③ Cf. Request dated November 4, 2011 (evidence file, folio 320).
④ Cf. Request dated November 8, 2011 (evidence file, folio 322). Additionally, following a request by the representative that he rule in this regard, on November 24, 2011, the Ombudsman sent a note to the Ministry of Justice asking it to forward the file of the provisional arrest so that he could decide the application for *habeas corpus* and asked the Vice Minister of Justice for "a report on the objective reasons why the official in charge of the sector had not responded to the note of the Seventh Court of El Callao [requesting the provisional arrest file], and had not forwarded this file." This request was answered on December 1, indicating that the court's request had already been answered and that "any evaluation of the reasonableness of the time taken by the extradition process could not be made without considering the procedural activity of the defense of the individual sought." Cf. Request dated November 21, 2011 (evidence file, folio 331); note of the Ombudsman of November 24, 2011 (evidence file, folios 315 and 316), and brief of the Ministry of Justice of December 1, 2011 (evidence file, folios 348 and 349).
⑤ Cf. Note of November 25, 2011, to the 30th Criminal Court of Lima (evidence file, folios 6469 and 6470), and communication of the Ministry of Justice of December 1, 2011 (evidence file, folios 348 and 349). The Office of Legal Advisory Services indicated that "it is necessary to comply with the request of the judge of the Seventh Criminal Court of the Superior Court of Justice of El Callao, consisting in forwarding the documentation of the provisional arrest that forms part of the case file related to the passive extradition request of the Chinese citizen, Wong Ho Wing, because this is an order or demand made by the judge who is hearing the corresponding criminal proceeding." In addition, it clarified that, as the Ministry of Justice does not have competence to deal with and/or decide release requests, the court's note "constitutes a document that should be dealt with by the Ministry of Justice, without this signifying that it has decision-making powers."

fice of Legal Advisory Services how to proceed. ① It also underlined that: (i) "it was not the Ministry of Justice that requested the arrest [⋯] and it [⋯] cannot decide his release"; (ii) "the arrest of [⋯] Wong Ho Wing was made with a view to an extradition process that has not ended," so that "no one can affirm that they know, or foresee, or state in advance, what decision the Peruvian State will take [⋯] on the extradition," and (iii) this "does not change the fact that a ruling of the Constitutional Court exists ordering that he not be extradited."②

107. On December 1, 2011, the Seventh Criminal Court ordered the return of the provisional arrest and extradition files to the Ministry of Justice, and denied the release request, because the final decision was still pending. ③

108. At the same time, on November 16, 2011, the representative filed afourth application for *habeas corpus* against the Ministry of Justice and the judge of the Seventh Criminal Court of the Court Superior of El Callao based on the initial forwarding of the file of the provisional arrest to the Ministry of Justice and the subsequent failure to forward it to the court. ④ On May 30, 2012, the application for *habeas corpus* was declared inadmissible, because it was not possible to observe "any harm to the constitutional rights of the beneficiary."⑤

109. On April 26, 2013, the representative filed asixth application for *habeas corpus* "asking [that] the immediate release of [Wong Ho Wing] without any restriction be ordered."⑥ On October 24, 2014, the corresponding court considered the application inadmissible, taking into account

---

① *Cf.* Note of November 24, 2011 (evidence file, folios 6466 and 6467).
② Note of November 25, 2011, to the Seventh Criminal Court of El Callao (evidence file, folios 6469 and 6470). On November 28, the Ministry of Justice sent another similar note to the 30th Criminal Court of Lima. *Cf.* Communication of November 28, 2011, to the judge of the 30th Criminal Court of Lima (evidence file, folio 346).
③ *Cf.* Decision of the Seventh Criminal Court of El Callao of December 1, 2011 (evidence file, folio 6472).
④ *Cf.* Application for *habeas corpus* of November 16, 2011 (evidence file, folios 325 and 326).
⑤ Decision of the 30th Special Criminal Court of Lima of May 30, 2012 (evidence file, folios 6443 to 6448).
⑥ Application for *habeas corpus* of April 26, 2013 (evidence file, folio 6086).

that the deprivation of liberty had already been changed to house arrest, and also that "the decision to release the beneficiary is currently before [the Inter-American Court, so that *lis pendens* applies]."①

110. On November 20, 2013, Wong Ho Wing requested a change in the provisional arrest.②

111. On January 24, 2014, the representative filed a brief before the Constitutional Court requesting that it "make the necessary requests to the corresponding authorities so that they archive the extradition process in Peru against Wong Ho Wing and order his immediate release, with the return of his passport and other personal document."③ On January 27, 2014, an order was issued to return the brief "to the appellant so that, if appropriate, he can defend it before the corresponding court."④

112. On March 10, 2014, the Seventh Criminal Court decided the request to change the provisional arrest in favor of Wong Ho Wing (*supra* para. 110), indicating that "the failure to establish a time limit for a provisional arrest with a view to extradition is incompatible with the principle of predictability and is also contrary to Article 7(5) of the American Convention."⑤ Furthermore, it indicated that:

> [I]t is unreasonable that, in a passive extradition process such as this one, an individual may endure imprison for more than the maximum time that [the] procedural norm has established for an ordinary criminal proceeding; particularly if, in the extradition process, as in this case, there is no particular evidentiary activity, and neither numerous agents nor numerous victims are involved.⑥

---

① Judgment of the 33rd Criminal Court of October 24, 2014 (evidence file, folios 8538 and 8539).
② *Cf.* Brief of the representative of November 20, 2013 (evidence file, folio 6450).
③ Brief of January 24, 2014 (evidence file, folio 6118).
④ Note of the Secretary-Rapporteur of the Constitutional Court of January 27, 2014 (evidence file, folio 8545).
⑤ Decision of the Seventh Criminal Court of El Callao of March 10, 2014 (evidence file, folio 6459).
⑥ Decision of the Seventh Criminal Court of El Callao of March 10, 2014 (evidence file, folio 6463).

113. The court concluded that "Wong Ho Wing [has been] deprived of his liberty for more than a reasonable time [⋯]; therefore, it is necessary [⋯] to impose on him a less severe measure that is less restrictive of his liberty, but that ensures that he remains in the country until the Executive Branch finally rules definitively on the extradition request."① The Court ordered "house arrest [⋯] in the custody of his brother."② On March 24, the Seventh Criminal Court executed this order.③

114. On March 3, 2015, the representative requested a change in the house arrest order, owing to the "urgency of an operation for the presence of neoplasia." He indicated that the change in the arrest warrant would mean that Wong Ho Wing could be treated promptly by the corresponding doctors. In addition, he underscored the length of time that the presumed victim's deprivation of liberty had lasted.④ On June 3, 2015, the court declared the request inadmissible, indicated that the need to undergo an operation, "was not sufficient for the effect of changing the legal status of the applicant."⑤ On June 11, the representative appealed this decision.⑥ The Court has no information on the result of this appeal.

7IX

RIGHTS TO LIFE AND PERSONAL INTEGRITY AND PRINCIPLE OF NON-REFOULEMENT, IN RELATION TO THE OBLIGATION TO ENSURE RIGHTS

115. In this chapter, the Court will examine the arguments of the Commission and of the parties concerning the extradition process in Peru

---

① Decision of the Seventh Criminal Court of El Callao of March 10, 2014 (evidence file, folio 6463).
② Decision of the Seventh Criminal Court of El Callao of March 10, 2014 (evidence file, folio 6464).
③ *Cf.* Decision of the Seventh Criminal Court of El Callao of March 24, 2014 (evidence file, folio 6453). See also, affidavit made by Wong Ho Wing on August 1, 2014 (evidence file, folio 6850).
④ *Cf.* Request of the representative of March 3, 2015 (merits file, folios 1240 to 1247).
⑤ Decision of the Seventh Criminal Court of June 3, 2015 (merits file, folios 1307 to 1311).
⑥ *Cf.* Appeal of June 11, 2015 (merits file, folios 1325 to 1331).

against Wong Ho Wing. In this regard, the Court takes note that Peru was asked to extradite the presumed victim by the People's Republic of China in 2008. To date, Wong Ho Wing has not been extradited. Under the laws of Peru, the extradition process has two parts, with the participation of the Supreme Court of Justice and of the Executive Branch. In this case, although the Supreme Court of Justice considered that the extradition was admissible, this determination constituted an advisory decision that, although favorable, was not binding. As has been shown and explained, the final decision in this regard falls to the Executive Branch and, to date, it has not ruled.

116. The Commission and the representative argue that, if he had been extradited, Wong Ho Wing would have been exposed – and still is to a certain extent – to different types of risk in the requesting State, particularly with regard to his right to life, owing to the possibility of the imposition of the death penalty; his right to personal integrity, owing to a presumed risk of being subjected to torture or other forms of cruel, inhuman or degrading treatment and, to a lesser degree, owing to a risk of presumed irregularities and violations of due process in the requesting State.

117. In this regard, in May 2011, the Constitutional Court issued a binding *prima facie* decision ordering the Executive Branch to refrain from extraditing Wong Ho Wing, considering that a risk to his life persisted if he was extradited, because the concerns about the possibility that the death penalty would be imposed if he was convicted had not been fully dispelled.

118. In principle this constitutional ruling would prevent the presumed victim's extradition, so that much of this dispute between the parties would be pointless. However, the Court notes that the position of the State before this Court questions the conclusions of that ruling, as well as the scope and interpretation that should be given to it. Therefore, the Court observes that, in this case, the dispute between the parties subsists in relation to the

possibility of extraditing Wong Ho Wing to the People's Republic of China, owing to the alleged risk of violation of his rights in the requesting State, as well as owing to the May 2011 order of the Constitutional Court.

119. This Court emphasizes, as it has in previous cases although in other contexts, the importance of the mechanism of extradition and the obligation of the States to collaborate in this regard. ① It is in the interests of the community of Nations that individuals who have been accused of certain offenses may be brought to justice. However, the Court notes that, in the context of extradition processes or other forms of international judicial cooperation, the States Parties to the Convention must observe the human rights obligations arising from this instrument. Thus, the international human rights obligations of the States and the requirements of due process must be observed in extradition proceedings, and this legal mechanism cannot be used as a path or impunity. ②

120. In order to determine the possible responsibility of the State for the eventual extradition of Wong Ho Wing, in this chapter the Court will analyze the obligation to ensure the right to life and to personal integrity of the presumed victim, together with the obligation to respect the principle of non-refoulement in case of extradition, when there is an alleged risk of harm to those rights.

A. Arguments of the parties and of the Commission

121. The Commission argued that, in this case there are three different levels of risk for Wong Ho Wing: a risk as regards the legal imposition

---

① *Cf. Case of Goiburú et al. v. Paraguay. Merits, reparations and costs.* Judgment of September 22, 2006. Series C No. 153, para. 132; *Case of La Cantuta v. Peru. Merits, reparations and costs.* Judgment of November 29, 2006. Series C No. 162, paras. 159 and 160; *Case of the Ituango Massacres v. Colombia. Monitoring compliance with judgment.* Order of the Court of July 7, 2009, *considerandum* 19, and *Case of the Mapiripán Massacre v. Colombia. Monitoring compliance with judgment.* Order of the Court of July 8, 2009, *consideranda* 40 and 41.

② *Cf. Matter of Wong Ho Wing. Provisional measures with regard to Peru.* Order of the Court of May 28, 2010, *considerandum* 16, and *Matter of Wong Ho Wing. Provisional measures with regard to the Republic of Peru.* Order of the Court of January 29, 2014, *considerandum* 13.

of the death penalty for one of the offenses for which his extradition was requested; a risk of the clandestine or secret application of the death penalty, and a risk of the application of torture or cruel, inhuman or degrading treatment. Consequently, it argued that the obligations to respect and ensure the rights to life and to personal integrity have "a procedural component" that "requires the State to request and assess diligently the assurances that the death penalty will not be imposed on him legally, and also a careful examination of the context in the requesting country, in terms of both the death penalty and of torture or cruel, inhuman or degrading treatment." It underlined that Peru has not taken "into account that the requesting State committed serious omissions" and irregularities in the initial request, and has an internationally-"known context as regard the application of the death penalty and reports of the use of torture." It indicated that the assurances given to date "only seek to respond to the first level of risk"; that is, that the death penalty would not be imposed legally, but "serious concerns [remain] in view of the inexistence of judicial mechanisms to implement them." The Commission concluded that the State had failed to comply with its obligation to ensure the rights to life and personal integrity of Wong Ho Wing.

122. The representative indicated that Peru had failed to comply with its obligation to ensure the rights to life and personal integrity of Wong Ho Wing at "two moments": (i) when twice approving the extradition of the presumed victim even though the authorities had not obtained "sufficient, clear and reliable assurances" that the death penalty would not be imposed on him and that he would not be subjected to torture or other forms of cruel, inhuman or degrading treatment, and (ii) by the "authorities' systematic failure [⋯] to take a final decision on the extradition of Wong Ho Wing in compliance with the judgment of the Constitutional Court." Regarding the second advisory decision, he indicated that "the supposed assurances

presented to the Peruvian State by the People's Republic of China that it would not impose the death penalty are not reliable. " He added that, owing to the context of torture that existed in the People's Republic of China, the Peruvian State "should also have requested [⋯] the assurance that torture or other cruel, inhuman or degrading treatment would not be applied. " In addition, he indicated "that the assurances alone are insufficient to provide adequate protection against the risk of ill-treatment"; the State should also examine the human rights situation in China and the special situation of Wong Ho Wing. Furthermore, the representative argued that the obligations arising from the American Convention and the Inter-American Convention to Prevent and Punish Torture were complemented by article 5 of the bilateral Extradition Treaty between Peru and the People's Republic of China and by article 517 of the new Code of Criminal Procedure that, interpreted together, establish that extradition shall not take place, among other reasons: (1) if the offense for which extradition is requested bears the death penalty in the requesting State and the latter fails to provide assurances that it will not be applied, and (2) if the proceedings to which the individual extradited will be subject do not comply with the international requirements of due process.

123. The State affirmed that it had complied with its international obligation to respect and ensure the rights to life, personal integrity and judicial guaranteesof the petitioner. It underlined that the Supreme Court of Justice and the Constitutional Court had assessed the guarantees that existed when they took their decision, but were unable to rule on the additional assurances provided by China and on the annulment of the death penalty as a criminal sanction for the offense of smuggling ordinary merchandise, which had also not been assessed by the Commission. The State emphasized that the Court should consider the circumstances at the time of the proceedings before it, and assess carefully the outdated or, at the very

least, incomplete sources of the Commission and the petitioner. The State also indicated that the principle of non-refoulement of Article 13(4) of the Inter-American Convention to Prevent and Punish Torture operates provided that there is a well-founded presumption (and not a mere unsubstantiated affirmation) about the risk that an individual's life could be harmed or that he could be subjected to torture or cruel, inhuman or degrading treatment. The State argued that, in this case, this well-founded presumption has not been proved and that, in the domestic courts, the burden of proof was on the presumed victim and/or his representative. Regarding the actions of the State authorities from the time of the extradition request and until the first advisory decision, the State argued that the Commission had not taken into account that the nullification of the ruling of the Supreme Court of January 20, 2009, rectified, in the domestic sphere, by means of effective and appropriate remedies, any possible errors or omissions that could have occurred during that first stage of the process. Regarding the second advisory decision of January 27, 2010, the State underlined that the Supreme Court of Justice had assessed the assurances that the death penalty would not be applied presented by the diplomatic authorities and the People's Supreme Court of China and considered them an incontrovertible commitment. It also indicated that "the present context in the requesting State is not as the [Commission] and the representative [⋯] seek to affirm."

B. Considerations of the Court

124. In order to examine the State's international responsibility owing to the alleged risk to violation of the rights of Wong Ho Wing in the requesting State, the Court will present some considerations on: (B. 1) the scope of the obligation to ensure rights and the principle of non-refoulement in relation to possible risk to the rights to life, to personal integrity and to due process in the context of extradition proceedings; (B. 2) the nature of

the international responsibility of the State in this case and the information that the Court must examine in order to analyze the specific circumstances with regard to (B. 3) the alleged risk of the application of the death penalty, and (B. 4) the alleged risk of torture and other forms of cruel, inhuman or degrading treatment in this case.

B. 1) General considerations on the obligation to ensure rights and the principle of non-refoulement in the face of possible risks to the rights to life, to personal integrity and to due process in extradition proceedings

125. The general obligation to respect and ensure rights gives rise to special duties, which are determined based on the particular needs for protection of the subject of law, owing to his personal situation or to the specific situation in which he finds himself. ① The Court considers that, in this case, the obligation of the State, faced with the request for Wong Ho Wing's extradition, gave rise to the obligation to ensure the rights recognized in Articles 4 (Right to Life)② and 5 (Right to Humane Treatment),③ in relation to Article 1(1) of the Convention,④ together with the principle

---

① Cf. Case of the Pueblo Bello Massacre v. Colombia. Merits, reparations and costs. Judgment of January 31, 2006. Series C No. 140, para. 111, and Case of the Pacheco Tineo Family v. Bolivia, Preliminary objections, merits, reparations and costs. Judgment of November 25, 2013. Series C No. 272, para. 128.
② The relevant part of Article 4 of the Convention establishes that: "Every person has the right to have his life respected. This right shall be protected by law and, in general, from the moment of conception. No one shall be arbitrarily deprived of his life. 2. In countries that have not abolished the death penalty, it may be imposed only for the most serious crimes and pursuant to a final judgment rendered by a competent court and in accordance with a law establishing such punishment, enacted prior to the commission of the crime. The application of such punishment shall not be extended to crimes to which it does not presently apply. 3. The death penalty shall not be reestablished in States that have abolished it. 4. In no case shall capital punishment be inflicted for political offenses or related common crimes."
③ The relevant part of Article 5 of the Convention establishes that: "1. Every person has the right to have his physical, mental, and moral integrity respected. 2. No one shall be subjected to torture or to cruel, inhuman, or degrading punishment or treatment. All persons deprived of their liberty shall be treated with respect for the inherent dignity of the human person."
④ Article 1(1) of the Convention establishes that: "The States Parties to this Convention undertake to respect the rights and freedoms recognized herein and to ensure to all persons subject to their jurisdiction the free and full exercise of those rights and freedoms, without any discrimination for reasons of race, color, sex, language, religion, political or other opinion, national or social origin, economic status, birth, or any other social condition."

of non-refoulement established in Article 13(4)① of the Inter-American Convention to Prevent and Punish Torture (hereinafter also "the ICPPT").②

126. Regarding the right to life, the Court recalls that, even though the Convention does not expressly prohibit the application of the death penalty, this Court has established that the relevant provisions of the Convention should be interpreted in the sense of "definitively limiting its application and its sphere, so that it is progressively reduced, until it is eliminated completely."③ Therefore, the provisions of the Convention in relation to the application of the death penalty should be interpreted in light of the *pro persona* principle; that is, in favor of the individual.④ The imposition of this punishment is subject to certain procedural guarantees and compliance with them must be strictly observed and reviewed.⑤ Owing to the exceptionally serious and irreversible nature of the death penalty, the possibility of imposing or applying it is subject to certain procedural requirements,

---

① Article 13 (paragraph 4) of the Inter-American Convention to Prevent and Punish Torture establishes that: "Extradition shall not be granted nor shall the person sought be returned when there are grounds to believe that his life is in danger, that he will be subjected to torture or to cruel, inhuman or degrading treatment, or that he will be tried by special or *ad hoc* courts in the requesting State."
② The State ratified the Inter-American Convention to Prevent and Punish Torture on March 28, 1991. In this case, only the representative argued a presumed violation of this provision. In this regard, the Court reiterates that the presumed victims or their representatives may cite the violation of other rights than those included in the Commission's Merits Report, provided that they abide by the facts contained in that document (*supra* para. 35).
③ *Case of Hilaire, Constantine and Benjamin. Merits, reparations and costs.* Judgment of June 21, 2002. Series C No. 94, para. 99, and *Case of Boyce et al. v. Barbados. Preliminary objection, merits, reparations and costs.* Judgment of November 20, 2007. Series C No. 169, para. 52. Cf. *Restrictions to the Death Penalty (Arts. 4.2 and 4.4 American Convention on Human Rights).* Advisory Opinion OC—3/83 of September 8, 1983. Series A No. 3, para. 57.
④ Cf. *Case of Boyce et al. v. Barbados, supra,* para. 52, and *Case of Dacosta Cadogan v. Barbados. Preliminary objections, merits, reparations and costs.* Judgment of September 24, 2009. Series C No. 204, para. 49.
⑤ Cf. *Case of Fermín Ramírez v. Guatemala. Merits, reparations and costs.* Judgment of June 20, 2005. Series C No. 126, para. 79, and *Case of Dacosta Cadogan v. Barbados, supra,* para. 47. See also *Restrictions to the Death Penalty (Arts. 4.2 and 4.4 American Convention on Human Rights), supra,* para. 55, and *The Right to Information on Consular Assistance within the Framework of the Guarantees of Due Process of Law.* Advisory Opinion OC—16/99 of October 1, 1999. Series A No. 16, para. 135.

compliance with which must be strictly observed and reviewed. ①

127. With regard to the right to humane treatment or personal integrity, this Court has already indicated that Article 5 of the American Convention, read in conjunction with the obligations*erga omnes* to respect and ensure respect for the norms for the protection of human rights, reveals the obligation of the State not to deport, return, expel, extradite or remove in any other way an individual subject to its jurisdiction to another State, or to a third State that is not safe, when there are grounds for believing that he would be in danger of being subjected to torture or cruel, inhuman or degrading treatment. ②

128. Additionally, the inter-American system includes a specific treaty, the Inter-American Convention to Prevent and Punish Torture, which refers to the principle of non-refoulement as follows: "Extradition shall not be granted nor shall the person sought be returned when there are substantial grounds to believe that his life is in danger, that he will be subjected to torture or to cruel, inhuman or degrading treatment, or that he will be tried by special or *ad hoc* courts in the requesting State." In addition, as it is regulated, the principle is also associated with protection of the right to life and certain judicial guarantees, so that it is not restricted merely to protection against torture. Added to this, it is not enough that States abstain from violating this principle, it is also essential that they adopt positive measures. In situations in which an individual is faced with a risk of torture the principle of non-refoulement is absolute. ③

129. Consequently, when an individual alleges before a State that he is

---

① *Cf. Case of Boyce et al. v. Barbados*, *supra*, para. 50, and *Case of Dacosta Cadogan v. Barbados*, *supra*, para. 84. *Cf. Restrictions to the Death Penalty* (*Arts. 4. 2 and 4. 4 American Convention on Human Rights*), *supra*, para. 55.

② *Cf. Rights and guarantees of children in the context of migration and/or in need of international protection.* Advisory Opinion OC—21/14 of August 19, 2014. Series A No. 21, para. 226.

③ *Cf. Rights and guarantees of children in the context of migration and/or in need of international protection*, *supra*, paras. 225, 227 and 236.

in danger if he is returned, the competent authorities of that State must, at least, interview him and make a preliminaryassessment in order to determine whether or not that risk exists if he should be expelled. ① This signifies that the aforementioned basic guarantees must be respected as part of the opportunity given to the individual to explain the reasons why he should not be expelled and, if that risk is verified, the individual should not be returned to the country where the danger exists. ②

130. This case represents the first occasion on which the Inter-American Court rules on the obligations of the States Parties to the Convention in the context of extradition proceedings. In this regard, the State contested the application of precedents in cases of deportation, asylum or expulsion. The Court notes that the obligation to ensure the rights to life and to personal integrity, as well as the principle of non-refoulement, when there is a risk of torture and other forms of cruel, inhuman or degrading treatment or risk to the right to life, "is applicable to all methods of returning a person to another State, even extradition."③

131. Based on the above, this Court finds it pertinent to take note of the extensive case law of the European Court on this matter, as well as the opinions and decisions of the Human Rights Committee of the International Covenant on Civil and Political Rights (hereinafter "the Human Rights Committee" or "the Committee") and of the Committee against Torture of

---

① *Cf. Rights and guarantees of children in the context of migration and/or in need of international protection*, *supra*, para. 232. See also, UN, Human Rights Committee, *Case of Jonny Rubin Byahuranga v. Denmark*, Communication No. 1222/2003, U. N. Doc. CCPR/C/82/D/1222/2003, December 9, 2004, para. 11. 3, and *Case of Jama Warsame v. Canada*, Communication No. 1959/2010, UN. Doc. CCPR/C/102/D/1959/2010, September 1, 2011, para. 8. 3.

② *Cf. Case of the Pacheco Tineo Family v. Bolivia*, *supra*, para. 136.

③ Affidavit made by Ben Saul on August 18, 2014 (evidence file, folio 6960), citing UN, Committee against Torture, *Case of Chipana v. Venezuela*, Communication No. 110/1998, U. N. Doc. CAT/C/21/D/110/1998, November 10, 1998, para. 6. 2, and *Case of G. K. v. Switzerland*, Communication No. 219/2002, U. N. Doc. CAT/C/30/D/219/2002, May 7, 2003, paras. 6. 4 and 6. 5. The European Court has ruled similarly. *Cf.* ECHR, *Case of Babar Ahmad and Others v. The United Kingdom*, Nos. 24027/07, 11949/08, 36742/08, 66911/09 and 67354/09. Judgment of April 10, 2012, para. 168 and 176.

the Convention against Torture and Other Cruel, Inhuman or Degrading Treatment or Punishment and its Optional Protocol (hereinafter "the Committee against Torture").

132. In general, the Human Rights Committee has indicated that States are obliged "not to extradite, deport, expel or otherwise remove a person from their territory where there are substantial grounds for believing that there is a real risk of irreparable harm, such as that contemplated in Articles 6 (right to life) and 7 (prohibition of torture or cruel, inhuman or degrading treatment or punishment) of the [International] Covenant [on Civil and Political Rights], either in the country to which removal is to be effected or in any country to which the person may subsequently be removed."① In particular, with regard to the death penalty, the Committee has indicated that: "For countries that have abolished the death penalty, there is an obligation not to expose a person to the real risk of its application. Thus, they may not remove, either by deportation or extradition, individuals from their jurisdiction if it may be reasonably anticipated that they will be sentenced to death, without ensuring that the death sentence would not be carried out."② Regarding the prohibition of torture, the Committee against Torture has stated that, under Article 3, paragraph 1, of the Convention against Torture and Other Cruel, Inhuman or Degrading Treatment or Punishment, the State Party has the obligation not to expel a person to another State when there are substantial grounds for believing that he

---

① Cf. UN, Human Rights Committee, General Comment No. 31, Nature of the General Legal Obligation on States Parties to the Covenant, CCPR/C/21/Rev. 1/Add. 13, May 26, 2004, para. 12.

② UN, Human Rights Committee, *Case of Roger Judge v. Canada*, Communication No. 829/1998, UN. Doc. CCPR/C/78/D/829/1998, October 20, 2003, paras. 10. 4 and 10. 6. Similarly, *Case of Yin Fong, Kwok v. Australia*, Communication No. 1442/2005, UN. Doc. CCPR/C/97/D/1442/2005, October 23, 2009, para. 9. 7.

would be in danger of being subjected to torture. ①

133. Meanwhile, the European Court has established repeatedly that the expulsion or extradition of a person under the jurisdiction of a State Party may engage its international responsibility "where substantial grounds have been shown for believing that the person in question, if expelled, would face a real risk of being subject to treatment contrary to" the prohibition of torture or other forms of cruel, inhuman or degrading treatment. ② Also, with regard to the death penalty, this Court has indicated that Article 2 of the European Convention for the Protection of Human Rights and Fundamental Freedoms which recognizes the right to life, and Article 1 of its Protocol No. 13 concerning the abolition of the death penalty in any circumstance, prohibit the extradition or deportation of an individual to another State when substantial grounds exist for believing that he could be subjected to the death penalty. ③

134. Taking into account all the preceding considerations and based on the facts of this case, the Court establishes that, pursuantto the obligation to ensure the right to life, States that have abolished the death penalty may not expose an individual under their jurisdiction to the real and foreseeable

---

① The application of Article 3 of the Convention against Torture is restricted to cases in which there are well-founded reasons to believe that the author would be in danger of being subjected to torture as defined in Article 1 of the Convention. *Cf.* UN, Committee against Torture. General Comment No. 1: Implementation of Article 3 of the Convention in the Context of Article 22, U. N. Doc. CAT, A/53/44, November 21, 1997, para. 1.

② *Cf.* ECHR, *Case of Shamayev and Others v. Georgia and Russia*, No. 36378/02. Judgment of April 12, 2005, para. 335, citing: *Case of Chahal v. The United Kingdom* [GS], No. 22414/93. Judgment of November 15, 1996, paras. 73 and 74; *Case of Soering v. The United Kingdom*, No. 14038/88. Judgment of July 7, 1989, paras. 34 to 36, and *Case of Cruz Varas and Others v. Sweden*, No. 15576/89. Judgment of March 20, 1991, paras. 69 and 70. Similarly, see *inter alia*, *Case of Saadi v. Italy* [GS], No. 37201/06. Judgment of February 28, 2008, para. 125; *Case of Nizomkhon Dzhurayev v. Russia*, No. 31890/11, Judgment of October 3, 2013, para. 105, and *Case of Othman (Abu Qatada) v. The United Kingdom*, No. 8139/09. Judgment of January 17, 2012, para. 185.

③ *Cf.* ECHR, *Case of Al-Saadoon and Mufdhi v. The United Kingdom*, No. 61498/08. Judgment of March 2, 2010, para. 123; *Case of Hakizimana v. Sweden*, No. 37913/05, Decision of March 27, 2008, and *Case of Kaboulov v. Ukraine*, No. 41015/04. Judgment of November 19, 2009, para. 99.

risk of its application and, therefore, may not expel, by deportation or extradition, persons under their jurisdiction, if it can be reasonably anticipated that they may be sentenced to death, without requiring guarantees that the death sentence would not be carried out. Furthermore, the States Parties to the Convention that have not abolished the death penalty may not jeopardize, by deportation or extradition, the life of any person under their jurisdiction who runs a real and foreseeable risk of being sentenced to death, unless this is for the most serious crimes for which the death penalty is currently imposed in the requested State Party. Consequently, States that have not abolished the death penalty may not expel anyone under their jurisdiction, by deportation or extradition, who may face the real and foreseeable risk of the application of the death penalty for offenses that are not punished with the same sanction within their jurisdiction, without requiring the necessary and sufficient assurances that this punishment will not be applied.

135. In addition, the obligation to ensure the right to personal integrity, together with the principle of non-refoulement recognized in Article 13 (4) of the ICPPT, imposes on States the obligation not to expel, by extradition, any individual under their jurisdiction when there are substantial grounds for believing that he will face a real, foreseeable and personal risk of suffering treatment contrary to the prohibition of torture or cruel, inhuman or degrading treatment.

136. The Court takes note that, during the domestic extradition process, the representative also alleged that certain characteristics of the judicial proceedings in China would constitute violations of due process. In this regard, the States Parties to the Convention also have the obligation to avoid the extradition, return or expulsion of any individual under their jurisdiction who has suffered or runs the risk of suffering a flagrant denial of

justice in the State of destination. ① However, this Court notes that the representative's arguments about a risk of violation of due process in the requesting State refer mainly to the presumed use of evidence obtained under torture and to the absence of the safeguards required by the American Convention in proceedings that could conclude with the imposition of the death penalty. Therefore, the Court will examine this alleged risk when making the relevant considerations on the presumed risk of torture and other forms of cruel, inhuman or degrading treatment, as well as on the alleged risk of the imposition of the death penalty and, if pertinent, it will include the corresponding conclusions in relation to a possible flagrant denial of justice in the requesting State.

137. In addition, this Court underlines that, for the purposes of this case, some of the said obligations arising from the Convention are also established in the Peruvian State's domestic laws. Specifically, article 517 of Peru's Code of Criminal Procedure establishes that extradition shall not be ordered when "[t]he offense for which extradition is requested bears the death penalty in the requesting State and the latter has not provided assur-

---

① In this regard, the European Court has indicated that: "It is established in the Court's case-law that an issue might exceptionally be raised under Article 6 by an expulsion or extradition decision in circumstances where the fugitive had suffered or risked suffering a flagrant denial of justice in the requesting country. [⋯] In the Court's case-law, the term "flagrant denial of justice" has been synonymous with a trial which is manifestly contrary to the provisions of Article 6 or the principles embodied therein. [⋯] [C]ertain forms of unfairness could amount to a flagrant denial of justice, includ[ing]: conviction *in absentia* with no possibility subsequently to obtain a fresh determination of the merits of the charge; a trial which is summary in nature and conducted with a total disregard for the rights of the defence; detention without any access to an independent and impartial tribunal to have the legality the detention reviewed; deliberate and systematic refusal of access to a lawyer, especially for an individual detained in a foreign country. [⋯] A flagrant denial of justice goes beyond mere irregularities or lack of safeguards in the trial procedures such as might result in a breach of Article 6 if occurring within the Contracting State itself. What is required is a breach of the principles of fair trial guaranteed by Article 6 which is so fundamental as to amount to a nullification, or destruction of the very essence, of the right guaranteed by that article." ECHR, *Case of Othman (Abu Qatada) v. The United Kingdom*, No. 8139/09. Judgment of January 17, 2012, para. 258 to 260.

ances that it will not be applied."①

138. Also, article 516 of this Code conditions granting extradition "to the existence of assurances that justice will be imparted fairly in the requesting State."② Meanwhile, although the Extradition Treaty between China and Peru does not establish specific rules with regard to the death penalty or possible risk of treatment contrary to personal integrity, its article 5 does establish, as a condition for the extradition, that: "Extradition shall only be carried out if it is not contrary to the legal system of the Requested Party."③

B. 2) Nature of the international responsibility of the State in this case and information to be considered by the Court

139. The parties differ as regards the moment and the information that must be examined by the Court in order to analyze this case. According to the Commission and the representative, the State's acts and omissions during the extradition proceedings constitute "violations that have been committed" of the American Convention and the situation must be examined based on the information obtained by the State that was available to the judicial authorities when the Supreme Court issued the opinion that the extradition was admissible and when the Constitutional Court ordered the State to refrain from extraditing Wong Ho Wing. Meanwhile, the State argues that the information obtained by Peru subsequently should be examined, including the new diplomatic assurances and explanations on the applicability of the death penalty to the case of Wong Ho Wing, and it is on this basis

---

① Code of Criminal Procedure, promulgated by Legislative Decree No. 957 of July 29, 2004, article 517. Available at: http://www.leyes.congreso.gob.pe/Documentos/Decretoslegislativos/00957.pdf, cited in the Commission's Merits Report, folio 24.
② Code of Criminal Procedure, promulgated by Legislative Decree No. 957 of July 29, 2004, article 516. Available at: http://www.leyes.congreso.gob.pe/Documentos/Decretoslegislativos/00957.pdf, cited in the Commission's Merits Report, folio 24.
③ Extradition Treaty between the Republic of Peru and the People's Republic of China, article 5 (evidence file, folio 1634).

that it indicates that is actions fall within its obligation to respect and ensure the rights to life and to personal integrity.

140. The consistent case law of the European Court concerning extradition establishes that, in order to determine the responsibility of a State, the information that the requested State was, or should have been, aware of at the time of the extradition should be analyzed and, in those cases in which extradition has not yet taken place, the information available when the European Court considers the case should be examined. ①

141. This Court agrees with this conclusion. The nature of the State's international responsibility in this type of case, according to the criteria established above, consists in exposing an individual under its jurisdiction to a foreseeable risk of suffering violations of the rights protected by the Convention. ② In this case, the eventual action of the State (the removal of Wong Ho Wing from Peru and his extradition to China) has not occurred, partly owing to the existence of the provisional measures ordered by this Court for the State to refrain from extraditing Wong Ho Wing. Therefore, when analyzing the possible risk that Wong Ho Wing would face in the requesting State, the Court will take into account and assess all the information available at this time, including the legislative developments in China following the second advisory decision of the Supreme Court, as well as the

---

① *Cf.* ECHR, *Case of Chahal v. The United Kingdom* [GS], No. 22414/93. Judgment of November 15, 1996, paras. 86 and 97; *H. L. R. v. France* [GS], No. 24573/94. Judgment of April 29, 1997, para. 37; *Mamatkulov and Askarov v. Turkey* [GS], Nos. 46827/99 and 46951/99. Judgment of February 4, 2005, para. 69. "The existence of the risk must be assessed primarily with reference to those facts which were known or ought to have been known to the Contracting State at the time of the expulsion […]. Where the applicant has not yet been expelled, the material point in time is that of the Court's consideration of the case." ECHR, *Case of Ryabikin v. Russia*, No. 8320/04. Judgment of June 19, 2008, para. 111.

② Similarly, see ECHR, *Case of Mamatkulov and Askarov v. Turkey* [GS], Nos. 46827/99 and 46951/99. Judgment of February 4, 2005, para. 69, which establishes that: "Since the nature of the Contracting States' responsibility under Article 3 in cases of this kind lies in the act of exposing an individual to the risk of ill-treatment, the existence of the risk must be assessed primarily with reference to those facts which were known or ought to have been known to the Contracting State at the time of the extradition […] However, if the applicant has not been extradited or deported when the Court examines the case, the relevant time will be that of the proceedings before the Court […]."

diplomatic assurances presented after the issue of the ruling of the Constitutional Court. The situation of risk that existed when that last ruling was issued will be taken into account, as pertinent and necessary, in the analysis of the alleged violation of the right to judicial protection (*infra* paras. 193 to 206).

142. The Court also notes that the examination of the State's responsibility in this case is conditional on the granting and implementation of the eventual extradition. According to Article 62 of the Convention, this Court has jurisdiction to hear all cases concerning the interpretation and application of the provisions of the Convention. Furthermore, Article 44 of the Convention establishes the right to "lodge petitions with the Commission containing denunciations or complaints of violation of this Convention by a State Party." Consequently, it is not normally for this Court to pronounce on the existence of potential violations of the Convention. However, when the presumed victim claims that, if he is expelled or, in this case, extradited, he would be subject to treatment contrary to his rights to life and personal integrity, it is necessary to ensure his rights and to prevent the occurrence of grave and irreparable harm.[①] Since the ultimate aim of the Convention is the international protection of human rights, it must be permissible to analyze this type of case before the violation takes place. Therefore, the Court must rule on the possibility that such harm may occur if the person is extradited. Thus, since the extradition has not occurred yet (which would constitute the internationally unlawful act if a foreseeable risk to the rights of Wong Ho Wing existed), the Court must examine the State's re-

---

① Similarly, see: ECHR, *Case of Soering v. The United Kingdom*, No. 14038/88. Judgment of July 7, 1989, para. 90. In this case, the European Court established that: "It is not normally for the Convention institutions to pronounce on the existence or otherwise of potential violations of the Convention. However, where an applicant claims that a decision to extradite him would, if implemented, be contrary to Article 3 by reason of its foreseeable consequences in the requesting country, a departure from this principle is necessary, in view of the serious and irreparable nature of the alleged suffering risked, in order to ensure the effectiveness of the safeguard provided by that Article 3."

sponsibility conditionally, in order to determine whether or not there would be a violation of the rights to life and personal integrity of the presumed victim should he be extradited.

143. The European Court of Human Rights and some United Nations committees, such as the Human Rights Committee and the Committee against Torture, have proceededsimilarly. ① Consequently, this Court establishes that, in cases in which extradition or expulsion has not occurred (but in which its acceptance or implementation is imminent), the analysis made by the Court consists in determining whether, based on the information available at the time the Inter-American Court considers the case, the State was, or should have been, aware that the extradition of the presumed victim, if granted and implemented, would be a violation of the American Convention.

144. The presumed harm to the right to judicial protection recognized in Article 25(2) (c) of the Convention (particularly based on compliance with decisions of the domestic courts), in view of the ruling of the Constitutional Court, will be examined in the following section (*infra* paras. 193 to 206), and separately from the presumed risk that Wong Ho Wing would face currently if he were to be extradited, for the reasons described *supra*.

145. Taking into account: (1) the protection standards in extradition

---

① In this regard, see: the European Court, inter alia, ECHR, *Case of Ryabikin v. Russia*, No. 8320/04. Judgment of June 19, 2008, para. 115; *Case of Hilal v. The United Kingdom*, No. 45276/99. Judgment of March 6, 2001, para. 68; *Case of Venkadajalasarma v. The Netherlands*, No. 58510/00, Judgment of February 17, 2004, para. 69, and *Case of Jabari v. Turkey*, No. 40035/98. Judgment of July 11 2000, para. 42. The Human Rights Committee, inter alia, *Case of Mehrez Ben Abde Hamida v. Canada*, Communication No. 1544/2007, U. N. Doc. CCPR/C/98/D/1544/2007, March 18, 2010, para. 8. 6, 8. 7 and 9; Case of *G. T. v. Australia*, Communication No. 706/1996, U. N. Doc. CCPR/C/61/D/706/1996, November 4, 1997, para. 8. 2 and 8. 3, and Case of *Thuraisamy v. Canada*, Communication No. 1912/2009, U. N. Doc. CCPR/C/106/D/1912/2009, October 31, 2012, para. 8. The Committee against Torture, inter alia, *Case of v. N. I. M. v. Canada*, Communication No. 119/1998, U. N. Doc. CAT/C/40/D/293/2006, November 12, 2002, para. 8; *Case of Attia v. Sweden*, Communication No. 199/2002, U. N. Doc. CAT/C/31/D/199/2002, November 17, 2003, para. 12. 3; *Case of Ke Chung Rong v. Australia*, Communication No. 416/2010, CAT/C/49/D/416/2010, November 5, 2013, para. 7. 5.

processes described above, and (2) the information and guarantees that are currently available, the Court will examine (3) the alleged risk of application of the death penalty, and (4) the alleged risk of torture or other cruel, inhuman or degrading treatment, in order (5) to determine whether the extradition of Wong Ho Wing would result in the State's international responsibility based on the possible violation of its obligation to ensure the presumed victim's rights to life and personal integrity.

B. 3) Alleged risk of application of the death penalty in this case

146. One of the offenses for which Wong Ho Wing issought called for the death penalty when he was arrested and his extradition was requested. Article 153 of the Chinese Criminal Code established:

> Smuggling merchandise and objects that are not mentioned in articles 151, 152 and 347 of this Law are punished pursuant to the following provisions, according to the severity:
>
> a. Smuggling merchandise and objects where the amount of the duty evaded is in excess of 500 000 yuans is punished by imprisonment for more than 10 years, or life imprisonment, and fines of from 100% to 500% of the amount of the duty evaded, or seizure of personal property; <u>in extremely serious cases, this will be punished pursuant to the provisions of paragraph 4 of [article] 151 of this Law</u> [⋯]. ①(Underlining added)

Then, paragraph 4 of article 151 stipulates:

> In the case of the offenses mentioned in paragraphs 1 and 2, if they are extremely serious,<u>they will be punished by life imprisonment or the death penalty</u>, and seizure of personal property. ②(Underlining added)

---

① Official translation of the Criminal Code of the People's Republic of China (evidence file, folio 1628).
② Official translation of the Criminal Code of the People's Republic of China (evidence file, folio 1627).

147. According to the expert witness in Chinese criminal justice, Bingzhi Zhao, "[b]efore the eighth amendment, a trial against Wong Ho Wing for his offense, would fall within the third category that ranges from more than 10 years' imprisonment to life imprisonment or the death penalty."① However, in May 2011, the eighth amendment to the Criminal Code of the People's Republic of China, promulgated in February 2011, came into force,② and this eliminated the possibility of the death penalty for smuggling ordinary merchandise for which Wong Ho Wing's extradition had been requested.③

148. The pertinent part of this amendment establishes:

Amendments to the Offense of Smuggling

Section XXVII

The first clause of article 153 of the Criminal Code is amended as follows: Anyone who shall smuggle merchandise and objects that are not mentioned in articles 151, 152 and 347 of this law shall be punished pursuant to the following provisions, according to the severity of the case:

[…]

---

① Statement made by Bingzhi Zhao during the public hearing held in this case. Similarly, a legal opinion prepared by the Max Planck Institute explains that the first paragraph of article 153 establishes the application of the death penalty "if the circumstances are especially serious." This opinion explains that "[a]ccording to a 'judicial interpretation' adopted by the People's Supreme Court in 2008, 'especially serious circumstances' include the fact that the amount of the payable duty evaded or avoided is more than 2.5 million yuans." Opinion of Experts in Chinese Criminal Law with regard to money-laundering, bribery, smuggling and customs duty evasion in the case of Wong Ho Wing (merits file, folio 815 and 816).

② According to an opinion of the Max Planck Institute, the eighth amendment eliminated 13 non-violent economic offenses from the list of 68 offenses punishable with the death penalty under the Criminal Code of the People's Republic of China. However, the death penalty continues to be applicable for smuggling "weapons and ammunition" or "nuclear material," or "counterfeiting currency" in especially serious circumstances. Cf. Opinion of Experts in Chinese Criminal Law with regard to money-laundering, bribery, smuggling and customs duty evasion in the case of Wong Ho Wing (merits file, folios 813, 815 and 816).

③ Cf. Statement made by Bingzhi Zhao during the public hearing held in this case, and Report of Experts on Chinese Criminal Law on money-laundering, bribery, smuggling and customs duty evasion in the case of Wong Ho Wing (merits file, folios 815 and 816).

c. Anyone who shall smuggle merchandise and objects where the amount of the duty evaded is extremely high or in very serious cases, <u>shall be punished by more than 10 years' imprisonment or life imprisonment</u> and fines of from 100% to 500% of the duty evaded [or] seizure of personal property. ①(Underlining added)

149. In addition, as explained by expert witness Bingzhi Zhao during the hearing,② and also in a legal opinion of the Max Planck Institute③ and the text of the norm, article 12 of the Criminal Code recognizes the principle of the retroactivity of the most favorable criminal law for the purpose of punishment. ④

150. Peru has not abolished the death penalty completely. The Peruvian Constitution accepts the possibility of the death penalty for crimes of

---

① Eighth amendment to the Chinese Criminal Code (evidence file, folio 7555). Expert witness Bingzhi Zhao explained that, in the case of Wong Ho Wing, "owing to the amount involved, it falls within the third category of imprisonment under article 153, which is imprisonment ranging from 10 years to life"; however, "in the trial of his [presumed] accomplices [...] they were sentenced to 13 years' imprisonment, thus [...] the court will take into consideration the effects on his accomplices for the same offense and the same amount in order to decide his sentence." Statement made by Bingzhi Zhao during the public hearing held in this case.
② Cf. Statement made by Bingzhi Zhao during the public hearing held in this case.
③ According to this opinion, "[t]he principle of legality (*nullum crimen sine lege, nulla poena sine lege*) is recognized in Chinese criminal law: according to article 12(1) of the Criminal Code, [...] the retroactive application of a new criminal provision is prohibited by article 12(1), unless the punishment contained in the new provision is more favorable (the *lex mitior* principle). In other words, if the new provision is more favorable, its application is compulsory." It also explained that, currently, "under Chinese criminal law, the death penalty is not applicable to the case of Wong Ho Wing for [any of the offenses for which his extradition is being requested]." Opinion of Experts in Chinese Criminal Law with regard to money-laundering, bribery, smuggling and customs duty evasion in the case of Wong Ho Wing (merits file, folio 820).
④ The said article 12 stipulates that: "For those acts committed after the founding of the People's Republic of China and before the application of this Code, the laws in force at that date shall be applied if the laws at that date did not define such acts as offenses; if those laws defined such acts as offenses and there are reasons to continue the proceedings as stipulated in the eight section of Chapter IV (General Aspects) of this Code, the laws in force at that time shall be applied; however, if this Code does not define such acts as offenses or defines them as acts that would involve a light punishment, this Code shall be applied. Sentences that have been handed down continue in effect according to the laws in force on the date they were delivered prior to the entry into force of this Code." Official translation of the Criminal Code of the People's Republic of China (evidence file, folio 7504).

treason and terrorism.① However, article 517 of the Peruvian Code of Criminal Procedure indicates that extradition shall not be ordered when "[t]he offense for which extradition is requested shall contemplate the death penalty in the requesting State and the latter shall not provide assurances that it will not be applied (*supra* para. 137). Since Wong Ho Wing is wanted for smuggling and other economic offenses, it is evident that Peru was obliged to demand the necessary and sufficient assurances that the death penalty would not be applied to him if his extradition was granted (*supra* para. 134).

151. Despite the foregoing, the Court considers that it has beenproved that, based on the principle of the favorable retroactivity of the criminal law and the annulment of the death penalty for the offense of smuggling ordinary merchandise, this punishment could not be applied to Wong Ho Wing, if he is extradited and subsequently sentenced and convicted in China. ② Although the death penalty was in force until May 2011 for one of the offenses for which Wong Ho Wing's extradition was requested, the Court reiterates that, in order to determine whether there is a real risk to the

---

① Article 140 of the Constitution establishes that: "The death penalty may only be applied for the crime of treason in case of war, and of terrorism pursuant to the laws and treaties to which Peru is a party and by which it is bound." 1993 Constitution of Peru. Available at: www. congreso. gob. pe/ntley/ConstitucionP. htm. Despite this, the Commission and the representative indicated that such punishments are not applied in practice because the death penalty is not contemplated for the said crimes in the substantive criminal laws in force. *Cf.* Merits Report of the Commission (merits file, folio 79), motions and arguments brief of the representative (merits file, folio 305). The Permanent Criminal Chamber of the Supreme Court of Justice, in its second advisory decision, indicated that "the punitive probability [of the death penalty] is contrary to Peru's extradition laws, because our domestic laws expressly prohibit the application of the death penalty. Indeed: (i) article 140 of the Constitution establishes that the death penalty is only applicable to the crimes of treason in case of war, and terrorism; (ii) article 517(3) (d) of the Code of Criminal Procedure indicates that extradition shall be denied when the offense for which extradition is requested contemplates the death penalty in the requesting State and the latter has not provided assurances that it will not be applied; (iii) article 55 of the Constitution establishes the supremacy and observance of the provisions of the human rights treaties, such as the American Convention on Human Rights, the Inter-American Convention against Torture, and the International Covenant on Civil and Political Rights and its Second Optional Protocol aiming at the abolition of the death penalty." Advisory decision of the Permanent Criminal Chamber of January 27, 2010 (evidence file, folio 170).

② Expert witness Bingzhi Zhao emphasized that "following the eighth amendment of the Criminal Code, even when diplomatic assurances are given that the death penalty will not be imposed, the death penalty would not be imposed for smuggling ordinary merchandise." Statement made by Bingzhi Zhao during the public hearing held in this case.

right to life of Wong Ho Wing if his extradition is granted, it is necessary to examine and assess all the information available at this time (*supra* paras. 140 and 141). Bearing this in mind, and based on the principle of the favorable retroactivity of the criminal law, the Court considers that, following the annulment of the death penalty for the offense of smuggling, there is no real risk that the death penalty will be applied legally to Wong Ho Wing if he is extradited to China.

152. Nevertheless, the Commission and the representative argue that there have already been autonomous violations of the right to life of Wong Ho Wing, owing to the failure to consider the risk of the application of the death penalty in the first advisory decision and to the absence of sufficient guarantees that it would not be applied in the second advisory decision of the Supreme Court, regardless of its subsequent annulment. Regarding the first advisory decision (dated January 20, 2009), the Court emphasizes that this decision was annulled as a result of an application for *habeas corpus*, so that it has no legal effects (*supra* para. 70). Regarding the second advisory decision (dated January 27, 2010), the Court reiterates that, inasmuch as the extradition process has not concluded and Wong Ho Wing has not been extradited, in order to determine whether, at this time, there is a risk to his right to life if he is extradited, the Court must assess all the information, including information subsequent to that judicial decision (*supra* paras. 140 and 141). When a possible risk to his right to life existed, the Court's provisional measures were effective to protect Wong Ho Wing. However, it would not be appropriate that, based on the information that the State had at the time of the second advisory decision, the Court determine that, at the present time, there is risk to the right to life of Wong Ho Wing if he is extradited, owing to the supposed possibility of the application of the death penalty, when subsequent measures and information have eliminated that possibility, as previously determined (*supra* para. 151).

153. In addition, the Court notes that the Commission also argued that there was "a risk of the clandestine or secret application of the death penalty" (*supra* para. 121). In this regard, the Court stresses that neither the Commission nor the representative have provided specific information on the alleged risk. In general, and as part of the contextual elements in relation to the application of the death penalty in the requesting State, the Commission and the representative indicated that data and statistics on its application are not public, they are presumable handled as State secrets, and there is no detailed information on the number of persons condemned to death,① and this has been confirmed by the requesting State itself.② Nevertheless, this Court considers that a real, foreseeable and personal risk that Wong Ho Wing could be subjected to extrajudicial execution if he is extradited to China cannot be derived from this information.

154. Furthermore, the Commission and the representative referred to information on reports concerning due process in trials for crimes punisha-

---

① In this regard, the case file contains reports of the Committee against Torture (2008); the Office of the United Nations High Commissioner for Human Rights (2009); the former United Nations Special Rapporteur on Torture, Manfred Nowak (2010), and the Periodic Universal Review Working Group (2013). *Cf.* UN, Committee against Torture, Concluding Observations on China, December 12, 2008, CAT/C/CHN/CO/4, paras. 17 and 34. Available at: http://www2.ohchr.org/english/bodies/cat/docs/CAT.C.CHN.CO.4.pdf; Human Rights Council, Compilation prepared by the Office of the High Commissioner for Human Rights, in accordance with paragraph 15(b) of the annex to Human Rights Council resolution 5/1. People's Republic of China (including Hong Kong and Macao Special Administrative Regions (HKSAR and MSAR)), January 6, 2009, A/HRC/WG.6/4/CHN/2, para. 16. Available at: http://lib.ohchr.org/HRBodies/UPR/Documents/Session4/CN/A_HRC_WG6_4_CHN_2_S.pdf; Special Rapporteur on torture and other cruel, inhuman or degrading treatment or punishment. Follow-up to the recommendations. China, February 26, 2010, A/HRC/13/39/Add.6, p. 45. Available at: http://www2.ohchr.org/english/bodies/hrcouncil/docs/13session/ A.HRC.13.39.Add%206_EFS.pdf, and Human Rights Council, Report of the Periodic Universal Review Working Group. China (including Hong Kong (China) and Macao (China)), December 4, 2013, A/HRC/25/5, p. 22. Available at: http://daccess-dds-ny.un.org/doc/UNDOC/GEN/G13/188/58/PDF/G1318858.pdf? Open Element.
② In answer to the conclusions and recommendations of the Committee against Torture, the People's Republic of China indicated that the statistics for cases involving the death penalty were consolidated with those involving life imprisonment and imprisonment for more than five years. *Cf.* Committee against Torture, Comments by the Government of the People's Republic of China concerning the conclusions and recommendations of the Committee against Torture, December 18, 2009, CAT/C/CHN/CO/4/Add.2, p. 20. Available at: http://www2.ohchr.org/english/bodies/cat/docs/followup/CAT.C.CHN.CO.4.Add2.pdf

ble by the death penalty, and the number of crimes to which it is applicable, as grounds for the alleged risk to the right to life of Wong Ho Wing in the requesting State, while Peru underscored the progress and improvements made in the requesting State. However, the Court considers that, inasmuch as, currently, the death penalty would not be legally applicable to the offense of smuggling ordinary merchandise in China, this information is not relevant or pertinent, and it is not incumbent on the Court to assess it in this case.

B. 4) Alleged risk of torture and other forms of cruel, inhuman or degrading treatment

155. When examining the principle of non-refoulement in relation to possible risks to the rights to life or liberty of an individual, this Court hasaffirmed that the risk "must be real; in other words, it must be a foreseeable consequence. Thus, the State must make an individualized analysis in order to verify and evaluate the circumstances cited by the individual which reveal that he may suffer harm to his life or liberty in the country to which it is sought to return him (that is, his country of origin), or that, if he is expelled to a third country, he runs the risk of the being sent to the place where he runs this risk. If his explanation that he could face a situation of risk is credible, convincing and coherent, the principle of non-refoulement should be observed."①

156. Furthermore, the Court reiterates that when an individual alleges before a State Party that there is a risk if he is returned, the competent authorities of that State should, at least, interview him, giving him the opportunity to explain the reasons why he contests the return, and make a prior or preliminary assessment in order to determine whether or not that risk exists and, if it is verified, the individual should not be deported to the country where the risk exists (*supra* para. 129).

---

① *Rights and guarantees of children in the context of migration and/or in need of international protection*, *supra*, para. 221.

157. In this type of situation, the Human Rights Committee has applied the standard of real risk, according to which any treatment contrary to the Covenant must be a necessary and foreseeable consequence of the extradition,① while the Committee against Torture has indicated that the risk must be foreseeable, real and personal. ② The European Court has affirmed this standard indicating that substantial grounds must be shown for believing that there is a real risk of suffering treatment contrary to the prohibition of torture and cruel treatment. This Court agrees with these criteria and considers that "to determine the existence of a risk of ill-treatment, the Court must examine the foreseeable consequences of sending the petitioner to the receiving State, bearing in mind the general situation of that State as well as the personal circumstances of the petitioner."③

158. Both the Commission and the representative argue that the extradition of Wong Ho Wing to China would expose him to treatment contrary to the prohibition of torture or other forms of cruel, inhuman or degrading treatment. However, in this case, the judicial authorities who intervened did not analyze this risk.

158. Based on the above, the Court will now examine: (a) the State's obligation to consider the argument concerning the risk of a violation of

---

① *Cf.* UN, Human Rights Committee, *Case of G. T. v. Australia*, Communication No. 706/1996, U. N. Doc. CCPR/C/61/D/706/1996, November 4, 1997, para. 8. 1, and *Case of Mahmoud Walid Nakrash and Liu Qifen v. Sweden*, Communication No. 1540/2007, U. N. Doc. CCPR/C/94/D/1540/2007, October 30, 2008, para. 7. 3.
② See, *inter alia*, UN, Committee against Torture, *Case of E. A. v. Switzerland*, Communication No. 28/1995, U. N. Doc. CAT/C/19/D/28/1995, November 10, 1997, para. 11. 5; *Case of U. S. v. Finland*, Communication No. 197/2002, U. N. Doc. CAT/C/30/D/197/2002, May 1, 2003, para. 7. 8; *Case of Zare v. Sweden*, Communication No. 256/2004, U. N. Doc. CAT/C/36/D/256/2004, May 12, 2006, para. 9. 3; *Case of Ke Chun Rong v. Australia*, Communication No. 416/2010, U. N. Doc. CAT/C/49/D/416/2010, November 5, 2012, para. 7. 4, and *Case of Y. G. H. et al. v. Australia*, Communication No. 434/2010, U. N. Doc. CAT/C/51/D/434/2010, November 14, 2013, para. 8. 3. See also, Affidavit made by Ben Saul on August 18, 2014 (evidence file, folio 6960).
③ ECHR, *Case of Ryabikin v. Russia*, No. 8320/04. Judgment of June 19, 2008, para. 112, and *Case of Vilvarajah and Others v. The United Kingdom*, Nos. 13163/87, 13164/87, 13165/87 13447/87, and 13448/87. Judgment of October 30, 1991, para. 108.

personal integrity, and (b) the existence of the alleged risk of treatment contrary to the prohibition of torture or other forms of cruel, inhuman or degrading treatment in the case of Wong Ho Wing, taking into account: (i) the alleged situation of risk in the requesting State, and (ii) the diplomatic assurances provided by the People's Republic of China in this regard.

B. 4. a) Obligation to consider the arguments concerning the risk of a violation of personal integrity

160. Regarding a possible risk of torture in case of return, the Committee against Torture has indicated that"the State party and the Committee are obliged to assess whether there are substantial grounds for believing that the author would be in danger of being subjected to torture were he/she to be expelled, returned or extradited, [thus,] the risk of torture must be assessed on grounds that go beyond mere theory or suspicion[, although] the risk does not have to meet the test of being highly probable."
It also indicated that the petitioner "must establish that he/she would be in danger of being tortured and that the grounds for so believing are substantial [⋯], and that such danger is personal and present."①

161. Although it is true that the main allegation of risk by the presumed victim and his representative throughout the extradition process has

---

① UN, Committee against Torture, General Comment No. 1: Implementation of Article 3 of the Convention in the Context of Article 22, U. N. Doc. CAT, A/53/44, November 21, 1997, paras. 6 and 7. To verify a substantial, personal and present danger of torture, the Committee against Torture has provided the following, non-exhaustive, guidelines, on some of the pertinent considerations to assess whether expulsion entails a real risk of torture: (a) Is the State concerned one in which there is evidence of a consistent pattern of gross, flagrant or mass violations of human rights? (b) Has the author been tortured or maltreated by or at the instigation of or with the consent or acquiescence of a public official or other person acting in an official capacity in the past? If so, was this the recent past? (c) Is there medical or other independent evidence to support a claim by the author that he/she has been tortured or maltreated in the past? Has the torture had aftereffects? (d) Has the situation referred to in (a) above changed? Has the internal situation in respect of human rights altered? (e) Has the author engaged in political or other activity within or outside the State concerned which would appear to make him/her particularly vulnerable to the risk of being placed in danger of torture were he/she to be expelled, returned or extradited to the State in question? (f) Is there any evidence as to the credibility of the author? (g) Are there factual inconsistencies in the claim of the author? If so, are they relevant? *Cf.* UN, Committee against Torture, General Comment No. 1: Implementation of Article 3 of the Convention in the Context of Article 22, U. N. Doc. CAT, A/53/44, November 21, 1997, para. 8.

been the possibleapplication of the death penalty, the Court notes that at different times during the extradition process, both the presumed victim and his representative have mentioned the possible violation of his right to personal integrity if he is extradited to China and, on one occasion, they even referred to Article 13(4) of the ICPPT. ① In addition, the file of the ex-

---

① In this regard: (i) in the second application for *habeas corpus*, of October 2009, the representative mentioned "the certain and imminent risk of violation of the rights to life and personal integrity that subsists against [⋯] Wong Ho Wing." He asserted that "[t]here is a certain and imminent risk to personal liberty and rights related to this, among which the rights to life and personal integrity are particularly significant; because, if he is extradited to the People's Republic of China, there are no guarantees that he will be subject to a fair trial and, consequently, he may be sentenced to death." Application for *habeas corpus* of October 12, 2009 (evidence file, folios 105 and 106); (ii) in the third application for *habeas corpus* of February 9, 2010, even though he made no specific allegations in this regard, the representative based himself on the principle of non-refoulement established in Article 13(4) of the ICPPT. Thus, he indicated that "Article 13(4) of the Inter-American Convention against Torture, to which Peru is a party, includes an article on non-refoulement that expressly prohibits extradition in cases in which the life of a person whose extradition is requested is in danger, and establishes that: *Extradition shall not be granted nor shall the person sought be returned when there are grounds to believe that his life is in danger, that he will be subjected to torture or to cruel, inhuman or degrading treatment.*" He also indicated that "[t]he rights affected include the rights to right to life and personal integrity, [⋯] because if passive extradition is granted and the Chinese citizen [Wong Ho Wing] is returned to the People's Republic of China, his life and physical integrity would be jeopardized, because there is no material possibility that the Peruvian authorities could monitor the execution of the sentence, owing, among other reasons, to the fact that not even international authorities can obtain access to the Chinese prison system, which is completely unreliable and discredited." He added that the presumed victim, "would be executed or kept in physical conditions that would entail a grave and progressive deterioration of his health in order to shorten his life." Application for *habeas corpus* of February 9, 2010 (evidence file, folios 189 and 192); (iii) in a statement made before the 42nd Special Criminal Court of Lima on February 11, 2010, the representative indicated that: "The possibility exists that [⋯] it is decided to extradite the said person, subject of the extradition request, to the People's Republic of China and, once he has been returned to that country, he will be sentenced to death in summary proceedings or else subjected to inhuman prison conditions that place his health and life in grave danger, as has happened on numerous occasions with thousands of people who are either executed or subjected to cruel and infrahuman treatment. What I have described has been reiterated in different reports of Amnesty International and other international agencies that indicate, among other matters, that last year more than 10 000 people were executed in China following summary proceedings during which their procedural guarantees were not respected, and in which the execution was carried out on the same day as the sentence." Preliminary statement by Luis Alberto Lamas Puccio on February 11, 2010, before the 42nd Special Criminal Court of Lima (evidence file, folios 8485 and 8486), and (iv) also, following the second advisory decision of the Supreme Court, during the hearing before the Constitutional Court of November 17, 2010, the representative indicated that "vast information can be found on the Internet about the precarious conditions of those deprived of their liberty in that country [China] and, in many cases, they are cut off, in a totally inhuman manner, from basic nutrition so that they weaken and can die sooner." He also indicated that he would be "unable to control whether or not this person [Wong Ho Wing] has been executed or subjected to inhuman treatment, which was also mentioned in the Inter-American Commission's report." Video of the hearing before the Constitutional Court of November 17, 2010 (evidence file, folio 7375).

tradition process contains news and reports of international and non-governmental organizations indicating and describing practices contrary to the prohibition of torture and other forms of cruel, inhuman or degrading treatment in China.①

162. In this regard, the Court takes note of the European Court's case law, according to which, although, "in principle, the petitioner must provide the evidence that proves the existence of substantial grounds for believing that, [if he is extradited] he would be exposed to a real risk of being subject to treatment contrary to Article 3," it is for the requested State "to dispel any concerns" when evidence has been presented in this regard. The European Court has also affirmed that "[i]n determining whether substantial grounds have been shown for believing that a real risk of treatment contrary to Article 3 exists, if he is extradited, the Court will assess the issue in the light of all the material placed before it and, if necessary, material obtained on its own motion."②

---

① The National Human Rights Coordinator, a coalition of Peruvian non-governmental organizations presented an *amicus curiae* brief to the Permanent Criminal Chamber of the Supreme Court noting some irregularities concerning the risk of the death penalty, as well as the way it was implemented, and about the alleged risk of torture and other forms of cruel, inhuman or degrading treatment. Cf. *Amicus curiae* of the National Human Rights Coordinator of Peru presented on October 2, 2009 (evidence file, folios 2095 to 2114). In addition, the representative provided relevant parts of 2007 and 2008 reports of Amnesty International in the domestic proceedings, which reveal information on the alleged risk of torture (evidence file, folios 8420 and 8422).

② ECHR, *Case of N. v. Finland*, No. 38885/02. Judgment of July 26, 2005, para. 167; *Case of Ryabikin v. Russia*, No. 8320/04. Judgment of June 19, 2008, para. 112; *Case of Nizomkhon Dzhurayev v. Russia*, No. 31890/11. Judgment of October 3, 2013, para. 108; *Case of Saadi v. Italy* [GS], No. 37201/06. Judgment of February 28, 2008, para. 128; *Case of Cruz Varas and Others v. Sweden*, No. 15576/89. Judgment of March 20, 1991, paras. 75 and 76; *Case of Vilvarajah and Others v. The United Kingdom*, Nos. 13163/87, 13164/87, 13165/87 13447/87, and 13448/87. Judgment of October 30, 1991, para. 107; and *Case of Mamatkulov and Askarov v. Turkey* [GS], Nos. 46827/99 and 46951/99. Judgment of February 4, 2005, para. 69. Also, the European Court has indicated that: "the Court must be satisfied that the assessment made by the authorities of the Contracting State is adequate and sufficiently supported by domestic material as well as by material originating from other reliable and objective sources such as, for instance, other Contracting or non-Contracting States, agencies of the United Nations and reputable non-governmental organisations. […] Accordingly, the Court will first assess in detail the relevant arguments raised by the applicant in the extradition proceedings and the consideration given to them by the competent authorities." *Case of Nizomkhon Dzhurayev v. Russia*, No. 31890/11. Judgment of October 3, 2013, paras. 108 and 114, and Cf. *Case of Salah Sheekh v. The Netherlands*, No. 1948/04. Judgment of January 11, 2007, para. 136, and *Case of Ismoilov and Others v. Russia*, No. 2947/06. Judgment of April 24, 2008. para. 120.

163. The Court considers that, owing to the absolute nature of the prohibition of torture, the specific obligation not to extradite when there is a risk of treatment contrary to personal integrity established in Article 13 (4) of the ICPPT and the obligation of all States Parties to the American Convention to take all necessary measures to prevent torture or other cruel, inhuman or degrading treatment, the States Parties to the Convention must assess this possibility effectively during their extradition proceedings when this risk is alleged by those subject to extradition.① The same reasons require this Court to examine the said arguments in this case with reference to current circumstances in the requesting State.

164. In the instant case, none of the judicial authorities that have intervened to dategave any consideration to the representative's arguments concerning a possible risk to the personal integrity of the presumed victim. As previously determined, States have the obligation to examine all the available information in order to determine the possible situation of risk of the person who may be extradited. If, having examined the information provided, the State determines that the arguments lack adequate grounds or the necessary evidence, then it may reject the situation of risk alleged by the presumed victim. This is the second step that requires or would have required the State, and now this Court, to assess the risks alleged by the presumed victim at that time, and then, if appropriate, reject them owing to lack of adequate grounds.

---

① The Human Rights Committee has ruled similarly in several decisions in individual cases, stating that it is not possible to extradite, deport, expel or remove in any way a person from the territory of a State if there are sufficient reasons to believe that there is a risk of irreparable harm to his rights, and without first taking into consideration that person's arguments concerning the existing risk. *Cf.* UN, Human Rights Committee, *Joseph Kindler v. Canada*, Communication No. 470/1991, UN Doc. CCPR/C/48/D/470/1991, November 11, 1993, para. 6.2; *Charles Chitat Ng v. Canada*, Communication No. 469/991, UN Doc. CCPR/C/49/D/469/1991, January 7, 1994, para. 6.2; *Jonny Rubin Byahuranga v. Denmark*, Communication No. 1222/2003, UN Doc. CCPR/C/82/D/1222/2003, December 9, 2004, para. 11.3; *Jama Warsame v. Canada*, Communication No. 1959/2010, UN Doc. CCPR/C/102/D/1959/2010, September 1, 2011, para. 8.3, and *Thuraisamy v. Canada*, Communication No. 1912/2009, November 2, 2012, para. 8.

165. In response to the Supreme Court's failure to consider the human rights situation in the requesting State, the State argued that there was no law that required the judicial organ to assess this, and that the alleged context could be taken into account at the political stage of the extradition process. In this regard, the Court notes that the State has presented contradictory arguments because, on the one hand, it has affirmed that the individual subject to extradition does not have the right to be heard at the political stage (*infra* paras. 226 to 234) and, on the other hand, it alleges that it is at that stage that any objections to the extradition request raised by the said individual or his representative could be decided. If the right to be heard of the individual whose extradition is sought is ensured by his participation at the judicial stage of the process, then it is at that stage where any objections to his extradition based on the contextual situation of possible human rights violations in the requesting State should be decided. In this case, at the judicial stage, Wong Ho Wing raised objections concerning the human rights situation in the requesting State and the possible risk to his life or personal integrity. Consequently, the Judiciary, in this case through the Supreme Court, should have responded to these allegations, especially bearing in mind that the Supreme Court found that the extradition was in order. The Court also underlines that, according to expert witness García Toma, offered by the State, "the Council of Ministers evaluates aspects relating to the political advisability of denying the extradition," and "if such political considerations against the extradition are uncertain [⋯], the extradition goes forward."① Therefore, despite the arguments put forward by the State, it is unclear whether the alleged situation of risk to the human rights of Wong Ho Wing in the requesting State could be examined during the political stage of the extradition process.

---

① Statement made by Victor García Toma during the public hearing held in this case.

166. Nevertheless, the Court notes that the mere failure to consider these allegations would not lead to a violation of the right to personal integrity of Wong Ho Wing, in the specific circumstances of this case. As mentioned previously, insofar as the extradition and, thus, the exposure to the alleged risk, has not happened, the Court must determine whether, in the actual circumstances, the extradition of Wong Ho Wing would result in a violation of the prohibition of torture or other cruel, inhuman or degrading treatment or punishment established in Article 5 of the American Convention and the principle of non-refoulement recognized in Article 13(4) of the ICPPT.

B. 4. b) Alleged risk to Wong Ho Wing in the requesting State

167. In order to determine whether the presumed victim would face a real, foreseeable and personal risk if he is extradited, the Court must examine all the information available and consider all relevant circumstances. To determine whether there is a risk of torture of other forms of cruel, inhuman or degrading treatment, it must examine the relevant conditions in the requesting State, the specific circumstances of the presumed victim and, as an additional factor, the diplomatic assurances, if these have been provided. [1] The Court will now analyze: (i) the alleged situation of risk in the requesting State and (ii) the diplomatic assurances provided.

168. The State has argued, with regard to the need to examine the human rights situation in the requesting State, as well as to how the diplomatic assurances are assessed that, "there are no international standards for extradition," and that it was in the Merits Report that the Commission

---

[1] In the *Othman* case, the European Court established that: In any examination of whether an applicant faces a real risk of illtreatment in the country to which he is to be removed, the Court will consider both the general human rights situation in that country and the particular characteristics of the applicant. In a case where assurances have been provided by the receiving State, those assurances constitute a further relevant factor which the Court will consider. ECHR, *Case of Othman (Abu Qatada) v. The United Kingdom*, No. 8139/09. Judgment of January 17, 2012, para. 187.

first "ruled on what it considered were the international standards as regards diplomatic assurances to guarantee the life and integrity of a person in relation to an extradition request." However, despite the inexistence of specific inter-American case law on extradition, this Court notes that the obligations of the States Parties to the Convention result from the American Convention and not from the Court's case law. ①

i) Alleged situation of risk in the requesting State

169. When examining the alleged situation of risk in the requesting State, the Court must necessarily examine the conditions in the destination country which are the grounds for the alleged risk, and compare the information presented with the standards derived from the American Convention. Nevertheless, the Court notes that this does not mean that it is judging the conditions in the destination country or signify that it is establishing responsibility with regard to the requesting State; particularly when the latter is not a State Party to the Convention. When establishing violations by means of this analysis in the context of processes of extradition, any liability incurred will correspond to the State Party to the Convention, whose act or omission exposed or would expose an individual under its jurisdiction to a risk contrary to the prohibition of torture or cruel, inhuman or degrading treatment. ②

---

① *Mutatis mutandi*, regarding the standards relating to military criminal justice, see: Case of Vélez Restrepo and family v. Colombia. Preliminary objection, merits, reparations and costs. Judgment of September 3, 2012. Series C No. 248, para. 241, and Case of Rodríguez Vera et al. (The Disappeared of the Palace of Justice) v. Colombia. Preliminary objections, merits, reparations and costs. Judgment of November 14, 2014. Series C No. 287, paras. 444 and 445.

② Similarly, the European Court has indicated that: "The establishment of such responsibility inevitably involves an assessment of conditions in the requesting country against the standards of Article 3 of the Convention. Nonetheless, there is no question of adjudicating on or establishing the responsibility of the receiving country, whether under general international law, under the Convention or otherwise. In so far as any liability under the Convention is or may be incurred, it is liability incurred by the extraditing Contracting State by reason of its having taken action which has as a direct consequence the exposure of an individual to proscribed ill-treatment". ECHR, Case of Mamatkulov and Askarov v. Turkey [GS], Nos. 46827/99 and 46951/99. Judgment of February 4, 2005, para. 67.

170. The State objected to certain information used by the Inter-American Commissionas grounds for the presumed situation of risk to human rights in the requesting State. Specifically, it noted that "the situations observed by some United Nations human rights treaty bodies, as well as some thematic rapporteurs, [cited by the Commission, refer to] previous years and not [⋯] necessarily to the reality today." When determining the relevant conditions in the People's Republic of China, the Court will take this observation by the State into account.

171. The Court considers that, toassess the possible situation of risk to the human rights of an individual under the jurisdiction of a State Party in a destination country, it can use domestic sources, as well as reports of international or non-governmental organizations. ①

172. When examining a possible situation of risk for an individual whose extradition has been requested in the destination country, the real conditions in that country must be taken into account, and notmerely the formal conditions, so that the ratification of treaties alone is insufficient to ensure that he will not be subjected to torture. ② Furthermore, the existence of domestic norms that ensure respect for human rights or the prohibition of torture and other forms of cruel, inhuman or degrading treatment, is insufficient, in itself, to ensure adequate protection against treatment contrary to the Convention. ③ However, the European Court has indicated that:

---

① Cf. ECHR, *Case of Saadi v. Italy* [GS], No. 37201/06. Judgment of February 28, 2008, para. 131; *Case of Chahal v. The United Kingdom* [GS], No. 22414/93. Judgment of November 15, 1996, paras. 99 and 100; *Case of Müslim v. Turkey*, No. 53566/99. Judgment of April 26, 2005, para. 67; *Case of Said v. The Netherlands*, No. 2345/02. Judgment of July 5, 2005, para. 54; *Case of Al-Moayad v. Germany*, No. 35865/03. Judgment of February 20, 2007, paras. 65 and 66, and *Case of Nizomkhon Dzhurayev v. Russia*, No. 31890/11, Judgment of October 3, 2013, para. 109.
② Cf. Affidavit made by Ben Saul on August 18, 2014 (evidence file, folio 6961).
③ Cf. ECHR, *Case of Saadi v. Italy* [GS], No. 37201/06. Judgment of February 28, 2008, para. 147; *Case of Muminov v. Russia*, No. 42502/06. Judgment of December 11, 2008, para. 96; *Case of Garayev v. Azerbaijan*, No. 53688/08. Judgment of June 10, 2010, para. 73, and *Case of Boutagni v. France*, No. 42360/08. Judgment of November 18, 2010, para. 44.

[I]n assessingwhether there is a risk of illtreatment in the requesting country, the Court assesses the general situation in that country, taking into account any indications of improvement or worsening of the human-rights situation in general or in respect of a particular group or area that might be relevant to the applicant's personal circumstances. ①

173. In addition, the Court notes that, when analyzing a possible situation of risk in the destination country, it is not sufficient to refer to the general situation of human rights in the respective State, but rather it is necessary todemonstrate the particular circumstances of the person to be extradited that would expose him to a real, foreseeable and personal risk of being subject to treatment contrary to the prohibition of torture or cruel, inhuman or degrading treatment if he is extradited, such as membership in a persecuted group, prior experience of torture or ill-treatment in the requesting State, and the type of offense for which he is sought, among other matters, depending on the specific circumstances in the destination country. In this regard, the European Court has indicated that:

[R]eference to a general problem concerning human rights observance in a particular country cannot alone serve as a basis for refusal of extradition [⋯]. Where the sources available to the Court describe a general situation, an applicant's specific allegations in a particular case require corroboration by other evidence, with reference to the individual circumstances substantiating his fears of ill-treatment [⋯]. The Court would not require evidence of such individual circumstances only in the most extreme cases where the general situation of violence in the country of destination is of such intensity as to create a real

---

① ECHR, *Case of Nizomkhon Dzhurayev v. Russia*, No. 31890/11, Judgment of October 3, 2013, para. 109. See also, *Case of Saadi v. Italy* [GS], No. 37201/06. Judgment of February 28, 2008, para. 131, and *Case of Shamayev and Others v. Georgia and Russia*, No. 36378/02. Judgment of April 12, 2005, para. 337.

risk that any removal to that country would necessarily violate Article 3. ①

174. Similarly, the Committee against Torture has indicated that "the existence of a consistent pattern of gross, flagrant or mass violations of human rights in a country does not, as such, constitute sufficient grounds for determining that the particular person would be in danger of being subjected to torture upon his return to that country; additional grounds must be adduced to show that the individual concerned would be personally at risk."②

175. In this case, regarding the possible risk of torture or cruel, inhuman or degrading treatment, the Commission and the representative argued that different international bodies, such as the Committee against Torture and the former Special Rapporteur on torture and other cruel, inhuman or degrading treatment or punishment, Manfred Nowak, as well as non-governmental organizations such as Amnesty International and Human Rights Watch have expressed concern owing to shortcomings in the legal framework with regard to torture,③ constant reports of the use of confessions

---

① ECHR, *Case of Nizomkhon Dzhurayev v. Russia*, No. 31890/11, Judgment of October 3, 2013, para. 110. See also: *Dzhaksybergenov v. Ukraine*, No. 12343/10. Judgment of February 10, 2011, para. 37; *Case of Mamatkulov and Askarov v. Turkey* [GS], Nos. 46827/99 and 46951/99. Judgment of February 4, 2005, para. 73.

② *Cf.* UN, Committee against Torture, *Case of G. K. v. Switzerland*, Communication No. 219/2002, UN. Doc. CAT/C/30/D/219/2002, May 12, 2003, para. 6. 4. Similarly, Affidavit made by Ben Saul on August 18, 2014 (evidence file, folio 6961).

③ In this regard, they underlined that the Committee against Torture, in its 2008 Concluding Observations on China, as well as the former Special Rapporteur on torture and other cruel, inhuman or degrading treatment or punishment, Manfred Nowak, in 2006, indicated shortcomings in the legal framework relating to torture, especially the failure to include its basic constituent elements. *Cf.* UN, Committee against Torture, Concluding Observations. China. CAT/C/CHN/CO/4, December 12, 2008, para. 32, Available at: http://www2. ohchr. org/english/bodies/cat/docs/CAT. C. CHN. CO. 4. pdf; UN, Report of the Special Rapporteur on torture and other cruel, inhuman or degrading treatment or punishment. Mission to China. E/CN. 4/2006/6/Add. 6, March 10, 2006, para. 17, Available at: http://daccess-dds-ny. un. org/doc/UNDOC/GEN/G06/117/50/PDF/G0611750. pdf? OpenElement. Also, in 2008, Amnesty International indicated that domestic law was not adapted to the provisions of the Convention against Torture, and, in 2012, several non-governmental organizations mentioned this to the former Special Rapporteur Manfred Nowak. *Cf.* Amnesty International, Summary presented to the Committee against Torture prior to its consideration of the fourth periodic report of China, November 3-21, 2008, p. 1, Available at: http://www2. ohchr. org/english/bodies/cat/docs/ngos/ AI_China_41. pdf; UN, Special Rapporteur on torture and other cruel, inhuman or degrading treatment or punishment. Follow-up to the recommendations. China. A/HRC/13/39/Add. 6, February 26, 2010, p. 38, Available at: http://www2. ohchr. org/english/bodies/hrcouncil/docs/13session/A. HRC. 13. 39. Add%206_EFS. pdf.

obtained by torture,① detention conditions in China,② and the failure to investigate, prosecute and punish those responsible for acts of torture.③ For its part, the State provided the opinion of expert witness Huawen Li to the case file to underscore the improvements or the new systems for the control, reporting on, and monitoring of the conditions and treatment received by persons detained in China in order to safeguard the prohibition of torture

---

① Regarding this use of confessions obtained by torture, in 2006, the former Special Rapporteur Manfred Nowak indicated that the use of confessions extracted through torture as evidence before the court was not explicitly prohibited, while, in 2008, the Committee against Torture, and the former Special Rapporteur Manfred Nowak in his 2010 report on the follow-up to his visit to China indicated that they had received continued allegations of the widespread use of the torture and ill-treatment of suspects in police custody, especially to extract confessions or information to be used in criminal proceedings. Non-governmental organizations had also emphasized the use of evidence extorted through torture which, according to Amnesty International is not specifically prohibited by domestic law. Cf. UN, Special Rapporteur on torture and other cruel, inhuman or degrading treatment or punishment. Report on mission to China. March 10, 2006, E/CN. 4/2006/6/Add. 6, paras. 37 and 73, Available at: http://daccess-dds-ny. un. org/doc/UNDOC/GEN/G06/117/50/PDF/G0611750. pdf? OpenElement; UN, Committee against Torture, Concluding Observations on China, December 12, 2008, CAT/C/CHN/CO/4, para. 11. Available at: http://www2. ohchr. org/english/bodies/cat/docs/CAT. C. CHN. CO. 4. pdf; UN, Special Rapporteur on torture and other cruel, inhuman or degrading treatment or punishment. Follow-up on recommendations. China. A/HRC/13/39/Add. 6, February 26, 2010, paras. 19 and 41, Available at: http://www2. ohchr. org/english/bodies/hrcouncil/docs/13session/A. HRC. 13. 39. Add%206_EFS. pdf; UN, Office of the High Commissioner for Human Rights, Compilation prepared by the Office of the High Commissioner for Human Rights, in accordance with paragraph 15(b) of the annex to Human Rights Council resolution 5/1. People's Republic of China (including Hong Kong and Macao Special Administrative Regions (HKSAR and MSAR)), January 6, 2009, para. 15, Available at: http://lib. ohchr. org/HRBodies/UPR/Documents/Session4/CN/ A_HRC_WG6_4_CHN_3_E. pdf; Human Rights Watch, World Report 2012. Evens of 2011. China, p. 2, Available at: http://www. hrw. org/sites/default/files/related_material/china_2012_0. pdf, and Amnesty International, Summary presented to the Committee against Torture prior to its consideration of the fourth periodic report of China, November 3-21, 2008, p. 16, Available at: http://www2. ohchr. org/english/bodies/cat/docs/ngos/AI_China_41. pdf.
② Cf. UN, Special Rapporteur on torture and other cruel, inhuman or degrading treatment or punishment. Report on mission to China. E/CN. 4/2006/6/Add. 6, March 10, 2006, para. 37 and 73, Available at: http://daccess-dds-ny. un. org/doc/UNDOC/GEN/G06/117/50/PDF/G0611750. pdf? OpenElement; UN, Committee against Torture, Concluding Observations. China. CAT/C/CHN/CO/4, December 12, 2008, para. 11, Available at: http://www2. ohchr. org/english/bodies/cat/docs/CAT. C. CHN. CO. 4. pdf; UN, Special Rapporteur on torture and other cruel, inhuman or degrading treatment or punishment. Follow-up on recommendations. China. A/HRC/13/39/Add. 6, February 26, 2010, para. 19, Available at: http://www2. ohchr. org/english/bodies/hrcouncil/docs/13session/A. HRC. 13. 39. Add%206_EFS. pdf.
③ Cf. UN, Committee against Torture, Concluding Observations. China. CAT/C/CHN/CO/4, December 12, 2008, paras. 20, 31 and 33, Available at: http://www2. ohchr. org/english/bodies/cat/docs/CAT. C. CHN. CO. 4. pdf; UN, Special Rapporteur on torture and other cruel, inhuman or degrading treatment or punishment. Follow-up on recommendations. China. A/HRC/13/39/Add. 6, February 26, 2010, para. 19, Available at: http://www2. ohchr. org/english/bodies/hrcouncil/docs/13session/A. HRC. 13. 39. Add%206_EFS. pdf.

and other forms of cruel, inhuman or degrading treatment, as well as to exclude evidence obtained by torture or other acts of violence. ①

176. This Court considers that the information on which both the Commission and the representative based themselves refers to the general situation of human rights in China. This is not sufficient to consider that Wong Ho Wing would be at real, foreseeable and personal risk of suffering treatment contrary to the prohibition of torture or other forms of cruel, inhuman or degrading treatment. Neither the representative nor the Commission offered arguments, evidence or grounds from which it can be inferred that this general situation creates a personal, individual and specific risk for Wong Ho Wing based on his particular circumstances. The representative referred to information on the human rights situation of individuals accused of terrorism, human rights defenders, those accused of political offenses, and the members of the Uyghur ethnic group, and this bears no relationship to the case of Wong Ho Wing.

177. In addition, and in view of the fact that diplomatic assurances were given in this case, the Court finds that any remaining concerns about the alleged risk of Wong Ho Wing suffering treatment contrary to Article 5 of the American Convention, should be satisfied by the last diplomatic assurance given by China in 2014, which will be examined below.

---

① This expert witness underscored that the Criminal Code, the Code of Criminal Procedure and the Law on the People's Police of the People's Republic of China contain explicit prohibitions of torture and ill-treatment, and the new Code of Criminal Procedure includes provisions that exclude evidence obtained unlawfully; for example, through torture or other acts of violence, such as threats. In addition, he reported that there are numerous norms which establish the steps to follow when investigating unlawful practices to obtain evidence or forced confessions or the physical punishment of detainees, such as the Code of Criminal Procedure, the Law on Administrative Supervision, the Law on the People's Police, the Commission for the Disciplinary Supervision and Control of the Public Security Body, and the Organic Law of People's Prosecutors. In addition, he clarified that rapid channels of communication exist for accusations or reports of torture or ill-treatment; that audio and video records are being promoted in investigation and interrogation procedures, and that frequent physical examinations are performed on detainees. He also highlighted several programs that are being implemented to prevent torture. *Cf.* Affidavit made by Liu Huawen on August 19, 2014 (evidence file, folios 6787, 6790, 6798, 6799, 6816 to 6818, 6824, 6830 to 6834, 6836 and 6837).

ii) Diplomatic notes and assurances provided by the People's Republic of China

178. Diplomatic assurances constitute a common practice among States in the context of extradition processes and it is usually presumed that they are given in good faith. Such diplomatic undertakings consist in promises or guarantees given by the requesting State to the requested State that the individual whose extradition is requested will received treatment or punishment in keeping with the international human rights obligations of the requested State.① When examining cases of return, deportation, extradition or any form of expulsion of individuals from the jurisdiction of a State Party, the European Court, and also the Human Rights Committee, have granted relative value to the diplomatic assurances provided by the States.② Moreover, when examining the relevance of the diplomatic assurances it is important to bear in mind:

> In a case where assurances have been provided by the receiving State, those assurances constitute a further relevant factor which the Court will consider. However, assurances are not in themselves sufficient to ensure adequate protection against the risk of ill-treatment. There is an obligation to examine whether assurances provide, in their practical application, a sufficient guarantee that the applicant will be protected against the risk of illtreatment. The weight to be given to

---

① According to expert witness Ben Saul, diplomatic assurances or guarantees "are typically political promises, rather than binding legal safeguards, and therefore they must be considered prudently." Affidavit made by Ben Saul on August 18, 2014 (evidence file, folio 6977). The United Nations High Commissioner for Refugees (UNHCR) has indicated that "the term 'diplomatic assurances,' as used in the context of the transfer of a person from one State to another, refers to an undertaking by the receiving State to the effect that the person concerned will be treated in accordance with conditions set by the sending State or, more generally, in keeping with its human rights obligations under international law." Cf. UNHCR Note on Diplomatic Assurances and International Refugee Protection, August 2006, para. 1.
② In this regard, see ECHR, *Case of Othman (Abu Qatada) v. The United Kingdom*, No. 8139/09. Judgment of January 17, 2012, para. 187, and the Human Rights Committee, *Mohammed Alzery v. Sweden*, Communication No. 1416/2005, U. N. Doc. CCPR/C/88/D/1416/2005, November 10, 2006, para. 11.5.

assurances from the receiving State depends, in each case, on the circumstances prevailing at the material time. ①

179. Both expert witnesses who testified on the use of diplomatic assurances, offered by the Commission and the State, agreed that diplomatic assurances are an additionalfactor that may be analyzed when there is a possible risk of violation of human rights in the context of the extradition of a person, so that they must be assessed and considered with prudence, taking into account all the circumstances of the case, on a case-by-case basis. ②

180. Following the case law of the European Court, the Court considers that, when assessing diplomatic assurances, the quality of the assurances and their reliability must be analyzed. ③ In the case of *Othman (Abu Qatada) v. The United Kingdom* ④ the European Court systematized some of the factors that are relevant when evaluating the quality and reliability of the diplomatic assurances:

(ⅰ) Whether the terms of the assurances have been disclosed to

---

① ECHR, *Case of Nizomkhon Dzhurayev v. Russia*, No. 31890/11. Judgment of October 3, 2013, para. 111. See also, *Case of Saadi v. Italy* [GS], No. 37201/06. Judgment of February 28, 2008, para. 148, and *Case of Othman (Abu Qatada) v. The United Kingdom*, No. 8139/09. Judgment of January 17, 2012, para. 187.
② *Cf.* Affidavit made by Ben Saul on August 18, 2014 (evidence file, folio 6977), and Affidavit made by Jean Carlo chos humanos del Estado requerido. erido de que la persona solicitada en exMejiaMMejia Azuero on August 15, 2014 (evidence file, folios 6566, 6592y 6593). chos humanos del Estado requerido. erido de que la persona solicitada en exchos humanos del Estado requerido. erido de que la persona solicitada en ex
③ In this regard, see, ECHR, *Case of Othman (Abu Qatada) v. The United Kingdom*, No. 8139/09. Judgment of January 17, 2012, para. 189. In addition, the Human Rights Committee has indicated that: "The existence of diplomatic assurances, their content and the existence and implementation of enforcement mechanisms are all factual elements relevant to the overall determination of whether, in fact, a real risk of proscribed ill-treatment exists". UN, Human Rights Committee, *Case of Mohammed Alzery v. Sweden*, Communication No. 1416/2005, U. N. Doc. CCPR/C/88/D/1416/2005, November 10, 2006, para. 11.5.
④ *Cf.* ECHR, *Case of Othman (Abu Qatada) v. The United Kingdom*, No. 8139/09. Judgment of January 17, 2012, para. 189.

the Court.①

(ⅱ) Whether the assurances are specific or are general and vague.②

(ⅲ) Who has given the assurances and whether that person can bind the receiving State.③

(ⅳ) If the assurances have been issued by the central government of the receiving State, whether local authorities can be expected to abide by them.④

(ⅴ) Whether the assurances concerns treatment which is legal or illegal in the receiving State.⑤

(ⅵ) Whether they have been given by a Contracting State.⑥

(ⅶ) The length and strength of bilateral relations between the

---

① ECHR, *Case of Othman (Abu Qatada) v. The United Kingdom*, No. 8139/09. Judgment of January 17, 2012, para. 189, citing, *inter alia*: ECHR, *Case of Ryabikin v. Russia*, No. 8320/04. Judgment of June 19, 2008, para. 119, and *Case of Muminov v. Russia*, No. 42502/06. Judgment of December 11, 2008, para. 97.

② ECHR, *Case of Othman (Abu Qatada) v. The United Kingdom*, No. 8139/09. Judgment of January 17, 2012, para. 189, citing: ECHR, *Case of Saadi v. Italy* [GS], No. 37201/06. Judgment of February 28, 2008, para. 147; *Case of Klein v. Russia*, No. 24268/08. Judgment of April 1, 2010, para. 55, and *Case of Khaydarov v. Russia*, No. 21055/09. Judgment of May 20, 2010, para. 111.

③ ECHR, *Case of Othman (Abu Qatada) v. The United Kingdom*, No. 8139/09. Judgment of January 17, 2012, para. 189, citing: ECHR, *Case of Shamayev and Others v. Georgia and Russia*, No. 36378/02. Judgment of April 12, 2005, para. 344; *Case of Kordian v. Turkey*, No. 6575/06. Decision of July 4, 2006; *Case of Abu Salem v. Portugal*, No. 26844/04. Decision of May 9, 2006, and, to the contrary, *Case of Ben Khemais v. Italy*, No. 246/07. Judgment of February 24, 2009, para. 59; *Case of Garayev v. Azerbaijan*, No. 53688/08. Judgment of June 10, 2010, para. 74; *Case of Baysakov and Others v. Ukraine*, No. 54131/08. Judgment of February 18, 2010, para. 51, and *Case of Soldatenko v. Ukraine*, No. 2440/07. Judgment of October 23, 2008, para. 73.

④ ECHR, *Case of Othman (Abu Qatada) v. The United Kingdom*, No. 8139/09. Judgment of January 17, 2012, para. 189, citing: ECHR, *Case of Chahal v. The United Kingdom* [GS], No. 22414/93. Judgment of November 15, 1996, paras. 105 to 107.

⑤ ECHR, *Case of Othman (Abu Qatada) v. The United Kingdom*, No. 8139/09. Judgment of January 17, 2012, para. 189, citing, *inter alia*: ECHR, *Case of Cipriani v. Italy*, No. 221142/07. Decision of March 30, 2010; *Case of Saudi v. Spain*, No. 22871/06, Decision of September 18, 2006; *Case of Ismaili v. Germany*, No. 58128/00, Decision of March 15, 2001; *Case of Nivette v. France*, No. 44190/98. Decision of July 3, 2001, and *Case of Einhorn v. France* No. 71555/01. Decision of October 16, 2001.

⑥ ECHR, *Case of Othman (Abu Qatada) v. The United Kingdom*, No. 8139/09. Judgment of January 17, 2012, para. 189, citing: ECHR, *Case of Chentiev and Ibragimov v. Slovakia*, Nos. 21022/08 and 51946/08. Decision of September 14, 2010, and *Case of Gasayev v. Spain*, No. 48514/06. Decision of February 17, 2009.

sending and receiving States, including the receiving State's record in abiding by similar assurances. ①

(ⅷ) Whether compliance with the assurances can be objectively verified through diplomatic or other monitoring mechanisms, including providing unfettered access to the applicant's lawyers. ②

(ⅸ) whether there is an effective system of protection against torture in the receiving State, including whether it is willing to cooperate with international monitoring mechanisms (including international human rights NGOs), and whether it is willing to investigate allegations of torture and to punish those responsible. ③

(ⅹ) Whether the applicant has previously been ill-treated in the receiving State. ④

(ⅺ) Whether the reliability of the assurances has been examined by the domestic courts of the sending/Contracting State. ⑤

181. Meanwhile, the Human Rights Committee has considered that:

---

① ECHR, *Case of Othman (Abu Qatada) v. The United Kingdom*, No. 8139/09. Judgment of January 17, 2012, para. 189, citing: ECHR, *Case of Babar Ahmad and Others v. The United Kingdom*, Nos. 24027/07, 11949/08, 36742/08, 66911/09 and 67354/09. Judgment of April 10, 2012, paras. 107 and 108; *Case of Al-Moayad v. Germany*, No. 35865/03. Decision of February 20, 2007, para. 68.

② ECHR, *Case of Othman (Abu Qatada) v. The United Kingdom*, No. 8139/09. Judgment of January 17, 2012, para. 189, citing, *inter alia*: ECHR, *Case of Chentiev and Ibragimov v. Slovakia*, Nos. 21022/08 and 51946/08. Decision of September 14, 2010, and *Case of Gasayev v. Spain*, No. 48514/06. Decision of February 17, 2009, and, to the contrary, *Case of Ben Khemais v. Italy*, No. 246/07. Judgment of February 24, 2009, para. 61; *Case of Ryabikin v. Russia*, No. 8320/04. Judgment of June 19, 2008, para. 119, and Case of *Kolesnik v. Russia*, No. 26876/08, Judgment of June 17, 2010, para. 73.

③ ECHR, *Case of Othman (Abu Qatada) v. The United Kingdom*, No. 8139/09. Judgment of January 17, 2012, para. 189, citing: ECHR, *Case of Ben Khemais v. Italy*, No. 246/07. Judgment of February 24, 2009, paras. 59 and 60; *Case of Soldatenko v. Ukraine*, No. 2440/07. Judgment of October 23, 2008, para. 73, and *Case of Koktysh v. Ukraine*, No. 43707/07. Judgment of December 10, 2009, para. 63.

④ ECHR, *Case of Othman (Abu Qatada) v. The United Kingdom*, No. 8139/09. Judgment of January 17, 2012, para. 189, citing: ECHR, *Case of Koktysh v. Ukraine*, No. 43707/07. Judgment of December 10, 2009, para. 64.

⑤ ECHR, *Case of Othman (Abu Qatada) v. The United Kingdom*, No. 8139/09. Judgment of January 17, 2012, para. 189 citing: ECHR, *Case of Gasayev v. Spain*, No. 48514/06. Decision of February 17, 2009; *Case of Babar Ahmad and Others v. The United Kingdom*, Nos. 24027/07, 11949/08, 36742/08, 66911/09 and 67354/09. Judgment of April 10, 2012, para. 106, *and Case of Al-Moayad v. Germany*, No. 35865/03. Decision of February 20, 2007, paras. 66 to 69.

"The existence of diplomatic assurances, their content and the existence and implementation of enforcement mechanisms are all factual elements relevant to the overall determination of whether, in fact, a real risk of proscribed ill-treatment exists."① This Committee, and also the Committee against Torture, have emphasized the need for mechanisms for monitoring the enforcement of the assurances and other provisions so as to ensure they are implemented.②

182. Expert witness Ben Saul emphasized the different nature of the diplomatic assurances provided in relation to non-application of the death penalty (a conduct that is not prohibited by international law) and those provided when there is a risk of torture and other forms of cruel, inhuman or degrading treatment (a conduct that is absolutely prohibited under international law).③ In this regard, the Court takes note of the critiques and difficulties as regards the use and support of diplomatic assurances when there is a possible risk of torture.④ Nevertheless, the European Court con-

---

① UN, Human Rights Committee, *Case of Mohammed Alzery v. Sweden*, Communication No. 1416/2005, U. N. Doc. CCPR/C/88/D/1416/2005, November 10, 2006, para. 11.3

② *Cf.* UN, Human Rights Committee, *Case of Mohammed Alzery v. Sweden*, Communication No. 1416/2005, U. N. Doc. CCPR/C/88/D/1416/2005, November 10, 2006, para. 11.5; the Committee against Torture, *Case of Agiza v. Sweden*, Communication No. 233/2003, U. N. Doc. CAT/C/34/D/233/2003, May 20, 2006, para. 13(4), and *Case of Elif Pelit v. Azerbaijan* Communication No. 281/2005, U. N. Doc. CAT/C/38/D/281/2005, May 1, 2007, para. 11.

③ *Cf.* Affidavit made by Ben Saul on August 18, 2014 (evidence file, folios 6979 and 6980).

④ In this regard, the former Special Rapporteur against torture, Manfred Nowak, "called attention to the importance of maintaining the focus and remaining vigilant on practices such as the use of diplomatic assurances, which attempt to erode the absolute prohibition on torture in the context of counter-terrorism measures. He reiterates that diplomatic assurances are not legally binding and undermine existing obligations of States to prohibit torture, are ineffective and unreliable in ensuring the protection of returned persons, and therefore should not be resorted to by States. *Cf.* Human Rights Council discusses reports on torture, arbitrary detention and independence of judges and lawyers, September 19, 2006. Available at: http://www.ohchr.org/EN/NewsEvents/Pages/DisplayNews.aspx? NewsID=1384. Furthermore, in 2006, Louise Arbour, the High Commissioner for Human Rights at the time, indicated that, [b]ased on the long experience of international monitoring bodies and experts, it is unlikely that a post-return monitoring mechanism set up explicitly to prevent torture and ill-treatment in a specific case would have the desired effect. These practices often occur in secret, with the perpetrators skilled at keeping such abuses from detection. The victims, fearing reprisal, often are reluctant to speak about their suffering, or are not believed if they do. *Cf.* Statement by Louise Arbour, United Nations High Commissioner for Human Rights, to the Council of Europe Group of Specialists on Human Rights and the Fight against Terrorism (DH-S-TER), March 29 to 31, 2006.

siders that it is not for that Court to reject the possibility of their use, when they constitute a usual practice of States,① even though their value and degree of reliability depend on the particular circumstances of the case, and the assurances offered.②

183. In this case, the Court notes that the assurances provided by the People's Republic of Chinagradually changed. Initially the assurances were addressed at the risk of the application of the death penalty, while the last ones, provided in 2014, cover aspects related to the alleged risk of torture or other cruel, inhuman or degrading treatment (*supra* paras. 92 and 93). This Court recalls that, at the present time, the possibility of Wong Ho Wing being tried and sentenced to death has been eliminated (*supra* para. 151), so that it does not find it necessary and pertinent to analyze the sufficiency of the diplomatic assurances provided in relation to the death penalty in order to determine the current circumstances of the risk for Wong Ho Wing. The Court also recalls that it has determined that the Commission and the representative have not proved that Wong Ho Wing faces a real, foreseeable and personal risk of suffering treatment contrary to the prohibition of torture or cruel, inhuman or degrading treatment if he is extradited

---

① In the case of *Othman (Abu Qatada) v. The United Kingdom*, the European Court "accepted that […] there is widespread concern within the international community as to the practice of seeking assurances to allow for the deportation of those considered to be a threat to national security. […] However, it not for this Court to rule upon the propriety of seeking assurances, or to assess the long term consequences of doing so; its only task is to examine whether the assurances obtained in a particular case are sufficient to remove any real risk of ill-treatment." ECHR, *Case of Othman (Abu Qatada) v. The United Kingdom*, No. 8139/09. Judgment of January 17, 2012, para. 186. It has also indicated that: "In extradition matters, Diplomatic Notes are a standard means for the requesting State to provide any assurances which the requested State considers necessary for its consent to extradition. In *Ahmad and Others*, the Court also recognised that, in international relations, Diplomatic Notes carry a presumption of good faith and that, in extradition cases, it was appropriate that that presumption be applied to a requesting State which has a long history of respect for democracy, human rights and the rule of law, and which has longstanding extradition arrangements with Contracting States". ECHR, *Cases of Harkins and Edwards v. The United Kingdom*, Nos. 9146/07 and 32650/07. Judgment of January 17, 2012, para. 85.
② *Cf.* ECHR, *Case of Othman (Abu Qatada) v. The United Kingdom*, No. 8139/09. Judgment of January 17, 2012, para. 142, and *Case of Rustamov v. Russia*, No. 11209/10. Judgment of July 3, 2012, para. 131.

(*supra* para. 176). However, in addition, it considers that the assurances provided in the eighth diplomatic note would help to eliminate any concerns about the presumed victim's situation of risk. The last assurance provided by the People's Republic of China was detailed and proposed a system for monitoring implementation, in keeping with several of the standards described above (*supra* paras. 180, 181 and 182). In this diplomatic note, the requesting State undertook to advise Peru about the possible place of detention of Wong Ho Wing, to give Peruvian diplomats access to and different means of contacting Wong Ho Wing during his detention; offered guarantees as regards his right of defense and the possibility of professional assistance and medical care, as well as granting the Peruvian diplomatic authorities authorization to monitor the proceedings eventually instituted against Wong Ho Wing (*supra* para. 93. h).

184. In addition to taking into account the standards of the European Court and other international bodies when assessing these assurances, the Court underlines that the terms of this last diplomatic note accord with what bothof the Commission's expert witnesses considered a sufficient guarantee in the context of an extradition. Expert witness Ben Saul emphasized as adequate characteristics of the diplomatic assurances that they were "solid, significant and verifiable"; that they "included an effective monitoring system that was prompt, regular and included private interviews," and also "prompt access to a lawyer, (video) recording of all interrogations sessions with a record of the identity of all those present, a prompt and independent medical examination, and the prohibition of solitary confinement or detention in clandestine places."[①] Meanwhile, expert witness Geoff Gilbert indicated that "[f]or the assurances to be sufficient to allow the return, they should refer specifically to the person whose extradition is re-

---

① Affidavit made by Ben Saul on August 18, 2014 (evidence file, folio 6980).

quested; they must depend on the circumstances (including the source and content of the assurances [...]), and they must be independently verifiable after the extradition."[1] The last guarantee provided by the People's Republic of China to Peru complies with these characteristics. Consequently, this Court finds that, in the circumstances of this case, the assurances provided may be considered sufficient to satisfy the concerns that remained about the alleged risk to Wong Ho Wing were he to be extradited.

185. The representative and the Commissioncontested assessment of this latest assurance, considering it time-barred. However, the Court notes that, under international law, there is no limit to the number of assurances that may be provided by the requesting State or required by the requested State. Moreover, there is no impediment to sufficient assurances being provided progressively and increasingly. As mentioned throughout this Judgment, in order to determine whether Wong Ho Wing would face a risk that would harm his right if he were extradited, this Court must examine and assess all the information currently available, because the extradition has not taken place yet. The possibility of obtaining the necessary and sufficient assurances progressively could be restricted by the guarantees of due process that protects every person under the jurisdiction of a State, if there was a limit in this sense in the domestic law of the State in question or, in any case, owing to the obligation to hold the trial within a reasonable time, but this does not mean that the Court cannot take these last assurances into account in order to determine Wong Ho Wing's presumed situation of risk in the requesting State if he were to be extradited. The possible consequences of the State's delay in obtaining appropriate assurances must be examined when analyzing the alleged violation of reasonable time made in another section of this Judgment (*infra* paras. 207 to 223)

---

[1] Affidavit made by Geoff Gilbert on August 16, 2014 (evidence file, folio 7024).

186. The representative also argued that the assurances provided by China were not reliable, because in three other cases where, presumably, the Chinese Government had provided assurances, these had not been fulfilled. ① In this regard, the Court notes that the representative did not provide any evidence for this affirmation. In addition, the representative's arguments refer to the presumed risk of the application of the death penalty, which, as the Court has reiterated, was eliminated with the eighth amendment to the Chinese Criminal Code (*supra* para. 151). The Commission argued that there are no judicial mechanisms to implement the said assurances. However, the Court takes note of the opinion of expert witness Ang Sun, according to which, "following the offer of diplomatic assurances by the Ministry of Foreign Affairs of China, such assurances are binding for all Chinese courts," pursuant to article 50 of the Chinese Extradition Law. ② This Court considers that, in the particular circumstances of this case, the assurances and the monitoring mechanisms offered are sufficient.

B. 5) General conclusion on the alleged risk of violation of the rights to life and personal integrity of Wong Ho Wing if he is extradited

187. Based on all the preceding conclusions, the Court finds that, at the present time, it would not be legally possible to impose the death penalty for the offense of smuggling ordinary merchandise, for which the extradition of Wong Ho Wing has been requested. In addition, it has not been proved that the extradition of Wong Ho Wing would expose him to a

---

① The representative referred to three cases mentioned in an Urgent Action of Amnesty International concerning the case of Wong Ho Wing. This organization indicated that: "China executed the Tibetan, Lobsang Dhondup, in January 2003, one month after it had assured the United States that his case would be subject to extensive review by the People's Supreme Court. Extraditions and expulsions implemented previously suggest that the Chinese assurances should not be relied on. In 1995, Wang Jianye was executed after he had been extradited from Thailand, despite the assurances given to the Thai authorities that he would not be sentenced to death. In June 2000, Fang Yong was sentenced to death after being returned from Canada. Unconfirmed reports suggest that China had provided assurances that he would not be sentenced to death. His sentence was commuted to life imprisonment on appeal."

② *Cf.* Statement made by Ang Sun during the public hearing held in this case.

real, foreseeable and personal risk of being subject to treatment contrary to the prohibition of torture or other cruel, inhuman or degrading treatment.

188. Therefore, the Court concludes that, if Wong Ho Wing is extradited in the current circumstances, the State would not be responsible for violating its obligation to ensure his rights to life and to personal integrity recognized in Articles 4 and 5 of the Convention, in relation to Article 1(1) of this instrument, or the prohibition of non-refoulement established in Article 13 (paragraph 4) of the Inter-American Convention to Prevent and Punish Torture.

X
RIGHTS TO JUDICIAL PROTECTION AND JUDICIAL GUARANTEES, IN RELATION TO THE OBLIGATION TO RESPECT AND ENSURE RIGHTS

189. Despite the Court's conclusion concerning the risk of violation of the rights to life and to personal integrity (*supra* para. 188), in this case, the relevant factor is that, following the Supreme Court's second advisory decision, the Constitutional Court ordered the Executive Branch to refrain from extraditing Wong Ho Wing to China (*supra* paras. 81 to 85). Therefore, this Court must decide whether, notwithstanding the inexistence of a risk at this time, the State may extradite Wong Ho Wing without being in non-compliance with other obligations derived from the Convention, such as the right to judicial protection and the enforcement of final judicial decisions, established in Article 25① of the American Convention, as argued by

---

① The relevant part of Article 25 of the American Convention establishes that: "1. Everyone has the right to simple and prompt recourse, or any other effective recourse, to a competent court or tribunal for protection against acts that violate his fundamental rights recognized by the constitution or laws of the state concerned or by this Convention, even though such violation may have been committed by persons acting in the course of their official duties. 2. The States Parties undertake: [⋯] (c) to ensure that the competent authorities shall enforce such remedies when granted."

the Commission and the representative. In this chapter, the Court will analyze this aspect of the dispute, as well as the alleged violations of the guarantees of a reasonable time and due process of law established in Article 8① of the Convention.

A. Arguments of the parties and of the Commission

190. The Commission indicated that "[t]he order of Peru's Constitutional Court [⋯] required that it was necessary that the final decision in the extradition process deny extradition." However, and even though Wong Ho Wing is still deprived of his liberty, the Executive Branch "has failed to take a final decision in the extradition process," abstaining from executing the judgment and actively seeking numerous legal mechanisms to modify the scope of this ruling that protects the rights of Wong Ho Wing. The Commission concluded that the State had failed to comply with its obligation to implement final judicial decisions. It also argued that "the legal time frames for the advisory procedure were not met in this case and, in addition, the absence of a legal time frame for the final decision of the Executive Branch encouraged the delay." Furthermore, in general, it objected to the "disproportionate time of six years that the extradition process has lasted." In this regard, it affirmed that this, "of itself, violates the guarantee of a reasonable time." It considered that "it was not [the] complexity [of the case] or the diligence in obtaining assurances that caused the delay" and that, "for long periods of time, the competent domestic authorities [⋯] had failed to issue the final decision in the extradition process." In addition, it clarified that the remedies filed by Wong Ho Wing formed part of the mechanisms established for his defense. Regarding the analysis of the legal situation of the person concerned, it underscored that "the delay in

---

① Article 8(1) of the American Convention establishes that: "Every person has the right to a hearing, with due guarantees and within a reasonable time, by a competent, independent, and impartial tribunal, previously established by law, in the substantiation of any accusation of a criminal nature made against him or for the determination of his rights and obligations of a civil, labor, fiscal, or any other nature."

the final decision in the extradition process [...] has meant that Wong Ho Wing remains deprived of his liberty."

191. The representative emphasized that there had been a "systematic failure by the authorities of the Executive Branch to take a final decision on the extradition of Wong Ho Wing that complied with the ruling of the Constitutional Court ordering the Peruvian State to refrain from extraditing him." He argued that the State had confused the provisional nature of the measures adopted by this Court with the final nature of the ruling of the Constitutional Court and concluded that Peru had violated Wong Ho Wing's right to judicial protection for the more than three years during which it had not executed the Constitutional Court's ruling. The representative indicated that there had been a lack of due diligence in the adoption of a final decision by the Executive Branch. In this regard, he argued that the Executive Branch "has been taking a series of delaying measures before adopting a final decision," despite the ruling of the Constitutional Court; among these, he mentioned the request to the Supreme Court to issue a complementary advisory decision, as well as the "request submitted to the 42nd Special Criminal Court of the Superior Court of Justice of Lima on November 25, 2011, that the Public Attorney responsible for the Judicial Matters of the Ministry of Justice present some 'clarifications' regarding compliance with the ruling of the Constitutional Court of May 24, 2011".

192. The State stressed that the Constitutional Court had ordered it to refrain from extraditing Wong Ho Wing, but had not decided on the denial of the extradition request. It noted that the ruling of the Constitutional Court was binding for the Executive Branch, but that "legal discrepancies or questions may exist regarding its execution." According to the State, the requests for clarification "in no way signify the intention to disregard a jurisdictional ruling or prevent its execution, but their purpose was to resolve any questions that arose." Regarding the reasonable time, the State

indicated that, "non-compliance with the reasonable time does not entail the immediate and direct harm to the right to a reasonable time for the duration of a process." In relation to the complexity of the matter, it asked that the Court take into account the "absence of case law of the inter-American system for the protection of human rights concerning the basic diplomatic assurances that a State should request in extradition matters; the absence of domestic case law on the constitutional control of acts of the Executive Branch in relation to extradition; the lack of clarify in the ruling of the Constitutional Court, and the fact that the provisional measures of the Inter-American Court were in force." With regard to the procedural activity of the person concerned, the State indicated that "[the applications for *habeas corpus*] were filed at each stage of the extradition procedure, preventing it from going forward normally." The State did not rule on the conduct of its judicial authorities, because it considered that this had "not been questioned" and that, "regarding the conduct of the authorities, the Commission only referred to those who were part of the Executive Branch." Thus, it affirmed that "the ruling of the Constitutional Court […] does not result in any obligation to issue a decision rejecting the extradition." The State also understood that the Commission's argument on the legal situation of the person involved in the process should "be rejected," because it was the result of its continuing confusion about the real scope of the ruling of the Constitutional Court. It underscored that "[t]he delay in the final decision in the extradition process has been the result of the actions of [the representative] in the domestic and international, and those of the Commission."

B. Considerations of the Court

193. The Court notes that, following the second advisory decision of the Supreme Court, the representative of Wong Ho Wing filed an application for *habeas corpus* in view of the certain and imminent risk that the pre-

sumed victim could be extradited, using the remedies established by Peruvian law. This *habeas corpus* was ultimately decided in May 2011 by the Constitutional Court, by means of a constitutional appeal, when that court considered that sufficient assurances that the death penalty would not be imposed had not been provided, and therefore: (i) ordered the State to refrain from extraditing Wong Ho Wing, and (ii) urged the State to try him in Peru (*supra* paras. 79 to 85).

194. Following that ruling, the State has not taken a final decision regarding the request for the extradition of Wong Ho Wing. Since then, the Executive Branch has tried different procedural channels to incorporate new information that would: (i) clarify or interest the scope of the Constitutional Court's ruling in order to permit the extradition of Wong Ho Wing; (ii) complement the Supreme Court's advisory decision so that it is admissible to extradite Wong Ho Wing, without infringing the literal text of the Constitutional Court's ruling, or (iii) interpret that it is possible to extradite Wong Ho Wing for the offense of bribery that was never subject to the death penalty.

195. Taking into account the arguments of the parties and of the Commission, the Court will now examine: (B.1) the alleged violation of the right to judicial protection, and (B.2) the alleged failure to comply with the guarantee of a reasonable time in the extradition process. Subsequently, the Court will examine: (B.3) the other presumed violations of judicial guarantees alleged by the representative.

B.1) The alleged violation of the right to judicial protection

196. Regarding the right to judicial protection, in the terms of Article 25 of the Convention it is possible to identify two specific State responsibilities. The first is to establish by law and to ensure the due application of effective remedies before the competent authorities that protect all persons subject to their jurisdiction against acts that violate their fundamental

rights or that lead to the determination of their rights and obligations. ① The second is to guarantee the means to executive the respective final decisions and judgments issued by those competent authorities, so that the declared or recognized rights are truly protected. ② The latter is required because a judgment that is *res judicata* grants certainty about the right or dispute discussed in the specific case and, consequently, one of its effects is its binding nature or the need to comply with it. ③ Otherwise, there would be a denial of the right concerned. ④

197. In this regard, Article 25(2)(c) of the Convention establishes the right "that the competent authorities shall enforce such remedies when granted."

198. The Court has indicated that State have the obligation to ensure the means to execute such final decision. ⑤ Effective mechanisms must exist to execute the decisions or judgments so that they truly protect the rights that have been declared. ⑥ In addition, the Court has established that the effectiveness of a judgment depends on its execution. The proceedings must attempt to implement the protection of the right recognized in the legal rul-

---

① Cf. Case of the "Street Children" (Villagrán Morales et al.) v. Guatemala. Merits. Judgment of November 19, 1999. Series C No. 63, para. 237, and Case of the Afrodescendant Communities displaced from the Cacarica River Basin (Operation Genesis) v. Colombia. Preliminary objections, merits, reparations and costs. Judgment of November 20, 2013. Series C No. 270, para. 405.

② Cf. Case of Baena Ricardo et al. v. Panama. Jurisdiction. Judgment of November 28, 2003. Series C No. 104, para. 79, and Case of the Afrodescendant Communities displaced from the Cacarica River Basin (Operation Genesis) v. Colombia, supra, para. 405.

③ Cf. Case of Acevedo Jaramillo et al. v. Peru. Preliminary objections, merits, reparations and costs. Judgment of February 7, 2006. Series C No. 144, para. 167, and Case of the Afrodescendant Communities displaced from the Cacarica River Basin (Operation Genesis) v. Colombia, supra, para. 405.

④ Cf. Case of Cantos v. Argentina. Merits, reparations and costs. Judgment of November 28, 2002. Series C No. 97, para. 54, and Case of Mémoli v. Argentina. Preliminary objections, merits, reparations and costs. Series C No. 265, para. 193.

⑤ Cf. Case of Baena Ricardo et al. v. Panama. Jurisdiction, supra, para. 79, and Case of the Afrodescendant Communities displaced from the Cacarica River Basin (Operation Genesis) v. Colombia, supra, para. 405.

⑥ Cf. Case of Acevedo Jaramillo et al. v. Peru, supra, para. 220.

ing by the appropriate execution of that ruling.①

199. The relevant part of the judgment of the Constitutional Court of May 24, 2011, indicated that:

> [...] the Inter-American Court of Human Rights has emphasized that Articles 4 and 1(1) of the American Convention on Human Rights recognize the international obligation of the States Parties "not to subject a person to the risk of the application of the death penalty via extradition" [...].
>
> Evidently, the Peruvian State has two obligations that, supposedly, it must meet. On the one hand, it has the obligation to extradite Wong Ho Wing based on the Extradition Treaty between the Republic of Peru and the People's Republic of China. On the other hand, it also has the obligation not to subject Wong Ho Wing to the risk of the application of the death penalty via extradition, and to try him for the offenses for which his extradition is sought.
>
> Apparently, the obligations described above are incompatible, because if Wong Ho Wing is extradited, the Peruvian State would be unable to try him. Conversely, if the Peruvian State decides to try Wong Ho Wing, it would be unable to extradite him, because it would prefer to safeguard the right to life.
>
> This apparent conflict between obligations must be decided bearing in mind the protection of the right to life of Wong Ho Wing, which is also an obligation imposed on the Peruvian State under Articles 4 and 1(1) of the American Convention on Human Rights.
>
> Indeed, should the death penalty be imposed on Wong Ho Wing, following his trial in the People's Republic of China, his right to life

---

① Cf. *Case of Baena Ricardo et al. v. Panama. Jurisdiction*, supra, para. 73, and *Case of Liakat Ali Alibux v. Suriname. Preliminary objections, merits, reparations and costs*. Judgment of January 30, 2014. Series C No. 276, para. 33.

would be evidently and truly harmed, and this could be attributed to the Peruvian State, because it had not assessed sufficiently and reasonably the sufficient and real assurances provided by the requesting State that it would not impose the death penalty on him.

In such cases, the European Court of Human Rights has emphasized that the Convention for the Protection of Human Rights and Fundamental Freedoms does not guarantee the right not to be extradited; however, if an extradition decision may affect the exercise of a right protected by the Convention, it is reasonable to require certain obligations of the Requesting State aimed at preventing the violation [⋯]. ①

200. The Court notes that, following the delivery of the judgment of the Constitutional Court in May 2011, that court issued a ruling clarifying it in which, regard the existence of new elements (the diplomatic assurances and the annulment of the death penalty for the offense for which the extradition of Wong Ho Wing was sought), it indicated that "the belated awareness of the content [of the diplomatic assurances] cannot change the sense of the decision adopted [⋯], because it is now constitutional *res judicata.* "② The court that decided to change the provisional detention of Wong Ho Wing ruled similarly,③ and the Supreme Court of Justice also④

---

① Judgment of the Constitutional Court of May 24, 2011 (evidence file, folios 278 and 279).
② Ruling of the Constitutional Court of June 9, 2011 (evidence file, folio 297).
③ *Cf.* Decision of the Seventh Criminal Court of El Callao of March 10, 2014 (evidence file, folio 6462).
④ The Supreme Court indicated, when it was asked to issue a complementary advisory decision, that, "in fact, there have been two final decision, one of an advisory nature (of the Judiciary) and the other of a binding nature (of the Constitutional Court), that the Executive Branch must comply with, taking into account the legal provisions (article 113 of the Code of Constitutional Procedure)." Decision of the Permanent Criminal Chamber of the Supreme Court of Justice March 14, 2012 (evidence file, folio 372 and 373). This article establishes: "Article 113. Effects of Judgments: The court's judgments are binding on the public authorities and shall have full effects for all of them. They determine the State branches or entities to which the disputed attributes and jurisdictions correspond, and annul unlawful provisions, decisions or acts. In addition, they decide, when appropriate, what is admissible in the legal situations produced by such administrative acts. When there is a negative conflict of jurisdictions or attributes, the judgment, in addition to deciding the appropriate responsibility, may indicate, as appropriate, a time frame within which the State branch or entity in question should exercise this." Code of Constitutional Procedure (evidence file, folio 8587).

201. In addition, in a ruling of March 12, 2013, the Constitutional Court rejected the possibility of extraditing Wong Ho Wing for the offense of bribery. When denying an appeal for interpretation filed by the Public Attorney responsible for Judicial Matters of the Ministry of Justice,① the Constitutional Court noted, regarding the possibility of extraditing Wong Ho Wing r the offense of bribery, that "with the pretext of 'clarifying' an element of its judgment" it was sought "to 'amend' its decision, so that it would express something that it had not done originally, also affecting the guarantee of *res judicata*." It indicated that "pursuant to the content of both the judgment and the clarifying ruling issued by the Constitutional Court, […] they did not make an individual or separate analysis of the offenses that the individual sought is accused of, not only because this was not in order […], but also because the relevant point was to determine whether the right to life of the beneficiary in the *habeas corpus* proceeding was threatened if the extradition request was declared admissible" (*supra* para. 90).

202. Nevertheless, the Court underscores that, at the date of the delivery of this Judgment, the Executive Branch has not taken a final decision in this case. According to Peru's domestic laws, although extradition involves a joint process, it corresponds exclusively to the Executive Branch to grant or reject extradition, in those cases where the Supreme Court has considered it admissible, such as in this one (*supra* para. 57). Expert witness García Toma explained that the judgment of the Constitutional Court has not been contravened, insofar as this decision consists merely in an ob-

---

① On that occasion, the said attorney expressly asked if it was possible to extradite Wong Ho Wing for the offense of bribery, for which the death penalty was not established, taking into account that "since the Constitutional Court's judgment makes no distinction between the offenses that result in protection by the judgment, the extradition can be carried out for the offense that does not entail the risk of the death penalty and, in that eventuality, the State's action would be aligned with the execution of the Constitutional Court's judgment." Judgment of the Constitutional Court of March 12, 2013 (evidence file, folio 376).

ligation "to refrain from extraditing Wong Ho Wing," and this has been complied with rigorously to date.

203. This Court considers that, in May 2011, Wong Ho Wing obtained a ruling of the Constitutional Court, which ordered the Executive Branch to refrain from extraditing him. However, the Court takes note that, in this decision, the Constitutional Court found that, according to the circumstances that existed at the time, a risk to the right to life of Wong Ho Wing persisted, in view of the absence of the necessary and sufficient assurances to safeguard it. ① In its decision of June 2011, the Constitutional Court clarified that, when issuing its decision, it was unable to take into account the assurances that had been provided up until that time, because they were not included in the case file, and that the diplomatic notes it had provided information on the annulment of the death penalty, but did not explain its applicability to the case of Wong Ho Wing. ② Thus, the Constitutional Court was unable to assess either the annulment of the death penalty for the offense of smuggling ordinary merchandise and it applicability to Wong Ho Wing's situation, or the subsequent diplomatic assurances provided by the People's Republic of China, which this Court has been able to assess (*supra* paras. 146 to 188).

---

① *Cf.* Ruling of the Constitutional Court of May 24, 2011 (evidence file, folio 280), and ruling of the Constitutional Court of June 9, 2011 (evidence file, folio 302).

② Regarding the reasons why the diplomatic assurances granted by the People's Republic of China had been considered insufficient, the Constitutional Court noted in its ruling of June 9, 2011, that "when the [Judgment] was delivered, the case file did not contain any of the diplomatic assurances to which [...] the public attorney petitioner referred"; rather, "[t]he only documents it had were informative diplomatic notes" on the annulment of the death penalty for the offense of smuggling ordinary merchandise. The Constitutional Court indicated that it became aware of the existence of diplomatic assurances through the Inter-American Court's order on provisional measures of May 28, 2010, but that these were "insufficient or inappropriate because, since it was unaware of the content of the said documents, and since the right to life was at stake, mere information on the amendment made in the objective criminal law of the People's Republic of China was not enough; rather, it was necessary that the People's Republic of China certify that, in no circumstance, would the death penalty be applied to the beneficiary of the *habeas corpus*. Therefore, in Decision No. 11 of the STC 2278 – 2010 – PHC/TC, it regret[ted] that the information provided concerning the legislative amendment did not specify 'whether the Constitution of the People's Republic of China recognized the favorable retroactivity of the criminal law.'" Ruling of the Constitutional Court of June 9, 2011 (evidence file, folios 295 and 296).

204. The Court notes that, following the decision of the Constitutional Court, the domestic judicial authorities have issued rulings indicating that it is not possible to review or amend the Constitutional Court's decision. However, it considers that the State must decide, pursuant to its domestic law, how to proceed with the request to extradite Wong Ho Wing, bearing in mind that, at this time, there would be no risk to his rights to life and personal integrity if he is extradited, but, at the same, that there is a Constitutional Court decision that, *prima facie*, cannot be amended and that, in principle, is binding for the Executive Branch.

205. In addition, the Court takes into account that, as indicated by the State and uncontested by the representative or the Commission, under the laws of Peru, the Executive Branch's discretionary acts may be subject to subsequent constitutional control. Expert witness García Toma expressed the same opinion, and explained that the decision of the Executive Branch, "although it is political, [⋯] is not exempt from control, and this is because, following this decision, any person subject to extradition may appeal that decision before the corresponding judge, using the constitutional procedures indicated in the Code of Constitutional Procedure."[①] Thus, Wong Ho Wing is still able to obtain a judicial review of the said decision if he does not agree with it. The Court notes that the review by a judge or court is a basic requirement to ensure an adequate control and scrutiny of administrative acts that affect fundamental rights.[②] In addition, it considers that the remedy used to contest the final decision in this matter must have suspensive effects, so that the measure is not implemented until the court

---

① Testimony of Víctor García Toma during the public hearing held in this case.
② *Cf. Case of Vélez Loor v. Panama. Preliminary objections, merits, reparations and costs.* Judgment of November 23, 2010. Series C No. 218, para. 126, and *Rights and guarantees of children in the context of migration and/or in need of international protection, supra,* para. 140.

hearing the appeal has issued a decision. ①

206. Based on the preceding conclusions, the Court finds that, in the actual circumstances of this case, it is not in order to issue a ruling on the alleged failure to comply with the decision of the Constitutional Court.

B. 2) Reasonable time of the extradition process

207. Regarding the guarantee of areasonable time, Article 8(1) of the American Convention establishes that "[e]very person has the right to a hearing, with due guarantees and within a reasonable time, by a competent, independent, and impartial tribunal, previously established by law, in the substantiation of any accusation of a criminal nature made against him or for the determination of his rights and obligations of a civil, labor, fiscal, or any other nature."

208. In principle, the jurisdictional function belongs preeminently to the Judiciary, notwithstanding the fact that other public authorities or bodies may exercise jurisdictional functions in certain specific situations. In other words, when the Convention refers to the right of every person to a hearing by "a competenttribunal" "for the determination of his rights," this expression refers to any public authority, whether administrative, legislative or judicial, which by means of its decisions determines rights and obligations of the individual. For this reason, the Court considers that any State organ that exercises functions of a materially jurisdictional nature has the obligation to adopt decisions that respect the guarantees of due process of law in the terms of Article 8(1) of the American Convention. ② Thus,

---

① *Cf.* ECHR, *Case of Conka v. Belgium*, No. 51564/99, Judgment of February 5, 2002, para. 79; *Case of Gebremedhin [Gaberamadhien] v. France*, No. 25389/05, Judgment of April 26, 2007, para. 58, and *Case of Hirsi Jamaa and Others v. Italy* [GS], No. 27765/09. Judgment of February 23, 2012, para. 199. See also, *mutatis mutandi*, *Rights and guarantees of children in the context of migration and/or in need of international protection*, *supra*, para. 142.

② *Cf. Case of the Constitutional Court v. Peru. Merits, reparations and costs.* Judgment of January 31, 2001. Series C No. 71, para. 71, and *Case of Argüelles et al. v. Argentina. Preliminary objections, merits, reparations and costs.* Judgment of November 20, 2014. Series C No. 288, para. 146.

the Court has establishes that, in proceedings such as those that may culminate in the expulsion or deportation of aliens, the State may not issue administrative acts or adopt judicial decisions without respecting certain basic guarantees, the content of which coincides substantially with those established in Article 8 of the Convention.① Although extradition processes are mechanisms for international cooperation between States in criminal matters, the Court reiterates that they must observe the States' international human rights obligations, insofar as the respective decision may affect the rights of the individual (*supra* para. 119). In particular, extradition proceedings must respect certain basic guarantees of due process, taking into account the political and legal aspects of such processes.

209. This Court has indicated that the "reasonable time" referred to in Article 8(1) of the Convention must be assessed in relation to the total duration of the proceedings, from the first procedural action until a final decision is delivered, including any appeals that may eventually be filed.② In this case, the extradition process has not concluded, so that it is necessary to take into account the time that has elapsed from the arrest of Wong Ho Wing on October 27, 2008, to date. In order to determine the reasonableness of the time that this process has lasted, the Court will proceed to analyze, in light of the facts of this case, the four elements that case law has established to determine where the time is reasonable: (i) the complexity of the matter; (ii) the procedural activity of the interested party; (iii) the conduct of the judicial authorities,③ and iv) the effects on the legal situa-

---

① *Cf. Case of Vélez Loor v. Panama*, *supra*, para. 142; *Case of the Pacheco Tineo Family v. Bolivia*, *supra*, para. 132, and *Rights and guarantees of children in the context of migration and/or in need of international protection*, *supra*, para. 112.

② *Cf. Case of Suárez Rosero v. Ecuador. Merits.* Judgment of November 12, 1997. Series C No. 35, para. 71, and *Case of Argüelles et al. v. Argentina*, *supra*, para. 188.

③ *Cf. Case of Genie Lacayo v. Nicaragua. Merits, reparations and costs.* Judgment of January 29, 1997. Series C No. 30, para. 77, and *Case of Argüelles et al. v. Argentina*, *supra*, para. 189.

tion of the person involved in the proceedings.① In this chapter, the Court will only analyze the reasonableness of the time of the extradition process and not of the proceedings resulting from the applications for *habeas corpus*, which will be examined in the chapter on the deprivation of liberty of Wong Ho Wing (*infra* Chapter XI). However, the applications for *habeas corpus* will be taken into account to the extent that they affected the duration of the extradition process.

B. 2. a) Complexity of the matter

210. This Court has taken different criteria into account to determine the complexity of a proceeding.② These include the complexity of the evidence,③ the number of procedural subjects,④ or the number of victims,⑤ the time elapsed since the violation,⑥ the characteristics of the remedies established by domestic law,⑦ the context in which the violation occurred,⑧

---

① *Cf. Case of Valle Jaramillo et al. v. Colombia. Merits, reparations and costs.* Judgment of November 27, 2008. Series C No. 192, para. 155, and *Case of Argüelles et al. v. Argentina, supra*, para. 189.

② *Cf. Case of Furlan and family members v. Argentina. Preliminary objections, merits, reparations and costs.* Judgment of August 31, 2012 Series C No. 246, para. 156, and *Case of Argüelles et al. v. Argentina, supra*, para. 190.

③ *Cf. inter alia, Case of Genie Lacayo v. Nicaragua, supra,* para. 78, and *Case of Anzualdo Castro v. Peru. Preliminary objection, merits, reparations and costs.* Judgment of September 22, 2009. Series C No. 202, para. 157.

④ *Cf. inter alia, Case of Acosta Calderón v. Ecuador. Merits, reparations and costs.* Judgment of June 24, 2005. Series C No. 129, para. 106, and *Case of López Álvarez v. Honduras. Merits, reparations and costs.* Judgment of February 1, 2006. Series C No. 14, para. 133.

⑤ *Cf. inter alia, Case of Baldeón García v. Peru. Merits, reparations and costs.* Judgment of April 6, 2006. Series C No. 147, para. 152; *Case of the Pueblo Bello Massacre v. Colombia, supra,* para. 184, and *Case of Kawas Fernández v. Honduras. Merits, reparations and costs.* Judgment of April 3, 2009 Series C No. 196, para. 113.

⑥ *Cf. inter alia, Case of Heliodoro Portugal v. Panama. Preliminary objections, merits, reparations and costs.* Judgment of August 12, 2008. Series C No. 186, para. 150 and *Case of Radilla Pacheco v. Mexico. Preliminary objections, merits, reparations and costs.* Judgment of November 23, 2009. Series C No. 209, para. 245.

⑦ *Cf. inter alia, Case of Salvador Chiriboga v. Ecuador. Preliminary objection and merits.* Judgment of May 6, 2008. Series C No. 179, para. 83, and *Case of Argüelles et al. v. Argentina, supra,* para. 190.

⑧ *Cf. inter alia, Case of the Pueblo Bello Massacre v. Colombia, supra,* para. 184, and *Case of the Ituango Massacres v. Colombia. Preliminary objection, merits, reparations and costs.* Judgment of July 1, 2006. Series C No. 148, para. 293.

and the number of remedies filed in the proceedings.① The Court affirms that, contrary to the State's assertions, the lack of clarity in the judgments of the local courts or the application of provisional measures ordered by the inter-American system for the protection of human rights cannot exempt the State from its obligation to ensure the reasonable time of the proceedings, or to justify their delay. However, in this case, the Court notes that the extradition process between Peru and China involves diplomatic relations and communications between two States with different legal systems and languages and that require the participation of numerous and different entities of both States. In addition, the absence of case law in this matter at the domestic or regional level and the diversity of remedies filed by both the presumed victim and the organs of the State (*infra* B. 2. b *and* B. 2. c) have contributed to make the process more complex and had an impact on prolonging it.② Therefore, the Court recognizes that the case is complex. However, the other elements of a reasonable time must be examined to determine whether the State has complied with this guarantee.

B. 2. b) Procedural activity of the interested party

211. The Court observes that the case file does not reveal that, during the extradition process, Wong Ho Wing or his representative failed to comply with any deadline that could have delayed the proceedings. The representative has filed six applications for *habeas corpus*; however, in this regard, it should be stressed that the presumed victim was making use of judicial remedies established by the laws applicable to the defense of his rights, which *per se* cannot be used against him.③ In this regard, this

---

① *Cf. Case of Mémoli v. Argentina*, *supra*, para. 173.
② *Cf. Case of Mémoli v. Argentina*, *supra*, para. 173. In this regard, see ECHR, *Case of Stoidis v. Greece*, No. 46407/99, Judgment of May 17, 2001, para. 18.
③ *Mutatis mutandi*, *Case of Genie Lacayo v. Nicaragua*, *supra*, para. 79. See also, *Case of Mémoli v. Argentina*, *supra*, para. 174; ECHR, *Case of Kolomiyets v. Russia*, No. 76835/01, Judgment of February 22, 2007, para. 29, and *Case of Eckle v. Germany*, No. 8130/78, Judgment of July 15, 1982, para. 82.

Court has considered that the filing of remedies is an objective factor that should not be attributed to either the presumed victim or to the defendant State, but should be taken into account as an objective element when determining whether the duration of the proceedings exceeded a reasonable time.① Also, following the Constitutional Court's decision, most of the briefs and remedies filed by the representative have sought the rapid resolution of the proceedings, requesting the adoption of a final decision.

212. Additionally, none of the applications for *habeas corpus* had suspensive effects on the extradition process, except the first application, where the court concerned ordered the suspension "of the processing of the extradition" from February 12, 2009, to April 24, 2009, when it annulled this suspension (*supra* para. 68). This period during which the proceedings were suspended will not be taken into account when determining whether the duration of the extradition process was reasonable.

213. The State referred to actions taken before the inter-American system and the fact that the provisional measures were in force as one of the factors that affected the prolongation of the process (*supra* para. 192). In this regard, the Court notes that, under the provisional measures, it had ordered the State to "refrain from extraditing Wong Ho Wing" until the case had been decided by the Inter-American Commission and subsequently by the Court. The purpose of those measures was to avoid Wong Ho Wing being physically removed from the jurisdiction of Peru and transferred to a jurisdiction outside the inter-American system, when violation of due process in his extradition proceedings and a possible risk to his life and per-

---

① *Cf. Case of Mémoli v. Argentina*, *supra*, para. 174. See also, ECHR, *Case of Eckle v. Germany*, No. 8130/78, Judgment of July 15, 1982, para. 82; *Case of Poiss v. Austria*, No. 9816/82, Judgment of April 23, 1987, para. 57, and *Case of Wiesinger v. Austria*, No. 11796/8, Judgment of October 30, 1991, para. 56.

sonal integrity if he was returned to the requesting State had been alleged. ① This order did not prevent the Executive Branch of Peru from taking a final decision for or against the extradition request; it merely sought to avoid the presumed victim being removed from the State's jurisdiction. To the contrary, on repeated occasions, the Court called attention to the delay in the adoption of a final decision in the extradition proceedings by the Executive Branch. ② Consequently, the Court does not find admissible the State's argument that the processing of this case before the inter-American system and, particularly, the fact that the provisional measures were in force, justify the delay in deciding the request for the extradition of Wong

---

① This is demonstrated by the orders of the Court in which it stated that: the requirement of extreme gravity was met in the case of Wong Ho Wing given "the inherent risk of extraditing an individual [⋯]", when this extradition may lead to the application of the death penalty in a State outside the inter-American system; the requirement of urgency was met because "the possible extradition of [Wong Ho] Wing could occur at any time," while the possible irreparable harm was related to the preventive aspect, because if Wong Ho Wing was extradited "the harm caused was irreparable. Thus, the right of petition established in Article 44 of the American Convention would be harmed irreversibly." *Matter of Wong Ho Wing. Provisional measures with regard to Peru*. Order of the Court of May 28, 2010, *consideranda* 12, 13, 14; *Matter of Wong Ho Wing. Provisional measures with regard to Peru*. Order of the Court of March 4, 2011, *consideranda* 11, 12 and 13; *Matter of Wong Ho Wing. Provisional measures with regard to Peru*. Order of the Court of June 26, 2012, *consideranda* 34, 35 and 36; *Matter of Wong Ho Wing. Provisional measures with regard to Peru*. Order of the Court of May 22, 2013, *considerandum* and note 19. These conclusions are not applicable merely to the decision in favor of extradition, but to the effective extradition and physical removal of Wong Ho Wing from Peru and his return to the authorities of the People's Republic of China. In addition, starting with the new adoption of provisional measures in June 2012, this Court emphasized that, "in this matter, the preventive dimension of the measures seeks to avoid obstruction of compliance with an eventual decision of the organs of the inter-American system [⋯], especially considering that, in this matter, the proposed beneficiary would be extradited to a State beyond the scope of the protection of the inter-American human rights system." *Matter of Wong Ho Wing. Provisional measures with regard to Peru*. Order of the Court of June 26, 2012, *considerandum* 40; *Matter of Wong Ho Wing. Provisional measures with regard to Peru*. Order of the acting President of the Court of December 6, 2012, *considerandum* 6; *Matter of Wong Ho Wing. Provisional measures with regard to Peru*. Order of the Court of February 13, 2013, *considerandum* 6; *Matter of Wong Ho Wing. Provisional measures with regard to Peru*. Order of the Court of May 22, 2013, *considerandum* 6, and *Matter of Wong Ho Wing. Provisional measures with regard to Peru*. Order of the Court of August 22, 2013, *considerandum* 7.

② Cf. *Matter of Wong Ho Wing. Provisional measures with regard to Peru*. Order of the Court of May 22, 2013, *considerandum* 19; *Matter of Wong Ho Wing. Provisional measures with regard to Peru*. Order of the Court of August 22, 2013, *consideranda* 5; *Case of Wong Ho Wing. Provisional measures with regard to Peru*. Order of the Court of January 29, 2014, *considerandum* 10, and *Case of Wong Ho Wing. Provisional measures with regard to Peru*. Order of the Court of March 31, 2014, *considerandum* 17.

Ho Wing.

B. 2. c) Conduct of the State authorities

214. In this case, the Court must analyze the actions of the judicial authorities responsible for the proceedings up until the issue of the second advisory decision, the authorities of the Executive Branch responsible for taking the final decision on the extradition request, as well as the other authorities who have intervened in the process. To facilitate the analysis, the process will be divided into two stages: (i) the first stage (from the arrest of Wong Ho Wing until the issue of the second advisory decision on January 27, 2010), and (ii) the second stage (from the issue of the second advisory decision on January 27, 2010, to date).

215. The first stage of the proceedings do not reveal periods of inactivity that can be attributed to the State and that could be considered the causes of the delay in obtaining a final decision. However, it does reveal negligent conduct by the State authorities who headed the proceedings, which resulted in their prolongation. Thus, on November 14, 2008, the Seventh Criminal Court of El Callao received the request to extradite Wong Ho Wing made by the People's Republic of China. ① However, the extradition request did not include article 151 of the Criminal Code of the People's Republic of China, which was applicable to the case and established the possibility of the death penalty for the smuggling offenses (*supra* para. 62). In this regard, both the Extradition Treaty and the laws of Peru require the extradition request to be accompanied by the "texts of the pertinent legal provisions of the criminal jurisdiction, with the offense and the punished

---

① *Cf*. Extradition request from General Directorate No. 24 of the Ministry of Public Security of the People's Republic of China of November 3, 2008 (evidence file, folio 28), and Decision of the Second Criminal Court of El Callao of November 14, 2008 (evidence file, folios 1737 and 1738). The request was sent under a note of the Embassy of the People's Republic of China dated November 13, 2008 (evidence file, folio 35).

imposed on it. "① The Extradition Treaty also establishes that:

> If the Requested Party considers that the information provided to support the extradition request is insufficient, this Party may require that additional information be provided within thirty days. When the Requesting Party provides justified reasons, the time frame may be extended by fifteen days. If the Requesting Party does not present the additional information within this period, it will be considered that it has voluntarily waived the extradition request. However, the Requesting Party shall not be prevented from making a new extradition request for the same offense. ②

216. Even though, in his first statement, Wong Ho Wing indicated that the offense he was accused of was punishable by the death penalty and, during the extradition hearing, his representative underlined that China had not provided a copy of article 151 of its Criminal Code, the authorities did not request this information from the requesting State. To the contrary, the Second Transitory Chamber of the Supreme Court of Justice issued the advisory decision in the extradition process, which was subsequently annulled by means of a *habeas corpus* (*supra* para. 70). Furthermore, neither did the authorities request the necessary and sufficient diplomatic assurances that the death penalty would not be imposed, which was

---

① Extradition Treaty between the Republic of Peru and the People's Republic of China, Article 7. 1. d (evidence file, folio 8299), and Code of Criminal Procedure, promulgated by Legislative Decree No. 957 of July 29, 2004, article 518. 1. d. Available at: http://www.leyes.congreso.gob.pe/Documentos/Decretoslegislativos/00957.pdf, cited in the Commission's Merits Report, folio 24.

② Extradition Treaty between the Republic of Peru and the People's Republic of China, article 8 (evidence file, folio 8299). See also, Supreme Decree No. 016 – 2006 – JUS. Norms on judicial and government conduct in matters relating to extraditions and prisoner transfers. Published on July 26, 2006, article 2 (evidence file, folio 8548), and Code of Criminal Procedure, promulgated by Legislative Decree No. 957 of July 29, 2004, article 518. Available at: http://www.leyes.congreso.gob.pe/ Documentos/Decretoslegislativos/00957.pdf, cited in the Commission's Merits Report, folio 24.

also grounds for the annulment of the first advisory decision. ①

217. Regarding these delays, the Permanent Criminal Chamber indicated in the second advisory decision that the delays in the processing of the request "were a result of the requesting State [⋯] failing to comply promptly with the presentation of the essential supporting documents [⋯] so as not to violate the supranational law on international agreements."② In this regard, it is important to point out that, even if the requesting State did not forward the complete documentation, it is the Peruvian State, as a State Party to the American Convention, that is obliged to conduct the extradition process in accordance with the obligations imposed by the American Convention, including that the process be conducted within a reasonable time.

218. Regarding the second stage of the process, once the annulment of the advisory decision was made final on June 15, 2009, a new decision was not issued until January 27, 2010 (*supra* para. 78). Between these dates, the Supreme Prosecutor gave his opinion on the request and several extradition hearings were held, the last on December 21, 2009. Nevertheless, the Court notes that the proceeding was twice as long as when the first advisory decision was issued, failing to comply with some of the legal deadlines. Thus, the Procedural Code establishes that, once the extradition hearing has been held, the Supreme Court has five days to issue the decision. In this case, the hearing was held on December 21, 2009, and the advisory decision was issued on January 27, 2010.

219. Following the issue of the advisory decision, the file was forwarded to the Ministry of Justice to start the procedure by which the Executive Branch would take a final decision on the extradition request. Over one

---

① *Cf.* Decision of the Second Special Criminal Chamber for proceedings with the accused in prison of the Superior Court of Justice of Lima of June 15, 2009 (evidence file, folio 6228).
② Advisory decision of the Permanent Criminal Chamber of January 27, 2010 (evidence file, folios 164 and 165).

year later, on May 24, 2011, the Constitutional Court "ordered the Peruvian State, represented by the Executive Branch, to refrain from extraditing Wong Ho Wing to the People's Republic of China."[①] Initially, the Executive interpreted that this decision meant that it could not extradite Wong Ho Wing. However, in November 2011, the Executive filed three different remedies or requests seeking a legal decision or interpretation that would allow it to extradite Wong Ho Wing without disregarding the decision of the Constitutional Court (*supra* paras. 86 to 90). Although, just as the presumed victim, the State authorities were using the remedies available under domestic law, it should be taken into account that all the remedies were declared inadmissible, considering that the Constitutional Court's decision was *res judicata*, could not be amended, and was binding. In addition, the remedies were filed by the Executive Branch, which is responsible for taking the pending decision on extradition, and related to the Executive Branch's options when deciding the extradition request. Therefore, contrary to the presumed victim, all the remedies filed directly affected the prolongation of the extradition process. Moreover, even though the last of these remedies was decided on March 12, 2013, more than two years later, the Executive Branch has still not decided the extradition request.

220. This delay in the final settlement of the extradition process, which can be attributed to the actions of the State authorities, must be examined together with the fourth and last element for determining the reasonable time analyzed below.

B. 2. d) Effects on the legal situation of the person involved in the proceedings

221. The Court recalls that, in order to determine whether the time is reasonable, it is necessary to take into account the effects caused by the du-

---

[①] Judgment of the Constitutional Court of May 24, 2011 (evidence file, folio 281).

ration of the proceedings on the legal situation of the personconcerned, considering, among other aspects, the matter that is the purpose of the dispute. Thus, this Court has established that, if the passage of time has a relevant impact on the legal situation of the individual, the proceedings must be advanced with greater diligence so that the case is decided rapidly. ①

222. The Court observes that the extradition process has lasted more than six and a half years and that, during this lapse, Wong Ho Wing has been deprived of his liberty (five and a half years in a detention center and one year under house arrest). In addition, the situation of uncertainty in which the presumed victim has been kept as regards his possible extradition to China should be mentioned. Despite this, throughout the extradition proceeding, the State has paid little or no attention to the effects on Wong Ho Wing of the delay in the final decision, and did not consider the possibility of tempering the impact of the duration of the proceedings on his individual rights until March 10, 2014, when house arrest was granted. In this regard, it should be emphasized that proceedings in which an individual is held in preventive detention should be held as rapidly as possible (*infra* para. 268). However, the Court does not find that this consideration has been taken into account in the processing of this extradition request.

B. 2. e) Conclusion concerning a reasonable time

223. The extradition proceedings against Wong Ho Wing have lasted more than six years and have not yet concluded. Once the Executive Branch has issued its decision, it can still be appealed (*supra* para. 205), which would add more time to the duration of the extradition process. The Court stresses that the extradition process represents a very preliminary stage in the possible criminal proceedings to which Wong Ho Wing may be subject

---

① *Cf. Case of Valle Jaramillo et al. v. Colombia*, *supra*, para. 155, and *Case of Argüelles et al. v. Argentina*, *supra*, para. 196.

and, more than six years have been invested in this stage alone, without it having concluded. Having analyzed the four elements to determine whether the time is reasonable (*supra* para. 209), the Inter-American Court concludes that the State authorities have not acted with due diligence and respecting the obligation of promptness required by Wong Ho Wing's detention, and the extradition process has therefore exceeded a reasonable time, which violates the right to the guarantees established in Article 8(1), in relation to Article 1 of the American Convention, to the detriment of Wong Ho Wing.

B. 3) Other guarantees of due process (right to be heard and right to a defense)

B. 3. a) Arguments of the parties and of the Commission

224. The Commission indicated that "the legal framework does not reveal any form of participation or defense for the requested person or his legal representative at the decision-making stage before the Executive Branch." The Commission considered that Peru had "failed to meet its burden of proof" as regards the presumed victim's arguments in relation to the impossibility of accessing the complete file of the extradition request. In this regard, it indicated that the State had not provided the complete file of the extradition process or of the different remedies it had filed in the domestic sphere, and had not submitted documentation indicating that it had made available to Wong Ho Wing the information he required to exercise his right to be heard or to file appropriate and prompt remedies during a proceeding in which his rights could be harmed.

225. The representative argued that "the procedural laws do not guarantee the right to be heard before [the authorities of the Executive Branch who exercise material jurisdiction to decide extradition matters] and they have not allowed Wong Ho Wing's defense counsel to explain his arguments against extradition, to the detriment of the right of every person to

be heard for the determination of his rights." According to the representative, this "has established a context of secrecy and lack of transparency in the access to documentation of vital importance for the preparation of Wong Ho Wing's defense against extradition, which has not been ensured by either the Judiciary or the Executive Branch during the proceedings," in a case where the presumed victim was at risk of being condemned to death or suffering torture other ill-treatment.

226. The State argued that ithad "not violated Wong Ho Wing's right to be heard and to have information and means to defend himself." In this regard, it underscored that, during the first stage of the extradition proceeding before the Judiciary, he was fully able to exercise his right of defense, while the second stage corresponded to a strictly political decision. Therefore, it considered that "[t]he responsibility of the State could only be involved if [the intervention of the person sought] was not established at any stage." It also indicated that "the alleged normative omission [to establish by law, channels or means of intervention for the representative in the extradition proceedings before the Executive Branch] c[ould] not be cited as grounds for harming the presumed victim's rights, since, in the practice, the extradition procedure before the Executive Branch was brought to a halt as a result of the legal actions filed by his procedural representative." Also, it clarified that "if a political decision to extradite [⋯] is considered to harm fundamental rights, the person concerned may contest it using the urgent mechanisms to protect fundamental rights." Lastly, with regard to the alleged lack of access to the documentation, the State indicated that the decision to deny the representative's request for access to information, "was not contested during the administrative proceeding, even though the possibility is established in the relevant law."

B. 3. b) Considerations of the Court

227. In Peru, the extradition process has a judicial stage and a political

stage. The arguments of the parties reveal that the dispute on the right to be heard refers to the political stage, while the dispute on the right of access to documents would appear to refer to both stages.

228. Regarding the right to be heard, the Court has indicated that this is protected in Article 8(1) of the Convention, in the general sense of including the right of every person to have access to the court or State body responsible for determining his rights and obligations.① In this regard, the Court has indicated that the guarantees established in Article 8 of the American Convention suppose that the victims should have extensive possibilities of being heard and acting in their respective proceedings,② so that they may indicate their claims and present probative elements and that these are analyzed in a complete and serious manner by the authorities before a decision is taken on the facts, responsibilities, punishments and reparation.③

229. The Court considers it necessary that the right to be heard is guaranteed in extradition proceedings. In this regard, expert witness Ben Saul asserted that the person must be allowed to explain the reasons why he or she should not be extradited.④ However, this does not mean that this should be guaranteed at all stages of the proceedings. In this regard, the Court notes that, in many of the States Parties to the Convention, extradi-

---

① *Cf. Case of Genie Lacayo v. Nicaragua, supra*, para. 74, and *Case of the Constitutional Tribunal (Camba Campos et al.) v. Ecuador. Preliminary objections, merits, reparations and costs.* Judgment of August 28, 2013. Series C No. 268, para. 181.
② *Cf. Case of the Constitutional Court v. Peru, supra*, para. 81, and *Case of the Constitutional Tribunal (Camba Campos et al.) v. Ecuador, supra*, para. 181.
③ *Cf. Case of Baldeón García v. Peru, supra*, para. 146, and *Case of the Constitutional Tribunal (Camba Campos et al.) v. Ecuador, supra*, para. 181.
④ *Cf.* Affidavit made by Ben Saul on August 18, 2014 (evidence file, folios 6938 and 6942).

tion proceedings have a political stage or element.① This circumstance or characteristic stems from the very nature of extradition processes, which constitute processes of international judicial cooperation between States.

230. Under the laws of Peru, during the judicial stage of the extradition proceedings, the stataement of the person sought is taken and the latter has the right to take part in any hearings that are held before the issue of the advisory decision of the Supreme Court. Subsequently, the person sought does not intervene at the political stage of the proceedings. Nevertheless, the Court recalls that, as argued by the parties, the discretionary actions of the Executive Branch may be subject to subsequent constitutional control (*supra* para. 205).

231. The Court considers that, insofar as Wong Ho Wing took part in the judicial stage of the proceedings and retains the possibility of obtaining judicial control of the final decision on extradition, the State has not failed to comply with its obligation to guarantee the presumed victim's right to be heard.

232. Furthermore, with regard to the alleged lack of access to docu-

---

① The following States have a judicial stage and a political stage similar to Peru: Argentina (Law on International Cooperation in Criminal Matters, articles 22, 34 and 36, Available at http://www.infoleg.gov.ar/infolegInternet/anexos/40000-44999/41442/norma.htm); Brazil (Aliens Statute, articles 66 and 83, Available at http://www.pge.sp.gov.br/centrodeestudos/bibliotecavirtual/dh/volume%20i/naclei6815.htm); Colombia (Code of Criminal Procedure, articles 491, 492, 501 and 503, Available at http://www.secretariasenado.gov.co/senado/basedoc/ley_0906_2004_pr012.html); Ecuador (Extradition Act, articles 13 and 14, Available at https://www.oas.org/juridico/mla/sp/ecu/sp_ecu-ext-law-leyext.pdf); Mexico (Constitution of the United Mexican States, article 119, Available at http://www.diputados.gob.mx/LeyesBiblio/htm/1.htm and International Extradition Act, articles 27 and 30, Available at http://www.diputados.gob.mx/LeyesBiblio/pdf/36.pdf) and Suriname (See Extradition system framework, Available at http://www.oas.org/juridico/mla/sp/sur/index.html#últimaactualización). In the following States, the decision on extradition corresponds exclusively to the Executive Branch, although judicial remedies are established to appeal the decision: Jamaica (The Extradition Act, articles 7, 8, 11 and 12, Available at http://www.oas.org/juridico/MLA/en/jam/en_jam-ext.pdf); Panama (Judicial Code of the Republic of Panama, articles 2504, 2510 and 2512, Available at http://www.oas.org/juridico/spanish/mesicic3_pan_cod_judicial.pdf), and Dominican Republic (Extradition Act, article 1, Available at http://www.oas.org/juridico/mla/sp/dom/sp_dom-ext-law-489.html).

mentation in the case file,① the Court notes that, since there is no obligation to allow the person sought to participate at the political stage of the extradition proceedings, there is no obligation to ensure access to the file during that stage. Regarding the subsequent information received during that stage, the Court considers that the State has an obligation to make available to anyone subject to extradition the necessary elements to exercise their right of defense or to explain their particular circumstances of risk in an adequate and effective manner. Nevertheless, in this case, the extradition process has not concluded and, as shown, the final decision is subject to subsequent judicial control. Therefore, the Court considers that, in this case, access to these elements could be ensured at that subsequent judicial stage, without the need to grant this access during the political stage of the extradition process having been proved. Regarding the alleged lack of access to documentation during the judicial stage, the Court notes that, although the representative argued that the Judiciary had not ensured access to "documentation of vital importance for the preparation of Wong Ho Wing's defense" (*supra* para. 225), he did not present clear and specific arguments in this regard; hence, the Court will not rule on this point.

233. The Court understand that the delay in the processing of the political stage has resulted in a situation of uncertainty for the presumed victim, particularly owing to the issue and reception of new diplomatic assurances during this stage, which he has become aware of incidentally, since

---

① On July 9, 2010, the Official Commission for Extraditions and Prisoner Transfers of the Ministry of Justice issued a new report on the request for the extradition of Wong Ho Wing, as a contribution to the decision of the Executive Branch. On September 28, 2010, the representative asked the Ministry of Justice for a copy of this report, but his request was refused indicating that, pursuant to article 17 of the Law on Access to Public Information, the right to public information cannot be exercised in the case of "information prepared or obtained by legal advisers or lawyers of the entities of the Public Administration, the publication of which could reveal the strategy to be adopted in processing an administrative or judicial proceeding or in the defense. *Cf.* Request for copy of reasoned report of September 28, 2010 (evidence file, folio 265); report No. 34-2010-DNJ/DICAJ of September 29, 2010 (evidence file, folio 2997), and Law on Transparency and Access to Public Information No. 27806 (evidence file, folios 3014 and 3015).

he has not had direct access to the case file at this stage. However, the Court finds that this uncertainty is an effect of the delay in obtaining a final decision from the Executive Branch, which the Court considered when analyzing and declaring a violation of the guarantee of a reasonable time (*supra* para. 223).

234. Based on the above conclusions, the Court finds that, in this case, the State has not violated the right to be heard, the right of defense, and the right of access to the case file, recognized in Article 8(1) of the American Convention.

XI

RIGHTS TO PERSONAL LIBERTY AND PERSONAL INTEGRITY, IN RELATION TO THE OBLIGATION TO RESPECT AND ENSURE RIGHTS

235. In previous cases, this Court has referred, among other matters, to deprivations of liberty carried out as a preventive measure and as a punitive measure in the context of criminal proceedings before the ordinary[1] or the military jurisdiction,[2] owing to an individual's migratory situation,[3] as well as to collective and planned detentions,[4] and those carried out totally unlawfully, which constituted the first act in the perpetration of extrajudi-

---

[1] Cf. *Case of García Asto and Ramírez Rojas v. Peru. Preliminary objection, merits, reparations and costs.* Judgment of November 25, 2005. Series C No. 137, paras. 115 and 134, and *Case of Yvon Neptune v. Haiti. Merits, reparations and costs.* Judgment of May 6, 2008. Series C No. 180, para. 100.

[2] Cf. *Case of Loayza Tamayo v. Peru. Merits, supra,* para. 61, and *Case of Argüelles et al. v. Argentina, supra,* paras. 128 and 137.

[3] Cf. *Case of Vélez Loor v. Panama, supra,* para. 106, and *Case of Expelled Dominicans and Haitians v. Dominican Republic. Preliminary objections, merits, reparations and costs.* Judgment of August 28, 2014. Series C No. 282, paras. 368, 370, 374, 379, and 380.

[4] Cf. *Case of Bulacio v. Argentina. Merits, reparations and costs.* Judgment of September 18, 2003. Series C No. 100, para. 38, and *Case of Expelled Dominicans and Haitians v. Dominican Republic, supra,* paras. 368, 374, 380 and 383.

*cial execution*① or enforced disappearance. ② In this case, the holder of the rights whose situation is examined is an alien detained owing to the existence of an international warrant for his arrest and a subsequent extradition request. However, regardless of the reason for his detention, insofar as it relates to a deprivation of liberty executed by a State Party to the Convention, this deprivation of liberty must be strictly in keeping with the relevant provisions of the American Convention and domestic law, provided that the latter is compatible with the Convention.

236. In this chapter, the Court will examine separately each of the arguments presented by the parties and the Commission in relation to the right to personal liberty. This Court recalls that Article 7③ of the American Convention includes two distinct types of regulations, one general and the other specific. The general one is found in the first paragraph: "Every person has the right to personal liberty and security." While the specific one consists of a series of guarantees that protect the right not to be deprived of liberty unlawfully (Article 7(2)) or arbitrarily (Article 7(3)), to know the reasons for the detention and the charges brought against the detainee

---

① *Cf. Case of the "Street Children" (Villagrán Morales et al.) v. Guatemala. Merits, supra,* paras. 132, 135 and 143, and *Case of Rodríguez Vera et al. (The Disappeared of the Palace of Justice) v. Colombia, supra,* paras. 368 and 369.

② *Cf. Case of Velásquez Rodríguez v. Honduras. Merits, supra,* para. 186, and *Case of Rodríguez Vera et al. (The Disappeared of the Palace of Justice) v. Colombia, supra,* paras. 322, 324, 368 and 369.

③ Article 7 of the Convention establishes that: "1. Every person has the right to personal liberty and security. 2. No one shall be deprived of his physical liberty except for the reasons and under the conditions established beforehand by the Constitution of the State Party concerned or by a law established pursuant thereto. 3. No one shall be subject to arbitrary arrest or imprisonment. 4. Anyone who is detained shall be informed of the reasons for his detention and shall be promptly notified of the charge or charges against him. 5. Any person detained shall be brought promptly before a judge or other officer authorized by law to exercise judicial power and shall be entitled to trial within a reasonable time or to be released without prejudice to the continuation of the proceedings. His release may be subject to guarantees to assure his appearance for trial. 6. Anyone who is deprived of his liberty shall be entitled to recourse to a competent court, in order that the court may decide without delay on the lawfulness of his arrest or detention and order his release if the arrest or detention is unlawful. In States Parties whose laws provide that anyone who believes himself to be threatened with deprivation of his liberty is entitled to recourse to a competent court in order that it may decide on the lawfulness of such threat, this remedy may not be restricted or abolished. The interested party or another person in his behalf is entitled to seek these remedies. […]".

(Article 7(4)), to judicial control of the deprivation of liberty (Article 7 (5)) and to contest the lawfulness of the detention (Article 7(6)).① Any violation of paragraphs 2 to 7 of Article 7 of the Convention necessarily results in the violation of its Article 7(1).②

237. Article 7(2) of the American Convention establishes that: "[n]o one shall be deprived of his physical liberty except for the reasons and under the conditions established beforehand by the Constitution of the State Party concerned or by a law established pursuant thereto." This Court has indicated that, in view of the reference to the Constitution and "a law established pursuant thereto," the examination of the observance of Article 7 (2) of the Convention entails the analysis of compliance with the requirements established as specifically as possible and "beforehand" in the said laws as regards the "reasons" for and the "conditions" of the deprivation of physical liberty. If the domestic law is not observed, both materially and formally, when depriving an individual of his liberty, this deprivation will be unlawful and contrary to the American Convention③ in light of Article 7(2).

238. With regard to the arbitrariness referred to in Article 7(3) of the Convention, the Court has established that no one may be detained or imprisoned for reasons and by methods that - although classified as lawful - may be considered incompatible with respect for the fundamental rights of the individual because, among other matters, they are unreasonable, unpredictable, or disproportionate.④ Thus, the arbitrariness referred to in

---

① Cf. Case of Chaparro Álvarez and Lapo Íñiguez v. Ecuador. Preliminary objection, merits, reparations and costs. Judgment of November 21, 2007. Series C No. 170, para. 51, and Case of Espinoza Gonzáles v. Peru. Preliminary objections, merits, reparations and costs. Judgment of November 20, 2014. Series C No. 289, para. 106.

② Cf. Case of Chaparro Álvarez and Lapo Íñiguez v. Ecuador, supra, para. 54, and Case of Espinoza Gonzáles v. Peru, supra, para. 106.

③ Cf. Case of Chaparro Álvarez and Lapo Íñiguez v. Ecuador, supra, para. 57, and Case of Argüelles et al. v. Argentina, supra, para. 116.

④ Cf. Case of Gangaram Panday v. Suriname. Merits, reparations and costs. Judgment of January 21, 1994. Series C No. 16, para. 47, and Case of Expelled Dominicans and Haitians v. Dominican Republic, supra, para. 364.

Article 7(3) of the Convention has its own legal content, which must be analyzed only in the cases of detentions that are considered lawful. ① Nevertheless, the domestic law, the applicable procedure, and the relevant general express or tacit principles must, in themselves, be compatible with the Convention. ② Thus, the concept of "arbitrariness" should not be equated to "contrary to the law," but should be interpreted more broadly in order to include elements of impropriety, injustice and unpredictability. ③

239. Article 9 of the Extradition Treaty between China and Peru establishes:

> Preventive detention
>
> 1. In urgent cases, before the presentation of the extradition request, the Requesting Party may require the preventive detention of the person sought. This request may be submitted in writing using the channels stipulated in article 6 of this Treaty, the International Criminal Police Organization (ICPO-INTERPOL), or other channels agreed between the Parties.
>
> [...]
>
> 4. The preventive detention shall conclude if the competent authority of the Requested Party has not received the formal extradition request within 60 days of the detention of the person sought. This period may be extended for a further 30 days when the Requesting Party provides reasons that justify this.
>
> 5. The conclusion of the preventive detention pursuant to paragraph 4 of this article shall not affect the extradition of the person

---

① *Cf. Case of Chaparro Álvarez and Lapo Íñiguez v. Ecuador*, supra, paras. 93 and 96, and *Case of Rodríguez Vera et al. (The Disappeared of the Palace of Justice) v. Colombia*, supra, para. 401.
② *Cf. Case of Chaparro Álvarez and Lapo Íñiguez v. Ecuador*, supra, para. 91, and *Case of Rodríguez Vera et al. (The Disappeared of the Palace of Justice) v. Colombia*, supra, para. 401.
③ *Cf. Case of Chaparro Álvarez and Lapo Íñiguez v. Ecuador*, supra, para. 92, and *Case of Rodríguez Vera et al. (The Disappeared of the Palace of Justice) v. Colombia*, supra, para. 401.

sought if the Requested Party subsequently receives the formal extradition request. ①

240. The relevant part of article 2. 24 (f) of the Constitution of Peru, in force at the time of the facts, establishes that:

> No one may be detained unless it is with a reasoned written order issued by a judge, or by the police authorities in case of *in flagrante delicto*. The detainee must be brought before the corresponding court within 24 hours or in accordance with the distance. ②

341. Meanwhile, Section II of the Seventh Tome of Peru's Code of Criminal Procedure (Legislative Decree No. 957), regulates the provisional arrestwith a view to extradition as follows:

Article 523. Provisional or pre-extradition arrest.

1. The provisional arrest of a person sought by foreign authorities shall be in order when:

a) This has been formally requested by the central authority of the interested country;

b) The person tries to enter the country while pursued by the authority of an adjoining country.

2. In the case of subparagraph (a) above, the formal request shall be sent to the Prosecutor General, either through the central authority or through INTERPOL. In urgent cases, a simple requisition made by any means, including telegram, telephone, radiogram or electronic mail, shall be required. The formal request shall contain:

a) The name of the person sought, with personal identity data and the circumstances why he is in the country;

---

① Extradition Treaty between the Republic of Peru and the People's Republic of China (evidence file, folio 1635).
② 1993 Constitution of Peru. Available at: www.congreso.gob.pe/ntley/ConstitucionP.htm, cited in the Commission's Merits Report, folio 19.

b) The date and place of the offense committed and its legal definition;

c) If the person sought has been accused, an indication of the punishment for the act perpetrated; and, if he has been convicted, an indication of the punishment imposed;

d) Mention of the existence of the court order for arrest or prison, and of absence or contempt of court, if appropriate;

e) The undertaking of the requesting State to present the formal extradition request within 30 days of the receipt of the requisition. If this time limit shall expire before the extradition request has been formally submitted, the person arrested shall be released immediately.

3. The Prosecutor General shall immediately forward this request to the competent preliminary investigation judge, advising the corresponding provincial prosecutor.

4. The judge will issue a provisional arrest warrant, provided that the act considered an offense is also an offense in Peru and a criminal punishment of any kind equal to or in excess of one year's imprisonment has not been established. If the perpetration of several offenses has been mentioned, it shall be sufficient that one of them complies with this condition in order for it to be in order for the other offenses. The decision issued shall be notified to the prosecutor and advised to the Prosecutor General and the local INTERPOL office.

5. In the case of paragraph 1(b), the border police shall immediately bring the detainee before the competent preliminary investigation judge of the place where the arrest is made, advising the provincial prosecutor. The judge, using the fastest means, which may be telephone, fax or electronic mail, shall advise the Prosecutor General and the diplomatic or consular official of the country seeking the detainee. The diplomatic or consular representative shall have two days to require the continuation of the provisional arrest, accompanying his request with the conditions established in para-

graph 2 of this article. If this is not done, the person arrested shall be released immediately.

6. Once the provisional arrest has been ordered, the preliminary investigation judge shall hear the person arrested within 24 hours, and shall appoint a defense lawyers *ex officio*, if that person does not appoint one of his own choice. The arrest shall be lifted if, initially, the judge notes that the conditions indicated in paragraph 4 of this article have not been met, becoming an order to appear in court periodically, with the prohibition to leave the country. The arrest shall cease if it is proved that the person arrested is not the person sought, or when 30 days have passed without the formal submission of the extradition request.

7. The person arrested who is released because the extradition request was not submitted in time may be arrested again for the same offense, provided that a formal extradition request is received.

8. While the provisional arrest lasts, the person arrested may consent to be transferred to the Requesting State. In this case, the provisions of article 521(6) shall be followed.

9. The person arrested may obtain provisional release, if the legal timeframes of the Treaty or of the law that justify the extradition request expire, or if the person whose extradition is requested meets the procedural conditions for this measure. In this case, an order of prohibition to leave the country shall be issued and his passport shall be retained, without prejudice to other measures of control that the judge may decide on a discretionary basis. The procedure established for the cessation of preventive detention shall be followed. [①]

242. The possibility of obtaining the provisional release indicated in

---

[①] Code of Criminal Procedure, promulgated by Legislative Decree No. 957 of July 29, 2004, Available at: http://www.leyes.congreso.gob.pe/Documentos/DecretosLegislativos/00957.pdf, cited in the Commission's Merits Report, folio 24.

paragraph 9 of article 523 (*supra* para. 241), is regulated in article 182 of the Procedural Code (Legislative Decree No. 638), which establishes that the accused who is detained may request provisional release when new evidence allows it to be reasonably envisaged that:

 1. The prison sentence to be imposed on him will be less than four years, or when the accused has been detained for more than two-thirds of the prison term requested by the prosecutor in the written indictment.

 2. The probability that the accused will evade prosecution or disrupt the probative activity has ceased.

 3. The accused provides the surety that has been established or, if applicable, the person who is insolvent offers a personal guarantee. ①

243. Based on the foregoing, the Court will analyze the alleged violations as regards: (A) the arbitrary nature of the provisional arrest; (B) the alleged unlawful and arbitrary nature of the detention following the decision of the Constitutional Court; (C) the duration of the provisional arrest, and (D) the right to appeal before a competent judge or court. Lastly, it will refer to (E) the alleged violation of the right to personal integrity.

A. Arbitrary nature of the provisional arrest

A. 1) Arguments of the parties and of the Commission

244. The Commission argued that, when determining the need for provisional arrest with a view to extradition, the concept of "procedural risk" should also be taken into consideration. Thus, it concluded that "the decision in the appeal of December 11, 2008, was arbitrary" since it indicated that "the concept of 'procedural risk' did not have to be examined, because this was not a criminal case instituted in Peru, but a 'provisional arrest made with a view to extradition.'" The Commission also argued that "the absence of a time limit expressly established for a provisional arrest with a

---

① Procedural Code promulgated by Legislative Decree No. 638 of April 27, 1991 (evidence file, folio 8623).

view to extradition [⋯] is incompatible with the principle of predictability."

245. The representative argued that the decision in the appeal concerning the detention of Wong Ho Wing did not take into account "whether [⋯] he would evade prosecution and interfere with the extradition process." He also underlined that the Chamber had not "verified the existence of other less onerous measures." Therefore, he argued that since the provisional arrest was "unreasonable, disproportionate and lacking appropriate grounds [⋯] Peru had violated the rights to personal liberty (Article 7(3)) and judicial guarantees (Article 8(1)) recognized in the Convention." He added that "the procedural laws with regard to extradition do not establish a time limit for deprivation of liberty during the extradition process or when they should conclude, [which] adds a degree of arbitrariness to the situation of Wong Ho Wing." Accordingly, he alleged the violation of Article 7(5) in relation to Articles 1(1) and 2 of the Convention.

246. The State indicated that "[t]he deprivation of liberty [of Wong Ho Wing] was the result of a duly founded provisional arrest warrant issued by the competent jurisdictional organ," so that it was in keeping with the laws of Peru. It also indicated that "the procedural risk was evaluated and his specific situation analyzed, and it was considered that his personal liberty should be limited to ensure that he could not interfere with the ongoing investigations or avoid prosecution." It emphasized that, during the appeal proceedings, "the presumed victim's defense counsel did not provide evidence in relation to the procedural risk." The State added that the representative had not filed any remedy against the second instance decision confirming the provisional arrest that could have been "contested by an application for *habeas corpus.*" Regarding the failure to regulate the time limit for detention, it argued that "the inter-American system does not have a standard or guidelines in its case law related to the 'principle of predictability' that can be used as a reference to determine international re-

sponsibility for violation of Article 7(5) ." On this point, it affirmed that the representative had alleged a violation of Article 2 of the Convention without providing grounds for this.

A. 2) Considerations of the Court

247. On October 27, 2008, Wong Ho Wing was detained based on an international arrest warrant. The following day, the special court ordered his provisional arrest and indicated that thisarrest had been made "in order to ensure the presence in the country [of Wong Ho Wing] while the extradition request was fully processed, because he had not proved that he had any known domicile or employment in the country and, because the offense of which he was accused was established in the laws [of Peru] under Customs Offenses: evasion of customs duty"①(*supra* para. 97). Wong Ho Wing's defense lawyer filed an appeal against this measure before the First Transitory Combined Superior Chamber. On December 11, 2008, the First Combined Superior Chamber confirmed the provisional arrest warrant②(*supra* para. 100). Both decisions were delivered taking into account article 523 of the Code of Criminal Procedure (*supra* para. 241). There is no dispute about the conformity of these decisions with Peruvian law.

248. The Inter-American Court has indicated that, notwithstanding the lawfulness of a detention, in each case an analysis must be made of the law's compatibility with the Convention, in the understanding that the law and its application must respect the following requirements to ensure that the deprivation of liberty is not arbitrary:③(i) that the purpose of the measures that deprive or restrict liberty are compatible with the Convention; (ii) that the measures adopted are appropriate to achieve the purpose

---

① Provisional arrest warrant of October 28, 2008 (evidence file, folio 18).
② *Cf.* Decision of December 11, 2008, delivered by the First Transitory Combined Superior Chamber (evidence file, folio 44).
③ *Cf. Case of Chaparro Álvarez and Lapo Íñiguez v. Ecuador*, *supra*, para. 93, and *Case of Argüelles et al. v. Argentina*, *supra*, para. 120.

sought; (iii) that they are necessary, in the sense that they are absolutely essential to achieve the purpose sought and that there is no less onerous measure, with regard to the right affected, among all those with the same ability to achieve the proposed purpose-which is why the Court has asserted that the right to personal liberty presumes that any restriction of this right must be exceptional,① and (iv) that the measures are strictly proportionate,② so that the sacrifice inherent in the restriction of the right to liberty is not exaggerated or excessive in relation to the advantages obtained from its restriction and achievement of the purpose sought.③ Any restriction of liberty that does not contain sufficient grounds which allow it to be evaluated to ensure that it meets these conditions will be arbitrary and, therefore, violate Article 7(3) of the Convention.④

249. The Court notes that the arguments of the Commission and the representative do not refer to the initial detention, or to the order of October 28, 2008. Therefore, the dispute between the parties does not relate to the lawfulness or arbitrariness of Wong Ho Wing's initial detention. This appears to have been carried out to meet the State's international obligations under the Extradition Treaty and also as a member of INTERPOL (*supra* para. 239), which has not been questioned before this Court. The dispute between the parties, regarding the alleged arbitrary nature of the detention of Wong Ho Wing, relates to the grounds for the decision on the appeal issued by the First Transitory Combined Superior Chamber of El Ca-

---

① Cf. *Case of Ricardo Canese v. Paraguay. Merits, reparations and costs.* Judgment of August 31, 2004. Series C No. 111, para. 129, and *Case of Norín Catrimán et al. (Leaders, members and an activist of the Mapuche Indigenous People) v. Chile. Merits, reparations and costs.* Judgment of May 29, 2014. Series C No. 279, para. 310.
② Cf. *Case of Ricardo Canese v. Paraguay*, *supra*, para. 129, and *Case of Argüelles et al. v. Argentina*, *supra*, para. 120.
③ Cf. *Case of Chaparro Álvarez and Lapo Íñiguez. v. Ecuador*, *supra*, para. 93, and *Case of Argüelles et al. v. Argentina*, *supra*, para. 120.
④ Cf. *Case of García Asto and Ramírez Rojas v. Peru*, *supra*, para. 128, and *Case of Argüelles et al. v. Argentina*, *supra*, para. 120.

llao on December 11, 2008, as well as the lack of a time limit for this detention. Consequently, the Court will analyze whether the grounds for the said decision reveal that it was necessary and proportionate (*supra* para. 248) and will then examine the arguments regarding the unpredictability of the duration of the detention.

250. As already established, States have the authority and, in some cases the obligation, to facilitate the extradition of citizens sought by another State using procedures that are compatible with the American Convention (*supra* para. 119). Therefore, implementation of the extradition may be a legitimate purpose pursuant to the Convention. In this regard, in cases relating to pre-trial detentions during criminal proceedings, the Court has indicated that the deprivation of the accused's liberty cannot be founded on general or special preventive objectives that can be attributed to the punishment, but only on a legitimate purpose, namely: to ensure that the accused does not interfere with the development of the proceedings or evade prosecution. [1] It has also underscored that procedural risk cannot be presumed, but must be verified in each case, based on the objective and evident circumstances of the specific case. [2]

251. This Court considers that these criteria are also applicable to detentions with a view to extradition. Therefore, detention of individuals sought in extradition processes will be arbitrary when the competent authorities order the individual's detention without verifying whether, in the objective and evident circumstances of the case, this is necessary to achieve the legitimate purpose of the measure; that is, the possibility that this person may evade extradition. This analysis must be made in each specific case

---

[1] *Cf. Case of Suárez Rosero v. Ecuador. Merits*, *supra*, para. 77, and *Case of Norín Catrimán et al. (Leaders, members and an activist of the Mapuche Indigenous People) v. Chile*, *supra*, para. 312.
[2] *Cf. Case of Barreto Leiva v. Venezuela. Merits, reparations and costs*. Judgment of November 17, 2009. Series C No. 206, para. 115, and *Case of Norín Catrimán et al. (Leaders, members and an activist of the Mapuche Indigenous People) v. Chile*, *supra*, para. 312.

and by an individualized and founded assessment.

252. In this case, the Court notes that article 523 of the Code of Criminal Procedure does not condition the admissibility of the provisional arrest to the existence of a procedural risk, but merely establishes the possibility that the individual arrested may request his provisional release if he meets the corresponding procedural requirements (*supra* para. 241). Nevertheless, the Court notes that the arrest warrant of October 28, 2008, does take the procedural risk into account (*supra* paras. 97 and 247). Following the provisional arrest warrant of October 28, 2008, the representative filed an appeal refuting the fact that Wong Ho Wing did not have any "known employment in the country" because he was the "founder and main shareholder of a company [that] he administers: the [···] 'Hotel Maury.'" Also, regarding the domicile, he pointed out that, "when he is in [Peru,] he stays at this hotel"①(*supra* para. 98). When deciding the appeal on December 11, 2008, the Chamber indicated with regard to the arguments of procedural risk that "regarding the procedural risk [···], it was not for the Chamber to analyze this for a provisional arrest with a view to extradition; rather it corresponded to a criminal proceeding instituted in [Peru] for a specific offense, which was not the case with [Wong Ho Wing]."②

253. The Court finds that, by failing to evaluate the procedural risk in relation to Wong Ho Wing, it was impossible for the Combined Superior Chamber to examine whether the deprivation of liberty was necessary or whether, in the specific case of Wong Ho Wing, less harmful measures ex-

---

① Appeal filed on October 28, 2008 (evidence file, folio 24). Similarly, on October 28, 2008, Wong Ho Wing had declared that he was in Peru "owing to a business investment of the Hotel Maur[y,] of which he was the majority shareholder, and also to see if he could invest in mines" and that, in Peru, he had "three hotels and a house that are the Hotel Maury and two small hotels and [his] house located in Camacho La Molina." Preliminary statement made by Wong Ho Wing on October 28, 2008, before the Special Criminal Court of El Callao (evidence file, folio 13).
② Decision of December 11, 2008, delivered by the First Transitory Combined Superior Chamber (evidence file, folio 44).

isted that would have ensured the implementation of the extradition. Consequently, the grounds for this decision were insufficient to justify the need for the measure of deprivation of liberty. Since it was not properly founded, following that decision the deprivation of liberty of Wong Ho Wing was arbitrary in violation of paragraphs 1 and 3 of Article 7 of the Convention, in relation to Article 1(1) of this instrument, to the detriment of Wong Ho Wing. Based on this conclusion, the Court considers it unnecessary to rule on the alleged violation of Article 8(1) of the Convention argued by the representative based on the same facts.

254. In addition, regarding the allegation of the detention's lack of predictability, this Court has established that the unpredictability of a deprivation of liberty may make it arbitrary (*supra* para. 238). Thus, the Court has indicated that the law on which the deprivation of personal liberty is based must establish as specifically as possible and "beforehand" the "reasons" for and "conditions" of the deprivation of physical liberty. [1] Compliance with these requirements is designed to protect the individual from arbitrary detention. [2] Among the conditions for deprivation of liberty, the applicable law should include criteria concerning the limits to its duration. [3]

---

[1] *Cf. Case of Chaparro Álvarez and Lapo Íñiguez v. Ecuador*, *supra*, paras. 56 and 57, and *Case of Argüelles et al. v. Argentina*, *supra*, para. 116.

[2] Similarly, the European Court has established that the protection of the individual from arbitrariness means that the law must be sufficiently precise and its application foreseeable. *Cf*. ECHR, *Case of Ryabikin v. Russia*, No. 8320/04. Judgment of June 19, 2008, para. 127; *Case of Baranowski v. Poland*, No. 28358/95. Judgment of March 28, 2000, paras. 50 to 52; *Case of Khudoyorov v. Russia*, No. 6847/02. Judgment of November 8, 2005, para. 125; *Case of Calovskis v. Latvia*, No. 22205/13. Judgment of July 24, 2014, para. 182; *Case of L. M. v. Slovenia*, No. 32863/05. Judgment of June 12, 2014, paras. 121 and 122.

[3] In this regard, the European Court has indicated that: "The Court observes that the domestic law regulated in detail 'detention pending investigation' in ordinary criminal proceedings and set specific time-limits for the pre-trial detention of criminal defendants. However, there was no provision in the domestic law concerning a timelimit specifically applying to detention 'with a view to extradition'. The Court notes that in the absence of clear legal provisions establishing the procedure for ordering and extending detention with a view to extradition and setting time-limits for such detention, the deprivation of liberty to which the applicant was subjected was not circumscribed by adequate safeguards against arbitrariness". ECHR, *Case of Garayev v. Azerbaijan*, No. 53688/08. Judgment of June 10, 2010, para. 99. See also, ECHR, *Case of Ryabikin v. Russia*, No. 8320/04. Judgment of June 19, 2008, para. 129.

Similarly, expert witness Ben Saul indicated that laws that do not include time limits for a detention cannot comply with the requirement of predictability. ① In addition, the Seventh Criminal Court, which decided the request to modify the provisional arrest, indicated that "the absence of a time limit expressly established for the mechanism of the provisional arrest with a view to extradition is incompatible with the principle of predictability."②

255. As the State has recognized, "there is no time limit for deprivation of liberty during the passive extradition proceedings, or a time limit for the final decision on it." This Court notes that neither the Extradition Treaty signed between China and Peru, nor the Peruvian Code of Criminal Procedure establish a time limit for the provisional detention in an extradition process once the formal extradition request is received or, if applicable, a time frame for the extradition process that could limit the duration of the detention. ③ The Court considers that the inclusion of time limits for a detention is a safeguard against the arbitrariness of the deprivation of liberty and, in this case, its omission also permitted the excessive duration of the detention of Wong Ho Wing, as the Court will analyze *infra* (paras. 267 to 275). In this case, the absence of a precise time limit to Wong Ho Wing's detention was used by the judicial authorities as an element to justify keeping him detained (*supra* para. 103). Thus, since it was used as a factor to continue his detention, the lack of predictability of the duration of the detention constituted an additional element of the arbitrariness of the detention, which has already been declared in paragraph 253 *supra*.

256. Nevertheless, the Court notes that, although it is not expressly

---

① *Cf.* Affidavit made by Ben Saul on August 18, 2014 (evidence file, folios 6904 and 6950).
② Decision of the Seventh Criminal Court of El Callao of March 10, 2014 (evidence file, folio 6459).
③ Regarding the length of the detention, the Extradition Treaty between China and Peru only establishes that: "The preventive detention shall conclude if the competent authority of the Requested Party has not received the formal extradition request within 60 days of the detention of the person sought. This period may be extended by a further 30 days when the Requesting Party provides reasons that justify this." Extradition Treaty between the Republic of Peru and the People's Republic of China (evidence file, folio 1635).

established in the pertinent laws, the duration of the proceedings was analyzed in at least three decisions concerning Wong Ho Wing's detention. ① Although only one of those decisions was in favor of the presumed victim, the representative has not provided sufficient arguments as to why the absence of express regulation would violate Article 2② of the Convention. Consequently, this Court finds that it is not in order to rule on the alleged failure to comply with the obligation to adopt domestic legal provisions established in Article 2 of the Convention.

257. Regarding the State's arguments in relation to the failure to file an application for *habeas corpus* (*supra* para. 246), it should be emphasized that these arguments refer to a discussion on admissibility and not on merits, so that it is not necessary to analyze them at this time.

B. The alleged unlawful and arbitrary nature of the detention after the decision of the Constitutional Court

B. 1) Arguments of the parties and of the Commission

258. The Commission argued that "Wong Ho Wing remains deprived of liberty without any legal justification [⋯] because the purpose of his arrest – that is, to ensure his eventual extradition – became pointless [⋯] following the order of the Constitutional Court not to extradite him," and "no criminal proceeding has been instituted in Peru [⋯], under which there would have to be a court order for his pre-trial detention in accordance with the Convention." Therefore, this "situation of legal limbo [⋯] constitutes an additional element of arbitrariness in light of Article 7(3) of the

---

① *Cf.* Vote of Supreme Justice José Antonio Neyra Flores of October 13, 2010, with regard to the decision of the Permanent Criminal Chamber of the Supreme Court of Justice of October 19, 2010 (evidence file, folios 1608 to 1611); Judgment of the 30th Criminal Court Lima of May 30, 2012 (evidence file, folios 6447 and 6448), and Decision of the Seventh Criminal Court of El Callao of March 10, 2014 (evidence file, folio 6463).

② Article 2 of the Convention establishes that: "Where the exercise of any of the rights or freedoms referred to in Article 1 is not already ensured by legislative or other provisions, the States Parties undertake to adopt, in accordance with their constitutional processes and the provisions of this Convention, such legislative or other measures as may be necessary to give effect to those rights or freedoms."

Convention." The Commission has not ruled on the alleged unlawfulness of the detention. Meanwhile, the representative argued that the State had violated Article 7(2) and 7(3) of the Convention "because, [following the decision of the Constitutional Court], there is no criminal proceeding or [⋯] extradition proceeding against Wong Ho Wing that would legally justify the restriction of his personal liberty." The State asked that the representative's "claim to include in the analysis of the case the presumed violation of the said Article 7(2) be disregarded, because it relates to facts that are outside the factual framework of the case delimited by the [Commission, which] has not raised the issue that the Peruvian State may have issued a detention order that was not in keeping with its domestic law." Furthermore, it indicated that the representative "confused [⋯] the exhortation of the [Constitutional] Court with a binding order to prosecute [Wong Ho Wing] in the domestic sphere," and stressed that "the judgment of the Constitutional Court [⋯] did not establish a mandate or order to release [Wong Ho Wing]."

B. 2) Considerations of the Court

259. First, the Court recalls that, contrary to what the State has indicated, the facts relating to Wong Ho Wing's detention following the decision of the Constitutional Court do fall within the factual framework of the proceedings. Also, the Court reiterates that the presumed victims and their representatives may claim the violation of rights other than those included in the Merits Report, provided these relate to the facts contained in that document (*supra* para. 35). Therefore, the Court will proceed to analyze the arguments of the representative and the Commission.

260. Regarding the detention of Wong Ho Wing following the Constitutional Court's judgment, the representative argued that it became unlawful and arbitrary, while the Commission only considered that the detention became arbitrary.

261. The analysis of whether a detention is lawful entails an examination of whether the domestic law was observed when a person was deprived of his liberty (*supra* para. 237). The Court must, therefore, verify whether, following the decision of the Constitutional Court, Wong Ho Wing's detention was in keeping with the laws of Peru.

262. The law in forceat the time of the facts reveals that a person could be deprived of liberty when his extradition was being sought by foreign authorities (*supra* para. 241). Also, according to the law, the extradition process concluded with the Executive Branch's decision on whether or not to grant the extradition.① Pursuant to this law, the Constitutional Court "order[ed] the Peruvian State, represented by the Executive Branch, to refrain from extraditing Wong Ho Wing to the People's Republic of China" (*supra* para. 83). But, accordingly, this decision did not signify the end of the extradition process, and thus the conditions that allowed the detention to be lawful remained in effect. Consequently, the State is not responsible for a violation of Article 7(2) of the American Convention.

263. Regarding the alleged arbitrary nature of the detention following the Constitutional Court's decision (*supra* paras. 258 and 260), the Court reiterates that the order of the Constitutional Court did not signify the end of the extradition process. Moreover, considering that, in the preceding section, this Court has already determined that the detention was arbitrary (*supra* paras. 247 to 255), the Court finds it unnecessary to analyze its alleged arbitrariness following the decision of the Constitutional Court.

C. The duration of the provisional arrest

C.1) Arguments of the parties and of the Commission

264. The Commission indicated that "aduration of four years and nine

---

① *Cf.* Code of Criminal Procedure, promulgated by Legislative Decree No. 957 of July 29, 2004. Available at: http://www.leyes.congreso.gob.pe/Documentos/Decretoslegislativos/00957.pdf, cited in the Commission's Merits Report, folio 24. See also, testimony of Victor García Toma during the public hearing in this case.

months to take a final decision in an extradition process, is *prima facie* problematic, and requires sufficient justification by the State of the reasons for the delay in the final decision." In this regard, it underlined that, while "receiving the diplomatic assurances," the State "was responsible for errors and omissions [⋯] that affected the duration of the process and, consequently, the personal liberty of Wong Ho Wing," and that "the delay was not justified in light of the factors analyzed when examining the guarantee of a reasonable time." It added that, following the Constitutional Court's decision, "a situation of legal limbo [was created that] has resulted in an excessive duration of the deprivation of liberty [⋯] in violation of Article 7(5) ".

265. The representative argued that "Wong Ho Wing [has been] deprived of his personal liberty without judicial control and for an excessive amount of time in violation of Article 7(5) of the Convention." He also indicated that, "in similar cases, [⋯] the assessment of the length of the detention has been made based on the due diligence with which the States had taken measures with a view to the extradition." In this case, "the Executive Branch has [taken] a series of measures that have delayed the adoption of a final decision, despite the existence of a Constitutional Court judgment [⋯] ordering it to refrain from extraditing him." He also stressed that the fact that "procedural law on extradition does not establish a time limit for the deprivation of liberty during the extradition process or a deadline for ending it [⋯] adds a degree of arbitrariness to Wong Ho Wing's situation."

266. The State responded that Article 7(5) of the Convention in relation Article 2 thereof had not been violated. Regarding due diligence, it argued that "in view of the fact that, in the opinion of the jurisdictional authorities, neither the conditions nor the procedural risk in this case had changed, the provisional arrest warrant was confirmed, [⋯] since it continued to seek the procedural purpose of passive extradition and grounds were provided for why the measure should not be modified." The State in-

dicated that, "the extradition process has not concluded, but this is because it has been extended owing to the domestic and international mechanisms for the protection of [Wong Ho Wing's] rights filed by his representative, which have raised concerns about the protection of his rights in relation to the offenses for which his extradition is sought." It added that, "the time that has passed without a final decision is an objective factor that, of itself, does not allow it to be concluded that due diligence has not been exercised, but it is necessary to analyze the specific situation in order to identify whether there are sufficient grounds to justify the delay." Regarding the proportionality of the delay, it claimed that "it is in keeping with the law, because no time limit exists for deprivation of liberty during the passive extradition process, or for the final decision in the process."

C.2) Considerations of the Court

267. Article 7(5) of the Convention establishes that: "[a]ny person detained [⋯] shall be entitled to trial within a reasonable time or to be released without prejudice to the continuation of the proceedings. His release may be subject to guarantees to assure his appearance for trial."

268. In cases relating to preventive or pre-trial detention in the context of criminal proceedings, the Court has indicated that this norm imposes time limits on the duration of preventive detention and, consequently, the authority of the State to ensure the purposes of the proceedings by means of this preventive measure. When the length of the preventive detention exceeds a reasonable time, the State may restrict the liberty of the accused with other less harmful measures that ensure his appearance at trial other than the deprivation of liberty. This right of the individual is accompanied by a judicial obligation to process the criminal proceedings during which the accused is deprived of his liberty with greater diligence and promptness. [1]

---

[1] Cf. *Case of Bayarri v. Argentina. Preliminary objection, merits, reparations and costs.* Judgment of October 30, 2008. Series C No. 187, para. 70, and *Case of Argüelles et al. v. Argentina, supra,* para. 129.

269. The American Convention does not establish a limitation to the exercise of the guarantee established in Article 7(5) of the Convention based on the reasons or circumstances why the person has been detained.① Consequently, the Court finds that this provisions is also applicable to detention for extradition purposes, as in this case.

270. The European Court of Human Rights has indicated, similarly, that detention with a view to extradition "will be justified only for was long as extradition proceedings are being conducted. It follows that if such proceedings are not being prosecuted with due diligence, the detention will cease to be justified under [the Convention]."② Thus, if the extradition proceedings are not conducted within a reasonable time, the person must be released, without prejudice to other less harmful measures than deprivation of liberty being adopted that ensure his appearance before the court.

271. In this case, Wong Ho Wing was detained in prison for more than five years following his initial arrest on October 27, 2008 (*supra* paras. 60 and 96). Subsequently, on March 10, 2014, the Seventh Criminal Court of El Callao changed this measure to "an order to appear in court periodically: house arrest" *supra* paras. 112 and 113), and he is currently detained in this way. Regarding the duration of the deprivation of liberty of Wong Ho Wing, first, the Court emphasizes that, from the time of his arrest and to date, the judicial authorities have committed different errors that have contributed to prolonging his detention (*supra* paras. 215 to 219). In this regard, the State has not acted with the greater diligence required when a person is detained (*supra* paras. 222 and 268).

---

① *Cf. Case of Vélez Loor v. Panama*, *supra*, para. 107.
② *Cf.* ECHR, *Case of Kolompar v. Belgium*, No. 11613/85. Judgment of September 24, 1992, para. 36; *Case of Quinn v. France*, No. 18580/91. Judgment of March 22, 1995, para. 48; *Case of Chahal v. The United Kingdom* [GS], No. 22414/93. Judgment of November 15, 1996, para. 113; *Case of Ryabikin v. Russia*, No. 8320/04. Judgment of June 19, 2008, para. 131; *Case of Akram Karimov v. Russia*, No. 62892/12. Judgment of May 28, 2014, para. 156, and *Case of Khomullo v. Ukraine*, No. 47593/10. Judgment of November 27, 2014, para. 52.

272. Second, the Court recalls that the applicable regulations do not establish atime limit for preventive detention in extradition proceedings, once the formal extradition request has been received, or a time frame for the extradition process that might limit the duration of the detention (*supra* para. 255). This absence of a time frame was used in judicial decisions concerning Wong Ho Wing's detention to justify its duration (*supra* paras. 103 and 255), preventing the analysis of the reasonable nature of the length of the presumed victim's detention and allowing it to be prolonged excessively.

273. Lastly, the Court reiterates that the existence of precautionary and provisional measures cannot be used to justify the excessive duration of the extradition proceedings or the detention of Wong Ho Wing.[①] In various orders on the provisional measures ordered in this case, the Court indicated that, "while this case is decided by the organs of the inter-American system, Peru may continue to adopt the necessary measures in relation to Wong Ho Wing to prevent his eventual extradition and the corresponding administration of justice in the requesting State from being ineffective or unrealistic."[②] This did not justify the deprivation of liberty of Wong Ho Wing indefinitely. Less harmful measures exist than imprisonment in a detention center that Peru could have adopted to avoid his eventual extradition becoming unrealistic, and this was not considered or analyzed by the State until March 2014. The Court stresses that orders for provisional measures must be interpreted taking into account the American Convention and this Court's case law. Therefore, due diligence in the extradition

---

① Similarly, see, ECHR, *Case of Ryabikin v. Russia*, No. 8320/04. Judgment of June 19, 2008, para. 132, and *Case of Gaforov v. Russia*, No. 25404/09. Judgment of October 21, 2010, para. 200.

② *Case of Wong Ho Wing. Provisional measures with regard to Peru.* Order of the Court of January 29, 2014, *considerandum* 14. See also, *Matter of Wong Ho Wing. Provisional measures with regard to Peru.* Order of the Court of May 28, 2010, *considerandum* 18; *Matter of Wong Ho Wing. Provisional measures with regard to Peru.* Order of the Court of August 22, 2013, *considerandum* 13.

process was required to ensure that the measures adopted were not arbitrary (*supra* paras. 248 and 255).

274. Similarly, in 2014, when examining the situation of Wong Ho Wing, the Ombudsman stated that:

> Although extradition proceedings do not have a legal time limit, the deprivation of liberty of the Chinese citizen for 39 months represented a delay that could not be justified by the fact that his defense had made use of constitutional or supranational proceedings. Consequently, [the State] was urged to adopt the corresponding measures that would allow the situation of [Wong] Ho Wing to be defined promptly.
>
> Also, it was recommended that the decision adopted must respect the Constitutional Court's arguments in the application for *habeas corpus* filed on behalf of Wong Ho Wing [⋯], ordering the Peruvian State to refrain from extraditing this individual. ①

275. Based on the preceding conclusions, the State violated Article 7 (1) and 7(5) of the Convention, in relation to Article 1(1) of this instrument, to the detriment of Wong Ho Wing. The arguments on the alleged lack of judicial control will be analyzed in the following section.

D. Right to appeal before a competent court

D. 1) Arguments of the parties and of the Commission

276. The Commission affirmed that "in the wake of the judgment of the Constitutional Court of May 24, 2011, [on October 18, 2011,] the representative [⋯] sought his immediate release based on the order in that judgment," but this "came up against several problems because the provisional arrest file was in the hands of the Ministry of Justice." In its Merits Report, the Commission indicated that, at that date, "Wong Ho Wing ha

---

① Note of the Ombudsman of September 4, 2014 (evidence file, folio 7293).

[d] not obtained a court ruling that, in the context of the remedies filed by his legal representative, decide[d] on the lawfulness of his detention after the judgment of the Constitutional Court," thus violating the "right recognized in Article 7(6) of the Convention".

277. The representative argued that, "[i]n this case, the Peruvian authorities have not ensured the effectiveness of the remedy of *habeas corpus*." In this regard, he indicated that "six applications for *habeas corpus* had been filed," and the third one "was declared admissible by the Constitutional Court"; however, "the Peruvian State has no complied with this decision, because it has not denied the request for Wong Ho Wing's extradition and ordered his release." In addition, he indicated that, with regard to the fourth, fifth and sixth application for *habeas corpus*, the judicial authorities had "not decided on their merits to ensure his personal liberty." In this regard, he stressed that, at the time of the submission of the motions and arguments brief, the "fourth application for *habeas corpus*, filed on November 16, 2011," had not been decided after two years and two months, "which evidently also violates the guarantee of a reasonable time established in Article 8(1) of the American Convention." He also indicated that the fifth and sixth applications for *habeas corpus* filed on March 13, 2012, and April 26, 2013, had also not been decided. In addition, he indicated that the response of the Permanent Criminal Chamber to the release request of October 10, 2011, "mean[t] that the Peruvian State did not guarantee, in the terms of Article 25(1) of the Convention [⋯], a simple and prompt remedy, but rather obliged the [presumed] victim [⋯] to use a series of remedies that, owing to the passage of time, make execution of the Constitutional Court's judgment unrealistic." In addition, he indicated that in the context of the release request of October 18, 2011, "officials of the Executive Branch [⋯] failed to forward the provisional arrest file to the Seventh Criminal Court of El Callao [⋯], even in response to two ur-

gent requests, so that it could take a decision on Wong Ho Wing's release in execution of the ruling of the Constitutional Court." He emphasized that this "serious omission [···] prevented the Seventh Criminal Court [···] from carrying out prompt judicial control for more than two years and eight month." He concluded that the Peruvian authorities had not ensured the effectiveness of the application for *habeas corpus* on behalf of Wong Ho Wing, in violation of Articles 7(6), 8(1), 25(1), 25(2) (a) and 25(2) (c) of the Convention, in relation to Article 1(1) of this instrument.

278. The State, with regard to the alleged violation of Article 7(6) of the Convention, denied that it had had "the intention not to provide the provisional arrest file to the courts in order to decide the release request filed following the judgment the Constitutional Court." It indicated that the "Ministry, at the appropriate moment, complied with the judge's request and, after he had ruled on the request, he ordered that the respective file be returned to the Ministry." Added to this, it indicated that, "on March 10, 2014, the Seventh Criminal Court of El Callao, declared the release request admissible [···], and therefore annulled the provisional arrest warrant and ordered the coercive measure of an order to appear in court periodically [···] because the Executive Branch had not yet taken a final decision on the extradition request." Regarding the relationship of this to the alleged violation of Articles 25(1) and 25(2) (a), Peru stressed that the representative was referring to the violation of these provisions in the sense that "the jurisdictional authorities before whom he had filed three applications for *habeas corpus* had not decided them favorably," considering that "the State does not fail to comply with its obligation to administer justice [···] if this does not provide a result that satisfies the petitioner's claims." Also, it asked the Court "to set aside the claim to [···] include this in the analysis of the case, [···] because [the facts described] are outside the factual framework of the case delimited by the [Commission], since the latter has

not questioned the specific situation of the [*habeas corpus*] or other release requests [⋯] (other than that [⋯] of October 18, 2011)."

D. 2) Considerations of the Court

279. First, the Court notes that the applications for *habeas corpus* filed on behalf of Wong Ho Wing do form part of the factual framework of this case (*supra* para. 35). In this regard, the Court reiterates that the representatives of the presumed victims may allege violations that differ from those described by the Commission in its Merits Report.

280. As can be seen, with regard to the applications for *habeas corpus*, the Commission argued the violation of Article 7(6), while the representative also argued the violation of Articles 8 and 25 of the Convention. The Court recalls that Articles 7(6) and 25 of the Convention refer to different spheres of protection. In this section, the Court will analyze whether the State gave Wong Ho Wing the possibility of appealing before a competent court "in order that the court may decide without delay on the lawfulness of his arrest or detention and order his release if the arrest or detention is unlawful," in accordance with Article 7(6) of the Convention. Given that Article 7(6) of the Convention has its own legal content and that the principle of practical effects (*effet utile*) crosscuts the due protection of all the rights recognized in this instrument, the Court finds it unnecessary to examine the alleged violation of Article 25 of the Convention. ①

281. Furthermore, the Court has established that, under Article 7(6) of the Convention, the authority that should decide of the lawfulness of the arrest or detention is a judge or court. Thus, the Convention is safeguarding the fact that control of the deprivation of liberty should be judicial. ② In addition, the Court has stated that it is not sufficient that remedies con-

---

① *Cf. Case of Anzualdo Castro v. Peru*, *supra*, para. 77, and *Case of Rochac Hernández et al. v. El Salvador. Merits, reparations and costs*. Judgment of October 14, 2014. Series C No. 285, para. 162.
② *Cf. Case of Chaparro Álvarez and Lapo Íñiguez. v. Ecuador*, *supra*, para. 128, and *Case of Espinoza Gonzáles v. Peru*, *supra*, para. 135.

cerning the judicial control of detention exist formally in the law, but they must also be effective; that is, comply with the purpose of obtaining a prompt decision on the lawfulness of the arrest or detention. ① Thus, this Court notes that the laws of Peru establish judicial remedies to control the lawfulness of the deprivation of liberty. Indeed, in this case, the representative filed four release requests and one request for a change in the provisional detention. He also filed six applications for *habeas corpus*. Not all of them have been decided in favor of his claims and only one of them resulted in effective control of the deprivation of liberty (in 2014, when the detention method was changed to house arrest owing to the time that had elapsed). However, this does not mean that the remedies filed were ineffective. To determine this, the Court must examine the arguments and the processing of each of these remedies.

282. The arguments of the Commission and the representative include specific allegations about the release requests of October 5 and 18, 2011 (*supra* para. 104), as well as about the applications for *habeas corpus* filed on February 9, 2010, November 16, 2011, March 13, 2012, and April 26, 2013 (*supra* paras. 79, 88, 108 and 109). The Court will now examine the effectiveness of each of these requests and remedies. It will not examine the first two applications for *habeas corpus* that were filed, or the other release requests the effectiveness of which has not been questioned.

D. 2. a) *Habeas corpus* of February 9, 2010

283. The Court notes that the application of February 9, 2010, was the third application for *habeas corpus* filed on behalf of Wong Ho Wing, and it was finally decided by the appeal based on constitutional injury admitted by the Constitutional Court on May 24, 2011 (*supra* paras. 79 and 81 to 83). In this regard, the Court notes that the alleged ineffectiveness of

---

① *Cf. Case of Acosta Calderón v. Ecuador*, supra, para. 97, and *Case of Espinoza Gonzáles v. Peru*, supra, para. 135.

this application for *habeas corpus* refers to the supposed lack of effectiveness of the appeal based on constitutional injury, owing to the alleged failure to comply with the Constitutional Court's decision of May 24, 2011. These arguments have already been analyzed in the preceding section (*supra* paras. 260 to 263). Moreover, the Court reiterates that the Constitutional Court did not order Wong Ho Wing's release (*supra* para. 262).

D. 2. b) Release request of October 5, 2011

284. The representative filed this request before the Permanent Criminal Chamber of the Supreme Court of Justice and, on October 10, 2011, the Chamber declared that the request should be "filed [⋯] before the corresponding court" (*supra* para. 104). The representative argued that this answer "mean[t] that the Peruvian State did not guarantee a simple and prompt remedy, in the terms of Article 25(1) of the Convention" (*supra* para. 277). In this regard, the Court notes that, although it is true that States must make adequate and effective remedies available to the persons under its jurisdiction, the presumed victims have the obligation to file such remedies or requests in keeping with the laws in force and before the authority with competence to decide them.① The representative has not argued that the Permanent Criminal Chamber was the competent court to decide this request. To the contrary, the evidence reveals that, following the decision of October 10, 2011, he filed another release request before the Seventh Criminal Court of El Callao (*supra* para. 104).

D. 2. c) Release request of October 18, 2011, and *habeas corpus* of November 16, 2011

285. The Court notes that the request of October 18, 2011, was filed before the Seventh Criminal Court of El Callao (*supra* para. 104). The representative based his request on the Constitutional Court's order to re-

---

① *Cf. Case of Velásquez Rodríguez v. Honduras. Merits, supra*, para. 67, and *Case of Brewer Carías v. Venezuela. Preliminary objections*. Judgment of May 26, 2014. Series C No. 278, para. 87.

frain from extraditing Wong Ho Wing. In this regard, he indicated that "[j]udgments delivered by the constitutional judges have prevalence over those of the other courts and must be executed on pain of incurring responsibility. Thus, the judgment that orders [the State ···] to refrain from extraditing [Wong Ho Wing] requires immediate execution." Therefore, he indicated that, following the decision of the Constitutional Court, "there is no legal pretext or provision that permits an individual to remain deprived of liberty." He also affirmed, in general, that preventive detention should not exceed a reasonable time. ①

286. The evidence provided reveals that, initially, the judge was unable to decide the release request because the provisional arrest file was with the Ministry of Justice. Following several requests, the Ministry of Justice forwarded the file to the Seventh Criminal Court on November 25, 2011 (*supra* paras. 105 and 106). On December 1, 2011, this court answered the request indicating that, "noting from a review of the extradition file forwarded by the Ministry of Justice that the issue of a final decision is still pending [it decided that the release request should be presented] opportunely and pursuant to the law"②(*supra* para. 107).

287. At the same time, on November 16, 2011, the representative filed a fourth application for *habeas corpus* against the judge's decision to return the provisional arrest file to the Ministry of Justice before deciding the release request (*supra* para. 108). In this application for *habeas corpus*, the representative indicated that "if the Constitutional Court has declared extradition inadmissible, the provisional arrest in this same context has no validity because it is a subsidiary measure of the extradition process."③ On May 30, 2012, the Special Criminal Court declared the application for *ha-*

---

① *Cf.* Request dated October 18, 2011 (evidence file, folios 306 and 310 to 312).
② Decision of the Seventh Criminal Court of El Callao of December 1, 2011 (evidence file, folio 6472).
③ Application for *habeas corpus* of November 16, 2011 (evidence file, folio 326).

beas corpus inadmissible. In this decision, the court referred to the different time limits for detention during a criminal proceeding established by law, and the ways in which these could be extended.① Nevertheless, it did not refer to the application of these provisions to the specific case. However, it did examine whether the proceedings had been conducted with due diligence and used this Court's criteria to examine the reasonable time. In this regard, it indicated that: (a) no delay by the judicial authorities could be noted that would affect the reasonable time; (b) regarding the complexity of the case, it considered that Wong Ho Wing "was deprived of his liberty based on a request made by the People's Republic of China, despite the [⋯] prohibition of his extradition [ordered by the Constitutional Court]." It also stressed that the extradition process had not concluded, because "the Executive Branch, in a duly motivated decision, must annul the extradition process," and (c) regarding the procedural activity of the interested party, it indicated that "even though it cannot be observed that this has obstructed the proceedings, based on the preceding arguments, the constitutional application must be rejected."②

---

① In this regard, the decision indicated that "[a]rticle 137 of the Code of Criminal Procedure (currently in force) amended by article 2 of Legislative Decree No. 983, published on July 22, 2007, has established that 'The detention shall not last more than nine months in the ordinary proceeding and eighteen months in the special proceeding, provided that the requirements established in article 135 of the Code of Criminal Procedure are met. In the case of proceedings for offenses of drug-trafficking, terrorism, spying and others of a complex nature against more than ten accused, that have harmed an equal number of persons or the State, the length of the detention shall be doubled. When the time limit has expired, without the delivery of a judgment in first instance, the immediate release of the accused shall be ordered, and the judge must establish the necessary measures to ensure his presence at the trial.' [⋯] The said article also established that 'When the circumstances are especially complex or result in a special prolongation of the investigation and the accused could evade prosecution, the detention may be extended for an equal length of time.' And "When the offense has been committed by a criminal organization and the accused may evade prosecution or interfere with the probative activities, the detention may be extended for an equal length of time. The extension of the detention shall be decided by a duly founded order, issued by the judge on his own motion, or requested by the prosecutor and notified to the accused. An appeal is admissible against this order, to be decided by the Chamber, following the opinion of the Superior Prosecutor, within 72 hours." Decision of the 30th Special Criminal Court of Lima of May 30, 2012 (evidence file, folios 6445 and 6446).
② Decision of the 30th Special Criminal Court of Lima of May 30, 2012 (evidence file, folios 6447 and 6448).

288. This Court has established that the competent authority's analysis of a judicial remedy contesting the lawfulness of deprivation of liberty cannot be reduced to a mere formality; rather the reasons cited by the applicant must be examined and referred to expressly, pursuant to the parameters established by the American Convention. ①

289. When examining the request release, the Seventh Court failed to rule on the allegation that, following the Constitutional Court's judgment there was no reason for the detention of Wong Ho Wing. Furthermore, it failed to rule on the reasonableness of the time that he had been detained. The same omissions can be observed in the decision on the application for *habeas corpus* filed on November 16, 2011. In this regard, the Court notes that the examination of a reasonable time made in this decision did not analyze whether the detention of Wong Ho Wing was still necessary and proportionate. To the contrary, this decision was based on the fact that the extradition process had not yet concluded.

290. Based on the foregoing, this Court finds that the release request of October 18, 2011, and the application for *habeas corpus* filed on November 16, 2011, were not effective to carry out an adequate control of the presumed victim's detention. Consequently, the State violated Article 7(6) of the Convention, in relation to Article 1(1) of this instrument, to the detriment of Wong Ho Wing.

D. 2. d) Failure to comply with a reasonable time when deciding these remedies

291. The Commission and the representative argued that a reasonable time had not been respected when deciding the release request of October 18, 2011, and the applications for *habeas corpus* of November 16, 2011, March 13, 2012, and April 26, 2013 (*supra* paras. 79, 88, 104, 108 and

---

① *Cf. Case of López Álvarez v. Honduras*, *supra*, para. 96.

109). In this regard, it should be underscored that the release request of October 18, 2011, was decided on December 1, 2011 (*supra* paras. 107 and 286).① The *habeas corpus* presented on November 16, 2011, was declared inadmissible on May 30, 2012 (*supra* paras. 108 and 287), and the *habeas corpus* presented on March 13, 2012, was still pending a decision on December 1, 2014, when the State's last report in this regard was forwarded.② Lastly, the *habeas corpus* presented on April 26, 2013, was declared inadmissible on October 24, 2014 (*supra* para. 109).

292. The Court recalls that, in general, it has considered the followingfactors to determine whether the time is reasonable: (a) the complexity of the matter; (b) the procedural activity of the interested party; (c) the conduct of the judicial authorities, and (d) the effects on the legal situation of the person involved in the proceedings (*supra* para. 209). However, the State did not present any evidence or information to justify the duration of these proceedings. The Court considers that taking one month to decide a release request that, by law, should be decided in 48 hours,③ and six months or more to decide the applications for *habeas corpus*, is clearly ex-

---

① During the proceeding, the judge and the representative of the presumed victim presented various requests for the Ministry of Justice to forward the provisional arrest file so that a decision could be taken; this was sent on November 25, 2011 (*supra* paras. 105, 106 and 286).

② *Cf*. The State's brief of December 1, 2014 (merits file, folio 1159). During this proceeding, on March 13, 2012, the application was declared "absolutely inadmissible." The decision was subsequently revoked on December 26, 2012. On April 29, 2013, the application was declared admissible (*supra note* 112). On August 4, 2014, the Public Attorney's Office presented its answering brief. *Cf*. Decision of the 41st Criminal Court of March 13, 2012 (evidence file, folios 8504 to 8507); Decision of the Second Special Criminal Chamber for Prisoners at Liberty of the Superior Court of Justice of Lima of December 26, 2012 (evidence file, folios 8508 to 8516), and Brief of the Public Attorney of the Judiciary of Peru of August 4, 2014 (evidence file, folio 8522).

③ In this regard, the Procedural Code in force under Legislative Decree No. 638 of April 27, 1991, establishes: "Article 184. Once the release request has been presented by the detainee, the prosecutor shall draw up the interlocutory motion within 24 hours and shall forward this to the judge, notifying the other parties to the proceedings. Article 185. The judge shall take a decision within 24 hours of receiving the interlocutory motion, shall notify the parties to the proceedings, and shall advise the prosecutor of his decision. The decision may be appealed within two working days." Code of Criminal Procedure, promulgated by Legislative Decree No. 638 of April 27, 1991 (evidence file, folio 8624).

cessive. Therefore, this constitutes an additional violation of Article 7(6) of the Convention, in relation to Article 1(1) of this instrument, to the detriment of Wong Ho Wing.

E. Alleged violation of the right to personal integrity of Wong Ho Wing

293. According to the representative, Wong Ho Wing "has suffered harm to his mental and moral integrity owing to the arbitrary deprivation of his liberty [⋯], and this constitutes a violation of his right to personal integrity." The State did not refer to this allegation by the representative, beyond contesting its inclusion in the factual framework of this case (*supra* para. 33).

294. In its case law, the Court has determined that, often, one of the inevitable consequences of deprivation of liberty is harm to the enjoyment of other human rights, such as the right to privacy and to family life, rather than merely the right to personal liberty.① However, this restriction of rights that results from the deprivation of liberty or is one of its collateral effects must be strictly limited because, under international law, any restriction of a human right can only be justified when it is necessary in a democratic society.② Although the Court has also stated that the restriction of the right to personal integrity, among others, is not justified based on the deprivation of liberty, and is prohibited by international law,③ an examination of the judgments in the relevant cases heard by this Court reveals that, in those cases, the detention conditions were cruel, inhuman or degrading, and even caused death or injuries, frequently of a very serious na-

---

① Cf. *Case of the Gómez Paquiyauri Brothers v. Peru. Merits, reparations and costs*. Judgment of July 8, 2004. Series C No. 110, para. 108, and *Case of Norín Catrimán et al. (Leaders, members and an activist of the Mapuche Indigenous People) v. Chile, supra*, para. 390.

② Cf. *Case of the "Juvenile Re-education Institute" v. Paraguay. Preliminary objections, merits, reparations and costs*. Judgment of September 2, 2004. Series C No. 112, para. 154, and *Case of Norín Catrimán et al. (Leaders, members and an activist of the Mapuche Indigenous People) v. Chile, supra*, para. 390.

③ Cf. *Case of the "Juvenile Re-education Institute" v. Paraguay, supra*, para. 155, and *Case of Norín Catrimán et al. (Leaders, members and an activist of the Mapuche Indigenous People) v. Chile, supra*, para. 390.

ture, to a significant number of inmates. ①

295. In this case, the representative based the alleged violation of the right to personal integrity of Wong Ho Wing on his arbitrary deprivation of liberty. The Court finds that these arguments refer to what the Court has called a collateral effect of the detention. ② In addition, the Court recalls that the facts relating to the detention conditions of Wong Ho Wing in Peru are not part of this case (*supra* para. 36). Consequently, the Court finds that the State did not violate Article 5 of the American Convention, in relation to Article 1(1) of this instrument, to the detriment of Wong Ho Wing. Notwithstanding the foregoing, when ordering any reparations that are in order, the Court will take into account, insofar as pertinent, the harm caused to Wong Ho Wing owing to his detention.

XII

REPARATIONS

(Application of Article 63(1) of the American Convention)

296. Based on the provisions of Article 63(1) of the American Convention, ③ the Court has indicated that any violation of an international obligation that has caused harm entails the obligation to make adequate reparation, and that this provisions reflects a customary norm that is one of the

---

① Cf. Case of the "Juvenile Re-education Institute" v. Paraguay, supra, para. 170, and Case of Norín Catrimán et al. (Leaders, members and an activist of the Mapuche Indigenous People) v. Chile, supra, para. 390.

② Cf. Case of the "Juvenile Re-education Institute" v. Paraguay, supra, para. 154, and Case of Norín Catrimán et al. (Leaders, members and an activist of the Mapuche Indigenous People) v. Chile, supra, para. 391.

③ Article 63(1) of the Convention stipulates that: "[i]f the Court finds that there has been a violation of a right or freedom protected by this Convention, the Court shall rule that the injured party be ensured the enjoyment of his right or freedom that was violated. It shall also rule, if appropriate, that the consequences of the measure or situation that constituted the breach of such right or freedom be remedied and that fair compensation be paid to the injured party."

basic principles of contemporary international law on State responsibility. [1]

297. The reparation of the harm caused by the violation of an international obligation requires, whenever possible, full restitution (*restitutio in integrum*), which consists in the re-establishment of the previous situation. If this is not feasible, as in most cases of human rights violations, the Court will determine measures that ensure the rights that have been violated and redress the consequences of the violations. [2] Therefore, the Court has found it necessary to award different measures of reparation in order to redress the harm integrally, so that in addition to pecuniary compensation, the measures of restitution and satisfaction, and also guarantees of non-repetition have special relevance for the harm caused. [3]

298. This Court has established that reparations must have a causal nexus to the facts of the case, the violations that have been declared, the harm proved, and the measures requested to repair this harm. The Court must observe the concurrence of these factors to rule appropriately and pursuant to law. [4]

299. Taking into consideration the violations declared in the preceding chapters, the Court will now examine the claims presented by the Commission and the representative, as well as the arguments of the State, in light of the criteria established in its case law concerning the nature and scope of the obligation to make reparation, [5] in order to establish measures to redress the harm caused to the victim.

---

[1] Cf. *Case of Velásquez Rodríguez v. Honduras. Reparations and costs.* Judgment of July 21, 1989. Series C No. 7, para. 25, and *Case of Cruz Sánchez et al. v. Peru*, supra, para. 451.

[2] Cf. *Case of Velásquez Rodríguez v. Honduras. Reparations and costs*, supra, para. 25, and *Case of Cruz Sánchez et al. v. Peru*, supra, para. 452.

[3] Cf. *Case of Cantoral Benavides v. Peru. Reparations and costs.* Judgment of December 3, 2001. Series C No. 88, paras. 79 to 81, and *Case of Cruz Sánchez et al. v. Peru*, supra, para. 452.

[4] Cf. *Case of Ticona Estrada v. Bolivia. Merits, reparations and costs.* Judgment of November 27, 2008. Series C No. 191, para. 110, and *Case of Cruz Sánchez et al. v. Peru*, supra, para. 453.

[5] Cf. *Case of Velásquez Rodríguez v. Honduras. Reparations and costs*, supra, paras. 25 to 27, and *Case of Cruz Sánchez et al. v. Peru*, supra, para. 454.

A. Injured party

300. The Court reiterates that, pursuant to Article 63(1) of the Convention, it considers the injured party to be anyone declared a victim of the violation of any right recognized therein. Therefore, this Court considers that Wong Ho Wing is the "injured party" and, in his capacity as victim of the violations declared in Chapters X and XI, he will be the beneficiary of the following measures ordered by the Court.

B. Measures of integral reparation: restitution and satisfaction

B. 1) Restitution

B. 1. a) Extradition process

301. The Commission asked the Court to order the State "[t]o establish the measures necessary to ensure that the extradition process is brought to a conclusion as soon as possible, in accordance with the procedures set forth in the Peruvian Code of Criminal Procedure, denying the extradition request in strict compliance with the judgment of the Constitutional Court of May 24, 2011." In addition, it asked that in compliance with this measure, the State ensure that none of its authorities implement mechanisms that would obstruct or delay execution of that judgment. The representative asked the Court to order the State to take a decision in the extradition process as soon as possible, "denying the extradition request." He also asked that, in no circumstance, should Wong Ho Wing be extradited to the People's Republic of China where his life and personal integrity were at risk and, as a result, the total disintegration of his immediate family." The State advised that the extradition process was at the final stage, so that the Commission's request would "be assessed by the corresponding entities, in accordance with the laws of Peru in force and the regular domestic procedures, based on the Court's decision" in this case.

302. The Court recalls that it has concluded that the State has not acted with the necessary due diligence in the extradition process, which has

resulted in the excessive duration of the extradition proceedings and of the deprivation of Wong Ho Wing's liberty. This constitutes a violation of the guarantee of a reasonable time in the processing of the extradition proceedings and of his detention in violation of Articles 7(1), 7(5) and 8(1) of the Convention, in relation to Article 1(1) of this instrument, as decided in Chapters X and XI of this Judgment. Consequently, the Court finds that the State should take the final decision in the extradition process as soon as possible, taking into account paragraphs 193 to 223 of this Judgment.

303. In addition, bearing in mind the nature of the provisional measures ordered in this case, the Court considers that the State's obligations under these measures is replaced by the measures ordered in this Judgment as of the dateof its notification.

B. 1. b) Review of the provisional arrest

304. The Commission asked that the Court order the State to review *ex officio* the provisional detention of Wong Ho Wing, taking into consideration his legal situation following the conclusion of the extradition proceedings. In particular, it asked that any judicial decision on the personal liberty of Wong Ho Wing should be made "in strict compliance with the principles of exceptionality, necessity and proportionality." The representative requested the immediate release of Wong Ho Wing. The State asserted that, on March 10, 2014, the Seventh Criminal Court of El Callao had revoked the provisional arrest warrant and issued the measure of an order to appear in court periodically: house arrest, establishing a financial surety and the prohibition to leave the country. It argued that the court had taken into consideration the time Wong Ho Wing had spent in the Sarita Colonia Prison, and considered it appropriate to modify the measures; hence, the State considered that it had complied with the Commission's request.

305. The Court recalls that Wong Ho Wing has been deprived of liberty since October 2008. Even though he has been kept under house arrest

since March 2014, the Court reiteratesits findings in this Judgment as regards the arbitrary nature of the detention, the excessive time taken to process the extradition proceedings, and the duration of the provisional arrest. The Court recalls that the purpose of the actual deprivation of liberty of Wong Ho Wing is his extradition. Therefore, taking into account the measure of reparation according to which the State must take a final decision in the extradition proceedings (*supra* para. 302), the Court orders the State to review, immediately, the deprivation of liberty of Wong Ho Wing, taking into account the standards established in Chapter XI of this Judgment. In addition, the State should take into consideration the time that he has remained deprived of his liberty to date and his actual situation and health care needs.

B.2) Satisfaction

B.2.a) Publication and dissemination of the Judgment

306. The representative asked that the Court order the publication of: (a) the official summary of this Judgment, once, in the official gazette; (b) the official summary of this Judgment, once, in a national newspaper with widespread circulation, and (c) the Judgment in its entirety, available for one year, on an official website. The State indicated that, if the Court so requests, it would not object to the publication of the Judgment.

307. The Court establishes, as it has in other cases,[①] that the State should publish, within six months of notification of this Judgment: (a) the official summary of this Judgment prepared by the Court, once, in the official gazette; (b) the official summary of this Judgment prepared by the Court, once, in a national newspaper with widespread circulation, and (c) the Judgment in its entirety, available for one year, on an official website.

B.3) Other measures requested

---

① *Cf. Case of Cantoral Benavides v. Peru. Reparations and costs*, *supra*, para. 79, and *Case of Cruz Sánchez et al. v. Peru*, *supra*, para. 466.

308. In addition, the representative asked that: (i) the authorities of the Judiciary and of the Executive Branch who have intervened in this case be investigated; (ii) a public act to acknowledge international responsibility be held, and (iii) medical, psychological and psychosocial treatment be provided to Wong Ho Wing. For its part, the Commission asked that the Court order measures of non-repetition. The State objected to these measures.

309. This Court does not find it necessary to order these other measures requested by the representative and the Commission, considering that the delivery of this Judgment and the reparations ordered in it are sufficient and appropriate.

C. Compensation

310. The Commission asked the Court to order that full reparation be made to Wong Ho Wing for the violations that were established.

311. The representative asked that the Court determine the consequential damages and the loss of earnings of Wong Ho Wing. In this regard, he indicated that, as a result of the arbitrary deprivation of his liberty for more than five years, the victim was unable to administer his businesses in the United States of America and, for this, he requested compensation of US $ 3,212,713.55, which corresponded to the value of two restaurants and the loss of their leasing rates. He also requested that the determination of the pecuniary damage be carried out in the jurisdiction of the Peruvian State in application of domestic norms. Furthermore, he indicated that, before being deprived of his liberty, Wong Ho Wing earned approximately US $ 10 000.00 a month from his business activities. Regarding the non-pecuniary damage, he asked that compensation be awarded for the suffering and affliction caused to the victim and asked the Court to determine the non-pecuniary damage taking into consideration the principle of *pretium doloris* of the victim, and establishing an amount, in equity.

312. The State reiterated that it had not violated the rights recognized in the American Convention, so that it had no obligation to make reparation. Nevertheless, it affirmed its opposition "to the elevated nature of the amounts requested, [and that] this type of claim sought to convert the Court into an economic entity, which was not in keeping with the object and purpose of its functions." It pointed out that the total requested by the representative amounted to a sum that "is evidently incompatible with the inter-American standards ineffect under the inter-American system and any other supranational system for the protection of human rights as regards reparations in favor of a single person." It also argued that the representative had not provided any evidence of the business losses, that the elements included as pecuniary damage were not included among the facts of this case, and that it would have been necessary to prove their causal nexus with facts of the case.

313. In its case law, this Court has developed the concept of pecuniary damage and the situations in which it should be compensated and has established that pecuniary damage supposes "the loss of, or detriment to, the income of the victims, the expenses incurred as a result of the facts, and the consequences of a pecuniary nature that have a causal nexus with the facts of the case."① In addition, the Court has developed the concept of non-pecuniary damage and has established that this "may include the suffering and affliction caused to the direct victim and his family, the impairment of values that have great significance for the individual, and also the changes of a non-pecuniary nature, in the living conditions of the victim or his family."②

314. From the information provided, the Court notes that Wong Ho

---

① *Case of Bámaca Velásquez v. Guatemala. Reparations and costs.* Judgment of February 22, 2002. Series C No. 91, para. 43, and *Case of Argüelles et al. v. Argentina, supra,* para. 286.
② *Case of the "Street Children" (Villagrán Morales et al.). Reparations and costs.* Judgment of May 26, 2001. Series C No. 77, para. 84, and *Case of Argüelles et al. v. Argentina, supra,* para. 286.

Wing and his wifeindicated that the family was in the hotel business in Peru. Also, in his affidavit, Wong Ho Wing indicated that he had two restaurants and an importing company in the United States of America, and that these businesses ceased operations because a building burned down and he "was unable to administer the company."① In addition, his wife asserted that "his businesses in the United States closed down owing to his absence; [but t]he family business in Peru remains, although the situation is not good."② Nevertheless, the evidence provided only authenticates the registration of the limited liability company "*Inversiones Turísticas Maury SAC*," founded by the victim. ③

315. Consequently, the Court notes that it does not have evidence authenticating the representative's calculation of pecuniary damage, or the income that Wong Ho Wing received before the events that resulted in the human rights violations declared in this case. However, the body of evidence reveals that Wong Ho Wing had several businesses before he was deprived of his liberty. Therefore, the Court finds it reasonable to consider that Wong Ho Wing suffered a loss of earnings during the time he remained detained.

316. Regarding the non-pecuniary damage, the Court notes that, in his affidavit, Wong Ho Wingstated that, while he was in prison, he "suffered immense emotional and physical devastation [⋯] as a result of the harsh environment of the prison, and also the constant fear that he would be extradited without any apparent reason." He also indicated that "if it

---

① Affidavit made by Wong Ho Wing on August 18, 2014 (evidence file, folio 6852).
② Affidavit made by Kin Mui Chan on August 18, 2014 (evidence file, folios 6865 and 6866).
③ *Cf.* Lima and Callao Registry Office. Registration of *Sociedades Anónimas Inversiones Turísticas Maury SAC*, of June 7, 1999 (evidence file, folio 6129).

was not for the fact that [he had] a family to maintain [⋯he] believe[d] that [⋯ he] would have lost the will to live."① Also, expert witness Carmen Wurst referred to the fact that Wong Ho Wing was "subjected to numerous stress factors during the time he spent in prison, owing to the prison conditions, [and this] has resulted in severe psychological effects and suffering," with depressive psychological tendencies, anxiety, dissociative disorder, and chronic anxiety among other symptoms. However, she indicated that "the symptoms have decreased slightly during his house arrest." In addition, regarding the risk of being extradited, she considered that this caused him sufferings, such as feeling a "permanent death threat [and he had encountered] situations of racial and personal abuse owing to the reactions of other prisoners to the possibility that he would be extradited."②

317. Based on the foregoing conclusions, the circumstances of this case, and the violations found, the Court considers it pertinent to establish, in equity, compensation for pecuniary and non-pecuniary damage in favor of Wong Ho Wing of US$ 30 000.00 (thirty thousand United States dollars). This amount must be paid within the relevant time frame established by the Court (*infra* para. 323).

D. Costs and expenses

318. The representative requested, for costs and expenses, the sum of US$ 10 000.00 as honoraria based on the professional services contract signed by the representative of Wong Ho Wing and He Long Huang; as well as US$ 6,651.44 for expenses related to the proceedings. With his final written arguments, the representative also forwarded vouchers for expenses incurred following the presentation of the motions and arguments

---

① Affidavit made by Wong Ho Wing on August 18, 2014 (evidence file, folio 6851).
② Expert opinion of Carmen Wurst provided by affidavit on August 18, 2014 (evidence file, folios 6885 and 6886).

brief. The State indicated that it was only in order to pay costs and expenses if receipts, travel vouchers, and other documents existed proving that the disbursements were made in relation to these proceedings. In particular, it argued that the need for, and the reasonableness, of the trips made by different persons, including the underage daughters of Wong Ho Wing, for the same event and on numerous occasions, referring to trips to Washington D. C, San José, and Lima.

319. The Court reiterates that, pursuant to its case law,[1] costs and expenses are part of the concept of reparation, insofar as the actions taken by the victims to obtain justice at both the domestic and the international level, involve expenditures that must be compensated when the international responsibility of the State has been declared in a sentence condemning it. The Court also recalls that the eventual reimbursement of costs and expenses is made based on the disbursements that have been duly proved before the Court.

320. The Court notes that the representative providedevidence corresponding to the expenses for: the professional services contract amounting to US $ 10 000. 00,[2] sending correspondence to the Inter-American Commission for US $ 138. 30,[3] payment of airfares for the family of Wong Ho Wing to take part in the hearing before the Court in February 2011 for US $ 2,751. 80,[4] accommodation in Washington, D. C. for his family and lawyer to take part in the hearing before the Inter-American Commission in

---

[1] *Cf. Case of Velásquez Rodríguez v. Honduras. Reparations and costs*, *supra*, para. 42, and *Case of Cruz Sánchez et al. v. Peru*, *supra*, para. 488.
[2] *Cf.* Contract for professional services (evidence file, folios 6083 and 6084).
[3] *Cf.* Mailing correspondence to the Inter-American Commission (evidence file, folio 6201).
[4] *Cf.* Payment of airline tickets to Costa Rica for the immediate family of Wong Ho Wing to take part in the hearing before the Inter-American Court of Human Rights in February 2011 (evidence file, folios 6202 and 6203).

October 2010 for US＄482.90,① payment of airfares for the family to participate in hearings before the Inter-American Commission in October 2010 and March 2012 for US＄1,982.80,② accommodation for Wong Ho Wing's brother to take part in a hearing before the Inter-American Commission for US＄429.60,③ and payment of airfares for Wong Ho Wing's family between Los Angeles and Lima for US＄4,905.55.④ Also, with his final written arguments, the representative provided evidence corresponding to the payment of legal advisory services in the amount of S/. 12,500.00,⑤ payment of US＄2 000.00 for a psychological opinion,⑥ and payment of S/. 1 875.00 for the professional fees of the lawyer María Eugenia Zegarra.⑦

321. In addition, the representative submitted the receipt for sending correspondence from Mercedes Wong Alza to Wong Ho Wing's wife and a certificate of a court surety bond. However, he failed to justify what this evidence related to;⑧ hence the Court has insufficient evidence to determine whether these amounts correspond to disbursements related to the proceed-

---

① Cf. Accommodation in Washington D.C. to participate in a hearing before the Inter-American Commission on Human Rights in October 2010 (evidence file, folios 6204 to 6209).
② Cf. Payment of airline tickets to Washington D.C. for Wong Ho Wing's family to take part in a hearing before the Inter-American Commission on Human Rights in March and October 2010 (evidence file, folios 6210 to 6214).
③ Cf. Accommodation in Washington D.C. for Wong Ho Wing's brother to take part in a hearing before the Inter-American Commission in March 2012 (evidence file, folio 6217).
④ Cf. Payment of airline tickets to Lima for Wong Ho Wing's family (evidence file, folios 6218 to 6221).
⑤ Cf. Receipt No. 001047 for professional honoraria of the lawyer, Luis Alberto Lamas Puccio, dated October 3, 2014 (evidence file, folio 7110.2).
⑥ Cf. Receipt No. 000707 for expert psychological opinion dated September 22, 2014 (evidence file, folio 7087).
⑦ Cf. Receipt No. 001079 for professional honoraria dated October 1, 2014 (evidence file, folio 7075).
⑧ Cf. DHL service for correspondence between Mercedes Esther Wong Alza and Kinmui Chan on May 19, 2014 (evidence file, folio 7071).

ings before the inter-American system. ①

322. Consequently, the Court orders the State to pay the representative, Luis Lamas Puccio, the sum of US $ 28 000.00 (twenty-eight thousand United States dollars) for costs and expenses. ② This amount shall be paid directly to the representative within the respective time frame established by the Court (*infra* para. 323). During the stage of monitoring compliance with this Judgment, the Court may decide that the State should reimburse the victim or his representative any subsequent reasonable and duly authenticated expenses. ③

E. Method of complying with the payments ordered

323. The State shallmake the payments of the compensation for pecuniary and non-pecuniary damage and to reimburse costs and expenses established in this Judgment directly to the persons indicated herein, within one year of notification of this Judgment, without prejudice to making full payment before this.

---

① In addition, the Court will not take into account the following evidence presented belatedly by the representative with the final written arguments: airfares in the name of Huang He dated May 22, 2010, from Lima to Los Angeles and June 6, 2010, from Los Angeles to Lima (evidence file, folio 7055); airfares in the name of Huang He dated May 23, 2010, from Los Angeles to Guangzhou, China, and June 4, 2010, from Guangzhou, China, to Los Angeles (evidence file, folio 7057); plane tickets in the name of Huang He Long dated May 25, 2011, to Lima, Peru, from Los Angeles (evidence file, folio 7058); plane ticket in the name of Huang He Long dated August 7, 2012, from Lima to Los Angeles and from Los Angeles to Lima; plane ticket in the name of Huang He Long dated June 18, 2013, from Lima to Los Angeles and from Los Angeles to Lima (evidence file, folio 7060); receipt for payment of October 29, 2008, to Rivera, Gervasi & Asociados for legal advisory services (evidence file, folio 7062); receipt dated December 28, 2010, for payment of professional honoraria of Luis Alberto Lamas Puccio for legal advisory services in 2010 (evidence file, folio 7063); receipt dated September 30, 2011, for payment of professional honoraria of Luis Alberto Lamas Puccio for legal advisory and defense services (evidence file, folio 7064); receipts for payments dated September 2 and October 2, 2013, to *Consorcio Trial S. A. C.* for legal advisory services (evidence file, folios 7065—7066), and invoices for sending correspondence from Lima, Peru, to the Inter-American Commission dated January 6, 21 and 30, February 17 and 29, March 6 and November 24, 2012, and March 30 and September 3, 2013 (evidence file, folios 7077 to 7085).

② The amounts presented in Peruvian new soles were converted to United States dollars using the bank exchange rate in force at the time of the payment receipt. *Cf.* Ministry of Economy and Finance of Peru, http://www.mef. gob. pe/contenidos/ tipo_cambio/tipo_cambio. php

③ *Cf.* Case of Ibsen Cárdenas e Ibsen Peña v. Bolivia. Merits, *reparations and costs*. Judgment of September 1, 2010. Series C No. 217, para. 291, and *Case of Rodríguez Vera et al. (The Disappeared of the Palace of Justice) v. Colombia, supra,* para. 608.

324. If the beneficiaries are deceased or die before they receive the respective amount, this will be delivered directly to their heirs, pursuant to the applicable domestic law.

325. The State must comply with the monetary obligations by payment in United States dollars or the equivalent in national currency, using the exchange rate in force on the New York Stock Exchange (United States of America), the day before the payment to make the calculation.

326. If, for reasons that can be attributed to the beneficiary of the compensation or his heirs, it is not possible to pay the amounts established within the time frame indicated, the State shall deposit these amounts in his favor in an account or certificate of deposit in a solvent Peruvian financial institution, in United States dollars, and in the most favorable financial termspermitted by the State's banking practice and law. If the corresponding compensation is not claimed, after 10 years the amounts shall be returned to the State with the interest accrued.

327. The amounts allocated in this Judgment as compensation for pecuniary and non-pecuniary damage and to reimburse costs and expenses shall be delivered to the persons indicated integrally, in accordance with this Judgment, without anydeductions arising from possible taxes or charges.

328. If the State shall incur in arrears, it shall pay interest on the amount owed corresponding to bank interest on arrears in the Republic of Peru.

XIII
OPERATIVE PARAGRAPHS

328. Therefore,

THE COURT

DECIDES,

By five votes to one,

1. To reject the preliminary objection filed by the State concerning the

exhaustion of domestic remedies, in the terms of paragraphs 21 to 30 of this Judgment.

Judge Vio Grossi dissenting.

DECLARES,

By five votes to one, that:

2. As described in paragraphs124 to 188, it would not be legally possible at this time to impose the death penalty, and it has not been proved that the extradition would expose Wong Ho Wing to a real, foreseeable and personal risk of being subject to treatment contrary to his personal integrity; thus, if he is extradited, the State would not be responsible for violating its obligation to ensure his rights to life and to personal integrity recognized in Articles 4 and 5 of the Convention, in relation to Article 1(1) of this instrument, or the obligation of non-refoulement established in Article 13(4) of the Inter-American Convention to Prevent and Punish Torture.

Judge Vio Grossi dissenting.

By three votes in favor and three against, and the deciding vote of the President, that:

3. The State is responsible for the violation of the guarantee ofa reasonable time, established in Article 8(1) of the American Convention in relation to Article 1(1) thereof, to the detriment of Wong Ho Wing, in the terms of paragraphs 207 to 223.

Judges F. Caldas, Pérez Pérez and Vio Grossi dissenting.

By five votes to one, that:

4. The State is responsible for the violation of the right to personal liberty, recognized in Article 7(1), 7(3), 7(5) and 7(6) of the American Convention in relation to Article 1(1) thereof, to the detriment of Wong Ho Wing, in the terms of paragraphs 247 to 255, 267 to 275 and 279 to 292.

Judge Vio Grossi dissenting.

By five votes to one, that:

5. The State is not responsible for the violation of the right to be heard and of the right of defense, established in Article 8(1) of the American Convention, in relation to Article 1(1) thereof, to the detriment of Wong Ho Wing, in accordance with paragraphs 227 to 234.

Judge Vio Grossi dissenting.

By, that:

6. The State is not responsible for the violation of Article 7(2) of the Convention, in relation to Article 1(1) of this instrument, to the detriment of Wong Ho Wing, in the terms of paragraphs 259 to 262.

Judges Pérez Pérez and Vio Grossi dissenting.

By five votes to one, that:

7. The State is not responsible for the violationof the right to personal integrity, recognized in Article 5 of the American Convention, in relation to Article 1(1) of this instrument, to the detriment of Wong Ho Wing, in the terms of paragraphs 294 and 295.

Judge Vio Grossi dissenting.

By five votes to one, that:

8. It is not necessary to issue a ruling on the alleged failure to comply with the right to judicial protection recognized in Article 25 of the Convention in relation to the alleged failure to comply with the decision of the Constitutional Court, in the terms of paragraphs 193 to 206.

Judge Vio Grossi dissenting.

By four votesto two, that:

9. It is not necessary to issue a ruling on the alleged failure to comply with the obligation to adopt domestic legal provisions, recognized in Article 2 of the Convention, in relation to the arbitrary nature of the detention of Wong Ho Wing, in the terms of paragraph 256.

Judges Pérez Pérez and Vio Grossi dissent.

AND ESTABLISHES,

By five votes to one, that:

10. This Judgment constitutes *per se* a form of reparation.

Judge Vio Grossi dissenting.

By five votes to one, that:

11. The State must take the final decision in the extradition process in the case of Wong Ho Wing as soon as possible, as established in paragraph 302.

Judge Vio Grossi dissenting.

By five votes to one, that:

12. The provisional measures ordered in this case are annulled, insofar as they are replaced by the measures of reparation ordered in this Judgment as of the date of its notification, as established in paragraph 303.

Judge Vio Grossi dissenting.

By four votes to two, that:

13. The State must immediately review the deprivation of liberty of Wong Ho Wing, as established in paragraph 305.

Judges Pérez Pérez and Vio Grossi dissenting.

By five votes to one, that:

14. The State must make the publications indicated in paragraph 307 of this Judgment, within six months of its notification.

Judge Vio Grossi dissenting.

By five votes to one, that:

15. The State must pay the amounts established in paragraphs 317 and 322 of this Judgment, as compensation for pecuniary and non-pecuniary damage and to reimburse costs and expenses, in the terms of these paragraphs and of paragraphs 323 to 328.

Judge Vio Grossi dissenting.

By five votes to one, that:

16. The State must, within one year of notification of this Judgment, provide the Court with a report on the measures taken to comply with it.

Judge Vio Grossi dissenting.

By five votes to one, that:

17. The Court will monitor full compliance with this Judgment, in exercise of its authority and in fulfillment of its obligations under the American Convention on Human Rights, and will consider this case concluded when the State has complied fully with all its provisions.

Judge Vio Grossi dissenting.

Judge Alberto Pérez Pérez advised the Court of his Partially Dissenting Opinion, which accompanies this judgment. Judge Eduardo Vio Grossi advised the Court of his Dissenting Opinion, which accompanies this judgment.

Done, at San José, Costa Rica, on June 30, 2015, in the Spanish language.

Judgment of the Inter-American Court of Human Rights. Case of Wong Ho Wing *v.* Peru. Preliminary objection, merits, reparations and costs.

Humberto Antonio Sierra Porto

President

Roberto F. Caldas   Manuel E. Ventura Robles

Alberto Pérez Pérez Eduardo Vio Grossi Eduardo Ferrer Mac-Gregor Poisot

Pablo Saavedra Alessandri

Secretary

So ordered,

Humberto Antonio Sierra Porto

President

Pablo Saavedra Alessandri

Secretary

PARTIALLY DISSENTING OPINION OF JUDGE ALBERTO PÉREZ PÉREZ
INTER-AMERICAN COURT OF HUMAN RIGHTS
CASE OF WONG HO WING v. PERU
JUDGMENT OF JUNE 30, 2015

(*Preliminary objection, merits, reparations and costs*)

1. I have issued a negative vote in relation to the following operative paragraphs of the judgment in the case of *Wong Ho Wing v. Peru*:

Operative paragraph 3:

"The State is responsible for the violation of the guarantee of a reasonable time, established in Article 8(1) of the American Convention, in relation to Article 1(1) thereof, to the detriment of Wong Ho Wing, in the terms of paragraphs 207 to 223."

Operative paragraph 6:

"The State is not responsible for the violation of Article 7(2) of the Convention, in relation to Article 1(1) of this instrument, to the detriment of Wong Ho Wing, in the terms of paragraphs 259 to 262."

Operative paragraph 9:

"It is not necessary to issue a ruling on the alleged failure to comply with the obligation to adopt domestic legal provisions, recognized in Article 2 of the Convention, in relation to the arbitrary nature of the detention of Wong Ho Wing, in the terms of paragraph 256."

Operative paragraph 13:

"The State must immediately review the deprivation of liberty of Wong Ho Wing, as established in paragraph 305."

2. I will now explain the reasons for these negative votes.

Non-violation of the right to a reasonable time

3. According to the judgment (para. 220, and also para. 223), the right to a reasonable time (Art. 8(1) of the Convention) was violated owing to the "delay in the final settlement of the extradition process, which

can be attributed to the actions of the State authorities." However, as of May 2010, this Court had ordered numerous provisional measures in favor of Wong Ho Wing[①] in which it had required the State to *"refrain from extraditing Wong Ho Wing until the organs of the inter-American human rights system had examined and ruled on the [case]."* That ruling has been made today by this Judgment; thus, up until this time, *there has been no delay in adopting the final decision on the extradition, and the time frame for adopting this decision has not yet commenced.* Abstract considerations regarding delays in extradition proceedings, the eventual possibility that these may be attributed to the State, and elements that may make these delays unreasonable are interesting, but are entirely inapplicable to this case.

4. Furthermore, the analysis of the requirement concerning the complexity of the matter, which concluded with the mere recognition that "the case is complex," does not accord with the extreme complexity of the case owing to the alternatives resulting from the determination of whether or not the offense for which extradition to the People's Republic of China could be granted was or is punished by the death penalty, and to the difficulties in obtaining an accurate translation from Chinese (paras. 60 to 93 of the Judgment).

---

① 401. On February 24, 2010, the Inter-American Commission, during the proceedings before this organ, asked the Court to adopt provisional measures in favor of Wong Ho Wing. The measures were granted for the first time in May 2010. Following orders of November 26, 2010, and March 4 and July 1, 2011, extending their effects, they were lifted in October 2011, after the decision of the Peruvian Constitutional Court of May 24 that year ordering the Executive Branch to refrain from extraditing Wong Ho Wing. Nevertheless, on June 26, 2012, the Inter-American Court again granted provisional measures in favor of Wong Ho Wing due to "the State's uncertainty" about the possibility of extraditing him, based on presumed "new facts." These measures were maintained by orders dated December 6, 2012, February 13, May 22 and August 22, 2013, and January 29 and March 31, 2014. In both May 2010 and June 2012, the provisional measures were *ordered to allow the inter-American system to examine and rule on this case, as well as to prevent thwarting compliance with an eventual decision by its organs. Based on the orders of January and March 2014, the measures remain in force"* (italics added).

Violation of Article 7(2) of the Convention

5. According to the Judgment (paras. 259 to 262), the State did not violate Article 7(2) of the Convention, which establishes that: "No one shall be deprived of his physical liberty except for the reasons and under the conditions established beforehand by the Constitution of the State Party concerned or by a law established pursuant thereto." The Judgment does not refer to any legal or constitutional provision that authorizes this deprivation of liberty. First, article 2.24 (f) of the Constitution (cited in para. 240 of the Judgment) contains no reference to an extradition request as a legitimate reason for deprivation of liberty. Second, both the legal provision cited in para. 241 (article 523 of the Peruvian Code of Criminal Procedure) and the Extradition Treaty between China and Peru (article 9, cited in para. 239) refer to a different situation to that of this case: to what Peru's domestic laws call "provisional or pre-extradition arrest" and the treaty calls "preventive detention" requested "before the presentation of the extradition request," which should cease when "30 days have passed without the formal submission of the extradition request" (article 523.6 of the Peruvian Code of Criminal Procedure) or "if the competent authority of the Requested Party has not received the formal extradition request within 60 days of the detention of the person sought," which "may be extended for a further 30 days when the Requesting Party provides reasons that justify this" (article 9.4 of the Extradition Treaty between China and Peru).

6. Consequently, there were no legal or constitutional grounds for the deprivation of liberty. For it to have been lawful, a legislative norm would have to have existed establishing the conditions for deprivation of liberty in the case of an extradition request. Thus, Article 7(2) of the Convention was violated.

Non-compliance with Article 2 of the Convention

7. The considerations in the previous section reveal that the Peruvian

State failed to comply with its obligation to adopt domestic legal provisions, inasmuch as its practice in relation to extradition includes the deprivation of liberty of the person whose extradition is requested, without establishing the conditions in which this detention can beimplemented, or the conditions of the deprivation of liberty, or its duration, or the possibility of securing the person using means other than deprivation of liberty or less harmful that this (such as the house arrest to which Wong Ho Wing is currently subject).

Inexistence of the obligation to make an immediate review of the deprivation of liberty of Wong Ho Wing

8. Lastly, I understand that the Peruvian State's obligation is not to "immediately review the deprivation of liberty of Wong Ho Wing," but rather to make a prompt final decision on the extradition request. If it is denied, Wong Ho Wing will be released automatically; if it is granted, Wong Ho Wing must be handed over to the Chinese authorities.

Alberto Pérez Pérez
Judge

Pablo Saavedra Alessandri
Secretary

SEPARATE DISSENTING OPINION OF JUDGE EDUARDO VIO GROSSI
INTER-AMERICAN COURT OF HUMAN RIGHTS
CASE OF WONG HO WING v. PERU
JUDGMENT OF JUNE 30, 2015
(Preliminary objection, merits, reparations and costs)

INTRODUCTION

This dissenting opinion① to the Judgment indicated above② is issued because the Judgment rejected the preliminary objection concerning failure to comply with the rule of prior exhaustion of domestic remedies filed by the Republic of Peru.③ The grounds for this dissent relate to the moment at which this rule should be complied with. The Judgment takes the view that this should be, at the latest, when the Inter-American Commission on Human Rights④ takes a decision on the admissibility of the petition or communication⑤ that has given rise to the corresponding case;⑥ to the contrary, in this opinion, I maintain that this rule should be complied with at the time the petition is lodged, and this should be verified by the Commission both when this occurs and when deciding on the petition's admissibility. In other words, while the Judgment considers that compliance with this rule is

---

① Article 66(2) of the American Convention on Human Rights (hereinafter "the Convention"): "[i]f the judgment does not represent in whole or in part the unanimous opinion of the judges, any judge shall be entitled to have his dissenting or separate opinion attached to the judgment." Article 24(3) of the Statute of the Inter-American Court of Human Rights (hereinafter "the Court"): "[t]he decisions, judgments and opinions of the Court shall be delivered in public session, and the parties shall be given written notification thereof. In addition, the decisions, judgments and opinions shall be published, along with judges' individual votes and opinions and with such other data or background information that the Court may deem appropriate." Article 65(2) of the Court's Rules of Procedure: "[a]ny judge who has taken part in the consideration of a case is entitled to append a separate concurring or dissenting opinion to the judgment. These opinions shall be submitted within a time frame to be established by the President so that the other judges may take cognizance thereof before notice of the judgment is served. The opinions shall only refer to the issues covered in the judgment."

② Hereinafter "the Judgment."

③ Hereinafter "the State."

④ Hereinafter "the Commission."

⑤ Hereinafter "the petition."

⑥ Cf. para. 26 of the Judgment.

a requirement for the admissibility of the petition, in this opinion, I consider that compliance with the rule is a requirement for its presentation and, consequently, to enable it to be processed.

Bearing in mind the provisions of Article 65(2) of the Court's Rules of Procedure, this opinion refers only and exclusively to the reasons why the undersigned considers that the Judgment should have admitted the preliminary objection concerning the lack of prior exhaustion of domestic remedies filed by the State and, consequently, must refrain from commenting on the merits of the case. Therefore, this opinions is limited to the operative paragraph on this point adopted in the Judgment.

Nevertheless, I wish to record that the undersigned, as in other cases,[①] has participated in both the deliberation and the voting by the Court with regard to each operative paragraph of the Judgment and has done so, however, without issuing a separate opinion on them.

Consequently, andpursuant to the provision of Article 65(2) of the Rules of Procedure that, if a separate concurring or dissenting opinion is issued, it should include the reasoning; then, to the contrary, if no separate opinion is issued, there is no obligation to provide the reasons for the positive or negative vote. Thus, considering that this opinion relates solely and exclusively to the operative paragraph adopted in the Judgment with regard to the said preliminary objection, the undersigned is not obliged to explain the reasons why he voted negatively with regard to the other paragraphs of the Judgment; namely, the operative paragraphs.

By adopting this course of action, the undersigned has proceeded in keeping with the principles of liberty and independence that should govern the actions of a judge, guaranteed by the Convention and the Court's Stat-

---

[①] Dissenting opinion of Judge Eduardo Vio Grossi, *Case of Cruz Sánchez et al. v. Peru. Preliminary objections, merits, reparations and costs.* Judgment of April 17, 2015. Series C No. 292, and Dissenting opinion of Judge Eduardo Vio Grossi, *Case of Díaz Peña v. Venezuela. Preliminary objection, merits, reparations and costs.* Judgment of June 26, 2012. Series C No. 244.

ute and Rules of Procedure, which impose no restriction as regards the reason he considers it appropriate to vote according to his conscience or, in particular, by not prohibiting him from explaining, if he so wishes, why he has proceeded in this way.

In addition, it should be borne in mind that this opinion is consistent; moreover, it diverges from the approach taken in the Judgment which simultaneously decided the preliminary objection and the merits of the matter, without first making a formal determination of whether the objection related to the merits and, if it considered that this connection existed, deciding to deal with both matters together. Conversely, the present opinion is based on the fact that the preliminary objection filed by the State regarding failure to comply with the rule of prior exhaustion of domestic remedies is not related to the merits of the case and, consequently, was essentially a preliminary matter that, as such, deserved to be decided before and separately from the merits, so that it could not be considered that the decision on the objection might be influenced, even indirectly, by the merits.

The reasons why the undersigned does not agree with the decision taken in this case concerning the objection filed by the State based on failure to exhaust domestic remedies are explained below, taking into account the applicable provision of the Convention, the facts of the case as they relate to this provision and, lastly, the part of the Judgment that refers to this objection.

1. PROVISION OF THE CONVENTION CONCERNING THE RULE OF PRIOR EXHAUSTION OF DOMESTIC REMEDIES

In the first part of this opinion, the undersigned will reiterate and complement some of the general comments made above[①] on the said rule and the procedure that should be followed in this regard; in other words,

---

[①] Dissenting opinion of Judge Eduardo Vio Grossi, *Case of Cruz Sánchez et al. v. Peru. Preliminary objections, merits, reparations and costs.* Judgment of April 17, 2015. Series C No. 292.

with regard to the petition, its study and initial processing by the Commission, the State's response to the petition, its admissibility, and the ruling that corresponds to the Court, to conclude with the consequences of considering the rule of prior exhaustion of domestic remedies to be a requirement of admissibility rather than of the petition.

A. General comments

Article 46 of the Convention recognizes the rule of prior exhaustion of domestic remedies and stipulates that:

"*1. Admission by the Commission of a petition or communication lodged in accordance with Articles 44 or 45 shall be subject to the following requirements:*

a. that the remedies under domestic law have been pursued and exhausted in accordance with generally recognized principles of international law;

b. that the petition or communication is lodged within a period of six months from the date on which the party alleging violation of his rights was notified of the final judgment;

c. that the subject of the petition or communication is not pending in another international proceeding for settlement; and

d. that, in the case of Article 44, the petition contains the name, nationality, profession, domicile, and signature of the person or persons or of the legal representative of the entity lodging the petition.

2. The provisions of paragraphs 1.a and 1.b of this article shall not be applicable when:

a. the domestic legislation of the state concerned does not afford due process of law for the protection of the right or rights that have allegedly been violated;

b. the party alleging violation of his rights has been denied ac-

cess to the remedies under domestic law or has been prevented from exhausting them; or

c. there has been unwarranted delay in rendering a final judgment under the aforementioned remedies."

As a preliminary observation, it should be noted that this provision is *sui generis*, exclusive to the Convention. For example, it does not appear in the same terms in the Convention for the Protection of Human Rights and Fundamental Freedoms or European Convention on Human Rights,[①] Article 35 of which refers to the requirement of prior exhaustion of domestic remedies more generally and, also, does not include the specific exceptions established in Article 46(2) of the American Convention.[②]

Furthermore, it should also be emphasized that the European Convention establishes that this requirement must be met prior to litigating before the European Court of Human Rights – a judicial body – while, in the case of the American Convention, it must be met prior to lodging the petition before the Commission – a non-judicial body it should be noted. And this is relevant insofar as "[t]*he main function of the Commission shall be to promote respect for and defense of human rights*"[③] and, in exercise of

---

① Nor is it established in the Statute or the Rules of Procedure of the International Court of Justice. Hence, in that sphere, it is only of a jurisprudential nature.
② "Admissibility criteria. 1. The Court may only deal with the matter after all domestic remedies have been exhausted, according to the generally recognised rules of international law, and within a period of six months from the date on which the final decision was taken. 2. The Court shall not deal with any application submitted under Article 34 that (a) is anonymous; or (b) is substantially the same as a matter that has already been examined by the Court or has already been submitted to another procedure of international investigation or settlement and contains no relevant new information. 3. The Court shall declare inadmissible any individual application submitted under Article 34 if it considers that: (a) the application is incompatible with the provisions of the Convention or the Protocols thereto, manifestly ill-founded, or an abuse of the right of individual application; or (b) the applicant has not suffered a significant disadvantage, unless respect for human rights as defined in the Convention and the Protocols thereto requires an examination of the application on the merits and provided that no case may be rejected on this ground which has not been duly considered by a domestic tribunal. 4. The Court shall reject any application which it considers inadmissible under this Article. It may do so at any stage of the proceedings."
③ Article 41 of the Convention, first phrase.

this function, *"to take action on petitions and other communications pursuant to its authority under the provisions of Articles 44 through 51 of this Convention,"*① including submission of the respective case to the Court. ②

Thus, the Commission should promote and defend human rights and can even act as a plaintiff before the Court and, accordingly, does notnecessarily share the impartiality that must characterize a judicial body. Consequently, Article 46(1) (a) of the Convention is also conceived as a limit to the actions of the Commission which may become a party in the consequent litigation that this non-judicial body has itself originated. Hence, the intention of this provision is to prevent the Commission from acting before the requirement or rule that it establishes has been duly complied with in a timely manner; in other words, from proceeding with the matter even though the domestic remedies have not been exhausted.

And it is in the same spirit that the said Article 46(2) of the Convention specifically establishes the cases in which the rule of prior exhaustion of domestic remedies is not applicable; namely, inexistence of due process of law to exercise the domestic remedies, impossibility of exercising them, and delay in deciding them. Thus, this norm does not establish any other exceptions than those indicated; therefore, it is not admissible to cite, or even admit, an exception that is not established in the said article, because, if it were, this could strip the general rule established in Article 46(1) (a) of the Convention of any meaning or practical effects and, above all, it would leave its application to the discretion and, perhaps, the arbitrariness of the Commission.

As a second general comment, it is worth calling attention to the reference made in Article 46(1) (a) of the Convention to the circumstance *"that the remedies under domestic law have been pursued and exhausted in ac-*

---

① Article 41(f) of the Convention.
② Articles 51 and 61(1) of the Convention.

cordance with generally recognized principles of international law." The allusion to such principles signifies that they are not the ones subsequently established in paragraph 2 of this article because, if they were, this allusion would not have been necessary. Accordingly, it is included in order to recall that the rule of prior exhaustion of domestic remedies is established by principles of international law, even prior to or irrespective of the provisions of any treaty, in this case the Convention, and that these principles involve other rules, such as the rule indicating that any objection that relates to the merits of the case in question is not strictly preliminary and must be decided when deciding on the merits.

403. Third, attention should be called to the fact that, with regard to the provision transcribed above, the Judgment indicates that "[t]he Court recalls that the rule of prior exhaustion of domestic remedies was conceived in the interests of the State, because it seeks to exempt it from responding before an international organ for acts it is accused of before it has had the occasion to remedy them by its own means."[①]

The foregoing appears to signify that the Court would follow the thesis according to which the said rule, since it is conceived in the interests of the State, without considering the attitude of the petitioner, would mean that the State's international responsibility for the violation of an obligation established by the Convention would be engaged from the time at which one of its organs committed an internationally wrongful act, even though it had not had the opportunity to redress this internationally wrongful act.

Now, whether this or any other thesis is followed, in the practice, the ultimate intention of the said rule is to enable the State to establish, as soon as possible, the effective exercise of, and respect for, the human

---

① Para. 27 of the Judgment.

rights that have been violated. This is the object and purpose of the Convention[①] and, consequently, should happen as soon as practicable in everyone's interests, making the intervention of the inter-American jurisdiction unnecessary.[②]

This means that, in situations in which it has been argued in the respective sphere of the domestic jurisdiction that the State has not complied with its undertakings as regards respecting and ensuring the free and full exercise of human rights, it is possible to claim the intervention of the international jurisdictional body and not before, so that, if admissible, the State is ordered to comply with the international obligations it has violated, to guarantee that it will not violate them again, and to make reparation for all the consequences of such violations.[③]

Therefore, this rule is also a mechanism to encourage the State to comply with its human rights obligations without waiting for the inter-American system to order it to do soas a result of litigation. Thus, its practical effect is that the State re-establish respect for human rights as soon as possible and, to that end, it could be said that this rule has been established also and, above all, to benefit the victim of human rights violations.[④]

Based on the above, it can be concluded that this rule has been estab-

---

① Art. 1(1) of the Convention: "[t]he States Parties to this Convention undertake to respect the rights and freedoms recognized herein and to ensure to all persons subject to their jurisdiction the free and full exercise of those rights and freedoms, without any discrimination for reasons of race, color, sex, language, religion, political or other opinion, national or social origin, economic status, birth, or any other social condition."
② Art. 33 of the Convention: "[t]he following organs shall have competence with respect to matters relating to the fulfillment of the commitments made by the States Parties to this Convention: (a) the Inter-American Commission de Human rights, referred to as the Commission, and (b) the Inter-American Court of Human Rights, referred to as the Court".
③ Art. 63(1) of the Convention: "[i]f the Court finds that there has been a violation of a right or freedom protected by this Convention, the Court shall rule that the injured party be ensured the enjoyment of his right or freedom that was violated. It shall also rule, if appropriate, that the consequences of the measure or situation that constituted the breach of such right or freedom be remedied and that fair compensation be paid to the injured party".
④ Hereinafter "the victim."

lished in the Convention as an essentialcomponent of the whole inter-American system for the promotion and protection of human rights, by stressing that, as indicated in the second paragraph of its Preamble, the *"international protection [...] reinforc[es] or complement[s] the protection provided by the domestic law of the American States."*[①]

And this relates to the international juridical structure that, fundamentally, is still based on the principle of sovereignty, which, in the case of the inter-American system, is embodied in Articles 1(1)[②] and 3(b)[③] of the Charter of the Organization of American States. Consequently, and in keeping with the principle of public law that one can only do what the law expressly authorizes, the provisions of the Convention that establish restrictions to State sovereignty must be interpreted and applied taking this reality into account.

Thus, the rule of prior exhaustion of domestic remedies is also an expression of the exercise of State sovereignty and of the need to give the State the preferential opportunity to take action with regard to the presumed human rights violations. Moreover, this has acquired greater relevance nowadays, when all the States Parties to the Convention abide by the

---

① Segundo paragraph of the Preamble of the Convention: "[r]ecognizing that the essential rights of man are not derived from one's being a national of a certain state, but are based upon attributes of the human personality, and that they therefore justify international protection in the form of a convention reinforcing or complementing the protection provided by the domestic law of the American States."Perhaps it is Article 25(1) of the Convention that best expresses the subsidiary nature of the inter-American human rights system, when it indicates that: "[e]veryone has the right to simple and prompt recourse, or any other effective recourse, to a competent court or tribunal for protection against acts that violate his fundamental rights recognized by the constitution or laws of the State concerned or by this Convention, even though such violation may have been committed by persons acting in the course of their official duties."
② "The American States establish by this Charter the international organization that they have developed to achieve an order of peace and justice, to promote their solidarity, to strengthen their collaboration, and to defend their sovereignty, their territorial integrity, and their independence. Within the United Nations, the Organization of American States is a regional agency."
③ "The American States reaffirm the following principles: [...] b) International order consists essentially of respect for the personality, sovereignty, and independence of States, and the faithful fulfillment of obligations derived from treaties and other sources of international law."

democratic rule of law; that is, they endorse democracy. ①

Consequently, based on the foregoing it can be inferred that compliance with the requirement establish in Article 46(1) (a) of the Convention, transcribed above, must take place before the petition is lodged before the Commission.

B. The petition

The first comment that should be made concerning the petition initiating the procedure before the Commission that may conclude before the Court is that compliance with the rule of prior exhaustion of domestic remedies is, essentially, an obligation of the presumed victim or the petitioner. It is the latter who must comply with the requirement of prior exhaustion of domestic remedies; in other words, to be able to allege a violation before the inter-American jurisdictional body,② the petitioner must previously do so before the corresponding domestic jurisdictional bodies. Otherwise, this would evidently prevent the prompt and timely achievement of the above-mentioned practical effects. Thus, rather than a benefit granted to the State, this rule is a requirement or obligation that must be met by the presumed victim or the petitioner.

This is why Article 28(h) of the Rules of Procedure of the Commission in force at the time the petition was lodged③(hereinafter "the Commission's Rules of Procedure") stipulates that the petition must contain information on "[a]ny steps taken to exhaust domestic remedies, or the impossibility of

---

① The Inter-American Democratic Charter adopted at the twenty-eighth special session of the General Assembly of the Organization of American States by a resolution dated September 11, 2001.
② Article 44 of the Convention: "[a]ny person or group of persons, or any nongovernmental entity legally recognized in one or more member states of the Organization, may lodge petitions with the Commission containing denunciations or complaints of violation of this Convention by a State Party.". Article 61(1) of the Convention: "[o]nly the States Parties and the Commission shall have the right to submit a case to the Court."
③ Approved by the Commission at its 109th special session held from December 4 to 8, 2000, and amended at its 116th regular period of sessions held from October 7 to 25, 2002, at its 118th regular period of sessions held from October 6 to 24, 2003, at its 126th regular period of sessions held from October 16 to 27, 2006, and at its 132nd regular period of sessions held from July 17 to 25, 2008.

doing so." It should be noted that, by referring to the said Rules of Procedure, attention is being drawn to how the Commission itself, by approving this legal instrument, has interpreted the provisions of the Convention and, in particular in this case, its Article 46(1) (a).

Clearly for the same reason, Article 31(3) of the Commission's Rules of Procedure refers to the situation in which *"the petitioner contends that he or she is unable to prove compliance with the requirement indicated in this article."* In other words, this provision indicates that the specific exceptions to the rule of prior exhaustion of domestic remedies are established in favor of the presumed victim or the petitioner. Consequently, it is the petitioner and no one else, not even the Commission, who may argue or assert some of the exceptions to the said rule and, evidently, this can only be done when the petition is drawn up.

The second comment regarding the petition relates to the fact that Article 46(1) of the Convention refers to it as *"lodged,"* which means that it should be considered just as it was submitted and if, at that time, it meets the requirements set out in this provision, it should be admitted. Accordingly, it is at that moment – the moment of its submission – when it should have complied with the requirement concerning the prior exhaustion of domestic remedies established in Article 46(1) (a) of the Convention and, only if this is so, the petition *"lodged"* may be *"admitted"* by the Commission.

Similarly, Article 46(1) (b) of the Convention is based on the same concept since it establishes that, for the petition to be admitted, it must have been *"lodged within a period of six months from the date on which the party alleging violation of his rights was notified of the final judgment."* Undoubtedly, it should be understood that this should be the judgment handed down on the last remedy that was filed, with no other remedies that may be filed. In other words, the time frame indicated for lodging the petition is calculated from the date of notification of the final decision of the domestic authorities or courts on the remedies that have been filed before them and, consequently, these may have resulted in the State's international responsibility, which evidently implies that they must have been exhausted when the petition was "*lodged.*"

Meanwhile, Article 26(1) of the Commission's Rules of Procedure stipulates that the initial processing is carried out of the petitions "*that fulfill all the requirements set forth,*" and such petitions must indicate, as established by the above-mentioned Article 28(h), the "*steps taken to exhaust domestic remedies, or the impossibility of doing so,*" and if they do not meet this requirement, "*the Commission[, as established in Articles 26(2) and 29(1) (b) of these Rules of Procedure,] may request the petitioner or his or her representative to fulfill them.*" Moreover, according to the said Article 46(1) (b) of the Convention, the Commission should consider, only those petitions "*lodged within a period of six months from the date*" of notification of the decision that exhausted the domestic remedies.

Based on all the above, it can beconcluded that, ultimately, compliance with the said rule of prior exhaustion of domestic remedies constitutes a requirement that the petition must meet in order to be "*lodged.*"

C. Study and initial processing by the Commission

However, in addition to benefitting both the State and the presumed victim or the petitioner and representing an obligation for the latter, the rule of prior exhaustion ofdomestic remedies also entails an obligation for the Commission. Indeed, according to Article 26(1) of the Commission's Rules of Procedure, "*[t]he Executive Secretariat of the Commission shall be responsible for the study and initial processing of petitions lodged before the Commission that fulfill all the requirements set forth in the Statute and in Article 28 of these Rules of Procedure.*" Meanwhile, and as already indicated, Articles 26(2) and 29(1) (b) of the text add that "*[i]f a* petition or communication does not meet the requirements set forth in these Rules of Procedure, the Executive Secretariat may request the petitioner or his or her representative to fulfill them."

Furthermore, Article 29(1) of those Rules of Procedure establishes that, "[t]he Commission, acting initially through the Executive Secretariat, shall receive and carry out the initial processing of the petitions presented" and adds that the Commission must register each petition and "record the date of receipt on the petition itself and acknowledge receipt to the petitioner." Lastly, according to Article 30(1) of this instrument, "[t]he Commission, through its Executive Secretariat, shall process the petitions that meet the requirements set forth in Article 28 of these Rules of Procedure."

Consequently, the steps taken by the Executive Secretariat, acting on behalf of the Commission, as regards the petition that has been "lodged" are not limited merely to verifying whether it includes the required information; rather it must carry out the "study and initial processing" of the petition, provided that it "fulfill[s] all the requirements set forth," including, evidently, the most important, namely, that "the remedies under domestic law have been pursued and exhausted in accordance with generally recognized principles of international law." Thus, the Commission, acting through its Executive Secretariat, must carry out an initial control of conventionality of the petition, ensuring that it meets the requirements established in the Convention in order to be considered "lodged."

Reasonably, the foregoing infers that the domestic remedies must have been exhausted before the petition is lodged before the Commission because, to the contrary, the logic and need for the "study and initial processing" by the Commission's Executive Secretariat cannot be understood, or the reason why the petitioner may be requested to complete it, or why the petitioner should indicate the steps taken to exhaust domestic remedies;

furthermore, the time frame indicated for its presentation would be meaningless.

Lastly, bearing in mind that the Commission's function consists in studying the petition, requesting its completion, and processing it, it must be concluded that all of this must be carried out in keeping with the terms in which the petition has been "*lodged.*" Thus, it can be affirmed that, just as "*it is not the task of the Court, or of the Commission, to identify* ex officio *the domestic remedies that remain to be exhausted, so that it is not incumbent on the international organs to rectify the lack of precision of the State's arguments,*"① it is not their task to rectify the petition or accord it a broader scope than the one it expresses and requires. Thus, the Commission must abide by what is requested of it.

This thesis issupported by the provisions established for the situation in which it is not necessary, or it is impossible, to exhaust such remedies previously. In this regard, Article 32(2) of the Commission's Rules of Procedure indicate that "[*i*]*n those cases in which the exceptions to the requirement of prior exhaustion of domestic remedies are applicable, the petition shall be presented within a reasonable period of time, as determined by the Commission. For this purpose, the Commission shall consider the date on which the alleged violation of rights occurred and the circumstances of each case.*" In other words, under that alternative, the Commission must also consider the date on which the alleged violation occurred, which obviously must have happened prior to the submission of the petition.

Consequently, the Commission's function when a petition is lodged confirms that the requirement of prior exhaustion of domestic remedies must be met before it acts.

---

① *Case of Cruz Sánchez et al. v. Peru. Preliminary objections, merits, reparations and costs.* Judgment of April 17, 2015. Series C No. 292, para. 49.

D. Response or observations of the State

Article 30(1) and (2) of the Commission's Rules of Procedure indicate that "*[t]he Commission, through its Executive Secretariat, [⋯] shall forward the relevant parts of the petition to the State in question.*"

Evidently, the relevant parts forwarded to the State must include, as indicated in Article 28(h) of these Rules of Procedure, information on "*[a]ny steps taken to exhaust domestic remedies, or the impossibility of doing so as provided in Article 31 of these Rules of Procedure.*" And Article 30(3) cited above adds that "*[t]he State shall submit its response within two months from the date the request is transmitted*"; a response that, evidently, must contain the preliminary objection of absence of prior exhaustion of domestic remedies by the presumed victim or the petitioner, if the State wishes to file this objection.

Moreover, similarly, Article 31(3) of the Commission's Rules of Procedure stipulates that "*[w]hen the petitioner contends that he or she is unable to prove compliance with the requirement indicated in this article, it shall be up to the State concerned to demonstrate to the Commission that the remedies under domestic law have not been previously exhausted, unless that is clearly evident from the record.*"

In other words, if the petitioner alleges in his petition that he is unable to prove that he has previously exhausted the domestic remedies, the State may contest this allegation, in which case it must prove that they have not been exhausted, provided that this is not evident from the case file. It is in relation to this possibility that the Court's assertion that, "*[w]hen arguing the failure to exhaust domestic remedies, the State must specify the domestic remedies that remain to be exhausted, and prove that these remedies were available, adequate, appropriate and effective,*"[①] should be under-

---

[①] *Case of Cruz Sánchez et al. v. Peru. Preliminary objections, merits, reparations and costs.* Judgment of April 17, 2015. Series C No. 292, para. 49.

stood.

Nevertheless, it should be recalled that, logically, also in the case – which is not expressly considered in the Commission's Rules of Procedure – that the petitioner indicates in his petition that he has previously exhausted the domestic remedies (that is, he has met the requirements of Article 46(1)(a) of the Convention), the State may file the objection that this has not occurred.

Thus, it is clear that compliance with the rule of prior exhaustion of domestic remedies or the impossibility of complying with it must be indicated in the petition, because, otherwise, the State could not respond to this. In other words, it is only if the petition indicates that this rule has been complied with or that it is impossible to do so, that the State may argue that it has not been complied with and, in this case, it must prove the availability, adequacy, appropriateness and effectiveness of the domestic remedies that were not exhausted, all of which shows, once again, that this requirement must have been met previously; that is, before drawing up the petition the relevant parts of which are forwarded to the State precisely so that it may respond to them.

Furthermore, Article 30(5) and (6) of the Commission's Rules of Procedure point in the same direction. Indeed, they establish that "*[p]rior to deciding upon the admissibility of the petition, the Commission may invite the parties to submit additional observations, either in writing or in a hearing, as provided for in Chapter VI of the [⋯] Rules of Procedure*," which leaves no margin of doubt that the said "*additional observations*" must relate to the petition, as it was "*lodged*" and not constitute a new petition or modify the original one, unless, as is logical, this entails its withdrawal.

Consequently, it is undeniable that this response by the State logically and necessarily must relate to the petition that was "*lodged*" before the

Commission, and that it is at that moment, and not afterwards, that the legal proceedings, or the adversarial proceedings, as regards the exhaustion of domestic remedies are instituted.

And, for the same reason, it is at that moment that the domestic remedies must have been exhausted or that the petitioner indicates the impossibility of exhausting them. To affirm that those remedies could be exhausted after the petition has been *"lodged"* and, consequently, notified to the State, would affect the essential procedural balance and would leave the State defenseless, because it could not file the pertinent preliminary objection in time and in due form.

It is in this context that the criterion *"consistently affirmed* [by the Court that] *an objection to the jurisdiction of the Court based on the supposed failure to exhaust domestic remedies must be filed at the appropriate procedural opportunity; that is, during the admissibility stage of the proceedings before the Commission"*[①] should be understood.

E. Admissibility of the petition

The preceding consideration is also evident from Article 31(1) of the Commission's Rules of Procedure, which establishes that *"[i]n order to decide on the admissibility of a matter, the Commission shall verify whether the remedies of the domestic legal system have been pursued and exhausted in accordance with the generally recognized principles of international law."*

This provision requires the Commission to *"verify,"* that is, to confirm [Note: *verificar-comprobar*[②] in the Spanish text], the filing and exhaustion of the domestic remedies, in order to *"decide"* on admissibility. And, this is logical, because that decision could be not to admit the petition

---

① *Case of Cruz Sánchez et al. v. Peru. Preliminary objections, merits, reparations and costs.* Judgment of April 17, 2015. Series C No. 292, para. 49.
② *Diccionario de la Lengua Española, Real Academia Española*, 23rd edition, October 2014.

because such remedies have not been exhausted. This means that, in order to take a decision on the admissibility of the petition, the Commission must verify whether the rule of prior exhaustion of domestic remedies has been complied with and, if not, the corresponding decision would be to declare the petition inadmissible. The essential requisite that enables the Commission to decide on the admissibility of the petition is, thus, the verification it must make that the petition has complied with the rule of prior exhaustion of domestic remedies, and not merely that this rule has been complied with.

In addition, it should be noted that, although it is logical that the preliminary objection of prior failure to exhaust domestic remedies should be filed during the procedure on the admissibility of the petition – which extends from the date the petition is received and processed by the Commission, through its Executive Secretariat, until the moment at which the Commission rules on its admissibility – this does not mean that it should be at this latter moment (that is, at the end of this procedure) when the said requirement should have been met. It only means that, at that moment, the Commission must rule on or rather "*verify*"① whether it was met when the petition was lodged.

This is evident if it is considered that Article 36 (1) of the Commission's Rules of Procedure establishes that "*[o]nce it has considered the positions of the parties, the Commission shall make a decision on the admissibility of the matter.*"

Hence, it is indisputable that the moment at which the Commission rules on the admissibility of the petition is distinct from the moment when it is lodged or completed. This is clear when it is recalled that the Commission's Rules of Procedure establish an "*initial processing*"② of the

---

① Article 31(1) of the Commission's Rules of Procedure.
② Article 29 of the Commission's Rules of Procedure.

petition, that the petition must be "*register[ed]*,"① and that the "*relevant parts*"② must be forwarded to the State. It is only after the State has submitted its observations that the Commission determines the admissibility of the petition and, to this end, "*shall verify*,"③ that is, confirm, that the corresponding requirements have been met – including those relating to the prior exhaustion of domestic remedies – and, consequently, "*shall decide*" on admissibility or inadmissibility.

In short, the Commission's Rules of Procedure do not establish that it is when the Commission decides on the admissibility of the petition that the domestic remedies should have been exhausted. Rather, to the contrary, they indicate that it is when the Commission "*shall verify*" whether such remedies were filed and exhausted in a timely manner or whether this was unnecessary and, on this basis, "*shall decide*" – in other words, make a second control of conventionality of the petition, checking it against the provisions of the Convention as regards the requirements that should have been met – and, thus, it may either be admitted or rejected.

F. The Court's ruling

Lastly, in relation to the Court's function as regards compliance with the requirements that the petition must meet, it should be recalled that, according to Article 61(2) of the Convention, "*[i]n order for the Court to hear a case, it is necessary that the procedures set forth in Articles 48 and 50 shall have been completed.*"

Thus, the Court must verify that the requirement of prior exhaustion of domestic remedies has been dulycomplied with before the Commission. As the Court has asserted, "*in matters that it is hearing, the Court has the*

---

① Idem.
② Article 30(2) of the Commission's Rules of Procedure.
③ Article 31(1) of the Commission's Rules of Procedure.

authority to carry out a control of the legality of the Commission's actions,"[①] *and that it* "*has the authority to review whether the Commission has complied with the statutory and regulatory provisions, as well as those of the Convention.*"[②]

And it could not be otherwise, because if it were not so, the Commission would be accorded the broadest possible authority to take an exclusive and final decision on the admission or rejection of a petition, which would clearly mean that this power would be discretionary and could even be arbitrary, undermining the jurisdiction of the Court, because, in this hypothesis, the Court would have no alternative but merely to be an entity that confirms or observes, without even ratifying, the actions of the Commission, and there can be no doubt that this is not in keeping with the letter and spirit of the said Article 61(2) of the Convention.

G. Consequences of considering the rule of prior exhaustion of domestic remedies as a requirement for the admissibility of the petition and nota requirement of the petition itself

In addition to the above considerations, it should be reiterated that if it were notcompulsory to have exhausted the domestic remedies before lodging the petition, it would be permissible that, at least for some time – that is, between the moment at which the petition is lodged and the moment at which the decision is taken on its admissibility (which in many situations may be considered extremely lengthy) – the same case could be dealt with simultaneously by both the domestic jurisdiction and the international jurisdiction. This would evidently render the statement in the second paragraph of the Preamble meaningless, and even the rule of prior exhaustion of domestic remedies as a whole. In other words, in this situation, the inter-A-

---

① *Case of Cruz Sánchez et al. v. Peru. Preliminary objections, merits, reparations and costs.* Judgment of April 17, 2015, para. 37.
② *Case of Cruz Sánchez et al. v. Peru. Preliminary objections, merits, reparations and costs.* Judgment of April 17, 2015, para. 75.

merican jurisdiction would not reinforce or be complementary to the domestic jurisdiction, but rather would substitute it or, at least, could be used to bring pressure to bear on the latter and, clearly, this is not what the Convention seeks.

Moreover, it might constitute an incentive, which could be considered perverse, to lodge petitions before the Commission when the said requirement has not been met in the hope that it can be complied with before the Commission decides on their admissibility and, evidently, this was not anticipated or sought by the Convention.

In addition, this begs the question of whether the *"study and initial processing"* of the petition is required, if it could be lodged without having previously exhausted the domestic remedies. Indeed, if this requirement was only compulsory when deciding on the admissibility of the petition, it is legitimate to question why it would be necessary to make an initial study of the petition and, furthermore, what would be the reason for and the practical effect of the Convention making a distinction between the moment of the lodging of the petition and the moment of its admissibility. Likewise, if it is considered that the said requirement or rule must be complied with when the decision on the admissibility of the petition is taken and not when it is lodged, it is logical to question the meaning of the petition itself.

It should also be noted that, if the criterion thatthis compliance should have taken place at the time the petition is lodged or completed is not respected and, to the contrary, the thesis is adopted that compliance is determined when the Commission decides on the admissibility of the petition, this would result in situations of evident injustice or arbitrariness, insofar as the moment of this compliance would ultimately depend not on the victim or the petitioner, but on the Commission's ruling when deciding on the admissibility or inadmissibility of the petition. Thus, the requirement would evidently not be the same in all cases, or known with due anticipation.

II. THE FACTSRELATING TO THE OBJECTION OF PRIOR FAILURE TO EXHAUST DOMESTIC REMEDIES

Based on the norms that have been mentioned, the relevant facts relating to the objection of non-compliance with the rule of prior exhaustion of domestic remedies are as follows.

A. Those set out in the petition

The petition of March 27, 2009, indicated that "[i]n this case, the petitioner ha[d] duly exhausted the ordinary remedies of the domestic jurisdiction because, as established in the third and fourth paragraphs of article 521 of the Code of Criminal Procedure, in extradition proceedings, there is a single entity that decides a request of this nature[.] In other words, the jurisdictional extradition proceedings had concluded with the final judgment delivered by the Second Transitory Criminal Chamber of the Supreme Court of Justice which declared that the extradition request was admissible."

As revealed by the above, the petitioner expressly indicated that, prior to the petition, he had exhausted the remedies established in the domestic jurisdiction, and did not make any mention of the situations indicated in Article 46(2) of the Convention in which it is unnecessary to apply the requirement under Article 46(1) (a) of this instrument. In other words, the situations in which it is not necessary to have previously exhausted the domestic remedies in order to lodge a petition before the Commission.

B. Those contained in the State's response or observations

Meanwhile, in its observations on this petition presented on April 29, 2009, the State indicated that "Wong Ho Wing ha[d] not complied with exhausting the remedies of the domestic jurisdiction; thus, this party ask[ed] the Inter-American Commission to declare the inadmissibility of this petition pursuant to Article 46 of the American Convention on Human Rights, because the 56th Criminal Court of Lima decided to declare that the application for habeas corpus *was well-founded in part and that the decision issued by the Second Transitory Criminal Chamber of the Supreme Court of Justice on January 20, 2009, was null, and that the Chamber should issue a new decision*" and that "*[t]his* habeas corpus *proceeding was still being processed.*"

The note added that "*[i]n addition, the extradition proceedings with regard to Wong Ho Wing have not concluded because, pursuant to article 515 of the new Code of Criminal Procedure, it is the Peruvian Government that takes the final decision on the extradition by means of a Supreme Decision issued with the agreement of the Council of Ministers, following a report of the Official Commission on Extraditions and Prisoner Transfers.*"

In this regard, the note ends by indicating that: "*[i]n a decision of February 12, 2009, the 56th Criminal Court of Lima ordered the temporary suspension of the extradition procedure against the Chinese citizen, Wong Ho Wing, until the* habeas corpus *proceeding had concluded.*"[①]

Thus, the State cited three reasons to support its position on the inadmissibility of the petition; namely, the ongoing processing when the petition was lodged of an application for *habeas corpus* filed by the petitioner himself; the processing of the extradition procedure, also at that time, and, lastly, the suspension of the procedure by a court order.

C. Those relating to the Admissibility Report

The Admissibility Report of November 1, 2010, indicates that "*the presumed victim first argued the failure to comply with the legal and constitutional requirements for admission of the extradition request throughout the advisory proceeding decided in the final instance by the Supreme Court of Justice on January 27, 2010*"; "[s]*econd, he submitted*

---

① See also paras. 18 and 22 of the Judgment.

two applications for habeas corpus *against the members of the Second Transitory Criminal Chamber and of the Permanent Criminal Chamber of the aforementioned Supreme Court, pointing to alleged defects in the advisory proceeding and an alleged inadequate evaluation of the guarantees provided by the Government of the People's Republic of China concerning the non-application of the death penalty,"* and added that *"[i]n addition, the presumed victim filed a preventive application for* habeas corpus *against the President of the Republic and the Council of Ministers, which has been pending a final decision on constitutional injury from the Constitutional Court since July 14, 2010."*

The Admissibility Report also adds that *"[b]ased on the foregoing considerations, the [Commission] consider[ed] that the presumed victim [had] exhausted the available remedies under domestic law aimed at rectifying the alleged irregularities in the advisory proceeding in which the final decision was taken by the Permanent Criminal Chamber of the Supreme Court of Justice on January 27, 2010."* Thus, the Commission concluded that, *"[c]onsequently, the requirement established in Article 46 (1) (a) of the American Convention has been met."*

First, attention should be drawn to the fact that the Admissibility Report refers to facts and/or judicial actions that took place after the petition had been lodged and to the corresponding observations of the State as grounds for the decision to admit the petition. In other words, it follows its consistent practice of determining whether the domestic remedies had been exhausted prior to this report, and not whether they had been exhausted prior to the petition. [1]

It should also be pointed out that, in order to found the decision issued in this report, the Commission does not refer to the provisional measures

---

[1] *Cf.* para. 19 of the Judgment.

that, on May 28, 2010, had ordered the State to refrain from extraditing Wong Ho Wing until December 17, 2010, to allow the Inter-American Commission on Human Rights to examine and decide on petition P－366－09 lodged before that organ on March 27, 2009. In other words, the report does not consider that the possible extradition of Wong Ho Wing, and therefore the corresponding proceedings, had been suspended on the orders of the Court at the request of the Commission itself.

Ⅲ. CONSIDERATIONS ON THE JUDGMENT

405. The Judgment refers to two of the arguments made by the State with regard to its preliminary objection. One consists in the fact that, when the initial petition was lodged, the domestic remedies had not been exhausted, and the other to the fact that, when deciding on admissibility, the Commission did not take into account that other applications for *habeas corpus* filed by the representative were being processed.[①] This opinion is only concerned with the first argument, regarding which the Judgment gives four reasons to reject the preliminary objection filed by the State based on the petitioner's failure to comply with the obligation to exhaust the domestic remedies before lodging the petition.

407. The first reason is stated as follows: "[a]s the State mentioned, *the decisions that, according to the Commission, exhausted the domestic remedies were adopted after the initial petition had been lodged. However, the Court notes that, by requiring that "<u>admission</u> by the Commission of a petition or communication [⋯] shall be subject to" the said exhaustion (underlining added), Article 46 of the American Convention, should be interpreted in the sense that exhaustion of the remedies is required when deciding on the admissibility of the petition and not when this is lodged.*[②]

[①] Cf. para. 23 of the Judgment.
[②] Para. 25 of the Judgment.

409. Thus, the Judgment is aligned with the Court's invariable position that the requirement of prior exhaustion of domestic remedies must be met at the time the Commission takes a decision on the admissibility of the petition and not when the latter is lodged; a position that, as indicated in Part I of this document – and especially in its sections B, C and D – this opinion does not share, above all, because it runs counter to the express provisions of Article 46(1)(a): by disregarding the qualifying term of *"lodged"* attributed to the petition in order to indicate that it is with regard to the petition as lodged that the admissibility or inadmissibility should be declared; by not weighing the State's observations and the fact that these could only refer to the petition as lodged, which established the adversarial proceedings on the matter, and regarding which the Commission should take a decision and, lastly, by not considering that, in order to decide on admissibility, the Commission should *"verify,"* – that is, confirm – that the requirement of prior exhaustion of domestic remedies has been met, which, undoubtedly and consequently, should have occurred before that moment.

411. It should also be noted that the Judgment appears to contain a contradiction because, when setting out the Court's second reason for rejecting the preliminary objection in question, it affirms that: *"[o]nce the petition has been forwarded to the State, the admissibility stage starts and, consequently, the adversarial proceedings on whether the petition meets the admissibility requirements, including the requirement of exhaustion of domestic remedies,"* and that *"it is when examining admissibility that the Commission decides whether or not the petition complies with this requirement, or whether any of the exceptions established in the Convention are applicable."* [1] This appears to suggest that the Judgment follows the thesis

---

[1] Para. 26 of the Judgment.

set out in this opinion; namely, that it is on the adversarial proceedings established or constituted by the petition and the corresponding observations of the State that the Commission's decision on the admissibility or inadmissibility of the "*lodged*" petition should be based.

413. However, this is not so. The second reason indicated in the Judgment to reject the said preliminary objection is that "*the Commission's Rules of Procedure make a distinction between the time at which the initial processing is carried out, when it only examines whether the petition includes information on 'any steps taken to exhaust domestic remedies, or the impossibility of doing so,' and the moment when it decides on admissibility, when it determines whether such remedies were exhausted, or applies an exception to this requirement.*"① Thus, the Judgment appears to lessen the obligation contained in Article 28(h) of the Commission's Rules of Procedure or to place the emphasis on the fact that the petition must include "*information*," rather than that this information must be specifically on "*any steps taken to exhaust domestic remedies, or the impossibility of doing so.*" In other words, it appears that, according to the Judgment, it is sufficient that a general mention is made of some information on such steps in order to meet the requirement to consider the petition, and not that the steps taken up until that time – that is, up until the lodging of the petition-to exhaust such remedies are indicated clearly and specifically.

To the contrary, this opinion affirms that the obligation established in Article 28(h) is not merely that of providing "*information*" that steps were taken, but rather to provide specific "*information*" on "*any steps taken to exhaust domestic remedies, or the impossibility of doing so.*" Hence, the obligation consists in describing the steps specifically taken which mean that the said remedies have already been exhausted or indicating the impos-

---

① Para. 26 of the Judgment.

sibility of exhausting them. This obligation does not consist, consequently, in providing general information that steps were taken, but in providing specific information on the steps that were taken and that prove that either the domestic remedies were exhausted, or that it was impossible to do this.

415. The third reason cited by the Judgment to reject the objection in question is indicated as follows: "*[t]he Court recalls that the rule of prior exhaustion of domestic remedies was conceived in the interests of the State, because it seeks to exempt it from responding before an international organ for acts it is accused of before it has had the occasion to remedy them by its own means. Nevertheless, the subsidiary nature of the inter-American system is not affected by the fact that the analysis of compliance with the requirement of exhaustion of domestic remedies is made based on the situation when a decision is taken on a petition's admissibility. To the contrary, if any domestic remedy is pending, the State has the opportunity to resolve the situation alleged during the admissibility stage.*"[①]

417. With this assertion, the Judgment forgets that compliance with the rule of prior exhaustion of domestic remedies is basically an obligation that, even though it may benefit the State or be in its interests, is essentiallyrequired of the petitioner; in other words, it is the petitioner who must comply with it. The Judgment, to the contrary, seems to understand that this rule is a State obligation, because it indicates that, if any remedy is pending, the State can resolve or rectify the situation. However, with this phrase, the Court is also providing an incentive for lodging petitions before the Commission even if domestic remedies have not been exhausted, because these can be exhausted later; thus making it possible for the domestic jurisdiction to co-exist with the inter-American jurisdiction in the same case.

---

① Para. 27 of the Judgment.

419. In addition, the Judgment appears to disregard the fact that it is not for the State to exhaust the remedies, but rather, when appropriate, it corresponds to the State to decide the situation alleged in the remedies that the petitioner has filed in its jurisdiction and, if the petitioner has not filed any remedies or if they are pending, it is not incumbent on the State to provide any solution, because its international responsibility has not yetbeen engaged.

421. The fourth reason cited by the Judgment for not admitting the objection in question is as follows: "*[i]n addition, the Court considers that it would be contrary to the principle of procedural economy if petitions were not admitted based on the fact that, at the time of the initial presentation, domestic remedies had not been exhausted and if, when the admissibility of these remedies was analyzed, they have been exhausted. The European Court of Human Rights [⋯] has ruled similarly in some cases, as has the International Court of Justice in relation to access to its jurisdiction.*"①

With the reference to procedural economy, the Judgment provides more direct encouragement. Hence, it is necessary to reiterate the assertion made previously in this opinion that, if was not compulsory to have exhausted domestic remedies before lodging the petition, it would be permissible that, at least for a time, the same case could be examined simultaneously by the domestic jurisdiction and the international jurisdiction, and this could constitute a perverse incentive to lodge petitions before the Commission even when the said requirement has not been met, in the hope that it can be complied with before the Commission takes a decision on their admissibility. Evidently, that possibility was not envisaged or sought by the Convention.

Furthermore, regarding the references to precedents in the case of the

---

① Para. 28 of the Judgment.

European Court of Human Rights and the International Court of Justice made by the Judgment in support of this decision,[1] it is sufficient to point out that neither the European Convention of Human Rights nor the Rules of Procedure of the International Court of Justice contain a provision such as that of Article 46(1)(a) of the Convention. In addition, both these bodies are courts rather than a non-judicial entity, as in the case of the Commission, before which compliance with the requirement in question must be substantiated. This means that, in the European case, the rule is that, before resorting to the European Court of Human Rights the remedies of the domestic jurisdiction must be exhausted. This is the general rule, admitting the exception only if this exhaustion is achieved shortly after the presentation of the case. And, in the case of the International Court of Justice, the cases referred to relate to recognition of that court's jurisdiction and not to the filing of a preliminary objection concerning the prior exhaustion of domestic remedies. Consequently, the cases referred to do not represent precedents.

CONCLUSION

In short and as pointed out previously, as Article 46(1)(a) of the Convention clearly states and based on the congruent understanding of Articles 26(1) and 2, 28(h), 30(1), (2) and (3), 31 and 32 of the Commission's Rules of Procedure, which interpret the said article of the Convention, it can be concluded, unequivocally, that compliance with the rule of prior exhaustion of domestic remedies must have occurred at the time the petition is lodged before the Commission, taking into consideration, also, any observations made by the State when responding to the relevant parts of the petition forwarded to it.

However, this was not considered to be so in the Judgment, which, to

---

[1] Idem.

the contrary, indicates that the decision on the objection filed by the State based on the petitioner's failure to comply with this rule was taken by verifying that this requirement had been met when the Commission took a decision on the petition's admissibility. Hence, the ruling infringes the provisions of Article 46(1) (a) of the Convention and the said regulatory provisions.

The undersignedalso dissents from the Judgment because, the *"reinforcing or complementing"* nature of the Convention that inspires the inter-American system of human rights as a whole is nullified, encouraging the lodging of cases before the system without the domestic remedies having been exhausted previously, which will result in such cases being examined simultaneously by the domestic jurisdiction and the inter-American jurisdiction.

Proceeding in this way not only makes the rule of prior exhaustion of domestic remedies meaningless and inapplicable, but is also contrary to the Court's affirmation that it *"must safeguard the just balance between the protection of human rights, the ultimate purpose of the system, and the legal certainty and procedural balance that ensure the stability and reliability of the international protection."*[①]

Consequently, it is in this sense that the undersigned sharesthe assertion of the Court itself as regards *"the tolerance of 'evident violations of the procedural rules established by the Convention itself* [and, it should be added, by the Rules of Procedure of the Court and of the Commission,] *would entail the loss of authority and credibility essential for the organs responsible for administering the system for the protection of human rights."*[②] And this is so, because it is precisely these rules that guarantee the impartiality and independence of the Court when imparting justice in cases relating to human rights.

[①] *Case of Cruz Sánchez et al. v. Peru. Preliminary objections, merits, reparations and costs.* Judgment of April 17, 2015. Series C No. 292, para. 37.

[②] *Case of Díaz Peña v. Venezuela. Preliminary objection, merits, reparations and costs.* Judgment of June 26, 2012. Series C 244, para. 43.

Strict compliance with the rule of prior exhaustion of domestic remedies is not, therefore, a mere legal formality. Rather, respect for this rule strengthens and enhances the inter-American human rights system, because it guarantees the principles of legal certainty, procedural balance and complementarity that sustain the system, leaving no margin or, at least, the smallest margin possible, for the perception that the Court's rulings do not respond, strictly and exclusively, to considerations of justice – beyond the explicable discrepancies that they may elicit, particularly from those who consider them adverse.

Considering that its case law is binding only for the State that has undertaken to comply with the *"judgment of the Court"* in the case to which it is a party,① and that, for the other States Parties to the Convention it is only a subsidiary source of public international law, in other words, a *"subsidiary means for the determination of rules of law*,② this dissenting opinion is evidently issued in the hope that it contributes to the reflection on the rule of prior exhaustion of domestic remedies and, thus, leads to the Court's case law in this regard adopting the criteria described above in the near future.

Moreover, this opinion evidently takes into account, asalso did another opinion,③ of the fact that one of the particular imperatives faced by a tri-

---

① Article 68 of the Convention: "1. The States Parties to the Convention undertake to comply with the judgment of the Court in any case to which they are parties. 2. That part of a judgment that stipulates compensatory damages may be executed in the country concerned in accordance with domestic procedure governing the execution of judgments against the State."
② Article 38 of the Statute of the International Court of Justice: "1. The Court, whose function is to decide in accordance with international law such disputes as are submitted to it, shall apply: a) international conventions, whether general or particular, establishing rules expressly recognized by the contesting states; b) international custom, as evidence of a general practice accepted as law; c) the general principles of law recognized by civilized nations; d. subject to the provisions of Article 59, judicial decisions and the teachings of the most highly qualified publicists of the various nations, as subsidiary means for the determination of rules of law. 2. This provision shall not prejudice the power of the Court to decide a case *ex aequo et bono*, if the parties agree thereto."Article 59 of this Statute: "[t]he decision of the Court has no binding force except between the parties and in respect of that particular case".
③ Record of complaint submitted to the Court on August 17, 2011, by Judge Eduardo Vio Grossi and Dissenting opinion of this judge, *Case of Barbani Duarte et al. v. Uruguay. Merits, reparations and costs.* Judgment of October 13, 2011. Series C No. 234.

bunal such as the Inter-American Court is that of acting with full awareness that, as an autonomous and independent entity, there is no superior authority that controls it, which means that, true to the important role assigned to it, it must strictly respect the limits of this role, and remain and evolve in the sphere inherent to a jurisdictional entity.

Without doubt, acting as indicated above is the best contribution that the Court can make to the development and consolidation of the inter-American system of human rights – a requirement *sine qua non* for the proper safeguard of those rights – an institutional framework within which it is incumbent on the Commission to promote respect for and to defend those rights,① on the Court to interpret and apply the Convention in the cases that are submitted to it,② and on the States to amend the Convention if they consider this necessary. ③ The development and strength of this system is rooted in compliance by each of them with their specific roles.

Eduardo Vio Grossi
Judge

Pablo Saavedra Alessandri
Secretary

---

① First phrase of Article 41 of the Convention: "[t]he main function of the Commission shall be to promote respect for and defense of human rights."

② Article 62(3) of the Convention: "[t]he jurisdiction of the Court shall comprise all cases concerning the interpretation and application of the provisions of this Convention that are submitted to it, provided that the States Parties to the case recognize or have recognized such jurisdiction, whether by special declaration pursuant to the preceding paragraphs, or by a special agreement."

③ Article 76 of the Convention: "1. Proposals to amend this Convention may be submitted to the General Assembly for the action it deems appropriate by any State Party directly, and by the Commission or the Court through the Secretary General. 2. Amendments shall enter into force for the States ratifying them on the date when twothirds of the States Parties to this Convention have deposited their respective instruments of ratification. With respect to the other States Parties, the amendments shall enter into force on the dates on which they deposit their respective instruments of ratification." Article 39 of theVienna Convention on the Law of Treaties: "General rule regarding the amendment of treaties. A treaty may be amended by agreement between the parties. The rules laid down in Part II apply to such an agreement except in so far as the treaty may otherwise provide."

黄海勇走私普通货物案一审判决书

湖北省武汉市中级人民法院刑事判决书 （2017）鄂01刑初83号

公诉机关湖北省武汉市人民检察院。

被告人黄海勇（又名黄贺永，英文名 WONG HO WING），男，1963年6月3日出生于辽宁省丹东市，身份证号码440301196306030934，香港永久性居民身份证号码PO61299(9)，汉族，大学文化，曾任深圳裕伟实业发展有限公司、深圳裕伟贸易实业有限公司、湖北裕伟贸易实业有限公司、武汉丰润油脂保税仓库有限公司等四家公司董事长兼法定代表人，深圳市亨润国际实业有限公司（上述五公司均已被工商部门吊销营业执照）董事、总经理，香港宝润集团有限公司执行董事，户籍所在地广东省深圳市南山区沙河东方花园F区31栋。1998年8月黄海勇出境，2001年3月16日湖北省武汉市人民检察院以走私普通货物罪对黄海勇批准逮捕，2001年6月海关总署通过国际刑警组织对黄海勇发出红色通缉令，2008年10月30日黄海勇在秘鲁入境时被秘鲁警方收押。2016年7月13日黄海勇被秘鲁政府移交我国，2016年7月17日黄海勇被武汉海关缉私局押解回国执行逮捕。现羁押于武汉市第二看守所。

辩护人冉慧军，湖北创智律师事务所律师。

湖北省武汉市人民检察院以武检公刑诉〔2017〕67号起诉书指控被告人黄海勇犯走私普通货物罪，于2017年4月18日向本院提起公诉。本院于当日立案，并依法组成合议庭，于2017年6月15日公开开庭进行了审理。公诉机关指派检察员朱明等出庭支持公诉，被告人黄海勇及其辩护人到庭参加诉讼。因案件重大复杂，经报请湖北省高级人民法院批准延长审理期限三个月，湖北省武汉市人民检察院建议延期审理二次，经最高人民法院批准四次延长审理期限各三个月。本案经合议庭评议并提交审判委员会讨论决定,现已审理终结。

湖北省武汉市人民检察院指控:1996年,被告人黄海勇在担任深圳裕伟实业发展有限公司、深圳裕伟贸易实业有限公司、湖北裕伟贸易实业有限公司、武汉丰润油脂保税仓库有限公司等四家公司董事长兼法定代表人,深圳市亨润国际实业有限公司董事、总经理,香港宝润集团执行董事期间,以上述公司名义伙同其他公司及自然人,利用虚假备案资料领取毛豆油进料加工手册,逃避海关监管,将本应用于加工的毛豆油未向海关申报并在不补证不补税的情况下直接销售牟利。

1996年,被告人黄海勇及其下属潘子牛(已判刑)前往上海,与香港荣成发展有限公司、上海润丰油脂食品有限公司总经理周永生商谈并签订联营协议解决了进口油源的问题。双方约定由上海润丰提供境外毛豆油油源,并协助深圳裕伟在上海外高桥保税区海关办理报关、转关手续;深圳裕伟负责办理毛豆油免税进口手续,进口后双方在国内各自销售一半。

1996年,被告人黄海勇通过刘国建的引荐,认识其胞兄武汉外贸经济贸易发展有限公司总经理刘国光(已故)。后双方商定,深圳裕伟支付给武汉外贸进料金额1‰的代理费委托其代理进料加工业务,双方准备了内容虚假的委托加工合同等备案资料,以武汉外贸的名义向武汉海关申领毛豆油加工贸易手册。1996年8月16日,黄海勇申领到2万吨毛豆油加工贸易的C47006100042号手册(以下简称42号手册),油源实际由香港荣成提供,实际进口19 925吨。为争取时间办理手续,涉案毛豆油由上海金环国际贸易有限公司(以下简称上海金环)办理区外保税,同年10月被告人黄海勇要求武汉外贸与上海金环补签进口合同,上海金环将保税油以42号手册进口,随后黄海勇安排潘子牛人办理了转关手续。同时,为了兑现联营协议中与上海润丰各自销售一半的约定,深圳裕伟以市场变化和加工能力不足为由,通过武汉海关货管处向上海外高桥保税区海关出具证明函,将42号手册项下的1万吨毛豆油中的5 000吨滞留上海。随后在未向海关申报许可证并补证补税的情况下,湖北裕伟将9 925吨毛豆油销售给武汉油脂集团有限公司(以下简称武汉油脂)和上海润丰。经武汉海关核定,上述9 925吨毛豆油完税价格人民币 46 013 585 元,偷逃关税、增值税等应缴税款人民币 64 485 576.44 元。

1996 年 12 月 31 日,被告人黄海勇以深圳亨润名义与香港兆光(中国)有限公司签订了假进口合同等备案资料,向武汉海关申领到 2 万吨毛豆油加工贸易的 C47006100175 号手册(以下简称 175 号手册),油源实际由香港荣成提供,实际进口 19942 吨。1997 年 1 月,黄海勇安排潘子牛到上海浦江海关办理毛豆油转关手续。随后深圳亨润再次通过武汉海关货管处向上海浦江海关出具证明函,将 1 万吨毛豆油滞留在上海。随后在未向海关申报许可补证补税的情况下,湖北裕伟将 19942 吨毛豆油销售给武汉油脂、武汉华捷油脂公司(以下简称武汉华捷)、上海润丰和上海金环。1997 年 2 月、3 月,175 号手册项下被倒卖的 19942 吨保税毛豆油,才以少报数量、低报价格在武汉海关申报进口。经武汉海关核定,上述毛豆油完税价格人民币 92 452 752 元,偷逃关税、增值税等应缴税款人民币 133 526 889.74 元。

1997 年 2 月 14 日,被告人黄海勇以湖北裕伟名义委托武汉外贸代理进料加工业务,双方准备了内容虚假的备案资料,以武汉外贸的名义申领到 2 万吨毛豆油加工贸易的 C47007100051 号手册(以下简称 51 号手册),油源实际由香港荣成提供,实际进口 18 851 吨。随后,湖北裕伟在上海外高桥保税区海关办理前述保税毛豆油转关手续,并再次通过武汉海关货管处向上海外高桥保税区海关出具将货物部分滞留上海的证明函,在办理转关手续过程中,湖北裕伟将前述保税毛豆油分别销售给武汉油脂、武汉华捷、上海润丰与上海市油脂公司进出口分公司。1997 年 5 月,51 号手册项下已被倒卖的 18 851 吨毛豆油,才以少报数量、低报价格分拆转至 42 号手册、丰润保税库向武汉海关申报。经武汉海关核定,上述 18 851 吨毛豆油完税价格人民币 87 393 742 元,偷逃关税、增值税等应缴税款人民币 122 231 269.61 元。

1997 年 3 月,湖北裕伟再次使用 51 号手册,在天津海关办理了从北海粮油工业(天津)有限公司(以下简称北海粮油)手册结转 2 万吨毛豆油的手续。1997 年 4 月,湖北裕伟再次通过武汉海关货管处向天津海关出具将 1 万吨毛豆油销售给武汉油脂、武汉华捷与北海粮油。经武汉海关核定,上述 2 万吨毛豆油完税价格人民币 92 720 320 元,偷逃关税、增值税等应税款人民币127 454 057.72元。

1997年5月,为便于走私牟利,香港宝润集团采取与武汉油脂假合资的方法,成立武汉丰润油脂保税仓库有限公司(以下简称丰润保税库)丰润保税库进口的37 709吨毛豆油,先后两次以南海油脂委托仓储名义申请办理转头手续,油源实际由香港荣成和建兴企业有限公司两公司提供。湖北裕伟在上海龙吴海关办理转关手续后,毛豆油没进入武汉丰润保税库,在向武汉海关报关前,将毛豆油已销售给武汉油脂、武汉华捷与湖北长江油脂有限公司。经武汉海关核定,上述37709吨毛豆油完税价格人民币174 822 647元,偷逃关税、增值税等应缴税款人民币262 947 246.93元。

为了掩盖犯罪事实,被告人黄海勇及潘子牛代表湖北裕伟、深圳裕伟与鹤山华侨商品供应公司商定后,由该公司代湖北裕伟、深圳裕伟为购买毛豆油的客户虚开增值税专用发票,并按照每吨90元向湖北裕伟、深圳裕伟收取了开票费。

综上,湖北裕伟、深圳亨润、深圳实业、丰润保税库等单位走私毛豆油共计10.64万余吨,完税价格共计人民币710 645 040.44元。2000年11月2日,湖北裕伟被工商行政管理部门吊销营业执照;2001年1月10日,深圳亨润、深圳裕伟、深圳实业被工商行政管理部门吊销登记;2002年5月19日,丰润保税库被工商行政管理部门吊销登记。

1998年8月被告人黄海勇出境,2001年6月海关总署通过国际刑警组织对黄海勇发出红色通缉令,2008年10月30日黄海勇在秘鲁入境时被秘鲁警方收押,2016年7月13日黄海勇被秘鲁政府移交我国,2016年7月17日黄海勇被武汉海关缉私局押解回国。

公诉机关当庭宣读出示的证据有:1. 受理刑事案件登记表、抓获经过、情况说明等;2. 合同、发票、凭证、银行账据、判决、报关单证、关税缴款书、核查传真、扣押清单、手册等书证材料;3. 海关关税部门核定走私案件偷逃税额表等鉴定结论;4. 证人周永生、刘卓尔、杨永昌、冯楠杰、刘国建、刘国光(已故)、向求亮、王阿才、周南岗、韩文杰、董铭、王绩成、桂绩金、李鸿雁、刘方锡、鄢海斌、张宝林、邵益先、陈正光、梁萍、赵伟娜、李福财、祁军、潘学俊、廉华、李伟锋等人证言;5. 同案犯潘子牛的供述和辩解等;6. 被告人黄海勇的供述及辩解等。

公诉机关认为,被告人黄海勇在担任深圳裕伟、深圳实业、湖北裕伟、丰润保税库、深圳亨润、香港宝润等公司高管期间,为了公司利益,以公司名义伙同其他公司、自然人,用虚假备案资料骗取三本进料加工手册,逃避海关监管,将本应用于加工后复出口的毛豆油未向海关申报并在不补证不补税的情况下直接销售牟利;成立丰润保税库后,将本应入库的保税毛豆油直接毛销售牟利,走私毛豆油10.64万余吨,偷逃应缴税款人民币710 645 040.44元,犯罪数额特别巨大,犯罪情节特别严重,使国家利益遭受重大损失。在单位犯罪中,被告人黄海勇系直接负责的主管人员,已触犯《中华人民共和国刑法》第三十条、第三十一条、第一百五十三条、第一百五十四条,应当以走私普通货物罪追究其刑事责任。

被告人黄海勇对公诉机关指控其犯走私普通货物罪的罪名及主要犯罪事实不持异议。其辩护人提出:1. 本案走私的金额应按同案犯潘子牛湖北省高级人民法院终审判决确定的走私金额认定;2. 黄海勇认罪坦白;3. 黄海勇在秘鲁羁押的时间应当折抵刑期。

经审理查明,1996年,被告人黄海勇在担任深圳裕伟实业发展有限公司(简称深圳裕伟)、深圳裕伟贸易实业有限公司(简称深圳实业)、湖北裕伟贸易实业有公司(简称湖北裕伟)、武汉丰润油脂保税仓库有限公司(简称武汉丰润)等四家公司董事长兼法定代表人,深圳市亨润国际实业有限公司(简称深圳亨润)董事、总经理,香港宝润集团执行董事期间,与其下属潘子牛(已判刑)、邵辉(在逃)等人谋划,采取申领进料加工手册和设立保税库的方式进口保税毛豆油,不经加工和复出口,通过补办能够享受外贸优惠税率的许可证,向外经委、海关等部门申请出口转内销,并向海关补缴关税、增值税等应缴税款后,将毛豆油在国内予以销售。为此,黄海勇、潘子牛等人以上述单位名义分别与武汉外贸经济贸易发展有限公司(简称武汉外贸)、上海润丰油脂食品有限公司(简称上海润丰)、武汉油脂集团有限公司(简称武汉油脂)、西藏外贸公司、鹤山华侨商品供应公司(简称鹤山华侨)商定合作经营毛豆油事宜,由武汉外贸代理深圳裕伟、湖北裕伟等涉案单位向外经委、海关等部门申领毛豆油进料加工手册、申报毛豆油出口转内销,涉案单位按进口毛豆油数量及比例向武汉外贸支付代理费;上海润丰提供境外进口油源,深圳裕伟、湖北裕伟等涉案单位负责办理进口通关、转关、内销、补证、补税手续,毛豆油入境后双方各销售一半;武汉油脂及其下属企业为深圳裕伟、湖北裕伟等涉案单位提供毛豆油加工手续,向涉案单位购买毛豆油,与涉案单位合伙成立保税库;西藏外贸以委托经营的方式为深圳裕伟、湖北裕伟等涉案单位提供毛豆油西藏许可证和配额,供涉案单位按外贸优惠政策缴纳税款;鹤山华侨代替深圳裕伟、湖北裕伟等涉案单位向购买毛豆油单位开具增值税专用发票,涉案单位按 90 元/吨向鹤山华侨支付开票手续费。1996 年 8 月至 1997 年 5 月,深圳裕伟、湖北裕伟等涉案单位以进料加工为名,分别以申领的 42 号手册、175 号手册、51 号手册和设立的武汉丰润保税库,向武汉海关等部门申报进口毛豆油共计 10.64 余万吨,其中,3 万吨毛豆油经海关批准以西藏许可证和配额缴税后予以销售,0.16 万吨毛豆油经海关批准以低于国家规定的价格缴税后予以销售,2.04 万吨在海关办理了结转加工手续,其余 5.44 万吨毛豆油均未经海关许可并且未补缴税款予以销售,走私偷逃应缴税款共计 379 524 829.28 元。案发前 175 号手册已核销,42 号、51 号手册至今未核销。

案发后,深圳裕伟、深圳实业、湖北裕伟、深圳亨润均被工商部门吊销工商登记。

1998 年 8 月被告人黄海勇出境,2001 年 6 月海关总署通过国际刑警组织对黄海勇发出红色通缉令,2008 年 10 月 27 日黄海勇在秘鲁入境时被秘鲁警方抓获,同月 30 日收押。2016 年 7 月 13 日黄海勇被秘鲁政府移交我国,2016 年 7 月 17 日黄海勇被武汉海关缉私局押解回国。

另查明,武汉海关缉私局查封、扣押涉案单位及被告人黄海勇用赃款购买的如下财产:1. 湖北裕伟贸易实业有限公司的轿车一辆,车牌号为鄂 A80103,该车已变卖,所得价款 25.4 万元扣押在武汉海关专门账户;2. 北京裕伟达经贸发展有限公司的轿车二辆,车牌号为京 CH6818、京 CH1965;3. 武汉丰润保税库的轿车一辆,车牌号为鄂 AF1458,该车已变卖,所得价款 13.8 万元扣押在武汉海关专门账户;4. 武汉丰润保税库的轿车一辆,车牌号为鄂 AF1799;5. 深圳市亨润国际实业有限公司的旅行客车一辆,车牌号为粤 BF1466;6. 深圳裕伟贸易实业有限公司的轿车一辆,车牌号为粤 B30298;7. 深圳市裕伟实业发展有限公司 1 200 万元,该笔款项已追回,暂存在武汉海关专门账户;8. 湖北裕伟公司转移走私毛豆油赃款给上海裕源实业有限公司 1 529 526.6 元,该笔款项已追回,暂存在武汉海关专门账户;9. 湖北裕伟公司转移走私毛豆油赃款给上海衡利贸易实业有限公司 273 841.94 元,该笔款项已追回,暂存在武汉海关专门账户;10. 深圳裕伟贸易实业有限公司在中国工商银行深圳市分行存款 33 091.54 元;11. 深圳市亨润国际实业有限公司在中国银行深圳市分行存款 39 927.17 元;12. 深圳裕伟贸易实业有限公司在中国工商银行深圳分行存款 144 436.85 元;13. 深圳裕伟贸易实业有限公司位于深圳市罗湖区外运路荔都大厦 20D、20E、20F 综合楼房屋三套,面积分别为 107.57 平方米、80.14 平方米、86.14 平方米;14. 深圳市裕伟实业发展有限公司位于深圳市罗湖区笋岗路同乐大厦同德阁 3006 号房屋一套,面积为 90.21 平方米;15. 深圳裕伟贸易实业有限公司位于上海市徐汇区襄阳南路 485-495 号金环大厦 12 层 C 房屋一套,面积 197.43 平方米,尚未办理房产证;16. 湖北裕伟贸易实业有限公司位于武汉市江岸区车站路 6 号怡东大厦 18 层 1 座房屋一套,面积为 228.72 平方米,尚未办理房产证;17. 湖北裕伟贸易实业有限公司位于武汉市同城广场同心大厦 2205 室房屋一套,面积为 104.89 平方米,尚未办理房产证;18. 北京裕伟达公司位于北京市朝阳区幸福一村幸福公寓 802 号房屋一套,面积为 132.09 平方米,尚未办理房产证。

还查明,位于深圳市罗湖区田贝一路华丽园南座 2A 面积为 112.64 平方米的房屋一套系被告人黄海勇作案之前购买。

认定上述事实,有下列经过庭审举证、质证的证据予以证明:

1. 身份资料、工商登记资料等书证证实:被告人黄海勇的身份、任职及深圳裕伟、深圳实业、湖北裕伟、深圳亨润成立时间、经营范围以及案发后均被吊销工商登记等情况。

2. 合同、发票、凭证、银行账据、报关单证、关税缴款书、核查传真、扣押清单、进料加工手册、西藏许可证和配额等书证证实:深圳裕伟、深圳实业、湖北裕伟、深圳亨润、武汉丰润保税库与有关单位合作,采取申领进料加工手册、设立保税库等方式进口保税毛豆油后予以销售、补税等情况。

3. 海关总署回复、武汉海关核定走私案件偷逃税额表、核税证明等书证证实：深圳裕伟、深圳实业、湖北裕伟、深圳亨润、武汉丰润保税库走私的毛豆油中，未缴税的有54428.245吨，偷逃关税、增值税等税款共计379 524 829.28元。

4. 鹤山华侨虚开的增值税专用发票、广东省江门市中级人民法院刑事判决书证实：1996年12月至1997年5月，鹤山华侨受深圳裕伟之托，先后为上海润丰、武汉油脂、上海金环国际贸易有限公司（简称上海金环）、上海市油脂公司进出口分公司（简称上海油脂）等单位虚开购销毛豆油增值税专用发票，数额共计34 750吨。

5. 湖北省武汉市中级人民法院刑事判决书、湖北省高级人民法院刑事裁定书证实：原武汉海关关长莫海涛同意黄海勇、潘子牛等人使用无效西藏许可证低价补税，以玩忽职守罪被判处刑罚等情况。

6. 湖北省武汉市中级人民法院刑事判决书、湖北省高级人民法院刑事判决书证实：同案犯潘子牛已因犯走私普通货物罪被判处刑罚及判决对涉案财产依法处置的情况。

7. 中国外交部条法司向海关总署缉私局出具的复函证明：秘鲁驻华大使馆向中国外交部条法司的照会证实：黄海勇在秘鲁期间被收押日期为2008年10月30日至2016年7月13日其被引渡回中国为止。

8. 武汉海关缉私局查封、扣押涉案财产的手续及情况说明。

9. 证人周永生（原上海润丰总经理）的证言：1996年，我与黄海勇、潘子牛合作经营毛豆油，我方提供境外油源，黄海勇方申领加工手册报关、转关，并提供许可证补税，进口毛豆油先后销售给黄海勇方指定的武汉外贸、深圳亨润后，再由我方向黄海勇方进行回购，发票由鹤山华侨开具。我方回购的毛豆油销给了上海金环。此外，我方还向黄海勇的丰润保税库提供了4万吨油源。潘子牛随同黄海勇参与了协议签订、货物转关、销售联络、商谈成立保税库、与鹤山华侨协商开票等事宜。1996年10月，我与潘子牛见面，潘说有经贸部签发的许可证；有一次，黄海勇、潘子牛到上海，潘拿出武汉海关关封，称毛豆油必须在武汉报关交税，先进料加工，再拿许可证顶出来；第一笔1万吨毛豆油转关武汉，是潘子牛带手册到上海金环和上海海关办理的；香港荣成与深圳亨润签订的2万吨毛豆油外贸合同,是潘子牛去报关的,我方经销的1万吨毛豆油由鹤山华侨开具发票,也是潘子牛转交给我们的;1997年初,我到武汉拿货款时,黄海勇、潘子牛与我商谈成立保税库事宜;同年四五月份,潘子牛、邵辉拿着丰润保税库的营业执照到上海进货,当时我方正好有2万吨毛豆油到码头,于是双方进行了交易。

10. 证人刘卓尔(原上海润丰副总经理)的证言:我公司与黄海勇、潘子牛合营的3本手册共进口毛豆油5万吨,武汉海关出具证明后,毛豆油留一半在上海由我方经销,我方将其中的1.5万吨销给了上海油脂;另一半毛豆油由黄海勇方经销,是武汉油脂、武汉华捷油脂有限公司(简称武汉华捷)等单位带款到上海提货。丰润保税库成立后,向香港荣成、香港建兴各购买2万吨毛豆油,都是武汉油脂提的货。以手册进口的毛豆油中第一次1万吨、第二次2万吨的转关手续都是潘子牛经办的,以保税库进口的4万吨毛豆油的手续是潘子牛和邵辉经办的。

11. 证人杨永昌(原上海金环总经理)的证言:我任职期间,经手卖给武汉2批毛豆油,由上海润丰提供提单,我公司发货。我公司还向上海润丰购买毛豆油1.5万吨左右,向鹤山华侨购买毛豆油1万吨左右,卖方提供的税单有些是在交易之前,有些是在交易之后,缴税单位为武汉外贸和深圳亨润。转关到武汉的毛豆油是武汉油脂、武汉华捷等单位到上海来提的货。我到深圳亨润与鹤山华侨签订合同时,黄海勇、潘子牛均在场。

12. 证人冯楠杰(原武汉油脂总经理)的证言:1996年,我经刘国建介绍与黄海勇、潘子牛相识,双方达成购买毛豆油意向。后我公司向湖北裕伟购买毛豆油6余万吨(其中1998年之后购买2余万吨),除在天津提货5 000吨外,其余均在上海提货,由鹤山华侨向我公司开具发票。丰润保税库于1997年建办公室和油柜,柜子里装的毛豆油都是我公司的。

13. 证人刘国建(原武汉外贸总经理刘国光的弟弟)的证言:我经人介绍与黄海勇相识,后通过黄海勇认识潘子牛。黄海勇想在武汉经营毛豆油进口加工业务,需要我帮忙联系外贸公司和加工厂。以武汉外贸名义申领的第一本手册,是我自已先行与南海油脂签订进出口合同并与沙鸥油厂签订加工协议申请的,但未获海关审批,认识黄海勇后,黄很快就让该手册在海关获批。1997年,我哥哥刘国光所在的武汉外贸又代理黄海勇方申领了一本2万吨毛豆油进料加工手册,由武汉外经委审批的事项是武汉外贸办理的,由武汉海关审批的事项是黄海勇办理的。毛豆油内销补税的手续由外经委审批的事项也是武汉外贸办理的。

14. 证人向求亮(原武汉外贸部门经理)的证言:1996年8月份,刘国建、刘国光和我在江汉饭店与深圳裕伟的黄海勇会面,商谈毛豆油进料加工业务,并签订了协议。此前,我与刘国建等人与沙鸥油厂签订了毛豆油加工协议,刘国建还办理了加工保函和出口合同,但后来办理手册(42号手册)未获审批,结识黄海勇后,手册很快获批。后我公司又接受湖北裕伟委托,申领了第二本手册(51号手册)。毛豆油内销审批手续是我公司到外经委办理的。内销时,潘子牛提出由我公司开具增值税发票和付汇的问题,但后来都没能落实,我公司只赚取代理费。

15. 证人刘国光(原武汉外贸总经理)的证言:我公司与深圳裕伟共签订2份毛豆油进料加工代理协议,进口毛豆油4万吨。

16. 证人祁军(原武汉华捷经理)的证言:我公司共从湖北裕伟购买4批毛豆油,数量17 467吨,除第一单5 000吨外,其余均未拿到增值税发票。我还以经营部名义与黄海勇签订过毛豆油加工合同,黄海勇持该合同申领了一本进料加工手册。

17. 证人廉华的证言:我公司与北海粮油和武汉外贸签订三方合同,由北海粮油结转2万吨毛豆油到武汉外贸,经补证、补税后,再由北海粮油向湖北裕伟购买1万吨毛豆油。我们同武汉外贸的约定是由北裕伟履行的。审批通过后,我方向湖北裕伟催要了补证、补税手续,再将该手续交给北海粮油,1万吨毛豆油通过我公司调汇。

18. 证人李福财(原鹤山华侨副经理)的证言:1996年,我公司冯福亨经理经人介绍认识潘子牛。同年八九月份,潘子牛打电话联系冯福亨,称他们进口了1万吨毛豆油,他们提供报关、清关资料和海关关税发票、海关代征的增值税发票,要我公司替他们公司开具内销的增值税发票,问冯福亨敢不敢做,冯把这件事告诉我后,打电话回复潘子牛说可以做。我公司按每吨90元收取手续费,共替深圳亨润、湖北裕伟为上海润丰、上海油脂、武汉油脂等单位开具 5 万吨毛豆油交易的增值税发票。

19. 证人周南岗（原安徽宇环储运公司上海办事处主任）的证言：1997年间，我公司受潘子牛等人委托，分别以安徽宇环储运公司和上海中艺国际储运公司的名义 3 次为其代办毛豆油报关转关业务。提单、发票等资料由潘子牛等人提供，代理费由潘子牛经手支付，申报后我方将海关的放行单交给潘子牛。第一单代理的是进料加工手册，第二单和第三单代理的是武汉某保税库。

20. 证人梁萍（原武汉丰润保税库员工）的证言：我于 1998 年在丰润保税库工作期间，按照黄海勇的吩咐，向海关写过几份补税申请，办理过湖北裕伟税务歇业等业务；按照潘子牛的通知，将湖北裕伟人民币 100 多万元转汇深圳。

21. 证人赵伟娜（原武汉丰润保税库财务人员）的证言：丰润保税库没有收入，支出的钱都是前期投入的注册资金，到企业年检时，就从湖北裕伟将钱打入以备检查，待会计师事务所验资后再把钱还给湖北裕伟。丰润保税库在武汉油脂设立的办公室建好不久，我带海关人员去看过，黄海勇向他们作了介绍，说目前是租用武汉油脂的油罐，以后还要扩建，海关人员没有实地察看。

22. 证人韩文杰（原湖北裕伟出纳员）的证言：湖北裕伟的老板是黄海勇和潘子牛，公司银行账户是潘子牛带我去开的。公司财务章由我保管，公司法人印章和黄海勇、潘子牛的私人印章由潘子牛保管。1997 年 1 月，邵辉接任公司经理。公司资金往来单位主要有武汉华捷、武汉油脂、深圳裕伟、上海润丰等单位。

23. 证人董铭（原湖北裕伟司机）的证言：1997 年 6 月，我受邵辉指派，将 1 枚印章送到上海交给潘子牛；同年 9 月，我再次受邵辉指派，将 1 张人民币 500 万元的汇票送到深圳交给潘子牛。

24. 证人王绩成（原武汉海关货管处负费人）的证言：1996 年底莫海涛调任武汉海关关长后，将黄海勇、潘子牛介绍给我们认识。此后，黄海勇在我处办理了 3 本毛豆油进料加工手册。货物转关过程中，我处给上海海关开过几次证明，给天津海关开过 1 次证明，内容是同意将部分进口毛豆油暂时留在上海或天津。1997年3月,黄海勇持报关单和西藏许可证申请补税内销,我请示莫海涛,他说西藏许可证可以用,后来我就批准黄海勇以每吨480美元的价格补税。黄海勇的保税库是1997年4月批准成立的,共进口毛豆油4.7万吨,都没有核销。

25. 证人桂继金(原武汉海关货管处保税科科长)的证言:1996年我和几名同事受邀到江汉饭店吃饭,席间王绩成处长将黄海勇、潘子牛介绍给我们认识,莫海涛关长让我们对黄海勇、潘子牛给予关照。此后,我按照王绩成的吩咐为黄海勇、潘子牛写了3份转关便函,第一份函是1996年10月写给上海外高桥保税区海关的,内容是同意先运5 000吨毛豆油到武汉,余下5 000吨留在上海;第二份函是1997年7月写给上海浦江海关的,内容是将1万吨毛豆油转运到武汉,余下1万吨留在上海;第三份函是1997年2月写给上海某海关的,内容是将51号手册项下1万吨毛豆油转运武汉,余下1万吨留在上海。这3份函的货主是深圳亨润和武汉外贸,但海关手续都是黄海勇、潘子牛前来联系办理的。此外,我还审核了175号毛豆油进料加工手册,数量2万吨,单耗20%,单价每吨400美元;经办了第一笔5000吨毛豆油内销补税手续,是黄海勇前来申请的,当时这些毛豆油在哪不知道。

26. 证人李鸿雁(原武汉海关江汉办事处综合科科长)的证言:我经办了黄海勇、潘子牛4单毛豆油报关手续。办理第一单毛豆油时,我见数额比较大,觉得应当实地验货,就将单子暂时放下,后王绩成处长把我叫到他办公室,货主潘子牛也在,王说这是莫关长的关系,不验货先放行,且由他先签字我后签字。后面3单和第一单办理的情况基本相同。42号手册的经营单位是武汉外贸,报关手续是黄海勇、潘子牛与该公司的人一起来办理的。175号手册的经营单位是深圳亨润,每次报关不是黄海勇来就是潘子牛来。

27. 证人刘方锡(原武汉海关员工)的证言:黄海勇、潘子牛是莫海涛到任后介绍给我们认识并吩咐给予关照的。有一次,王绩成处长把我叫到他办公室,拿了几份黄海勇公司进口货物的报关单,他签字后给我,我不敢得罪他们,没有查验就在单子上签了字。有3张报关单是后来改过的,每年国家审计署来检查前,我们海关内部要自查,在自查的过程中发现报关单的进口货物数量与手册不一致而作的修改,如42号手册只批2万吨毛豆油,但是报关单记载毛豆油进口数量却多于2万吨。

28. 证人张宝林(原武汉海关机场办事处综合科副主任)的证言:黄海勇是王绩成介绍我认识的,后我通过黄海勇认识潘子牛。1997年1月30日,黄海勇拿着手册的一些单证和许可证找我,要求核销手册,申请补税,我见许可证是西藏经贸厅发的,说西藏许可证恐怕不行,这种情况以前没有办成。他说怎么不行,王绩成处长和桂继金科长都批了,关长也同意。我拿西藏许可证去莫海涛关长办公室,询问是否可以使用。莫看后说可以用,许可证签发日期在前,海关总署规定在后,可以打擦边球。第二天上午,我拿着西藏许可证去找王绩成,王也说可以用,他已经审批了。我见黄海勇申报的每吨400美元的补税价格偏低,又请示王绩成,结果遭王斥责。

29. 证人陈正光(原武汉海关副关长)的证言:1996年下半年,莫海涛介绍我认识了黄海勇。关于西藏许可证补税之事,莫的意见是黄海勇公司所持西藏许可证的签发日期是在海关总署下发不准使用西藏许可证的日期之前,可以打擦边球使用,我当时没有提出不同意见。我印象中西藏经贸厅无权签发毛豆油的许可证。关于深圳亨润1万吨毛豆油内销补税的情况,我跟莫海涛讲补税价格太低,莫说我们有5%至10%的下浮权,我说毛豆油是一级价格,如要下浮需报海关总署批准,我也把这个情况告诉了王绩成,说每吨400美元的补税价格太低,不能这样征税。后在1997年4月中旬,莫关长打电话给我,问起深圳亨润毛豆油补税价格之事,要我当时作出决定,我说那就先按实际成交价格报价受理,不能按每吨400美元征税,以后还有可能补税。

30. 同案犯潘子牛供述:我曾任深圳裕伟、深圳实业董事和总经理、湖北裕伟总经理、深圳亨润事和副总经理、香港宝润集团董事。任职期间,香港荣成的蔡诚广、周永生找黄海勇商谈经营进口毛豆油生意,商定由蔡诚广和周永生组织货源、黄海勇负责通关,毛豆油进口后双方各自销售一半,各自按照比例支付货款、税费及相关费用,我也参加了洽谈,并按照黄海勇的授意代表深圳裕伟与周永生(代表上海润丰公司)在协议上签字。当时,业内一般都是以进料加工的名义进口毛豆油,然后再办理补证、补税手续,直接在国内予以销售。采取这种方式经营进口毛豆油,办理手续和资金周转都有缓冲,黄海勇和蔡诚广、周永生他们就是这种经营思路,根本没有打算进口毛豆油后进行加工和复出口。但问题是配额（许可证）很难拿到，而有了配额（许可证）之后税率也要低得多，所以蔡诚广、周永生和黄海勇谈好要以补证、补税的方式经营进口毛豆油。

刘国建是武汉外贸总经理刘国光的弟弟，第一本进料加工手册是经他介绍办理的。我和黄海勇通过刘国建介绍认识刘国光后，以深圳裕伟的名义与武汉外贸签订了合作协议，商定由武汉外贸申领手册，黄海勇负责沟通，手册办好后给我们使用。手册虽然以武汉外贸名义办理，但实际上外商、货源、货物品名、数量、规格等相关内容都是黄海勇确定的，与海关人员的沟通、海关方面手续的办理也是由黄海勇负责，有些手续是我按照黄海勇的指示经办的，如我到上海海关办理毛豆油转关事宜等。

武汉丰润保税库的设立都是黄海勇直接经办的，我参与不多，但经办过以保税库名义进口的毛豆油的报关和转关业务。

毛豆油进口到上海后先入保税库，办好转关或者清关手续后直接转卖，用手册进口的毛豆油货款一般先由周永生垫付，之后再按照各自销售毛豆油的比例来结算，购油客户由周永生和黄海勇各自联系。黄海勇的资金由他自己掌控。

报关和清关的手续有些是黄海勇拿着手册到海关办理的，有些是报关员或是武汉外贸、武汉油脂等公司的人去海关办理的，我按照黄海勇的吩咐也到海关办过几次。手册核销有些是以海损名义报损，有些是以质量问题压低价格报税清关，还有些是补证、补税清关，后来在美国我听黄海勇说还有一些毛豆油以假手续、假核销的方式清关，根本没有缴税。我向周永生或者刘卓尔提交过以西藏许可证补税的税单。向海关申报补税核销毛豆油在销售之前或销售之后都有。

黄海勇和我商量后，让我具体与鹤山华侨联系，向他们支付一定的费用，通过他们向购油客户开具增值税票。每次都是黄海勇告诉我客户名称、价格、数量等内容后，我再转告鹤山华侨的李福财和冯福亨，他们开好税票交给我，我再转交给购油客户。

31. 被告人黄海勇的供述：我1994年前后与潘子牛在深圳注册了深圳裕伟贸易公司、之后在香港注册成立香港宝润集团公司，还在国内先后成立了湖北裕伟贸易实业有限公司、深圳市亨润国际实业有限公司、武汉丰润保税库、北京裕伟达公司、上海衡得等公司。这些公司都是为了在国内做生意先后成立的,我在公司是股东或法人代表。1996年,周永生通过潘子牛找到我,和我谈了毛豆油进口的生意。周永生提供国外的货源,我负责毛豆油的进口清关。我与周各自负责销售一半。我在武汉办好相关手续,前后总共申领了3本进料加工毛豆油的手册,总量6万吨。申领企业分别是以深圳亨润和武汉外贸贸易经济发展公司。我用加工手册在进口口口岸报关,口岸海关会根据加工手册转关至武汉海关,从口岸清关之后我便将毛豆油销售了。一开始我们低报毛豆油进口价格,在内销的时候就可以少缴税款,后来就直接用进料加工手册免税进口毛豆油后直接出售,也就不核销了。这样就不用交税了。我以进料加工名义进口了6万吨毛豆油,还以保税库的名义进口了4万吨,都出售了。

我和潘子牛到武汉后,原准备以亨润公司名义在武汉申请加工贸易手册,恰好武汉外贸的刘国光和他弟弟刘国建找到我,他们知道我跟武汉海关很熟,武汉外贸当时有本毛豆油手册,我就要他们将手册卖给我,就拿他们的手册到武汉海关备案,这本手册(42号手册)是2万吨。备案的资料都是武汉外贸提供的。这些都是潘子牛与武汉外贸确定好细节,最后我签的字。我和潘子牛就拿手册去上海找周永生,谈好由周永生负责油源,我负责进口清关报关,各自负责1万吨的销售,然后我以深圳裕伟公司名义、周永生以他们公司名义签订了协议。我与武汉外贸谈好后,我就当面向武汉海关的莫海涛关长汇报,说我拿了一本武汉外贸的加工手册,需要海关办理备案手续,然后莫海涛关长当我面向武汉海关陈关长交待同意武汉外贸的加工手册,并要求通知货管处办理手续。后来周永生通知我油到货了,我就按约定办理了2万吨油的转关武汉手续,同时还在武汉海关办了同意1万吨油留在上海海关的函,随后周永生在上海将油卖了,因为武汉外贸手册备案的加工厂是武汉油脂,所以我在武汉将油卖给了武汉油脂。油销售完后,我就在武汉海关办理补税手续,补税时低报了价格。后来潘子牛联系鹤山华侨,按销售价格给我武汉的客户开具了增值税票,鹤山华侨按进出项差额按一定比例收取费用。在办手册后不久,我在湖北注册了湖北裕伟公司,这本手册的

2万吨油销售完后,我就用西藏许可证在海关办理内销补税手续。我在买西藏许可证之前就向莫海涛汇报过,他说可以用,我们才买的。我们实际并不是做进料加工业务,也没有打算出口,我们一直是准备把油转到武汉来清关,在武汉海关报税,我负责确定业务开展方式,与海关沟通,具体操作细节一般是潘子牛来经手。海关相关部门应该知道这些手册进口油准备内销,因为我们在办理结转手续的时候,每次都留一半在上海和天津等口岸,实际上都是准备内销。我补税清关是以每吨400美元,每吨480美元的价格补税清关,这些都是海关同意的,我之所以在武汉海关清关,一是我能出具部队公函,二是我和莫海涛熟,海关也认可这个价格。

第二本手册(175号手册)是以深圳亨润的名义办理的,都是我出面协调好,具体业务是潘子牛去操作的,申领这本手册,也不是为了开展进料加工业务,只是为了在武汉清关,进口后在国内销售。第三本手册又用武汉外贸的名义申领的。再后来就申请丰润保税库了。实际上保税库的油进口就卖了,油都没有实际入保税库,当时是以租用武汉油脂的油库的名义申请保税库。后来这些进口的油本来想按之前的方式核销,但海关总署要求按照每吨680美元的价格报税,我们发现按这个价格赚不到钱,就没有核销,后来转过2万多吨到湛江、南宁等地去补税核销。

销售毛豆油的利润都在国内买了房产、固定资产、投资等。在武汉、上海、深圳、北京等地都有,都是以公司的名义买的,以及后来在国内投资和购买汽车等固定资产的钱,我参与设立的北京裕伟达公司在北京购买过房产。我在深圳和武汉以公司名义都购买有房产。深圳华丽园12A这一套房产是我前妻刘露的房子,这是我们1995年离婚时分给刘露的房产。

本院认为,深圳市亨润国际实业有限公司、深圳裕伟贸易实业有限公司、深圳市裕伟实业发展有限公司、湖北裕伟贸易实业有限公司、武汉丰润油脂保税仓库有限公司未经海关许可并且未补缴应缴税款,擅自将批准进口的进料加工保税毛豆油在境内销售牟利,偷逃应缴税款共计人民币379 524 829.28元,其行为均构成走私普通货物罪,且数额特别巨大。被告人黄海勇作为上述单位直接负责的主管人员,应对上述单位所犯走私普通货物罪承担罪责,其行为已构成走私普通货物罪,且犯罪情节特别严重。鉴于上述涉案单位均被吊销营业执照,依法对上述涉案单位不再追诉。公诉机关指控被告人黄海勇犯走私普通货物罪的犯罪事实成立,但指控的犯罪数额有误,应按照湖北省高级院人民法院对同案犯潘子牛走私普通货物案终审判决确定的走私金额认定。关于被告人黄海勇的辩护人提出本案走私的金额应按北省高级院人民法院终审判决确定的走私金额认定、黄海勇在秘鲁羁押的时间应当折抵刑期的辩护意见成立,本院予以采纳;关于其辩护人提出黄海勇认罪坦白的辩护意见成立。鉴于被告人黄海勇犯罪情节特别严重,且案发后潜逃境外多年,对其不予从轻处罚。涉案单位及被告人黄海勇用赃款购买的财产依法应予追缴,因前案生效判决已对涉案财产作出处理,本院不再重复判处,海关部门可根据该生效判决依法对涉案财产进行处置。依照《中华人民共和国刑法》第十二条第一款,第三十条,第三十一条,第一百五十三条第一款第(三)项、第二款、第三款,第一百五十四条第(一)项以及最高人民法院、最高人民检察院《关于办理走私刑事案件适用法律若干问题的解释》第二十四条第二款的规定,判决如下:

被告人黄海勇犯走私普通货物罪,判处有期徒刑十五年。

(刑期从判决执行之日起计算。判决执行以前先行羁押的,羁押一日折抵刑期一日,即自2008年10月30日起至2023年10月29日止)。

如不服本判决,可在接到判决书的第二日起十日内,通过本院或者直接向湖北省高级人民法院提出上诉。书面上诉的,应当提交上诉状正本一份,副本二份。

审判长　汪海燕
审判员　张　青
审判员　林　林

湖北省武汉市中级人民法院
二零一九年六月十二日

书记员　李　祎

潘子牛走私普通货物案二审判决书

湖北省高级人民法院刑事判决书 （2013）鄂刑一终字第00001号

原公诉机关湖北省武汉市人民检察院。

上诉人（原审被告人）潘子牛，又名潘禹任，曾任广东省深圳市亨润国际实业有限公司董事、副总经理、深圳裕伟贸易实业有限公司、深圳市裕伟实业发展有限公司董事、总经理、湖北裕伟贸易实业有限公司总经理、香港宝润集团有限公司董事。因本案于2001年3月16日被批准逮捕，2010年9月29日被抓获归案，同年10月9日被逮捕。现羁押于湖北省武汉市第二看守所。

辩护人陈威良，湖北九畴律师事务所律师。

湖北省武汉市中级人民法院审理武汉市人民检察院指控原审被告人潘子牛犯走私普通货物罪一案，于2012年10月17日作出（2011）武刑初字第00280号刑事判决。原审被告人潘子牛不服，提出上诉。本院依法组成合议庭，公开开庭审理了本案。湖北省人民检察院指派检察院刘仁鼓、代理检察员蒋建宇出庭履行职务。原审被告人潘子牛及其辩护人陈威良到庭参加诉讼。本案经合议庭评议并提交审判委员会讨论决定，现已审理终结。

原审判决认定：1996年至1998年，被告人潘子牛在担任广东省深圳市亨润国际实业有限公司（简称深圳亨润）董事、副总经理、深圳裕伟贸易实业有限公司（简称深圳裕伟）、深圳市裕伟实业发展有限公司（简称深圳实业）董事、总经理、湖北裕伟贸易实业有限公司（简称湖北裕伟）总经理、香港宝润集团有限公司（简称香港宝润集团）董事期间，伙同其上司黄海勇，以上述公司名义，与武汉对外经济贸易发展公司（简称武汉外贸）、上海润丰油脂食品有限公司（简称上海润丰）、武汉油脂集团有限公司（简称武汉油脂）、鹤山市华侨商品供应公司（简称鹤山华侨）等单位合作，先后申领C47006100042毛豆油进料加工手册（简称42号手册）、C47006100175毛豆油进料加工手册（简称175号手册）、C47007100051毛豆油进料加工手册（简称51号手册）和成立武汉丰润油脂保税仓库有限公司（简称武汉丰润保税库），进口保税毛豆油10.64余万吨，未经海关许可全部倒卖。事后，潘子牛等人使用无效西藏许可证补税3万吨、低报价格补税0.16万吨，其余毛豆油均未补税（其中假结转湛江、蛇口、南宁海关核销2.04万吨，编造假海损、假损耗事故核销0.66万吨，编造理由申请延期0.94万吨），走私偷逃税款共计人民币7.1余亿元。

上述事实，原审人民法院根据工商登记资料、合同、发票、已生效的刑事判决书等书证，证人周某甲、杨某、刘某甲、刘某乙、祁某、梁某、王某、陈某、李某甲等的证言，被告人潘子牛的供述确认。

原审人民法院认为，深圳亨润、深圳裕伟、深圳实业、湖北裕伟和武汉丰润保税库违反海关法规，逃避海关监管，共同走私毛豆油10.64万余吨，偷逃国家税款人民币710 645 040.44元，其行为构成走私普通货物罪。被告人潘子牛系单位犯罪的直接责任人员，其行为构成走私普通货物罪，且情节特别严重。遂判决：一、被告人潘子牛犯走私普通货物罪，判处有期徒刑十三年。二、武汉海关缉私局扣押的上海金环国际贸易公司账上原湖北裕伟贸易实业有限公司的走私赃款人民币8 775万元由武汉海关缉私局依法没收，上缴国库。其余涉案单位的资金、房产、车辆等财产，由武汉海关缉私局依法予以处理。

原审被告人潘子牛上诉及其辩护人辩护提出：1、走私犯罪系黄海勇个人实施，不是单位行为；潘子牛没有参与黄海勇实施的走私犯罪，只是执行上司的指示，不是单位犯罪的直接责任人员。2、黄海勇等人低价补税及使用西藏许可证按优惠税率补税后，将进口保税毛豆油转内销，得到海关认可，不是走私行为，原审判决将已经补税的毛豆油认定为走私货物不当。3、原审判决认定黄海勇等人将部分毛豆油"假结转"至湛江、蛇口、南宁，仅凭当地海关一纸文书，证据不足；4、海关以每吨560美元核定应缴税款错误，依法应以毛豆油的进口价格核定税款。

湖北省人民检察院认为,原审判决认定的事实清楚,证据确实、充分,定罪准确,量刑适当。潘子牛提出的上诉理由及其辩护人提出的辩护意见均不能成立。建议驳回上诉,维持原审判决。

经审理查明:1996年,上诉人潘子牛在担任深圳裕伟、深圳实业、湖北裕伟总经理、深圳亨润副总经理、香港宝润集团董事期间,与其上司黄海勇、同事邵辉(均在逃)等人谋划,采取申领进料加工手册和设立保税库的方式进口保税毛豆油,不经加工和复出口,通过补办能够享受外贸优惠税率的许可证,向外经委、海关等部门申请出口转内销,并向海关补缴关税、增值税等应缴税款后,将毛豆油在国内予以销售。为此,黄海勇、潘子牛等人以上述单位名义分别与武汉外贸、上海润丰、武汉油脂、西藏外贸、鹤山华侨商定合作经营毛豆油事宜,由武汉外贸代理深圳裕伟、湖北裕伟等涉案单位向外经委、海关等部门申领毛豆油进料加工手册、申报毛豆油出口转内销,涉案单位按进口毛豆油数量及比例向武汉外贸支付代理费;上海润丰提供境外进口油源,深圳裕伟、湖北裕伟等涉案单位负责办理进口通关、转关、内销、补证、补税手续,毛豆油入境后双方各销售一半;武汉油脂及其下属企业为深圳裕伟、湖北裕伟等涉案单位提供毛豆油加工手续,向涉案单位购买毛豆油,与涉案单位合伙成立保税库;西藏外贸以委托经营的方式为深圳裕伟、湖北裕伟等涉案单位提供毛豆油西藏许可证和配额,供涉案单位按外贸优惠政策缴纳税款;鹤山华侨代替深圳裕伟、湖北裕伟等涉案单位向购买毛豆油单位开具增值税专用发票,涉案单位按90元/吨向鹤山华侨支付开票手续费。同年8月至1997年5月,深圳裕伟、湖北裕伟等涉案单位以进料加工为名,分别以申领的42号手册、175号手册、51号手册和设立的武汉丰润保税库,向武汉海关等部门申报进口毛豆油共计10.64余万吨,其中,3万吨毛豆油经海关批准以西藏许可证和配额缴税后予以销售,0.16万吨毛豆油经海关批准以低于国家规定的价格缴税后予以销售,2.04万吨在海关办理了结转加工手续,其余5.44吨万吨毛豆油均未经海关许可并且未补缴税款予以销售,走私偷逃应缴税款共计379 524 829.28元。案发前175号手册已核销,42号、51号手册至今未核销。案发后,深圳裕伟、深圳实业、湖北裕伟、深圳亨润均被工商部门吊销工商登记。其间,潘子牛参与以进料加工为名进口毛豆油转内销的预谋;代表深圳裕伟、湖北裕伟涉案单位参与合作项目的洽谈,并与上海润丰、武汉外贸等合作单位签订合同;联系海关、报关公司并传递报关材料;与海关人员沟通、协调转关事宜;联系鹤山华侨等公司向购油单位开具增值税发票等。

上述事实,有下列证据证明:

1. 身份资料、工商登记资料等书证,证实潘子牛的身份、任职及案发后深圳裕伟、深圳实业、湖北裕伟、深圳亨润均被吊销工商登记等情况。

2. 合同、发票、凭证、银行账据、报关单证、关税缴款书、核查传真、扣押清单、进料加工手册、西藏许可证和配额等书证,证实深圳裕伟、深圳实业、湖北裕伟、深圳亨润、武汉丰润保税库与有关单位合作,采取申领进料加工手册、设立保税库等方式进口保税毛豆油后予以销售、补税等情况。

3. 海关总署回复、武汉海关核定走私案件偷逃税额表、核税证明等书证证实:深圳裕伟、深圳实业、湖北裕伟、深圳亨润、武汉丰润保税库走私的毛豆油中,未缴税的有54 428.245吨,偷逃关税、增值税等税款共计379 524 829.28元。

4. 鹤山华侨虚开的增值税专用发票、广东省江门市中级人民法院刑事判决书证实:1996年12月至1997年5月,鹤山华侨受深圳裕伟之托,先后为上海润丰、武汉油脂、上海金环国际贸易有限公司(简称上海金环)、上海市油脂公司进出口分公司(简称上海油脂)等单位虚开购销毛豆油增值税专用发票,数额共计34 750吨。

5. 湖北省武汉市中级人民法院刑事判决书、湖北省高级人民法院刑事裁定书,证实原武汉海关关长莫海涛同意黄海勇、潘子牛等人使用无效西藏许可证低价补税,以玩忽职守罪被判处刑罚等情况。

6. 证人周某甲(原上海润丰总经理)的证言:1996年,我与黄海勇、潘子牛合作经营毛豆油,我方提供境外油源,黄海勇方申领加工手册报关、转关,并提供许可证补税。进口毛豆油先后销售给黄海勇方指定的武汉外贸、深圳亨润后,再由我方向黄海勇方进行回购,发票由鹤山华侨开具。我方回购的毛豆油销给了上海金环。此外,我方还向黄海勇的丰润保税库提供了4万吨油源。潘子牛随同黄海勇参与了协议签订、货物转关、销售联络、商谈成立保税库、与鹤山华侨协商开票等事宜。1996年10月,我与潘子牛见面,潘说有经贸部签发的许可证;有一次,黄海勇、潘子牛到上海,潘拿出武汉海关关封,称毛豆油必须在武汉报关交税,先进料加工,再拿许可证顶出来;第一笔1万吨毛豆油转关武汉,是潘子牛带手册到上海金环和上海海关办理的;香港荣成与深圳亨润签订的2万吨毛豆油外贸合同,是潘子牛去报关的,我方经销的1万吨毛豆油由鹤山华侨开具发票,也是潘子牛转交给我们的;1997年初,我到武汉拿货款时,黄海勇、潘子牛与我商谈成立保税库事宜;同年四五月份,潘子牛、邵辉拿着丰润保税库的营业执照到上海进货,当时我方正好有2万吨毛豆油到码头,于是双方进行了交易。

证人刘某丙(原上海润丰副总经理)的证言:我公司与黄海勇、潘子牛合营的3本手册共进口毛豆油5万吨,武汉海关出具证明后,毛豆油留一半在上海由我方经销,我方将其中的1.5万吨销给了上海油脂;另一半毛豆油由黄海勇方经销,是武汉油脂、武汉华捷油脂有限公司(简称武汉华捷)等单位带款到上海提货。丰润保税库成立后,向香港荣成、香港建兴各购买2万吨毛豆油,都是武汉油脂提的货。以手册进口的毛豆油中第一次1万吨、第二次2万吨的转关手续都是潘子牛经办的,以保税库进口的4万吨毛豆油的手续是潘子牛和邵辉经办的。

7. 证人杨某(原上海金环总经理)的证言:我任职期间,经手卖给武汉2批毛豆油,由上海润丰提供提单,我公司发货。我公司还向上海润丰购买毛豆油1.5万吨左右,向鹤山华侨购买毛豆油1万吨左右,卖方提供的税单有些是在交易之前,有些是在交易之后,缴税单位为武汉外贸和深圳亨润。转关到武汉的毛豆油是武汉油脂、武汉华捷等单位到上海来提的货。我到深圳亨润与鹤山华侨签订合同时,黄海勇、潘子牛均在场。

8. 证人冯某(原武汉油脂总经理)的证言:1996年,我经刘某甲介绍与黄海勇、潘子牛相识,双方达成购买毛豆油意向。后我公司向湖北裕伟购买毛豆油6余万吨(其中1998年之后购买2余万吨),除在天津提货5 000吨外,其余均在上海提货,由鹤山华侨向我公司开具发票。丰润保税库于1997年建办公室和油柜,柜子里装的毛豆油都是我公司的。

9. 证人刘某甲(原武汉外贸总经理刘某乙的弟弟)的证言:我经人介绍

与黄海勇相识,后通过黄海勇认识潘子牛。黄海勇想在武汉经营毛豆油进口加工业务,需要我帮忙联系外贸公司和加工厂。以武汉外贸名义申领的第一本手册,是我自己先行与南海油脂签订进出口合同并与沙鸥油厂签订加工协议申请的,但未获海关审批,认识黄海勇后,黄很快就让该手册在海关获批。1997年,我哥哥刘某乙所在的武汉外贸又代理黄海勇方申领了一本2万吨毛豆油进料加工手册,由武汉外经委审批的事项是武汉外贸办理的,由武汉海关审批的事项是黄海勇办理的。毛豆油内销补税的手续由外经委审批的事项也是武汉外贸办理的。

证人向某(原武汉外贸部门经理)的证言:1996年8月份,刘某甲、刘某乙和我在江汉饭店与深圳裕伟的黄海勇会面,商谈毛豆油进料加工业务,并签订了协议。此前,我与刘某甲等人与沙鸥油厂签订了毛豆油加工协议,刘某甲还办理了加工保函和出口合同,但后来办理手册(42号手册)未获审批,结识黄海勇后,手册很快获批。后我公司又接受湖北裕伟委托,申领了第二本手册(51号手册)。毛豆油内销审批手续是我公司到外经委办理的。内销时,潘子牛提出由我公司开具增值税发票和付汇的问题,但后来都没能落实,我公司只赚取代理费。证人刘某乙(原武汉外贸总经理)的证言:我公司与深圳裕伟共签订2份毛豆油进料加工代理协议,进口毛豆油4万吨。

10. 证人祁某(原武汉华捷经理)的证言:我公司共从湖北裕伟购买4批毛豆油,数量17 467吨,除第一单5 000吨外,其余均未拿到增值税发票。我还以经营部名义与黄海勇签订过毛豆油加工合同,黄海勇持该合同申领了一本进料加工手册。

11. 证人廉某的证言:我公司与北海粮油和武汉外贸签订三方合同,由北海粮油结转2万吨毛豆油到武汉外贸,经补证、补税后,再由北海粮油向湖北裕伟购买1万吨毛豆油。我们同武汉外贸的约定是由湖北裕伟履行的。审批通过后,我方向湖北裕伟催要了补证、补税手续,再将该手续交给北海粮油,1万吨毛豆油通过我公司调汇。

12. 证人李某甲(原鹤山华侨副经理)的证言:1996年,我公司冯福亨经理经人介绍认识潘子牛。同年八九月份,潘子牛打电话联系冯福亨,称他们进口了1万吨毛豆油,他们提供报关、清关资料和海关关税发票、海关代征的增值税发票,要我公司替他们公司开具内销的增值税发票,问冯福亨敢不敢做,冯把这件事告诉我后,打电话回复潘子牛说可以做。我公司按每吨90元收取手续费,共替深圳亨润、湖北裕伟为上海润丰、上海油脂、武汉油脂等单位开具5万吨毛豆油交易的增值税发票。

13. 证人周某乙(原安徽宇环储运公司上海办事处主任)的证言:1997年间,我公司受潘子牛等人委托,分别以安徽宇环储运公司和上海中艺国际储运公司的名义3次为其代办毛豆油报关转关业务。提单、发票等资料由潘子牛等人提供,代理费由潘子牛经手支付,申报后我方将海关的放行单交给潘子牛。第一单代理的是进料加工手册,第二单和第三单代理的是武汉某保税库。

14. 证人梁某(原武汉丰润保税库员工)的证言:我于1998年在丰润保税库工作期间,按照黄海勇的吩咐,向海关写过几份补税申请,办理过湖北裕伟税务歇业等业务;按照潘子牛的通知,将湖北裕伟人民币100多万元转汇深圳。

证人赵某(原武汉丰润保税库财务人员)的证言:丰润保税库没有收入,支出的钱都是前期投入的注册资金,到企业年检时,就从湖北裕伟将钱打入以备检查,待会计师事务所验资后再把钱还给湖北裕伟。丰润保税库在武汉油脂设立的办公室建好不久,我带海关人员去看过,黄海勇向他们作了介绍,说目前是租用武汉油脂的油罐,以后还要扩建,海关人员没有实地察看。

证人韩某(原湖北裕伟出纳员)的证言:湖北裕伟的老板是黄海勇和潘子牛,公司银行账户是潘子牛带我去开的。公司财务章由我保管,公司法人印章和黄海勇、潘子牛的私人印章由潘子牛保管。1997年1月,邵辉接任公司经理。公司资金往来单位主要有武汉华捷、武汉油脂、深圳裕伟、上海润丰等单位。

证人董某(原湖北裕伟司机)的证言:1997年6月,我受邵辉指派,将1枚印章送到上海交给潘子牛;同年9月,我再次受邵辉指派,将1张人民币500万元的汇票送到深圳交给潘子牛。

15. 证人王某(原武汉海关货管处负责人)的证言:1996年底莫海涛调任武汉海关关长后,将黄海勇、潘子牛介绍给我们认识。此后,黄海勇在我处办理了3本毛豆油进料加工手册。货物转关过程中,我处给上海海关开过几次证明,给天津海关开过1次证明,内容是同意将部分进口毛豆油暂时留在上海或天津。1997年3月,黄海勇持报关单和西藏许可证申请补税内销,我请示莫海涛,他说西藏许可证可以用,后来我就批准黄海勇以每吨480美元的价格补税。黄海勇的保税库是1997年4月批准成立的,共进口毛豆油4.7万吨,都没有核销。

证人桂某(原武汉海关货管处保税科科长)的证言:1996年我和几名同事受邀到江汉饭店吃饭,席间王某处长将黄海勇、潘子牛介绍给我们认识,莫海涛关长让我们对黄海勇、潘子牛给予关照。此后,我按照王某的吩咐为黄海勇、潘子牛写了3份转关便函,第一份函是1996年10月写给上海外高桥保税区海关的,内容是同意先运5 000吨毛豆油到武汉,余下5 000吨留在上海;第二份函是1997年7月写给上海浦江海关的,内容是将1万吨毛豆油转运到武汉,余下1万吨留在上海;第三份函是1997年2月写给上海某海关的,内容是将51号手册项下1万吨毛豆油转运武汉,余下1万吨留在上海。这3份函的货主是深圳亨润和武汉外贸,但海关手续都是黄海勇、潘子牛前来联系办理的。此外,我还审核了175号毛豆油进料加工手册,数量2万吨,单耗20%,单价每吨400美元;经办了第一笔5 000吨毛豆油内销补税手续,是黄海勇前来申请的,当时这些毛豆油在哪不知道。

证人李某乙(原武汉海关江汉办事处综合科科长)的证言:我经办了黄海勇、潘子牛4单毛豆油报关手续。办理第一单毛豆油时,我见数额比较大,觉得应当实地验货,就将单子暂时放下,后王某处长把我叫到他办公室,货主潘子牛也在,王说这是莫关长的关系,不验货先放行,且由他先签字我后签字。后面3单和第一单办理的情况基本相同。42号手册的经营单位是武汉外贸,报关手续是黄海勇、潘子牛与该公司的人一起来办理的。175号手册的经营单位是深圳亨润,每次报关不是黄海勇来就是潘子牛来。

证人刘某丁(原武汉海关员工)的证言:黄海勇、潘子牛是莫海涛到任后介绍给我们认识并吩咐给予关照的。有一次,王某处长把我叫到他办公室,拿了几份黄海勇公司进口货物的报关单,他签字后给我,我不敢得罪他们,没有查验就在单子上签了字。有3张报关单是后来改过的,每年国家审计署来检查前,我们海关内部要自查,在自查的过程中发现报关单的进口货物数量与手册不一致而作的修改,如42号手册只批2万吨毛豆油,但是报关单记载毛豆油进口数量却多于2万吨。

证人张某(原武汉海关机场办事处综合科副主任)的证言:黄海勇是王某介绍我认识的,后我通过黄海勇认识潘子牛。1997年1月30日,黄海勇拿着手册的一些单证和许可证找我,要求核销手册,申请补税。我见许可证是西藏经贸厅发的,说西藏许可证恐怕不行,这种情况以前没有办成。他说怎么不行,王某处长和桂某科长都批了,关长也同意。我拿西藏许可证去莫海涛关长办公室,询问是否可以使用。莫看后说可以用,许可证签发日期在前,海关总署规定在后,可以打擦边球。第二天上午,我拿着西藏许可证去找王某,王也说可以用,他已经审批了。我见黄海勇申报的每吨400美元的补税价格偏低,又请示王某,结果遭王斥责。

证人陈某(原武汉海关副关长)的证言:1996年下半年,莫海涛介绍我认识了黄海勇。关于西藏许可证补税之事,莫的意见是黄海勇公司所持西藏许可证的签发日期是在海关总署下发不准使用西藏许可证的日期之前,可以打擦边球使用,我当时没有提出不同意见。我印象中西藏经贸厅无权签发毛豆油的许可证。关于深圳亨润1万吨毛豆油内销补税的情况,我跟莫海涛讲补税价格太低,莫说我们有5%至10%的下浮权,我说毛豆油是一级价格,如要下浮需报海关总署批准,我也把这个情况告诉了王某,说每吨400美元的补税价格太低,不能这样征税。后在1997年4月中旬,莫关长打电话给我,问起深圳亨润毛豆油补税价格之事,要我当时作出决定,我说那就先按实际成交价格报价受理,不能按每吨400美元征税,以后还有可能补税。

16. 上诉人潘子牛供述:我曾任深圳裕伟、深圳实业董事和总经理、湖北裕伟总经理、深圳亨润董事和副总经理、香港宝润集团董事。任职期间,香港荣成的蔡诚广、周某甲找黄海勇商谈经营进口毛豆油生意,商定由蔡诚广和周某甲组织货源、黄海勇负责通关,毛豆油进口后双方各自销售一半,各自按照比例支付货款、税费及相关费用,我也参加了洽谈,并按照黄海勇的授意代表深圳裕伟与周某甲(代表上海润丰公司)在协议上签字。当时,业内一般都是以进料加工的名义进口毛豆油,然后再办理补证、补税手续,直接在国内予以销售。采取这种方式经营进口毛豆油,办理手续和资金周转都有缓冲。黄海勇和蔡诚广、周某甲他们就是这种经营思路,根本没有打算进口毛豆油后进行加工和复出口。但问题是配额(许可证)很难拿到,而有了配额(许可证)之后税率也要低得多,所以蔡诚广、周某甲和黄海勇谈好要以补证、补税的方式经营进口毛豆油。

刘某甲是武汉外贸总经理刘某乙的弟弟,第一本进料加工手册是经他介绍办理的。我和黄海勇通过刘某甲介绍认识刘某乙后,以深圳裕伟的名义与武汉外贸签订了合作协议,商定由武汉外贸申领手册,黄海勇负责沟通,手册办好后给我们使用。手册虽然以武汉外贸名义办理,但实际上外商、货源、货物品名、数量、规格等相关内容都是黄海勇确定的,与海关人员的沟通、海关方面手续的办理也是由黄海勇负责,有些手续是我按照黄海勇的指示经办的,如我到上海海关办理毛豆油转关事宜等。

武汉丰润保税库的设立都是黄海勇直接经办的,我参与不多,但经办过以保税库名义进口的毛豆油的报关和转关业务。

毛豆油进口到上海后先入保税库,办好转关或者清关手续后直接转卖,用手册进口的毛豆油货款一般先由周某甲垫付,之后再按照各自销售毛豆油的比例来结算,购油客户由周某甲和黄海勇各自联系。黄海勇的资金由他自己掌控。

报关和清关的手续有些是黄海勇拿着手册到海关办理的,有些是报关员或是武汉外贸、武汉油脂等公司的人去海关办理的,我按照黄海勇的吩咐也到海关办过几次。手册核销有些是以海损名义报损,有些是以质量问题压低价格报税清关,还有些是补证、补税清关。后来在美国我听黄海勇说还有一些毛豆油以假手续、假核销的方式清关,根本没有缴税。我向周某甲或者刘某丙提交过以西藏许可证补税的税单。向海关申报补税核销毛豆油在销售之前或销售之后都有。

黄海勇和我商量后,让我具体与鹤山华侨联系,向他们支付一定的费用,通过他们向购油客户开具增值税票。每次都是黄海勇告诉我客户名称、价格、数量等内容后,我再转告鹤山华侨的李某甲和冯福亨,他们开好税票交给我,我再转交给购油客户。

上列证据,均经一、二审庭审质证,来源合法,所证内容客观、真实,本院予以确认。

针对控辩意见,根据已查明的事实和已查证属实的证据,依照有关法律规定,本院评判如下:

一、关于上诉人潘子牛及其辩护人提出黄海勇等人低价补税及使用西藏许可证按优惠税率补税后,将进口保税毛豆油转内销,得到海关认可,不是走私行为,原审判决将已经补税的毛豆油认定为走私货物不当的上诉理由及辩护意见

经审查:走私普通货物罪侵犯的客体是国家对普通货物进出口监管、征税的制度。刑法规定,未经海关许可并且未补缴税款,擅自将批准进口的来料加工的原材料等保税货物在境内销售牟利的,以走私普通货物罪定罪处罚。据此,构成本罪必须同时具备两个条件:一是逃避海关监管,二是偷逃税款。本案中,首先,深圳裕伟、湖北裕伟等涉案单位的补税行为系其主动向海关申报,主观上没有逃避海关监管的故意;其次,西藏许可证和配额都是真实的,涉案单位使用西藏许可证和配额按优惠税率补税得到海关审批,不属于偷逃税款;第三,深圳裕伟、湖北裕伟等涉案单位是否弄虚作假,故意低报价格,没有证据证实,其补税价格得到海关审批确认;第四,没有证据证实深圳裕伟、湖北裕伟等涉案单位与海关人员内外勾结实施走私犯罪,武汉海关原关长莫海涛同意涉案单位使用西藏许可证和配额补税的行为,已被生效的刑事判决、刑事裁定确认为玩忽职守罪。综上,原审判决认定深圳裕伟、湖北裕伟等涉案单位低价补税及使用西藏许可证优惠补税的行为构成走私犯罪,事实不清,证据不足。上述上诉理由及辩护意见成立,本院予以采纳。

二、关于上诉人潘子牛及其辩护人提出原审判决认定黄海勇等人将部分毛豆油"假结转"至湛江、蛇口、南宁,仅凭当地海关一纸文书,证据不足的上诉理由及辩护意见

经审查:结转申请表、报关单、合同等证据证实,深圳裕伟、湖北裕伟等涉案单位将进口毛豆油中的8 000吨转关至蛇口、2 400吨转关至湛江、1万吨转关至南宁。案发后,侦查机关武汉海关分别向湛江、蛇口、南宁海关发

出电传,调查上述申请转关加工的毛豆油委托加工合同是否真实,湛江、蛇口、南宁海关分别答复是虚假的。但上述转关手续不只有委托加工合同,还有双方海关签署确认的转关报关单以及结转申请表,对于报关单、结转申请表的真伪,侦查机关未进一步查实;对于受托加工方是否存在、受托加工行为是否真实,侦查机关也未查证。故证实上述毛豆油属于假结转的证据只有海关出具的证明,不足以认定深圳裕伟、湖北裕伟等涉案单位实施了假结转行为。上述上诉理由及辩护意见成立,本院予以采纳。

三、关于上诉人潘子牛及其辩护人提出海关以每吨560美元核定应缴税款错误,依法应以毛豆油的进口价格核定税款的上诉理由及辩护意见

经审查:本案中,进口毛豆油油源由深圳裕伟、湖北裕伟等涉案单位相关联的公司提供,故进口合同上记载的毛豆油进口成交价格的真实性存疑,故应按海关总署核定的价格每吨560美元作为征税标准。上述上诉理由及辩护意见不能成立,本院不予采纳。

四、关于上诉人潘子牛及其辩护人提出走私犯罪系黄海勇个人实施,不是单位行为;潘子牛没有参与黄海勇实施的走私犯罪,只是执行上司的指示,不是单位犯罪直接责任人员的上诉理由及辩护意见

经审查:1.周某甲、刘某甲、杨某等人的证言及合同、工商登记资料等书证证实,黄海勇、潘子牛等人以深圳裕伟、湖北裕伟等涉案单位名义与合作单位签订合同,以涉案单位名义申领进料加工手册进口毛豆油,以涉案单位名义将保税毛豆油予以倒卖,销售所得通过涉案单位账户流转,且部分赃款用于涉案单位购房、购车、投资等业务,故黄海勇和潘子牛的行为应当认定为单位行为。2.上述证据还证实,潘子牛在深圳裕伟、湖北裕伟等涉案单位中均担任要职,参与了与上海润丰、武汉外贸等有关单位合作经营毛豆油的洽谈;代表涉案单位与合作公司签订合同;联系海关、报关公司并传递报关材料;与海关人员沟通、协调转关事宜;联系鹤山华侨等公司向购油单位开具增值税发票等,足以认定潘子牛参与了走私犯罪,且系单位犯罪的直接责任人员。上述上诉理由及辩护意见不能成立,本院不予采纳。

综上所述,本院认为,广东省深圳市亨润国际实业有限公司、深圳裕伟贸易实业有限公司、深圳市裕伟实业发展有限公司、湖北裕伟贸易实业有限

公司、武汉丰润油脂保税仓库有限公司未经海关许可并且未补缴应缴税款,擅自将批准进口的进料加工保税毛豆油在境内销售牟利,偷逃应缴税款数额特别巨大,其行为均构成走私普通货物罪。上诉人潘子牛作为上述单位直接负责的主管人员,应对上述单位所犯走私普通货物罪承担罪责,且其犯罪情节特别严重。鉴于上述涉案单位均被吊销营业执照,依法对上述涉案单位不再追诉。原审判决认定上诉人潘子牛犯走私普通货物罪成立,但认定其犯罪数额不当,对其量刑偏重,本院予以纠正。依照《中华人民共和国刑法》第十二条第一款、第三十条、第三十一条、第一百五十三条第一款第(三)项、第二款、第三款、第一百五十四条第(一)项和《中华人民共和国刑事诉讼法》第二百二十五条第一款第(一)、(二)项的规定,判决如下:

一、维持湖北省武汉市中级人民法院(2011)武刑初字第00280号刑事判决中对上诉人潘子牛的定罪部分以及财物处置部分;撤销该判决中对上诉人潘子牛的量刑部分。

二、上诉人潘子牛犯走私普通货物罪,判处有期徒刑十年。

(刑期从判决执行之日起计算。判决执行以前先行羁押的,羁押一日折抵刑期一日,即自2010年9月29日起至2020年9月28日止。)

本判决为终审判决。

审　判　长　柯武松
代理审判员　邓海兵
代理审判员　郭　鹏

二〇一四年八月十五日
书　记　员　唐　鹭

延伸阅读

习近平反腐败追逃追赃思想研究*

赵秉志　张　磊

一、前言

党的十八大以来,以习近平同志为核心的党中央团结带领全国各族人民谋篇布局、励精图治、砥砺奋进、万众一心,围绕实现"两个一百年"奋斗目标和中华民族伟大复兴的中国梦,统筹国际国内两个大局,开创了党和国家事业发展的新局面,开启了坚持和发展中国特色社会主义的新篇章,赢得了全国广大干部群众的衷心拥护,在国际社会引起了重大影响。2017年10月,党的十九大在北京召开,习近平总书记代表第十八届中央委员会,向大会作了题为《决胜全面建成小康社会　夺取新时代中国特色社会主义伟大胜利》的报告,这是我们党面向新时代的政治宣言和行动纲领,标志着在以习近平总书记为核心的党中央的领导下,中国特色社会主义已经进入了新时代。

在十八大以来治国理政的新实践中,以习近平同志为核心的党中央以巨大的政治勇气和强烈的责任担当,提出一系列新理念新思想新战略,出台一系列重大方针政策,推出一系列重大举措,推进一系列重大工作,解决了许多长期想解决而没有解决的难题,办成了许多过去想办而没有办成的大事,推动党和国家事业发生了历史性变革。② 反腐败工作就是十八大以来我

---

* 本文系赵秉志教授主持的教育部阐释党的十九大精神专项任务课题"习近平反腐败追逃追赃思想研究"的最终成果。
② 参见习近平总书记在党的十九大上代表十八届中央委员会所作的题为《决胜全面建成小康社会　夺取新时代中国特色社会主义伟大胜利》的报告。

们党和国家重点推进的一项重要战略措施,反腐败追逃追赃工作则是反腐败战略的重要组成部分,对于推动反腐败的顺利进行,遏制腐败行为的发生具有重要意义。习近平总书记高度重视反腐败追逃追赃工作,围绕反腐败追逃追赃问题发表了一系列重要讲话,提出了一系列新的重要理论、重要论断、重要观点,从而形成了习近平反腐败追逃追赃思想。习近平反腐败追逃追赃思想紧密结合当代中国实际,探索出了中国特色反腐败追逃追赃道路,回答了当前为什么进行反腐败追逃追赃、如何进行反腐败追逃追赃等一系列重大理论和现实问题,对于我国当前正在开展的反腐败追逃追赃工作具有重大指导意义。也正是在习近平反腐败追逃追赃思想的指引下,我国反腐败追逃追赃工作取得了突出成绩,从2014年全面开展反腐败追逃追赃工作至今,全国共追回外逃人员5 974人,其中党员和国家工作人员1 425人,"百名红通人员"58人,追回赃款142.48亿元人民币。通过追逃追赃布下天罗地网,切断腐败分子后路,有效遏制住了外逃多发势头,为反腐败斗争取得压倒性胜利提供了有力支撑。① 本文拟在简要梳理习近平反腐败追逃追赃思想的主要内容的基础上,详细论述习近平反腐败追逃追赃思想的科学定位,并就如何在实践中贯彻习近平反腐败追逃追赃思想提出若干建议。

二、习近平反腐败追逃追赃思想的科学定位

（一）习近平反腐败追逃追赃思想是习近平新时代中国特色社会主义思想的重要组成部分

习近平总书记指出,"党的十八大精神,说一千道一万,归结为一点,就是坚持和发展中国特色社会主义。"中国特色社会主义,是中国共产党和中国人民团结的旗帜、奋斗的旗帜、胜利的旗帜,是当代中国发展进步的根本方向。坚持和发展中国特色社会主义,是实现中华民族伟大复兴的必由之路。② 中国特色社会主义是实践、理论、制度紧密结合的,包括中国特色社会

---

① 姜洁、江琳:《布下反腐败追逃追赃天罗地网——中央追逃办成立五周年工作回眸》,载《人民日报》2019年6月27日第7版。
② 参见中共中央宣传部编:《习近平总书记系列重要讲话读本》,学习出版社、人民出版社2016年版,第18页。

主义道路、中国特色社会主义理论体系和中国特色社会主义制度。其中,中国特色社会主义道路是实现途径,中国特色社会主义理论体系是行动指南,中国特色社会主义制度是根本保障,三者统一于中国特色社会主义伟大实践,这是中国特色社会主义的最鲜明特色。

中国特色社会主义是不断发展、不断前进的。习近平总书记指出:"坚持和发展中国特色社会主义是一篇大文章","我们这一代共产党人的任务,就是继续把这篇大文章写下去。"① 在建设中国特色社会主义的伟大征途中,特别是十八大以来,围绕新时代坚持和发展什么样的中国特色社会主义、怎样坚持和发展中国特色社会主义的重大时代课题,我们党坚持以马克思列宁主义、毛泽东思想、邓小平理论、"三个代表"重要思想、科学发展观为指导,坚持解放思想、实事求是、与时俱进、求真务实,坚持辩证唯物主义和历史唯物主义,紧密结合新的时代条件和实践要求,以全新的视野深化对共产党执政规律、社会主义建设规律、人类社会发展规律的认识,进行艰辛理论探索,取得重大理论创新成果,形成了习近平新时代中国特色社会主义思想。习近平新时代中国特色社会主义思想,是对马克思列宁主义、毛泽东思想、邓小平理论、"三个代表"重要思想、科学发展观的继承和发展,是马克思主义中国化最新成果,是党和人民实践经验和集体智慧的结晶,是中国特色社会主义理论体系的重要组成部分,是全党全国人民为实现中华民族伟大复兴而奋斗的行动指南,必须长期坚持并不断发展。②

习近平新时代中国特色社会主义思想,是以习近平总书记为代表的中国共产党人围绕坚持和发展中国特色社会主义、实现中华民族伟大复兴的中国梦,围绕推进经济、政治、文化、社会和生态文明建设,围绕从严管党治党、全面提高党的建设科学化水平等所提出的一系列富有创见的新思想新观点新论断新要求,深刻回答了新的历史条件下党和国家发展的一系列重大理论和现实问题,是马克思主义中国化最新成果的集中体现,闪耀着马克思主义真理的光辉,是全党全国各族人民为实现中华民族伟大复兴而奋斗的行动指南和基本遵循。习近平新时代中国特色社会主义思想中关于反腐

---

① 中共中央宣传部编:《习近平总书记系列重要讲话读本》,学习出版社、人民出版社2016年版,第25—26页。
② 参见《中国共产党章程》(中国共产党第十九次全国代表大会部分修改,2017年10月24日通过)。

败追逃追赃的部分,是习近平反腐败追逃追赃思想的重要内容。习近平反腐败追逃追赃思想与习近平总书记其他领域的思想一道,都是在新的历史条件下习近平新时代中国特色社会主义思想的重要组成部分,是马克思主义与中国实践发展相结合的最新发展。

(二)习近平反腐败追逃追赃思想是"四个全面"战略思想的有机蕴含

党的十八大以来,以习近平同志为核心的党中央从坚持和发展中国特色社会主义全局出发,立足中国发展实际,坚持问题导向,逐步形成并积极推进全面建成小康社会、全面深化改革、全面依法治国、全面从严治党的战略布局。"四个全面"战略布局确立了新的历史条件下党和国家各项工作的战略目标和战略举措,是我们党在新形势下治国理政的总方略,是事关党和国家长远发展的总战略,为实现"两个一百年"奋斗目标、实现中华民族伟大复兴的中国梦提供了重要保障。① 2014 年 12 月,习近平总书记在江苏调研时,第一次明确提出"四个全面"的总体布局。强调要主动把握和积极适应经济发展新常态,协调推进全面建成小康社会、全面深化改革、全面推进依法治国、全面从严治党,推动改革开放和社会主义现代化建设迈上新台阶。② 2015 年 2 月 2 日,在省部级主要领导干部学习贯彻十八届四中全会精神全面推进依法治国专题研讨班的开班仪式上,习近平总书记集中论述了"四个全面"战略布局的逻辑关系。习近平总书记指出,四个全面战略布局,既有战略目标,也有战略举措,每一个"全面"都具有重大战略意义。③ 全面建成小康社会是重大战略目标,在"四个全面"战略布局中居于引领地位。全面深化改革、全面依法治国、全面从严治党是三大战略举措,为如期全面建成小康社会提供重要保障。④

我国的反腐败追逃追赃工作与"四个全面"战略布局具有密切联系,习

---

① 中共中央宣传部编:《习近平总书记系列重要讲话读本》,学习出版社、人民出版社 2016 年版,第 41 页。
② 参见霍小光、华春雨:《习总书记首谈"四个全面"意味着什么》,载 http://news.xinhuanet.com/politics/2014—12/16/c_1113661816.htm。
③ 习近平:《领导干部要做尊法学法守法用法的模范 带动全党全国共同全面推进依法治国》,载《人民日报》2015 年 2 月 3 日。
④ 参见中共中央宣传部编:《习近平总书记系列重要讲话读本》,学习出版社、人民出版社 2016 年版,第 45—46 页。

近平反腐败追逃追赃思想是"四个全面"战略思想的有机蕴含:(1)全面从严治党。在"四个全面"当中,反腐败追逃追赃与全面从严治党关系最为密切。习近平总书记指出:"加强反腐败国际追逃追赃工作是坚持党要管党、从严治党,遏制腐败现象蔓延势头的重要举措。""要以零容忍态度惩治腐败,不管腐败分子跑到天涯海角,也要把他们绳之以法,决不能让其躲进'避罪天堂'、逍遥法外。要把追逃追赃工作纳入党风廉政建设和反腐败斗争总体部署,把反腐败斗争引向深入。"①从这些重要论述可以看出,加强反腐败追逃追赃工作,把追逃追赃工作纳入党风廉政建设和反腐败斗争总体部署,将潜逃海外的腐败分子绳之以法,把转移至境外的赃款赃物追缴归案,既是以零容忍的态度惩治腐败的重要措施,更是全面从严治党的重要体现。(2)全面依法治国。全面依法治国是我们党领导人民治理国家的基本方略,是全面建成小康社会、加快推进社会主义现代化的重要保证。全面依法治国要求把党和国家的工作纳入法治化轨道,坚持在法治轨道上统筹社会力量、平衡社会利益、调节社会关系、规范社会行为,依靠法治解决各种社会矛盾和问题。反腐败追逃追赃是我们党和国家反腐败工作的重要组成部分,当然也应当纳入法治化轨道,依法追逃追赃。对此,2015 年 10 月 18 日习近平总书记在接受采访时候指出:"中国是一个法治国家,无论是在国内惩治腐败,还是开展反腐败国际合作,都依法办事,坚持以事实为依据、以法律为准绳。"②习近平反腐败追逃追赃思想也是全面依法治国思想的重要体现。(3)全面深化改革。全面深化改革的总目标是完善和发展中国特色社会主义制度、推进国家治理体系和治理能力现代化。反腐败追逃追赃制度的完善、能力的提高,依赖于国家司法体制改革的顺利进行,依赖于国家反腐败体制机制改革的全面展开,依赖于各有关部门工作的协调配合,只有全面深化改革,才能促进国家反腐败追逃追赃工作全面而高效地展开。(4)全面建成小康社会。全面建成小康社会是实现中华民族伟大复兴的重要基础、关键一步,

---

① 《在十八届中央政治局常委会第七十八次会议上关于加强反腐败国际追逃追赃工作的讲话》,载载中共中央纪律检查委员会、中共中央文献研究室编:《习近平关于党风廉政建设和反腐败斗争论述摘编》,中央文献出版社、中国方正出版社 2015 年版,第 23、100 页。
② 参见李晓珍、施希茜:《坚持党的领导总书记在国际上是怎么讲的》,载 http://politics.people.com.cn/n1/2016/0216/c1001—28128730.html。

在中华民族发展史上和社会主义发展史上，都具有极为重大的意义。作为我们党向人民、向历史做出的庄严承诺，全面建成小康社会需要风清气正的政治生态，需要更加科学、更加有效地惩治腐败，需要以零容忍态度严惩腐败，需要全面开展反腐败追逃追赃工作，不论腐败分子逃到哪里，都要将他绳之以法，决不让外逃腐败分子逍遥法外。

（三）习近平反腐败追逃追赃思想是社会主义核心价值观的重要体现

在当代中国，我们应该坚守的社会主义核心价值观，就是党的十八大提出要倡导的富强、民主、文明、和谐，自由、平等、公正、法治，爱国、敬业、诚信、友善等一系列理念。习近平总书记指出，"社会主义核心价值观是当代中国精神的集中体现，凝结着全体人民共同的价值追求"，①我们要"用社会主义核心价值观凝魂聚力，更好构筑中国精神、中国价值、中国力量，为中国特色社会主义事业提供源源不断的精神动力和道德滋养"。② 近年来，随着我国经济社会的发展和国际地位的提高，国际社会对中国的关注度越来越高，但是国际社会对于我国的误解也不少，"中国威胁论""中国崩溃论"等论调不绝于耳，一些西方媒体仍然在"唱衰"中国。在这样复杂的形势下，要集中讲好中国故事，传播好中国声音，向世界展现一个真实的中国、立体的中国、全面的中国。③ 根据上述论断，我们不仅要积极倡导、践行社会主义核心价值观，利用社会主义核心价值观为中国特色社会主义事业提供精神动力和道德滋养，而且要通过向世界讲好中国故事，传播中国声音，宣传社会主义价值观，向世界展现一个真实的中国。

习近平反腐败追逃追赃思想是社会主义核心价值观的重要体现：（1）贯彻习近平反腐败追逃追赃思想需要践行社会主义核心价值观。在实践中贯彻习近平反腐败追逃追赃思想，就是要在与他国开展刑事司法合作过程中，体现文明、和谐、自由、平等、公正、法治、爱国、敬业、诚信等社会主义核心价值观的精神意蕴。例如，追逃追赃是追逃国与腐败分子出逃目的国之间在

---

① 习近平总书记在党的十九大上代表十八届中央委员会所作的题为《决胜全面建成小康社会 夺取新时代中国特色社会主义伟大胜利》的报告。
② 中共中央宣传部编：《习近平总书记系列重要讲话读本》，学习出版社、人民出版社2016年版，第189—190页。
③ 参见中共中央宣传部编：《习近平总书记系列重要讲话读本》，学习出版社、人民出版社2016年版，第209页。

遵循主权原则的前提下,和谐、平等开展司法合作的过程,需要依法进行,充分保障外逃人员的各项诉讼权利,在追回国之后,追逃国需要信守在追逃过程中对于对方国家做出的庄严承诺,对外逃人员进行公证审判,只有在合作过程中充分体现双方之间的诚信、敬业,才可能实现境外追逃追赃的良性循环。(2)贯彻习近平反腐败追逃追赃思想是弘扬、宣传社会主义核心价值观的重要途径。毛主席曾说:"长征是宣言书,长征是宣传队,长征是播种机"。在反腐败追逃追赃国际合作实践中贯彻习近平反腐败追逃追赃思想,也是"宣言书,宣传队,播种机":通过与他国开展合作,向世界庄严宣告中国坚决不让外逃腐败分子逃脱惩罚的坚定信念,是向外逃腐败分子发出的宣言书;在与他国开展合作中,宣传中国刑事法治的发展进步,宣传中国人权保障事业的伟大进展;在与他国开展合作中,要通过我方人员一言一行、一举一动弘扬社会主义核心价值观,通过讲好中国反腐败的法治故事,赢得他国对于中国法治事业、中国核心价值观的信任、赞许,埋下友谊和信任的种子。

(四)习近平反腐败追逃追赃思想是我国反腐败追逃追赃实践的理论升华和指导思想

习近平总书记指出,社会存在决定社会意识。我们党现阶段提出和实施的理论和路线方针政策,之所以正确,就是因为它们都是以我国现时代的社会存在为基础的。习近平反腐败追逃追赃思想也以我国现时代的社会实践为基础。改革开放以后,伴随着我国与国际社会交流的频繁,我国开始出现腐败分子携款外逃的现象,并由此开启了反腐败追逃追赃的实践。十八大以后,以习近平总书记为核心的党中央掀起了反腐败高潮,特别是 2014 年以后,启动了以"天网行动""猎狐行动"等为代表的追逃追赃专项行动,取得了突出的成绩。作为"天网行动"标志性行动的"公布 100 名涉嫌犯罪的外逃国家工作人员、重要腐败案件涉案人等人员的红色通缉令(百名红通人员)",[①]截止到 2019 年 6 月 29 日,已经归案 59 人[②],引起社

---

① 参见张磊:《从"百名红通人员归案"看我国境外追逃的发展》,载《北京师范大学学报》2017 年第 3 期。
② 《第 59 名!外逃 18 年"百名红通人员"刘宝凤回国投案》,载 https://www.thepaper.cn/newsDetail_forward_3806841。

会各界的广泛关注和赞许。习近平反腐败追逃追赃思想形成于我国反腐败追逃追赃的实践当中,是对于我国以往特别是十八大以来我国反腐败追逃追赃实践的经验总结和理论升华,是马克思主义基本原理与中国反腐败追逃追赃具体实践结合的产物,饱含着习近平总书记长期以来对于我国反腐败追逃追赃工作的思考、提炼、总结和创新,具有鲜明的中国特色、时代特征与实践品质。

习近平总书记指出,中国特色社会主义是实践、理论、制度紧密结合的,既把成功的经验上升为理论,又以正确的理论指导新的实践,还把实践中已见成效的方针政策及时上升为党和国家的制度。坚持和发展中国特色社会主义,必须高度重视理论的作用,增强理论自信和战略定力,对经过反复实践和比较得出的正确结论,要坚定不移坚持。① 运用马克思主义基本原理指导中国实践是我们的看家本领,作为马克思主义与中国反腐败追逃追赃实践结合的产物,作为中国特色社会主义理论在当代中国的最新发展成果,习近平反腐败追逃追赃思想科学总结了我国以往追逃追赃实践中的经验与教训,集中体现了对国际国内反腐败形势的深刻洞察和准确把握,蕴含着丰富的思想内涵和牢固的理论根基,②是经过我国反腐败追逃追赃的长期、反复实践和比较得出的正确结论,不仅是对以往反腐败追逃追赃实践的理论升华,而且是我国反腐败追逃追赃新的实践的指导思想、科学指南和根本遵循,为开展反腐败追逃追赃工作指明了方向,我们一定要坚定不移地坚持,一定要在反腐败追逃追赃实践中全面贯彻执行。

三、习近平反腐败追逃追赃思想的主要内容

习近平反腐败追逃追赃思想着眼于我国反腐败追逃追赃新的实践和新的发展,着眼于对追逃追赃实践中突出问题的理论思考,内涵深刻、博大精深、体系完整、逻辑严谨,蕴含着反腐败追逃追赃各个领域的重要战略思想、

---

① 中共中央宣传部编:《习近平总书记系列重要讲话读本》,学习出版社、人民出版社2016年版,第25、33页。
② 参见黄树贤:《把惩治腐败的天罗地网撒向全球——深入学习习近平总书记关于反腐败国际合作和追逃追赃工作的重要论述》,载《求是》2016年第11期。

基本立场和理论观点,具体可以区分为反腐败追逃追赃的意义和原则、工作方法、国际视野和配套措施等四个方面的内容,从而构成了习近平反腐败追逃追赃思想的理论体系。下面我们就其要点进行简明梳理:

(一)反腐败追逃追赃的意义、原则和立场

反腐败追逃追赃的现状、意义与工作原则是反腐败追逃追赃的基础理论问题,习近平总书记指出,我国反腐败追逃追赃工作任务艰巨、意义重大,在实践中应当坚持法治原则和平等互信、包容互鉴、合作共赢原则,并进行了深入论述:

1. 反腐败追逃追赃任务艰巨,意义重大

反腐败追逃追赃工作,是全面从严治党、推进党风廉政建设和反腐败斗争的重要组成部分,关系党和国家工作大局。习近平总书记从政治和全局的高度,坚持理论和实践相结合,深入而全面地论述了这项工作的重要性和紧迫性:

(1)追逃追赃工作任务艰巨

习近平总书记指出,"近年来,党员干部携款外逃事件时有发生。有的腐败分子先是做'裸官',一有风吹草动,就逃之夭夭;有的跑到国外买豪车豪宅,挥金如土,逍遥法外;有的跑到国外摇身一变,参与当地选举。这些年,我们追回了一些重要外逃人员,但总体看,还是跑出去的多,抓回来的少,追逃工作还很艰巨"。① 在以上论述中,习近平准确揭示了当时我国腐败分子外逃现象严重的客观现实。通过洗钱将巨额资金汇出境外,准备护照,将家属转移出境,自己做"裸官",做好充分准备,然后择机潜逃境外,这已经成为是腐败分子出逃的经典公式。② 到了国外之后,不少腐败分子凭借已经转移到境外的巨额资金,过着纸醉金迷的奢华生活。有的还凭借各种渠道,融入当地的居民的政治生活中去,甚至参与当地的政治选举。虽然近些年,我们经过努力追回了一些外逃人员,但客观来说,还有很多没有追回来,而且与逃出去的总数量相比,已经追回来的比例也较小。"党员干部携款外

---

① 《在十八届中央政治局常委会第七十八次会议上关于加强反腐败国际追逃追赃工作的讲话》,载中共中央纪律检查委员会、中共中央文献研究室编:《习近平关于党风廉政建设和反腐败斗争论述摘编》,中央文献出版社、中国方正出版社2015年版,第23页。
② 参见张磊:《反腐败零容忍与境外追逃》,法律出版社2017年版,第23—24页。

逃,就是叛党叛国,严重损害党和国家形象。腐败分子偷走了国家和人民的钱财,人民群众痛恨至极。不将他们缉拿归案、绳之以法,党纪国法不容,党和人民决不答应。"①所以,当前我国反腐败追逃追赃的任务非常艰巨,也正是在此背景下,2014年我国开展了以"天网行动""猎狐行动"等为代表的追逃追赃专项行动。

(2) 加强追逃追赃能够对腐败分子形成震慑

全面开展反腐败追逃追赃行动,追回逃往境外的腐败分子,追缴转移到境外的赃款,能够对于腐败分子形成威慑。习近平指出,"加强追逃追赃工作是向腐败分子发出断其后路的强烈信号,能够对腐败分子形成震慑,遏制腐败现象蔓延势头。"②腐败分子携款外逃的主要目的是逃脱惩罚,在国外享受在国内实施腐败行为所得收益。所以,全面开展反腐败追逃追赃工作,表明党和国家要追回一切腐败分子和追缴一切腐败收益的坚定决心,将有利于遏制腐败行为的发生,具体来说:(1) 对于企图外逃但尚未外逃的腐败分子,如果看到外逃的腐败分子都已经被追回,腐败犯罪的赃款赃物也都被追缴,就会意识到即使是逃到海外也不能逃脱惩罚,进而放弃携款外逃的幻想。(2) 对于已经外逃的腐败分子,看到我国反腐败追逃追赃工作卓有成效,在国外也会惶惶不可终日,无处藏身,在巨大的压力面前,迷途知返。(3) 对于想要实施腐败的党员干部,看到在追逃追赃中体现出来的党中央以零容忍的态度严厉惩治腐败的坚强决心,也会掂量自己实施腐败的代价,断了念头、放弃侥幸。总之,加强反腐败追逃追赃工作,就是向腐败分子表明,只要实施腐败行为,不论逃到天涯海角,都将难逃法律的制裁,从而威慑腐败分子,遏制腐败现象的发生。

(3) 反腐败追逃追赃有利于争取人民群众的支持

党的十八大以来,以习近平总书记为核心的党中央坚持以零容忍态度惩治腐败,要求"老虎""苍蝇"一起打,坚定不移把党风廉政建设和反腐败斗

---

① 参见《反腐败国际追逃追赃之一 决不让腐败分子躲进避罪天堂》,载《中国纪检监察报》2016年6月6日第1版。
② 《在十八届中央政治局常委会第七十八次会议上关于加强反腐败国际追逃追赃工作的讲话》,载中共中央纪律检查委员会、中共中央文献研究室编:《习近平关于党风廉政建设和反腐败斗争论述摘编》,中央文献出版社、中国方正出版社2015年版,第100页。

争引向深入,使不敢腐的震慑作用充分发挥,不能腐、不想腐的效应初步显现,反腐败斗争压倒性态势正在形成。习近平总书记指出,党的十八大以来,我们把党风廉政建设和反腐败斗争作为全面从严治党的重要内容,推动党风廉政建设和反腐败斗争取得新的重大成效。我们严明党的政治纪律,夯实管党治党责任,创新体制机制,扎牢制度笼子,持之以恒纠正"四风"、党风民风向善向上,强化党内监督、发挥巡视利剑作用,严惩腐败分子,加强追逃追赃工作。民心是最大的政治,正义是最强的力量。反腐败增强了人民群众对党的信任和支持,人民群众给予高度评价。[①] 腐败分子特别是党员干部,盗窃了国家和人民的财产之后携款外逃,严重损害党和国家形象,将他们缉拿归案依法制裁,是反腐败的应有之义。反腐败追逃追赃是我国反腐败战略的重要组成部分,加强反腐败追逃追赃工作,对于严惩腐败分子,争取党心民心,具有重要意义。

2. 反腐败追逃追赃工作的原则

反腐败追逃追赃工作是一项系统工程,必须坚持一定的基本原则,才能保障各项工作的顺利进行,从而既实现追逃追赃,又与他国保持良好的互利互信合作关系。

(1) 法治原则

习近平总书记指出:"中国是一个法治国家,无论是在国内惩治腐败,还是开展反腐败国际合作,都依法办事,坚持以事实为依据、以法律为准绳。"[②] 在党的十九大报告中也明确指出"全面依法治国是中国特色社会主义的本质要求和重要保障。必须把党的领导贯彻落实到依法治国全过程和各方面,坚定不移走中国特色社会主义法治道路,完善以宪法为核心的中国特色社会主义法律体系,建设中国特色社会主义法治体系,建设社会主义法治国家。"[③]作为我国社会主义法治建设和反腐败战略的重要组成部分,反腐败追逃追赃工作当然也应当坚持法治原则,严格依法进行。具体来说,追逃追赃

---

① 参见《习近平在接见军委机关各部门负责同志》,载《人民日报》2016年1月12日第1版
② 参见李晓珍、施希茜:《坚持党的领导总书记在国际上是怎么讲的》,载 http://politics.people.com.cn/n1/2016/0216/c1001—28128730.html,登陆日期2017年9月2日。
③ 习近平总书记在党的十九大上代表十八届中央委员会所作的题为《决胜全面建成小康社会 夺取新时代中国特色社会主义伟大胜利》的报告。

需要依据以下几个方面的法律:(1) 双方国内法律。境外追逃追赃是我国与他国开展国际合作,必须要遵守双方国内法律。对于在我国境内开展的程序,主要依据我国法律。对于在他国境内开展相应的诉讼程序,则要严格遵守当地国的法律和我国的法律。如在中国与加拿大合作开展的赖昌星遣返案中,我们配合加拿大方面,依据加拿大《移民与难民保护法》等法律展开了非法移民遣返程序。① 在此过程中,我们依据中国国内法的相关规定,向加拿大方面做出不判处赖昌星死刑的庄严承诺,最终将赖昌星于2011年遣返回国,并依据中国《刑法》和《刑事诉讼法》之规定进行审判。(2) 双边国际条约。双边国际条约指两国就特定事项签订的国际协议,缔约双方都有履行条约的义务。截至2018年9月,我国已与76个国家缔结司法协助条约、资产返还和分享协定、引渡条约和打击"三股势力"协定共159项(128项生效),②这些条约、协议是我国与他国开展追逃追赃合作的重要依据。比如我国和秘鲁合作开展的黄海勇引渡案,最为重要的依据就是双方签署的《中秘引渡条约》。③ (3) 多边国际公约。规定有国际刑事司法合作内容的多边国际公约也是我们开展追逃追赃工作的法律依据。例如我国和新加坡合作合作开展的李华波遣返案,就是两国依据《联合国反腐败公约》、践行《北京反腐败宣言》开展追逃追赃的成功案例。④

(2) 平等互信、包容互鉴、合作共赢原则

党的十八大报告指出:"在国际关系中弘扬平等互信、包容互鉴、合作共赢的精神,共同维护国际公平正义。"2013年4月13日,习近平总书记在人民大会堂会见美国国务卿克里的时候表示:"希望双方坚持从战略高度和长远角度把握两国关系,以积极态度和发展眼光推进对话合作,以相互尊重、求同存异精神妥处分歧矛盾,不断充实合作伙伴关系的战略内涵,走出一条

---

① 关于赖昌星遣返案的详细情况,请参见赵秉志、张磊:《赖昌星案件法理问题研究》,载《政法论坛》2014年第4期。
② 《司法协助类条约缔约情况一览表》,载 https://www.fmprc.gov.cn/web/ziliao_674904/tytj_674911/tyfg_674913/t1215630.shtml.
③ 关于黄海勇引渡案的详细情况,请参见赵秉志、张磊:《黄海勇引渡案法理问题研究》,载《法律适用》2017年第4期。
④ 关于李华波遣返案的详细情况,请参见戴佳:《跨国缉贪:逃之夭夭?回头是岸!——李华波案追逃追赃工作纪实》,载《检察日报》2015年5月10日第1版。

平等互信、包容互鉴、合作共赢的新型大国关系之路"。① 党的十九大报告也指出:"中国将高举和平、发展、合作、共赢的旗帜,恪守维护世界和平、促进共同发展的外交政策宗旨,坚定不移在和平共处五项原则基础上发展同各国的友好合作,推动建设相互尊重、公平正义、合作共赢的新型国际关系。"② 上述论述标志着平等互信、包容互鉴、合作共赢已经成为我们对于国际关系的一贯主张,是我国发展国际关系的重要原则,符合各国人民的共同利益和愿望。十八大以后,以习近平总书记为核心的党中央将反腐败国际合作上升到国家政治和外交层面,倡议构建国际反腐败新秩序,将平等互信、包容互鉴与合作共赢作为反腐败国际合作的重大原则。习近平总书记主张平等互信,指出反腐败是各国面临的共同任务和致力于现代化的必然举措;主张包容互鉴,指出中国愿意借鉴国际反腐败经验,与各国相互支持、相互协助;主张合作共赢,指出构建务实合作网络,营造风清气正的商业环境。这些主张得到国际社会的广泛支持与认可,使中国成为全球反腐败治理的重要力量。③ 我们在反腐败追逃追赃国际合作的工作中,一定要坚持上述原则,与世界各国共同努力,接续奋斗,携手并肩,互相支持,共同打击腐败分子。

3. 反腐败追逃追赃工作的基本立场

党中央对反腐败追逃追赃工作高度重视,党的十八届三中、四中、五中全会和中央纪委三次、五次、六次全会以及党的十九大等,都对加强反腐败追逃追赃作出重要部署。习近平总书记指出:"国际追逃工作要好好抓一抓,各有关部门要加大交涉力度,不能让外国成为一些腐败分子的'避罪天堂',腐败分子即使逃到天涯海角,也要把他们追回来绳之以法,五年、十年、二十年都要追,要切断腐败分子的后路。"④党的十九大上,习近平总书

---

① 参见《习近平会见克里纵论中美新型大国关系 平等互信 包容互鉴 合作共赢》,载《人民日报(海外版)》2013年4月15日第1版。
② 习近平总书记在党的十九大上代表十八届中央委员会所作的题为《决胜全面建成小康社会 夺取新时代中国特色社会主义伟大胜利》的报告。
③ 参见黄树贤:《把惩治腐败的天罗地网撒向全球——深入学习习近平同志关于反腐败国际合作和追逃追赃工作的重要论述》,载《求是》2016年第11期。
④《在第十八届中央纪律检查委员会第三次会议上的讲话》(2014年1月14日),载中共中央纪律检查委员会、中共中央文献研究室编:《习近平关于党风廉政建设和反腐败斗争论述摘编》,中央文献出版社、中国方正出版社2015年版,第98页。

记再次强调:"当前,反腐败斗争形势依然严峻复杂,巩固压倒性态势、夺取压倒性胜利的决心必须坚如磐石……不管腐败分子逃到哪里,都要缉拿归案、绳之以法,"①不仅如此,习近平总书记在出访他国或者参加国际会议时,都会同有关国家领导人商谈加强追逃追赃合作,既为我追逃追赃工作寻求到更多国际支持,也大力宣传了我们反腐败特别是追逃追赃工作取得的成果。除了习近平总书记亲自做出指示以外,我们党中央政治局常委会会议也专门听取追逃追赃工作汇报,对于相关工作实施强有力的领导,做出专门决策。中央反腐败协调小组及其相关单位认真贯彻中央决策部署,取得重要追逃成果,向腐败分子发出断其后路的强烈信号。以上都表明,全面和深入反腐败国际追逃追赃工作,是全面从严治党、推进党风廉政建设和反腐败斗争的重要组成部分,凸显了党和国家以零容忍的态度惩治腐败,强力推进反腐败追逃追赃工作的坚定决心、鲜明态度和严正立场。不论腐败分子逃到哪里,逃出去多久,即使是天涯海角,即使是五年、十年、二十年甚至再长的时间,都一定将其追回来绳之以法,绝不让一人逃脱惩罚。

(二)反腐败追逃追赃的工作方法

习近平总书记不仅对反腐败追逃追赃的基础理论问题进行论述,还特别关注反腐败追逃追赃的工作方法,对于在纷繁复杂的国际社会中如何开展反腐败追逃追赃提出了具体工作建议,具有很强的可操作性:

1. 摸清外逃腐败分子底数,强化追逃追赃工作基础

反腐败追逃追赃,只有清楚外逃人员和外流资金有多少,在哪里,工作才能目标清晰,更有针对性。过去我们追逃追赃工作面临的最为突出的问题就是底数不清。到底有多少人通过什么渠道逃出去了,携带或者转出去了多少资金,怎么转出去的,现在藏在哪里等等,都不是很清楚。这就是基础性工作没有做好,严重影响了我国追逃追赃工作的开展。针对这种情况,习近平总书记明确指出:"要强化基础工作,摸清外逃腐败分子底数,建立和完善外逃人员数据库。要建立统计数据动态更新机制,对外逃腐败分

---

① 习近平同志在党的十九大上代表十八届中央委员会所作的题为《决胜全面建成小康社会 夺取新时代中国特色社会主义伟大胜利》的报告。

子的情况做到数字准、情况明,并及时上报中央。要对掌握的情况深入分析,从个案中发现规律,寻找一些途径和方法。要加强对党员干部的日常监督管理,严格执行对配偶子女移居国外的国家工作人员的相关管理规定,加强党员干部出入境证照、出入境资金监控等方面的管理。重大事项报告制度不能摆在那,要抽查,抽查以后有问题的就要追究处理,这样这个制度才有用,而且才能如实报"。[①] 在上述论述中,习近平总书记一针见血地看到我国追逃追赃工作存在的问题,提出一定要强化追逃追赃的基础性工作,摸清外逃人员的数量、情况,为开展追逃追赃工作夯实基础。根据上述论述,追逃追赃的基础性工作有以下内容:(1)摸清底数。境外追逃追赃,对象在国外,基础在国内,只有国内基础性工作扎实、完善,摸清楚多少腐败分子外逃,多少腐败资金外流,建立完善的外逃人员数据库,根据情况及时更新,随时掌握外逃人员的最新动态,对相关情况了然于胸,实时把握准确的数字和真实的情况,为有针对性地开展追逃追赃工作奠定基础。(2)对于所掌握的情况进行分析,从中发现规律。在搞清楚外逃人员、外流资金的基本数字、基本情况,以及大致流向之后,要认真对于这些原始资料进行分析,得出外逃人员、外流资金的基本特点,流向的国家,从中梳理出一定的规律,有针对性的采取措施,阻断人员的外逃和资金的外流,及时追回外逃人员和外流资金。(3)加强对于党员干部及其配偶子女的监督管理,充分发挥重大事项报告制度的作用,随时了解党员干部及其资金的出入境情况。腐败分子出逃前,一般都会有向境外转移资金,办理虚假护照等异常举动,一旦发现这些情况,要立即采取措施,防止腐败分子外逃。总之,只有加强统一领导,打牢基础工作,做到数字准、情况明、底数清,才能掌握主动,抓出成效。[②]

2. 加大交涉力度,突破一批重点个案

近年来我国腐败外逃人员和外流资金数量巨大,在短时间内将所有人员追回既不可能也不现实,在此背景下,如何既稳步推进追逃追赃工作的开

[①]《在十八届中央政治局常委会第七十八次会议上关于加强反腐败国际追逃追赃工作的讲话》,中共中央纪律检查委员会、中共中央文献研究室编:《习近平关于党风廉政建设和反腐败斗争论述摘编》,中央文献出版社、中国方正出版社2015年版,第131页。
[②] 参见《反腐败国际追逃追赃之三 对象在国外 基础在国内》,载《中国纪检监察报》2016年6月20日第1版。

展,又能够遏制更多腐败分子外逃,就成为我们必须面对的问题。对此习近平总书记指出:"加大交涉力度,突破一批重点个案,使企图外逃分子丢掉幻想、望而却步。"①也就是说,在一时不能追回所有外逃人员的前提下,我们必须进一步加大工作力度,甄选一批外逃人员职位较高、国际国内影响较大、外逃时间较长、追逃追赃具有一定难度的案件进行重点突破,适当宣传,形成威慑和示范效应,使外逃人员丢掉外逃或者继续潜逃的幻想,回国自首。我们在实践中办好一个有影响的案件,胜过做千百个人的工作。只有办理一些有影响的案件,我们的反腐败追逃追赃工作才具有说服力,才能形成强大的震慑和示范效应。所以,我们一定要明确追逃追赃的主要方向和重点对象,集中时间、集中力量,追回一批有影响腐败分子,以成功案例增强广大群众信心,带动追逃追赃工作整体推进。②也正是在此思想的指导下,我们开展了对于一批重点案件的追逃追赃,取得了良好的效果。例如,2014年4月,按照"天网"行动统一部署,国际刑警组织中国国家中心局集中公布了针对100名涉嫌犯罪的外逃国家工作人员、重要腐败案件涉案人等人员的红色通缉令,加大全球追缉力度。这次集中公布的100人包括外逃国家工作人员和重要腐败案件涉案人,都是涉嫌犯罪、证据确凿的外逃人员,已经由国际刑警组织发布红色通缉令,正在全球范围追捕。③相对于其他犯罪嫌疑人来说,"百名红通人员"主要是腐败犯罪涉案人员,他们出逃准备多比较充分,拥有丰厚的资金聘请律师为自己提供法律帮助,多逃往西方发达国家,由于自身身份而容易提起政治避难请求,所以对这些人员的追逃将遭遇更为复杂的环境,面临更多的挑战,任务更为艰巨。④但是,经过我方工作人员的努力,截止到2019年6月29日,"百名红通人员"已经归案59人,取得了以杨

---

① 《在十八届中央政治局常委会第七十八次会议上关于加强反腐败国际追逃追赃工作的讲话》,载中共中央纪律检查委员会、中共中央文献研究室编:《习近平关于党风廉政建设和反腐败斗争论述摘编》,中央文献出版社、中国方正出版社2015年版,第132页。
② 参见《反腐败国际追逃追赃之四 追逃追赃既是内政又是外交》,载《中国纪检监察报》2016年6月27日第1版。
③ 参见《"天网"行动重拳出击全球通缉百名外逃人员》,http://www.ccdi.gov.cn/xwtt/201504/t20150422_55183.html。
④ 参见张磊:《从"百名红通人员"归案看我国境外追逃的发展》,载《北京师范大学学报(社会科学版)》2017年第3期。

秀珠(百名红通头号嫌犯)劝返案,①李华波(百名红通二号嫌犯)遣返案,②闫永明(百名红通五号嫌犯)劝返案③等为代表的一系列影响较大的典型案件。而且,我们每成功一个标志性的案例,都由媒体配合进行适当的宣传,并在"百名红通人员"发布两周年的时候进行集中宣传,取得了良好的效果。这都向世界昭示着,我国惩治腐败的天罗地网已撒向全球,外逃人员逃到哪里都将被追回。习近平总书记"突破一批重点个案,使企图外逃分子丢掉幻想、望而却步"的指示,正逐步变成现实。

3. 加快与外逃目的地国家签署引渡条约,建立执法合作

反腐败追逃追赃需要依法开展,这就要求善于运用法治思维和法治方式,健全配套法规制度。在完善立法的基础上,与他国尽快建立执法合作。对此,习近平总书记指出:"要加快与外逃目的地国家签署引渡条约,建立执法合作。"④具体来说,包括两方面内容:

第一,尽快与主要外逃目的国签订引渡条约。引渡是境外追逃中最为传统的国际刑事司法合作形式。但是由于各国引渡相关立法对引渡多规定了一些前提条件(如条约前置主义、互惠原则、双重犯罪原则),并受到死刑不引渡、政治犯不引渡等原则的限制,引渡合作往往不能顺利实现。截止到2018年9月,我国已经对外缔结了54项引渡条约(37项生效),⑤但是受多种因素影响,与我国缔结引渡条约的多是发展中国家,发达国家较少。而且我国尚未与我国外逃人员主要目的国,如美国、加拿大、澳大利亚等签订双边引渡条约(或者还没有生效),这就难以与其开展引渡合作。例如,美国在引渡问题上一直严格坚守引渡的"条约前置主义"(只有在行为人在外国受

---

① 关于杨秀珠劝返案的详细情况,请参见张磊:《境外追逃中的引渡及其替代措施研究——以杨秀珠劝返案为切入点》,载《法学评论》2017年第2期。
② 关于李华波遣返案的详细情况,请参见黄风主编:《中国境外追逃追赃经验与反思》,中国政法大学出版社,第151—172页。
③ 关于闫永明劝返案的详细情况,请参见吉追逃:《"百名红通人员"闫永明归案纪实》,载《中国纪检监察》2017年第16期。
④ 《在十八届中央政治局常委会第七十八次会议上关于加强反腐败国际追逃追赃工作的讲话》,载中共中央纪律检查委员会、中共中央文献研究室编:《习近平关于党风廉政建设和反腐败斗争论述摘编》,中央文献出版社、中国方正出版社2015年版,第132页。
⑤ 《司法协助类条约缔约情况一览表》,载 https://www.fmprc.gov.cn/web/ziliao_674904/tytj_674911/tyfg_674913/t1215630.shtml。

到指控的犯罪属于针对海外美国国民的暴力犯罪的情况下才可能有所例外),①要求开展引渡合作的双方签订有双边引渡条约。加拿大虽然由于1999年《引渡法》的规定,而在引渡问题上一定程度上放弃了对于条约前置主义的限制,但是我国和其在引渡问题上至今还没有实质性的突破。澳大利亚虽然和我国于2007年签订了双边引渡条约,但是该条约迄今尚未得到澳大利亚国会的批准,因此一直没有生效。由此,与西方发达国家双边引渡条约的缺位是影响境外追逃的一个重要因素。② 在此背景下,习近平总书记提出尽快与外逃目的国签订引渡条约,是推动我国反腐败追逃追赃顺利进展的一项关键性措施,具有非常重要的实践意义,一旦我国与外逃主要目的国签订了引渡条约,将为我国境外追逃扫除了立法上的一大障碍。

第二,加强与主要外逃目的国反腐机构和执法机构的合作。习近平总书记指出:由于各国在法律制度等方面存在差异,通过国际合作打击腐败犯罪需要解决一些法律技术性问题。这需要有关各方共同探讨解决方案,特别是要加强反腐败机构和执法机构在个案调查和信息交流等方面合作。相信只要有打击腐败的政治意愿,反腐败国际合作一定能够取得更多成果。③由于各国历史文化、法律传统、基本国情不同,各国的法律体系和司法制度也有很大区别,在实践中也存在一些法律技术性问题,这都给追逃追赃司法合作带来很多挑战。对此,习近平总书记提出有关各方应当通过共同协商进行解决,特别是加强双方反腐败机构和执法机构在个案调查和信息交流等方面的合作,坚持具体问题具体分析,针对不同个案的特点,灵活运用遣返、劝返、引渡、异地追诉等方式,逐一突破。例如,我国和美国不存在于双边引渡条约,法律制度存在较大差异,双方就是通过执法机构之间的合作,逐步确立了固定的追逃合作机制:1998年5月,中美执法合作联合联络小组(JLG)成立,就特定案件进行磋商。2005年JLG反腐败工作组成立。党的十八大之后,特别是2014年开展反腐败追逃追赃专项行动以来,中美JLG机制逐步成为两国执法合作的主要主渠道。在中央反腐败协调小组的直接

---

① 参见黄风:《国际刑事司法合作的规则与实践》,北京大学出版社2008年版,第6页。
② 参见张磊:《腐败犯罪境外追逃追赃的反思与对策》,载《当代法学》2015年第3期。
③ 参见李晓珍、施希茵:《坚持党的领导总书记在国际上是怎么讲的》,载 http://politics.people.com.cn/n1/2016/0216/c1001—28128730.html,登陆日期2017年9月2日。

指挥下,中央追逃办通过 JLG 机制与美国有效推动了反腐败执法合作,成功追回了王国强、杨进军、邝婉芳、赵世兰等腐败分子。2015 年 9 月习近平总书记应邀对美国进行国事访问所取得的一个重要成果,就是双方决定继续以中美执法合作联合联络小组(JLG)为主渠道,进一步落实好两国领导人达成的有关共识,采取切实措施,推进双方共同确定的重大腐败案件的办理。双方同意加强在预防腐败、查找腐败犯罪资产、交换证据、打击跨国贿赂、遣返逃犯和非法移民、禁毒和反恐等领域的务实合作。在追赃领域,双方同意商谈相互承认与执行没收判决事宜。① 除了中美以外,习近平总书记在同其他外逃主要目的国领导人会晤的时候,也分别就加强双方执法合作,推动反腐败追逃追赃的开展达成共识。如 2014 年 11 月 9 日,习近平在北京会见加拿大总理哈珀时表示,中国正在加大反腐败斗争,中加双方应该在执法领域包括追逃追赃问题上加强合作。② 同年 11 月 17 日,习近平在访问澳大利亚同澳大利亚总理阿博特举行会谈时强调,中方重视同澳方加强司法执法、追逃追赃合作,共同打击腐败犯罪。③ 同年 11 月 20 日,习近平在访问新西兰同新西兰总理约翰·基举行会谈时表示,双方要加强防务、执法交流,在打击腐败、追逃追赃等方面开展合作。④ 在以习近平同志为核心的党中央的部署下,我国与各外逃主要目的国反腐机构和执法机构的双边执法合作机制正在逐步建立、完善,为推动反腐败追逃追赃的全面开展铺平道路。

(三)反腐败追逃追赃的国际视野

我们的事业是同世界各国合作共赢的事业。党的十八大以来,面对国际形势的深刻变化和世界各国同舟共济的客观要求,以习近平同志为核心的党中央,统筹国内国际两个大局、统筹发展安全两件大事,坚持独立自主的和平外交方针,推动构建以合作共赢为核心的新型国际关系,打造人类命

---

① 参见《习近平主席对美国进行国事访问中方成果清单》,载《人民日报》2015 年 9 月 26 日。
② 参见赵成:《习近平分别会见印度尼西亚总统、加拿大总理、泰国总理和新加坡总理》,载《人民日报》2011 年 11 月 10 日第 1 版。
③ 参见《习近平同澳大利亚总理阿博特举行会谈一致决定建立中澳全面战略伙伴关系 宣布实质性结束中澳自由贸易协定谈判》,载《人民日报》2014 年 11 月 18 日 1 版。
④ 参见陈赞、田帆、刘华:《习近平同新西兰总理会谈强调:双方要在打击腐败、追逃追赃等方面开展合作》,载 http://cpc.people.com.cn/n/2014/1120/c87228—26063705.html。

运共同体,开启了中国特色大国外交新征程。① 打击腐败是世界各国面临的共同任务,反腐败国际合作是各国反腐败斗争的重要组成部分。习近平总书记指出:"没有哪个国家能够独自应对人类面临的各种挑战,也没有哪个国家能够退回到自我封闭的孤岛。"②世界上任何国家都无法免受腐败困扰,任何政府都无法单独对抗腐败,反腐败追逃追赃是与他国合作追回我国逃往境外外逃人员和外流资金,更需要与其他国家开展国际合作,需要具有国际视野:

1. 坚定不移反对腐败,占据国际道义制高点

我们开展的反腐败追逃追赃国际合作,是我国反腐败斗争的重要组成部分,是针对腐败现象和腐败分子的正义之战,在国际社会上占据了道义制高点,得到了国际社会的广泛支持。习近平总书记指出:"我们坚定不移反对腐败,使我们占据了国际道义制高点。""我们主动提出一系列反腐败国际合作倡议,倡议构建国际反腐新秩序,特别是加大对美国等西方国家在反腐败合作方面的压力,要求他们不要成为腐败分子的'避罪天堂'。原来他们认为那些犯罪嫌疑人是他们手中的牌,现在都成了手里的烫山芋。各方面对我们敢于向腐败亮剑是佩服的,我们的反腐行动赢得了国际社会尊重。"③得道多助,失道寡助,是永恒不变的真理。我们开展的反腐败追逃追赃行动,对象是腐败分子和被腐败分子贪污的国家和人民的财产,他们伪造国际旅行证件潜逃他国,通过洗钱的手段将巨额资金汇往境外,这些行为不论在世界哪个国家都是严重犯罪,都将得到人民群众的强烈谴责,受到国家法律的严厉惩罚。近年来,我国以零容忍的政策重拳反腐,在国内深得民心党心,回应了人民群众的反腐败期望,赢得了人民群众的高度赞誉。例如,2015年,国家统计局在22个省区市开展的全国党风廉政建设民意调查结果显示,91.5%的群众对党风廉政建设和反腐败工作成效表示满意,比2012年提高16.5个百分点,90.6%的群众认为当前腐败案件高发势头得到遏制,

---

① 中共中央宣传部编:《习近平同志系列重要讲话读本》,学习出版社、人民出版社2016年版,第260页。
② 习近平同志在党的十九大上代表十八届中央委员会所作的题为《决胜全面建成小康社会 夺取新时代中国特色社会主义伟大胜利》的报告。
③《在第十八届中央纪律检查委员会第六次全体会议上的讲话》,载中共中央文献研究室编:《习近平同志重要讲话文章选编》,中央文献出版社、党建读物出版社2016年版,第361—362页。

90.7%的群众对遏制腐败现象表示有信心。① 在国际社会,我们的反腐斗争引起了广泛关注与充分尊重,反腐败所取得的显著成效引起了国际社会的强烈反响与高度肯定。许多国外专家表示,观察近几年的反贪污、反腐败行动,"中国反腐"展现的定力和毅力让他们吃惊,从掀起国内反腐败高潮到影响波及国际的反腐败行动,中国展现的高压态势和累累硕果不仅仅显示了大国能量,也塑造了大国形象。② 欧洲委员会前副主席皮埃尔·德福安在中纪委网站的访谈中表示,他认为严格的程序使"老虎苍蝇一起打"成效显著,中国为公众通过社交网络和网站进行举报提供机会,这对那些受到腐败诱惑的人能够发挥非常有效的震慑作用。印度中国研究所副主任郑嘉宾认为,空前规模的反腐行动,不仅让中国人民看到了决心,也让世界对中国共产党产生新的期待。③ 我们主动提出的一系列反腐败国际合作倡议,呼吁构建国际反腐新秩序,希望一些国家不要成为腐败分子的"避罪天堂"的提议,也得到了国际社会的广泛支持和积极回应。由此可见,我国当前全面开展的反腐败斗争,为我们的境外追逃追赃提供了坚强的道义基础,我们反腐败越是坚决、彻底,越通过证据充分揭露腐败分子违法乱纪、经济贪婪、生活腐化、作风专横、盗窃国家和人民财产的真实面目,在开展境外追逃追赃工作的时候,越能把握国际道义制高点,越能够理直气壮、底气十足。所以,我们一定要将反腐败斗争坚定不移地推向前进,经常抓、长期抓,以锲而不舍、驰而不息的决心和韧劲,坚决遏制腐败蔓延势头,将反腐败斗争进行到底,直到取得反腐败斗争的压倒性胜利,也只有这样,我们才能在反腐败追逃追赃的国际舞台上,旗帜鲜明、立场坚定,永远占领国际道义制高点,高举"正义"的旗帜,凝聚起一切可以凝聚的力量,牢牢把握主动权和话语权。

2. 倡议构建国际反腐新秩序,在多边框架下加强追逃追赃国际合作

习近平总书记高度重视反腐败追逃追赃工作,倡议构建国际反腐新秩

---

① 《吴玉良:去年91.5%群众对党风廉政建设和反腐败工作成效满意》,载 http://fanfu.people.com.cn/n1/2016/0115/c64371—28057745.html.
② 参见陈定定:《中国反腐收获国际赞誉》,载《中国纪检监察报》2017年8月25日第4版.
③ 参见《"打虎拍蝇猎狐":铁腕反腐交出沉甸甸的成绩单》,载 http://fanfu.people.com.cn/n1/2016/1022/c64371—28798692.html.

序,搭建全球追逃追赃国际合作平台,得到了世界各国的充分认可和高度肯定。习近平总书记指出:"我们主动提出一系列反腐败国际合作倡议,倡议构建国际反腐新秩序,特别是加大对美国等西方国家在反腐败合作方面的压力,要求他们不要成为腐败分子的'避罪天堂'"。①我们"要搭建追逃追赃国际合作平台","继续推动在二十国集团、亚太经合组织、《联合国反腐败公约》等多边框架下加强追逃追赃国际合作。"②十八大以来,习近平总书记在重大外交活动中近80次就反腐败和追逃追赃发表重要论述,站在构建国家间政治与外交关系的战略高度推动,有效凝聚了国际共识,强调和号召国际社会积极推进国际反腐国际合作,搭建追逃追赃国际平台,使我国与有关国家开展反腐败合作、强化追逃追赃有了坚实的政治基础。③例如,2014年11月8日,亚太经合组织(APEC)部长级会议通过了《北京反腐败宣言》,习近平总书记在随后举行的APEC领导人非正式会议发表闭幕词指出,我们大力推动亚太反腐败合作,建立亚太经合组织反腐败执法合作网络,就追逃追赃、开展执法合作等达成重要共识。④2014年11月16日,习近平总书记出席二十国集团(G20)领导人第九次峰会会议时指出,中国坚持有腐必反、有贪必肃,以零容忍态度惩治腐败,加强反腐败国际合作,中方支持二十国集团加强国际追逃追赃务实合作。⑤2016年9月4至5日,二十国集团(G20)杭州峰会成功召开,习近平总书记在闭幕词中指出,"我们就继续深化反腐败合作达成多项共识,决心让腐败分子在二十国乃至全球更大范围无处藏身、无所遁形。"⑥在此次会议上,G20各国领导人一致批准通过《二十国集团

---

① 《在第十八届中央纪律检查委员会第六次全体会议上的讲话》,载中共中央文献研究室编:《习近平同志重要讲话文章选编》,中央文献出版社、党建读物出版社2016年版,第361—362页。
② 《在十八届中央政治局常委会第七十八次会议上关于加强反腐败国际追逃追赃工作的讲话》(2014年10月9日),载中共中央纪律检查委员会、中共中央文献研究室编:《习近平关于党风廉政建设和反腐败斗争论述摘编》,中央文献出版社、中国方正出版社2015年版,第132页。
③ 参见窦克林:《占领道义制高点 推动构建国际反腐新秩序》,载《中国纪检监察》2017年第16期。
④ 《习近平在亚太经合组织第二十二次领导人非正式会议上的闭幕词》,载《人民日报》2014年11月12日第2版。
⑤ 《习近平:中方支持二十国集团加强国际追逃追赃务实合作》,http://news.sina.com.cn/c/2015—11—17/doc-ifxksqku3158720.shtml。
⑥ 《习近平在二十国集团杭州峰会上的闭幕词》,载http://politics.people.com.cn/n1/2016/0905/c1001—28692951.html。

反腐败追逃追赃高级原则》、在华设立 G20 反腐败追逃追赃研究中心、①《二十国集团 2017—2018 年反腐败行动计划》等重要反腐败成果。2017 年 5 月 14 日,习近平总书记出席"一带一路"国际合作高峰论坛开幕式的主旨演讲中强调要加强国际反腐合作,让"一带一路"成为廉洁之路。② 2017 年 9 月 4 日,习近平总书记主持金砖国家领导人第九次会晤,与会领导人就加强反腐败合作达成重要共识并写入《金砖国家领导人厦门宣言》,该宣言强调"我们支持加强金砖国家反腐败合作,重申致力于加强对话与经验交流,支持编纂金砖国家反腐败图册。""我们支持加强资产追回合作。""我们支持包括通过金砖国家反腐败工作组机制加强国际反腐败合作和追逃追赃工作。"③从 APEC 北京会议、G20 杭州峰会,到"一带一路"高峰论坛,再到金砖国家领导人会晤,从《北京反腐败宣言》到《二十国集团反腐败追逃追赃高级原则》,再到金砖国家反腐败图册,我国国际反腐的路径越走越宽,所提出的一系列"中国方案""中国主张"正引领国际反腐合作向纵深发展,所倡导和引领的国际反腐新秩序正逐渐建立,为进一步拓宽国际反腐合作格局打下了基础。

(四)反腐败追逃追赃的配套措施

反腐败追逃追赃工作是一项系统工程,需要在理论研究、舆论宣传等多个方面的配合,对此习近平总书记也进行了深入论述:

1. 加强国际规则研究,深入了解他国立法

如前所述,反腐败追逃追赃应当坚持法治原则,严格依照国际规则和有关国家的法律进行,所以必须要加强对于国际规则和有关国家法律制度的研究,对此,习近平总书记从两个方面提出了明确要求:

第一,加强对于国际规则和有关国家法律制度的研究。习近平总书记指出:"要加强对国际规则和国际组织情况的研究,深入了解和掌握有关国

---

① G20 反腐败追逃追赃研究中心是在中央纪委支持下于 2016 年 9 月 23 日依托于北京师范大学刑事法律科学研究院成立的,旨在开展 G20 成员国的反腐败追逃追赃相关问题研究,加强 G20 国家反腐败追逃追赃合作,促进构建国际反腐败新秩序的学术机构。该研究中心在中国成立,是 2016 年 9 月 4—5 日在中国杭州召开的 G20 峰会所取得的重要国际合作成果之一。

② 参见李忠发、王慧慧、李舒:《习近平:要加强国际反腐合作,让"一带一路"成为廉洁之路》,载 http://www.jcrb.com/anticorruption/ffpd/201705/t20170519_1754852.html。

③ 参见赵林:《〈厦门宣言〉蕴含成果:反腐败国际合作续写新篇章》,载 http://www.ccdi.gov.cn/yw/201709/t20170907_106681.html。

家的相关法律和引渡、遣返规则。要及时了解和掌握国际反腐败最新动态,提高追逃追赃工作的针对性。"①知己知彼,方能百战不殆。反腐败追逃追赃是在他国境内追回我国外逃人员和外流资金,需要依据追逃追赃的国际规则和当地的法律制度。如果不对当地法律法规和国际规则了然于胸,追逃追赃根本就寸步难行。所以我们必须加强对于当地法律法规和有关国际规则的研究,比如外逃目的国的引渡法、国际刑事司法协助法、犯罪收益追缴法、刑法、刑事诉讼法、民法、民事诉讼法等国内法;我国与该国缔结的双边引渡条约、国际刑事司法协助条约,犯罪收益分享相关协议等双边国际条约、协议;我国与该国共同参加的国际公约如《联合国反腐败公约》《联合国打击跨国有组织犯罪公约》等。特别是我国腐败分子外逃的主要目的国(例如美国、加拿大、澳大利亚、新西兰、新加坡等)和世界主要国家(如英国、法国、德国等)的相关法律和制度,同时了解和掌握国际社会反腐败追逃追赃的最新立法规定,司法动态,针对他国出现的新情况、新问题提早准备,尽早熟悉,有针对性地开展追逃追赃工作。

第二,加强对于有关国家证据规则的研究。② 习近平总书记指出:"中国司法机关在进行反腐败国际合作时,对具体案件都应该提供确凿证据。"③在追逃追赃国际合作中,想要追回腐败分子和外流资金,必须向对方提供确凿证据证明该外逃人员实施了腐败犯罪,该外流资金是来源于腐败行为的赃款赃物。只有提供的证据符合对方法律的要求,对方才可能提供相应的刑事司法协助,为成功追逃追赃奠定基础。实际上,证据问题是我国反腐败追逃追赃合作中的一个重要而且亟需解决的问题。在以往的国际合作中,由于各国司法制度差异较大,对于司法协助请求所要求提供的证据材料不统一,而我国办案机关又多来自基层,对于国际司法合作和不同国家的具体标准欠缺经验,在准备、翻译所需证据和材料方面不太熟练,难以在短时间内

---

① 《在十八届中央政治局常委会第七十八次会议上关于加强反腐败国际追逃追赃工作的讲话》载中共中央纪律检查委员会、中共中央文献研究室编:《习近平关于党风廉政建设和反腐败斗争论述摘编》,中央文献出版社、中国方正出版社2015年版,第101页。
② 严格来说,证据规则也是外国法律制度的重要组成部分,但由于习近平总书记对于证据问题进行专门论述,而且证据问题在国际合作中具有关键作用,所以这里单独进行论述。
③ 参见李晓珍、施希茜:《坚持党的领导总书记在国际上是怎么讲的》,载http://politics.people.com.cn/n1/2016/0216/c1001—28128730.html。

提供符合对方要求的证据,从而导致降低了国际合作的效率。习近平总书记准确地看到了这一点,明确提出要求加强证据规则的研究,在具体案件中提交确凿的证据,反映出习近平总书记对于反腐败追逃追赃不仅从大处着眼,而且从小处入手,对于具体工作提出了明确要求,对于推动追逃追赃工作的开展具有重要的指导意义。

2. 开展舆论宣传,揭露外逃腐败分子真面目

关于反腐败追逃追赃的配套宣传工作,习近平总书记指出:"中央媒体要及时发声,揭露外逃腐败分子违纪违法、逃避惩罚的真面目。对一些证据确凿、定性清晰地外逃腐败分子,可以考虑向全世界公布,点名道姓公开曝光,是指在世界上任何一个角落都成为过街老鼠,人人喊打。这样震慑力就会更强"。① 这些重要论述,为反腐败追逃追赃的配套宣传工作指明了方向,凸显了媒体宣传对于我们赢得在追逃追赃战争中的舆论战的重要意义。根据习近平总书记的上述论述,我们在开展反腐败追逃追赃工作的同时,一定要一边干一边说,加强舆论宣传工作,打好反腐败追逃追赃的舆论战。具体来说,要配合追逃追赃工作的开展,选择合适时机,以适当方式向国际社会揭示腐败分子贪污腐败的违法犯罪事实,让世界知道,这些人员是在中国实施了严重腐败行为的腐败分子,应当为自己的行为承担法律责任。向世界表明,我们的反腐败追逃追赃,是正义之战、法治之战。对于一些证据确凿、违法犯罪性质清晰明确的腐败分子,向世界公布其姓名和可能的藏身地点,让他们成为随时可能被"打"、随时可能遭到举报的过街之鼠,丧家之犬,让腐败分子无处可逃。例如,2015 年 4 月我们公布了"百名红通人员"的主要信息,②加大全球追缉力度,③得到了媒体的广泛转发和报道。在"百名红通人员"公布两周年之际,也就是 2017 年 4 月,中央反腐败协调小组国际追逃追赃工作办公室又通过媒体发布了 22 名涉嫌职务犯罪和经济犯罪的部分外

---

① 《在十八届中央政治局常委会第七十八次会议上关于加强反腐败国际追逃追赃工作的讲话》,载《习近平关于党风廉政建设和反腐败斗争论述摘编》,中央文献出版社、中国方正出版社 2015 年版,第 101 页。
② 具体包括姓名、性别、原工作单位及职务、外逃所持护照信息、外逃时间、可能逃往国家和地区、立案单位、涉嫌罪名、发布红色通缉令时间,红色通缉令号码等十类信息。
③ 参见《"天网"行动重拳出击全球通缉百名外逃人员》,http://www.ccdi.gov.cn/xwtt/201504/t20150422_55183.html。

逃人员藏匿线索,公布举报网址,希望国际社会提供在逃人员线索,积极举报新逃人员,使外逃人员无处遁形,并将根据追逃追赃工作需要,通报更多外逃人员线索。① 据统计,近年来在追逃追赃中,我们已经及时曝光100多名被追回人员涉及的犯罪事实。② 上述舆论宣传,一方面表明我们对于外逃腐败分子一追到底的决心,无论腐败分子跑到哪里,都将被缉拿归案,另一方面形成全球追逃的氛围,给外逃人员施加压力,形成震慑,促使其早日归案。

四、坚决贯彻、落实习近平反腐败追逃追赃思想

习近平总书记关于反腐败追逃追赃工作的重要论述,集中体现了对国际国内反腐败追逃追赃形势的深刻理解和准确把握,具有很强的理论性、实践性和针对性,是我们在新的历史条件下开展反腐败追逃追赃工作的思想武器和行动指南。

(一)强化"四个意识",坚决以习近平反腐败追逃追赃思想为指导

习近平反腐败追逃追赃思想是中国特色社会主义理论体系的最新发展,是"四个全面"战略思想的重要组成部分,是社会主义核心价值观重要体现,是我国反腐败追逃追赃实践的理论升华和指导思想。贯彻习近平反腐败追逃追赃思想,我们首先要坚持正确的政治方向,不断增强政治意识、大局意识、核心意识、看齐意识:(1)不断增强政治意识。反腐败追逃追赃不仅是法治问题、外交问题,更是政治问题,要将其看作一项重要的政治任务,站在政治的高度来看待、分析和认识。在反腐败追逃追赃工作中坚定政治信仰、把握政治方向、站稳政治立场,严守政治纪律,保持政治清醒和政治定力,提高政治敏锐性和政治鉴别力,切实增强做好反腐败追逃追赃工作的政治责任感和历史使命感。要认识到反腐败国际追逃追赃工作是遏制腐败蔓延的重要一环,是党风廉政建设和反腐败斗争的重要组成部分,是全面从严

---

① 参见《中央反腐败协调小组国际追逃追赃工作办公室关于部分外逃人员藏匿线索的公告》,载http://www.ccdi.gov.cn/special/ztzz/ztzzjxs_ztzz/201704/t20170428_98256.html。
② 参见窦克林:《占领道义制高点 推动构建国际反腐新秩序》,载《中国纪检监察》2017年第16期。

治党的重要举措,既是法纪问题,更是政治问题。坚持从政治的高度去认识、思考、谋划和推进追逃追赃工作,充分发挥制度优势,将反腐败追逃追赃工作纳入党风廉政建设和反腐败工作总体部署,坚决完成这项神圣而光荣的重要政治任务。①（2）不断增强大局意识。习近平总书记强调,"必须牢固树立高度自觉的大局意识,自觉从大局看问题,把工作放到大局中去思考、定位、摆布,做到正确认识大局、自觉服从大局、坚决维护大局"。我们要将反腐败追逃追赃工作放到建设新时代中国特色社会主义的大局中,放到"四个全面"战略布局中,特别是从全面依法治国、全面从严治党中去认识、去定位、去把握。要准确把握反腐败追逃追赃与建设新时代中国特色社会主义、全面依法治国、全面从严治党之间的关系。只有这样才能明确内涵、厘清责任,使我们反腐败追逃追赃的工作更好地服务于建设中国特色社会主义、坚持依法治国和全面从严治党的大局,更好地服务于党风廉政建设和反腐败斗争的大局。（3）不断增强核心意识。所谓核心意识,就是要坚持中国共产党的领导,坚决听从党中央的决策部署,坚决维护习近平总书记的威信。增强反腐败追逃追赃工作中的核心意识,就是要始终坚持、切实加强党对于反腐败追逃追赃工作的领导,与以习近平总书记为核心的党中央保持高度一致,把思想统一到习近平总书记反腐败追逃追赃的重要论述上来,更加扎实地把党中央关于反腐败追逃追赃工作的各项部署落到实处。（4）不断增强看齐意识。习近平总书记强调:"必须有很强的看齐意识,经常、主动向党中央看齐,向党的理论和方针政策看齐"。无论是坚持政治意识、大局意识,还是增强核心意识,最终都要落脚于看齐意识,在思想上政治上行动上同中央保持高度一致。"群力谁能御,齐心石可穿"。反腐败追逃追赃工作必须要向党中央有腐必反、有贪必肃的鲜明立场态度看齐,向全面从严治党的顽强意志品质看齐,把看齐的要求落到反腐败追逃追赃的实际行动中,坚决保证以习近平总书记为核心的党中央的各项部署的贯彻执行。

（二）坚持法治反腐,将反腐败斗争进行到底

贯彻习近平反腐败追逃追赃思想要求坚持我们依法将反腐败斗争进行

> 延伸阅读

---

① 参见杨晓超:《推动反腐败国际合作和追逃追赃向纵深发展——写在"一二·九"国际反腐败日之际》,载《人民日报》2016年12月09日。

到底,依法开展追逃追赃。(1) 将反腐败斗争进行到底。习近平总书记指出:"人民群众最痛恨腐败现象,腐败是我们党面临的最大威胁。只有以反腐败永远在路上的坚韧和执着,深化标本兼治,保证干部清正、政府清廉、政治清明,才能跳出历史周期律,确保党和国家长治久安。"①我们正在进行的反腐败追逃追赃主要是针对外逃腐败分子和外流腐败资金的,也正因为我们反腐败斗争的正当性,才使得我们的反腐败追逃追赃在国际社会上占据了道义制高点,得到了国际社会的广泛支持。十八大以来,以习近平总书记为核心的新一届中央领导集体以巨大的政治勇气和历史担当,加大反腐败斗争力度、严肃查处腐败分子,"老虎""苍蝇"一起打,坚持以零容忍的态度惩治腐败,取得了突出的成绩。但是我们也要看到"当前,滋生腐败的土壤依然存在,反腐败形势依然严峻复杂,一些不正之风和腐败问题仍然影响恶劣",②"一些领域消极腐败现象仍然易发多发,一些腐败分子一意孤行,仍然没有收手,甚至变本加厉"。③ 我们必须更加清醒地认识反腐败斗争的长期性、复杂性、艰巨性,"巩固压倒性态势、夺取压倒性胜利的决心必须坚如磐石",④继续"深入推进反腐败斗争,持续保持高压态势,做到零容忍的态度不变、猛药去疴的决心不减、刮骨疗毒的勇气不泄、严厉惩处的尺度不松。"⑤只有持续不断地开展党风廉政建设和反腐败斗争,继续保持惩治腐败高压态势,才能为反腐败追逃追赃提供源源不断的正义之基和道义支持,也只有一个努力实现干部清正、政府清廉、政治清明的中国,才有能力为共同提升打击腐败犯罪的国际合力提供新经验、作出新贡献。⑥(2) 坚持法治反腐。反腐败追逃追赃工作对象在国外,但是基础在国内。在追逃追赃国际合作中,能否取得相关国家的支持与配合,一个关键问题在于相关国家对于中国刑

---

① 习近平总书记在党的十九大上代表十八届中央委员会所作的题为《决胜全面建成小康社会 夺取新时代中国特色社会主义伟大胜利》的报告。
② 中共中央宣传部编:《习近平同志系列重要讲话读本》,学习出版社、人民出版社2016年版,第122页。
③ 《在中共十八届四中全会第二次全体会议上的讲话》,载中共中央纪律检查委员会、中共中央文献研究室编:《习近平关于党风廉政建设和反腐败斗争论述摘编》,中央文献出版社、中国方正出版社2015年版,第25页。
④ 习近平总书记在党的十九大上代表十八届中央委员会所作的题为《决胜全面建成小康社会 夺取新时代中国特色社会主义伟大胜利》的报告。
⑤ 《在中共十八届四中全会第二次全体会议上的讲话》,载中共中央纪律检查委员会、中共中央文献研究室编:《习近平关于党风廉政建设和反腐败斗争论述摘编》,中央文献出版社、中国方正出版社2015年版,第102页。
⑥ 参见陈治治:《反腐败国际合作,从"道"与"术"看大势》,载《中国纪检监察报》2016年5月12日第1版。

事法治制度的评价问题。也就是说,站在对方的视角,目前中国的法治是否符合国际标准,外逃人员回国之后,诉讼权利能否得到充分的保障,能否得到公正的审判。① 由此,中国自身的法治发展状况,是否严格依法惩治腐败犯罪,将对于中国境外追逃追赃的顺利开展产生重要影响。所以,在反腐败斗争中,我们一定要坚持法治原则,严格遵循法治反腐。对此,习近平总书记强调:"要善于以法治思维和法治方式反对腐败,加强反腐败国家立法,加强反腐倡廉党内法规制度建设,让法律制度刚性运行"。② "在新的起点上持续深化党的纪律检查体制和国家监察体制改革,促进执纪执法贯通,有效衔接司法,推进反腐败工作法治化、规范化,为新时代完善和发展中国特色社会主义制度、推进全面从严治党提供重要制度保障。"③ 而且,也只有坚持法治反腐,才是反腐败最有效的手段,是解决腐败问题的根本方式。要使反腐败取得根本的成效,就应当在法治的框架下,以法治思维和法治方式推进反腐败,使反腐败走向规范化、制度化。④ 只要我们坚持法治反腐,依法充分犯罪嫌疑人和被告人的各项诉讼权利,对其进行依法公开审判,公正判决,在遭遇国际社会的质疑和外逃人员的污蔑时,才能够镇定自若、底气十足,向对方提供扎实、充分的证据,彻底揭露他们违法犯罪的真实面目。

(三)加强法治建设,推动反腐败追逃追赃良性循环

习近平总书记在十九大报告中指出:"全面依法治国是国家治理的一场深刻革命,必须坚持厉行法治,推进科学立法、严格执法、公正司法、全民守法。"⑤ 贯彻习近平反腐败追逃追赃法治思想,同样需要坚持法治原则,需要积极推进我国刑事法治建设,完善反腐败追逃追赃相关立法,严格依法开展反腐败追逃追赃。我们要善于运用法治思维和法治方式开展追逃追赃工作,深入了解和掌握有关国家法律和引渡、遣返规则,提高追逃追赃工作的

---

① 参见赵秉志、张磊:《赖昌星案件法理问题研究》,载《政法论坛》2014年第4期。
② 参见中共中央国家机关工作委员会编著:《学习习近平同志关于机关党建重要论述》,党建读物出版社2015年版,第111页。
③ 《习近平:持续深化国家监察体制改革 推进反腐败工作法治化规范化》,载 http://www.xinhuanet.com//politics/2018-12/14/c_1123855139.htm。
④ 参见赵秉志:《开启法治反腐新时代》,载《光明日报》2015年3月15日第6版。
⑤ 习近平总书记在党的十九大上代表十八届中央委员会所作的题为《决胜全面建成小康社会 夺取新时代中国特色社会主义伟大胜利》的报告。

针对性。追逃防逃追赃既要做好对内的法法衔接,确保协调一致、高效顺畅;又要注重与国(境)外法律的衔接,确保程序的合法性和证据的有效性:①

1. 完善反腐败追逃追赃相关立法。具体来说包括以下内容:(1)加快限制和废除腐败犯罪死刑的步伐。当前我国刑法对于腐败犯罪(如贪污罪、受贿罪等)还在立法上保留有死刑。而我国外逃人员主要出逃目的国大多已经废除死刑(如加拿大、澳大利亚)或者基本不执行死刑(如美国),并坚持死刑不引渡(遣返)的原则,由此我国不论是引渡还是遣返的请求,都可能被对方以死刑不引渡、不遣返为理由搁置或者拒绝。所以,我们应当顺应世界范围内限制和废除死刑的国际趋势,结合我国国情,切实推进死刑改革进程,尽早废除非暴力犯罪特别是腐败犯罪的死刑,②并为最终废除死刑而努力。在当前我国还不具备完全废除死刑的条件下,如果在引渡、遣返等国际合作中遭遇死刑问题,应当根据案件情况,及时、果断作出并严格信守不判处死刑的承诺,避免死刑成为外逃者的免责盾牌,以尽早将外逃者缉捕归案,切实推动我国境外追逃工作的开展。③(2)缔结追逃追赃类双边条约。相对于国际公约来说,双边国际条约能够针对两国的情况进行较为具体的规定,也更能够得到双方的遵守与履行,所以我们应当重视双边条约在反腐败追逃追赃中的作用。除了尽快与外逃目的地国家签署引渡条约之外,我们还应当积极缔结资产追缴类协定,刑事司法协助条约等双边条约、协议,为追逃追赃提供法律依据。在缔结引渡条约之前,则可以采取引渡替代措施进行追逃,或者是通过国际公约和个案协议开展引渡合作。④(3)完善其他立法。我们还要积极进行其他追逃追赃配套法规制度建设,完善违法所得特别没收程序,实现国内法律与国际规则的有效衔接,为国际追逃追赃提供法律保障和制度支撑。⑤

2. 严格依法开展反腐败追逃追赃。具体包括内容:(1)充分发挥制度

---

① 姜洁、江琳:《布下反腐败追逃追赃天罗地网——中央追逃办成立五周年工作回眸》,载《人民日报》2019年6月27日第7版。
② 赵秉志:《论我国反腐败刑事法治的完善》,载《当代法学》2013年第3期。
③ 赵秉志:《关于进一步推动我国境外追逃工作的几点思考——我在美洲人权法院巡回法庭黄海勇引渡案中出庭作证的体会》,载《刑法评论》2016年卷,法律出版社2016年版。
④ 张磊:《腐败犯罪追逃追赃的反思与对策》,载《当代法学》2015年第3期。
⑤ 参见《反腐败国际追逃追赃之二占领道义制高点》,载《中国纪检监察报》2016年6月13日第1版。

的优势。反腐败追逃追赃涉及多个部门,我们应当充分发挥我国的制度优势,在党中央的统一领导下,落实党的十八届三中全会提出的"改革和完善各级反腐败协调小组职能"的要求,发挥各级反腐败协调小组的组织协调作用,统一部署纪检、组织、政法、外交、金融和立法等机关和部门各司其职、各尽其责,形成上下联动、内外配合、齐抓共管、合成作战的工作机制,把这项跨领域、跨部门的重要工作抓紧抓实。① (2)继续深化司法体制改革。我们应当继续深化司法体制改革,严格规范司法行为,优化司法权力配置,更好地尊重和保障人权,不断提高执法办案水平和司法公信力,②完善包括量刑承诺制度在内的各项追逃追赃制度建设,③全面推进中央所确定的以审判为中心的诉讼制度改革,充分保障犯罪嫌疑人、被告人的诉讼权利,切实减少甚至杜绝刑讯逼供,增强国际社会对于中国刑事法治的认同,奠定我国在境外追逃中的底气。④ 事实一再证明,我国近年来能够反腐败追逃追赃取得突出成绩的一个重要原因就是我国对通行的国际刑事司法合作规则的采纳和顺应,对先进法治理念和人权保障原则的落实。⑤ (3)严格依照国际规则和双方法律追逃追赃。在追逃追赃的过程中,严格遵循国际规则和对方法律要求提交司法协助请求和相关证据材料,根据对方要求,在不违背中国法律原则的基础上,慎重而又果断作出外交承诺。⑥ 在外逃人员回国之后,一定要严格遵循法治程序,充分保障其各项诉讼权利,完全兑现之前我国作出的外交承诺,向他国和国际社会表明,中国政府一诺千金、言而有信、言出必行,增强他国对于我国刑事法治的信心,实现我国反腐败追逃追赃的良性循环。⑦

---

① 参见黄树贤:《把惩治腐败的天罗地网撒向全球——深入学习近平同志关于反腐败国际合作和追逃追赃工作的重要论述》,载《求是》2016年第11期。
② 参见赵秉志:《中国反腐败刑事法治重大现实问题研究》,载《法学评论》2014年第3期。
③ 参见张磊:《境外追逃中的量刑承诺制度研究》,载《中国法学》2017年第1期。
④ 参见张磊:《反腐败零容忍与境外追逃》,法律出版社2017年版,第186页。
⑤ 参见黄风:《境外追逃需宽严相济》,载《人民日报》2013年1月15日。
⑥ 实践中的外交承诺主要指承认不判处死刑或者不执行死刑,同时还包含承诺充分保障外逃人员的诉讼权利,承诺外逃人员不会遭受酷刑等非人道的待遇,承诺外逃人员在享有医疗服务等内容。关于外交承诺的详细论述可参见 赵秉志、张磊:《黄海勇引渡案程序问题研究(下)》,载《法学杂志》2018年第2期。
⑦ 赵秉志、张磊:《黄海勇引渡案法理研究》,载《法律适用》2017年第3期。

(四)站稳国际平台,引领国际反腐新秩序

反腐败追逃追赃,既是内政又是外交,基础在国内,关键在国外。近年来,习近平总书记在重大外交活动中,数十次就反腐败问题发表重要论述,表明中国共产党坚定不移反对腐败的鲜明态度,呼吁世界各国共同打击跨国腐败犯罪,为反腐败国际合作奠定了坚实政治基础。① 贯彻习近平反腐败追逃追赃思想,既要完善本国刑事法治建设,又要积极融入全球治理,加强国际交流,深化多边和双边合作,站稳国际平台,引领国际反腐新秩序。具体来说,包括以下几个方面的工作:

第一,加强以《联合国反腐败公约》等为基础的反腐败追逃追赃合作。《联合国反腐败公约》是旨在预防和打击腐败、加强国际合作、促进跨国流动的腐败资产追回的反腐败国际法律文件,该公约专章规定了国际社会打击腐败犯罪的国际合作和资产追回问题,②为我国逐步解决涉外腐败犯罪案件中的"调查取证难、人员引渡难、资金返还难"提供了国际法依据。③ 而且,在缺少双边条约的情况下,我们可以依据该公约与相关国家开展合作,例如李华波遣返案就是我国和新加坡在没有双边条约的情况下依据《联合国反腐败公约》开展国际合作的典型案例。④ 再如,我国和加拿大之间虽然没有双边条约,但是根据加拿大 1999 年《引渡法》关于国际公约也可以成为开展引渡合作的依据之规定,我们可以依据《联合国反腐败公约》与其开展引渡合作。⑤

第二,提高通过国际平台开展国际合作的效率。区域性国际合作平台是我们加强追逃追赃国际合作、倡导国际反腐新秩序的重要平台。展望未来,我们一定积极参与二十国集团反腐败工作组会议,健全交流机制,畅通沟通渠道,推动各国落实《二十国集团反腐败追逃追赃高级原则》与《二十国

---

① 参见杨晓超:《推动反腐败国际合作和追逃追赃向纵深发展——写在"一二·九"国际反腐败日之际》,载《人民日报》2016 年 12 月 09 日。
② 《联合国反腐败公约》第四章是国际合作,第五章是资产的追回。
③ 参见倪四义、孟娜:《〈联合国反腐败公约〉提请全国人大常委会审议》,载 http://news.xinhuanet.com/politics/2005—10/22/content_3667887.htm。
④ 参见戴佳:《跨国缉贪:逃之夭夭?回头是岸!——李华波案追逃追赃工作纪实》,载《检察日报》2015 年 5 月 10 日第 1 版。
⑤ 赵秉志、张磊:《赖昌星案件法理问题研究》,载《政法论坛》2014 年第 4 期。

集团 2017—2018 年反腐败行动计划》的规定，推动 G20 反腐败追逃追赃研究中心的积极运作，为二十国集团反腐败境外追逃追赃理论研究、国际合作、人才培养作出积极贡献；采取各种措施推动《北京反腐败宣言》的落实，促使亚太经合组织反腐败执法合作网络发挥实质作用；促进"一带一路"国际反腐合作机制的构建，助推"一带一路"成为廉洁之路；加快金砖国家反腐败机制建设，努力提高新兴市场国家和发展中国家在国际反腐败领域的话语权；从而逐步推动中国倡导和引领的国际反腐新秩序的确立，推动中国反腐败追逃追赃的全面开展。

第三，实现与重点国家之间的合作共赢。纵观以往实践，我国反腐败追逃追赃工作的难点主要在于美国、加拿大、澳大利亚、新西兰等若干西方发达国家。我们一定要在用好已经建立的中美执法合作联合联络小组反腐败工作组这个平台的基础上，重点推动建立中加、中澳、中新等双边反腐败执法合作机制，搭建联合调查、信息共享、快速遣返等便捷通道，构建司法执法合作法律体系，①在平等互信、包容互鉴的基础上，开展务实合作，实现合作共赢。

（五）讲好反腐故事，全面提升中国国际法治形象

落后就要挨打，失语就要挨骂。当前世界范围内的舆论格局总体是西强我弱，西方社会掌握主动权。由于我们的话语体系还没有建立起来，不少方面还没有话语权，甚至处于"无语"或"失语"状态，所以别人就是信口雌黄，我们也往往有理说不出，或者说了也传不开。② 改革开放以来，我国积极推进社会主义法治建设，确立了依法治国基本方略，基本形成以宪法为核心的中国特色社会主义法律体系，人权得到可靠的法治保障。但是部分西方发达国家对于我国刑事法治建设不断进步，人权保障不断完善的现状置若罔闻、视而不见，极端贬低中国刑事法治制度。③ 在他们眼中，中国并没有完善的刑事法治制度，相关审判缺乏公正性，外逃人员一旦会被引渡（遣返）回国，很可能会受到不公正对待，甚至遭受酷刑、死刑等严刑峻法，并且在不同

---

① 《反腐败国际追逃追赃之六深化合作互利共赢》，载《中国纪检监察报》2016 年 7 月 11 日第 1 版。
② 参见中共中央宣传部编：《习近平总书记系列重要讲话读本》，学习出版社、人民出版社 2016 年版，第 210 页。
③ 赵秉志：《我在加拿大赖昌星聆讯庭上作证》，载《凤凰周刊》2011 年第 23 期。

的国际媒体、国际场合中污蔑中国法治制度。部分外逃腐败分子在逃到他国之后,为了抗拒追逃,也往往将中国的依法反腐诬蔑为政治迫害,极力丑化中国的刑事法治制度,这往往使得我们的反腐败追逃追赃工作人员在实践中有口难言,百口莫辩。这都反映出,虽然近年来我国的法治发展取得了重要进展,但是已经取得的法治优势并没有转化为话语优势。所以,我们在开展反腐败追逃追赃工作的同时,一定要加强配套的宣传舆论工作,通过中央媒体、国际媒体等各种媒体主动发声,利用各种平台宣传中国刑事法治的全面进展,宣传中国反腐倡廉的主张,讲好中国反腐败的法治故事,全面展示我们坚定不移反对腐败的理念、做法和成效,驳斥西方社会对于中国法治建设的错误言论,消除国外民众对于中国法治建设的误解与偏见,努力营造有利于反腐败追逃追赃的良好国际舆论环境。实践也证明,在反腐败全球治理的舞台上,反腐败国际合作和追逃追赃充分彰显了中国共产党"有腐必应、有逃必追"的坚定决心,[①]对外树立了中国共产党和中国政府坚定不移打击腐败的良好形象,成为推进中国特色大国外交、构建人类命运共同体的重要内容。[②]

在对反腐败追逃追赃的成绩进行宣传的时候,我们一定要注意报道的专业性、大局性、客观性,在报道成绩的同时,多宣传我国追逃追赃工作在准备证据材料,与当地国政府沟通,严格遵守当地法律和司法主权,切实保障犯罪嫌疑人权利等方面所做出的努力,避免由于过度宣传取得成绩的高效性而引起他国对我国追逃追赃程序是否正当的质疑,影响境外追逃追赃的大局。而在我国对于回国以后的外逃人员进行公正审判以后,特别是在完全兑现了之前对于他国做出的外交承诺之后,要对我们如何保障外逃人员的诉讼权利,如何进行公正审判,如何兑现外交承诺的情况进行充分宣传,用铁的事实向国际社会表明,中国政府值得信赖,中国法治值得信赖,提高他国对于我国刑事法治的信心,全面提升中国的国际刑事法治形象。

---

① 王卓:《写在中央追逃办成立五周年之际:有逃必追 一追到底》,载《中国纪检监察报》2019年6月27日。
② 姜洁、江琳:《布下反腐败追逃追赃天罗地网——中央追逃办成立五周年工作回眸》,载《人民日报》2019年6月27日第7版。

五、结语

十八大以来,我国反腐败追逃追赃不断取得新成就,开创新局面,根本就在于以习近平总书记为核心的党中央的坚强领导,根本就在于习近平总书记关于反腐败追逃追赃思想的科学指导。深入学习、研究和贯彻习近平反腐败追逃追赃思想,对于全面推进依法治国,建设法治中国具有重要意义;对于推动全球反腐新格局的建立,提升中国法治国际话语权具有重要意义;对于推动新时代中国特色社会主义法学理论创新具有重要意义。深入学习和研究习近平反腐败追逃追赃思想,要着力全面准确理解基本观点和精神实质,深刻领会把握思想精髓和核心要义。要坚持实事求是,弘扬理论联系实际的作风,强化问题导向、实践导向、需求导向,紧密结合我国反腐败追逃追赃的伟大实践,紧密结合我国反腐倡廉和反腐败斗争的伟大实践,紧密结合我国建设新时代中国特色社会主义的伟大实践,在实践中贯彻落实习近平反腐败追逃追赃思想。让我们紧紧团结在以习近平总书记为核心的党中央周围,高举中国特色社会主义伟大旗帜,以习近平新时代中国特色社会主义思想为指导,锐意进取、团结奋进、攻坚克难,为推动反腐败斗争和追逃追赃事业的顺利进行而努力奋斗,为推动建设法治中国伟大事业的全面开展而努力奋斗。

(本文主要内容曾发表于《吉林大学社会科学学报》2018年第2期和《河南大学学报(社会科学版)》2018年第2期)